THE FALSIFICAT␣␣␣␣␣␣␣ HISTORY

Our Distorted Reality

By

John Hamer

To Danny
With best wishes
John Hamer
(dad)

RB

Rossendale Books

Published by Rossendale Books

11 Mowgrain View, Bacup,

Rossendale, Lancashire

OL13 8EJ

England

http://www.rossendalebooks.co.uk

Published in paperback 2012

Category: Politics & History

Copyright © John Hamer 2012

ISBN: 978-1-906801-78-6

Dedication

First and foremost, I would like to thank my wonderful, long-suffering wife Linda for all her unstinting support, encouragement and love and without whom I could not have completed this lengthy project. Her down-to-earth advice and pragmatic common-sense whenever the going got tough, was the difference between my finishing this book and it remaining a mere pipe-dream.

This book is dedicated to her.

Thanks and Acknowledgements

Indeed I should like to express my gratitude to all my close family. My sons Danny and Ryan and John and his lovely wife, Carrie (not forgetting my beautiful granddaughters, Charlie and Katy) have all been especially supportive and encouraging, despite on occasions being subjected to demands upon their patience well above and beyond the call of family duty. And whilst my eldest son Chris and I have not enjoyed the closest of relationships down the years, he and his family are often in my thoughts, nevertheless.

I should also like to place on record, my thanks to our very good friends, John and Nicola Eastwood, who despite being subjected night after night to my inane ramblings and rants against all the injustices in the world and their causes, still somehow managed to remain on speaking-terms with me, the following day!

And also Richard Morson, my good mate, who in the early days of our joint ventures into the world of alternative history and reality, was a great 'sounding-board' and helped me get much of this into perspective. In short, I believe that we 'came of age' in this field, together. Thank you, Rich.

A special mention should also go to Adam Leak whose imagination and great artistic skills were responsible for the cover design of this book. His achievement being all the more commendable due to a distinct lack of guidance, direction and input from myself! Adam's blog may be found at this address:
http://ivebeenherethiswholetime.tumblr.com/

Lastly, but not least, I would like to thank those courageous, great champions of alternative history and reality, two of whom ultimately died for their beliefs. It was they who firstly introduced me to the subject, thus changing my life and ultimately taught me all I know, through their writings, lectures and in some cases their personal conversations and communications with me. There are too many to mention them all by name but include primarily (in no particular order)... Dr. Henry Makow, Ian R. Crane, Alan Watt, John Kaminski, David Irving, David Icke, the late William (Bill) Cooper, Jay Weidner, Jordan Maxwell, the late Phil Schneider, David Wilcock, Terry Boardman, Paul Craig Roberts, Dr. Michael Newton and Chris Everard.

To you all, I am and will remain eternally grateful.

Contents

PART 1 – The Prologue

Introduction

"History is created, manipulated and written by those who are predominantly on the victorious side of the nation which has supreme political, and especially military, dominance. Any 'truth' which has the slightest potential of weakening their total hold over the masses is not tolerated. Any truth which can impact their power is squelched or cunningly hidden by them, usually in a manufactured media release to the unsuspecting public, often in a jovial manner to render the information a laughing matter and display it as harmless." Former NASA astronaut, Clark C McClelland

"History is a lie, commonly agreed upon." Voltaire, French philosopher

The ongoing, deliberate, systematic falsification of both ancient and modern history and thus by default, our present reality, is undoubtedly taking place as part of a conspiracy by the ruling Elite. I do not intend by this statement to suggest that the whole of recorded history is false, but it is clear that at the very least, the framework of our past and present is certainly distorted and manipulated to present a deliberately misleading picture of reality in order to benefit a tiny minority of humanity. This is no wild, unsubstantiated claim, it is a well-established fact and I believe it to be no great exaggeration to say that almost everything you think you know about history and the present-day is wrong.

However, I use the word 'conspiracy' guardedly. The very word itself conjures up an image of tin-foil-hat-wearing geeks, suffering from extreme paranoia and irrationality. This engendered image in itself is an appropriate illustration of how we have been systematically socially-engineered into believing the Orwellian 'double-think' that war is peace, freedom is slavery, ignorance is strength, truth is lies, black is white, up is down, 2+2=5 and anyone even suggesting a conspiracy is simply crazy or outrageous. However as 'conspiracy' is indeed what it is, I shall continue to use the word.

"In fact, 'conspiracy' is very plausible. People who control a grossly disproportionate share of the world's wealth will take extreme measures to consolidate their position." Dr. Henry Makow, author of 'A Cruel Hoax'

"How many times have you heard the mainstream media dismiss certain points of view as 'conspiracy theories'? It seems as though one of the easiest ways to brush something off is to label it as something that only 'conspiracy theorists' would believe. Well, you know what? A whole lot of the time, the 'conspiracy theorists' are right and the mainstream media is wrong. In fact, we owe a great debt to 'conspiracy theorists' because they will go places and investigate things that the mainstream media would never even touch. The reality is that the mainstream media only tells us what the government and the big corporations want us to hear, and much of the time it is those in the alternative media that are left with the task of trying to figure out what the real truth is. So don't look down on conspiracy theories or conspiracy theorists. In a world where almost everything we are told is a lie, the truth can be very difficult to find." Michael Snyder, Blacklisted News. August 2011

In my view, when anyone says "I do not believe in conspiracy theories", what they actually mean is... "I have already made-up my mind based upon what I have been told to think by the mainstream media conspiring to propagandise us through TV, radio and newspapers, so please do not confuse me with the truth".

Unfortunately, the society described in George Orwell's dystopian novel, '1984' is not some distant future improbability, it is already here. More than one quarter of a century later than the author anticipated, but here it is nevertheless. George Orwell and Aldous Huxley were both members of the inner sanctum of the Fabian Society; an integral part of the Elite secret society network and this is whence they derived the insider knowledge for their prophetic novels, '1984' and 'Brave New World'. This is also the reason that these works are now proving to be so accurate in their 'predictions'.

In order to comprehend why and how the entire history of the human race as related by politicians, scientists, historians and educators, is very largely a manufactured falsehood, one has to attempt to understand and interpret a pattern which only becomes evident upon the closer analysis of world events today and their root causes. One is naturally faced with the greatest difficulty in coming to terms with all the various and diverse facets of this whole conspiracy and understanding the many different phases of this monstrous plan, as it is staggering in its interconnectedness and complexities. The purpose of this book is to facilitate the linking of all these at first glance, unrelated facets and thus lead to a better, more complete understanding of the insidious plight currently facing the human race.

"Our Western history is every bit as distorted, censored and largely useless as that of Hitler's Germany, the Soviet Union or Communist China." Dr. Anthony Sutton, historian

It is a truism to state that in the Western world, we all grew up with mainstream media stories of Soviet and Communist Chinese governments who were able to fool all their naïve citizens into believing that they lived in some sort of 'socialist' paradise, not realising themselves that they suffered a kind of 'living hell', whilst we were all assured that we lived in a blissful state of democratic freedom and we, for our part were only too happy to believe this lie. How many times have you personally used the expression 'it's a free country' in proclaiming your right to express an opinion or perform a specific action? How ironic it is then that it turns out that the joke is actually on us?

In fact, the citizens of both those aforementioned countries knew the real situation exactly. They watched the state news broadcasts and read the state newspapers and treated them as some kind of sick comedy show at worst, whilst at best trying to ignore them and live their lives as well as they were able, under the circumstances. How different to our experience in the 'free world', then. We were subjected to much the same kind of lies and propaganda as were our Soviet and Chinese counterparts, but the big difference is that we believed that we were being told the truth and worse yet, we for the most part *still do* believe it. Our so-called 'news' and history and indeed much else of what we are conditioned to believe is nothing but outright propaganda and lies, broadcast as part of the ongoing, insidious Elite conspiracy. Propaganda is similar to rat poison in that 99% of it is tasty and wholesome, the purpose of which is to disguise the remaining 1% that will kill you.

"Coexistence on this tightly knit earth should be viewed as an existence not only without wars... but also without the government telling us how to live, what to say, what to think, what to know and what not to know". Aleksandr Solzhenitsyn, from a speech on the 11th September 1973

If you still believe you live in a free country and not an Orwellian police-state, try one of these actions for yourself...

— Take a photograph or video of a public building or a public servant (a police or traffic officer, for example) going about his duty.

— Ask politely for a police officer's name and number after feeling you have been unfairly treated by him / her or a colleague.

— Take a perfectly innocent photograph of your baby or toddler in his / her natural state (ie. naked) and then attempt to get the picture developed at a high street photo-processing outlet.

— Take a photograph of your *own* child at a school or other organised children's event.

— Post a small 'flyer' on a wall offering a reward for returning a missing pet cat.

— Wear a t-shirt or badge (button) bearing an anti-government or anti-establishment slogan.

— Attempt to provide food and drink to a small group of homeless people in a public park.

— Stand in a public place peacefully making non-confrontational, anti-government or anti-royalty statements or handing out leaflets regarding the same.

— Make a public statement, verbal or written, to the effect that you do not believe that as many as six million Jews were systematically exterminated in gas chambers in World War II.

— Place the wrong kind of trash in the wrong bin.

— Post a stupid, insensitive, joking statement on a social networking website about blowing-up an airport.

— Take a small paring knife to school in your lunchbox to peel your lunch apple.

— Drop bio-degradable 'litter' on an area of public grass (for example an apple core).

— Politely refuse to submit to an outrageous, invasive body search when attempting to board a plane.

— Verbally defend someone you believe is being treated unfairly by police / figures of authority.

— Write and publish a poem on the Internet about assassinating the US president.

I am sure you get the picture and these are just a few examples, but suffice to say that people have been harassed, verbally and physically assaulted by police, arrested, fined and jailed in the UK, US and elsewhere in the so-called 'free world' for these and similar activities and these are not just isolated incidents. The last named action above, in fact resulted in a three year jail sentence in America in 2010.

In addition to this, in our glorious so-called, western 'free world' society in 2010/11 the following horrendous 'felonies' were recorded:

In America, a 6 year old boy was sentenced to 45 days in reform school for taking to school a camping utensil best described as a combination of a knife, fork and spoon.

A 7 year old boy, described as 'a nice kid' and 'a good student' by his school was charged by police for simulating a gun in the traditional way by bending back two fingers under the thumb and pointing the remaining two fingers at another student.

Also, in Britain in June 2011, a 13 year old boy was dragged out of bed at 11.30pm by police who had unceremoniously burst into his house issuing threats to his parents. His 'crime'? He *allegedly* threw an apple core at another boy – an allegation that was only the word of one thirteen year old against another. Despite protests from the boy's parents that he was asleep in bed, the police threatened arrests if their demands were not met.

And horrifically, in November 2010 a 14 year-old boy was shot dead in America by a school-district officer for becoming involved in a schoolboy fight with another boy of the same age. The boy, when confronted, ran away, was pursued by the officer and found to be hiding in fear in a nearby garden shed. The officer simply took out his gun and summarily executed the boy on the spot. And this was not the first time apparently that he had resorted to unnecessary, extreme violence and yet had nevertheless been allowed to keep his job.

"There's no way to rule innocent men. The only power any government has is the power to crack down on criminals. Well, when there aren't enough criminals, one makes them. One declares so many things to be a crime that it becomes impossible for men to live without breaking laws. Who wants a nation of law-abiding citizens? What's there in that for anyone? But just pass the kind of laws that can neither be observed nor enforced nor objectively interpreted and you create a nation of law-breakers and then you cash in on guilt." Ayn Rand, 'Atlas Shrugged'

It is now said that there are so many laws, rules and regulations in the first world that each person breaks at least one law per day, if not many more – without even knowing it. But governments are now becoming more obvious and blatant in how they go about making everyone a criminal and fining them ridiculous amounts of money in doing so. Recently, an American family who said they were simply trying to teach their son about responsibility and entrepreneurship was fined **$90,000** by the USDA because the teenager sold $4,600 worth of rabbits he had bred and reared himself, in one calendar year *without a licence*. Not only were they ordered to pay $90,000, but were told that if they did not pay within a short period of time the fine could increase to as high as $4 million. This one case alone goes to show how easy it now is, within the system, to take any small transgression and in effect blackmail someone for every penny they have – and much more.

This situation is being exploited to the full by authorities who openly state that *'ignorance of the law is no excuse for breaking it'*. This is in itself a very dangerous state of affairs for the ordinary 'man in the street' as it is now possible for surreptitious, pernicious new laws to be passed solely with the intention of entrapment. Who among us is aware of every law and statute passed by our governments in the last two years, let alone the last one hundred years? However this lack of knowledge may well be used against us at any time it suits, in order to 'protect us' by curbing our freedoms.

"When even one American who has done nothing wrong is forced by fear to shut his mind and close his mouth, then all Americans are in peril." Former US President, Harry S. Truman

In May 2011 in a decision that shocked the independent media community but went entirely unreported in the mainstream, the Indiana Supreme Court ruled that citizens have no right to block a police officer's entry into their home, even if the officer does not have a warrant. The officer also does not have to give any clear indication as to why he wishes to enter their home, meaning he can enter without just cause or suspicion. So, if he wishes to walk into a house, for any reason, he may do so, without a warrant and without even knocking. The householder may not block his path, cannot close his door and lock it and cannot physically restrain him. The householder cannot even discuss the matter calmly with him beforehand, he can simply walk in and he is fully legally protected. If the good citizens of Indiana are not even aware of this law then how dangerous might it be to attempt to physically prevent a police officer from entering their homes? I submit that this policy could well lead to many of them being shot dead on the spot for what amounts to nothing at all.

"The USA PATRIOT Act, the Military Commissions Act, the TSA, the FDA, the CIA, renditions, assassinations, multiple and continuous wars, torture, bailouts, inflation, false flag events, secrecy, illegal searches, spying on citizens, private property confiscations and much, much more is now commonplace. It is now considered to be a crime to grow your own food, to film the police, to sell lemonade on the street corner, to protest and in many cases just to speak out against the State". Gary D. Barnett, September, 2011

I am afraid that in Britain now at least, with the rest of the world rapidly following in our wake, we live in a 'surveillance-based' police-state with cameras in every shop, bank and public building and at virtually every street corner in our towns and cities as well as every few hundred yards along our highways. This situation has been imposed upon us by stealth, ostensibly 'for our own protection' whilst we all watch our favourite soap operas and game shows, play mind-numbingly violent computer games around the clock or spend 90% of our waking lives wearing headphones blocking out the world around us whilst listening to the latest appalling trash masquerading as music and worship at the altar of the great 'celebrity cult'. The result of which, over time has been the systematic but nevertheless steady loss of most of our basic freedoms today – all as planned and facilitated partly by the fake 'war on terror' of course, that perversely seeks to enslave us in order to 'preserve our freedoms' and which has gone-by un-noticed by the majority. And now we have the great 'global warming' latterly re-branded as 'climate change' scam which is designed to surreptitiously impose even more onerous taxation and curb our rapidly diminishing freedoms.

"Through clever and constant application of propaganda, people can be made to see paradise as hell and also the other way around, to consider the most wretched sort of life as paradise." Adolf Hitler, 'Mein Kampf', 1923

In late 2010, amidst a veritable blaze of zero publicity for obvious reasons, the US Senate passed Senate bill S-510 (the Food Safety and Modernisation Act) by 74 votes to 25, which effectively banned the growing of any foodstuff, vegetables or fruit on one's OWN land or garden and the sale of any such produce at farmers' markets or at the roadside – all under the frankly laughable pretext of preventing food smuggling and enabling 'food safety'. Ever heard of food smuggling? I didn't think so, neither have I, but anyway this bill will definitely prevent it, whatever it is. This quasi-fascist piece of legislation, provably written by *Monsanto* lobbyists, also makes illegal the saving and storing of fruit or vegetable seeds for future use in propagating next year's crops, seriously detrimentally affecting the livelihoods of farmers and independent food producers. Also, believe it or not, it is now illegal to save and/or store rainwater that falls on one's own house roof or land in that wonderful 'land of the free'. After all, the profits of the water companies must be protected and we wouldn't want anyone to escape their daily dose of 'soma', sorry, fluoride, would we?

LOBBYISTS
Helping corporations run America since 1869

So why do you think these frankly draconian, invasive laws have come to pass? The answer, as always is complex, but to try and simplify it into three distinct reasons may help. Firstly it is about control, the control of populations and also the control of the food supply. Should the Elite decide to restrict food or water supplies in any way or in any specific geographical area as a population control mechanism (and they will, one day very soon, see section on *Agenda 21*), then it will now be much simpler to achieve. Secondly it drastically reduces or eliminates the opportunities for us to source local, organic, healthy, untainted produce. And last but certainly not least, it is also about boosting the corporate profits and furthering the agenda of such horrendous organisations as *Monsanto*, in their sick and demented quest to 'corner the market' of the entire world's food supply.

Now Americans are being *forced* by this legislation which was of course bought and paid for by Elite corporate lobbyists to eliminate competition and boost profits substantially, to buy food from the huge corporate food conglomerates (Big Food) and supermarket chains only. This is now food, which if the Elite desired (and they certainly do) can be tainted in any way they choose, be it with dangerous pesticides, harmful chemicals, genetically modified organisms or even if they wished with mind-altering chemicals. First, America and then the rest of the world will follow as always. How long before this abomination is foisted on all of us? If this is living in a 'free country' give me tyranny any day.

"Control the food and you control the people." Henry Kissinger, 1973

The last Labour Government in Britain 1997-2010, was responsible for more new legislation being instigated, than in the *entire previous history of Britain as a nation*. Much of this legislation has been introduced to curb our freedoms in the guise of 'anti-terrorist' policies as a by-product of the fictional war on terror. So yes, we are 'free' in a sense. Free to do as we are told – or else suffer the consequences.

"In Britain, there is no need for tanks in the streets. In its managerial indifference to the freedoms it is said to hold dear, bourgeois Britain has allowed parliament [this century] to create a surveillance state with 3,000 new criminal offences and laws: more than for the whole of the previous century. Powers of arrest and detention have never been greater. The police have the impunity to kill; asylum seekers can be 'restrained' to death on commercial flights and should fellow passengers object, anti-terrorism laws will deal with them. Abroad, British militarism colludes with torturers and death squads." John Pilger, investigative journalist, 2010

Each element of this great conspiracy to totally subjugate humanity, when taken in isolation is often made to appear an individual, isolated anomaly, which as a result may be easily dismissed by those who wish to deceive us, as nonsense or at worst an unfortunate 'coincidence'. It is only the unification of all these individual elements that presents us with a clear and undeniable, composite picture of the truth. A partially-completed jigsaw puzzle does not reveal the whole picture and indeed until the puzzle is almost complete, it is difficult to connect the subject matter with that depicted on the box lid. This is in fact, the very essence of the struggle between those of us who have actually mentally completed the jigsaw puzzle as it were and those who are aware of none, one or just some of the component parts of the conspiracy. The latter will simplistically dismiss the former as 'conspiracy theorists', encouraged and cajoled all the while by our masters and further dismiss the individual pieces of the whole, as random aberrations in the overall grand scheme of things.

Significantly, in this case, the whole is indeed greater by magnitudes than the sum of all its parts.

It is extremely important to accept and understand that despite every fibre of your being denying that it could possibly be true, the world has indeed been hijacked by a satanic cult, better known as the Illuminati, whose nefarious plans, in place for at least 235 years (and probably millennia), are almost at fruition. They have taken every possible safeguard and spared no expense to ensure that you are not aware of this, but should you become aware of even a small part of their master-plan, through the resulting wholesale denial and ridicule from both your masters and your peers, your deliberately pre-conditioned mind will immediately reject it as impossible or insane.   This is an acknowledged psychological condition known as 'cognitive dissonance', during which state your mind is subjected to an attempt to displace the truths in which you have always believed, by a conflicting ideal which you subconsciously concede has great merit, resulting in extreme confusion and distress. This state of mind can itself often cause irrational anger and occasionally, violence among its sufferers.

My many years of research have led me to conclude that what they are doing is actually totally senseless and in fact, is pure evil. It is destruction of all that is good, wholesome and natural simply to reap short-term profit and to further their sick agenda. There can be no other logical explanation. No amount of reasoned logic can explain the utter stupidity of the seemingly deliberate destruction of the planet on which we all have to live, its finely balanced eco-systems and its indigenous species to the extent that is happening today. The only vaguely plausible reason for world events of today, can be a staggering disregard not just of the welfare of those they seek to oppress and enslave or eliminate, but also their own wellbeing and that of their descendants.   Through their wars and corporate exploitation they are succeeding in destroying the rainforests, the natural weather cycles, land and oceanic eco-systems, polluting rivers and fresh water systems beyond the point of no return, destroying whole species such as the honey-bees that are essential for pollinating food-crops worldwide and latterly the bat population, poisoning the entire atmosphere and oceans with deadly chemicals and radiation, undermining the entire food-chain with genetic modifications, artificial growth hormones and poisonous pesticides and generally creating a kind of 'hell on Earth'. They then have the sheer audacity to blame the state of the planet on 'overpopulation' and/or 'global warming', now re-invented and re-branded as 'climate change' as it becomes more apparent that the world climate is actually growing noticeably cooler. It would be funny if it wasn't so serious.

"This is what we are experiencing today: Perpetual War, created illegally, to invade and destroy other countries and steal their natural resources; pestilence created in black ops bio-weapons labs; extensive famine in Africa, India, and now Haiti; millions of American children, too, are without adequate daily food; a contaminated food supply created by corporate chemical production and dangerous husbandry practices foisted on us by greed. The soil is destroyed, because genetically engineered and carcinogenic plants can only grow in soil that must be loaded with pesticides. This is now part of a globally poisoned food chain. Medicine is no longer the practice of doing NO harm, but rather radiating critically ill patients and injecting young and old with poisoned vaccines that have created two generations of children with compromised cognitive function (ADD, ADHD, and autism) and damaged immune systems. The list goes on and on. In all of it, precaution is hardly ever used, and harm is the avenue chosen." Dr. Ilya Sandra Perlingieri 'The Allegories of Good and Bad Government', January 2011

If and when their master-plan ever comes to fruition and the world is completely under their jackboots, I am afraid it will have been a pyrrhic victory and I sincerely hope that I am no longer around in our desolated Earth to witness their hollow triumph.

So then, if all this is even remotely true, how is it possible to keep such a vast conspiracy secret, especially as it encompasses every aspect of our lives? For instance, would there not be 'whistle-blowers' by the thousand, coming forward to expose it?

The answer is complex. Firstly, let me say that there have been and no doubt will continue to be, many, many people who come forward to expose this or that individual aspect of the plot. These people for the most part are not generally aware of the whole picture and so are fairly easy to dismiss and ridicule as 'conspiracy nuts' or even ignore completely. Secondly and more importantly, the hierarchical structure of the Elite network is similar to that of any individual company or corporation, in that it is pyramidal and self-contained, albeit huge in its scope. Contained within the larger, overall structure is a series of smaller and smaller, pyramids within pyramids each with its own individual hierarchy reporting upwards as in a typical corporate scenario.

In a corporate structure for example, the top of the pyramid is the CEO or managing director who has overall responsibility for the entity as a whole and he is served directly by a board of directors or vice-presidents. Within that small cabal of these corporate 'leaders'; instructions, orders and information are passed down, strictly on a 'need to know' basis and nothing that is privy to that small group is released down the 'food chain' unless it has some importance in the smooth operation of the organisation. Similarly, proceeding down the hierarchy, senior management will be made aware of certain facts or situations that are for their ears only and these will not be passed down to middle management, junior management and so on to the very bottom of the pile, the base of the pyramid where the armies of clerks, assistants, assorted labourers and wage-slaves ply their trades, unless vital to the company's needs. For example, a cashier in a bank has no idea and is not made aware of the ultimate goals and strategic financial policies of the bank, other than what she needs to know to perform her duties efficiently, which is therefore, in effect virtually nothing. This construct of pyramids within pyramids and 'divide and rule' is the ultimate tool by which secrecy is maintained.

There have of course, been many instances of Elite, Illuminati defectors who attempt to expose what is happening behind the scenes, but these people are comfortably contained by denying them a mainstream platform and thus any form of credibility in the eyes of the 'masses' and the 'useful idiots' who control them for their Elite masters. They may well be given air-space on occasions in order to ridicule the information they impart or enable their being labelled as crazy or 'madmen' and indeed many of them disappear forever after their brief moment in the spotlight. This may often be attributed to the *'if it's not in the mainstream, it cannot be true'* viewpoint, we have been conditioned all our lives to believe. Our completely impartial news media would of course tell us all if there was anything untoward going-on in the world would they not?

"This `cabal` of evil is best known as `the Illuminati` and includes a core of thirteen bloodlines, all interconnected, intermarried and tracing their lineage back to the Near East in ancient times. They are worshippers of `Lucifer` and see themselves as `Gods` on a planet filled with `cattle`. They number amongst their members, the Royal families of Europe, the leading bankers, industrialists, media tycoons and political elites. They operate through a dazzling array of `front groups` and secret societies such as the

Freemasons, The Council for Foreign Relations, Bilderbergers, Trilateral Commission, Common Purpose and many, many more. Their tentacles are everywhere and the major intelligence agencies of the world are in the pockets of these self-styled `Gods`". Philip Jones, 'Playing God', 13th March 2009

"The world is governed by far different personages from what is imagined by those who are not behind the scenes." Benjamin Disraeli, former British Prime Minister

"The individual is handicapped by coming face-to-face with a conspiracy so monstrous he cannot believe it exists." J. Edgar Hoover, former head of the FBI

ILLUMINATI

Indeed the very fabric of our so-called 'democracy' can be shown to be a complete sham as may be witnessed by the examination of the corrupt two-party state of affairs prevalent today, both elements of which immediately, quietly backtrack on all election promises the moment they come to 'power' and proceed to implement very largely the same policies as their supposed opposition would have done, should the puppet-masters have declared that it be they whose 'turn' it is to be 'in power'. In Britain, the hugely corrupt 'first past the post' political electoral system ensures that we regularly get governments voted in by a small minority of the population. Indeed, we really need to closely scrutinise the extent of the political spectrum covered by the 'free democratic choice' we are given in elections. In the US there are the Democrats and the Republicans and in the UK, we have the Labour and Conservative parties (with the odd token interjection by the almost irrelevant Liberal Democrats). We all need to ask ourselves, how much of the full political spectrum do these 'choices' encompass? I would strongly suggest that the answer is 'a miniscule amount'. In all cases, these political parties are almost identical bar one or two minor differences in their views and policies, despite what the mainstream press will contend to the contrary.

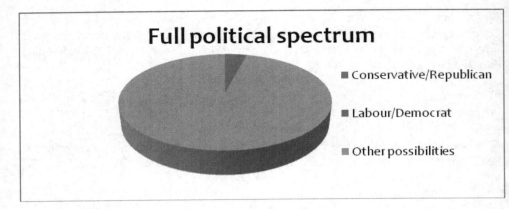

Example of mainstream politics versus other possible political alternatives

"Obama campaigned longer than anyone else in American history, for the office of the Presidency. For over two years this half-white, half-black man 'ran' for the presidency. During that impossibly-long campaign he was running against everything that George W. Bush had done or was doing. Once he was anointed as 'president' however, he began to break every campaign-promise he made to all of us, about everything that Cheney-Bush had done." Jim Kirwan, political researcher, May 2011

"I'll show you politics in America. Here it is, right here. 'I think the puppet on the right shares my beliefs.' 'I think the puppet on the left is more to my liking.' 'Hey, wait a minute, there's one guy holding out both puppets!'" Bill Hicks, late US comedian

Indeed, the very minor differences exhibited by our major political parties and their continuing, utter failure to have any positive impact whatsoever on the quality of life of us 'ordinary' people, should be enough to demonstrate to us all that there is a major background conspiracy in operation to convince us that we live in a country where freedom of choice reigns supreme. But of course, most people are unaware of this, largely due to the complicit media puppets and their relationships to the controlling Elite who blatantly perpetuate this great myth of freedom. The enormous power of the propaganda generated by our controlled media cannot be over-estimated.

"Democracy is two wolves and a sheep voting on what to have for dinner. Liberty is a well-armed lamb contesting the vote." Former US President, Thomas Jefferson

"Republicans ousting Democrats is like the Gambinos replacing the Bonnanos." Gerard Celente, trends forecaster

"Sooner or later people will wake up. First we have to dump the trap of right and left. This is a Hegelian trap to divide and control. The battle is not between right and left; it is between us and them." Dr. Anthony Sutton, historian

The Democratic and Republican parties offer the masses of everyday Black, White, Brown, Red, and Yellow people the de facto non-choice of either euphemistic death by drowning or death by hanging. Thus, no real choice is offered at all. As the politicos of the Democratic Party foxes and the Republican Party wolves feed, like swine, from the bottomless blood-drenched financial trough of the corporate/military elite, democracy is rendered null and void. Larry Pinkney, 'Online Journal', 15th October 2010

From the food we eat, to the air we breathe, from our so-called healthcare systems to covert genocide, humanity is under siege. This truth is of course concealed at every turn by the 100% compliant, Elite-owned mainstream media (written press and TV / radio) who spare no expense in covering-up the real truth behind world events whilst presenting a completely distorted view of the same. Indeed the popular image projected and carefully nurtured by these organisations is one of a caring government, doing its level best under trying circumstances to maintain a fair society for all and to keep its citizens safe from harm in this dangerous world. And yet whence does this 'dangerous world' spring? I would venture to suggest that it originates from those same governments, who hand-in-hand with multi-national corporations and the military, all controlled of course by bloodline, Elite families, far from protecting us, actually *intentionally cause* all of the extensive misery, poverty and ills existing in the world today whilst maintaining a pretence of trying to end it.

"Unfortunately, most people have believed the line that government exists to take on the responsibility of looking after the People. The People have been sold an image of government as some kindly entity which somehow looks after everyone in the nation no matter if they be young or old. This is the result of aeons of propaganda which has been perpetrated by the royal-political elite, who use pomp and circumstance, parades, fly-bys, flag-waving, national anthems, patriotism, royal weddings and the kissing of babies as a tool to fool people into thinking that they have some kind of group membership to a nation which has at its head either a king, queen or president that represents their wishes and protects their families. It's a lie." Chris Everard, British researcher and film director

We are moving rapidly now into an era where the gap between the haves and have-nots is not only increasing at a staggering rate but, as is intended by the hidden, prevailing agenda, the truth is that the so-called 'middle-classes' are being systematically eliminated. The ultimate goal of a tiny Elite minority, their every need being catered for and served by an army of mind-controlled drones and slaves, is drawing ever closer as each year goes by. I firmly believe that the only reason that we, the 'huddled masses, yearning to breathe free' are allowed to exist is for the same reason we were 'created' in the first place – to fulfil our eternal roles as economic slaves to the system, built, maintained and run for the sole benefit of the tiny Elite minority. Once we have outlived our usefulness and we are now fast approaching that point, then we will literally be systematically 'phased-out' and replaced by modern technology. This I suggest is the real reason for all the current wars, 'natural' disasters, diseases and destruction. Of course they cannot do this overtly as they well know that we are far too numerous and powerful as a group were we ever to get our collective act together, so they must contrive various other covert methodologies with which to dispose of us.

America, once hailed as the great bastion of freedom and the land of opportunity, is now being rapidly subsumed into a fascist-communitarian state totally controlled by corrupt corporate and banking cartels. The role of American president, once dubbed the 'most powerful role on Earth' is now no more than that of a puppet, manipulated, cajoled and coerced by vested interests to fulfil their own private agendas and sick ambitions of global conquest in the name of profits. Western armed forces have become the private mercenaries of the super-rich Elite whose media lackeys spin us fairy tales of 'global terrorism', 'global warming', 'weapons of mass destruction' and the great 'Muslim threat' in order to justify the subjugation of us all and the conquest, financial exploitation, rape and destruction of third world countries and their helpless populations in reckless pursuit of their obscene profits.

I would also venture to suggest that it is no coincidence that it is the Muslim *economies* and their total rejection of usury (lending money at interest), rather than their so-called terrorism that offer the bigger threat to Western capitalist interests and world domination by their financial Elite. Does not this latter statement alone impart sense to much of what is happening in the world today?

"Somewhere in our own inner darkness, thinking the worst that we can about ourselves, we still are hard pressed to reach the depths of depravity we confront daily in the stark facts of the world. All the big news items of history, when analysed at a later date, turn out to be hoaxes, false-flag operations conducted for an ulterior motive always hidden from the public. And those bits of common knowledge we always accepted as 'gospel' as children almost always, when analysed from the perspective of a future we did not know at the time, turn out to be quite different from what we thought they were and would be." John Kaminski, political researcher, December 2010

Our physical health and mental welfare is also under systematic attack from this Elite group, one of whose *clearly stated and documented* goals is the reduction of the world population by more than 95%. It is certainly not by accident that the giant, multi-national pharmaceutical companies have completely infiltrated all of the important healthcare organisations from cancer research charities such as the huge American Cancer Society (ACS) to the American Food and Drug Administration (FDA), to the British and American Medical Associations (BMA and AMA) and even medical education establishments across the Western world. Indeed, many of the pharmaceutical super-giants (Big Pharma) have at their disposal, substantially more financial power and resources than many medium to large-sized countries and the totally corrupt FDA, far from acting as the protector of people's health and well-being from greedy corporate interests, as is its mandate, is provably culpable for allowing highly-profitable yet highly-toxic, substances into the food chain in what can only be described as at best, irresponsible and at worst, criminal activities. The upper echelons of the FDA and Big Pharma / Big Food would also appear to operate a 'revolving door' policy whereby senior executives from both sides of the supposed 'divide' regularly trade positions in both organisations. No conflict of interest to be seen there then.

'Big Pharma' is also responsible for the wholesale, mass propaganda affecting not just the layman, but even medical personnel – from the highest-paid professor of medicine to the lowliest trainee nurse. It is this propaganda which implants the now 'received wisdom' that cure is better than prevention and illness and disease can only be effectively treated by artificially manufactured chemical, pharmaceutical products (which they are of course, very happy to supply at grossly inflated prices), rather than natural foodstuffs and a healthy diet. Unfortunately there are no vast profits to be made in the prevention of disease by proper nutrition and nor would a happy, healthy population be in their best interests. Vitamins and mineral supplements and other 'natural' and dietary remedies are under such severe attack by these organisations and their lackeys, that we are now seeing them increasingly being made illegal or legislated against as 'untested' or 'un-approved drugs' via organisations such as the Codex Alimentarius committee and the aforementioned FDA. It can even be shown from readily available evidence that indeed, Big Pharma is actually responsible for 'inventing' many new diseases simply in order to profit from their 'cures'. Impossible? It is not only possible, but absolutely true (as outlined in the section on health).

*"I would like to dispel the myth that the pharmaceutical industry is in the business of health care and healing. Because, in fact, what the pharmaceutical industry is in the business of, is disease maintenance and symptoms management. They are not in the business of curing cancer, Alzheimer's or heart disease because if they were, they would be in the business of putting themselves out of business and that does not make sense.... The pharmaceutical industry does **not** want to cure people."* Gwen Olsen, former pharmaceutical industry insider and author of *'Confessions of a Drug Pusher'*

However, perhaps the single, greatest criminal act of the pharmaceutical cartel is the great cancer hoax. Cancer is not incurable or unpreventable as their propaganda makes widely believed, but all forms of cancer can be treated and prevented very effectively, easily and inexpensively using simple, readily available nutritional supplements and vitamins and if this statement is untrue, why then would they cause such unnecessary suffering on such a grand scale by spending millions fighting and suppressing these proven remedies as they do? Several reasons spring to mind. Firstly, we cannot exclude the fact that cancer is a huge destroyer of human life and as such is a valuable tool in their *self-admitted* goal of large-scale human population reduction. There is also much truth in the premise that ageing populations are extremely expensive for governments to maintain and so how much better for them that people should die on average ten to twenty years sooner than they naturally would and thus reduce the overall financial burden on the state? However, the primary reason for this cruel deception is the great god of profit.

Cancer is absolutely without doubt a multi-trillion-dollar industry employing millions worldwide in the form of researchers, charity workers and carers, before we start on the vast armies of medical personnel dependent on cancer for their careers or livelihoods. Take away the disease and you remove the huge annual profits associated with its useless and deadly drugs in the form of chemotherapy, radiotherapy and also surgical procedures. Significantly, in a recent, mainstream-ignored (of course) survey, 91% of oncologists said that they would not undergo chemotherapy or radiotherapy if they were ever diagnosed with the disease or indeed allow family members to do so as these treatments 'poison the system'. In addition, there is also the vast, vast amount of money that is siphoned from us through our generous contributions to cancer research 'charities' each year, often in the face of extreme emotional blackmail, the vast majority of which never even reaches the medical research teams anyway. Big Pharma spends many millions per annum in the perpetuation of this hoax through the infiltration and 'incentivising' of such organisations as medical societies, the medical profession itself, medical education and ACS, Cancer Research, MacMillan etc. I have no doubt that there are many decent, caring people in these organisations who are striving hard to discover a pharmaceutical-based cure against all odds, but they and humanity as a whole are being duped by these truly evil organisations on a grand scale.

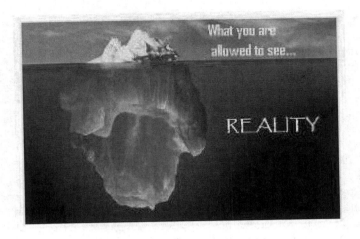

We are also kept in perpetual slavery by our rigged monetary system, designed to maintain us in a permanent state of debt and thus under easier control. We are now drowning in debt on a never-before-seen scale, in the form of student loans, credit cards, store cards, personal loans, mortgages and the like and it could be convincingly argued that we are indeed now defined as individuals by our personal credit rating, all determined by our financial masters of course in the form of the banksters (banker-gangsters), which either allows or denies us the ability to live the lives we choose. The overall control of finance unsurprisingly has also been wrested from public control into private hands (in the Western world at least) in a series of planned moves dating back to the formation of the Bank of England in 1693, under the orders of King William III of England who supplanted James II in 1688, in a plot hatched by senior Freemasons and carried out by Elite forces in both England and Holland.

"Give me control of a nation's money and I care not who makes its laws." Mayer Amschel Rothschild, 1790

"History records that the money-changers [bankers] have used every form of abuse, intrigue, deceit, and violent means possible to maintain their control over governments by controlling money and its issuance." Former US President, James Madison

The long-term Elite-driven plan was essentially to remove from elected governments, the creation and printing of paper money, backed by equivalent amounts of gold to maintain its intrinsic value, with a 'fiat' currency of worthless paper, whose value is not fixed and can therefore be adjusted upwards or downwards to suit any agenda the Elite decide to impose upon us, but otherwise known as the financial 'boom and bust cycle'. The result of this has also been the introduction of 'fractional reserve' banking by which decidedly dubious tactic, banks can lend money that they do not even possess and better yet, charge interest on this non-existent money from day one.

The charging of interest on loans is otherwise known as usury and up until the Middle-Ages had long been banned by the Christian and Muslim worlds as an abomination. The introduction of usury, the system heavily promoted by Jews was the reason for their being expelled from most Christian, European countries at many different points in history and this practice is depicted (and derided) most famously in the Shakespeare play, 'The Merchant of Venice' whereby the Jewish moneylender, Shylock demands his 'pound of flesh' for default of interest payment even after the original debt has finally been repaid.

By way of illustrating this important point, consider this; should you wish to take out a mortgage or a loan with a bank or other financial institution, once you have been vetted and approved for the loan, the bank will then simply key into your account the amount of the mortgage/loan and create the 'money' with several simple keystrokes, 100,000, 200,000, 500,000 or even more – it really does not matter to them as this is not actual money that they possess, it is just 'created out of nothing' by simple, but nevertheless utterly fraudulent book-keeping. To make it clearer, imagine you have 'hacked' into your online bank and have devised a way to key in figures directly to your account. You just sign in and then key into the relevant place £1,000,000.00 and suddenly you are an instant millionaire!

"Wealth is simply ones and zeros in the computers of the international banking system. When we borrow money to buy a house (or whatever) the bank gives us permission to pretend that they gave us money to give to the seller. The bank in fact created the money out of nothing, altered their computer records accordingly, and printed out some hard-copy evidence to support the notion that real money is now being dealt with." Judith Moriarty, political researcher.

This is *exactly* what they *do*. This figure does not have a pile of notes or coins in a vault somewhere that is attached to it and earmarked for you, it is simply summoned into existence arbitrarily. Not another single note or coin is printed or minted. Not a single note or coin is shuffled from one physical place to another. Not a single 'paper' transaction occurs to theoretically move that amount from one account to another in the form of 'double-entry book-keeping'. That sum is just an 'imaginary' figure which is then utterly fraudulently added to the credit side of the bank's accounts.

You now immediately owe them that amount of money, which you must of course, pay back to them in 'real' money, so not only are they benefitting to the tune of whatever extortionate amounts of interest they see fit to charge, they are also gaining the actual capital amount too – and all this from *nothing at all*.

The real crowning glory for the banksters though, is that should you default on the payments of the loan of this 'money' that never existed in the first place, they will come along and in collusion with the Elite controlled, corrupt legal and court systems, perfectly 'legally' take away your property, which quite plainly does exist and does have an intrinsic value. Indeed many sub-prime, less-reputable lenders, those who prey like vultures on those poor souls with less than perfect credit ratings, will do all they can to ensure that you do default, thus giving them the court-granted authority to remove your property from you. By any standards, all of this should be regarded as gross deception and fraud. If we, the people behaved in this way with our own finances, we would very quickly end up in jail. Ever thought you were in the wrong business?

"I sincerely believe that banking institutions are more dangerous than standing armies. If the American people ever allow private banks to control the issue of their money, first by inflation and then by deflation, the banks and corporations that will grow up around the banks, will deprive the people of their property until one day their children will wake up homeless on the continent their fathers conquered." Former US President, Thomas Jefferson

How prophetic! This is exactly what is happening today in America and throughout the first world. In the USA alone, more than one million properties are being repossessed and standing empty *each year* – and rising. There are at the time of writing, approximately 150,000 homeless people living on the streets of Los Angeles alone and there are tent villages continually springing-up all over the country, with whole families living under crude canvas shelters or actually in their cars, with no electricity, sanitation or cooking facilities. And now many states are passing legislation to make it illegal to live in cars and tents in addition to making it illegal to feed and clothe homeless people. How long will it be before the dispossessed are actually legislated out of existence altogether? In November 2011 it was stated by reliable, alternate media sources that only 45% of Americans were actually in gainful employment and that 48% of the population are below the poverty-line. All these facts of course are concealed from the majority by the simple expedient of not being reported in the mainstream media.

In 1913 the United States acquired its own 'Bank of England' type organisation with the surreptitious passing of the Federal Reserve Act through Congress in the early hours of the morning of 23rd December whilst opposition was at a minimum, most Congressmen having already left for their Christmas holiday break. Congressman Charles Lindbergh Sr., the father of the famous flier was offered a $2m dollar 'incentive' not to publish his book *'Banking and Currency and the Money Trust'* which exposed the threat posed by the Federal Reserve System. In fact, shortly before the end of his political career, Lindbergh formally moved to impeach the members of the Federal Reserve Board and offered a 15-count indictment of their conspiracy. The motion however, was unsurprisingly buried and 'forgotten' by the Congressional Judiciary Committee.

As with the formation of the Bank of England, this Act in effect gave the power to create money to a group of *private* individual bankers outside of elected

Government. Therefore, the Federal Reserve is not 'federal' (ie. of the government) at all and neither does it have any reserves. Another gross deceit.

"Whosoever controls the volume of money in any country is absolute master of all industry and commerce... and when you realise that the entire system is very easily controlled, one way or another, by a few powerful men at the top, you will not have to be told how periods of inflation and depression originate." Former US President, James Garfield, 1881

Within weeks of making this statement, President Garfield was assassinated.

And slightly more recently...

On the 4th June 1963, Presidential Executive Order 1110 was signed by President John F. Kennedy, directing the US Treasury to issue a new US currency. This new currency was to be backed by the precious metal silver, in effect by-passing and isolating the Federal Reserve, in control of currency issuance since 1913. President Kennedy's signing of Executive Order 1110 effectively returned the power to issue currency back to the US Treasury and therefore 'the people', thereby ending the then fifty-year monopoly of private bankers and the Federal Reserve Bank over US currency. Five months later on 22nd November 1963, JFK was famously shot and killed in Dallas, Texas, supposedly by Lee Harvey Oswald, a known-to-be CIA agent but described as a 'deranged lone gunman' by the lackeys of the media, who was conveniently 'disposed of' himself two days later by yet another 'deranged lone gunman', Jack Ruby who just *happened* to be a CIA colleague of Oswald. Ruby later developed a particularly fast-acting cancer whilst awaiting trial which literally killed him in days rather than months or years. All a coincidence? You decide, but just before you do so, consider that the new President, Lyndon B. Johnson's first official action as President was to immediately revoke the decision to implement EO 1110, literally within hours of taking office. The law in fact still stands on the US statute books but unsurprisingly no President since that time has chosen to use it.

In addition, when the Warren Commission was formed to whitewash, sorry 'investigate' Kennedy's death, one of the Commission members was none other than John J McCloy, President of the Chase Manhattan Bank and the World Bank and member of the Federal Reserve board. Now why would this be? What on earth has a presidential murder investigation to do with banking? I really do wonder.

These are but a few small examples and are representative of a tiny fraction only, of the prevailing, insidious agenda. These and many other issues will be covered in more detail throughout this book, leading to the inescapable conclusion that they are all deeply and intrinsically connected and not as they are made to appear, merely a series of unrelated, independent anomalies.

It has become a cliché, but it is nevertheless a truism to say that 'history is written by the victor'. However, it is also true to say that history is written and often surreptitiously re-written by those who own the printing presses and the rights of broadcasting information, which they use as a means of control and modification of the behaviour of populations. The significance of the fact that a mere six Elite families own and control 96% of the entire world's media organisations should not be lost here. All of the Western world's media obtain their versions of the news from two major sources only – Associated Press (AP) and Reuters, both owned by the usual suspects in the form of two related Elite families. How simple is it then to control the news and tell us only what they want us to know or believe and to mould our opinions to suit their agenda? Trust me; it is an absolute 'piece of cake' so to do.

But what if virtually the *whole* of the history of our species was distorted and inaccurate as well as our current reality not being as portrayed? What if so-called mainstream science, history and education could not be trusted to give us truthful interpretations of the universe around us? What if we humans were not whom we have been portrayed as being, by the prevailing wisdom, for centuries? What if we have all been lied-to on a scale that beggars belief, all our lives, not just about history and science, but also religion, politics, archaeology, anthropology and many other subjects?

This may seem like a bizarre series of rhetorical questions, but as strange as it sounds, many respected researchers outside the mainstream whose numbers are growing daily, believe that these questions are pertinent exactly to the state of affairs in existence today. Why are they outside the mainstream? Simply because as with most, if not all elements of modern life, mainstream thinking is under the strict control of this insidious, largely invisible Elite group who protect and enhance their own positions of money, power and influence by fabricating and maintaining a hugely distorted version of history and reality that suits their own agenda and keeps the 'huddled masses' in a tiny box of totally manufactured ignorance.

The world is a far, far different place to what one imagines or is conditioned to believe. We have in place as our 'norms', rigid, immutable laws of physics and the five-sense reality that most of us believe is the be-all-and-end-all of the universe, but our reality absolutely does not work in the way it is popularly portrayed. Anything at all is possible, yet we are all conditioned and mind-controlled from cradle to grave, to believe that the lies and distortions we are given by figures of authority and teachers are sacrosanct and unquestionable. However, there is much evidence emerging now that proves that the received wisdom regarding the nature of our 'reality' is false. For example, the power of thoughts and human consciousness to physically affect material substances, the interconnectedness of all physical and non-physical matter, remote-viewing and also the interchange-ability of cause and effect are areas to consider in this regard and these are but four small examples from a long list of potential others.

Also consider the fact that matter itself is far from being as is popularly described. An atom (of which all 'solid' matter in the universe is composed) consists of 99.999999%+ empty space with just a tiny nucleus in the centre and several even smaller electrons orbiting this insignificant nucleus. To illustrate this point, imagine that an atom is the size of a cathedral and then understand this; on the same scale, the nucleus would be the size of an apple seed, the electrons the size of grains of sand and the rest... empty space.

And all this is what 100% of the matter in the universe consists of? How can this arrangement possibly present an appearance of solidity? Everything is indeed all an illusion, but as Albert Einstein himself noted, "...the Universe is an illusion, but a persistent one, nevertheless".

In addition there is much compelling evidence emerging from many different scientific sources that human souls, far from existing only in spiritual or religious fantasies are in fact a real entity and live on after death, to be re-incarnated in another body, life after life for millennia as we all experience the learning process leading ultimately to perfection, that each individual life on Earth or indeed countless other worlds in other Universes gives us. I refer to the pioneering work of Dr. Michael Newton in this respect. It was Michael Newton who 'discovered' that our souls do live on after death by entering a different dimension known colloquially as 'spirit world' and he has backed-up this work by the meticulous recording of many thousands of individuals' hypnotherapeutic regressions into the spirit world itself and our 'lives between lives'. As outlandish as this may seem to anyone unfamiliar with his work, the evidence he and his colleagues have painstakingly amassed over four decades of research is virtually irrefutable, but as always completely ignored by the mainstream.

"Step by step and day by day, the claims of what must be real have become increasingly outrageous, as the history and excuses used to defend them have become more fragile, ridiculous and indefensible." Les Visible, musician and researcher

So, presenting us with a false version of reality is an intrinsic part of the way we are controlled. We are all part of an 'infinite consciousness' linking all sentient and indeed non-sentient entities together at a very basic, sub-atomic level. This is not simply my own speculation but the opinions of a growing number of independent-thinking 'mainstream' scientists and researchers. If we knew what power we really have as individuals and collectively as a species and what infinite possibilities exist it would be impossible to control us effectively, so a system has been devised and evolved which keeps us in ignorance in our narrow little 'box of reality' and if we question it or try to move outside of it, we are instantly slapped-down or ridiculed, not just by our masters but also by all the other 'sheeple', our peers and our 'gatekeepers'. And thus within this self-policing paradigm we find it difficult – if not impossible – to accept anything that is not part of our pre-programmed reality. Anything that appears to fall outside the narrow boundaries of what we have been told and accepted as absolute fact all our lives is regarded and treated as simply ludicrous by the 'ignorant masses' and I include in this term even those supposedly well-educated persons who 'benefitted' from a 'first-class education' at the world's premier Universities. Actually no, allow me to revise that, I would say *especially* those supposedly well-educated persons who 'benefitted' from a 'first class education' at the world's premier Universities, usually followed by a career in politics or an Elite corporate, scientific, medical or educational environment.

And of course any evidence presented, even backed by substantiated research and proof, that contradicts the official position is either blatantly ignored, subtly swept aside or ruthlessly destroyed to protect current, accepted wisdom and knowledge and thus the positions of those in whose best interests it is to deceive and manipulate us for their own nefarious ends.

As already stated, the world has been co-opted by a covert group, generally known as the Illuminati, or as I will refer to them in this book, the 'Elite'. This group has been in existence under several names and guises for several millennia and its central 'core' comprises of the same thirteen bloodlines that have remained virtually unchanged since Sumerian times and probably long before that. Since those times, these people have infiltrated and hijacked almost every aspect of human life, including governments and the multi-national corporations, to ensure that they remain in control of all humanity and they have lied on a grand scale, cheated, stolen, manipulated, murdered and committed genocide throughout all recorded history, in order to facilitate, sustain and further the continuance of their own power-base and immense wealth.

"At present, more than 90 percent of the world's wealth, in a world of six billion people, is controlled by less than 10,000 individuals, mostly from two dozen families who can trace their blueblood lineage back many hundreds of years. At the head of the line is the Rothschild family, which controls all the others. It has been estimated that the aggregate Rothschild wealth is at a minimum 5,000 times greater than the annual gross national product of the United States, although it's difficult to calculate, because the Rothschild octopus (and its loyal lieutenants of the Rockefeller family) literally own the US money supply, the Federal Reserve and all the major banks of the Western world. Henry Kissinger is the chief lieutenant of David Rockefeller, who is the American commissar of the Rothschild Empire which runs just about everything. There are no real enemies, only those created by the powers that be to create the chaotic conditions to both cull the population and profit from the sales of weapons to both sides. It has been that way throughout the 20th century, and doubtless long before." John Kaminski, independent researcher

These people do not represent any single country, race, political persuasion or religion. Rather they are a hybrid of all of these elements, transcending all countries, races and religions. In fact a good case can be made for suggesting that countries, racial divisions, political divides and religions were actually manufactured by them as part of a plan to 'divide and conquer' which has long been a central plank of their strategy for the total subjugation of mankind.

If you believe that senior politicians, prime ministers and presidents control the destiny of the world, think again. These people are merely puppets of the Elite, bought-and-paid-for lackeys who occupy the lower fringes of the Elite pyramid. They are often groomed from birth, often because of bloodline, to fulfil their apparent positions of 'power' and are controlled by the threat of losing their lucrative positions of apparent influence (and worse); such is the forward and long-term strategic planning of this cabal. They are nothing if not extremely patient in the pursuit of their master-plan for absolute and total world domination.

"I have this feeling man, cos you know there's a handful of people actually run everything. That's true, it's provable. A handful, a very small elite group run and own these corporations, which include the mainstream media. I have this feeling whoever's elected President, ...no matter what you promise on the campaign trail, 'blah, blah, blah', when you win, you go into this smoky room in the basement of the White House with the twelve industrialist, capitalist scum-f**ks who got you in there and you're in this smoky room and the little screen comes down and a big guy with a cigar says 'roll the film'. And it's a shot of the Kennedy assassination from an angle you've never seen before... that looks suspiciously off the grassy knoll. And then the film ends, the screen goes up and the lights come on and they say to the new guy, 'Any questions Mr. President?'" Bill Hicks, comedian, shortly before his premature death from cancer in 1994

"World events do not happen by accident, they are made to happen. Whether it is to do with national issues or commerce, they are staged and managed by those who hold the purse strings". Denis Healey, former British deputy Prime Minister, Chancellor of the Exchequer and member of the secretive Elite-run and controlled Bilderberg group who are in effect the *real* world political policy-makers.

So what exactly is their clearly-stated and documented 'master-plan'? It is actually nothing less than total control of all of the Earth's resources, finances, military and populations. Their aim is to create a society that would make the world described by George Orwell in '1984' and Aldous Huxley in 'Brave New World', look like a summer Sunday afternoon picnic. They plan to impose a world-wide military dictatorship via the mandatory micro-chipping of all, a reduction of population to less than 500 million (95% less than the current figure), a fascist-communitarian one-world government, a one-world-bank cashless-society linked to your implanted micro-chip and a society of slaves (the ones 'lucky' enough to survive the cull) controlled by mind-altering chemicals and both subcutaneously implanted and remote electronics, to serve them and their families. All this of course would then be controlled and enforced by a one-world army. This is exactly where we are headed and soon, unless the world wakes up to their sordid scheme.

Everything that happens in the world is but one tiny step further down the road to achieving this hellish scenario. They are not so stupid as to make the mistake of trying to achieve their nefarious ends by making radical changes in a series of giant leaps, rather they use the tactic of metaphorically speaking, 'keeping the frog in the pot' by heating the water one degree at a time instead of throwing the frog straight into the boiling water, as it would very quickly escape, albeit badly scalded. This is a tactic described aptly and succinctly by researcher David Icke as the *'totalitarian tiptoe'*.

It is probably worth relating at this point that the protection of the mainstream view is also self-policing to a very large extent. Most research of a scientific nature, indeed most research of any kind is usually funded by *either* government *or* more often by private commercial interests. In either case, scientists will not receive research funding unless they are prepared to produce results that reflect the desired outcome of the paymaster. This may be a cynical view, but it is one which has been proven to be absolutely true over the long term. Indeed, given the circumstances, it would only be remarkable if the truth was the diametric opposite of this.

There is a large group of people out there who do not believe anything that contradicts their own, already-established world-view, despite what evidence can be brought to bear that shows it to be incorrect.

'No credible evidence' and 'where is the proof?' are the constant weapons used against whatever argument is put forward. This is an almost classic position for a 'sceptic' or 'skeptic' if you prefer and as well as being used by those who automatically gainsay anything and everything that does not match their belief system, is a classic tactic used by professional shills and gatekeepers in their attempts to prevent the real truth from seeping into the mainstream.

If you have never encountered the term 'shill' before, this is someone who is an agent of disinformation, someone who deliberately plants or promotes false information or provides false evidence to discredit so-called 'conspiracy theories' in order to deceive and deflect from the truth. For example they may inhabit Internet forums to hijack discussions or even have their own TV/radio shows to spread false 'truths' that have the appearance of being anti-establishment in order to apportion the blame away from those really responsible. They are usually paid handsomely for doing so and all shills worth their name, or at least their paymasters, know that 'proof' is an illusion and use this to their advantage at every given opportunity. The problem with this constant demand for proof is that as any first year student of philosophy will tell us, absolute proof of anything is a completely unattainable goal.

By way of an example, if someone is shot in the chest and dies how do we know that it was the actual bullet entering the body that killed them? Stupid question you may say perhaps, but in reality the best we can hope for is to say that on the greater **balance of probability** it was the bullet that killed them. Other possibilities, no matter how negligible are that they were killed by the utter shock of being shot before the bullet could inflict any physical damage or that they were killed by a blood clot to the heart at exactly the same time as the bullet hit and which was subsequently destroyed by the bullet, creating an impression that it was the bullet impact that caused death. Highly unlikely obviously, but **not** impossible and that is the key issue. All this may be a little tenuous perhaps, but the point I am attempting to make is that 100% absolute, cast-iron proof of anything is an illusion. What we all believe to be true is based purely on our own personal experience and belief system and also what we believe to be the balance of probability – sometimes an exceptionally high 99:1 and sometimes 51:49, but I do not believe that 100:0 is ever possible, in-line with the basic tenets of philosophy. However most people's lifetime of programming does not allow them to consider or even be aware of this fact.

This pre-programmed mind-set is exceptionally prevalent in academia also. Supposedly 'intelligent', well-educated members of the scientific, political, commercial, media and educational communities possess opinions that have been moulded by decades of propaganda from primary school through University, backed up by the self-over-estimation of their own intelligence, influenced in no small measure by society's misleading norm that presents 'knowledge' as synonymous with 'intelligence'. To try to break that programming by offering up strong circumstantial evidence and alternative, considered hypotheses about anything that contradicts their mind-set, is often an impossible task.

For example, in recent 'research', performed by Chris French BA PhD CPsychol FBPsS FRSA of Goldsmith's College, University of London (impressive credentials eh?) he determined that; *"Those who trust authority are less likely to believe in conspiracies and those who distrust authority are more likely to believe in conspiracies."* Money and time well spent there, then Chris.

Obvious really is it not? If anyone distrusts authority then it is common-sense to assume that they are less likely to believe what they are told by them, but is not this all really missing the point? Surely the real question should be not under what circumstances are people more or less likely to believe in 'conspiracies', but whether or not those 'conspiracies' are supported by credible evidence. However in the fantasy-world according to the likes of Dr. French, 'conspiracies' are obviously not real, they exist only as a result of a fault in their believers' psyches.

According to French also, believers in conspiracies were "more likely to be delusional" than those who did not believe in them. French defined 'delusional' as for example those people who answered 'yes' when asked questions such as 'do you believe you are being tracked by your mobile phone'? Again, is that not a circular 'proof' of what is after all only his opinion, or is it just me who is marching out of step?

There is no attempt made to even consider the question of whether it is possible to be tracked by mobile phones or even whether it is actually happening, which are the real issues to my mind, but then I do not have an impressively long list of letters after my name, accompanied by a position at one of the world's premier seats of education, so it naturally follows in the mind-sets of these people (and indeed most people per se, who have been conditioned to believe that educational qualifications equal intelligence) that it must be my logic that is faulty.

When French was confronted on his illogical views by a well-known so-called 'conspiracy' researcher and author, French told him that there was 'no evidence' for what this researcher was saying in his many well-researched books on the topic of a global conspiracy to impose a 'New World Order'. The response to this by the said researcher was to ask if he had ever read any of his books (which by the way contain an absolute mountain of evidence to support his assertions) and was told 'no'. How very typical. These people are not interested in circumstantial proof or evidence if it goes against their set-in-stone mind-sets or presents a viewpoint that contradicts their unassailable opinions and yet they will openly accuse their detractors of exactly the same tactics.

In my experience, people who refuse to look at both sides of the argument have no high moral ground or even credibility at all. I have met dozens of these people over the years, people who have only ever seen the view of reality as propounded by the mainstream and yet dismiss one's own position as being 'ludicrous' or 'crazy' despite the fact that I am the one who has looked at two sides of the coin in order to formulate my opinion and not simply just one side, as they have.

There is a famous organisation known as the 'Sceptics Society' devoted to 'promoting scientific scepticism and resisting the spread of pseudoscience, superstition and irrational beliefs'. It is an assumption among most people that it is 'healthy' to be sceptical, but I believe that to be untrue, if not downright misleading.

It is healthy to question and research controversial issues, but that is not the same as scepticism whose adherents maintain a fixed position and then filter-out all evidence that does not fit that stance. They will always attempt to find another means of explaining away something that challenges their immutable beliefs and it is almost irrelevant whether or not that argument is illogical or contradicted by the evidence or not, just so long as it allows them a 'get-out clause' to maintain their fixed view.

In any case, we should ask who decides what is 'pseudoscience, superstition and irrational beliefs'? The answer is that they themselves do, of course and so we find ourselves back within the circular logic-trap again. They devote themselves to protecting the so-called scientific and societal norms and received wisdom, to which they cling with almost touching loyalty and vociferously attack anyone who dares to question them and/or put forward an alternative viewpoint, no matter how well-researched or pertinent it may be.

"That's what a closed mind does for you. You don't research to discover anew; you research to confirm your current beliefs. Most of academia is another religion, another belief system repelling all boarders. Academia often condemns and ridicules religion when it is one [itself] and operates in the same way. What unites all religions? Concrete minds." David Icke, geopolitical researcher

Unfortunately, all of academia has almost completely abandoned the core principles of good science in their disturbing quest to make money at all costs for their corporate paymasters, ultimately the Elite bloodlines. Rather than asking pertinent questions of nature and relating and accurately interpreting the answers provided by the data, these 'scientists' plot the desired outcome based on pre-determined criteria and then defend it at all costs, even if this necessitates the misrepresentation, falsification and distortion of data and thus results, to achieve their ends.

"The downfall of 'science' is upon us. Eroded by the intellectual dishonesty of those who promote GMOs, pesticides, vaccines and fluoride in the name of 'science', the reputation of science itself has lost tremendous ground over the last few years. Even though I am scientifically educated, I believe today's misappropriation of 'science' for corporate greed is perhaps the most destructive, pathological force that has yet been unleashed upon human civilization." Mike Adams, Natural News, January 2011

To say that this approach to research is entirely *unscientific* is an understatement of some magnitude. It would appear to be that in all disciplines, Elite, corporate profits, personal prestige and maintaining the 'illusion' are far more important than accurate conclusions. Whether we are discussing archaeology, astronomy, mathematics, anthropology, physics, biology, chemistry, history or virtually anything else you can name, the huge majority of scientists and academics will do whatever it takes to defend their pre-determined positions and protect their own livelihoods and interests and of course, those of their employers, ultimately the Elite families when traced to the top of the pyramid. No wonder it is virtually impossible to penetrate the barriers erected by medical professionals with the real facts about vitamin D, sunscreen lotion and cancer for example. These 'scientific-thinkers' have already had their 'beliefs' instilled by the Elite-owned pharmaceutical cartel's propaganda and they will steadfastly defend those beliefs even to the detriment of the health and well-being of their patients and the human race as a whole.

Today's scientists unfortunately, are not even *trained* to be truly scientific thinkers. They are often just indoctrinated followers of a particular vested interest's own private cult (usually the Elite's, when traced back to source). For example, some 'scientists' belong to the Cult of Pharmacology and they believe (or so they would have *us* believe) that pharmacological solutions are the answer to all health issues and that natural remedies are mere 'quackery'. Whilst others belong, for example, to the Cult of Climatology, where scientific evidence proving that global-warming is not human-caused or linked to CO_2 emissions, is ignored or replaced with 'facts' that are not allowed to be questioned and are repeated ad nauseum by the controlled media and complicit corporate interests, until we poor, deluded souls assume that they must be true.

Science rarely advances based entirely on new research, new ideas and data. Instead, these new discoveries often founder against an impenetrable barrier erected by the established scientific community in protection of their own positions and at the behest of their all-powerful masters. Sometimes, new ideas may be consigned to the background for decades or even centuries before finally being seriously considered by the scientific community as worthy of being adopted as 'truth' and so the cycle continues on. A classic example of this was the ruthlessly enforced 'Earth as the centre of the Universe' belief that was eventually replaced with the current sun-centric solar system model but not before many scientists and philosophers were condemned and even killed for their unacceptable belief that the Earth was not the centre of the Universe. Indeed it appears to be the case that 'new' ideas, provable or not, are only accepted once the surrounding infrastructure is adjusted accordingly over time to accommodate them within the controlled paradigm.

"It is often the case that the more you know, the more you realise you don't know. In other words, you see that so many assumptions of knowledge were just that - assumptions. This is the same for everyone to an extent, because there is so much to know, but with mainstream science it is part of the very fabric of the way it operates. The disease of tuberculosis used to be known as consumption, but science is infected with the disease of 'assumption'. The assumptions are then constantly repeated; appear in the school books, technical and science journals, and morph, simply through repetition, into accepted 'everybody-knows-that, fact'. But it's not; and if we are going to understand anything about reality, who we are and where we are, we don't need textbooks full of assumptions - we need blank sheets of paper and open minds. We live on a planet orbiting the sun with a few others, but we know next to nothing about any of it. The more technology explores the Solar System the clearer it becomes that

previous scientific (actually unscientific) assumptions were wrong and often way out."
David Icke, researcher, June 2011

For good examples of 'assumption' becoming de facto reality, consider the following **non-facts;** the 'Big Bang' theory, human evolution from apes and the dinosaurs being wiped-out by a meteorite, theory. Ask almost anyone in the world how the Universe came about, how our species developed or how the dinosaurs died-out and they will invariably spout the above 'party-lines' without even considering that these are not established, proven-beyond-all-doubt facts but merely theories – and all fairly insubstantial ones at that. And please bear in mind that these are just three small examples of the information taught to our children in school as indisputable 'facts'.

The 'Big Bang' theory for example, is based upon the premise that gravity is the strongest of the 'universal' forces known to physicists (the Standard Model) and yet even a small fridge magnet can lift-up a paperclip in defiance of the gravitational pull of the entire Earth. If we were to imagine our Sun as a speck of dust, the next nearest star would be another speck of dust around four miles away and yet if we consider the gravitational attraction between two grains of dust four miles apart, that is the miniscule force which the Standard Model relies upon to account for most of the workings of our universe.   It all seems somehow more than a little unconvincing to me, but if any mainstream scientist speaks out on that or any other 'accepted truth', he will be dismissed from his position, denied research funding and will find it difficult if not impossible to secure gainful employment anywhere.

All of this totally discredits the widely-accepted, but in my view at best, highly debatable idea that science is the ultimate fount of knowledge. There are many ways to gain knowledge about the world around us and mainstream science is but one of the least convincing of them. Other less conventionally accepted methods include such as meditation, communing with nature, hypnosis, astrology (true astrology and not the execrable, popularised version) or even spiritual journeys with the help of psychotropic plant extracts and I for one would humbly venture to suggest that these routes to personal knowledge and wisdom are the more reliable ones, regardless of the fact that all of these methods are either ridiculed and/or legislated against by the mainstream.   In short, science has totally failed us, deliberately so I believe as it concentrates its efforts solely on the physical and it has never so much as attempted or even come close to providing answers on important, esoteric issues such as the meaning of life, the nature of human consciousness and the nature and purpose of the human soul. To do so would only jeopardise the power of the Elite by imparting knowledge of our true natures and thus empowering the masses.

*"The Universe is not only stranger than you may suppose, it is stranger than you **can** suppose."* J P S Haldane, geneticist

Science will *never* answer our questions as long as it is run by a profit-focused, Elite-controlled scientific community that has no real interest in truth-seeking and really only exists in any case, to serve the interests of the Elite families in the generating of obscene profits and to maintain the false reality they have carefully created and nurtured and not as they would have you believe, for the furtherance of human knowledge or to create a 'better world' for us all.

So, where does all this radical and possibly confusing information leave us? To discover the complete truth, please read the rest of this book. I am sure you can now see that a chillingly different picture of the world as it is really is beginning to emerge as the ancient bloodlines' desperate race to complete their great 'work of ages' now shifts into high gear.

But, if this all sounds like the ramblings of a lunatic, then this book is probably not for you and I would respectfully suggest that you replace it back in its place on the shelf and go 'back to sleep' along with the rest of the populace. Before you take that drastic step though, it may just be worthwhile to investigate some of the claims I have made in the preceding pages. Since the advent of the Internet, this task has been made much easier for us all and even a cursory search of the topics I have touched-upon will prove extremely revealing.

If however, these words have stirred something within your soul and awakened an interest or a desire to find out more and/or actually do something about it, even if only for the sake of the future of your own children and *their* children, then please read on. By adopting a completely open-minded approach to the many, often deeply disturbing aspects of the huge conspiracy I am about to reveal in the forthcoming pages, the truth will indeed set you free, to paraphrase what someone once famously said......

Evolution – the greatest deception of our times?

"Of course, only a fool would question the theory of evolution, even though the theory is most closely associated with a man who, along with other members of his clan, was a key figure in the eugenics movement and even though the concept of natural selection just happens to nicely compliment the eugenics agenda, which in turn, dovetails nicely with the agenda of the 'peak oil' crowd, whose theory, as we all know, rests upon the notion of oil as a 'fossil fuel,' which is taken as a given by most of the scientific community, which just goes to show you, I suppose, that you shouldn't always listen to the scientific community." David McGowan, 25th July 2006

Are the origins of the human race really what we have been taught and assumed all our lives to be true? The received wisdom, relayed to our grand-parents, parents, ourselves and our children, is that we all evolved from single-celled organisms, born of amino acids combining together in the 'primordial soup', through a series of greater and more complex organisms to the ape-like creatures that were our supposed ancestors and thence to human beings. No arguments or discussions as to the veracity or proof of this proposition are tolerated. It is a fact, end of story – period. Accept it or be ridiculed and worse.

I believe that this is an absurd and monstrous deception and that we are no more descended directly from single-celled creatures or even apes than we are from unicorns or goblins. Evolution, or to be more precise the '**theory** of evolution' is exactly that, a theory and an extremely tenuous one at that. There is a veritable mountain of evidence to contradict this premise and also to suggest that Darwin was part of the overall conspiracy and grand deception that continues to this day. He is even rumoured by some sources to have confessed in anguish in his last days, to the hoax he was instrumental in inflicting on a gullible humanity and indeed some of his quoted statements late in his life directly bear-out that premise.

My research has personally led me to believe that evolution was conceived and promoted deliberately as a way of discrediting and thus replacing organised religion as a belief system. By the second half of the nineteenth century, organised, mainstream religion was just beginning to lose its vice-like grip as a control mechanism of the subdued masses and there was a small but growing band of people who were questioning the unthinkable – was Christianity or indeed any religion, the truth after all? To combat this dangerous turn of events, what was needed was another false creed to supplant organised religion. It does not matter to the Elite what false paradigms we believe in, just so long as we believe in *something*, anything that will lead us away from the real truth. So, in the mid-nineteenth century, they simply decided to replace their fading, old-fashioned myth of faith-based creationism with something more in line with the fashionable, brave new world of scientific discoveries, hence the more credible, modern, 'scientific' myth of evolution. As alluded-to previously, it is also, I believe, more than coincidence that the theory of evolution was not only originally propounded by Elite eugenicists but also that the tenets of evolutionary dogma nicely complement the fundamental principles of eugenics.

"The model of human prehistory built-up by scholars over the past two centuries is sadly and completely wrong, and a deliberate tool of disinformation and mind control." Michael Cremo and Richard L Thompson, 'The Hidden History of the Human Race'

This extremely revealing book, exhibits in great detail and with literally thousands of case studies and examples, how we have been duped into believing that homo-sapiens as a species is much less than one million years old and is a product of macro-evolution from apes. However Cremo and Thompson have uncovered literally hundreds of examples of mainstream archaeological cover-up operations, to prevent the truth becoming widely known. And that truth is simply that there are in existence many, many examples of human remains, **some dating back several hundred million years**! One simple example:

"In Macoupin County, Illinois, the bones of a human were recently found on a coal-bed capped with two feet of slate rock, ninety feet below the surface of the Earth. The bones, when found, were covered with a crust or coating of hard glossy matter, as black as coal itself, but when scraped away left the bones white and natural." 'The Geologist' magazine, December 1862

This coal was at least 286 million years old and may be as old as 320 million years, way, way beyond any timescales admitted by the mainstream regarding the possible antiquity of our species. Any such discoveries these days are never reported in the mainstream media, despite there being thousands of examples constantly occurring.

Interestingly, this distortion of facts in an attempt to 'prove' a huge falsehood to be the truth, has resulted in the classic, Hegelian 'evolution versus creation' argument to keep us all busy and distracted from searching for the actual truth. In other words, never mind the real facts, let's all waste our time arguing the rights and wrongs of two false creeds. Strange is it not that if one does not subscribe to the religion of evolution, then one is automatically dubbed a 'creationist' with all the negative connotations and inherent stupidity and ignorance that this has been manipulated and engineered to imply?

It is also known that Dr. Thomas Henry Huxley, a stalwart of the Elite establishment, Fellow of the Royal Society and a prominent Freemason, strongly encouraged and even cajoled Charles Darwin to publish his theory. Huxley would eventually become the 'official spokesman' for Darwin and even became known as 'Darwin's Bulldog', such was his forceful assertions of the truth of the theory. He was also the grandfather of Aldous Huxley, the author of *'Brave New World'* a novel written in the 1930s that demonstrates an uncannily accurate depiction of a future society of oppressed masses in a similar vein to Orwell's '1984'. Another grandson was Julian Huxley, famous as the first secretary-general of UNESCO, a branch of the Elite-controlled United Nations. Coincidence? I shall let the reader draw his/her own conclusions.

Already I can almost hear the calls for me to be burned at the stake for daring to question the great religion of evolution – for that is what it has become to so many people. I do not suggest for one moment that localised evolving of bodily features and functions of certain creatures (micro-evolution) does not take place over millennia in order to adapt to surroundings and for example, fine-tuning defences against predators. To suggest that, would be just as absurd. However, to believe that whole new species are created from others or from virtually nothing (macro-evolution) when the abundant, contrary evidence is examined seems too far-fetched and unscientific to be anything but an elaborate hoax and a deliberate deception, perpetuated by wholesale propaganda.

"The known fossil record fails to document a single example of evolution accomplishing a major transition - every palaeontologist knows that most species don't change." Stephen Gould, evolutionary biologist, Harvard University 1980.

"I am not satisfied that Darwin proved his point or that his influence in scientific and public thinking has been beneficial. The success of Darwinism was accomplished by a decline in scientific integrity." W.R. Thompson, Canadian scientist.

"... as by this theory, innumerable transitional forms must have existed. Why do we not find them embedded in the crust of the earth? Why is not all nature in a confusion of halfway species instead of being, as we see them, well-defined species?" Charles Darwin.

Darwin's own answer to this particular question was that there had been insufficient time since his theory was espoused to thoroughly check the available fossil records. Interesting hypothesis yes, but now proven to be totally incorrect. We have now had almost another 150 years since the death of Darwin to rectify this inconvenient fact, but evolutionary 'science' is no further forward in this respect than it was in the 1860s.

"Just as pre-Darwinian biology was carried out by people whose faith was in the Creator and His plan, post-Darwinian biology is being carried out by people whose faith is in, almost, the deity of Darwin. They've seen their task as to elaborate his theory and to fill the gaps in it, to fill the trunk and twigs of the tree. But it seems to me that the theoretical framework has very little impact on the actual progress of the work in biological research. In a way some aspects of Darwinism and of neo-Darwinism seem to me to have held back the progress of science." Colin Patterson, senior palaeontologist, the Museum of Natural History, London

"Not many scientists are willing to risk their livelihood to point out the facts. They remain mute, mouthing the party line when necessary in order to keep their positions. Those illogical arguments mouthed by the scientists then fuel misunderstanding among those who are unable to double-check the truth and logic behind the theory of evolution." Duncan Long.

And, remarkably...

"Not one change of species into another is on record. We cannot prove that a single species has changed into another." Charles Darwin, 'My Life and Letters', Vol. 1, page 210

That contemporary, great champion of evolutionary myth and dogma, Professor Richard Dawkins, latterly of the Elite-funded and controlled, great educational propaganda machine, Oxford University and author of 'The Selfish Gene' and 'The God Delusion', wastes no time in denouncing, belittling and even insulting anyone who dares question the great pseudo-religion of evolution. Why would this be? Why is it such a crime or heresy to question or debate widely-held scientific beliefs? Is Dawkins an evolutionist per se or simply anti-religion, choosing evolution as the only viable alternative? This of course is the classic Hegelian trap. Present two options to choose from, neither of them correct, whilst encouraging the masses to pick their favourite and debate the pros and cons until we lose sight of the real issue. We should ask why the mainstream media even allows Dawkins a platform for his mostly disingenuous tirades, whilst denying it to those who espouse the contrary view in a more considered, rational or scientific way. Dawkins' ironically, somewhat evangelical–type arguments have brought him largely unreported ridicule from many quarters with even the hard-line Darwinian, Michael Ruse suggesting that Dawkins' rants make him feel *"embarrassed to be an atheist"*.

"When you find issues/controversies which people love to debate endlessly, which are emotionally inflammatory and which divide the masses into oppositional stances/groups, it is a pretty strong possibility that the controlling elites might be busy behind the scenes, fomenting these quarrels and keeping them alive." kennysideshow.blogspot.com 15th November 2011

Could Dawkins, knowingly or un-knowingly be a puppet of the Elite, a so-called 'shill' or 'useful idiot' who is discreetly encouraged to spread his dis-information to as wide an audience as possible? If so, he certainly would not be the first nor the last, one suspects.

Richard Milton was initially an ardent believer in Darwinian doctrine until he began to investigate the myths and legends of evolutionary theory in depth. After 20 years of studying and writing about evolution, he realised that there were many anomalous elements in the theory. He therefore decided to put every main classic 'proof' of Darwinism to the test. His results left him stunned at first. He found that the theory could not even stand up to the rigours of even rudimentary investigative journalism. Eventually, he published a book titled *"The Facts of Life: Shattering the Myths of Darwinism"*.

"I experienced the witch-hunting activity of the Darwinist police at first hand – it was deeply disappointing to find myself being described by the prominent Oxford zoologist, Richard Dawkins, as 'loony', 'stupid' and 'in need of psychiatric help' in response to purely scientific reporting." Richard Milton

Do we detect shades of the Soviet Union in the 20th century, when so-called dissident scientists there began speaking out against the diktats and manufactured reality of Stalin's regime?

If all the preceding assertions are true, this all begs the question, 'what is the point of the deception'? If someone goes to all that trouble to make sure we believe something that is not and cannot be proven, there must be a reason for it and a hidden agenda behind it. Indeed, this simple test can be applied to anything but in this case the overwhelmingly obvious conclusion is that it is done in order to deceive and therefore impose and maintain control by taking advantage of the lack of knowledge of the real truth of our origins and purpose as a species.

Fossil records constitute the primary source for the evolutionists in searching for evidence for the theory of evolution. The fossil records certainly contain the remains of past human beings but when these are examined objectively, it may be seen that the records themselves are in no way in favour of evolutionary theory, but rather against it, contrary to the assertions of the evolutionists. However, since these fossils are incorrectly portrayed by the evolutionists and presented for public opinion with the intent of fulfilling pre-conceived ideas; many people are fooled into incorrectly believing that the fossil records actually *verify* the theory of evolution.

The evolutionists disingenuously use the fact that findings of fossil records are open to many different interpretations, to their own advantage and as 'proof' of their own assertions. The discovered fossils are usually not sufficient to make a firm analysis, but are generally comprised of incomplete and fragmented bone pieces. This is why it is so simple for them to distort the available data and use them fraudulently to portray the desired objectives.

Belief in the theory of evolution has come to be seen as almost a life-style choice, a mode of thinking, even an ideology rather than just simply a theory like any other by its evangelical defenders who do not deem it necessary to take steps to prevent the distorting of data or even the committing of more serious, deliberate forgeries. Indeed, extremist advocates of evolutionary ideology do not hesitate to undertake any kind of distortion necessary in order to interpret the fossil records in favour of evolutionary theory. It is a classical scientific mistake to build any kind of theoretical framework from the basis of an incorrect initial assumption and yet I believe that this fundamental 'mistake' is made time after time by the proponents of evolutionary theory.

"Theory shapes the way we think about, even perceive, data... We are unaware of many of our assumptions. In the course of rethinking my ideas about human evolution, I have changed somewhat as a scientist. I am aware of the prevalence of implicit assumptions and try harder to dig them out of my own thinking. Theories have, in the past, clearly reflected our current ideologies instead of the actual data... I am more sombre than I once was about what the unwritten past can tell us." David Pilbeam, anthropologist, Harvard University

It is true that ideological expectations can and do influence the interpretation of any given data set and the fact that fossil records are open to many different interpretations raises doubts on the reliability of the whole science of paleo-anthropology which is mostly under the control of the evolutionists. Certain prejudices and expectations will undoubtedly have an impact on the veracity of data extrapolation.

"...We then move right off the register of objective truth into those fields of presumed biological science, like extra-sensory perception or the interpretation of man's fossil history, where to the faithful anything is possible - and where the ardent believer is sometimes able to believe several contradictory things at the same time." Sir Solly Zuckerman, palaeontologist at Birmingham University, England

Since fossil records are usually unorganised and incomplete, the estimations based on them are inevitably totally speculative. As a matter of fact, the reconstructions (drawings or models) made by evolutionists based on the fossil remains are often treated in a speculative way in consort with the evolutionary theory. Since most people are more easily influenced by visual rather than written data, the aim of evolutionists is to entice them to believe that these reconstructed creatures have really existed in the past.

For this reason alone, the reconstructions of fossils and skulls are always designed to meet the needs of the evolutionary theory. Evolutionist researchers often set out from a single tooth, a mandibular fragment or even a tiny bone of the arm, draw semi-human-like imaginary creatures and then present these to the public sensationally as a link in the evolution of man. These drawings and reconstructions have indeed played an important role in the visualisation of the 'primitive man' image in the minds of people.

Reconstructions based on the bone remains can only reveal the general characteristics of the object at hand. Yet, the real defining details are soft tissues often muscles or tendons that do not leave an impression in the rocks as they decay too rapidly. Therefore, with the speculative interpretation of the soft tissues, the reconstructed drawing or model becomes totally dependent upon the imagination of the person constructing it.

"To attempt to restore the soft parts is an even more hazardous undertaking. The lips, the eyes, the ears, and the nasal tip, leave no clues on the underlying bony parts. You can with equal facility, model on a Neanderthaloid skull the features of a chimpanzee or the lineaments of a philosopher. These alleged restorations of ancient types of a man have very little if any scientific value and are likely only to mislead the public... So put not your trust in reconstructions." Ernst A. Hooten, Harvard University

Indeed, evolutionists invent such ridiculous stories that they even ascribe different faces to the same skull. For example, three different reconstructed drawings made for the fossil named *Australopithecus robustus*, is a famous example of such a forgery.

A group of evolutionists who could not find any substantial evidence in the fossil records to support their at best, tenuous beliefs, actually decided to create their own evidence themselves. Some of these studies were even included in text books under titles such as 'evolution conspiracies' and this is probably a good clue to the fact that the theory of evolution is an ideology or a life philosophy that has to be contrived to be kept alive by considerable effort.

A well-known doctor and amateur palaeontologist, Charles Dawson announced in 1912 that he had found a jaw bone and a cranial fragment in a pit in Piltdown, Sussex, England. Despite the fact that the jaw bone was ape-like, the teeth and the skull were similar to a human's. These specimens were designated by science as 'Piltdown Man', determined to be dated to half a million years ago and depicted as absolute 'proof' of the evolution of man for more than 40 years. Many scientific articles were written about the artefacts, many interpretations and drawings were made and it was presented as important evidence and taught as undeniable proof of the macro-evolution of mankind.

The discovery of 'Piltdown-man' engendered massive enthusiasm in paleo-anthropological circles and gave birth to many new debates which automatically assumed that evolution was absolute fact.   For example, the famous English anthropologist, G. E. Smith pondered... "Did the brain or body of man evolve first?"

In 1949, Kenneth Oakley from the palaeontology department of the British Museum in London devised the 'fluorine test' to determine the date of fossils. When the test was performed on the Piltdown-man fossil, the subsequent result was shocking. It was proved conclusively that the jaw-bone of Piltdown-man contained no fluorine and this therefore indicated that the bone was underground no more than a relatively few short years and was therefore obviously a fraud. In addition, the skull itself contained a small amount of fluorine, enough to determine that it was a few thousand years old, only. It was also proved by the tests that the jaw-bone and the skull came from two entirely separate creatures and time-periods and must therefore be a deliberate hoax.

"The latest chronological researches made with the fluorine method revealed that the [Piltdown] skull was only a few thousand years old. It was manifest that the teeth in the jaw bone belonging to an orang-utan were worn out artificially and the primitive tools found next to the fossils were simple imitations sharpened by steel devices."
Kenneth Oakley, palaeontologist, the British Museum, London

Alongside these fossils were found some extinct elephant fossils and some tool remains made out of the bones of the same elephant species. These elephant fossils were used in the dating of the skull and in the tests it was understood that these elephant fossils were indeed very ancient. However, the jaw bone and the skull were much more recent than the elephant fossils. What then was the significance of these facts? It was surmised that the Piltdown ivory fossil had probably been found in

Africa and then deliberately placed in the Piltdown site to give the impression that the false skull was as old as the elephant fossil in order to mislead. As the researchers studied the other animal fossils found in the same region in more depth, they found that these were also placed there with the deliberate intention of deception and the Piltdown bone tool was eventually discovered to be an elephant fossil shaped with a steel knife.

However, the hoax could still be regarded as a raging success by the evolutionists in as much as it had propagandised the population for almost half a century into a definitive belief of evolutionary myth and the Elite know very well that once any beliefs become deeply entrenched in the human psyche then even subsequent absolute proof to the contrary will not necessarily remove or diminish them.

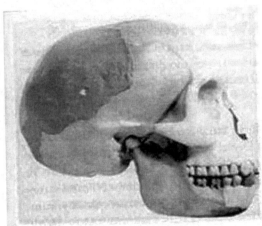

Piltdown man skull

This fake fossil that occupied the evolutionist circles for a many years, demonstrates the lengths to which those who desire to prove the theory of evolution at all costs are prepared to go. Why would this be? Why would anyone fake scientific evidence? I suggest that it is done (in this case at least) to provide hard evidence of the proof of evolutionary theory in the absence of any other real or tangible facts that would verify it. This in itself speaks volumes to my mind.

After the detailed analysis completed by Kenneth Oakley, William le Gros Clark and J. S. Weiner, this forgery was eventually made public in 1953. The skull was discovered to be human and was a mere 500 years old and the jaw-bone was from a recently deceased ape. The teeth had been specially arranged and added separately to the jaw and the tooth sockets were set in such a way as to resemble those of a human. All these individual elements were then deceptively stained with potassium-dichromate to give them the false appearance of great age. These stains disappeared when the skull was dipped in acid.

There was also much evidence of artificial abrasion that in hindsight was so obvious that it begged the question; how had it escaped the notice of experienced palaeontologists for forty years? Sir Solly Zuckerman's view was...

"As I have already implied, students of fossil primates have not been distinguished by caution when working within the logical constraints of their subject. The record is so astonishing that it is legitimate to ask whether much science is yet to be found in this field at all."

However, in my view, the story of the Piltdown-man fraud provides a pretty good answer to that question.

So, the 'theory' of evolution is based on the hypothesis that contemporary man today has evolved from his primate ancestors, diversifying from them between 4 and 10 million years ago. Although no definitive consensus has yet been reached by the evolutionary researchers, the generally accepted list of ancestors of humans reads as follows:

Australopithecus or 'southern ape'
Homo habilis or 'tool using man'
Homo erectus or 'upright man'
Archaic Homo Sapiens or 'old modern man'
Homo sapiens or 'modern man'

According to the evolutionists the first ape ancestors of man, *Australopithecus* were creatures which had some human-like but possessed mostly ape-like characteristics. Some branches of the *Australopithecus* have allegedly become extinct and the others developed into the Homo (human) strain. Evolutionists also insist that *Homo erectus* and its subsequent incarnations were almost identical with contemporary man.

Today there are over 200 species of apes still extant. However, it is claimed that there were in total, more than 6500 species of primates that lived in ancient times but are now extinct. According to the estimates of scientists, only 3% of these primates are known. The species *Australopithecus* named by evolutionists are actually extinct apes which share some common structural characteristics with today's apes.

The primary criteria used by evolutionists in categorising and evaluating human fossils are; bipedalism (upright walking), cranial capacity (the volume of the brain-pan) and cranial shape. Various classifications are evaluated according to those criteria.

Yet, some of these criteria, especially the cranial capacity are extremely unreliable. For example, the generally accepted cranial capacity figure for a contemporary ape is a maximum of 750 cubic centimetres (cc). The cranial capacity of humans is said to

The Falsification of History: Our Distorted Reality

range between 900-2200cc, but among the Australian Aborigine natives, there are quite a number of individuals who have a capacity of around 850cc and furthermore cranial capacity is obviously subject to huge variations, depending on age, sex, race and other criteria. Cranial capacity can therefore never be a reliable means of measurement.

The crania of ape fossils and the crania of today's apes are very similar to each other, being narrow and long. However, human crania are more voluminous with wide foreheads, the skull is flat with no protrusions, eyes are wide apart and the shape of the eyebrow ridges above the eyes change according to racial traits. In addition, the mandibles of humans are very much different from that of apes, bearing a distinctly parabolic shape.

To continue the argument, the arms of apes are longer in relation to the body and their legs are shorter, both toes and fingers of apes have grasping abilities and they are all quadrupeds – all true of both primitive and modern species. Indeed their entire skeleton is designed for a quadrupedal-type body structure. They stand on two feet only rarely, for example when reaching upwards to grasp tree branches or pick fruit, but generally spend most of their time on all-fours.

Bipedalism is a characteristic exclusive to humans (in primates) and this quality is the factor that most distinguishes human beings from other mammals. A human hip, pelvis, back-bone and spinal cord are designed only for a biped and could not function correctly in a quadrupedal frame. In short therefore, when analysing the 'proof' of evolution, one could realistically say that the most important and binding criterion should be bipedalism. Bipedalism is the critical factor that distinguishes humans from apes and therefore the focal point of the argument should be the question of whether our so-called 'ancestors' walked upright or not.

One of the most enduring chapters of the apocryphal human evolution story is *Neanderthal man*. Neanderthals, whom even the evolutionists deem to be 'real' human beings were regarded for some considerable time as 'a primitive human race' by the evolutionists and are considered by them as an intermediate, transitional form from ape to man, possibly in an attempt to solve the 'missing-link' conundrum which haunts evolutionary theory to this day and which has never been adequately explained.

The story of Neanderthal man began in the Neander valley in what is now modern Germany, where a local schoolteacher discovered a skull fragment, a thighbone and other small pieces of a skeleton in 1856. These pieces were subsequently studied by an anatomy professor named Schaafhausen at Bonn University and were eventually considered, after many surveys and comparisons, to be a typical human male with no anatomical abnormalities. According to Schaafhausen who made the first study, the bones belonged to an old human race, possibly to a Barbarian tribe who resided there before the Germanic races moved into the region.

- 55 -

Some years later however, the fossils were sent to the University of Berlin and re-examined there by Professor Rudolf Virchow. Virchow who later in life came to be regarded as the 'father of pathology', made a diagnosis which still holds validity today; that these bones belonged to a *Homo sapiens* (modern human) who had suffered from severe arthritis in his childhood and who had died from what appeared to be several blows to the skull.

Nevertheless, William King an anatomy professor from Queens University in Ireland who studied the fossils after Virchow, produced a totally new interpretation of the facts, which was in effect responsible for the Neanderthal man 'legend'. As a long-time passionate advocator of the theory of evolution, King drew his conclusions from the structure of the bones in accordance with evolutionist prudence. He pronounced that this fossil was more 'primitive' than modern man and therefore could not be classified as such. He also assigned to the fossil, it's now ubiquitous scientific name, *Homo Neanderthalensis*. According to King, it was a member of the Homo (human) species; but at the same time too primitive to be a human.

Two years later, similar skeletons were found in Belgium. These skeletons, which did not attract much attention initially, were subsequently brought to the attention of those who were looking for the supposed ape-ancestors of man, influenced strongly of course by Darwin's book, *'The Origin of Species'*.

In 1908, further Neanderthal skeletons were found in Moustier in the region of La Chapelle-aux-Saints, France. These were studied by Professor Boule from the Paleo-anthropology Institute in Paris, himself a dedicated and passionate supporter of evolutionary theory. Professor Boule himself was indeed responsible for creating the popular, primitive Neanderthal man image in our minds. Boule described his findings as follows:

"Neanderthals seem to be closer to apes than any other group of man and their intelligence is not wholly developed. The composition, position and the order of the cerebellum and spinal cord are the same as the apes. Besides, the feet have the same grasping attribute as in chimpanzees and gorillas. The anatomical structure of Neanderthals indicates that they walk in an awkward and clumsy way."

At the same time, Professor Boule was responsible for the first Neanderthal face and body shape reconstruction. According to this reconstruction, which he made whilst relying upon his own preposterous pre-conceptions, *"Neanderthal man is a half-man and half-ape being. He cannot walk upright and stoops, as do apes."* This utterly baseless theory made by Boule in accordance with his subjective interpretation of the Neanderthal fossils he had in his possession is responsible for the popular mental image we have of Neanderthal man, which still abides to this day.

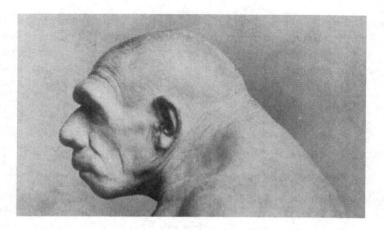

Popularised depiction of a Neanderthal

Despite all the unstinting efforts of the evolutionists, this subjective approach to Neanderthals began to change in the 1950s. Advanced technology began to confirm that Neanderthals were by no means primitive humans, in sharp contrast to the prevailing view. In light of the advent of this new data, these questions were still pertinent; was Neanderthal man, alleged to live only 30,000 years ago, really as primitive as the evolutionists claimed and were Neanderthals primitive creatures who had no civilisation and unable to even walk upright?

These questions were answered by two researchers who examined the La Chapelle-aux-Saints fossils in 1957. These anatomists whose names were Straus and Cave discovered exactly why the fossil man found in 1908 and depicted in a reconstruction by Boule, stooped. As Professor Rudolf Virchow from Berlin University had pointed out originally, this fossil had also suffered from chronic arthritis, just as had the original Neanderthal man who was found in 1856. This insidious bone disease was deforming the shape of the spinal column and led to stooping due to the gradual decaying of the bones. His mandible bone was also deformed and in short, the reason why the Neanderthal fossil possessed a bent posture was the simple fact that he suffered from nothing more uncommon than severe arthritis and not as had been proffered by the evolutionist dogma, his relationship to a primitive species of man.

In all other aspects, 'Neanderthal man' possessed human characteristics. His big toe was not bent as Boule claimed; his thighbone was exactly the same as that of modern man and the report prepared by Straus and Cave culminated with the following words:

"If they had come back to life today, most probably they would not be discriminated from the other people in the New York subway, provided that they had bathed, were shaved and wore modern suits."

Today, evolutionists remain evasive on the subject of Neanderthal man. It has been proven beyond reasonable doubt that the reason why the fossil was stooped as illustrated in Boule's crude and deceptive reconstruction, was the presence of severe arthritis. An authority on this subject, Erik Trinkaus of The University of New Mexico, remarked...

"Detailed comparisons of Neanderthal skeletal remains with those of modern humans have shown that there is nothing in Neanderthal anatomy that conclusively indicates locomotive, manipulative, intellectual or linguistic abilities inferior to those of modern humans."

The evolutionists deliberately ignore the difference between the average 1400cc cranial volume of modern man and the 1750cc volume of Neanderthals. They know very well that the announcement of this fact would pose another serious problem to their weak thesis. Since the evolutionists interpreted the cranial volumes they found, as evidence of evolution, accepting the fact that Neanderthal man had an even larger cranial volume than modern man would imply a regression in the evolutionary process as this would simply mean that Neanderthals were more intelligent than modern humans.

Today Neanderthal man, as indeed is the case with many other subjects, is an assumed truism, an 'assumption' that has been deceptively transmuted into hard fact. The mainstream media and the film industry routinely discuss and treat the topic as though it were absolute, proven fact and not just a flimsy, insubstantial theory at best, as do educators and scientists. This is a recurring theme that as will become apparent, we find in many, many topics from history to astronomy, biology to physics and chemistry alike.

There are many other examples of fatal flaws in the theory of evolution, indeed far too numerous to cover in any detail or to do justice to in a volume such as this. However, even using the small amount of evidence presented here, there now would appear to be only one possible conclusion:

The evolutionary theory asserting that humans came into existence by macro-evolution from single-celled life-forms and latterly from other primates is not supported by any convincing, concrete evidence whatsoever and indeed is invalidated completely by much evidence to the contrary. The whole premise of the evolution of man is actually based on extremely subjective interpretations, poor or bad science, deliberate distortions and even the outright forgeries of many unscrupulous evolutionists who seek to convince us that yet another huge falsehood is the truth.

"Why doesn't the scientific community abandon Darwin's failed hypotheses? Simple: The Jewish-dominated media and educational establishment are determined that, like

unconditional support of Israel, Holocaust mythology, hate laws, and 'civil rights' favouritism, there will be no end to the relentless force-feeding of evolution. Belief in evolution is a prerequisite for Jewish supremacism's new-world order." Reverend Ted Pike, researcher 16th May 2011

There are undoubtedly some genuine, well-meaning scientists who firmly believe in the evolutionary model but they have been duped just as the rest of us, by the deliberate subterfuge of those who are determined to perpetuate a lie. Or could they simply be victims of the Hegelian trap of mainstream religion-based creation versus evolution, believing as they do in the more 'plausible', scientific alternative?

Whatever the answer to that particular poser may be, it seems clear to me that macro-evolution is a huge deception, a pseudo-science and just one of many in a long list of deceptions emitting from the forces of evil, that we are forced to endure on a daily basis.

The Real Origins of the Human Race

"Almost everything they teach us about the ancient history is wrong: origins of men, civilisations and pyramids. Homo sapiens are not a result of evolution and biologists will never find a 'missing link', because intelligent man is a product of genetic engineering. Sumerians are not the beginning of civilised man, but rather the beginning of another cycle of humanity." Dr. Sam Semir Osmanagich, Professor of Anthropology at the American University, Bosnia

So, if we can eliminate evolution as a prime suspect in our search for the true origins of life on Earth, where does that leave the argument? In my humble estimation that would leave but two alternatives, the biblical story of creation by a supreme being or one other possibility. I will exclude this former option for the simple reason that everyone reading this book already has at least a rudimentary knowledge of the Adam and Eve story in the book of Genesis and quite frankly the absurdity of the entire proposition should be very apparent.

Surprisingly to most people, the Elite of this Earth firmly believe that they are the direct descendants of a race of extraterrestrial beings who visited the Earth millions of years ago. This is not mere speculation on my part, but one of their stated, well-documented albeit not well-publicised, beliefs. Again, the evidence that the planet was visited and seeded by extraterrestrials in the dim and distant past, is widespread but nevertheless as far as is possible, is generally concealed from the un-thinking general public who seem to accept lies at face value with no question when given them by the mainstream, but vehemently defend the status quo and decry other mooted alternatives, when these are presented to them from other, 'discredited' sources, whether accompanied by substantial proof or not. All as a natural consequence of course, of the aeons of propaganda and social engineering performed on us, the masses, by the ruling Elite.

If the assumption of an extraterrestrial origin of humanity and all life on Earth is correct, I am aware that this does not categorically answer the 'creation or evolution' question, it merely deflects it much further back in time to the origins of extraterrestrial life, but that particular argument falls outside the scope of this book, our true origins being much, much older presumably than the Earth and indeed very possibly, our Solar System.

There are countless stories and pictorial depictions passed down from ancient civilisations about strange 'visitors' and unearthly beings. One of the more prominent ones being for example, that in the mid-nineteenth century in what is now modern-day Iraq; a huge find of clay tablets was made by Sir Austen Henry Layard, an English archaeologist. Thought to be from the Sumerian culture, these tablets depict an extraordinary story that absolutely contradicts in every way the 'official' history of our species. Unsurprisingly, this is given no credence whatsoever by modern historians, archaeologists and educators as it does not fit the 'accepted' view of history and human evolution decreed, cultivated and ruthlessly and relentlessly enforced by our Elite masters. I feel it somewhat significant to my point that these views are rarely considered or rationally argued against by the mainstream, they are simply ignored, presumably in the hope that they will simply go away or be regarded as unbelievable, if left un-discussed and unacknowledged.

Zecharia Sitchin, who could read Aramaic, Sumerian, Babylonian and several other less well-known, long-dead Middle Eastern languages was the most famous translator of these tablets and he was convinced that the tablets tell a story of extraterrestrial visitors creating the Sumerian civilisation as a 'gift from the gods'. These gods are referred to as the 'Annunaki' or 'those who from Heaven to Earth came'. They are considered by some researchers to be one and the same as the biblical 'Nephilim', the race of giants who probably were around 8 feet tall, according to some researchers. However opinions do vary on this.

The tablets also describe how the Annunaki arrived here from a planet they named Nibiru, which allegedly has a huge elliptical orbit taking it 3600 years to travel around the sun, but whilst at its closest approach point, is situated between the orbits of Mars and Jupiter. A possible sighting was briefly reported in 1983 and then immediately forgotten and buried by the mainstream media...

"A heavenly body possibly ... so close to Earth that it would be part of this solar system has been found in the direction of the constellation Orion by an orbiting telescope aboard the US infrared astronomical satellite. So mysterious is the object that astronomers do not know if it is a planet ... so close in fact that it would be the nearest

heavenly body to Earth beyond the outermost planet Pluto." Washington Post, 31st December 1983.

These clay tablets are the written accounts of traditions that go back many tens of thousands of years but much credence can be given them not least due to their incredibly accurate depiction of the solar system as we now know it. All the planets are in their correct positions (for the era) with relative sizes and orbits, all accurately charted.

How could this knowledge have been available in those times, when most of that information has only been known to us for about 200 years or so? The answer of course is that it is the current view of history which is inaccurate. Ancient cultures and civilisations knew far more about the universe and its secrets than modern science and history will give them credit for. This is why many ancient cultures and cultural traditions such as native American, native African – Zulu for example and Australian aborigines were all ruthlessly suppressed and their ancient artefacts destroyed by forces representing the world Elite. We can also add to this list, the Mayan, Inca and Aztec civilisations in South and Central America, brutally subjugated and systematically eliminated by the Conquistadors, sponsored by the European Elite in the 16th and 17th centuries and charged with the destruction and devastation of these ancient cultures that in fact held a much more accurate world-view than we do today.

Arguably, the most important aspect of the contents of the Sumerian tablets is their description of the creation of humankind. Sitchin estimates the timescales as around 400,000 years ago, but I personally believe that it could be much longer ago than this. According to the story within the tablets, The Annunaki landed originally in Southern Africa to mine the mineral deposits abundant in that area, primarily gold, but other minerals were also involved. According to Sitchin's translation, there was, for want of a better description, a sort of ongoing 'worker's revolt' involving the Annunaki mine labourers or slaves and so the rulers in order to avoid further inconvenience, eventually decided to generate a new race of slaves to replace the truculent labourers. This new race was a hybrid created from the genes of the Annunaki and those of the native, early humanoid species who roamed the plains of the African continent and the Middle East at that time and whose remains have been found in rock strata dating back millions, not simply hundreds of thousands of years as we are led to believe is the case. This hybrid was destined to become modern man, Homo sapiens.

Could this event also be linked to the appearance in archaeological records of a new, distinct form of humanoid which even mainstream anthropology admits appeared suddenly, from nowhere about 200,000 years ago in this region of Africa? If true, nothing much changes does it? We began as a slave race and are still fulfilling the same role 200,000 years later. It is in fact this 'new' species that causes the evolutionists' search for the so-called 'missing link', the infamous huge hole in evolutionary theory, in a vain attempt to explain the gap in the records, the appearance of an hitherto unknown species and thus to 'fit in' with contemporary scientific, evolutionary dogma.

The creators of humanity according to Sitchin's translation were two Annunaki 'scientists' known as Enki (a male) and Ninkharsag (a female). She was also known as 'Mammi' and this is very likely the source of the root word meaning 'mother' and from which we also derive the word 'mammal', still prescient in many ancient and modern languages today. The leader of the Annunaki on Earth was Enlil, the half-brother of Enki. Eventually after many abortive (literally) attempts, as the story goes, Enki and Ninkharsag found the correct formula and the human race was born (created) making 'test tube' babies of us all in the process!

Could this also be the origin of the biblical story of Adam and Eve? Was Eve created symbolically perhaps, from Adam's rib in an ancient description of the cloning process? Also within the tablets is a description of the 'abode of the righteous ones', where humans were said to have first been created, known as E.DIN. Similarly, is this the origin of the Garden of Eden legend in the Bible? It would certainly make some sense of an unlikely 'legend'.

This all dovetails neatly with the Elite's belief system, that they are indeed 'the masters of the Universe', with a special genetic connection back to these ancient 'gods' who seeded and engineered the human race and the rest of us are fit only for slavery and to serve their every need. The 'useless eaters' as Henry Kissinger, one of the more prominent, contemporary Elite pawns has been known to refer to us.

"I will demonstrate that virtually every current belief system that delves into the origins and development of humanity is full of untruths and distortions that serve to keep the reality of human origins concealed." 'Humanity's Extra-Terrestrial Origins'. Dr. Arthur David Horn.

After a huge amount of research and reflection, Dr. Horn came to realise that the belief systems we have been taught regarding the origins of our physical bodies are not true. Rather, they serve an agenda that, for the most part, Western religious institutions and governments have propagated for their own selfish purposes and in order to control the minds of the 'sheeple'. Upon arriving at this conclusion, Dr. Horn, in a totally selfless action which he believed retained his personal and professional integrity, resigned from his professorship. He simply felt that he could no longer, morally speaking, teach the inaccurate, establishment views of humanity's physical origins to his students. He then authored the above quoted book whilst living a simple life in Mt. Shasta, California with his wife.

Based upon his extensive knowledge of evolutionary patterns and forces, Dr. Horn tells us that there were unexplained sudden 'jumps' or 'explosions' in the distant past, which caused new categories of life forms to appear, including pre-humans.

Furthermore, there have been instances in which various life forms have appeared simultaneously, or in parallel with one another, rather than in a gradual step-by-step fashion as is usually propounded by the totally unscientific, *theory* of evolution. These incidents cannot be explained by today's scientific theories, including evolution, rather, it is as though an 'other-worldly' force influenced these natural processes by speeding-up what would normally take millions of years to occur and this applies to the physical bodies we, as spiritual beings, occupy today. How could this be?

These same sudden 'spurts' in evolutionary time may also be found more recently in early civilisations, such as the Sumerian civilisation, which appeared approximately 5000 years ago in the area known today as southern Iraq and which left many archaeological artefacts for study. Horn makes the point that the Sumerian culture did not gradually evolve into existence, their civilisation appeared almost 'overnight' in archaeological terms, complete with mathematics, language, irrigation systems, farming, the written word and an extensive knowledge of the heavens. Who helped them achieve this monumental feat?

The people of Sumer were not primitive savages as much of mainstream history leads us to believe but amazingly, one of their surviving pictorial depictions (below) shows that they knew even at that time that all the planets in our solar system revolve around the sun; something according to mainstream science, that was only 'discovered' 4-500 years or so ago.

Furthermore, the Sumerians were aware of the distant planets in our solar system, Pluto, Neptune and Uranus, which cannot be seen with the naked eye and they also knew that Neptune contained liquid water. How could they know this, given the 'primitive' state of knowledge we are led to believe was in existence at that time? In the same drawing depicting their celestial knowledge, the Sumerians also include a 12th planet in our solar system. Could this be the mysterious Planet X or Niburu, referred to in many ancient texts and as referred to above in the writings of Zecharia Sitchin? In the below image, made approximately 5000 years ago by the Sumerians, one can clearly see our solar system with *twelve* planets revolving around the sun.

Sitchin's book, *The 12th Planet* (now in its 45th printing and translated into 23 languages, millions of copies sold), tells a very credible story of how the Annunaki from the 12th planet (Nibiru) in our solar system created the forerunners of the Sumerians and then interacted with their descendants more than 5000 years ago.

Below, is an ancient Sumerian cylinder seal showing an Annunaki flying machine or space-ship.

Another of the most credible pieces of evidence indicating extra-terrestrial visitation and interaction with human affairs comes from the Dogon tribe of West Africa. The credibility of the Dogon oral history is greatly enhanced by the fact that they have long had extensive knowledge of the planets and stars that modern 'scientists' have only recently acquired.

The Dogon have known for thousands of years that Sirius, the brightest star in the sky, is a binary star-system. This is in itself remarkable, simply because Sirius A, the main star is visible to the naked eye, whereas its neighbour Sirius B which orbits Sirius A, can only be detected with modern-day telescopes. The Dogon also knew that the orbit of Sirius B around Sirius A is elliptical rather than circular and this was also only discovered very recently indeed by mainstream science. In the oral histories of the Dogon that span thousands of years, they speak of entities from the vicinity of Sirius, who visited their ancient ancestors in an 'airship' and taught them many things including how to live in harmony with their own divine nature. Incidentally Sirius is known as the 'Dog' star in some quarters. Coincidence?

Other civilisations such as the Egyptians had a strong connection with the star Sirius and were most likely visited and assisted by 'ETs' from that area of the galaxy. Also possibly significantly, the most important female god of the ancient Egyptians, Isis, was identified with Sirius. In addition, the very basis of Mayan beliefs and legends is the book, Popul Vuh. It contains a creation story of humans, which is similar to that told by the Sumerians, specifically that there were 'creator gods' that 'came down from the heavens' and created mankind to be slaves and serve them. It is also known that the advanced Mayan civilisation seems to have appeared out of nowhere some 3,500 years ago in the jungles of Mexico and interestingly, this was yet another elaborately developed culture with no discernible evolution from a primitive society into a more and more advanced one. Mayan artefacts tell us in no uncertain terms that they were master astronomers with an intimate knowledge of the heavens. From where did this knowledge emanate?

There is a very credible case for the argument that planet Earth has been visited time and time again by 'ETs' from other star systems. Some have visited, stayed for a while and left whilst yet others have created living things, including human physical bodies, which resemble their own. A strong case can be made for the fact that humanity's real origins were in the constellation Lyra; specifically from the star system Vega. From there our ultra-ancient ancestors branched out to other areas of the galaxy, including the Pleiades. Some of them over aeons became aggressive and war-like, whilst some became more spiritually advanced and benevolent.

The net effect of all this upheaval and disruption is a constant, ongoing battle between good and evil, here on this planet and upon reflection; this would partly explain why the world is in constant turmoil. Without this struggle between the dark and the light factions, the yin and the yang, we would not have an opportunity to grow, learn and thereby facilitate the evolution of our souls.

There are many unexplainable artefacts in existence that lend credence to these beliefs and which strongly support the argument that Earth was and continues to be visited by ETs and that other visitors and civilisations existed here from millions of years ago – all evidence which is refuted by Elite-controlled mainstream science and archaeology as such an admission would reveal the real knowledge of who we are as a species and where our real origins lie and of course that would not be in the best interests of our lords and masters.

There is much irrefutable evidence to suggest that we humans were first created through genetic engineering, then nurtured and controlled by alien races or other life forms, that are not originally of this Earth. For example, how is it possible to explain that the ancient Egyptians and Sumerians of more than 5000 years ago were much more advanced in many ways, than the Romans and the Europeans in the Dark Ages of 1000-1500 years ago, despite the vast difference in time periods?

Erich Von Daniken in his oft-criticised by the mainstream, yet stunning work, 'Chariots of the Gods?' suggested that the ancient astronauts or extraterrestrials, had somehow given biological evolution a 'boost' that would allow humans to be able to maintain a civilisation. Considering all the abundance of evidence in favour of this theory of extra-terrestrial origins, I would suggest that it is of many magnitudes more credible than its usurper, the theory of evolution. Indeed, macro-evolution (the transition of one species into another distinctly different one) could even be said to be the most un-scientific, unbelievable, far-fetched, implausible theory of human origins and development ever promoted by humankind.

As outlined in the previous section, the theory of evolution is simply a major part of a massive cover-up operation by the ruling Elites regarding our extra-terrestrial origins and influence on humanity in their ongoing attempts to subjugate and enslave us, as they firmly believe is their birthright.

Many historical records and other esoteric sources, strongly indicate that ETs genetically engineered modern humans and instigated the rise of civilisation. Both positively-oriented and negatively-oriented ETs were involved in this development of mankind from the beginnings of this Earth, but it is unfortunately the negatively-oriented ETs that have largely been in control of the Earth for the past several thousand years via their direct descendants, the Elite, Illuminati, thirteen bloodline families.

Unfortunate also, is the fact that the primary methodology utilised by these darkly negative entities to maintain a divided and thus controlled humankind is through the distorting and concealment of both spiritual truth and also significantly by the distortion of history and our present reality.

Within the last few years, a small group of researchers working on the Human Genome Project, which was completed in 2003, announced that they have made an astonishing scientific discovery. They firmly believe that the so-called 'junk DNA', the 97% non-coding sequences in human DNA *is no less than the genetic code of extraterrestrial life forms.*

The non-coding sequences are common to all living organisms on Earth, from single-celled organisms through plants, insects, lizards, birds and fish to humans. In human DNA, they constitute a larger part of the total genome, admitted Professor Sam Chang, the group leader. These non-coding sequences, originally known as 'junk

DNA', were discovered several years ago, yet their function remained a mystery and indeed they were totally dismissed by mainstream scientists as having no significance whatsoever, as the thoroughly misleading term 'junk DNA' would imply. The conclusion that these scientists are now seriously endorsing and promoting is that **the overwhelming majority of human DNA is extra-terrestrial in origin**, passed-on from parent to child down through millions, if not billions of years.

Following much research, contemplation and scientific analysis with the assistance of other scientists, including computer programmers and mathematicians, Professor Chang wondered if this apparent 'junk DNA' was created by some kind of 'extraterrestrial programmer'. The alien portion of human DNA, Professor Chang further observed, 'has its own veins, arteries and even its own immune system'.

The most logical hypothesis for this, according to Chang is that an extraterrestrial life-form was involved in creating new life and seeding it on various planets, for whatever greater purpose this may serve, one of those planets of course being our own Earth. Perhaps our 'creators' nurtured our race in much the same way we grow bacteria in Petri dishes. We cannot possibly know or understand the motivation behind this act, but maybe it is an ongoing scientific experiment or a way of preparing new planets for colonisation, or even simply the way by which all life is propagated throughout the universe as 'receptacles' for our immortal souls.

Chang further suggests that these apparent 'extraterrestrial programmers' were possibly working on a much larger project consisting of several sub-projects, all of which are concerned with producing various life-forms for various planets. Indeed, Chang and his team are only one of many groups of scientists and other researchers who have discovered and propounded the theory of the apparent extra-terrestrial origins of humanity.

"*Soon or later, we have to come to grips with the unbelievable notion that every life on Earth carries genetic code for his extraterrestrial cousins and that evolution is not what we think it is.*" Professor Sam Chang.

The implications of these ground-breaking scientific finds, staggering as they appear to be, would certainly reinforce claims by many other scientists and observers of having contact with other-worldly, humanoid extraterrestrial entities. These humanoid beings are claimed to have provided some of the genetic material for human evolution by some researchers and it has also been concluded by others, that many of these extra-terrestrials have allowed some of their souls to incarnate as 'star-seed' on Earth in human families. These 'star-children' are described by Brad and Francie Steiger as individuals whose souls were formerly incarnated on the planets of other star-systems and then travelled to Earth and decided to incarnate here in order to enhance the spiritual, evolutionary development of humanity. This theory would also seem to sit well with the discoveries of Dr. Michael Newton, a prominent American psychiatrist, who has uncovered evidence of this fact himself, whilst conducting regressional therapy on thousands of patients. Michael Newton's work is also covered in more detail in later chapters of this book.

Most of humanity would consider this group of extra-terrestrials to be 'benevolent' as described by several prominent 'contactees' such as George Adamski, Orfeo Angelucci, George Van Tassell, Howard Menger, Paul Villa, Billy Meier and Alex Collier all of whom explain the nature of their voluntary interactions with these humanoid extraterrestrials. These 'contactees' also often provide physical evidence in the form of photographs, film and/or witnesses of their contact with extra-terrestrial races. The most extensively documented and researched contactee is Eduard 'Billy' Meier from Switzerland, who has provided much physical evidence for investigators to consider albeit, as one would expect, largely unreported by the compliant mainstream.

Indeed, many 'ancient astronaut' writers and researchers believe that a race of intelligent extra-terrestrial beings visited and/or colonised Earth in the remote past, whereupon they 'upgraded' the primitive hominid *Homo erectus* by means of genetic engineering to create the human race as we know it, *Homo sapiens*. Evidence for this idea may be found in the improbability of *Homo sapiens* emerging so suddenly, according to the principles outlined in the theory of evolution and also significantly in the 'myths and legends' of ancient civilisations, passed down the generations which tell a similar story, no matter how physically far apart in time and distance they may have occurred. Many of these legends describe human-like gods 'descending' from the heavens and creating mankind 'in their own image'. *Homo sapiens* is thus regarded as a hybrid being, incorporating a mix of terrestrial genes from *Homo erectus* and extraterrestrial genes from an ascribed 'race of gods'. This would also of course fit neatly with Zecharia Sitchin's research of Layard's clay tablets.

Prior to the modern-age phenomena of space travel and genetics, this theory of the origins of humanity could not have been conceived or even have been remotely believable and even now in the 21st century, there are many people who would regard it as nothing more than science fiction. However, in the light of the substantial evidence against the orthodox theory of human evolution, the idea of genetic intervention by an alien, intelligent species should be taken very seriously I believe, as a potential solution to the mystery of life on Earth itself.

Whatever the truth of the matter, and I absolutely concede that we may never have definitive proof either way, I believe strongly that the evidence is stacked disproportionately in the favour of Earth being seeded by an alien race of beings, whose descendants in the form of bloodline, Elite families, still rule us to this day. And furthermore it is of course very much in their interests that the real truth of this and many other aspects of our long, chequered history as a species should remain hidden in order that they may retain control of our lives in every conceivable way.

We will now examine how this control has developed and evolved since humans' first attempts at developing a civilised society.

Atlantis – The Legend

Where do the myths and legends of Atlantis, the lost, submerged continent said to have existed between Africa / Europe and America, come from and why are they so persistent if, as we are led to believe by the mainstream, there is no truth in them whatsoever? Could the stories possibly be true and this is simply yet another case of concealment to maintain the ongoing, grand deception?

According to the consensus of this multiplicity of legends, the island city of Atlantis disappeared beneath the waves around 9600BC after a huge global cataclysm, which incidentally some sources say, was caused by the seismic disturbances engendered by the close passing-by of the Planet Nibiru at that time upon one of its infrequent returns to the Solar System.

Plato, the ancient Greek was a most serious philosopher and historian and as such was not given to 'flights of fancy'. He has never been shown to have been guilty of any kind of hoax or fabrication or indeed of the writing of any fiction and so therefore his comprehensive account of the destruction and disappearance of the city / island of Atlantis, far from being treated as a myth, deserves serious consideration.

Plato stated that, *"The island has a small central mountain surrounded by ripples or water filled depressions. There are many fissures, not man-made, in the ground. There are lakes surrounding this cone. Hot and cold springs are evident. The lands surrounding this central mountain are very fertile and there are cliffs at the edge of the sea."*

This is a very accurate description of a volcanic island. The central cone could be an ancient, dormant volcano. Hot springs are positive indications of geothermal activity and lands surrounding volcanoes are often very fertile. Finally, volcanic islands, particularly those of the Atlantic often have steep cliffs where they meet the sea.

If Atlantis existed in the middle of the Atlantic Ocean, it would have almost acted as a land-bridge between the continents of Africa and America, allowing animals and plants to migrate more easily from one to the other. Non-Atlantis experts in several different fields of research have independently stated that there must have been an intermediate land-mass connecting the distant continents together in some way. Plato actually said Atlantis was *"the way to other islands and from these you might pass to the whole of the opposite continent"*. He also said it was *"… an island situated in front of the straits which are by you called the Pillars of Hercules."* The Pillars of Hercules being the ancient name for the Straits of Gibraltar

The important point of this description of Atlantis is not just what it describes, but it is the fact that the components are consistent with each other. In other words, it sounds like the depiction of a real place rather than one sprung entirely from the imagination. More importantly, Plato did not have the benefit of modern research methods; he merely described them as he understood them and as passed down the ages through his family. This lends his work even more credibility. The very fact that Atlantis was in all probability of volcanic origin, lends great credence to its existence in the first place and subsequent destruction in the second place. Volcanic forces were not understood at this period of history and so his descriptions could not have been undertaken with the intent of deception.

Plato also describes a more modern and technologically advanced society than is currently regarded as possible by mainstream thinking at this stage of human history. There are descriptions of advanced architecture and advanced skills and knowledge, particularly of engineering. These include sophisticated irrigation systems and canals or channels as described by Plato. I believe that it is a strong possibility that the Atlanteans were the original pyramid builders and they shared their knowledge with their neighbours. Pyramids are extremely sophisticated structures, often built so that their angles align perfectly with constellations in the heavens, so can it be simply coincidental that several ancient cultures seem to have spontaneously and independently acquired certain knowledge and skills that were apparently beyond their level of development at the time, the ability to build a perfect pyramid, for example?

This skill could not possibly have been developed by several different cultures independently of each other in such a short period of time and yet this is demonstrated in the Egyptian civilisation as well as South American and certain Asian cultures. Maybe the truth of the matter is that they inherited this knowledge from a previous culture – Atlantis?

The Swiss author of *'Chariots of the Gods'*, Erich von Däniken, believes these 'coincidences' can be linked to *'ancient astronauts'*, aliens who visited Earth in ancient times and shared technologies with the ancient humans. And several researchers also conclude that the inhabitants of Atlantis were in fact aliens (the Annunaki?). They were said to be taller than the average person and of 'fairer features'.

There have also been suggestions from several sources that the Atlanteans may have been aliens visiting Earth to collect minerals to supplement their own planet's dwindling resources. They arrived on Earth and colonised Atlantis and Africa and possibly several other locations also. Is this beginning to sound familiar yet?

Edgar Cayce, the famous American psychic of the late nineteenth and early twentieth centuries undertook psychic readings on thousands of people, investigating their previous lives. He concluded that some of the people he interviewed had previously been alive during the heyday of Atlantis and from them he collated incredibly detailed and coherent descriptions of their civilisation at that time. He also made several uncannily accurate predictions regarding future evidence coming to light. Although Cayce died in 1945, he predicted that in 1968 or 1969... *"A portion of the temples may yet be discovered under the slime of ages and sea water near Bimini"*

Incredibly, in 1968, twenty three years after Cayce's death, the Bimini Road was discovered on the floor of the Atlantic Ocean at North Bimini Island in the Bahamas. The Bimini Road is a half-mile long road of perfectly aligned limestone rocks, most spectacular when viewed from the air. Although some people believe that these rocks are a natural phenomenon, new evidence has shown this not to be the case.

In fact some truly amazing discoveries have actually been made. The most significant one being that beneath the precisely placed giant stones is another layer of stones, exactly the same. Could this be a wall and not a road as previously surmised? It also seems to completely destroy the 'natural formation' argument. A research team has also discovered markings on some of the rocks that seem to be man-made holes or possibly tool marks. In taking all this and much other evidence into account it is perhaps no surprise that the Bimini Road is believed by many credible researchers, to be part of the ruins of Atlantis.

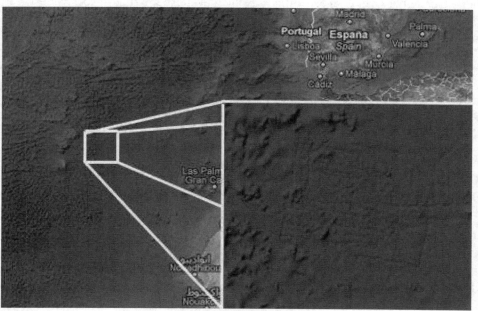

The Bimini Road

Is the Atlantis story regarded as a 'myth' by contemporary history because it does not fit in with existing theories of the state of development of mankind at this particular juncture in time? It would seem likely given the evidence and if so is yet another example of the ongoing deceit that maintains us in our present state of ignorance of real history.

There are also numerous reports of other possible sites of Atlantis all around both sides of the Atlantic seaboard and even into the Mediterranean Sea itself but they are all broadly consistent in their descriptions of an island containing a people whose civilisation was not only more advanced than the Earth had hithertofore seen but was widely believed to have been in some respects even more advanced than we are today.

Many ancient artefacts are in existence, some found on the Atlantic and Mediterranean sea-beds which bear more than a passing resemblance to modern machinery and even computers and yet have been dated to more than 5000 years old. How is this possible? How can a civilisation from so long ago in time, relatively speaking, be more advanced technologically speaking than civilisations which followed thousands of years later?

It is eminently possible if that civilisation was destroyed by some natural or even un-natural cataclysmic event which destroyed it an instant or even in the space of a few days. Maybe some lucky few Atlanteans were fortunate to escape the wrath of the huge tsunami or earthquake or other unknown event that wrought such widespread destruction and just maybe those people found landfall in Spain or North Africa or even North America where they were able to pass-on tales of the destruction of their 'world' and all its knowledge. Indeed a few survivors would in no way necessarily ensure the perpetuation of that superior technology.

How many among us now in the event of a similar cataclysm could re-start civilisation and re-construct all the modern conveniences that we just take for granted in our world today? Speaking personally, I have never been practically-minded and indeed I am almost an 'idiot' where practical matters such as car maintenance, carpentry, metalwork and DIY tasks are concerned. I would not know where to begin to construct a simple refrigerator for example or even to describe to someone with more advanced technical skills and knowledge than myself how the principle of refrigeration works. And the same holds true with almost anything else we could mention; a car, a jet-plane or even a humble bicycle for that matter!

So to summarise, Atlantis was in my view much, much more than a legend, a mere figment of the over-productive imaginations of our forebears. I believe that Atlantis did exist and indeed it was the cradle of our civilisation, the remnants of which were utilised in re-building a version of society which whilst may not be as advanced as Atlantis itself, at least became more advanced once again with the passing of the millennia. And maybe now, at this point in our history we are just reaching a level whereby we can match the technological achievements of that long-gone age.

The Ancient Bloodlines

From out of the ashes of Atlantis arose several new civilisations, the Babylonians and Sumerians, closely followed by the Phoenicians, the Egyptians, the Ancient Greeks and then the Romans, as the dominant world societies.

There are so many ongoing new discoveries pertaining to our ancestors and their civilisations that much of what was current and regarded as the indisputable truth, even ten years ago, is now considered to be false. Mainstream archaeologists who are ingrained with specific immutable beliefs and theories are now finding it increasingly more difficult to continue to justify and defend them and to compound those difficulties, many new discoveries and interpretations of old ideas are being promulgated by those who collate knowledge from several different, alternative disciplines outside mainstream archaeology, such as astronomy, scientific and social studies. As always, the political motivations of the ruling Elite, in their desperate attempts to maintain their own prime position within the status quo has a huge bearing on this. In many instances, where new proofs are discovered to back-up certain theories, there is a huge impetus building to supplant the old beliefs with the new.

This is very clearly a consequence of the intransigence of contemporary scientific thinking. If it doesn't fit the existing, acceptable framework then it cannot possibly be correct. No questions, no debate, it is just plain wrong – end of discussion. There is no doubt in my mind that this state of affairs has been deliberately engineered to stifle possible, alternate hypotheses from seeping into the mainstream and polluting the purity of the official storyline. Under no circumstances can this be allowed to happen as humanity would then possess the knowledge of whom and what we really are and as a result become a huge threat to the prevailing powerbase. After all, as we all know well, knowledge is power.

So, were the Sumerian 'gods' just mythical stories or, as related earlier in this volume, were they very real beings who were regarded as different and superior to the everyday Sumerians because they could do unexplainable things that even today we would no doubt refer to as god-like?

I strongly contend that all the evidence points to the fact that the 'gods' of this period were the original ancestors of the thirteen Elite bloodline families that even to this day own disproportionately large swathes of the Earth, its resources and wealth and have painstakingly set in place a huge spider-web of control spanning the entire globe in order to safeguard and protect their extensive interests. This tiny group own and control either directly or via proxy, all the major media outlets, banking and financial corporations, industrial conglomerates, pharmaceutical companies, food production and service industries. And as a result of this truly staggering wealth, they also have a huge controlling influence over the world's central and local governments, military capabilities, legal and policing systems, the medical professions and education systems which they use as a valuable propaganda tool in conjunction with the mainstream media.

It is vitally important that we do not fall victim to the Elite lies and distortions that state that people who lived ten thousand years ago or even longer, had the same priorities, concepts, thoughts and world-view that we have today. And we absolutely must reject any thoughts that lead us to believe that we are somehow superior in intellectual, social, spiritual and cultural matters to our distant forebears. The facts show that the ancient civilisations and their mysterious predecessors, were indeed just as advanced and intelligent as we are today and surprisingly, much evidence also exists that demonstrates that they were in possession of certain knowledge and technology that may not even exist, at least overtly, today.

Why would the Elite want to turn the world into their own personal fiefdom when they already have all the money and power anyone could ever wish for? Using the principle of *Occam's Razor*, that is that the most simplistic answer is usually the correct one, they firmly believe it is their 'birthright'. They believe themselves, like their remote ancestors, to be the 'gods', true masters of their domain and we are the serfs, slaves created by them in the distant past to serve their every whim and what we are seeing now in the second decade of the twenty-first century is the culmination of many thousands of years of them striving to redress the balance back to as it was in those long-gone Atlantean/Sumerian/Babylonian times. They would like to see and indeed are working towards a return to the days when they were the true, uncontested 'masters of the universe', living in obscene luxury, their every need catered-for and served by an army of mind-controlled drones composed of the few remaining humans still around after their planned, genocidal cull of 95% of the world's population. The truth is that technological advances have now brought us to a situation where they no longer need vast armies of people to 'make the world go around' or generate their profits for them, any more. Their luxurious, pampered lifestyles could now easily be served with the overt technology available today, the 'hidden' technology that they have already developed and successfully concealed plus a much-reduced human population to perform the few still remaining non-automatable tasks. This is in fact the reason for their proposed depopulation agenda – they simply do not need us any longer.

Down through the millennia, beginning with the Sumerian 'gods', these bloodlines have incorporated and included (among other civilisations now long gone) the Babylonian ruling classes, Atlanteans, the Pharaohs of ancient Egypt, the ancient Greeks including Alexander the Great, Phillip of Macedonia, Roman Emperors and

Cleopatra the Great (who married Julius Caesar and bore Mark Antony twin sons). We also can include such notables as Herod the Great and the kings and princes of the Middle East, Assyria and Turkey. These lines once firmly established in the Near and Middle East began migrating north and west into Central and Northern Europe seeding the diverse royal families that existed then and now, through the Merovingian bloodline. One of the great Roman families involved, was the influential Piso family of whom it is thought, wrote large parts of the biblical New Testament and were responsible for the mythology of the 'Jesus' story.

Throughout all of history it has not always been the case that these families have plotted and conspired together in a co-ordinated sense. There have been many, many internal conflicts, feuds and power struggles along the way, but the basic premise has always been the shared goal of world domination to a greater or lesser degree.

You may think that in these 'modern' days the thirteenth Illuminati bloodline, Royalty, has no power at all and that they are merely figureheads, kept in obscene luxury for the sake of tradition and to 'promote tourism', as we are always told by the controlled and corrupted media. Unfortunately, I can expose this as being a huge deception. It does not take much in the way of detailed research to easily discover that this is far from being the case. Indeed there is much evidence to support the assertion that the Royal families of the world still rule with almost the same rod of iron and cold-blooded callousness that they always have. It is just that these days, they have learnt from their past mistakes, how to keep the peasants in their place without risking revolts and outright revolution by overt displays of force or blatantly obvious autocratic behaviour. It is a far, far better solution for them to create the illusion of rule by supposedly democratic government than risk outright rebellion and over time, this illusion is exactly what they have managed to achieve.

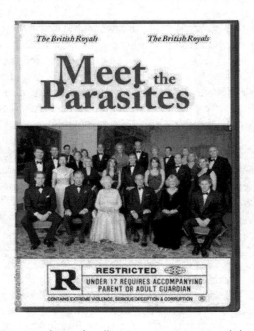

For example in the UK, to whom do all MPs, government ministers and members of the House of Lords swear their allegiance in their investiture oaths? Is it to the country, the people or to the government itself? No, it is to the *Queen*. Likewise the armed forces, police, local government officials, secret societies et al, swear their loyalties to one person, the head of state, regardless of any arguments contesting the validity of that idea.

Our armed forces are in effect, the 'Crown's' private mercenaries who despite the lies propagated by the Elite media, far from fighting distant wars in dirty, foreign 'hell-holes' to 'defend democracy' and our 'way of life' are simply there to expand commercial markets or facilitate and enhance Royal and Elite corporate profits and indeed fulfil the ongoing 'agenda'. This myth of 'fighting for our freedoms' is constantly perpetuated by the media, partly by the expedient of branding anyone who has been a part of the armed forces, as a 'hero', especially those who are unfortunately maimed for life or killed in the process. It makes me literally sick to my stomach to see these poor unfortunates and their families, periodically wheeled-out into the media spotlight to be publicly worshipped and fêted, whilst the sheep-like masses applaud or fawn and weep over them, as they have been encouraged if not outright programmed to do. In many cases, these poor souls, once they have fulfilled their propagandistic roles are brutally discarded by the very society that makes pretence of their 'hero' or 'heroine' status, by denying them a fair pension or compensation and thus anything approaching a 'normal' life, even though in many instances they are unable to support themselves and their families ever again due to severe physical injuries or debilitating mental scars.

"Military men are just dumb, stupid animals to be used as pawns for foreign policy." Henry Kissinger.

Often in the case of mental disorders caused by battle stress, shell-shock or post-traumatic stress disorder, the armed forces medical staff are instructed and pressurised by the hierarchy to wherever possible, diagnose that the victims' states of mind are not caused by their service in the forces and thus deny them a decent standard of life after their discharge from duty. Even the survivors of long-past conflicts are not immune to being discarded after use, as witness the now elderly WWII veterans, who totally abandoned by the government long, long ago, have to find their own fares and accommodation costs on annual pilgrimages to pay respect at the graves of their many fallen friends, before they themselves die, often un-mourned and forgotten by a society they allegedly 'saved' from the forces of evil. However, try propounding this view in public and you would probably be metaphorically torn to pieces by your peers and the media wolf-pack, such is the power of extreme propaganda.

"I always get that crawling sensation on my skin when I hear about the noble troops defending our freedoms, as if our freedoms were ever challenged by anyone but bankers and politicians, who send them out to die in place of themselves." Les Visible, researcher, September 2011.

"None of them know the real reason for the bloodbaths in which they lost their friends. They only know they followed orders as best they could, some suffered and some survived. But whose orders they really were is something all those people under all those white tombstones never knew. Even now, precious few people know. You think it's the presidents and prime ministers. It isn't." John Kaminski, researcher, October 2011.

The very fact that 'charities' such as 'Help for Heroes' actually exist at all should be enough to demonstrate that those who rule over us care nothing whatsoever for wounded ex-servicemen and women and their families who have outlived their usefulness to their twisted ambitions, leaving their welfare and support at the mercy of 'charitable' donations. It is seemingly not enough that these people are 'used' to further the ongoing bloody, corporate expansion of the Royal-Elite empires, but through the existence of these charities, these same Elite are somehow absolved of their social and financial responsibilities to care for their victims. Why can most people not see through this charade? Why do we allow these psychopaths to abdicate their responsibilities and pass them on to the gullible public, with never so much as even a murmur of dissent from the brainwashed proletariat, let alone the complicit media?

"Yesterday around 750 people paid their respects to deceased Marine, James Wright of the 42 Commando, who lost his life while serving in Afghanistan. The media call him a

hero, but with the facts about the Afghan invasion firmly on the record, maybe it's time we started calling these young men 'victims'." wideshut.co.uk, 31st August 2011.

In fact, 'victim of US, British and Israeli imperial hegemony' may well be a much more accurate description than 'hero'.

'Head of State' is absolutely not an honorary title, the Queen has the power should she choose to use it, to over-rule any government policy, block any legislation or indeed to dismiss the Prime Minister or dissolve the government should she wish, not just in Britain but in any of the so-called 'Commonwealth' nations. But of course this rarely happens as usually only those who are pre-determined to be unquestioningly loyal to her wishes are considered for 'election' in the first place, having been screened, groomed and nurtured from birth in most cases.

"Don't be fooled by the mainstream press, the British royal family are the BIGGEST despots on this planet and UK voters have a choice only of her personally selected masonic goons who head the dodgy political parties that masquerade as some sort of fabricated democracy. No-one can be a British Prime Minister without the blessing of the tyrannical Royals. She and her loyal, judicial mafia rule Britain with an evil, wicked and brutal iron fist." International Men's Organisation.

I have often heard people ask, '... how can a frail old lady (the Queen) in her late-eighties, possibly wield that amount of power and influence?' Queen Elizabeth may now indeed be an old lady, but she is still the matriarch of the wealthiest and most powerful family the world has ever seen. She may be just a figurehead in some respects but she still holds the ultimate executive power that may be questioned or challenged only at one's extreme peril. Obviously she does not physically enforce that ultimate power personally, she has her legions of loyal 'retainers' to do that for her, such as MI5, MI6, the 'elected' government of the day, the armed forces, police services, backed by a corrupt legal system. In the event of an attempted insurrection or usurpation of her authority of any kind, these forces would collectively act to swiftly physically enforce and protect her undemocratic power, as they are sworn so to do.

For example, an instance of the use of this undemocratic power occurred in Australia in the 1970s. The then Labour Prime Minister, Gough Whitlam upon his 'democratic' election and entirely in line with his election mandate, immediately ended military conscription and Australia's military commitment in Vietnam, promised Papua New Guinea independence, officially recognised Communist China, provided greater services and freedoms for aboriginal, native Australians, abolished the Imperial honours list and supported equal pay for women. And probably most significantly, it was Whitlam who exposed the head of the Pine Gap secret military underground facility in the Northern Territories as a CIA agent and furthermore demanded that the entire CIA operational staff in Australia at that time be identified and named. The rest of his three-year reign (including re-election in 1974) was characterised by tension resulting from further sweeping reforms and the emergence of forces undermining his programmes.

In other words, he had been a little too liberal for the liking of the ruling Royals in introducing social measures designed to benefit the masses to a greater degree than was deemed acceptable by the Queen and her advisors and also by exposing the covert military agenda being undertaken by the CIA in after all what is a *foreign country* to them. So, what did she do? She simply intervened, as is her prerogative and ordered the Australian Governor-General, John Kerr (the Queens figurehead and the *real* but unelected political power in Australia), to dismiss Whitlam. This was achieved simply and with the minimum of fuss and barely a passing comment in the compliant media as to the rights, wrongs or otherwise of this action. Even had a storm been provoked, it was perfectly 'legal' and nothing could have been done via the corrupt judicial system to change it or prevent it happening. I would ask simply, how can this be regarded as democracy in any shape or form? Rest assured that should a British Prime Minister ever stand against the royal agenda in a similar manner, then his fate would be identical.

So specifically who are these people? The thirteen bloodlines now consist of the following families; Astor, Bundy, Collins, Du Pont, Freeman, Kennedy, Li, Onassis, Reynolds, Rockefeller, Rothschild, Russell and last but most definitely not least, the Merovingian bloodline which consists of all the European royal families including Elizabeth Windsor-Saxe-Coburg-Gotha-Battenberg-Mountbatten, her utterly appalling, inbred family et al.

This is the ultimate 'conspiracy theory', the fact that the world is secretly governed by a small group of people who operate behind the scenes and through 'elected politicians'. 'Conspiracy theory' is now an accepted turn of phrase but sometimes one hears the expression, 'The Illuminati'.

What does this mean? Who are the Illuminati or the 'Elite' as I refer to them throughout this book?

Freemasonry, the Illuminati and the New World Order

It is a scientifically accepted fact that approximately 1% or one hundredth of the world's population is psychopathic, and that at least 4% of lower management in corporate organisations has that same attribute. However it is perhaps a less well-known fact that the closer to the top of any Elite pyramid we venture, the greater the proportion of psychopaths to 'normal' people there are until at the very top, almost 100% of senior management in any corporate sphere, also including politics, the law, the armed forces, the police etc. etc., possess psychopathic tendencies and this fact in itself explains much about how the world operates today.

"At one major investment bank for which I worked, we used psychometric testing to recruit social psychopaths because their characteristics exactly suited them to senior corporate finance roles." A senior UK Investment Banker, quoted in the UK newspaper, *The Independent*, 1st January 2012.

Of course, this does not necessarily mean that all psychopaths are mass-murderers or totally insane, simply that they suffer from a physical-cum-psychological disorder that sets them apart from the rest of us 'normal' people. Psychopaths are by their nature, cunning, subtle and manipulative but most importantly lack the one human trait that gives us our identity as a species above all else – empathy. Empathy may be broadly defined as the ability to recognise and share the emotions, feelings or sufferings of other people and therefore to experience their grief or joy along with them. In short a psychopath has no compassion, no conscience and has no inherent ability to feel guilt or shame for their own actions. This is why so many psychopaths are extremely violent and even mass-murderers, as they are always able to self-justify their actions as being reasonable.

Physically speaking, psychopathy is the lack of a gene in human DNA that controls and engenders feelings towards other people. Although psychopaths lack compassion and guilt, they do however feel the emotion of fear and they are well aware of what the consequences would be of them ever being caught-out in their selfish, often criminal actions. It is in fact 'fear' that is the only limiting factor in inhibiting their behaviour and which could otherwise result in them becoming totally 'out of control', so it would naturally follow that if this fear could be overcome or removed then a psychopath has no need of self-restraint whatsoever. Sadly, this is exactly what has happened over the millennia. The dominant, psychopathic families/bloodlines were able to assume control of the rest of us by the expedient of being utterly ruthless, merciless and uncaring as to the fate of anyone else and this state of affairs has persisted since almost the beginning of time. If one has enough money, power and influence (which they have in abundance) then one can do anything and ignore the consequences. This situation has also been exacerbated by the constant inter-breeding of the bloodlines within themselves across the centuries and thus deliberately keeping the psychopathic traits in the genes of those who rule us with utter brutality.

The possession of unlimited finances provides the ability to do almost anything to protect their position of power and removes the inhibiting element of fear. They can arrange for wars to further their fortunes through bribery, blackmail and corruption. They can buy-off governments and countries whilst subtly promoting their own agenda through propaganda in the media which they own in one form or another in its entirety. They can place their own puppets in strategic, influential positions, arrange for expedient political assassinations for the disposing of unsympathetic 'world leaders' or anyone disloyal to their goals or whom they may see as a potential threat. They can re-write history to their own script to aid their future agendas, manipulate current events to their own advantage and in short, they can do anything they wish to ensure that their power-base is protected and enhanced, in fact exactly what is happening all around us in the world today.

It is this uninhibited, uncaring, pitiless, utterly ruthless attitude that leads to all the ills of the world today and in the sending of thousands (millions?) of propagandised young men (and now even women) to fight their wars and in the process, maim, kill and bomb helpless, innocent men, women and children in the name of corporate profits and wealth. They have no shame or feelings of guilt but what they do have however is a strong sense of self-justification running contrary to the feelings and emotions inherent in most 'normal' people.

A recent peer-reviewed theoretical paper entitled *'The Corporate Psychopaths' Theory of the Global Financial Crisis'*, details how highly-placed psychopaths in the banking sector almost brought down the entire world economy (and may yet still) through their own inherent inability to truly care about the consequences of their actions. The author of this paper, Clive Boddy, formerly of Nottingham Trent University in England, believes that this theory would go a long way towards explaining how and why senior managers in the banking industry acted in ways that were disastrous for the institutions for which they were employed, the investors they represented and the global economy at large. If true, this also means that the astronomically expensive public bailouts would never have solved the problem anyway, since many of the morally-impaired individuals who caused this mess still remain in positions of power. Worse still, they are actually the same people advising governments on how to resolve this crisis.

When employed in senior positions, their psychopathy also means that they are biochemically incapable of something they are legally required to do, that is act in good faith on behalf of other people. The banking and corporate sector is built on the ancient principle of 'fiduciary duty' which is a legal obligation to act in the best interest of those with whose money or property you are entrusted. Asking a psychopath to act in another's best interests is tantamount to recruiting a pyromaniac to become a fire-fighter.

"With a total disregard for traditional culture, the ruling elites have turned our schools, universities, arts and mass media into a giant propaganda machine promoting political correctness, pseudo-history and economics and the new world religion: debt-based consumerism. Anyone who questions their version of science, world history, or monetary policy is immediately branded as a malcontent and removed from the public discourse. They control the message by controlling the money. Many look at the twentieth century as a time of great economic and technical advance, but history, while recognising the technical innovation, will condemn this century as the most vile in human history. The miracle that began in Greece, expanded in Rome, flourished in the

Renaissance and Enlightenment and finally found its modern form in the Western liberal democracy has been gutted by a century of materialism, enslavement, slaughter and greed." Robert Bonomo, activistpost.com 13th October 2011

And so this is the background to the Illuminati, who are today in essence a cartel of international bankers and corporate industrialists primarily but not exclusively based in Western Europe and North America, the family lines of whom have persisted over long, long periods of time. The most important names are Rothschild and Rockefeller along with the royal lines, but the rest are as noted in the previous section. These are the same bloodlines that have ruled over us with varying degrees of despotism for aeons. At least 45 US presidents were provably descended from William the Conqueror (King William I of England) as are the entire British and all the European Royal families. William himself was descended from the Viking rulers of the 'Dark Ages' who in turn had been spawned from Greek and Roman nobility back through to the ancient times of antiquity, the Sumerians and Babylonians et al, before their mass-migration North-westward through Europe.

In more recent times, 1776 to be precise, a man named Adam Weishaupt in Bavaria, in what is now part of Germany, became interested in Freemasonry. However, he was disappointed in what he discovered, believing that the Freemasons did not understand Masonry's occult significance and refused to accept its roots in the ancient pagan religions – hence his subsequent takeover of a society which he transformed into the Illuminati. In 1777, he finally joined the Masonic Lodge of the Strict Observance Rite in Munich, which practiced a form of neo-Templar-Masonry.

At around this time in 1776, the Order of Perfectibilists also became known as the Order of Illuminists or the Order of the Illuminati, sometimes known to its members as the Society of the Hidden Hand. 'Illuminati' is the plural of the Latin Illuminatus, from *illumino* meaning lighten or enlighten, or 'enlightened one', a term used to describe the initiates of the Pagan Mysteries. Initially the Order had only five members, who were radical freethinkers, but they soon attracted the attention of Bavarian society and within ten years of its foundation there were over 2,000 members.

Illuminism spread from Ingolstadt all over Bavaria and then to other German dukedoms such as Saxony, Westphalia and Franconia that were at the time ruled by feudal princes and dukes. It was also exported abroad to the Austro-Hungarian Empire, France and Italy. The Illuminati's membership was largely drawn from the middle and upper classes and with this in mind it is ironic to note that revolutionary movements are seldom started by the working-classes. Instead, they are usually led by intellectuals and disenchanted members of the ruling power Elite. Members of the Illuminati included doctors, teachers, lawyers, judges, university professors, priests, police and military officers and aristocrats such as Duke Ferdinand of Brunswick, Duke Ernst of Gotha, Duke Karl of Saxe-Weiner, Prince Augustus of Saxe-Gotha, Prince Carl of Hesse, and Baron Dalberg.

The inclusion of these aristocratic and royal rulers in its membership roll seems strange considering the methods of the Illuminati. Adam Weishaupt's personal vision was a utopian, pacifist society without monarchy, private property, social inequality, national identity and religious affiliation – in other words, what we would now refer to as 'communism'. In this new state people would supposedly live together in harmony in a universal brotherhood based on peace, free love, spiritual wisdom, intellectual and scientific knowledge and equality. According to Weishaupt's doctrine in his own words: *"Salvation does not lay where strong theories are defended by swords, where the smoke of censers ascends to heaven or where thousands of strong men pace the rich fields of harvest. The revolution which is about to break [the French Revolution] will be sterile. It is not complete".*

Eventually, the Illuminati was infiltrated and usurped by the Rothschilds who introduced the element of Satanism which is still practiced extensively today by these people and their wide ranging networks. These Satanic psychopaths believe that Lucifer and Satan are two distinctly separate entities. Lucifer is their god of light, knowledge, science, logic and philosophy whereas Satan is their god of chaos and destruction and Jehovah, the Christian god, is their sworn enemy. The Illuminati practice a combination of Luciferianism and Satanism as well as a form of communitarianism (a kind of communism/fascism hybrid) which they are currently attempting to foist upon the world.

Luciferianism is embodied in Freemasonry, with its intentionally obscured symbolism and ordinances. It is also symbolised by the 'All-Seeing Eye' at the top of an uncapped pyramid which they often use symbolically as a 'calling-card' or a mark of the fact that they are behind some given event. At the highest level of the Illuminati are the Philosopher kings that seek to bring about the Luciferian ideal of 'Atlantis', as described by Plato. The second level is reserved for the military ruling class, which worship destruction and are hard-core Satanists whilst the third level is reserved for the International Bankers and other business leaders which merely manage the resources of the organisation.

Both the York and Scottish Rites of Freemasonry are designed to lead mankind to the worship of Lucifer, although this is hidden to the majority of the members of the organisation, the so-called 'blue degrees' (levels 1-3) which are considered 'useful idiots' by the hierarchy. The top three degrees (31-33) correspond to the above leadership pattern (Philosopher Kings, Military Ruling Class and Merchant Class). Interestingly enough, the Knights Templar were organised in this fashion and also worshipped both Lucifer and Satan (Baphomet). They were also the founders of the Rosicrucians and Freemasonry.

Solomon, the son of David, is believed by the Illuminati to have rejected the one true God for the above practices. This is evidenced by the fact that he was led away from God by his foreign wives and even went so far as to sacrifice his own son to Moloch (Satan).

The pivotal family, royalty aside is probably the house of Rothschild, the descendants of Mayer Amschel Rothschild (1743–1812) of Frankfurt. The male descendants of this family, for at least two generations and often more, generally married first cousins or even nieces in order to 'keep it in the family'. The family established banking institutions in Vienna, London, Naples and Paris as well as Frankfurt and ever since the Middle Ages, these families have been building and consolidating their power by lending money at various rates of interest to the monarchies and governments of Europe who were forever in debt, particularly in times of war. Sooner than tax the population to raise funds, always an unpopular measure, they usually preferred to borrow money from these corrupt money-lenders. This was the birth of the concept of 'the national debt'. The countries of the world are forever in debt, all of it unpayable because of interest mounting upon interest and where there is a debtor there is also a creditor. So to whom is this money owed? It is owed to this coterie of international bankers or banksters (banker–gangsters) for such they are.

By the nineteenth century the power of the Rothschild family had become immense. They constantly increased their wealth with great cunning and fortitude whilst always endeavouring to maintain a low public profile. A notable example of their methods was their exploitation of the outcome of the Battle of Waterloo to gain vast profits and further extend control. The Rothschilds had spies watch the course of the battle and as soon as it became evident that Wellington had won the day, a Rothschild agent travelled at maximum speed to London, arriving hours before Wellington's own messenger. Rothschild received the news of the battle's outcome and began conspicuously selling his stocks. The whole stock exchange assumed that the battle was lost and so everyone started selling. At this point however, other Rothschild agents bought massive amounts of shares at greatly reduced prices and in this way an already incalculable fortune was massively increased.

The Rockefeller family is almost equally important. They are the loyal lieutenants of the Rothschilds on the American continent. The pivotal figure in this family was J. D. Rockefeller, who made his fortune out of Standard Oil in Ohio and Pennsylvania and also controlled the American railways. When rival, road transport systems were established he attempted to block them by parking his trains across the roads at level crossings and his basic business technique was the elimination of competitors at all costs, the establishment of a monopoly, followed by extreme profiteering. He rapidly acquired a name for huge wealth, secrecy and hard and dirty business practice. In his later years he had a harsh and gaunt appearance, so to counter his bad 'public image', JD Rockefeller effectively invented the PR industry. He had short films of himself made, calculated to charm the public, for example playing golf with a cute little child. This was very effective with the less conspicuously 'aware' public of the day in promoting his own image as one of a 'benevolent', caring person.

The Rockefellers currently have controlling interests in the oil company Exxon (the world's largest corporation) and the Chase Manhattan Bank, which turns over trillions of dollars *every week.* Strange is it not, that names such as Rockefeller,

Rothschild, Windsor et al never appear in the popular 'rich lists' of the world's most wealthy? Why is that? What do the media not want us to know? I would venture to suggest that they do not want us to know who **really** runs the world and exactly how wealthy and powerful these families really are. With so many trillions under their direct control already, what does more money mean? Obviously it means more power and even more control over other human beings, but to what end and in whose name?

Apparently, one would assume, in the name of Lucifer, the 'fallen angel' also known as the bringer of light, hence the name 'Illuminati' which literally means 'the enlightened ones'. Lucifer is also known for the characteristics of pride, deception and impermanence. As previously stated, the Illuminati were founded in Bavaria in 1776 by Adam Weishaupt, a student of the Jewish philosopher Mendelsohn and backed by both the Rothschild and European royal families. The Illuminati has always been based on and maintained strong links with Freemasonry, which was taken over at the highest levels during the course of the eighteenth and nineteenth centuries by agents of Weishaupt's Illuminati. Freemasonry is an extremely secretive institution, to the extent that members at one level do not know what members at another level are doing and hence it is commonly known as an organisation concerned with charitable events and money raising for worthwhile causes at the lower levels, whilst its motives and deeds at the higher levels manifest an extremely dark side indeed. Anyone of any 'importance' in the world today such as senior police officers, members of the judiciary and local as well as central government officials can only attain the highest positions through Freemasonry, such is its insidious grip on the lives of us all. Indeed anyone deemed as an outsider will not be accepted for high office without being a member and depending on the exact position, a member at a certain level.

Both Freemasonry and Judaism have strong roots in the ancient Egyptian systems of religious belief and it was this very similarity which attracted the illuminati to Freemasonry, for most of them were Jewish originally and many senior people still are to this day. However, It is a source of controversy today to speculate whether or not they are still predominantly Jewish. Obviously it is evident that they are not all Jewish. Both George Bushes for instance, are prominent illuminati figures and yet overtly not Jewish, nevertheless they are Zionists despite their lack of 'Jewishness' as are the overwhelming majority of all politicians, the significance of which will be covered in greater detail in a later chapter.

The United States of America itself is no less than a creation of Freemasonry. The symbol of Freemasonry was placed on the cornerstone of the White House, while the assembled Freemasonic lodges stood and watched the ceremony. The famous 'all-seeing eye in the pyramid' appears on the US one dollar bill and is one of the main symbols of Freemasonry and the Illuminati. This $1 bill also bears the inscription, in Latin, '1776, the year of inception of a secular new world order' (Novus Ordo Seclorum) and significantly this does not refer to the date of American independence as assumed by most but simply to the date of the founding of the Illuminati. Also significantly, the dots formed by the stars of the thirteen original states depict an exact 'Star of David'.

As briefly alluded to previously, the goal of the Illuminati is total, absolute control of the world for the benefit of themselves and their families. They wish to see a one-world government, a one-world religion (theirs) and a one-world bank, all enforced by a one-world army who will police and subjugate the micro-chipped, remaining slave population who survive the proposed cull of 95% of the current population in line with their stated aims. The only nations currently resisting their power are the middle eastern, Islamic nations and China but this resistance is very limited purely because the Illuminati have vast economic power and influence and as can be observed in world events today, the western nations led by the USA and Britain primarily are currently systematically subjugating those remaining few nations not yet under their jackboots, one by one. The dominoes are falling all across the middle east as Afghanistan, Iraq and now Egypt and Libya fall under their spells with Syria, closely followed by Iran widely expected to be the next ones to succumb to their irresistible military machine.

There are certain methods of subjugation and control which are indispensable to this power, in addition to overt brute force. The first is, of course, complete control over all financial systems, all borrowing and lending. All banks, all building societies (mortgage providers) and all insurance companies will be completely under their control as one single entity in their proposed New World Order. It is an interesting if not widely known fact that both the Federal Reserve Bank and its British counterpart, the Bank of England are currently controlled by these Elite, Illuminati dynasties, in spite of the names of these banks deceptively suggesting that they are publicly run for public benefit. Both Abraham Lincoln and John F. Kennedy most famously attempted to change this system, along with several other US presidents such as James Garfield. They were of course all disposed of by the usual expedient of blaming 'lone-nut' assassins, but we all know who were the real culprits and they were certainly not those who purportedly 'pulled the triggers'.

The second essential component of maintaining ultimate power is total control of the media. This is achieved simply through standard business protocols. If a board meeting, a management meeting or a sales meeting for example, suggests or recommends that facts should be presented in a certain way, who is going to present them differently or even challenge this decree within a corporate entity without seriously jeopardising their own positions? In commerce, there is always an implied or even overt threat to jobs and livelihoods for the heinous crime of challenging the status quo and therefore few people would gladly risk unemployment for standing-up for a principle and indeed many people are so ambitious or desperate to enhance their standards of living that they will do almost anything at all 'reasonable', to court favour with their superiors. This is how all commerce and business activity is controlled and the media is at the forefront of the Elite control structure as it strongly influences the way we all think and what we believe to be real and unreal, true or false. Humans are very suggestible animals and this factor itself, is used by the Elite to the full. For example, Lenin's primary objective after the Russian revolution was the capture of the radio stations as he knew it was important to be able to influence and preferably win 'the hearts and minds' of the masses through propaganda broadcasts. Where have we heard that before?

The third element in the quest to wield total control of a population is 'education'. From the Elite-controlled universities down through the entire spectrum of the education system, there must be a paradigm in place which constantly churns out generation after generation of programmed 'system-servers'. Particular emphasis is placed on the teaching of sociology, politics, economics and education itself in order to affect full control. Elite place-men are inserted into the universities through the power of funding by big business and thus do they then spread their influence downwards from tertiary to secondary and primary education.

The fourth factor is the enormous influence wielded by two similar organisations, the Council on Foreign Relations (CFR) in the USA and the Royal Institute of International Affairs (RIIA) in the UK (see later chapters for more details). These institutions are training-schools for statesmen, Elite-controlled statesmen. They are the spawning grounds of men such as Henry Kissinger, Zbigniew Brzezinksi and Lord Carrington and exert a pernicious influence on all US and British governments, no matter which party is currently pretending to be 'in power'. The statesmen produced by these institutions can and do decide the fate of nations and even the whole world as well as fixing future policies with extremely long-term agendas through such methodologies as 'The Report from Iron Mountain' covered elsewhere in this book, totally regardless of supposed political affiliations. There are also many tax-exempt foundations which are also instruments of Elite power-broking. The Ford foundation and the Rockefeller foundation are two prominent examples of this type of 'charitable' institution and both of these organisations were heavily involved in supporting various communist powers when the 'Cold War' of 1945-90 was at its height. This communism versus capitalism arms race was simply a ploy by which more money and power for the Illuminati could be engendered, whilst at the same time causing most of the world to cower in fear at the thought of an imminent nuclear attack, referred to at every given opportunity by the media moguls of the world, as with the fake 'war on terror' in operation today. Fear is a most valuable weapon in their arsenal as fear renders populations easier to control and manage, but fear is only one simple method by which we are controlled, amongst many others.

Artificially creating conflicts using a theory devised by Hegel (the Hegelian dialectic), which is: thesis versus antithesis = synthesis. Sometimes more commonly referred to as 'problem, reaction, solution'. Every force tends to have an opposite counterforce and the conflict between the two results in a new situation, the synthesis. The Elite make it their business to be the synthesis and thus no problem situation is ever solved early but it is rather encouraged, exacerbated and used for their own ends.

After a time, the masses will cry out for a solution to the problem and of course our Elite masters will then come to our rescue with a plan to resolve it, thus engendering the exact situation that they wanted in the first place. A simple example would be this; the Elite decide that they want to impose more police powers to say, stop and search civilians at random. They will then engineer a scenario where several terrorist attacks take place which they deem could have been prevented by random street searches. The media will then make a huge 'play' of this fact and then the public will in turn and as planned all along, clamour for the very thing the Elite wanted, to be brought into law. Q.E.D.

Another ploy is that of 'divide and rule'. This takes so many forms and is utterly rampant in all its manifestations. Instead of promoting the similarities between all the diverse peoples of the world, the Elite emphasise the differences at every opportunity The encouragement of large scale immigration into first world countries is one great example of this 'divide and rule' strategy. Firstly, make a race of people appear to be the enemy through the usual methods of demonisation through the media and then encourage that race of people to undertake large scale immigration to the country in question. The newspapers and TV/Radio stations news programmes will then be full of comments such as '... these people, coming over here, taking OUR jobs' etc. all of which creates severe resentment, tension, unease, possibly violence and even murders. Create enough of this type of situation to keep us all engrossed and then by this expedient the Elite are left free to continue their agenda 'under the radar' as it were.

Even more common examples of the 'divide and rule' strategy are such basics as religion, race, gender, sexual orientation, age, class and skin colour. All these are used against us by encouraging us to concentrate on the differences between our fellow men and women, rather than the similarities and things we all have in common as members of the same species on the same planet.

'Double-speak' and 'double-think' were George Orwell's creations in his hugely prophetic novel, '1984'. Orwell was from an Elite, insider family who was broadly aware of the proposed future agenda for mankind. An example of double-speak would be; 'I categorically deny it will happen' really meaning 'it will happen a little later whilst you are all distracted by something else' or 'peace equals war by another means'. To say one thing and actually do the opposite is fundamental to Elite methods and practices. They believe that the public will accept these lies through apathy, ignorance, laziness and wishful thinking. Unfortunately they are usually correct – on all counts.

Keeping us all busy is another crucial aspect of their control. We are kept so busy working longer and longer hours and then afterwards with social distractions such as mass communication devices that allow us to be in almost constant contact with friends, computer games, music and 24/7 sports and entertainment broadcasting so that we do not have the energy left to care about, understand or participate in the decisions and events that will crucially affect our future. This of course allows them the clear route through to fulfilling their vile agenda almost un-noticed.

When a real move is made to grab even more power, it is usually done secretly and suddenly, often with the pretence that nothing has happened. There is preparation for opposition, but conflict is often not necessary as most people have been programmed to be so passive that they will probably not raise any effective opposition and often bad news for the masses can be buried in the fallout of other tragedies that now, to my mind at least, suspiciously take place in ever greater frequency. One example of this was the announcement of the Pentagon 'misplacing' $2.6 trillion dollars on the 10th September 2001 which was very convenient and largely responsible for the birth of the phrase 'a good day to bury bad news'. Also digressing slightly, but strange was it not that the missile, sorry, plane that allegedly hit the Pentagon on 9/11 just happened to hit the audit department where the search for the missing money was in feverish full-swing at the time. It was indeed the audit department that suffered the 120+ casualties sustained by employees of the Pentagon in the attacks of that day. This was obviously just another coincidence though, so please do not be at all alarmed.

The use of 'front men' in important positions is another important tactic. These 'front men' are in all cases, slavishly obedient to their Elite masters, usually because of their reputations being previously compromised by financial irregularity or indiscreet 'honey-traps' which they are anxious to conceal and often also because they are afraid of losing their positions of importance and influence and even sometimes they and their families' lives. Most of the Presidents of the USA and western senior politicians in general, fall into this category and they have in many cases, been groomed for this position almost from birth. Men like Tony Blair, David Cameron, Henry Kissinger, Zbigniew Brzezinski, Bill Clinton and George Bush are good examples.

Often the assassination of dissenting leaders is ordered, as quietly and as secretly as possible, so as to simulate a natural death or sometimes via the tried and tested 'lone-nut gunman' method. If this is not appropriate or possible due to circumstances, surrogates are used and the lines of suspicion are covered by deception, false accusation and if necessary, multiple assassinations to eliminate all those with the knowledge of what actually occurred. Undetectably induced heart attacks (eg. Robin Cook), fake 'accidents' (eg. Princess Diana) and contrived suicides (eg. Dr. David Kelly) constitute some of their favoured methods of assassination, besides the more overt assassinations such as those of Kennedy, John Lennon or Martin Luther King. It is rumoured that the secret services (MI5, MI6 and CIA etc.) are in possession of a type of gun that will fire deadly, bullet-like, thin slivers of ice that can penetrate the heart instantly and then melt, leaving no trace whatsoever.

An easily manipulated, compliant, un-thinking population is highly desirable and mixed population groups with weak morals, weak traditions, low educational standards and weak group-willpower are the aim. Those with special aptitudes, especially blind, unquestioning loyalty, will be groomed and trained to serve the Elite for technical purposes, security purposes or as part of the propaganda apparatus. Through skillful, patient social engineering, the middle classes are being systematically engineered to become surplus to requirements, reduced to relative poverty and eventually, over time to be part of the planned 'cull'.

Undermining the virtues and morals of society, control of the media, the fashion industries and the education systems are essential components in this strategy. 'Free love' otherwise known as extreme sexualisation – especially homosexuality, perverted sex, sexualisation of children, the cult of youth, overt and sustained mockery of religious faiths also fall into this category. By these means of subtle subversion, societies and nations are conquered from within and open confrontation is usually rendered unnecessary. It is the overt encouragement of homosexuality, increasingly-vile pornography, perversion and paedophilia etc., which is being used at an ever-increasing pace to attempt to bring about the destruction of human society and the traditional family and its values, thereby weakening humanity's last bastion of defence, the security inherent in the philosophy of 'sticking together against the odds', against these extreme psychopathic predators.

The concept of unrelenting economic warfare is yet another weapon in their armoury and the recent economic crashes and the widely expected worldwide financial catastrophe at the time of writing still-to-come, is in reality an assertion of the Elite's economic power, an expression of economic dominance and a weapon to cause maximum fear and disruption and the extending of their power, money and influence still further. Also as we will see in a later chapter, the Elite now own the means to control the worldwide weather and even geological upheaval and are not averse to using it for their own nefarious ends. (see chapter on HAARP).

We are also suffering from the extreme control and exploitation and a general lowering of the standards of public health. The sale of prescription drugs is a huge business, generating obscene profit levels, whilst seriously debilitating our physical and mental health and thus affecting further our ability to recognise how we are being duped on a grand scale. In fact, big business, particularly the big drug companies, have a vested interest in the ill health of the population. These companies, working through the US Food and Drug Administration, (FDA) are wilfully suppressing the health food industry in order to own and control it so that healthy and nutritious foods will only be available to the Elite few.

It is perhaps pertinent at this stage to point-out the great deception taking place on a worldwide scale regarding political labels, in order to confuse and obfuscate the hidden goals of the Elite. To clarify here are some political terms, their perceived meanings and their actual meanings...

Communism. Believed to be and painted as the 'evil' doctrine devised by the Elite puppet Karl Marx as a means of equalising and sharing power between all levels of society and portrayed by its exponents as a legitimate way of ending all the inequality and poverty in the world. Often described as unworkable as it 'runs contrary to human nature'.

Actually no different in practice to Socialism. More accurately described as Communitarianism consisting of totalitarianism and overt control by the Government instead of by 'the people', the exact opposite to that implied.

Socialism. Generally thought by 'the people' to be a form of watered-down Communism. A sort of acceptable 'half-way house' which enables the 'lower classes' to participate in the governmental decision-making process without the full descent into anarchy that Communism is perceived as being. The antithesis of Capitalism.

No different in practice to Communism, but this perceived difference allows the Elite to subtly promulgate Socialism where Communism would be unacceptable.

Fascism. The overt control of the people and all of capitalist industry by the Government rather than the capitalist interests. Another 'no-no' as far as the masses are concerned.

There is absolutely no difference whatsoever between any of these three terms in a practical, working sense. These perceived opposites, Fascism and Communism have been used to divert us from the truth and control us for more than a century, whilst the Elite work towards their ultimate goal of a Fascist / Socialist / Communist One World Government. They do not really care what it is referred to as in respect of the above terms – only that it comes about as quickly as possible.

"Under Capitalism, man exploits man while under Communism; it's the other way around." 20th century Russian saying.

So, there is no fundamental difference between the perceived polarities of Fascism and Communism and its little brother, Socialism. It is simply a ruse to keep us all debating and thus lose sight of the real issues. In other words it is a typical 'Hegelian trap'. Under Communism, the state owns the corporations and the bankers own the state. Under Fascism, the corporations own the state and the bankers own the corporations. Both 'systems' are absolutely dedicated to providing the Elite bankers (who are the real rulers) with a total political, cultural, economic and spiritual monopoly, otherwise known as the New World Order. This is the real reason for the existence of deliberately manufactured, false paradigms such as 'racism', 'anti-Semitism' 'hate speech' and 'political correctness'. It is not about protecting the 'freedoms' and rights of minorities as it is portrayed to be, it is really about the restriction and ultimately the enslavement of the majority. Do you think the likes of Cameron, Obama, Sarkozy, Merkel, Gillard and their ilk (or any of the so-called 'loyal opposition' for that matter) give a damn about protecting the rights of blacks, Jews, homosexuals and other 'oppressed minorities'? Unfortunately, it is just another control mechanism.

What we casually refer to as 'racism' is so blatantly one-sided in any case. What actually constitutes racism and where do we draw the line? An obvious example of racism would be calling someone a 'black bastard' for example, but why is that now accepted and reviled universally as being a crime worse than simply calling someone a 'Welsh bastard', a 'ginger bastard' or even just simply a 'bastard'? Referring to someone of a white-majority race such as a Welshman by his race is less unacceptable is it? It certainly would not invoke the same outrage as the use of his skin colour would. We need to look between the lines and ask why this has been engineered to be the case, as it most certainly has and not just over-react to conveniently arbitrary, artificial distinctions.

For example in late 2011 / early 2012 the world of British sport was thrust into the spotlight with a series of 'racism' scandals which dominated the sports and the standard news broadcasts for weeks on end, with accusations and counter accusations flying around and a series of 'talking heads' being employed to emphasise the evil inherent in these heinous crimes (as they have been engineered to become). One of the incidents culminated in the English FA removing John Terry (the England soccer captain) from his duties simply because he was *accused* (not convicted or proven mind you, simply accused) of using racist language to another player, in turn resulting in the resignation of the England team manager, Fabio Capello in protest and in a show of allegiance to Terry. Now, I am not condoning what he allegedly did at all. Any form of verbal abuse of anyone is unacceptable in my opinion, but the fact that the tag 'racism' has been attached to it, somehow puts it on a par with first degree murder, such is the ensuing outcry. Why should this be? We need to ask ourselves honestly if the same degree of 'horror' would have resulted from Terry or anyone else abusing one of his colleagues because he was a 'northerner' or had ginger hair, but I think we all already know the answer to that question. Please do not be fooled by this hypocrisy.

However, getting back on topic, the huge difference in the 'first world' as opposed to the rest of the world is that there is an illusion of freedom and democracy. Groomed servants of the bankers are chosen to lead governments and corporate organisations, whilst unwitting dupes and shills perpetuate the illusion of a free, democratic society. The masses meanwhile are deliberately kept in a deep coma through the education system and the mass media and with engineered distractions such as the above-described racism debate.

To conclude this section, it is growing increasingly evident that a world government, otherwise widely referred-to as the *New World Order* is being promulgated by the Elite as rapidly as they dare. The consequences of World Government (or some of them) will be as follows:

Increasing profits for big business whilst further centralising power into the super-corporations.

Increasing poverty for and dissolution of the middle classes.

A rapid decline in moral standards and the promotion of social decay resulting in extreme social instability.

Extreme transience including but not exclusive to, jobs that do not last and communities that do not survive long.

Increasing levels of crime and violence to cause maximum fear and disruption.

The decline and ultimate demise of public services which will be replaced by private enterprise. Good service only for those few that can afford it.

Ongoing ill health for the bulk of the population because of stress, poor quality foods, food additives, genetic engineering, vaccinations, environmental and atmospheric pollution and pharmaceutical drugs. There will be good health only for those who can afford it and it will be priced well beyond the means of us ordinary mortals.

The gradual phasing out of national governments, which will have powers more similar to the regional/local governments of today. This is already happening through organisations such as the United Nations, the EU and NAFTA.

The appointment (note, not the election) of a new 'world leader' wielding supreme executive power over the whole of the planet.

This then will comprise their much-vaunted and oft-cited 'New World Order', a world of utter, abject misery and slavery for the few non-Elites still remaining after the proposed super-genocide to come.

The Great Library of Alexandria

Perhaps the very first known major example of an attempt to facilitate the systematic falsification of history was the deliberate burning of the great Library of Alexandria, established in the third century BC as a central archive for all the knowledge of the known world, in what is now modern day Egypt. This library was the repository of most of the ancient knowledge passed down from the previous millennia and stored there in the form of scrolls, meticulously copied from the originals by an army of scribes. Had we access now to the knowledge deliberately destroyed at this time, then this world would be a vastly different place today, where false versions of history are the norm and grand deception is very much the order of the day.

In much the same way, a false version of reality has been protected ever since throughout history by the destruction of ancient tribal knowledge as empire-building nations such as the British, Spanish, French, Dutch and latterly the Americans have spread their various doctrines throughout the world utilising the bloodiest methods imaginable. In this way, ancient civilisations such as the Incas, Aztecs, Mayans, Zulus, native Australians and native Americans were firstly subjected to brutal conquest, annihilation and then 'westernisation' whilst their ancient knowledge, passed down meticulously from generation to generation for millennia, was systematically eliminated to protect the status quo.

The museum at the Library of Alexandria was a place of study which included lecture areas, gardens, a zoo and shrines for each of the nine ancient Greek muses as well as the Library itself. It has been estimated that at one time the Library held more than half a million documents from Assyria, Greece, Persia, Egypt, Rome, India, China and many other nations. Over 100 scholars lived at the Museum full-time to perform research, write, lecture or translate and copy documents.

The actual date of the destruction is still debated to this day. Some sources regard it as being as early as the 3rd century AD whilst others consider it to be as late as the 7th century AD, these dates being wholly dependent upon who is apportioned the blame for the tragedy. However, most credible historians and commentators generally ascribe the act to the Holy Roman Emperor Theodosius I, a violent and fanatical Christian in 391AD, as he was almost certainly responsible for the destruction of the daughter library nearby at the Serapeum in that year.

The destruction of all that ancient knowledge by Christians, supposed men of peace and 'love', is actually quite plausible. Christianity was born of extreme violence and indeed kept alive by the same despicable methods for many centuries, even up to the present time, almost. Indeed, by what better expedient could its myths and lies be perpetuated, if not the destruction of all the knowledge that would no doubt prove it to be the outright deception it most certainly was and is? The deception surrounding one of the greatest hoaxes inflicted upon the masses by the Elite of the day, had to be protected somehow and by burning all the ancient knowledge, Theodosius and his fanatical supporters performed a great service to the cause. Now Christianity could reign supreme with little or no ancient knowledge surviving to contradict its many myths, lies and distortions of the truth.

Since time immemorial, this same modus operandus has constantly been used to deceive. Destroy the conflicting knowledge in order to enable what remains to stand-alone as the truth with no competition remaining to dilute its purity. It is in fact this one significant, documented event that has set the scene for the future. Mankind's destiny has been determined almost by this one major incident alone. The burning of the library and its priceless, utterly irreplaceable contents has indeed set a precedent to be repeated over and over during the following 1600+ years of misery for those millions and billions unfortunate enough to have been born outside of the Elite families.

False Flag Operations

A false flag operation may be loosely defined as an act or series of acts that is designed to fool the victims and / or the unsuspecting public into believing that it was carried out by totally different entities to those who were the actual perpetrators. The name is derived from the fact that the perpetrators were apparently operating under a country's flag different from the one of whom it appeared on the surface to have carried out the attack.

"Covert operations designed to deceive the public in such a way that the operations appear as though they are being carried out by other entities." Wikipedia

For example, the incident that purportedly sparked WWII, the supposed dressing-up in Polish uniforms of German soldiers and attacking their own borders. And more recently the case of the 'inside job' now simply referred to as '9/11' whereby a group of 19 young Saudi Arabians (at least 12 of whom are proven to be still alive), controlled and funded by a dying man in a cave in Afghanistan, that we are meant to believe overwhelmed the defences of the strongest, most security-conscious nation on Earth and managed to hijack not one, but four planes in the most heavily secured airspace in the world and fly three of them into buildings with flying skills, many commercial airline pilots have publicly stated to be way beyond their own capabilities, let alone those of one who has merely had twelve lessons in a single-engined turbo-prop plane.

These are both popular, well-known examples of false flag attacks.

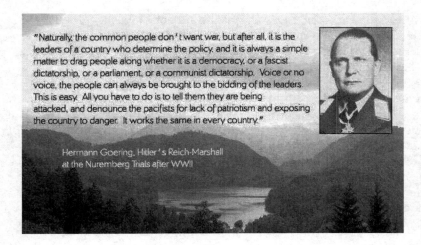

"Naturally, the common people don't want war, but after all, it is the leaders of a country who determine the policy, and it is always a simple matter to drag people along whether it is a democracy, or a fascist dictatorship, or a parliament, or a communist dictatorship. Voice or no voice, the people can always be brought to the bidding of the leaders. This is easy. All you have to do is to tell them they are being attacked, and denounce the pacifists for lack of patriotism and exposing the country to danger. It works the same in every country."

Hermann Goering, Hitler's Reich-Marshall at the Nuremberg Trials after WWII

So, 'false flag' is one of the major propaganda weapons of choice for our Elite friends. They use it all the time – and to be brutally frank, why would they not continue to use it? It works perfectly time after time. From the *'USS Maine'* incident used to provoke the Spanish-American war at the turn of the 20th century, to the 'Gulf of Tonkin' incident that sparked the Vietnam War, to the bombing of the Alfred P Murrah building in Oklahoma, 9/11 itself, the Madrid railway station bombing and 7/7 in London. Many of these incidents (and these are just a few prime examples) were perpetrated by the Elite run CIA / MI6 / Mossad group which pretends to be three separate entities, but in reality is one and the same at the top echelons, in league with the relevant governments, all controlled by the same Elite group of course.

The real 'Axis of Evil'

Why? Why would they do this? What is there to gain for a country and its ruling Elite, from pre-meditated, cold-blooded mass-murder of its own citizens?

The highly simplified answer of course is 'to further their agendas'. However, as is always the case, the reasons are far more complex than this.

"Past US false flags provided pretexts for militarism, wars, occupations, domestic repression, and national security state extremism, antithetical to democratically free and open societies." Stephen Lendman, researcher, *'False Flags – An American Tradition'*, May 2011

In the case of 9/11 (see relevant chapter), this was used to further the ambitions of subjugation of the people to even greater degrees through such insidious legislation as the *Patriot Act* (2001) which had obviously been prepared well in advance of the 9/11 attacks and which further served to severely limit freedom of speech and freedom of movement, to generally spread fear – a fearful population is easier to control than a happy one – and to increase governmental control of the American population. 9/11 was also used as a pretext to invade Iraq and later Afghanistan along with the now discredited and falsified evidence for the presence of 'weapons of mass destruction'. However it is yet to be satisfactorily explained as to why Iraq bore any responsibility for 9/11 even if we temporarily assume that it was the work of a terrorist group and not, as was actually the case, the Mossad in co-operation with American insiders in the form of Neo-Conservatives and American-Israeli dual-citizen Zionists. Of course that is all highly irrelevant in a sense. The facts are not important to these people as long as they can create an impression in the public's minds that Iraq was to blame (easy when you use the power of the controlled media) – that is all that matters.

It can also be argued that we should always look, in these situations, to who had the most to gain from the event (cui bono – who benefits?). Once again the Israeli connection rears its head. Israel is always looking for excuses to attack and further subjugate its Muslim neighbours, as is its mandate and indeed, raison d'être and how better to achieve this end than to unite the American public in its hatred of both the general Muslim world and specifically Iraq who had long been targeted as the next for annihilation by these Satanic entities?

False flag operations have been a strategic method of Elite governments to gain control on many platforms throughout history. One of the earliest accounts of a False Flag operation taking place is in 47BC when Julius Caesar used a series of riots and arson attacks that he paid for and commanded, to destabilise the Roman Republic before marching his legions across the Rubicon and into Rome, where he seized power and declared himself Emperor.

That may indeed be the earliest known example, but since this type of operation is so effective it seems plausible to speculate that even earlier in human history there may have been many others.

Indeed, much of history is littered with False Flag operations since almost the beginning of time. There is compelling evidence of such operations from as long ago as the English Wars of the Roses in the 15th century and continuing through the English and US Civil Wars, Spanish-American War and every conflict since then up to the present time. Were we to have asked most people prior to 9/11 if they had heard of the term 'False Flag operation' the answer would most likely have been a negative, very probably due to the fact that an operation of that size had not taken place since the US government purposely ignored the military intelligence received regarding the fact that the Japanese were planning an attack on Pearl Harbor.

False flag operations fall under the umbrella of Black Operations and these Black Ops are of course 'Above Top Secret' covert operations performed by such special forces as the US Navy SEALS, Delta Force, CIA, MI5, MI6, Mossad and the rest of the military branches as well as other government agencies in many countries. They are utilised for a number of reasons and it is important to understand that most Black Operations are executed solely through government but occasionally it may be a military-industrial-complex co-operation. By that I mean that the government will work jointly with a private multinational company or corporation if there is the opportunity for both sides to gain. Such Black Operations can be assassinations, industrial espionage, force reconnaissance, psy-ops, abductions, drug trafficking, false flag operations and more.

Let us briefly examine the 9/11 situation as an example. This operation was engineered for a number of reasons ranging from financial to a further clampdown on personal liberties as well as justification for the illegal invasion and occupation of two sovereign states (Iraq and Afghanistan). The day before the attack it was reported that the Pentagon had somehow 'lost' $2.6 trillion and could it therefore have been simply coincidence that the attack on the Pentagon occurred in the area where hundreds of auditors were feverishly searching for the missing trillions, over one hundred of whom died?

Then literally within days of the attacks, the 'Patriot Act' was rushed through Congress allowing no time whatsoever for Senators to even read the massive document, let alone form an opinion as to its validity or efficacy. It also begs the question as to how such a weighty document could have been collated in such a short space of time after the attacks. The answer of course is obvious and that is simply that the document was authored long before the event and the event had been in the planning for several years, if not actually decades.

Immediately, following the Patriot Act was the integration of dozens of Federal agencies to form the Department of Homeland Security and also the Transportation Security Administration. The 'attack' also caused a public outcry which through the expedient of 'problem, reaction, solution', allowed the Elite to deploy the might of the American military in *Operation Enduring Freedom* in 2001 and then *Operation Iraqi Freedom* in 2003. And last but certainly not least was the crucial 'fear factor' which is designed to keep the population in a permanent state of trepidation and thus easier to control and manipulate.

As former President George W. Bush discovered, attacking America is the surest way to raise the popularity of the President. In the aftermath of 9/11, Bush's popularity soared beyond 70% and gave him the political momentum to pass almost any law he desired. Out of that was born the Patriot Act, one of the most dangerous freedom-crushing laws in US history, a law which absolutely dismantles the Bill of Rights and is now being successfully used against animal rights protestors, farmers and anyone who has a legitimate grievance with authority and other 'dissident' groups, as a by-product.

As previously related, false flag terror attacks have been part of governments' game plans for the last several centuries. *Operation Northwoods*, whose documents have now been made public under the 'fifty year' rule, revealed that in the early 1960s, the US government plotted to stage attacks on US cities in order to blame Fidel Castro and justify an invasion of Cuba. This is a well-documented historical fact, so please do not assume that this is all just some bizarre conspiracy theory. This was official, strategic policy at the highest levels of government and is most assuredly conspiracy fact and not theory.

So, to repeat for the avoidance of doubt, the US government was willing to kill many innocent American citizens in order to garner public support for a war against Cuba to further the Elite agenda. One of the proposed target-cities of this operation was Miami, which would have suffered countless civilian casualties under this plan. This was all spelt-out by the US Department of Defence and the Joint Chiefs of Staff in a document entitled, *'Justification for US Military Intervention in Cuba'* and is important to consider in the light of the events of 9/11, especially by those among us who are firmly of the opinion that their governments would simply just 'not be capable' of such an act.

"Operation Northwoods, which had the written approval of the Chairman and every member of the Joint Chiefs of Staff, called for innocent people to be shot on American streets; for boats carrying refugees fleeing Cuba to be sunk on the high seas; for a wave of violent terrorism to be launched in Washington DC, Miami, and elsewhere. People would be framed for bombings they did not commit and planes would be hijacked. Using phony evidence, all of it would be blamed on Castro, thus giving Lemnitzer and his cabal the excuse, as well as the public and international backing, they needed to launch their war." James Bamford, journalist

So, false flag attacks are routinely used by government around the world as pretexts for war. They are also quite convenient for boosting the popularity of the President and/or the government. Slumping in the polls? Stage a mass-shooting, or better still, why not poison the water supply of an entire city. In the aftermath of this terror, the sheeple will go along with just about anything, including military troops on the streets, even in total violation of *Posse Comitatus* which prohibits the military from engaging in law enforcement actions on US soil.

Janet Napolitano, the most prolific of the propagandists of fear at the Department of Homeland Security, is constantly busy warning people about further impending terrorist attacks. However, what she has omitted to mention in all this is that it is the US government itself that is the terrorist group that is most likely to be organising these attacks for its own political ends. Having a terrorist group take over a nuclear power plant on say a 9/11 anniversary would remind Americans to 'be very afraid' and surrender to government authority in order to feel a little safer. This is classic problem-reaction-solution.

The US government needs to be able to keep control of hundreds of millions of people but many people are now beginning to question authority. They are tired of the thugs of the TSA groping and ogling at their sons, wives and daughters in the name of air security, tired of extreme police brutality, tired of the government bailing out the banks and are currently engaged in an online groundswell of disobedience toward Washington. One way to silence all these people and portray anti-government speech as 'acts of terrorism' would be to plant a bomb somewhere such as the New York subway and blame it on white American extremists. The Department of Homeland Security (DHS) is already preparing the US for this or similar with propaganda ads that depict ordinary white people as terrorists after whites have complained about the extent to which their activities are being curtailed despite the fact that their physical appearance is nothing like the previously stereotypical 'Muslim terrorists'.

The most likely targets for new false flag attacks are ones that have lots of eye-catching visuals that can be shown on the news channels 24/7 so that they can almost literally burn the fear into the eyeballs of the sheeple. The bloodier it all is, the better, in the eyes of the Elite conspirators because blood and gore creates fear that can be harnessed to pass yet more freedom-crushing legislation or simply to install the military on the streets, in yet another furtherance of the wider agenda. So the government needs something that has a strong visual element, such as a destroyed building, piles of bodies or thousands of people becoming sick and dying from radiation unleashed from a dirty bomb, for example.

Therefore these possible false flag terror scenarios would appear to be the most likely to be invoked:

• Blowing-up trains carrying either nuclear materials and/or extremely dangerous chemicals, probably near a large population area in order to cause mass casualties.

• Setting-off a dirty bomb in a major city, causing widespread radiation poisoning of millions.

• A mass shooting massacre at a sporting event or shopping mall. This one has the added benefit of also instigating a call for national gun confiscation.

• Taking-over and exploding an oil refinery. They will wait for all the TV cameras to arrive before setting off the explosions, of course.

• There is also a possibility that the Elite will try to use a disgruntled farmer as the patsy, rigging up some sort of explosion using large volumes of fertilizer and a white farmer wielding a firearm. This would be an expedient way to attack food freedoms by portraying farmers as terrorists. A farmer could easily be made to target a government building (as with the Oklahoma City bombing in 1997) and the explosion would help spread fear and instill even more government control and restrictions over farms and food production, again in line with the wider objectives.

This would play directly into the hands of the FDA which is already in the process of grabbing more control over the food supply. What better way to accomplish that than to portray farmers as terrorists?

The whole point of these operations is to paint patriots as terrorists and thereby convince the rest of the sheeple in the country to strip away whatever remaining rights and protections free people might expect to enjoy.

But the question remains, how does the government get 'patsies' to co-operate with them? How does the government get people like Timothy McVeigh (Oklahoma bombing) or Lee Harvey Oswald (Kennedy assassination) the London 'tube bombers' on 7/7 2005 or the Saudi 'terrorists' on 9/11, to play their roles? The answer is deceptively simple. Undercover intelligence agents find and nurture people (sometimes for years) who are disgruntled and a little 'unconventional'. Then they convince them or literally 'programme' them to take action against the country and actually provide them with the money, materials, logistics and know-how they need to pull off 'their' operations.

This is the reason that government agents 'helped' the infamous Christmas Day 'underwear bomber' board an aircraft even though he had no identification. The FBI has also admitted to having been caught trying to arm a terrorist in Portland, Oregon with a 'fake bomb'. In the UK the Muslim 'bombers' of 7/7 fame were known-to-be government sympathisers helping out the government in what they (the patsies) thought was an anti-terrorism exercise.

"Why does the FBI orchestrate fake 'terror plots'? The latest one snared Osman Mohamud, a Somali-American teenager in Portland, Oregon. The Associated Press report is headlined, 'Somali-born teen plotted car-bombing in Oregon'. This is a misleading headline as the report makes it clear that it was a plot orchestrated by federal agents. Two sentences into the news report we have this: 'The bomb was an elaborate fake supplied by the [FBI] agents and the public was never in danger, authorities said'. The teenager was supplied with a fake bomb and a fake detonator and the FBI's staging of 'fake terror' in Portland resulted in a mass of angry citizens storming the Portland city hall to protest." Paul Craig Roberts, former member of the Reagan government

In all probability, the FBI, CIA, Mossad, MI5 and MI6 are currently, as you read this, trying to recruit disgruntled 'lone-nuts' to carry out 'terror attacks' on home soil and the DHS is busily spreading lies in America that the next terror attack will come from white American terrorists. (Meanwhile, hilariously, the leader of the Libyan rebels who have been strongly aided by the US and the United Nations is admittedly an 'al-Qaeda' operative, once again proving that the US government openly funds terrorists.)

We should all realise that all these individual actions of government tyranny and intimidation make up the puzzle-pieces of a much larger picture and that that picture clearly depicts governments as something that has long forgotten any sense of serving the people through civic duty and, instead, now views itself as the **controller** of the people. Government today views itself as the police state authority over every detail of our lives.

The government of America has become the very same freedom-crushing monstrosity that the founding fathers originally warned about and exists solely to keep the American people in line. Indeed, this is the reality of all governments today and so we need to take back our freedoms to prevent violence from being committed by our governments against its own citizens.

This is why we can now expect the next so-called 'terrorist' attacks to be false flag operations. Now that rule of law has been almost totally abandoned, terror is the one remaining tactic they can use to keep the sheeple in line. George Bush used it effectively to partially dismantle the Bill of Rights and now Obama (and his successor) will continue the work of George Bush just as he already has with secret prisons, illegal wars, economic destruction and empty rhetoric that only distracts the people from the reality of what is being committed upon them. All at the behest of course of the unseen, hidden hand that rules us all. eg. In December 2011 it was reported in the alternative media, backed up with documentary proof, that the Homeland Security agency and FEMA are currently recruiting staff for the staffing of and issuing tenders for the fitting-out of the hundreds of concentration camps currently lying empty all over the US, in conjunction with passing the legislation required to fully dismantle the Bill of Rights and create a martial-law governed state with the power to detain dissenters, indefinitely.

Truly Orwellian stuff indeed and all achieved without a murmur of protest from the unknowing, uncaring, unthinking masses as they watch their TV soaps, read the latest celebrity scandals and sports scores in the so-called 'newspapers' and incessantly chatter inanely with their friends using the latest gadgets and technology. Machiavelli, Hitler, Mussolini and Stalin would be very proud.

Examples of major false flag operations in the last 400 years, some of which are covered in detail in this book:

The Gunpowder Plot 1605
The English Revolution (Civil War) 1642
The American Revolution 1776
The French Revolution 1789

The assassination of Lincoln 1865
The 'Jack the Ripper' murders 1888
The USS Maine incident sparking the Spanish-American war of 1898
The sinking of the Titanic 1912
The sinking of the Lusitania 1915
The Russian Revolution 1917
The burning of the Reichstag building 1938
The Polish attack on Germany 1939
The attack on Pearl Harbour 1941
The bombing of the King David Hotel 1948
The installation of the Shah of Iran 1952
Operation Northwoods 1962
The assassination of JF Kennedy 1963
The 'Gulf of Tonkin' incident 1965
The assassination of RF Kennedy 1968
The Apollo moon landings 1969-72
The Birmingham and Guildford pub bombings 1974
The Jonestown 'suicides' 1979
The Lockerbie bombing 1989
The burning of the compound at Waco 1993
Hurricane Andrew 1993
The Omagh bombing 1995
The Oklahoma City bombing 1997
The assassination of Princess Diana 1997
The attacks on the World Trade Center and the Pentagon (9/11) 2001
The Bali bombing 2004
The Madrid train bombing 2004
The Indian Ocean Tsunami 2004
The London tube bombings (7/7) 2005
Hurricane Katrina 2005
The China earthquake 2009
The Haiti earthquake 2010
The Polish 'government' plane crash 2010
The Japanese earthquake and Tsunami 2011

So now let us now begin the rocky journey towards the present day whilst focussing upon some of the most important historical events and those perhaps 'hidden histories', concealed truths and incidents that have served to shape the world in which we all live today...

PART 2 – The Dark Ages to the End of the Second Millennium

The Discovery of the American continent

If you believe that Christopher Columbus 'discovered' America in 1492, I would urge you to think again.

America is well known to have been visited more than a thousand years ago by the Vikings who actually named it 'Vinland' and even set-up several permanent settlements there. However, perhaps a little less well-known is the fact that travellers from the British Isles sailed to and colonised parts of the American landmass more than fifteen hundred years ago and are even said to be the original ancestors of some (but not all) of the native tribes such as the Mohicans and the Mohawks amongst others.

But then of course, the American land mass has 'always' been there, even before it was occupied by the ancestors of the 'Native American' Indians, the Aztecs, the Maya and the Incas et al. So as to who actually 'discovered' it in the sense of being the first humans to set foot upon its soil, is really a moot point.

Again we are the victims of a grand deception if we believe erroneously that Christopher Columbus (aka Christophe Colon) actually accidentally discovered America, allegedly in a quest to sail to India, by sailing westwards and thus prove that the world was round (spherical) and not flat. Firstly, Columbus never actually set foot on the American mainland, he merely encountered the island group now known as the West Indies (hence the name – Indies – India).

The information which we are constantly fed by mainstream history and which is perpetuated by the controlled media is typical of the systematic re-writing and invention of history and is incorrect on several levels. Columbus never intended to sail to India by sailing westward. The Elite of that era knew very well that the continent of America existed and that the world was round, as did all the ancient cultures of the time. Columbus was in fact sponsored by the Spanish royal family to go forth and conquer and bring back as much booty as his little ship(s) would carry, in order to swell the royal coffers. This he did very successfully. In addition, the only people who believed that the Earth was flat at that time were the poor, suppressed, illiterate masses who had no option but to believe everything that their rulers and the Catholic Church told them as they had no other means of educating themselves with the truth or indeed of acquainting themselves with a diametrically opposing viewpoint. There was at the time, of course, no media of ANY kind, no education or access to books for the poor underclasses and absolutely no other means of contradicting whatever garbage the powers-that-be should foist upon the unfortunate, 'great unwashed' of the time. It is fairly easy therefore to understand how these myths were able to be propagated and sustained in perpetuity.

In the sixteenth century, the Turkish cartographer Piri Reis published over 200 maps of the world. In preparing these maps, Reis stated that he had used as the basis for them, 20 old charts depicting the entire known landmasses of the Earth (including Antarctica which was purportedly unknown as a landmass at that time and also the Americas) believed by him to have been drawn-up during the time of Alexander the Great. These ancient charts he had discovered in the Imperial Library in Constantinople, a repository of surviving ancient knowledge and the scholars there told him that apparently these had been based-upon even older charts, some said from Sumerian sources. These maps also depicted the exact position of the Falkland Islands, allegedly not discovered until 1592 and fully documented the entire lengths of the major South American rivers, the Orinoco, Parana and Amazon which were not fully charted in modern times until the advent of satellite technology!

Again, clear evidence that ancient knowledge far surpassed that of our immediate forebears – or at least knowledge that was commonly-known by all.

In 2002, a team of historians and researchers headed by the British historical researchers, Alan Wilson and Baram Blackett, announced that radio-carbon dating evidence and the presence of ancient British–style artefacts and inscriptions liberally scattered in the North American continent, provide virtually irrefutable evidence that ancient British (Welsh) explorers under Prince Madoc ap Meurig, arrived there during the 6th Century AD and established several settlements.

Wilson and Blackett had previously been aware of the location of burial sites of Madoc's family members in Wales for many years and they have been attempting to get this information out into the mainstream, for the most part unsuccessfully due to the intransigence of mainstream history, which refuses to acknowledge the truth despite an abundance of evidence being offered in proof of their discoveries. DNA evidence may eventually be the key to the mystery and could help identify the human remains found at Bat Creek, Tennessee and which currently reside at the Smithsonian Institute in Washington DC. These remains may even turn out to be those of Madoc himself. The British researchers were contacted by Jim Michael of the 'Ancient Kentucke Historical Association' in 1989 with a view to sharing knowledge and to learn from each other's detailed research on the subject.

Several tumuli (grave mounds) discovered in the American mid-West, including ones at Bat Creek are almost certainly ancient British in origin and design, Wilson confirmed and Jim Michael added that the stone-tablet found at Bat Creek in 1889 included an inscription written in Coelbren, an ancient British alphabet, primarily of Welsh origin but similar in appearance to Celtic and extensively recorded and studied by historians through the ages.

Alan Wilson's research had previously included the investigation of similar alphabetic inscriptions in Britain, Europe and the Middle East, the components of which derived from the earliest days of the Khumric (Welsh) people and were known to have been used all along their migration routes from Babylon into Wales, going back literally thousands of years. Baram Blackett commented, *"Once we discovered the cipher for the alphabet recorded in texts dating to the 1500s we knew we were in business. We have translated many of these inscriptions and they all make perfect sense."* Jim Michael also added that the final translation of the Bat Creek tablet provided the researchers with the stunning revelation, *'Madoc the ruler he is'.*

Most mainstream historians have disregarded all this evidence for Prince Madoc, the Welsh Prince having sailed to America circa 562AD, as to acknowledge this work would virtually demolish all of current mainstream Dark Age history and thus the reputations and livelihoods of many researchers. Indeed, Wilson and Blackett have been constantly subjected over the years to concerted smear campaigns, common insults and 'stonewalling' by the establishment. Fortunately however, due mainly to Wilson and Blackett's persistence, there exists a substantial body of evidence to prove their hypotheses.

"I think they're afraid that an independent group such as ours has made such progress. They prefer to ignore and neglect ancient British history rather than to deal with it. The Welsh people have suffered and the opportunity to boost the economy, to bring thousands of jobs to Glamorgan and Gwent, where Madoc and his brother Arthur II ruled, has not been exploited." Alan Wilson.

There are numerous ancient British Coelbren inscriptions in the American mid-West including skulls of definite European or Caucasian origin, unlike most other Native American ancient remains.

Prince Madoc was the brother of King Arthur II and lived during the 6th Century. This is fact and not mere speculation and is confirmed by many ancient British manuscripts and genealogies. If it can be proved beyond all lingering doubt that he and many of his followers indeed emigrated en masse to the Americas almost 1500 years ago then history will need to be re-written to embrace the truth.

Of course, the Columbus story is simply a myth, a convenient cover story to deflect us from the truth and protect those who would deceive us. The main significance of the date 1492 is that it marked the beginning of the rape and pillage of the American continent. After Columbus' exploits, he was followed by a huge influx of invaders from all over Europe, all eager to gain their share of the spoils to be had in abundance from a previously 'virgin' territory. The Spanish conquistadors infamously succeeded in all but destroying the ancient Inca, Aztec and Mayan cultures in South and Central America in an action that was coldly calculated to destroy any vestiges of ancient knowledge which would have proved harmful if not fatal to the Christian creed, as well as facilitate the theft of all their valuable, ancient gold artefacts.

Then just over 100 years later in the early seventeenth century, the mass immigration to North America commenced, initially by the persecuted Puritans from England who subsequently proceeded to inflict the same fate that they had endured upon the ancient native tribes they encountered upon settlement there. The English were joined by first the French and the Dutch and then in the succeeding centuries by the 'huddled masses yearning to breathe free' from all over Europe and indeed the world and thus from such small beginnings was born what was to become 'the greatest Empire the world has ever known', to the great misfortune of us all, but especially those millions if not billions of innocents who have suffered and died at the hands of that great 'superpower', the United States of America.

Ancient British History

Alan Wilson, the author and researcher has been researching ancient British history, latterly along with his colleague, Baram Blackett, for more than 50 years and his amazing discoveries and revelations have absolutely revolutionised British 'Dark Ages' history.

Of course, as with any truths which do not fit the manufactured history of the Elite and/or go against the heavily protected mainstream view, his work has been undermined, subjected to lies, disinformation and even threats from the establishment. Primarily however, it has simply been ignored (another successful tactic employed by the powers that be) despite Wilson's entreaties to historians and archaeologists to examine the abundance of evidence he has uncovered and which offers virtually irrefutable proof that his hypotheses are correct. He has even begged for open debate on the subject, contacted governments, universities and academia in general, simply to be met with a deafening silence, lies or the aforementioned, veiled threats.

Why would this be? What do these people have to hide or to lose?

As ever, reputations are at stake. Most mainstream archaeologists and historians must 'toe the party line' in order to gain employment and funding and if they were to embrace or espouse a viewpoint which goes against the accepted version of events, then they will naturally be shunned and denounced by the majority who do so in order to protect their own livelihoods and positions of power.

Of course, the bigger picture is that there are also powerful vested interests, the Elite, who do not want the real truth to be known as it goes against their manufactured version of reality, put in place to deceive and cover-up the truth of who we really are and from whence we originated.

The 'Legend' of King Arthur

Ask most people about King Arthur and the response you will likely elicit is that he never really existed and is simply 'a legend'. I should like to ask in all seriousness, how are these 'legends' propagated in the first place? It is far too simplistic to dismiss as a legend anything that does not fit the accepted version of history, in my view. These 'legends' do not spontaneously erupt from nowhere and I strongly submit that there is never 'smoke without fire' in these cases. Indeed, Wilson and Blackett have spent many years researching this one topic alone and have uncovered a plethora of documentary and archaeological evidence to prove beyond question that not only did Arthur exist, but there were actually two King Arthurs, several centuries apart and that the famous legend is likely a composite of those two distinctly separate entities.

King Arthur, son of Uther Pendragon and his Knights of the Round Table in Camelot, his advisor Merlin the magician or sorcerer and his sword Excalibur, has been a popular fable for many centuries. In this legend, Arthur is married to Guinevere and he waged war against the Saxons of South East Britain under their ruler Hengist (who significantly did actually exist – even according to mainstream history). In these fables, Hengist (a Saxon) was invited into Britain by Vortigern, a traitor who had killed many of the aristocracy of Britain of the time. The stories also relate a stirring tale of how Arthur also planned a successful military campaign against all of Britain, Europe, and even the might of Rome itself which culminated in the death of the Roman Emperor.

It has always been puzzling to scholars that the myths and legends of King Arthur have defied all logical attempts to identify and pin upon him an identity of any kind. In reality the confusion may well be ascribed to the fact there are definitely two separate entities involved and this duality is no doubt partly responsible for all the confusion surrounding the attempted identification of Arthur. There were actually several Arthurs of Britain but only two who match the exploits recounted in the classic myths. The first one was a General and the son of the British Emperor Magnus Maximus, who in the late 4th Century with his army, left for Europe and eventually confronted the power of Rome, in the process killing the Emperor Gratian.

Arthur mark II was a King of the 6th Century AD. He was the son of Meurig ap Tewdrig and it was this Arthur that successfully defeated the Saxons. The confused histories by later writers such as the medieval historian Geoffrey of Monmouth accidentally (or possibly even deliberately) merged these two distinct Arthurs into one and this has caused much confusion and obfuscated the authentication of British history of this period. This has also been further compounded by the deliberate falsification of British heritage by entities whose interests are not best served by the truth. The ramifications of the Arthur revelations are negatively significant for the religious and political powers that be.

King Arthur I, the son of Magnus Maximus of the 4th Century AD and King Arthur II of the late 6th Century AD, can both trace their ancestry back to the British, Holy Roman Emperor Constantine and (according to Wilson and Blackett) back even as far as the 'Holy Family' itself which allegedly arrived in Britain in 37AD and for which event there is plenty of documented evidence. They can also both trace their lineage back to King Brutus, one of the great-grandsons of Aeneas of Troy. Brutus apparently arrived in Britain around 500BC.

The 'Khumry' people (the origin of the Welsh word 'Cymru' meaning Wales) were also part of this huge migration into Britain at this time and were the original lost 'Ten Tribes' who migrated north-westwards after the murder of Sennacherib, the King of Assyria in the early 7th century BC. These people, over a long period of time, travelled through Asia Minor and they are recorded in Assyrian texts as the 'Khumry' and are believed to be the same tribe that ancient Greek writings also refer to as the 'Cimmeroi'.

According to Wilson and Blackett's stunning research and as outlined in their subsequent book, published in 2007, 'The Discovery of the Ark of the Covenant', these people actually brought the Ark of the Covenant with them to the island of Britain and here it lies still, buried in a field in Wales, the precise location of which has been identified by Wilson and Blackett although unsurprisingly, they have been denied permission by the authorities to instigate an archaeological dig. However they did conduct a geophysical survey and metal detector investigation of the plot and a 'non-ferrous' metal object, four to four and a half feet long by one foot by one foot, has been located precisely in that spot, a few feet down below the surface.

According to Wilson and Blackett, the Khumric people were originally to be found living in Egypt before Moses famously led them away, sometime in the middle of the 14th Century BC and their ancient Khumric alphabet, Coelbren is still evident today and is utilised with incredible accuracy in the translation of Egyptian hieroglyphs.

Unsurprisingly, another major source of opposition to these incredible revelations is the Roman Catholic Church, another protector of the status quo at all costs, not least because of what Wilson and Blackett's research has revealed regarding Christianity. When Augustine arrived Britain in 597AD he was apparently astounded to learn that the British already had Christian churches as well as priests and in fact the British Apostolic Christian religion was even more advanced than that of Rome and again according to documented history, arose from the fact that a man who went by the name of 'Jesus the Nazarene' who did not die on a cross in 33AD, apparently arrived in Britain in 37AD. All this information is of course, still regarded as highly heretical by the Church hierarchy, even today.

Obviously this version of events completely demolishes mainstream Christianity's view and renders it completely unsurprising that this research has been rejected out of hand by the establishment, both religious and political. Whether or not one believes that Jesus Christ was indeed the son of, or the earthly incarnation of 'God' or Jehovah, there does appear to be much evidence that such a person did actually exist and indeed many other so-called 'legends' from several diverse sources also propound the story of Jesus visiting Britain, *after* the alleged crucifixion event, a fact which lends more credence to this hypothesis.

In fact, Christianity was not introduced into Britain from Rome as is popularly ascribed to be the case, but was actually exported to Rome from Britain in 51AD by King Caradoc (also sometimes referred to by his Latinised name of Caractacus) who was taken to Rome and held there for several years.

The truth is that real British history is the most comprehensively recorded history in all Europe and had it not been for the 'Holy family' arriving here in 37AD, none of this 'taboo' history would be an issue. Indeed, it is only since the beginning of the 19th Century that the suppression of real British history has been actively and widely taking place. Up until that point in time, much of this knowledge was widely available to anyone with access to books and the ability to read and research. This obviously excluded, as ever, the ordinary man-in-the-street of the times and thus was it possible to hide this knowledge from the masses until such a juncture whereby a sustained cover-up was rendered necessary by the steady increase in literacy of the population.

The academic community today acknowledges only its own invented versions of Roman Britain, Saxon Britain and Viking Britain and any major artefact discoveries made by archaeologists are inevitably categorised as belonging to one of those alternatives and never, ever under any circumstances ascribed to being Khumric-British, despite there being an abundance of these already in existence and many, many more being unearthed, constantly.

The Comet of 562AD

In 562AD, a little-known, virtually unrecorded, catastrophic natural disaster occurred, which almost completely destroyed the islands of Britain and Ireland, causing a terrible conflagration, destroying towns, villages and forests throughout and resulting in major widespread flooding as a result of a massive Tsunami being generated by the colossal amounts of rock or ice falling from the sky. There must also have been a horrendous death toll amongst the inhabitants, although the true extent of this will probably never be known for sure. This disaster is now known to have been caused by a comet, which either struck directly or passed close enough to earth that the impact damage was a direct result of the debris contained within the 'tail' of the comet coming into contact with the land.

The reason that this episode has never been included in mainstream history books or acknowledged by historians is that up until the early nineteenth century, it was strictly forbidden by the Christian religion, indeed heretical even, to acknowledge that it was possible for stones and rocks to fall from the sky. This is why the entire event has been airbrushed from history and has remained virtually unacknowledged by historians. In 1986, when Wilson and Blackett first brought this event to the notice of the mainstream, they were unsurprisingly subjected to much scorn and ridicule and yet now this event is slowly becoming accepted as reality and is just beginning to be incorporated into history texts.

This widespread destruction was recorded in several authenticated, contemporary records. Gregory of Tours, the French writer relates that Britain was one of the points of impact in a straight line running from the North East in a South Westerly direction from Norway, through Britain and Ireland and into the Atlantic Ocean, thence to the South American continent and on to what is now Bolivia where similar ancient records relate a parallel tale of destruction and mayhem. Vast tracts of Britain were rendered uninhabitable for as long as eleven years, with poisonous and noxious gases in abundance and mud-covered landscapes meaning that no crops of any kind could even be attempted to be grown anywhere. Virtually every living thing was either killed instantly or died shortly afterwards and those lucky few that did somehow survive, abandoned the country altogether, leaving behind an entirely unpopulated, empty land.

This barren wilderness lay empty for around eleven years according to contemporary reports but eventually, people slowly began to venture into the devastated land as nature took its course and life once again started to regain a foothold in the previously barren earth. It was indeed the emptiness of Britain that led to the Saxon invasion at this time and to their colonisation of most of the British mainland as conditions slowly returned to normal and plant and animal life re-asserted itself once more.

It was also as a direct result of the disaster of 562AD, that as related in the earlier chapter on the discovery of the American landmass, that Prince Madoc ap Meurig led expeditions to seek out new homelands for the Khumry and resulted in his settlement of certain areas of what is now the United States.

Prince Madoc's Colonisation of America

Whilst many of the few survivors among the population of the British Isles made the short sea journey to sanctuary in France or Gaul as it was still known at this time, as stated, a large group of hardy people under the leadership of the Khumric Prince Madoc ap Meurig, the brother of Arthur II, embarked on what must have been at the time a formidable and dangerous expedition westwards across the mighty Atlantic Ocean to the Americas. Were they aware that this landmass existed and were determined to escape the devastation they left behind by travelling to the furthermost known outpost of the earth or did they simply depart more in hope than expectation that they would find a more hospitable environment somewhere? We will never know for sure, but to simply head in a westward direction not knowing when or even if they would ever reach their 'promised land' would seem rather a prohibitive risk to take, to my mind. However, this is what they indeed did.

There are several detailed references to Madoc's voyage in epic Khumric poetry of the time and also significantly in 1625, George Abbott, the Archbishop of Canterbury wrote a history in which he describes in detail the fact that a Welsh prince discovered America in the late 6th century. This was also the date ascribed to the event by Reuben T. Durrett of Kentucky in his book on ancient voyages to the Americas published in 1908.

In 1981 Wilson and Blackett decided to switch their focus from Ancient Egypt and Asia Minor to America in order to investigate Madoc's alleged presence in that country and the results were absolutely conclusive. Evidence of Madoc and his people was to be found almost everywhere they looked. Their American colleague, Jim Michael of the *'Ancient Kentucke Historical Association'* supplied a mass of information and data, photographs of likely sites and inscriptions upon rocks, cave walls and cliffs relating to the possible influence of the Khumry presence. These were inspected, examined and translated by Wilson and Blackett from the ancient British Coelbren alphabet which each site was found to possess in abundance. Michael also supplied many examples of ancient Native American records of a tribe or nation of 'powerful White Men' who seized their lands in what is now Kentucky. In addition to all this documentary evidence there were also the abundance of earth-banked hill-forts designed in typically British style that added their weight to the argument as also did the many Khumric-style tumuli, liberally scattered around the areas in question.

And as if that were not enough evidence to form an opinion as to the veracity of the story, many artefacts and rock-carvings were also discovered, written in Coelbren, bearing what were obviously Christian inscriptions and symbols, all of which were carbon-dated to the sixth and seventh centuries AD.

Madoc did not stay in America, however. He returned in about 572AD when the effects of the comet devastation were slowly starting to subside. His account of this vast new 'unknown' land were disbelieved by many and so the King sent out Admiral Gwenon to check Madoc's incredible story of a land of huge rivers, mountains and plains. Gwenon indeed returned a year or two later and verified everything that Madoc had claimed to be true. As a result of this, a major expeditionary force was raised and set out in 574AD to return to the American continent.

So this is the account discernible from both the written records and the surviving artefacts of how America was really discovered by the Europeans, but the Normans and their successors, inhibited by the restrictions of fundamental Christianity imposed upon them by their Elite masters conspired to conceal the truth for a millennium to protect a huge lie. For the truth being brought into focus we owe much to the oft-maligned, Wilson and Blackett along with their colleagues such as

Jim Michael. The catastrophe that was the Comet of 562AD and its aftermath were inconvenient episodes which did not fit into the decreed history and therefore were always dismissed out of hand or simply ignored. The pattern continues apace.

The Knights Templar

From the beginning of the Middle Ages, around the 11th century onwards, many sects and secretive organisations began to establish themselves. These were soon infiltrated by the Elite and many were in fact commandeered in order to further oppress and control the masses surreptitiously as was the case with the Knights Templar, to quote but one small example.

Early in the 12th century, a group of knights led by Hugh de Payens offered their services to the Patriarch of Jerusalem to serve as a military force. This group, generally regarded as being nine in number, had the mandate of protecting Christian pilgrims who were en route to the Holy Land to visit the shrines sacred to their faith.

The Templars were the first 'bankers'. They acquired and accumulated vast sums of money from the Christian pilgrims they purported to protect on their crusades and also from people who simply wished to buy their way into paradise by the way of bequests and legacies left to the Templars. They became the wealthiest organisation in every country in which they had a presence and their 'temples' in London and Paris eventually morphed into medieval versions of financial centres in much the same way as todays financial empires began. Of course this vast wealth gave them disproportionate power, as with today's banksters and this extreme wealth in turn led to avarice from certain factions of Elite society at the time and opened up the opportunity for greedy profiteers such as the Catholic Church and King Phillip IV of France to conspire against them with the intention of redistributing the wealth into their own already substantial coffers.

Eventually the Templars were destroyed by Phillip in league with Pope Clement V and all their assets were seized. Jacques de Molay was burnt at the stake (actually he was roasted alive rather than consumed by flames) and the organisation continued, albeit 'underground' from that point onwards.

At this time, the Christian world had a strict moratorium on usury, the lending of money at interest, but of course as time passed and the centuries rolled-on, this was conveniently forgotten and the banking system based on the Templar model began to emerge, eventually becoming part of the control process under which we all now suffer.

In fact the Knights Templar are often regarded as being the role model for today's secret society network as well as banking and even the Illuminati itself is said to be a direct result of the strong, continuing influence of the Templars from the 11th century up to the present day, both as an independent organisation and also more importantly perhaps as a part of other secret societies such as freemasonry which has a branch still named 'The Knights Templar'. Many researchers believe that the Scottish Rite of Freemasonry is indeed simply a pseudonym for the Knights Templar, which went 'underground' at the time of its alleged disbandment rather than simply a borrowed name.

These apparently disconnected groups are all part of the same overall organisation and include such as the Knights of Malta and the Arab Brotherhood and continue to be a force of evil working against the best interests of the majority of the human race.

Secret Societies

Freemasonry

Of all the secret societies, probably the most famous as well as being the most misunderstood, by both outsiders and even its adherents at its lower levels, is freemasonry.

Freemasonry probably had its original roots in the mediaeval crafts, whereby each trade had its own 'guild' or 'union' in modern parlance, to protect the interests of its members. In return for this protective presence the craftsman had to submit to the most rigorous regulation. He had to serve as an apprentice, usually without pay, for two to ten years (depending on the trade), live with and obey the master craftsman who taught him and then finally once this long induction process was complete, the apprentice was free to start out alone, frequently taking one of his master's daughters as a wife.

With the expansion of economics often came the need of the craftsman to borrow money to finance long-term or long-distance undertakings and his willingness to pay interest for this benefit. The Christian Church condemned usury and money-lending was permitted only by and to Jews, who were barred from guild membership by dint of their religious practices.

Stonemasons, by the very nature of their trade, were itinerant, constantly moving between villages and towns seeking employment. Their membership of the masonic craft guild was a reassurance to potential customers and employers that here was a bona fide craftsman who could be relied upon to provide a fair days work for a fair days pay. The insignia of their guild displayed representations of the tools of their trade and where language or literacy was a barrier to communication, served as a visual guarantee of ability. It was from these humble beginnings that secret symbols, restricted membership, oaths of secrecy and mutual aid evolved but eventually the guilds became entities that were no longer necessarily populated by those skilled in the crafts and trades their societies purported to represent, becoming almost entirely symbolic and totally unrepresentative of the craft or trade.

In 1645, the Royal Society, founded either in Oxford or in London depending on source, was created with the intention of promoting scientific enquiry rather than the simple, unthinking acceptance of received wisdom. Many facets of the society were based on the tenets of freemasonry and indeed many of the founders were freemasons – a state of affairs that still exists to this day.

It was the brother-in-law of Oliver Cromwell, the future 'Lord Protector' of the Commonwealth of Great Britain who became its first chairman. Cromwell's uncle, Thomas Cromwell during the reign of Henry VIII a century earlier had already severed the ties between the Roman Catholic Church and the English monarchy and Oliver himself managed to complete the job by engineering the severing of King Charles I's head from his body.

In 1717, Freemasonry, now a new form of cult entirely distinct from the various existing creeds of Europe, spread rapidly to Paris, Florence, Rome and Berlin, where its deliberately syncretic rituals and décor, Solomon's temple's signs and symbols made it thoroughly cosmopolitan and religiously neutral. Nothing could better encapsulate the early spirit of the 'enlightenment'.

Andrew Ramsay, a Scottish Jacobite exiled in France, who was Chancellor of the French Grand Lodge in the 1730s, claimed that the first Freemasons had been stonemasons in the crusader states who had learned the secret rituals and gained the special wisdom of the ancient world. According to the German Freemasons, the Grand Masters of the Order had learned the secrets and acquired the treasure of the Jewish Essenes.

Either way, Freemasonry had escaped its earlier guise of stonemasonry and in its new incarnation appealed to the intellectuals and the nobility. The early membership of masonic lodges included merchants and financiers, notaries and lawyers, doctors, diplomats and gentry, in other words men of substance or sound reputation. By the middle of the eighteenth century these included members of the French royal family, Frederick the Great, Maria Theresa's husband, Francis of Lorraine and her son, Joseph. Voltaire was admitted with great pomp into a publicity-hungry masonic lodge in Paris.

Freemasonry not only played an important role in the French Revolution, but also with regard to the American Revolution, in particular the lodges affiliated to the Grand Lodge of Scotland. Scottish Rite Freemasonry blossomed in the North American soil and indeed Freemasonry could be found on both sides of the looming war between the colonists and the Crown and although there is no clear evidence of collusion amongst masons from opposing camps, the fact that the British made some extraordinary military errors arouses my suspicions in this regard.

Sir William Howe's failure to pursue Washington after expelling him from New York and Sir Henry Clinton's wilful failure to link up with Burgoyne's army marching south from Montreal in 1777 are the two most conspicuous examples. The Grand Master for North America was Joseph Warren and the Green Dragon coffee house in Union Street, Boston, purchased by the Provincial Grand Lodge is generally considered to be the site where one of its offshoots 'The Sons of Liberty' plotted the Boston Tea Party and carried it out in the guise of 'Red Indians', now re-branded for the sake of political correctness as 'Native Americans'.

So already there was an infiltration of the 'hidden hand', as a secret society is an ideal vehicle for undercurrents and for control. It was however, an infiltration of which many of its members were unaware.

However, one of the little known and least advertised facts about Freemasonry and the Masonic Lodge is its Jewish origin and nature. The religion of Judaism based on the Babylonian Talmud and the Jewish Kabbalah formed the basis for the Scottish rites 33 ritual degree ceremonies.

"Masonry is based on Judaism. Eliminate the teaching of Judaism from the Masonic ritual and what is left?" The Jewish Tribune of New York, 28th October 1927

"Freemasonry is a Jewish establishment, whose history, grades, official appointments, passwords and explanations are Jewish from beginning to end." Rabbi Isaac Wis

Undoubtedly already under Jewish influence, Judeo-masonry in Europe became popular with the rise to power of the House of Rothschild. Adam Weishaupt who formed the 'Illuminati' in 1776, founded the Lodge of Theodore in Munich and was befriended and funded by Meyer Rothschild, whose clerk Sigmund Geisenheimer in his Frankfurt office had wide Masonic contacts and was a member of the French Grand Orient Lodge called l'Aurore Naissante Lodge. With the help of Daniel Itzig (Court Jew to Frederick William II) and the merchant Isaac Hildesheim (who changed his name to Justus Hiller) he founded the Judenloge.

In 1802 the old established Jewish families including the Adler, Speyer, Reiss, Sichel, Ellison, Hanau and the Goldsmid families became members of the Judenloge and in 1803 Nathan Rothschild joined the Lodge of Emulation in England whilst his brother James Rothschild became a 33rd degree Mason in France.

The book on the Masons 'Morals and Dogma', authored by the late Sovereign Grand Commander of the Scottish rite, Albert Pike, states...

"Masonry conceals secrets from all except the adepts and sages and uses false explanations and myth interpretation of its symbols to mislead."

The rise of Masons to political power in Israel dates back to the state's origins in 1948. David Ben Gurion, Israel's first Prime Minister, was a Freemason. Every Prime Minister since then has been a high level Mason, including Golda Meier who was a member of the women's organisation, the Co-Masons. Most Israeli judges and religious figures are masons and the Rothschild-supported Hebrew University in Israel has erected an Egyptian obelisk, symbol of Freemasonry in its courtyard.

Indeed today, it is virtually impossible to obtain a state of high office in any sphere without membership of this all-pervasive body. From politicians to law-makers, to police and security agencies, they are all heavily populated at the upper echelons by high-ranking Freemasons. All of which makes claims of democracy for our society, almost laughable if it were not so serious a subject. Freemasons must always and under all circumstances put their own kind first. How then can one conclude that any election, from political by-elections to the election of political party leaders to the appointment of company directors and high-level civil servants, could possibly be fairly conducted?

The simple answer of course is that they cannot and thus we have as our default a system whereby exploitation and corruption is the norm and not the exception, whatever we may try to convince ourselves to the contrary.

The Bilderberg Group

The Bilderberg group is yet another Elite group, intrinsically connected to Freemasonry. In 1954 Dr Joseph Retinger, communist Poland's Charge d'Affaires, was supposed to have set up this group, probably in the role of agent. Alongside him were Prince Bernhard of the Netherlands, Colin Gubbins (former director of the British Special Operations Executive) and General Walter Bedel-Smith (former American Ambassador to Moscow and director of the CIA).

Bilderberg's membership is liberally inter-mingled with members of the Council on Foreign Relations, the Pilgrims Society, the Trilateral Commission and the infamous 'Round Table', a British, Oxford-Cambridge Elite group founded in 1910. The Round Table, which also denies its existence as a formal group, called for a more efficient form of global empire so that Anglo-American hegemony could be extended throughout the 20th century. In other words, the New World Order.

Its governing council was made up of Robert Ellswort (Lazard Freres), John Loudon, (N. M. Rothschild), Paul Nitze (Shroeder Bank), C. L. Sulzberger (New York Times), Stansfield Turner (later to become CIA Director) Peter Calvocoressi, (Penguin Books), Andrew Schoenberg, Daniel Ellsberg and Henry Kissinger.

The first meeting of these unelected yet highly influential people took place at the Hotel de Bilderberg in the Netherlands, hence the name of the group. Lord Rothschild and Laurence Rockefeller handpicked one hundred of the world's richest and most influential people and the group has met annually in great secrecy and with massive security arrangements in place, in different parts of the world since then. Their principle goal is world government but it is they who are also the main political policy makers of the entire world and NOT individual governments as the liars and cowards of the mainstream media would have us all believe.

Past attendees have included several US presidents, Ben Bernanke, Timothy Geithner, Prince Charles, current British Prime Minister David Cameron, former British Prime Minister Tony Blair, German Chancellor Angela Merkel, Hillary Clinton, Bill Gates and current Texas governor Rick Perry.

Unfortunately, the mainstream media largely ignores the Bilderberg Group meetings and even if they do cover them it is only to dismiss it all as a 'conspiracy theory' and the real agenda is completely ignored.

Under any other circumstances, a gathering of executives from Google, Facebook and Microsoft would have the media in raptures as would a gathering of some of the most important international politicians on the globe. So why is this not the case with the Bilderberg Group? I am sure we all know the answer to that by now.

Every year, over a hundred of the most powerful, yet mainly unelected people on the planet will meet in complete secrecy and will plan and discuss the future of the world. Even those elected individuals are not there upon the mandate of the people; they only ever attend in a 'private' capacity. They have all been sworn to absolute secrecy as to what is discussed and yet this has no interest for the mainstream media at all?

It is only in recent years that the alternative news media has brought so much attention to the Bilderberg Group that everyone finally admits that the Bilderberg Group really does exist, but now the controlled mainstream media does everything it possibly can to downplay the importance of the organisation by suggesting that anyone that believes that there is anything wrong with dozens of the most powerful people on the planet meeting in utter secrecy to discuss the future course of world events is 'crazy'.

If the Bilderberg Group is so unimportant, then why would people like Bill Clinton, Prince Charles, David Cameron, Tony Blair, Henry Kissinger, Bill Gates, Angela Merkel, Ben Bernanke, Tim Geithner, Rick Perry, David Rockefeller, Herman van Rompuy, Jean-Claude Trichet, Jeff Bezos, Chris R. Hughes, Eric Schmidt, Craig J. Mundie, Anders Fogh Rasmussen, Richard Perle, Paul Volcker, Lawrence Summers, Hillary Clinton and Joe Biden take the time to attend?

Below is a list of some others who have attended Bilderberg Group meetings over the years...

NATO Secretary Generals:

Joseph Luns (1971-84)
Lord Carrington (1984-88)
Manfred, Werner (1988-94)
Willy, Claes (1994-5)
Javier, Solana (1995-99)
Robertson, Lord (1999-2003)
Scheffer, Jaap de Hoop (2003)

European Commissioners:

Barroso, Jose Manuel - President of the European Commission (2004-09)
Prodi, Romano - Head of State - Europe (1999-2004)
Bolkestein, Frits - International Markets Commissioner, European Commission (1999-2004)
Lamy, Pascal - European Trade Commissioner (1999-2004)
Fortescue, Adrian, Director General, Justice and Internal Affairs (1999-2004)
Fischler, Franz - Member of the Commission Agriculture and rural development & Fisheries (1999-2004)
Monti, Mario - Member of the European Commission responsible for competition (1999-2004)

Banking Governors and other fiscal elites:

King, Mervyn - Governor, Bank of England
Trichet, Jean-Claude - President, European Central Bank
Schwab, Klaus,- President, World Economic Forum
Wallenberg, Jacob - Chairman of the Board, Skandinaviska Enskilda Banken
Wolfensohn, James - President, The World Bank
Kielholz, Walter - Former Chairman of the Board, Credit Suisse
Soros, George - President and Chairman of Soros Fund Management
Kopper, Hilmar - Chairman of Deutsche Bank
Greenspan, Alan - former Chairman, Federal Reserve System
McDonough, William - President, Federal Reserve Bank of New York
Moscow, Michael - President and CEO of the Federal Reserve Bank of New York
Pearl, Frank - Chairman and CEO, Perseus, L. L.C.
Kist, Ewald - Chairman of the Board ING

Petroleum, Chemical, Genetic Engineering:
Shapiro, Robert - Chairman and CEO, Monsanto Company

Vasella, Daniel - Chairman and CEO, Novartis AG Pepsico Inc.
Pragnell, Michael - CEO Syngenta AG: Director, AstraZeneca plc
Sutherland, Peter - Non-executive Chairman of BP plc
Hubbard, Allan - President, E&A Industries
Veer, Jeroen van der - President of the Royal Dutch Petroleum Co.

Annual meetings are held in locations all over the world and are closed to the public and the press. The resort areas and hotels where they meet are cleared of residents and visitors and surrounded by soldiers, armed guards, the Secret Service, state and local police. All conference and meeting rooms are scanned for bugging devices before every single meeting.

Prior to the 1971 meeting in Woodstock, Virginia, Prince Bernhard of the Netherlands (one of the founding members) said that the subject of the meeting was the 'change in the world role of the United States'. After the weekend conference, Kissinger went to Red China to open up trade relations and an international monetary crisis developed, which prompted the devaluing of the dollar by 8.5% (which made a tremendous profit for those who converted to the European currency.

In 1976, fifteen representatives from the Soviet Union attended the meeting which was held in the Arizona desert and it was believed that at that time the plans were formulated for the break-up of the Soviet Union. At the 1990 meeting held at Glen Cove, Long Island, they decided that taxes had to be raised to pay more towards the debt owed to the International Bankers (the IMF and World Bank), whilst at the 1991 meeting at the Black Forest resort in Baden Baden, Germany, they discussed plans for a common European currency and European central banking and discussed a 'shake-up' of the Middle Eastern countries to the benefit of their corporate friends. This all came to pass shortly afterwards without need for consultation among individual countries.

At their 1992 meeting the group discussed the possibility of 'conditioning the public to accept the idea of a UN army that could, by force, impose its will on the internal affairs of any nation'.

Bilderbergers meekly justify their existence as 'simply a place to discuss ideas', an innocent forum where anyone can 'speak frankly' and other assorted clichés. However, any group that conducts its activities under the cloak of secrecy can be regarded as conspiratorial. It may hide under a figurehead who may or may not know the true aims of the body he/she represents but without doubt the Bilderberg Group is a group of politicians, financiers and industrialists under the command of unelected and undemocratic Elite individuals who through their enormous power and the money behind them dictate the political policy of the entire world to their own benefit.

Skull and Bones, Scroll and Key and Phi Beta Kappa

These are the names of the major American 'Ivy League' Universities' secret society groups. Their influence is felt disproportionately throughout all of American politics, banking and industry and its members are extremely influential and yet for the most part, unelected individuals who nevertheless through the power wielded by the senior members of these groups are able to short-circuit the normal, democratic routes to the top levels of American society.

Skull and Bones is the most well-known of the 'University' secret societies and is based at Yale University in America. It has numbered among its members many famous political figures throughout the last almost two hundred years, its most famous, recent 'son' being George W. Bush who despite an obvious lack of intellect or talent of any kind has managed to become President of the USA on two occasions as well as becoming a multi-millionaire in his own right. Skull and Bones is almost an offshoot of Freemasonry, with adherents of S&B often being also senior, high-level Freemasons.

Members of the Skull and Bones Society at Yale, meet twice weekly at their headquarters, a windowless mausoleum of a building known colloquially as 'the tomb' to members. It was founded in 1832 by William Russell and was 'incorporated' in 1856 as the 'Russell Trust'. The Russell family derived its fame and fortune from the opium trade in the nineteenth century, illegally transporting opium from Turkey to China and indeed the Russells soon became the centre of the US opium-supply trade making absolutely mind-boggling fortunes for the family members. The head of the Russell firm in China at this time was Warren Delano, the grandfather of Franklin Delano Roosevelt, who was of course destined to be President of the US in the 1930s and 1940s. And other famous names of the Skull and Bones have been such notables as Prescott Bush (the grandfather of Bush the lesser), and his son George H. W. Bush, the father of the lesser one. We also encounter within the membership lists such names as Rockefeller, Harriman. Whitney, Payne, Vanderbilt etc., in other words a veritable who's who of American society throughout the ages.

The late historian and researcher, Anthony Sutton somehow acquired the records of all the members of the society going back to 1832 and confirmed that around twenty prominent families from American high society totally dominate these lists. These prominent families all unsurprisingly have genetic links to the English aristocracy via the Puritan settlers in the American continent in the early seventeenth century and have remained in prominence ever since, with the help and assistance of their comrades in the societies named above as well as several other less famous ones.

Skull and Bones is also a popular recruiting ground for secret service agents for the CIA, much as are the British counterparts to Yale and Harvard universities, Oxford and Cambridge. George H. W. Bush was head of the CIA for a spell in the 1980s in the Reagan administration and was no doubt originally recruited whilst still attending Yale. It was George H. W.'s father, Prescott who was responsible for the theft of the skull of the Native American chief, Geronimo from his grave in 1919 for use in the society's bizarre and depraved rituals, before eventually S&B were forced to return it whence it came, many years later.

It was also prominent 'bonesmen', as they are known, who were behind the secret funding of the Bolshevik revolution in 1917, providing millions of dollars in backing for their 'front-men' Trotsky, Lenin and Stalin.

In a fair, just and democratic society, how can such organisations be allowed to exist? The obvious answer of course is that they should not be allowed to exist, but at least if they are in existence, as they most certainly are, let us pretend no longer that we all live in anything approaching a democratic society or nation.

The Round Table

The Round Table also has strong links with Freemasonry. Although centred in Britain, this financial empire extends its influence through a worldwide network, whose supreme council is headed by the Rothschilds of Britain and France. A generational seat is accorded to a descendant of the Habsburgs, and to the ruling families of England and France. In America, the Illuminati were represented by old-money families, such as the Rockefellers, Mellons and Carnegies.

The siphoning of the British people's wealth into the coffers of the Illuminati in the City of London, created severe economic inequalities and stifled the nation's ability to adapt technologically at a pace similar to that of the rapidly expanding nation of Germany. And so, by the 1870s, the British Empire attained its zenith and Britain began the longest economic depression in its history, one that it was not to recover from until the 1890s. Therefore, the country of Britain no longer provided the economic capacity to support the global ambitions of the Illuminati and so it was at that point that the Illuminati sought to confer increasing power to its branches in the United States, which it could rule by proxy in the coming century, while still based financially in Britain.

The son of Baron Lionel Rothschild, Nathaniel Mayer, also known as 'Natty' de Rothschild, became head of NM Rothschild and Sons upon his father's death in 1879. In 1876, he had succeeded to the Baronetcy, created for his uncle Anthony Rothschild, who died without a male heir and in 1884 Nathaniel Mayer became the first Jew elevated to the House of Lords. Following the Rothschild's funding of the Suez Canal, Natty de Rothschild developed a close relationship with Prime Minister Benjamin Disraeli and affairs in Egypt. Rothschild also funded Cecil Rhodes in the development of the British South Africa Company and the De Beers diamond conglomerate. He administered Rhodes's estate after his death in 1902 and assisted in the setting-up of the 'Rhodes Scholarship' at Oxford University.

In the first of seven wills, Cecil Rhodes called for the formation of a 'secret society', devoted to 'the extension of British rule throughout the world'. Rhodes posited that only the 'British elite' should be entitled to rule the world for the benefit of mankind, in other words, the Illuminati of the City of London would exploit the expansion of British imperialism, to increase their control over gold, the seas, the world's raw materials, but most importantly, after the turn of the century, a new precious commodity: oil. The goals Rhodes articulated included the 'ultimate recovery of the United States as an integral part of the British Empire', and would culminate in '...consolidation of the whole Empire, the inauguration of a system of Colonial Representation in the Imperial Parliament which may tend to weld together the disjointed members of the Empire and finally the foundation of so great a power as to hereafter render wars impossible and promote the best interests of humanity'.

In his third will, Rhodes left his entire estate to the senior Freemason Lord Nathaniel Rothschild as trustee. Rhodes had also been initiated into Freemasonry in 1877, shortly after arriving at Oxford, and joined a Scottish Rite Lodge. To chair Rhodes' secret society, Lord Nathaniel Rothschild appointed Alfred Milner, who then recruited a group of young men from Oxford and Toynbee Hall. All were well-known English Freemasons, among them Rudyard Kipling, Arthur Balfour, also Lord Rothschild and several other Oxford graduates, known collectively as 'Milner's Kindergarten'. And so, with a number of other English Freemasons, they founded what became known as 'The Round Table'.

The man charged by the Round Table with bringing the United States within the financial control of the Rothschilds was German-born Jacob Schiff. In America, Schiff bought into Kuhn and Loeb, a well-known private banking firm and shortly after he became a partner, he married Loeb's daughter, Teresa. Then he bought-out Kuhn's interests and moved the firm to New York, where it became Kuhn, Loeb, and Company, international bankers, with Schiff, agent of the Rothschilds, ostensibly as sole owner. Then, following the Civil War, Schiff began to finance the great operations of the Robber Barons. Thus, Jacob Schiff financed the Standard Oil Company for John D. Rockefeller, the Railroad Empire for Edward R. Harriman, and the Steel Empire for Carnegie.

However, instead of monopolising all the other industries for Kuhn, Loeb, and Company, Schiff opened the doors of the House of Rothschild to bankers like JP Morgan. In turn, the Rothschilds arranged the setting up of London, Paris, European and other branches for these bankers, but always in partnerships with Rothschild subordinates and with Jacob Schiff in New York as head. Thus, at the turn of the nineteenth into the twentieth century, Schiff exercised firm control of the entire banking fraternity on Wall Street, which by then with Schiff's help, included Lehman brothers, Goldman-Sachs, and other internationalist banks that were headed by men chosen by the Rothschilds.

John D. Rockefeller Sr. was tasked by the Rothschilds, through their agents John Jacob Astor and Jacob Schiff, to gain control of the American oil industry. The Rockefellers are themselves an important Illuminati family, being Marranos, who initially moved to Ottoman Turkey and then France, before arriving in America.

John D. Rockefeller Sr. founded Standard Oil, which through the second half of the nineteenth century, achieved infamy for its ruthless practices towards its competitors. Growing public hostility toward monopolies, of which Standard Oil Trust was the most egregious example, caused a number of states to enact anti-monopoly laws, leading to the passage of the Sherman Antitrust Act by Congress in 1890. In 1892, the Ohio Supreme Court decided that Standard Oil was in violation of its monopoly laws but Rockefeller evaded the decision by dissolving the trust and transferring its properties to companies in other states, with interlocking directorates, so that the same men continued to control its operations. In 1899, these companies were brought back together in a holding company, Standard Oil Company of New Jersey, which existed until 1911 when the U.S. Supreme Court declared it in violation of the Sherman Antitrust Act, and therefore illegal. The splintered company under various names, continued to be run by the Rockefellers.

Thus, the fate of the world would be guided by the Round Table, headed by the Rothschilds in London and their various subsidiaries, aided by the control Rockefeller would come to exercise over the United States through his monopoly of its crucial oil supply.

"There does exist, and has existed for a generation, an international Anglophile network which operates, to some extent, in the way the radical Right believes the Communists act. In fact, this network, which we may identify as the Round Table Groups, has no aversion to cooperating with the Communists, or any other groups, and frequently does so. I know of the operations of this network because I have studied it for twenty years and was permitted for two years, in the early 1960s, to examine its papers and secret records . I have no aversion to it or to most of its aims and have, for much of my life, been close to it and many of its instruments". Carroll Quigley, 'Tragedy and Hope: A History of Our Time'

Quigley further confirmed that the far-reaching aim of this network *"is nothing less than to create a world system of financial control in private hands able to dominate the political system of each country and the economy of the world as a whole. The system was to be controlled in a feudalistic fashion by the central banks of the world acting in concert, by secret agreements arrived at in frequent private meetings and conferences."*

The Council on Foreign Relations (CFR)

In the late 19th century, several Elite insiders, namely Rockefeller, JP Morgan and others, mostly Jewish, established an organisation designed to consolidate their control of America and eventually, the entire world. This was named the Council on Foreign Relations. Offshoots, such as the Bilderbergers, have been established since then, but the objective has never slipped from their sight.

One of the first acts of the CFR was to survey the newspaper field, the only mass medium of the time and from this survey they concluded that purchasing control of only 25 major newspapers would give them effective, overall control of news dissemination. They consequently bought those newspapers and since then, many, many more. Today, members of these shadowy organisations literally run virtually all of the media, control the political structure of the western world, much of world business and are totally in control of world banking.

This is the reason why the two political-party systems in America and Europe have become identical, to provide us mere mortals with the illusion of being able to oust the underperformers at election time, with the overall agenda being unaffected. Was there really a difference from Bush I to Clinton to Bush II to Obama in America or from Major to Blair to Brown to Cameron in Britain? Blair, Brown and Cameron knew exactly what the real agenda of the EU is and what it would do to Britain's nationhood and its economy, yet both Conservatives and Labour embraced it fully as the next step down the path to one-world government and the New World Order so dear to their hearts.

There is a sinister agenda under the surface of world politics and that is the plot to destroy the sovereignty of the United States and all of Europe and undertake the enslavement of all the people within a one-world dictatorship. This is completely unknown by the vast majority of the people of the world and the reason for this unawareness of the threat to our countries and to the entire free world is simple; the masterminds behind this great conspiracy have absolute control of all of our mass media, especially television, radio, the printed press and Hollywood. Governments have already brazenly proclaimed that they have the right and the power to manage the news, to not tell us the truth but only what they want us to believe and they have also seized that power on orders from their masters, the Elite and the final objective is to brainwash the people into accepting the transformation of the individual countries of the world into an enslaved unit of the proposed one-world government.

There is a similar branch of the Illuminati in Britain operating under the name of the Royal Institute of International Affairs. There are similar secret Illuminati organisations in France, Germany, and other nations operating under different names and all these organisations, including the CFR, continuously set up numerous subsidiary or front-organisations that are infiltrated into every phase of the various nations' affairs. But at all times, the operations of these organisations were and are masterminded and controlled by the International Banksters whilst, they in turn were and are controlled by the Rothschilds.

Immediately after the Napoleonic wars, the Illuminati assumed that all the nations were so destitute and so weary of wars that they would be glad of almost any solution, so the Rothschild stooges set up what they called the Congress in Vienna and at that meeting they tried to create the first League of Nations, their first attempt at one-world government, based on the theory that all the crowned heads of European governments were so deeply in debt to them that they would willingly or unwillingly serve as their stooges. But the Tsar of Russia uncovered the plot and completely sabotaged it. The enraged Nathan Rothschild, then the head of the dynasty, vowed that sooner or later, he or his descendants would destroy the Tsar and his entire family and his descendants did accomplish that very threat, a century later in 1917. Please bear in mind that the Illuminati were never set-up to operate on a short-term basis. Normally conspiracies of any type are entered-into with the expectation of being fulfilled reasonably quickly, but that was most definitely not the case with the Illuminati. The Illuminati operates on a very long-term basis. Whether it will take scores of years or even centuries, they have dedicated their descendants to keep the 'pot boiling' until the conspiracy is finally achieved.

Those who today comprise the CFR in the United States and the RIIA in Britain direct our governments whom they hold in usury through such methods as the Federal Reserve System in America and the Bank of England in Britain, to fight wars such as those currently being fought in the Middle East in order to further Illuminati plans to bring the world to that stage of the conspiracy whereby it will be forced into an all-out third world war. Unfortunately, we are very close today, to that frightening spectre becoming a reality.

The Trilateral Commission

Unfortunately, the Council on Foreign Relations is not the only group proposing an end to the sovereignty of the United States. In 1973, another organisation which is now prominent in covert US politics first saw the light of day. Also based in New York City, this one is called the Trilateral Commission.

The Trilateral Commission's roots stem from the book 'Between Two Ages', written by Zbigniew Brzezinski in 1970. The following quotations from that book show how closely Brzezinski's thinking parallels that of CFR founder Edward Mandel House.

On page 72, Brzezinski writes: "*Marxism is simultaneously a victory of the external, active man over the inner, passive man and a victory of reason over belief.*"

On page 83, he states: "*Marxism, disseminated on the popular level in the form of Communism, represented a major advance in man's ability to conceptualize his relationship to his world.*"

And on page 123, we find: *"Marxism supplied the best available insight into contemporary reality."*

Nowhere does Brzezinski tell his readers that the Marxism 'in the form of Communism', which he praises, has been responsible for the murder of at least 100 million human beings in the Twentieth Century, has brought about the enslavement of over a billion more, and has caused want, privation and despair for all but the few criminals who ran the communist-dominated nations.

On page 198, after discussing America's shortcomings, Brzezinski writes: *"America is undergoing a new revolution"* which *"unmasks its obsolescence."*

On page 260, he proposes *"Deliberate management of the American future...with the...planner as the key social legislator and manipulator."* The central planning he so desires is a cardinal underpinning of communism and the very opposite of how a 'free' country is organised. But then of course Brzezinski and his ilk do not wish to see a free country. Rather, they would prefer a one world communitarian super-state, run by and for the Elite, with the rest of humanity merely slaves to their every whim.

On page 296, Brzezinski suggests piecemeal *"Movement toward a larger community of the developed nations...through a variety of indirect ties and already developing limitations on national sovereignty."* Here, we see the same proposal that has already been offered by Richard Gardner in the CFR publication 'Foreign Affairs'.

Brzezinski then calls for the forging of community links among the United States, Western Europe, and Japan and the extension of these links to more advanced communist countries. And finally, on page 308 of his 309-page book, he finally admits that what he really wants is *"the goal of world government"*.

This then is the real picture of the society in which we are forced to live. Not exactly how the world is presented to us by the mainstream media is it? Instead of a democratic world run by governments elected by the people using the democratic election process, we have a world run by puppet governments at the behest of such organisations as Freemasonry, Skull and Bones, the Bilderberg group, the Trilateral commission, the Council on Foreign Relations, the Royal Institute of International Affairs and the Round Table, in conjunction with the corporate-military-industrial complex whose constant lobbying of government combined with the their incalculable financial resources, buys them the world they wish for, to the detriment of us all.

Let us now examine how our economic and financial slavery has been engendered.

Money, the Great Confidence Trick

"...the most astounding piece of sleight of hand ever invented". Sir Josiah Stamp, former Chairman of the Bank of England.

"It is well enough that people of the nation do not understand our banking and monetary system, for if they did, I believe there would be a revolution before tomorrow morning." Henry Ford

The mandate for the creation of money has been surreptitiously removed from Governments and thus 'the people' by a private banking cartel owned and run in its entirety by the Elite. It is generally assumed by the layman that all money is issued by and under the control of government, but this is not so. With the exception of coins, which comprise less than 0.05% of the total money in circulation, *all* money is now created by *private corporations ie, banks.* In the USA, the Federal Reserve Bank a *private* banking corporation is responsible for the issuance of notes and in the UK it is the Bank of England (also, perhaps surprisingly to many, a privately owned corporation) whose responsibility is the creation of our money.

This currency is then astoundingly, *lent* to governments and must be repaid along with interest accrued. This then is the real reason for massive and ever-increasing National Debts and not as our controlled governments tell us deceitfully, due to excessive public spending or anything else of that ilk, for that matter. The only way that this debt can ever be repaid is by the printing (and thus borrowing) of more and more money from the banking monopoly all with its own portion of interest attached. All of the taxes paid by all of us to the Government go towards servicing this debt to the banksters (banker-gangsters) and not as they would have you believe, towards public services and the running of the country. Thus the huge and growing percentage of our salaries that is defrauded from us in the form of direct and indirect taxation is being used to further line the pockets of the already immensely wealthy Elite banking families, including Royalty who are strongly suspected to be major shareholders in the Bank of England. And so it continues, on and on down the decades and centuries.

"Interest has always been the Money Power's main instrument. It took control of the planet by starting wars, financing both sides, and having Governments go deeply into debt. Interest is a wealth transfer from the poorest 80% to the richest 10%. The global numbers are not known, but in Germany a billion dollars a day is paid by the poorest 80%. Extrapolated to the world, this means the Plutocracy drain anywhere between $5 trillion and $10 trillion dollars per year." Anthony Migchels (henrymakow.com) 5th January 2012

However, banknotes and coins together comprise only around 3% of the money supply. The other 97% is created by commercial banks as loans, these days by the expedient of creatively typing numbers into a computer screen and in the past by creative book-keeping, all of which of course carries its own imbedded debt in the form of interest payable.

"When a bank makes a loan, it simply adds to the borrower's deposit account in the bank by the amount of the loan. The money is not taken from anyone else's deposit; it was not previously paid in to the bank by anyone. It is new money, created by the bank for the use of the borrower". Robert B. Anderson, Secretary of the US Treasury, August 31, 1959. *'US News and World Report'*

"We are completely dependent on the commercial Banks. Someone has to borrow every dollar we have in circulation, cash or credit. If the Banks create ample synthetic money we are prosperous; if not, we starve. We are absolutely without a permanent money system. When one gets a complete grasp of the picture, the tragic absurdity of our hopeless position is almost incredible, but there it is. It is the most important subject intelligent persons can investigate and reflect upon". Robert H. Hemphill, Credit Manager of the Federal Reserve Bank of Atlanta, 1934

How has this dangerous and criminal state of affairs come about without publicity and with no questions raised? Unsurprisingly, the power and wealth of the corporate Elite and their compliant media and propaganda mills have served them well yet again. With the unlimited resources available to them, it is an absolutely simple process to deceive 99.99% of the trusting populations as to the real situation and smooth the way for the scam of this or indeed any other millennium.

"Capital must protect itself in every possible way, both by combination and legislation. Debts must be collected, mortgages foreclosed as rapidly as possible. When, through process of law, the common people lose their homes they will become more docile and more easily governed through the strong arm of the government applied by a central power of wealth under leading financiers. These truths are well known among our principal men, who are now engaged in forming an imperialism to govern the world. By dividing the voter through the political party system, we can get them to expend their energies in fighting for questions of no importance. It is thus, by discrete action, we can secure for ourselves that which has been so well planned and so successfully accomplished." Montagu Norman, Governor of The Bank of England, addressing the United States Bankers' Association, New York, 1924

The story of modern money begins in Renaissance Europe, around five hundred years ago. At that time the currency consisted mainly of gold and silver coinage, with no paper money. Gold coins of course were very durable and had intrinsic value in themselves (unlike paper currency), but they were heavy, difficult to transport in large quantities and they were open to theft if not stored securely. As a result of this, the general population therefore deposited their coins with goldsmiths who had strong-rooms and safes in which to store the coins securely and without fear of theft. These goldsmiths issued paper receipts which could be redeemed at any time for the stated amount of gold. Eventually these convenient receipts began to be traded themselves instead of the less convenient coins they represented.

With the passage of time, the goldsmiths realised that only about 10% of these receipts were ever redeemed in gold at any one time and they could quite comfortably lend the gold in their possession, with interest, time after time as long as they ensured that they retained the 10% of the value of their outstanding loans in actual physical gold to meet any demand. By this process, paper money (notes) which were in reality receipts for loans of gold was born. Notes could now be issued and loans made in amounts that were up to ten times their actual gold holdings. At interest rates of 20%, the same gold could be lent 10 times over yielding a 200% return every year and this was backed by gold that did not even exist! Of course, the goldsmiths were careful not to overextend themselves and thus became very wealthy at the expense of the rest of the populace without producing anything of intrinsic value.

Since only the principal was lent into the money supply, more money was eventually owed back in principal plus interest than the people as a whole, possessed. They had to continually take out loans of new paper money to cover the shortfall, causing the wealth of the towns and eventually of the country to be diverted into the vaults of the goldsmiths, by this time now 'bankers', whilst the country began to progressively drown in debt.

As related briefly in the introduction to this book, the Bank of England was formed in 1694 as a long-planned coup of the Elite, to set in motion the eventual world-wide appropriation by them, of the money creation process.

The Dutch branch of the Elite was the first to create a 'central' bank to facilitate this scam. The Bank of Amsterdam, the first ever 'central bank' was formed in 1609. In 1688, following the usurping of the Catholic King James II by English Elite forces conspiring with their Dutch counterparts to re-introduce a Protestant monarchy, William III, the Prince of Orange and his wife Mary (the daughter of James), were installed on the British throne. This was facilitated by the landing of William's invasion force at Brixham harbour in Devon, South West England and his claims to the throne being supported by high-ranking English Protestants, including Parliament. James was eventually forced to flee to France, where he lived until his death in 1701.

However, once installed as King of England, one of William's briefs was to create the same financial conditions, ripe for exploitation, as had been in existence in Holland for almost a century. The Elite banking classes were clamouring for an opportunity to procure the same obscene profits in England, that were available to the Dutch bankers and so the Bank of England was conceived and came into being by 1694.

William Paterson, a London merchant banker and initiate of the Merovingian bloodline secret society, the Order of the Orange, was sponsor of the scheme. He petitioned Parliament in 1693 "to form a company to lend one million, two hundred thousand pounds to the government at 8% interest plus the right of note issue". After a few false-starts and some objections were overcome, this was duly approved after "great debate" and the formation began of the institution that has contributed more than any other to the economic slavery of the people of not just Britain, but also the world.

"I care not what puppet is placed upon the throne of England to rule the Empire on which the sun never sets. The man who controls Britain's money supply controls the British Empire and I control the British money supply." Nathan Mayer Rothschild, 1815

Can anyone please explain to me why any government would agree to such terms and in doing so forfeit the right to create interest-free money, whilst agreeing to pay a private corporation 8% interest on a loan that it did not even need had it retained the power to create its own currency? There can be only one reason and this speaks volumes to my mind.

"The modern banking system manufactures money out of nothing. The process is perhaps the most astounding piece of sleight of hand that was ever invented. Banking was conceived in inequity and born in sin . . . . Bankers own the earth. Take it away from them but leave them the power to create money and, with a flick of a pen, they will create enough money to buy it back again. . . . Take this great power away from them and all great fortunes like mine will disappear, for then this would be a better and happier world to live in. . . . But, if you want to continue to be the slaves of bankers and pay the cost of your own slavery, then let bankers continue to create money and control credit." Sir Josiah Stamp, Chairman of the Bank of England and the second richest man in Britain in the 1920s

Following the Bank of England model, in nineteenth century America, private banks issued their own bank-notes in sums up to ten times their actual reserves in gold. This is known as 'fractional reserve' banking, meaning that only a fraction of the total deposits managed by a bank are kept in reserve to meet the demands of depositors. But, 'runs' on the banks when the customers all demanded their gold at the same time, caused several banks to go bankrupt and made the system unstable. In 1913, the private bank-note system was therefore consolidated into a national bank-note system under the Federal Reserve Bank, a privately-owned corporation, given the right to issue Federal Reserve Notes and lend them to the US government at interest. These notes, which were issued just for the cost of printing them, came to form the basis of the American national money supply.

Prior to the formation of the Federal Reserve Bank, there had been a previous attempt at forming a Central Bank in the US, in the early 19th century and this was known as the Bank of the United States. Here is what the US President (at the time) had to say about it...

"Gentlemen, I have had men watching you for a long time and I am convinced that you have used the funds of the bank to speculate in the breadstuffs of the country. When you won, you divided the profits amongst you and when you lost, you charged it to the bank. You tell me that if I take the deposits from the bank and annul its charter, I shall ruin ten thousand families. That may be true, gentlemen, but that is your sin! Should I let you go on, you will ruin fifty thousand families, and that would be my sin! You are a den of vipers and thieves. I intend to rout you out, and by the eternal God, I will rout you out. If only people understood the rank injustice of our banking and money system, there would be a revolution before morning." Andrew Jackson, former US President

Shortly after this statement and the subsequent annulment of the Bank of the US, Jackson survived an assassination attempt, when the would-be assassin's gun jammed. There was no arrest made.

As previously stated, The Federal Reserve Act was passed through Congress in the early hours of the morning of the 23rd December 1913 whilst opposition was at a minimum, most Congressmen having already left for their Christmas holiday break. The Act itself was a lengthy document and had in fact only been introduced to Congress earlier that previous evening, allowing no time whatsoever for the document to be even read in full, let alone studied in detail.

"I am a most unhappy man. I have unwittingly ruined my country. A great industrial nation is controlled by its system of credit. Our system of credit is concentrated. The growth of the nation, therefore, and all our activities are in the hands of a few men. We have come to be one of the worst ruled, one of the most completely controlled and dominated Governments in the civilized world. No longer a Government by free opinion, no longer a Government by conviction and the vote of the majority, but a Government by the opinion and duress of a small group of dominant men." Former US President, Woodrow Wilson, several years after signing the Federal Reserve into existence

Inflation is nothing less than theft. Inflating the money supply by continually printing more money to pay the interest on the money that already exists has the disastrous effect of inflating prices. More money in competition for the same goods sends prices skywards and therefore the currency buys less, robbing people of the value of their money and savings. Inflation is then blamed on the government by the financial Elite, which is accused of printing money to fuel its excessive spending. However, the only money that governments actually issue is coins. This is a nice little deception and another sleight of hand by the 'banksters' and their media poodles.

At the time of writing, the US National debt (ie. to the Banksters) is $15 trillion and increasing by $1.5 trillion per year in interest alone! How can these sums ever be paid back? The simple unambiguous truth is that they cannot – in any way shape or form – ever. This in effect means that we and our descendants are in debt to and are slaves to the banksters forever and ever, giving them the 'right' to basically do whatever they see fit with our lives. By way of an illustration what these 'monopoly money' sums look like, please the illustrations below.

Believe it or not, this small pile is $1 million dollars. You could easily hold it in your hands and carry it around with you.

Although $1 million looks a little unimpressive, $100 million is a little more respectable. It fits neatly on a standard pallet...

And $1 BILLION dollars...

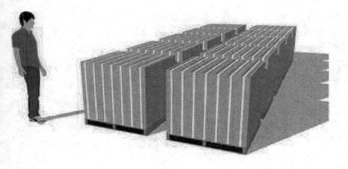

Next let us examine ONE TRILLION dollars. This is that number that we have been hearing so much about. A trillion is a million millions, a thousand billions. It is a one followed by 12 zeros.

So here we are.... $1,000,000,000,000 (one trillion dollars).......

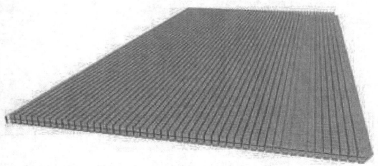

(And notice the pallets are double stacked.)

So if you hear someone casually mention the phrase 'one trillion dollars/pounds'... that is what they are talking about.

In addition, to put these figures into perspective even further, would it surprise you to learn that, despite the fact that figures of one million and much, much more are casually tossed around these days, an average human lifetime is considerably less than one million hours – at 657,000 for a span of 75 years? Or put another way, just under 40 million minutes. And since the alleged birth of Christ over 2000 years ago, less than 0.75 million days have passed.

As we now know, banks create the principal in the form of currency, but not the interest owed on their 'loans' to government. This creates an ever-spiralling shortfall as more money is printed just to pay the interest owed to the banksters. One pound lent at 5% becomes two pounds in 14 years which in effect means that the money supply has to double every 14 years just to cover the interest payments alone. Or to put it another way; every 14 years, banksters take as much money in interest payments from the government as comprised the entire economy 14 years previously! Easily the biggest deception ever perpetrated on a helpless humanity. This is the real reason for inflation and the fact that a loaf of bread which now costs around £1.00 cost about 2 pence in 1911.

"World bankers, by pulling a few simple levers that control the flow of money, can make or break entire economies. By controlling press releases of economic strategies that shape national trends, the power elite are able to not only tighten their stranglehold on this nation's economic structure, but can extend that control worldwide. Those possessing such power would logically want to remain in the background, invisible to the average citizen." Aldous Huxley

The seizure of the power to create money, by these arch-criminals is the absolute cause of all the global poverty and economic slavery that defines the sad state of the world today. These Elite that control the world's purse strings, causing the death of millions by starvation and disease whilst wielding ultimate power over us all are culpable of genocide on a grand scale. There can be no denial of this fact whatsoever.

"The Federal Reserve was set up in 1913 to finance both sides of two subsequent world wars. In other words, these wars were funded by the credit of the US taxpayer. Apart from profiting from it, the Illuminati bankers use war to enslave us with debt, enact social change and consolidate their power". Dr. Henry Makow, researcher and author, 2011

So, where are all the riots in the streets, the public storming of the Bank of England and the Federal Reserve Bank in New York, the loud demands from government and the media for financial reform? Unfortunately, through the mind-control process otherwise known as state education, mass media propaganda and the self-policing syndrome that infects the entire population from top to bottom, we are controlled and manipulated to believe that all is well and our current system is the 'only way'. Even when it becomes patently obvious that all is not well, we are still conditioned to believe that we are helpless and cannot make effective changes to the 'way of the world'. ...Go back to work everyone, nothing to see here. Everything is under control.

"The banks are allowed to create the money out of nothing and charge interest for turning the trick, while the masses have to earn it. The right to create money is the right to leverage, and it's that financial leverage that hoists them to the top of the pyramid. Without this leverage they would not be able to create such massive amounts of wealth and control. The only way to destroy this system and create fair money is by creating awareness. Once people understand the 'trick', the whole house of cards begins to collapse". Robert Bonomo, activistpost.com 13th October 2011

This problem can only be rectified by governments wresting back the constitutional power to print and issue currency. Fractional reserve banking should be eliminated, limiting banks to lending only existing funds. If the power to create money was returned to governments, all national debts could be paid off instantly, taxes could be reduced or even eliminated and government-sponsored social programmes could be instigated, benefitting the people as a whole and not just some tiny Elite clique. 100% of all our taxes go towards servicing the debt to the bankers and not, as we are widely led to believe, to providing services for the people.

It is worth relating the true story of a landmark court case in Minnesota, USA in 1969. *First National Bank of Montgomery vs. Daly* was an epic courtroom drama and although unsurprisingly, not widely reported either at the time or subsequently, is actually extremely significant. The defendant Jerome Daly a lawyer, defended himself against the bank's attempted foreclosure on his $14,000 mortgage on the grounds that there was no 'consideration' for the loan. 'Consideration' in legal-ese is a way of saying, 'the item exchanged' and is an essential element of any legal contract. Daly contended that the bank offered no consideration for his loan on the grounds that they had 'created' the money by bookkeeping, 'out of thin air' and had therefore not suffered a loss (another relevant point of law) by his refusal or inability to pay back the money.

The proceedings were recorded by Associate Justice William Drexler, who had given no credence whatsoever to the defence, until Mr. Morgan, the bank's president, took to the witness stand. To Drexler's and indeed everyone's surprise, Morgan casually admitted in cross-examination that the bank routinely created money 'out of thin air' for all its loans and mortgages and that this indeed was standard practice in all banks. Presiding Justice, Martin Mahoney declared that *'It sounds exactly like fraud to me'*, accompanied by nods and murmurs of assent from all the jury members. In his summary of the case, Justice Mahoney reported that; *"Plaintiff (the bank) admitted that it, in combination with the Federal Reserve Bank of Minneapolis, did create the entire $14,000.00 in money and credit upon its own books by bookkeeping entry. That this was the consideration used to support the Note dated May 8, 1964 and the Mortgage of the same date. The money and credit first came into existence when they* created it. (my emphasis - JH) Morgan admitted that no United States Law or Statute existed which gave him the right to do this. A lawful consideration must exist and be tendered to support the Note."

The court duly rejected the bank's claim for foreclosure, and the defendant kept his house. The implications of this case should have been enormous. If bankers are indeed extending credit *without* consideration ie without backing their loans with real money they actually had in their vaults and were entitled to lend, a decision declaring their loans void, could topple the financial and banking systems worldwide.

Jerome Daly subsequently wrote in a local news article; "This decision, which is legally sound, has the effect of declaring all private mortgages on real and personal property, and all US and State bonds held by the Federal Reserve, National and State banks to be null and void. This amounts to an emancipation of this Nation from personal, national and state debt purportedly owed to this banking system. Every American owes it to himself to study this decision very carefully . . . for upon it hangs the question of freedom or slavery."

Perhaps needless to say, the decision utterly failed to change prevailing practice, even though it was never legally challenged or over-ruled. Justice Mahoney actually threatened to prosecute and expose the bank and as a result, somewhat unsurprisingly, he died less than six months after the trial, in an extremely suspicious 'accident' that involved poisoning of some kind. Beware anyone who stands in the way of these people and their nefarious practices.

Since this precedent, quite a number of other defendants have attempted to have mortgages and loans nullified using the same defence as Daly, but there has been limited success only. In fact, one judge said off the record; "If I let you do that, you and everyone else, it would bring the whole system down. I cannot let you go behind the bar of the bank. . . . We are not going behind that curtain!"

At this point in the story it is also worth noting that the way that money creation has been engineered to operate, means that believe it or not, the simple action of completing a mortgage or loan application form with a signature, actually creates the amount of money being applied-for. It then does not matter to the finance company whether or not they loan-out the money, the only tangible difference being that should they deem the applicant to have a sufficiently high credit rating for them to risk lending the money that was created by the process in the first place, then they can also benefit from the interest that this will generate. Otherwise, if the application is declined, they have to content themselves merely with the capital sum. This then is why it is by no means 'immoral' to renege on the payments of mortgages or loans. Had the application not been made in the first place, then the money would not have been arbitrarily summoned into existence. To be clear, it is actually the signature of an applicant that creates the 'money' from nothing.

"When plunder becomes a way of life for a group of men living together in society, they create for themselves, in the course of time, a legal system that authorises it and a moral code that glorifies it." Frédéric Bastiat, 1801-1850

"Some people think the Federal Reserve Banks are U.S. government institutions. They are not ... they are private credit monopolies which prey upon the people of the U.S. for the benefit of themselves and their foreign and domestic swindlers, and rich and predatory money lenders. The sack of the United States by the Fed is the greatest crime in history. Every effort has been made by the Fed to conceal its powers, but the truth is the Fed has usurped the government. It controls everything here and it controls all our foreign relations. It makes and breaks governments at will." Congressman Charles McFadden, Chairman, House Banking and Currency Committee, 10th June 1932

So where are the armies of politicians, economists, financial experts, City analysts and media financial pundits, lining-up to expose this crime? The answer is that there are none because...

Most of them cannot see beyond the ends of their noses and just believe the powerful and convincing hype passed down from above by the propaganda mill, which is our so-called 'education' system and the complicit media.

Those that are aware of it have already been convinced that this is just a ridiculous conspiracy theory espoused by 'crazies' or 'loony lefties', and...

Those small few that are really aware will not make waves for fear of jeopardising their own well-paid positions. This is how the system really works. We all need to 'wake-up' as a species – and soon.

This fraudulent monetary system eventually created the prevailing conditions for the Elite to perpetrate a further heinous scam upon the unsuspecting masses, that of extreme consumerism.

The Descent into the Dark Abyss of Extreme Consumerism

The Industrial Revolution began in Britain in the mid to late 18th century with the invention and subsequent widespread utilisation of the steam engine, which enabled the automation of many previously, exclusively manual tasks and facilitated the invention of new labour-saving devices such as the power-loom. Within fifty years the country had changed dramatically. The quiet, serene, rural landscape had been replaced by noise, smoke and pollution and the living and working practices of the masses had changed forever from a relatively healthy, albeit physically-demanding life of fresh air and exercise, tending the fields and livestock, into a life of complete, utter slavery and drudgery in countless mills and factories breathing in the acrid smoke and filth under the yoke of the new age of the machines.

The lot of the poor, the weak and the working classes has always been one of slavery and exploitation by the wealthy, but by this point in time it was being practiced literally on a global, 'industrial scale' as the Elite spread their new economic culture throughout the world. The formerly rural-based economy was now almost abandoned as the millions of former farmworkers and their long-suffering families descended on the now overcrowded, squalid conurbations into which most rural townships were being transformed, in a desperate attempt to improve their standard of living. People spilled into these new towns and cities from the countryside in search of an escape route from the grinding poverty they had endured on the farms only to encounter even worse, utter desperation in the filthy, rat and disease-infested slums in which they were now forced to reside. They were made to work cripplingly long hours in inhuman conditions for starvation-level wages as the new spirit of industrialisation took over the world with its philosophy of raping the world's natural resources and turning them into consumer goods before discarding them and starting the cycle over again.

The great 'god' of 'economic growth to the detriment of all else' had arrived, producing and consuming more and more raw materials to manufacture goods, constantly improving them and then discarding their previous, perfectly usable forerunners to make repeat sales, all in the name of boosting the bank balances of those who own the means of production (the Elite) plus of course the Elite-owned banks. The fact that they were destroying the only home we have and/or are ever likely to have in the process is of course of no consequence to these psychopathic people of zero-conscience.

To facilitate these huge technical advances taking place at breath-taking speed, a new religion was born and foisted upon the world, 'modern science'. Christianity still held sway, especially in Europe and North America, but its influence was now in almost terminal decline as science began to take-over its mantle. Science was the instigator of the 'brave new world' of the machine-age and as the 19th century gave way eventually to the 20th century, the twin gods of science and profit had now taken over much of human consciousness. Indeed science had by now determined that life after death was a complete myth and that everything could be explained by its cold logic, in the process decreeing that we are all a 'cosmic accident', a chance occurrence, the mere product of complex chemical interaction in the primordial soup of the infant Earth. Of course this obviously proved to be a problem for mainstream religion, but it proved to be a greater one for humanity as life then, according to scientificism, the new religion, was utterly pointless. One was born, lived in poverty, in abject misery and wage-slavery to one's master and then died. Indeed the lives people were now being forced to endure in the slums and filthy, dangerous prison-like factories, seemed to bear-out this rationale which overall was yet another nail in the coffin of the human spirit and spirituality, crushed as it was then and still is now, by the Elite's relentless drive for profits to the detriment of all else.

In one sense, Christianity was now beginning to 'reap what it had sown' in terms of refusing to deviate from all its dogma and contentions that the Bible was one hundred percent the undeniable truth in the precise format that had been decided at Nicaea in 325AD (The Nicene Creed) and brutally enforced in the succeeding centuries by the Roman Catholic Church. The 'real' view of creation, life and re-birth had been suppressed for millennia by religious leaders and their predecessors, but now this view was also being suppressed by science too. Religion and science therefore formed a deadly, two-pronged assault on reality, despite the outward illusion of them being each other's sworn enemies. This indeed, as I mention elsewhere in this book is a classical Hegelian trap favoured by the Elite. Provide two alternatives, both of them false, to enable the masses to choose their favourite and then spend the rest of their pointless lives arguing the merits or otherwise of two entirely false premises, whilst the real truth goes by un-noticed or ignored completely.

Religion and science therefore enjoyed a mutual interest which was essential to the survival of both and the suppression of reality. This then ensured that as few people as possible understood the fundamental truths of eternal human consciousness and the reincarnation of the soul into new bodies after each death on its long, long journey to perfection. The widespread realisation of this fact would no doubt end the power of mainstream religion forever as well as precipitate the demise of cold scientific logic, both of which contribute greatly to the Elite's control system imposed upon the world and by which method it rules over us all with its iron fist in a velvet glove.

The overall result of this ascent of science is the emergence of a different world to that known and understood by our ancient ancestors. This is a world of 'five sense' reality, propounded by our masters and their shills and 'useful idiots' such as Professor Richard Dawkins, who decrees in effect, that anything that cannot be detected by human senses and/or explained by current scientific knowledge simply does not exist or at best has no value. It has been mooted however by the more free-thinking of those among the scientific community that the five human senses can only detect something like 0.05% of the entire 'spectrum of reality' but that does not deter Dawkins and his ilk from publicly 'rubbishing' everything that falls outside their narrow little world-view. According to mainstream science, God does not exist because it is not 'provable' and spirituality is all a fantasy of the 'ignorant' ancients, a primitive superstition. This view is frankly hypocrisy of the highest degree. Science would appear to have no problem accepting and expounding other unproven myths such as the Big Bang theory, the dinosaurs-extinction-by-meteorite-impact theory and the theory of evolution and also ridiculous assumptions about 'dark matter' and 'dark energy' which exist simply to conveniently fill a gap in scientific knowledge and which are all disingenuously taught to our children and students, amongst other myths, as absolute fact with no room for argument or debate. Newtonian and

Einstein-ian physics are simply guesses at best and dis-information of the most sinister kind at worst and nothing else. Additionally, does mainstream science ever actually attempt to use its methods to prove or disprove the existence of the other 99.95% of reality we are unable to detect with our human senses? No and nor will it, ever, as long as science is dominated by the Elite, whose very tenuous position is wholly dependent upon you and I believing their dis-information, lies and distortions. I submit that indeed science as we know it today is simply just another religion, populated, controlled and expounded by 'believers of the faith' just like any other.

"This time it is the creed of scientism and the pseudo-religion of the big bang that stands in the way of progress. In truth, we have no real understanding of matter, light, magnetism, gravity, quantum behavior, subatomic particles, stars, galaxies, or... need I go on? Stories of creation and what did and did not happen in the universe over the past 13.7 billion years are crackpot schemes by celebrities of less talent than many in the Natural Philosophy Alliance but of greater prestige. We have too much information and too little real understanding. Many of the things we are taught 'just ain't so'. This realization frees the mind to view everything afresh. It is the spark required to rekindle enthusiasm for science and drive progress. There is so much to be discovered." Wal Thornhill, September 2011.

The Elite themselves know that their five-sense universe is a complete fabrication. The universe, one suspects, is infinite; not merely in terms of the three dimensions plus time, as science tells us, but also in infinite numbers of inter-relating dimensions, pervading all. There is however still a spiritual vacuum which is only now beginning to be filled, as an understanding of who and what we really are begins slowly to emerge in our collective consciousness and the 'hundredth monkey syndrome' begins to take effect in earnest.

When scientificism originally began to emerge as a dominant force and a few members of the profession attempted to challenge some of its dogma, they were ruthlessly ridiculed or simply destroyed, as they still are today. The Elite do not want some inconveniently free-thinking, independent-minded scientist challenging their decreed 'truths', even less them being able to prove them as untrue. Notice the common theme here between the way this system operates and the way of extremist mainstream religion in previous centuries? Organisations such as the Spanish Inquisition existed to root-out and destroy those who were either 'unbelievers' or simply propounded a different view, no matter how innocuous and this is also the method of the scientific religion. To succeed in science one must toe the Elite-decreed party line, no independently-minded persons need apply. The way forward for science has thus been very slow and ponderous as it is obsessed with the purely physical whilst making little or no attempt at exploring the spiritual, the direction wherein most significant, valuable and life-enriching knowledge lies. Science serves the Elite 'system' by suppressing true knowledge and imprisoning humanity. This is almost exactly the same role fulfilled by religion in past centuries.

Exploitation is the key to all this. Exploitation underpins the whole control system we have in place as our reality today, exploitation of the planet and its resources and also the entire human population outside of the thirteen bloodline families.

This then was also the real reason for the huge expansion of the British Empire from the eighteenth century onwards, to gain control of and suppress the indigenous populations and take control of a country's natural resources and its peoples with a view to appropriating them for and on behalf of the British Elite families in their pursuit of profits. Britain and other dominant European countries literally stole these resources, turned the inanimate variety into consumables and simply used them and/or sold them back whence they had originated for enormous profits. And as for the animate variety, they were kidnapped and sold into a life of slavery on the other side of the world, to work in the plantations and fledgling factories of the ultra-rich. This indeed is exactly what still happens today on a much larger scale and predominantly by the American military-industrial empire, except today's slaves are now paid starvation wages and forced to feed and clothe themselves on the relative pittances they are paid, instead of their every need being provided by their owners. One could reasonably debate the idea that in many ways 18th and 19th century slaves were better-off than their modern counterparts. This looting of the world's resources has also had the unfortunate side-effect of destroying weaker, third-world countries' ability to feed themselves effectively and so they are now utterly dependent on their conquerors' benevolence in providing them with the resources they need to subsist, obviously at a price.

"I have heard that people are dependent upon us for food. I know that was not supposed to be good news. To me that was good news, because before people can do anything else, they have to eat. And if you are looking for a way to get people to lean on you and to be dependent on you, in terms of their co-operation with you, it seems to me that food dependency would be terrific." Former US Senator, Hubert Humphrey.

This policy leads directly to the famines and starvation existing in the world today, compounded by the exploitation of land for the production of cash-crops in ways which destroy soil fertility in the name of maximisation of short-term profit and also by the political and internal strife within these countries, caused by the overthrow of regimes which do not suit the Elite's geo-political interests. The USA leads the world in this respect today, changing political regimes at will where those in 'power' threaten any aspect of the Elite corporations' ongoing profit streams, often using the excuse of defending democracy by removing unelected 'dictators' using its armed forces, who despite outward appearances are nothing more than the mercenaries of those corporations. Unsurprisingly, these dictators have often been previously installed by the USA in the first place to further its own ends in the past, but have outlived their usefulness to the Elites. This is all disguised and misrepresented of course by the mainstream media at the behest of the rich and powerful families who currently own the Earth.

The speed at which the world has become 'industrialised' is absolutely staggering. Only just over one hundred years ago, we were still largely dependent on horse-power for transport and steam engines powered by coal and water were the only machines in existence capable of challenging the horse's superiority in this regard. Indeed, as a species we progressed from steam-power and horses to jet engines and space-travel in around 60 years. A monumental technological feat that had it been used for the benefit of humanity as a whole instead of a tiny minority, would have led to a world of peace and plenty for all instead of the truly appalling state of affairs we see today.

The last two hundred years have seen us shift from being the servants of Mother Nature to being its masters. We have behaved in the past, and are still today behaving in ways that seriously threaten the very existence of the Earth upon which we depend, whilst over 100,000 people die of starvation each day. Starvation caused directly by Elite profiteering.

Our so-called economic system depends wholly on the fact that we need to consume the Earth's resources at an ever-increasing rate simply to maintain and increase the profits and margins of the corporations. Economic growth, we are constantly told by the Elite-controlled economists, media pundits and financial analysts, is the only meaningful measure of a strong economy and as such is portrayed forcibly to be inherently desirable despite the fact that it is this very 'economic growth' that results in the wholesale destruction of the planet we see today and the constant widening of the gap between those who 'have' and those who do not.

"Somehow, we have come to think the whole purpose of the economy is to grow, yet growth is not a goal or purpose. The pursuit of endless growth is suicidal." David Suzuki

If a country has to produce and consume more and more to effect this growth, then a point is soon reached whereby that cannot be sustained within that country's own borders. It becomes necessary to sell abroad and export goods and technology and in order to do this effectively, often means converting other cultures and societies to the ethics (and I use the term loosely) of extremist capitalist consumerism. This can only be achieved by making them dependent upon the consumer goods and designer, junk foodstuffs of the originating country, through the use of thoroughly misleading, manipulative and often subliminal advertising. This then in turn has the long-term effect of destroying that country's self-sufficiency in food and further increasing its dependency upon the imports of the goods and food-types now newly in demand. The need to expand and increase production year on year means that everyone has to compete or die – literally in the case of many third world nations. The obvious exception to this rule being the banking cartels which never lose, whichever way the dice may fall.

We hear much idle talk and empty rhetoric about 'economic co-operation' and 'pulling in the same direction' in order to cure the ills of the world but the very basis of our corrupt economic system is to turn people against people and country against country as they fight among themselves for the metaphorical crumbs from the banksters' tables. 'Every man for himself', 'greed is good' and 'survival of the fittest' are the watchwords by which we are all really forced to live in order to survive in this artificially engineered world of utterly brutal, dog-eat-dog competitiveness.

"In order to give the Goyim* no time to think and take note, their minds must be diverted towards industry and trade. Thus, all the nations will be swallowed-up in the pursuit of gain and in the race for it will not take note of their common foe. But, again, in order that freedom may once and for all disintegrate and ruin the communities of the Goyim, we must put industry on a speculative basis; the result of this will be that what is withdrawn from the land by industry will slip through the hands and pass into speculation, that is, to our classes." Protocol 4. The Protocols of the Learned Elders of Zion.

*Hebrew word for 'cattle' and a derogatory term for a non-Jew, ie. 'the masses'.

The impetus for expansion is then promulgated by scientific research into new inventions and improvements of existing technology. Little by little we have been propagandised into the belief that we simply must have the latest technologies, gizmos and gadgets and that it is desirable to be seen as one who wears the most expensive clothing, jewellery and shoes or the person who buys the most expensive cars, watches, perfumes, colognes and visits the world's most desirable locations – all in the name of expanding the bank accounts and boosting the 'bottom lines' of the Elite corporations in catastrophic expense to the quality of our environment. But still, who cares eh? As long as the already filthy-rich continue to get richer and richer by enticing us to give them all our money plus some that we do not even have, to buy things that we do not even want or need and as a result remain in an almost permanent state of poverty and therefore slavery, as a result, that's OK.

Indeed, shopping and buying things – anything – seems to be a modern-day 'hobby'. Visit a shopping mall in any town anywhere in the Western world and people-watch for a while to see what I mean. These places are usually thronged with people at all hours of the day and night – buying consumer goods they do not need with money they do not even possess (credit granted by the banksters) and this, more often than not is stuff that we would not miss if we were not 'sold' it at every given opportunity by subtly persuasive and invasive marketing and advertising. Most of it anyway is used for a short time only and then when the updated version is released three months hence; it will be thrown away, even though it still more than adequately fulfils the function for which it was originally intended. We are made to feel worthless or like pariahs by both our masters and peers if we do not own the latest and 'best' versions of any given technology or possession.

It is exactly the same with clothes. How many suits, dresses, shirts, sweaters and t-shirts does one really need? How many pairs of shoes can one reasonably wear in a week or a month? I would even admit that I have myself on occasions, bought an item of clothing that I never got around to wearing even once, before deciding to dispose of it. Our forebears would probably have had one suit of clothes, perhaps two shirts, two pairs of underwear and socks and one pair of shoes (more likely, boots) to their name, two if they were very lucky and whilst I am not advocating that we return to this opposite extreme, surely there is a happy medium? We do not realise it, but we are being constantly enticed though subtle and subliminal advertising techniques to part with most of the money we earn as soon as it hits our bank accounts and the ongoing damage that this philosophy is wreaking, not only upon the environment, but to our own psychological well-being, beggars belief. The prevailing system ensures that we are given money with one hand, in exchange for our hard labours month on month and then have it taken from us with the other, whilst the Elites take ownership of and control the entire process and reap the vast profits to be had from this circular-process methodology. This is the 'religion' of extreme consumerism – criticise it only at your peril – you will very quickly be put in your place by your masters and peers, should you do so!

"An enormous, dictatorial corporate cartel is ruling the world through its proxies in government, banking, academia and media. Our entire Western culture has become an insidious farce with the sole purpose of maintaining the enslaved masses in their conjured up democracies, religions and histories". Robert Bonomo, activistpost.com 13th October 2011

The car licence/registration system in Britain is one good example of how consumers are subtly enticed to spend money unnecessarily by being peer-pressured into replacing their cars more often than they would under normal circumstances. Within the licence plate number is a code which tells everyone exactly the age of any car, to within 6 months. For example, a car may have a registration mark of RK05ZDP. 'RK' is the area code for the town of Reading, so that is the place of registration of the vehicle, 'ZDP' is the 3 digit unique identifier consisting of any combination of three letters from AAA to ZZZ and finally, the '05' is the giveaway. This denotes to everyone that the car was first registered between the 1st March 2005 and 31st August 2005, which has given rise to a 'keeping-up with the Joneses' mentality amongst British car buyers. When the neighbours suddenly appear with a brand new '11' (the code for March to August 2011) registered car, to many people an '05' car will begin to look a little dated and mark them down as inferior, such is the power of ostentation and peer pressure. Of course this system was lobbied for and 'paid' for by the car manufacturers' lobbyists, probably in the form of party donations, making a mockery of so-called democracy in the process. What other possible reason could there be for devising such a system in the first place?

According to government it is in order that people cannot easily fake the age of their cars when selling them, but that is abject nonsense. To get around this problem is simple – buy a cheap private, dateless plate from pre-1963 or even a dated plate from say the 1980s that is obviously not the year of manufacture of the car and yet in any case, the vehicle's registration document will tell a potential buyer the age of the car in an instant. One more example of how governments are dictated to by the mega-corporations at the expense of the people and in this case, the environment.

We are also bombarded with propaganda in the form of advertising, trying to convince us at every opportunity that banks and other large corporations are really quite benevolent entities who are here to serve you, care about the welfare of you and your family and cater for your every need – all at a price, of course. How often do we see TV and billboard ads proclaiming such things as '... *the bank that cares*' or '... *let us look after you and your family*', '... *you deserve only the best...*' or '... *we are here to help*'? All absolute lies and extremely subtle psycho-babble of course, designed to lull you into a false sense of security, convince you of the benevolence of Elite corporations and generally make you believe that the world is a completely different place to the one you know is real, deep-down.

"*The more money most people earn, the more they want and expect. In fact, for some it becomes a pathetic, obsessive way of life. Their version of God becomes the accumulation of worthless Federal Reserve notes stuffed in their pocket. Or running up insane balances for credit card junk purchases, for which greedy banks freely extend more and more credit until the person is buried too deep to get out. It proves the old expression – 'give someone enough rope and they will hang themselves'.*" Ted Twietmeyer, 'Are People Really Stupid or is it Something Else?' 2007

But, we always hear the cry... '*What is the alternative?*' A ridiculous question if ever I heard one, because there are so many alternatives. The reason that this question never gets a sensible, coherent answer, in my opinion is three-fold. This is firstly, because any alternative would probably destroy the current status-quo to the detriment of the Elite powers-that-be and their fat bank accounts. Secondly we are falsely encouraged to believe that no alternative is feasible because of the inherent human traits of greed and selfishness. However, anthropological science has long suggested that unbridled greed is not in fact a universal attribute of humanity, merely a personality blemish – usually applicable only to the psychopaths who freely walk among us and dictate our every movement and thought. And the third reason is, simply because it is the kind of question that is not possible to answer in an instant, succinct sound-bite. It is almost akin to abruptly asking someone in the street 'what is the meaning of life?' and expecting a precise, scientific and concise assessment of the issue.

The neatest answer to this largely rhetorical question I ever heard was this;

"*What's the alternative to a world in which the few control the many for the benefit of the few? Where billions get up every day to go to some joyless, soulless job that they hate - just to survive? Where every month is a daily challenge to pay the bills and there is no time for living, just survival? Where millions die of hunger in a world of plenty and millions more die in manufactured wars? Where billionaires run a system that makes them ever-richer while staggering numbers of people live on less than a dollar a day? Where people suffer and die from illnesses that could be cured if the means were not suppressed? Where children are conditioned from birth to serve the system that controls them their entire lives? What's the alternative to that? I don't know - you got me."* David Icke, political researcher

Although it does not, strictly speaking, answer the question, it at least illustrates the futility of asking it in the first place whilst also emphasising in what a crazy, upside-down world we all live. The system itself is almost a caricature, a mockery of how things ought to be. It is so utterly self-defeating and unsustainable and only by simply stepping-back a pace or two, 'outside the box' as it were, for a moment and observing it critically is it possible to recognise the sheer ludicrousness of it all. Only when we do this is it possible to perceive the fact that we are being fooled on a huge scale. The only reason that this system was propagated in the first place is simply to make the rich, richer and the poor, poorer and to maintain and enhance that status quo at all costs. It is absolutely not the result of an accidental evolution of society or the natural 'way of things' as we are led to believe by the liars and charlatans of all forms of the media whenever this philosophy is questioned.

We are subjected to 'education', and I use the term loosely, which is little more than outright indoctrination and propaganda designed to perpetuate the system at whatever detriment to people and the environment. The result of this has been to render the masses ignorant of what is really happening to them on a daily basis, thus securing the Elite few, virtually a free run-through to their perverted goals.

In third world countries, where people live on the land and by their wits and have not been subjected to our western 'education', we take away their lands and their forests by force and coercion and thus, their culture and way-of-life destroyed, they are then forced to embrace our own insidious consumer-culture and 'educational' programmes, perpetuating and extended the corrupt system exponentially. This is just another way that the system devours more and more until eventually there will be nothing left to consume.

With each passing decade, the technology used to further the system becomes ever more efficient and produces more and more 'things' with less and less reliance on people. This then has the effect of dramatically increasing unemployment and thus conversely increasing the lust for consumer goods and services. The more that people can be artificially induced to want (desire or even covet), the easier it is to ultimately control them by manipulating the symbols of human success to relate to material possessions. The word 'want' in itself is an interesting example of this subtle manipulation. Until around 150 years ago, to 'want' something was to lack or be in need of something, whereas now it has been construed to mean that you 'desire' something. For example; in 1850, the statement, 'I want a warm coat' simply meant that you did not have one. Now it actually means that you strongly desire to possess one. Although the change is subtle, it is I believe highly significant and symptomatic of on-going social engineering.

So, in order to control the masses, the Elite needed to develop a system whereby when people are dissatisfied with their lot, they are induced to seek happiness by buying and owning 'things' – anything at all, it does not really matter just so long as the money that the people have been given in wages finds its way back to the Elite's bank accounts as quickly as possible, usually in exchange for some intrinsically worthless yet over-priced bauble, in order that this cycle can continue.

Below is an excerpt from a book, which succinctly describes the way we are manipulated by the system and despite the fact that it was written over one hundred years ago, is still pertinent to the world of today:

"'Money is the real cause of poverty', said Owen.

'Prove it', said Crass.

'Money is the cause of poverty because it is the device by which those who are too lazy to work are enabled to rob the workers of the fruits of their labours'.

'Prove it', repeated Crass.

Owen slowly folded up the piece of newspaper he had been reading and put it into his pocket. 'All right', he replied. 'I'll show you how the Great Money Trick is worked'.

Owen opened his dinner basket and took from it two slices of bread but as those were not sufficient, he requested that anyone who had some bread left would give it to him. They gave him several pieces, which he placed in a heap on a clean piece of paper and, having borrowed the pocket knives they used to cut and eat their dinners with, from Harlow, Easton and Philpot, he addressed them as follows;

'These pieces of bread represent the raw materials which exist naturally in and on the Earth for the use of mankind; they were not made by any human being, but created by the Great Spirit for the benefit and sustenance of all, the same as were the air and the light of the sun.'

'You're about as fair-speakin' a man as I've met for some time', said Harlow, winking at the others.

'Yes, mate', said Philpot. 'Anyone would agree to that much, it's as clear as mud.'

'Now', continued Owen. 'I am a capitalist; or rather, I represent the landlord and capitalist class. That is to say, all these raw materials belong to me. It does not matter for our present argument how I claimed possession of them, or whether I have any real right to them; the only thing that matters now is the admitted fact that all the raw materials which are necessary for the production of the necessities of life are now the property of the Landlord and Capitalist class. I am that class; all these raw materials belong to me.'

'Good enough', agreed Philpot.

'Now you three represent the Working Class; you have nothing – and for my part, although I have all these raw materials, they are of no use to me – what I need is – the things that can be made out of these raw materials by work; but as I am too lazy to work myself, I have invented the Money Trick to make you work for me. But first I must explain that I possess something beside the raw materials. These three knives represent – all the machinery of production; the factories, tools, railways and so forth, without which the necessaries of life cannot be produced in abundance. And these three coins...' – taking three halfpennies from his pocket – '...represent my Money Capital'. 'But before we go any further...', said Owen interrupting himself, '...it is most important that you remember that I am not supposed to be merely a capitalist, I represent the whole of the Capitalist Class. You are not supposed to be just three workers – you represent the whole Working Class'.

'All right, all right', said Crass, impatiently. 'We all understand that. Git on with it'.

Owen proceeded to cut up one of the slices of bread into a number of little square blocks. 'These represent the things which are produced by labour, aided by machinery, from the raw materials. We will suppose that three of these blocks represent a week's work. We will suppose that a week's work is worth one pound and we will suppose that each of these halfpennies is a sovereign [a gold coin worth one pound – a significant sum 100 years ago – JH]. We'd be able to do the trick better if I had real sovereigns but I forgot to bring any with me'.

'I'd lend you some...' said Philpot regretfully '...but I left me purse on our grand pianner'.

As by a strange coincidence, nobody happened to have any gold with them, it was decided to make shift with the halfpennies.

'Now this is the way the trick works...'

'Before you goes on with it...' interrupted Philpot, apprehensively, '...don't you think we'd better 'ave someone to keep watch at the gate in case a slop [police officer] comes along? We don't want to get runned-in, you know'.

'I don't think there's any need for that', replied Owen. 'There's only one slop who'd interfere with us for playing this game and that's police constable Socialism'.

'Never mind about Socialism...' said Crass irritably. '...git along with the bloody trick'.

Owen now addressed himself to the working classes as represented by Philpot, Harlow and Easton.

'You say that you are all in need of employment and as I am the kind-hearted Capitalist Class, I am going to invest all my money in various industries, so as to give you Plenty of Work. I shall pay each one of you, one pound per week and a week's work is that you must all produce three of these square blocks. For doing this work you will each receive your wages; the money will be your own, to do as you like with and the things you produce will of course be mine, to do as I like with. You will each take one of these machines and as soon as you have done your week's work, you shall have your money'.

The Working Classes accordingly set to work and the Capitalist Class sat down and watched them. As soon as they had finished they passed the nine little blocks to Owen, who placed them on a piece of paper by his side and paid the workers their wages.

'These blocks represent the necessaries of life. You can't live without some of these things, but as they belong to me, you'll have to buy them from me. My price for these blocks is – one pound each.'

As the Working Classes were in need of the necessaries of life and as they could not eat, drink or wear the useless money, they were compelled to agree to the kind Capitalist's terms. They each bought back and consumed one third of the produce of their labour. The Capitalist Class also devoured two of the square blocks and so the net result of the week's work was that the kind Capitalist had consumed two pounds worth of the things produced by the labour of others and reckoning the squares at their market value of one pound each, he had more than doubled his capital, for he still possessed the three pounds in money and in addition, four pounds-worth of goods. As for the Working Classes, Philpot, Harlow and Easton, having each consumed the pound's worth of necessaries they had bought with their wages, they were then in precisely the same condition as when they started work – they had nothing.

This process was repeated several times. For each week's work the producers were paid their wages. They kept on working and spending all their earnings. The kind-hearted Capitalist consumed twice as much as any one of them and his pile of wealth continually increased. In a little while – reckoning the little squares at their market value of one pound each – he was worth one hundred pounds and the Working Classes were still in the same condition as when they began and were still tearing into their work as though their lives depended upon it.

After a while the rest of the crowd began to laugh and their merriment increased when the kind-hearted Capitalist, just after having sold a pound's worth of necessaries to each of his workers, suddenly took their tools – the machinery of production – the knives, away from them and informed them that owing to over-production, all his store-houses were now glutted with the necessaries of life, he had decided to close down the works.

'Well and wot the bloody 'ell are we to do now?' demanded Philpot.

'That's not my business', replied the kind-hearted Capitalist. 'I've paid you your wages and provided you with Plenty of Work for a long time. I have no more work for you to do at present. Come round again in a few months and I'll see what I can do for you'.

'But what about the necessaries of life?' demanded Harlow. 'We must have something to eat'.

'Of course you must...', replied the Capitalist affably. '...and I shall be pleased to sell you some'.

'But we ain't got no bloody money!'

'Well, you can't expect me to give you my goods for nothing! You didn't work for nothing, you know. I paid you for your work and you should have saved something. You should have been thrifty like me. Look how I have got on by being thrifty'.

The unemployed looked blankly at each other, but the rest of the crowd only laughed. And then the unemployed began to abuse the kind-hearted Capitalist, demanding that he should give them some of the necessaries of life that he had piled-up in his warehouses or; to be allowed to work again and produce some more for their own needs; and even threatened to take some of the things by force if he did not comply with their demands. But the kind-hearted Capitalist told them not to be insolent and spoke to them about honesty and said if they were not careful, he would have their faces battered-in for them by the police or if necessary he would call out the military and have them shot down like dogs, the same as he had done before at Featherstone and Belfast.

'Of course...', continued the kind-hearted Capitalist, '...if it were not for foreign competition I should be able to sell these things that you have made and then I should be able to give you Plenty of Work again, but until I have sold them to somebody or other or used them all myself, you will have to remain idle'.

...Philpot held out his cap for [charitable] subscriptions... and the kind-hearted Capitalist was so affected by the sight of their misery that he gave them one of the Sovereigns he had in his pocket; but as this was no use to them, they immediately returned it to him in exchange for one of the small squares of the necessaries of life, which they divided and greedily devoured. And when they had finished eating, they gathered around the philanthropist and sang, 'For he's a jolly good fellow' and afterwards Harlow suggested that they should ask him if he would allow them to elect *him to Parliament." 'The Great Money Trick' from 'The Ragged-Trousered Philanthropists' by Robert Tressell, 1910*

It is this very system that leads to those who 'have' living in greater and greater opulence whilst those who 'have not' are consigned, at best, to being wage-slaves for their entire lives. A small percentage thus benefits from every possession they could possibly ever want or need whilst a rapidly increasing under-class of the permanently deprived, live in tent-villages or even in their cars and in cardboard boxes on the filthy streets of our cities. In America it has recently been reported that of the one million homes currently being repossessed each year, and growing, the banks that now 'own' them are literally burning and demolishing tens of thousands of them each month in order to maintain the balance of supply and demand in their favour and thus artificially fix house prices at grossly-inflated levels. Yet another example of how twisted and sick the system has become.

And what is the world's greatest consumer feeding-frenzy now inflicted upon us by those who enslave us? None other than Christmas, that wonderful festival of love, warmth and family bliss. Christianity commandeered an originally pagan festival, 'Yuletide' and imposed its own version of events upon it and slowly by degrees, this supposed festival of 'love one another', has been manipulated into becoming an orgy of consumerism. Originally, Christmas was a time for families, a time of quiet contemplation, celebration and rest and a time to think about and where possible, help those less fortunate than ourselves. Now it is a living nightmare for millions. Bombarded for weeks on end by ruthless and incessant advertising and coerced and harried into buying ridiculously expensive gifts and toys by the huge propaganda mill that usually starts turning around early October, many parents borrow money at extortionate interest rates simply to buy their children throw-away consumables and soon-to-be-obsolete electronic gadgets. The result of this action usually results in their struggling all through most of the following year paying-off their debts to banks and corporate interests. The only alternative to this for many is a feeling of extreme guilt throughout what is supposed to be the happiest time of the year, because they have been unable to buy what their children most wanted. This is emotional blackmail of the highest degree and engineered solely for the purpose of making huge, obscene amounts of money for the Elite few.

"How can we, as a nation, wrestle our economy from the grip of greedy corporations when we play into their hands every year? Why do we buy their lies this time of year while rejecting them the rest of the year? How can we stop the cycle of debt? How about this: a nationwide boycott of Christmas purchases. Boy, wouldn't that put a crimp in corporate profits." Barbara H. Peterson, farmwars.info, November 2011

Significantly, this huge spend-fest every November / December becomes more and more desperate and frenzied with each passing year as more and more corporations become utterly dependent on Christmas-time profits and as their desperation increases, the effects of this are felt by us all in the shape of their concerted assault on all five of our senses in an attempt to convince us to spend, spend, spend.

The main waste-product of all this craziness is humanity itself. When people are forced to live and work in an utterly destructive, soulless system, it causes extreme distress and misery. As humans our potential is limitless, bounded only by the extent of our own imaginations, but under the present regime we are little more than manufacturing and consuming machines, slaves to the system and as demonstrated in the excerpt from *The Ragged-Trousered Philanthropists* above, a medium by which those who 'own' us body and soul, can perpetuate their 'cycle of profitability' by using we humans as the manufacturers and then in turn, the consumers of those manufactured goods.

This cycle has been responsible for the destruction of the human spirit and the cause of most illnesses, which are, despite all the propaganda to the contrary, mainly psychologically induced and I include in this all the so-called physical ailments, which are exacerbated by poor, destructive western diets, high in fat and sugar and low in essential vitamins and nutrients. Thus, 'the system' in conjunction with science and religion has combined to ensure that billions are tired of living and yet terrified of dying.

Another serious by-product of extreme consumerism is the huge increase in crime. We are all programmed from birth to see our success or failure as people, in terms of the abundance or lack of material possessions we have accumulated. She lives in a tiny, rundown house, therefore she is a failure. He has a high-powered job, holding the power of life and death over hundreds, with a huge salary and therefore he is a success. Is it surprising therefore when more and more people turn to crime to further their own Elite-seeded ambitions of self-aggrandisement, by taking things that are not theirs and even worse, by actually killing people to acquire more money or possessions?

In early August 2011 England was rocked by violent rioting and looting in many of its major cities. The large-scale riots fuelled by a combination of a corrupt, broken society and disaffected youth broke-out countrywide and thus threatened the well-being of us all. Not through fear of being physically attacked or being actually caught-up in the mindless violence, but simply due to the fact that this is exactly what the government wants as an excuse to further curb our freedoms in the guise of 'security', in effect, to enslave us for our own protection. This is borne out by many independently corroborated reports of both police and fire-services actually being ordered to 'stand-down' and let the mayhem continue unhindered. There was also talk of military intervention and curfews, but fortunately these did not come to pass, at least on this occasion but they will in future, only time will tell. In any event, they have certainly now been 'set-up' in the public's minds as a future possibility by the actions of the mob in conjunction with the policy of police non-intervention. These are classic 'problem–reaction–solution' tactics as usual, of course.

I'm just like you. I grew up on an estate as well.

The looting, thievery and lawlessness that the British PM, David Cameron condemned at the time is simply the reflection at street-level of British society of what is taking place on a much greater scale in the upper echelons of government, commerce and the economy. Despite their pinstripe suits and upper-class accents, we have been subjected to decades of looting and thievery of economic and financial resources by the corporate and banking Elite, aided and abetted by a long succession of alternating, corrupt Labour and Conservative governments. The taxpayer bailout of corrupt, failed banks initiated by the former Labour PM, Gordon Brown and now overseen by Cameron, paid for in large part by austerity from public spending cuts, is but the latest manifestation of the official theft from the majority, to further enhance the already outrageous wealth of the Elite.

Cameron and his gang of super-rich criminals are currently advocating £100 billion in public spending cuts to pay for the criminal enterprise known as British banking. This is racketeering on a scale that looters in our inner cities could only stand in-awe of and indeed, as we see, only attempt to emulate it on a much smaller, albeit far more visible, scale. Where is the mainstream media condemnation of all this upper-class, 'white-collar' crime? They are certainly not slow in condemning the 'mindless violence' perpetrated by the 'have-nots' in our society and calling, almost in unison for totally disproportionate sentences for those found guilty and this attitude is now unsurprisingly reflected in the attitude now prevailing amongst the unthinking 'sheeple'.

"The cause of this mayhem cannot be traced to any legitimate political grievance; it is almost entirely the product of a diseased culture, fostered by multinational corporations and the celebrity-obsessed entertainment industry that brainwashes young people to aspire to lifestyles they can never possibly attain. The social decline of young people becomes a self-fulfilling prophecy as a result of constant media fascination with demonising youngsters and presenting them with a putrid diet of 'heroes', vacuous footballers and drug-addled musicians, whose behaviour makes impressionable kids

think that life revolves around being constantly trashed, engaging in amoral sexual conquests and proving their manhood by pointless displays of animal-like aggression. MTV-manufactured rap icons, movies and video games have trained an entire generation of disadvantaged kids to grow up as wannabe gangsters, marauding around town with their jeans half-way down their thighs in huge mobs intimidating the public. Rampant consumerism is also to blame. Deprived kids on benefits cannot afford the iPods and laptops they are told they must own to be accepted by their peers, so an opportunity like this cannot be wasted. Where we used to be defined by what we did, now we are defined by what we buy." Paul Joseph Watson, prisonplanet.com, 10th August 2011, commenting upon the British riots of August 2011

This prevailing system of extreme consumerism, conditions us all and especially the more impressionable among us, to believe that we need to indulge in regular, ongoing 'spending sprees' in order to be accepted and to 'feel good' about ourselves. But in times of high unemployment and economic depressions, more people are denied the opportunity to 'succeed' through their own efforts and even to be able to feed their families adequately, let alone partake in the so-called luxuries of life. Is it such a shock then that in this situation the dispossessed turn to crime to satisfy those artificially engendered wants or needs? Resentment at being cast-aside by the system is rife today and this then leads to resentment of anything and anyone. In this state of mind, people have murdered defenceless old ladies for the few pounds in their purse, their inherent reasoning being that the state and society has no respect for me so therefore why should I have any respect for anyone else?

This attitude is becoming more and more prevalent today and I refuse to believe that is because these people are inherently evil, as is strongly suggested and portrayed by the media in all its forms. In my view, it is simply a natural consequence of the way society is strongly biased towards those who have more than their fair share of power, influence and money. Maybe you or I would not commit murder for a few pounds, but we are all a product of a combination of our genes and upbringing and it is I believe, hypocritical to assume that had our own personal circumstances been the same as those disaffected, that we would not have followed exactly the same course, as we can never know for sure.

Living as we all do in a quasi-police-state-cum-dictatorship, what do the powers-that-be need to further pursue their agenda of greater security and control of populations? I would strongly suggest that they need a crime-ridden society very much like the one we have today. How convenient, not to mention coincidental. This is just what is needed to sway public opinion in their favour; 'the streets are not safe to walk at night' = 'more police and security surveillance cameras please' and yet again, these are classic 'problem–reaction–solution' strategies.

Each year the system is faced with ever-growing bills for crime, medical services, policing and social benefits etc. This is an inevitable consequence of ultra-consumerism and all its many side-issues. And the solution to this as proposed by those who believe they 'know best' is simply to propagate and facilitate a greater expansion of consumption and production to generate more money by 'growth' of the economy and thus the cycle continues, ever onwards to its own inevitable destruction.

In order to disguise the shortcomings of and protect this system-from-hell, the Elite need strong police and security forces and other such abominations as 'secret services' like MI5, MI6, CIA and the Mossad. These are there ostensibly to 'protect' us all from foreign powers who covet our country, our 'freedoms', our 'wealth' and lifestyles and also to guard against the extreme terrorism that we are told exists and is a great threat to our lives and freedom. In reality, these secret-service organisations actually exist to hide the truth of what is really going on in the world from their own citizens and to protect the Elite from those who would dispossess them. These so-called security services actually spend far more time spying on us, who their masters fear may be challenging the status quo, than they do protecting the country from outside attacks from so-called terrorist groups, who are usually infiltrated and controlled, if not actually created in the first place by these very same security organisations themselves, anyway.

There are a multitude of tactics that they use to further these ends, such as phone-tapping, the bugging of rooms, hidden cameras, agents provocateurs, computer-hacking, framing suspects and assassinations. These tactics are all used by the wonderfully benevolent country in which you live – against its own citizens – yes, that means you too.

I have often heard it said that 'if you are not doing anything wrong then you have nothing to fear'. This glib, oft-quoted statement is misguided in the extreme on so many levels. Firstly, who decides what is wrong or right? One man's terrorist is another man's freedom fighter. Is it wrong for example to peacefully challenge the government if you believe that it is acting illegally or against the best interests of its citizens? Is it wrong to write books such as this that challenge the status quo and expose what is really happening throughout the world?

You may say 'yes' and you may well be right, I do not have a personal monopoly on the truth, but I do believe that it is everyone's right to peacefully challenge any form of injustice or suppression, as I am attempting to do in writing this book. But would my own (or any other) government agree with those sentiments that challenge its very authority to dictate to its citizens what is and is not acceptable? I doubt that very much. In fact the very writing of this book probably would expose me to covert surveillance and may already have done so, but I do not believe I am doing wrong by writing such a volume as this and nor I suspect do most free-thinking, fair-minded individuals, whether or not they agree with the bulk of what I have written, per se.

Also, do we actually trust the entity that has the power to suppress us if we deviate from their decrees? According to the above quote, I would have nothing to fear unless I was doing wrong. But do we trust our government to decide whether I am doing wrong or not? What if it was decided by them arbitrarily that you or I were doing something wrong when we patently were not, by any standards? Do we trust the government to always act in the best interest of its individual citizens? I think not. No. I am afraid that that statement is at best misguided and at worst, a deceit of great magnitude. All governments will do 'whatever it takes' to maintain control and stay in power, without exception and are far from being the benevolent yet bumbling, monolithic institutions that they overtly appear to be and are portrayed to be by the compliant media. Any one of their own citizens who is perceived either as an actual physical or even a passive threat to their supreme power will not be tolerated and will be dealt with severely, either overtly or covertly. This is the very embodiment of fascism/communism/socialism (communitarianism) and is precisely what we have in place today in our so-called but grossly mis-named 'democratic' societies.

Also, if politicians believe that they have the right to impose any 'law' they wish and police and security forces maintain the attitude that as long as anything is deemed 'lawful', they will enforce it rightly or wrongly, what is there to prevent complete tyranny? Not the consciences of the 'law-makers' or their legal enforcers obviously and not even peaceful petitions to the politicians will be effective. Politely asking oppressors not to be oppressive has a very poor track-record of success, historically. When tyrants define what constitutes 'law', then by definition it is up to the 'law-breakers' to combat tyranny and sometimes the end will justify the means.

Those who are proud to be 'law-abiding' would not agree and may even decline to think rationally about this, but what is the alternative? If we do not have the right to resist injustice, even if that injustice is called 'law', that logically implies that we have an obligation to allow governments to do to us whatsoever they may choose and also to our homes and families. Realistically, there are only two alternatives; we are either slaves, the property of the Elite, the politicians and their lackeys, with no rights at all or we have the right to resist government or Elite attempts to oppress us. There can logically be no other options.

"When the law has deviated from common sense and become an evil tool used for the robbery of others, do you obey it?" John Kaminski, researcher

So is the terrible state of affairs and of the planet in which we find ourselves living, simply the consequence of human nature as we are always led to believe? We are constantly fed the tired old line of '… well, its human nature to behave this way, nothing can ever change that'. The Elite cabal that rules our every moment are themselves clinical psychopaths, as discussed in a previous section. They exhibit every psychopathic trait known to man and indeed it is only by being psychopathic that they can possibly perpetuate this most unnatural state in which we all live. Psychopaths have no conscience; feel no remorse for their actions and no empathy for their fellow beings. They are ultra-manipulative and habitually lie whilst convincing themselves that they are in the right at all times.   In short, for a psychopath, the end always justifies the means, no exceptions.

Now please think about your family, your neighbours, your friends and indeed most people that you know. Think about those people from other cultures or countries that you may have briefly met whilst travelling through life. What is your overall impression of 90% of the people with whom you come into contact and socialise? Although none of them may be perfect, are they not for the most part, decent, honest, caring, compassionate people who share other's joys and sadnesses alike? Would they not offer their help to you in a crisis, and vice versa? What about the so-called foreigners and immigrants who live in this country and with whom you may have occasionally had cause to interact? Are they the monsters that our wholly-engendered prejudices are induced to paint them to be or would you say that deep down we are all really the same?

The truth is that we are a social animal, we are naturally programmed to co-operate and co-exist in peace and harmony, but the divisions between sex, races, religions, colours and cultures are constantly emphasised and exaggerated by the psychopathic Elite to cause dis-harmony and conflict. It is by this very methodology that they generate all of the unease and unrest, wars and conflicts in the world, partly as a means of controlling us through fear and of course in order to make their utterly obscene profits, usually by arming (and controlling) both sides.

It does not have to be like this. Humanity is by nature, decent, caring and good and not inherently evil as we are made to believe. We are all capable of expressing that goodness and by doing so, can change the world. When the time is right, the transformation that is imminent will free us all from the current state of economic slavery in which we all reside and it will not come a moment too soon.

Let us now depart from the generalised themes of this book for a moment to closely examine some specific examples of how many well-known historical events have been presented and given a cosmetic 'face-lift' and a completely different slant for the purposes of mass-consumption and manipulation. I will also demonstrate how easy it is to accomplish this seemingly impossible feat.

Who really wrote the works of William Shakespeare?

Did William Shakespeare really write such immortal works as 'Romeo and Juliet', 'Macbeth' or the 'Merchant of Venice'? How about 'Hamlet' and 'Twelfth Night'? And are we really sure that he wrote all the sonnets and countless other poems attributed to him? There would appear to be little doubt that all his works, stylistically speaking, were the product of one individual, but who was that individual?

Let us start at the beginning, then. Who was the character known as William Shakespeare and what was his story?

Shakespeare was born in 1564 in the English midlands market town of Stratford-upon-Avon, in the early years of the reign of Queen Elizabeth I. He was a contemporary of such notables as Sir Walter Raleigh, of Sir Francis Drake and the literary giant Christopher Marlowe but for someone of such apparent great stature in the literary world, almost nothing is known about Shakespeare's life.

We know that he was the son of a master glover (glove maker), John Shakespeare and Mary Arden, an aristocrat's daughter and had seven siblings (four sisters and three brothers) about whom nothing is known and he married Anne Hathaway in 1582 at the age of eighteen, with Hathaway giving birth to their first child just six months later in May 1583. Despite several sources claiming that he attended King Edward VI Grammar School in Stratford, this is pure conjecture as the school records from that period have not survived. From his marriage at age eighteen until his sudden appearance on the London acting circuit more than ten years later, nothing at all is recorded or known of his actions and whereabouts.

It is intriguing for example, that during his assumed 25 years of living in London, with as many as eight addresses quoted in a range of sources, he is never recorded in church attendance lists, even though attendance was compulsory at that time and therefore had to be recorded by law.

The origins of Shakespeare's professional career are also still debatable. For example, we do not know where or with which company he first became an actor and writer but after 1592 however, his life in London suddenly does become a little clearer. Shakespeare's early fame came through history plays, his first being a trilogy on the 'Wars of the Roses' and by the end of 1592 he had supposedly written the sequel, *Richard III*. His first definite address is documented as Bishopsgate in tax records and he is thought to have lived there from 1592, maybe earlier.

Shakespeare's supposed 'rival' Christopher Marlowe was murdered in May 1593 and this event, perhaps significantly, marks the point in time at which Shakespeare's almost 'overnight success' began.

For many years there has been much conjecture and intrigue surrounding the writing of those masterpieces of English literature ascribed to the pen of William Shakespeare. On the one hand, those people who revel in controversy and the attribution of conspiracy theories to almost anything we can name, gleefully add the name of William Shakespeare to the list whilst those of a more prosaic nature tend to hold the opposite, traditionalist view of the world and cling rigidly and sometimes blindly to the mainstream position, regardless of evidence to counter their views. The facts in all cases such as these should be examined thoroughly before jumping to wild, unsubstantiated conclusions. So, let us begin...

The belief that Shakespeare did not write the works attributed to him, may seem at first glance to be both bizarre and unbelievable. How and why could this be? What would be the purpose of, or the motive behind, such a deception? Surely it would defy any kind of logic? However, Shakespeare's doubters are by no means cranks or so-called 'conspiracy nuts', they number amongst them such well-respected literati as Mark Twain, Charles Dickens, Henry James, Walt Whitman and Daphne du Maurier, to name just a small selection. Their view was most definitely that there is a real and compelling 'authorship' issue.

For starters, there is a total lack of evidence in biographical records that a man by the name of William Shakespeare the 'Bard' of Stratford-upon-Avon was ever a writer. The only positive identification between the man himself and the works bearing his name came posthumously, as noted by Sir Hugh Trevor Roper...

"Of all the immortal geniuses of literature, none is personally so elusive as William Shakespeare. It is exasperating and almost incredible that he should be so. After all, he lived in the full daylight of the English Renaissance, in the well-documented reigns of Elizabeth and James I. Since his death and particularly in the last century, he has been subjected to the greatest battery of organised research that has ever been directed upon a single person. Armies of scholars, formidably equipped, have examined all the documents that could possibly contain at least a mention of Shakespeare's name. One hundredth of this labour applied to one of his insignificant contemporaries would be sufficient to produce a substantial biography."

So exactly what has all this intensive research revealed about the man? It is fairly certain that he was an actor, a shareholder in a theatre, a tax defaulter, a malt dealer, a commercial moneylender, a landlord, a litigant, a mean husband and a churlish father. However there is no existing evidence connecting him, however tenuously with the profession of writer, let alone indicating that he was the greatest dramatist that ever lived. If a psychologist were to undertake a psychological profile of the man, he would without doubt declare him to be a most undistinguished and ordinary individual, totally removed from the image one would expect of the genius who created the magnificent works which bear his name.

There is an absolute abundance of incongruity surrounding the life of this strange, mysterious character. As previously stated, for example, there are no records of the education of Shakespeare in existence. In fact, on the contrary, it is known for certain that he did not attend university and left no trace regarding a school education. It is also extremely surprising and possibly significant that he did not leave a single manuscript of even one of his plays or poems in his own handwriting, nor is there any evidence that he ever wrote a single piece of correspondence. All in all, very odd indeed.

It is also surprising to learn that both of Shakespeare's parents were illiterate, as was his daughter Judith, who could only sign her name with a virtually indistinguishable mark. Would a profoundly intelligent, educated and enlightened person such as one who was able to produce the wonderful masterpieces he allegedly did, treat his children in such a way, even a girl child? Was he perhaps of the view that the education of girls was a waste of time? This does not fit the picture of his supposed character at all.

It is also extremely clear from what we do know of the man and his family background that even very basic literary competence and/or a tradition of education was not a priority in any way for his family. And yet, in spite of this fact, Shakespeare was apparently immensely well-read and worldly-wise in an age where information was not 'on tap' instantly to those who wished to enjoy its benefits. Indeed books were a rare commodity to which virtually none but the wealthy and privileged had access and significantly Shakespeare's will makes no mention at all of any books, nor any of his literary works whose potential values, even at that time must have been immense.

Also significantly, of the six surviving alleged signatures of Shakespeare, only two are generally regarded as emanating from the same hand.

"It is obvious at a glance that these signatures, with the exception of the last two, are not the signatures of the same man. Almost every letter in each is formed in a different way." Shakespeare in the Public Records by Jane Cox, 1985

So, was the greatest writer in all history so intellectually and manually challenged that he was barely able to write his own name? Another disturbing fact is that Shakespeare appeared to be almost senile by 1612. His deposition to the Bellott vs. Mountjoy court case in that year reveals that he is very confused and capable of expressing himself only in very basic and crude English. Hardly what one would expect of the great man himself.

Another puzzling anomaly is that his death passed entirely unnoticed. There was no recognition of loss and no-one bothered to even acknowledge the fact, let alone pay any tributes to him. There was no state funeral as there had been for his peers Ben Jonson, Francis Beaumont and Edmund Spenser. Beaumont indeed died a few months before Shakespeare and received a fulsome national tribute whereas all Shakespeare's departure mustered was a deafening silence. Who today other than scholars and devotees of English literature has even heard of Francis Beaumont?

In fact his departure from this life was as mysterious as his sudden appearance upon the scene in 1593, shortly after the death of Christopher Marlowe, a fact to which we will return later. The newly-arrived poet from the backwaters of rural Warwickshire, managed to so cleverly disguise his regional background and what must have been an ear-wrenching midlands accent and dialect to the refined souls of the capital city, as to illicit no comment from his contemporaries whatsoever. But also significantly I believe, not once does his use of language in writing ever betray that homely, rural dialect he must surely have possessed, given the geography and nature of his upbringing.

Shakespeare's work reveals its writer as an 'insider', a man totally at ease with the intellectual and social elite of his day and most definitely not as a gauche countryman, which given his background and the age in which he lived, should almost certainly have been the impression he conveyed to his London contemporaries. Also, people who are highly gifted individuals, as was whoever wrote Shakespeare's works, naturally attract attention and praise wherever they go, whereas Shakespeare most certainly did not. In fact he was all but anonymous apart from in name.

His works demonstrate an intimate, detailed knowledge of geography, history, the classics, international politics and diplomacy, a first-hand experience of Italian ways and customs as in such works as The Merchant of Venice, Two Gentlemen of Verona and Romeo and Juliet as well as an intellectual level of the highest order. However, despite this his only friends would appear to have been lowly actors and theatre people and there is no evidence whatsoever linking him to the intelligentsia of the day. Despite his gargantuan intellectual capacity, was he just simply a boring non-entity of a man?

This strange lack of connection with the literary hierarchy of the time is compounded by the curiously reticent way in which he refers to himself throughout his sonnets. To whom were the sonnets addressed and dedicated and to what events in the life of their author do they refer? Nothing that is known of the man seems to fit the description and this compounds the issue somewhat.

"Why did Shakespeare, apparently never averse to any transaction that would financially benefit him, defer publication of his sonnet series until many years after the Elizabethan sonneteering vogue had spent itself? So that, whereas all other sonnet sequences went into many editions, his made only one very limited edition, never to be reprinted for over thirty years? Was their publication in fact, suppressed? To date, not a single one of these questions has been satisfactorily answered, although theories abound." A.D.Wraight, 1993

Sonnets 71 to 76 are the ones wherein the poet's identity is most strongly revealed. This series makes repeated references to its author's name and more significantly, to the danger of its being revealed.

Apart from literary references, the evidence linking the actor Shakespeare to the writer Shakespeare is also scant and it is partly for this reason that attempts have been made to assign an alternate identity to the writer from that of the actor. The three most common names in the frame are Francis Bacon, the Earl of Oxford and Christopher Marlowe, but they all would appear at first glance to have a serious drawback and therefore strong reasons to suggest they are incorrect. Francis Bacon did not possess the literary acumen and skill that Shakespeare's works would have demanded, the Earl of Oxford likewise would be disqualified on similar grounds and also by the fact that he died in 1604, well before the final works were known for certain to have been written. Christopher (Kit) Marlowe on the other hand would certainly have had the education, literary track record, writing skill and life experience to have written them but the problem with this assumption is that as Marlowe was murdered in 1593, this would seem to rule out that particular possibility.

Countering the premise that the actor William Shakespeare was not the man who wrote the works attributed to that name, is almost the entire Elite literary and historical establishment whose vested interest in protecting the knowledge that has been the received wisdom for almost 400 years, is obvious. Should it ever be proven that Shakespeare was not the author of Shakespeare's works, then the entire bedrock of academic orthodoxy would be shaken to its foundations by such a revelation and as we see in other areas of Elite orthodoxy being unwilling to yield to the truth, the entire 'house of cards' may well come crashing-down upon the heads of its upholders.

As with other areas of accepted knowledge, challenges to the 'powers that be' are never very welcome nor treated as a basis for rational debate. In order for the incumbents to retain control, potential usurpers of the status quo must be strongly resisted at all costs by the expedients of; wholesale denial, treating them with utter contempt or ignoring them completely is the usual recourse. The simple act of questioning the authorship of 'Shakespeare's' works is enough to engender extreme hostility from the establishment as with the questioning of other 'sacred cows' of the powers that be and this in itself speaks volumes.

In 1994, the historian A. D. (Dolly) Wraight postulated that Christopher Marlowe did not die in 1593 as has been widely claimed, but that his so-called murder in May of that year was a ruse to enable him to escape his imminent arrest, torture and execution on the grounds of his well-known atheistic views. After 1593, Marlowe, according to Wraight's theory, went into voluntary exile in France and Italy but continued to write his literature under the pseudonym of 'William Shake-speare'.

Kit Marlowe was indeed a genius and had fate not intervened in the form of his being persecuted by the fundamental Christianity that was rife throughout society at that time, it may well have been he who was regarded as 'the Bard' and the greatest literary icon that ever lived rather than the man who now bears those accolades. From 1587 until his alleged death in 1593 he was the author of a series of wonderful literary works to rival even the best that 'Shakespeare' himself could manage. There had been nothing in literature to challenge his superiority before and only Shakespeare since, has been remotely comparable to the genius that was Marlowe.

Christopher Marlowe

Marlowe's biographer, Dr. John Bakeless noted without irony that Shakespeare's work is replete with allusions to and quotations from Marlowe's work, whilst almost entirely ignoring his other literary contemporaries. There are numerous comparisons between the two and even contemporary literary critics were often known to have confused the works of both on occasion, such was the stylistic similarity.

"All the blank verse in Shakespeare's early plays bears the stamp of Marlowe's inspiration." Sir Sidney Lee.

"Marlowe is the greatest discoverer, the most daring pioneer in all our poetic literature. Before Marlowe there was no genuine blank verse and genuine tragedy in our language. After his arrival, the way was prepared, the path made straight for Shakespeare. Compared with his contemporaries such as Greene, Peele and Lodge, Marlowe differs from such people not in degree, but in kind; not as an eagle differs from wrens and tit-mice, but as an eagle differs from frogs and tadpoles. He first and he alone, gave wings to English poetry; he first brought into its serene and radiant atmosphere the new strange element of sublimity... Among all English poets he was the first full-grown man. Only young and immature by comparison with such disciples and successors as Shakespeare and Milton; but the first-born among us of their kind." Algernon Swinburne

I believe that this makes clear that in Swinburne's view that had Marlowe lived to fulfil his potential, he would have matched the achievements of Shakespeare.

The 20th century literary critic Edward Dowden also believed that in terms of ability, Marlowe was at least Shakespeare's equal...

"If Marlowe had lived longer and accomplished the work that lay clearly before him, he would have stood beside Shakespeare."

A more than significant point also is that a number of Shakespeare's early plays were, until recently, 'erroneously' attributed to Marlowe and there is an almost seamless transition from Marlowe's final work to the first one attributed to Shakespeare. Marlowe 'died' on the 30th May 1593 and Shakespeare made his first documented mark on the literary world two weeks later with the publication of the poem '*Venus and Adonis*'. As the scholar Arthur Acheson, noted; *"No atom of proof exists to show that previous to the publication of 'Venus and Adonis', Shakespeare had done any serious literary work"*.

This poem, to which Marlowe's *'Hero and Leander'* seems to be a prequel as it refers quite explicitly back to it, was entered at the Stationer's Register on 18th April 1593 without author. The printed version, appearing in June, contained a dedication and authorial attribution on a page that had been separately printed and interleaved with the main text as though it were an afterthought. This was most certainly not normal practice and was not the way that Shakespeare's subsequent (second) work was produced (*The Rape of Lucrece*). Thus do the circumstances around Marlowe's demise as a literary icon and Shakespeare's rise from obscurity, dovetail extremely neatly together – overwhelming circumstantial evidence I would suggest.

There are several ways to attempt to determine common authorship of literary works. There is the subjective method and the more objective, statistical methodology. Regarding the latter, one popular technique is to monitor the distribution curve of words and word-types so as to produce a 'fingerprint' for each individual writing style and thus provide a comparison with others. This method was devised by the famous, respected physicist Thomas Mendenhall at the turn of the nineteenth into the twentieth century. Mendenhall was very interested in identifying the authorship of Shakespeare's works, not for reasons of proving any particular pet theory; he merely wished to apply his methodology to an area of popular interest.

He and his specially gathered team of researchers set about counting the more than two million words in Shakespeare's work, plus those of his contemporaries – a monumental task in the days before information technology and the results of this project were pretty-well unambiguous. The resulting curves for Shakespeare and Bacon were entirely different as were the ones produced for Jonson, Beaumont and Fletcher. However, when the curves of Marlowe and Shakespeare were compared the results were astonishing to say the least.

"Something akin to a sensation was produced among those engaged in the work. In the characteristic curve of his plays, Marlowe agrees with Shakespeare about as well as Shakespeare agrees with himself!" Thomas Mendenhall

In the intervening century or so since Mendenhall's project, his methodology, if anything, has been further perfected. Louis Ule and John Baker updated Mendenhall's work using computer technology to analyse both word-length frequency distribution and the pace of new word uptake in both Shakespeare's and Marlowe's work. Based on analysis of every single piece of work known to have been produced by the hands of these 'two' authors, Ule and Baker were able to determine beyond reasonable doubt that they were statistically indistinguishable from one another.

So it is apparent that Marlowe was more than capable of producing Shakespeare's works, but perhaps a more apposite question may be, who else besides Marlowe would have had the ability and the wherewithal to do so? No-one else would seem to 'fit the bill' at all – if the reader will pardon the unintentional pun.

But perhaps a more important issue to address at this point would be the fact that Marlowe was murdered in 1593, was he not and so how could he possibly have written the works attributed to the Bard of Stratford? This is where the plot seriously thickens.

Ten days prior to Marlowe's death on the 30th May 1593, he had been arrested on a warrant from the Star Chamber on a charge of 'atheism'. This pseudo 'court' was established to ensure enforcement of laws against prominent people, those so powerful that ordinary courts could never convict them of their crimes. Court sessions were held in camera, with no indictments, no right of appeal, no jury of peers and no witnesses. Over the years it evolved into a political weapon, a symbol of the misuse and abuse of power by the English establishment and judiciary. Indeed 'Star Chamber' has become a byword today for a corrupted court.

From the first day, Marlowe had in effect been out 'on bail' and had to appear before the court on a daily basis whilst in the meantime, evidence against him was being collated by his informers. He had been under suspicion of atheism for some time prior to his arrest, being a known member of the 'School of Night' who openly discussed taboo issues of the day such as the accuracy of the bible etc. In those days, if something was stated in the bible, such as for example, Methuselah living to the age of 963, then that is exactly what happened – it was not up for question or debate. Anyone espousing a contradictory opinion was an atheist, pure and simple and the penalty for atheism was torture and death, no exceptions.

Marlowe's play, *Tamburlaine* had long been held to exhibit atheistic tendencies and was it not the author who was totally responsible for the contents of any work of literature, no matter how brilliant that work may be? His contemporary Robert Greene actually wrote a scathing accusation of atheism directed at Marlowe from his deathbed and this almost certainly contributed to the severe difficulties in which Marlowe found himself.

Then in early 1593, an author and erstwhile friend of Marlowe by the name of Thomas Kyd was found to be in possession of a copy of a 'heretical' piece which earned him an acquaintanceship with the rack and all the agony associated with that sorry experience. Under this horrific torture he implicated Marlowe in the writing of the said piece and explained that it must have somehow become mixed-up with his own papers in some way. This statement was enough to precipitate the arrest of Marlowe and his previously far-from-perfect past meant that he would potentially be in far greater danger (indeed probably mortal danger), than was the relative 'small-fry', Thomas Kyd.

Thus was engendered a situation whereby Marlowe's friends decided to act in concert to save him from his almost certain fate at the hands of the torturers and this would entail his complete disappearance in one form or another. Fortunately, Marlowe counted amongst his friends, two very influential Elizabethan gentlemen, Lord Burghley and Sir Thomas Walsingham. Walsingham was Marlowe's patron and it was at Walsingham's house in Kent where Marlowe was staying upon the event of his arrest. They were both employed as government intelligence agents in what was in effect a forerunner of today's MI5 and MI6 and as such were well acquainted with the methodology of executing covert operations – a fact which would become extremely important, especially to Marlowe.

The 'murder' itself was very strange, to which anyone who has investigated the facts will bear witness. It involved three men, all known to Marlowe, all of whom had worked under Walsingham and all of whom were well versed in espionage tactics. In fact if one was to hand-pick a team with which to pull-off the alleged plot, then these would certainly have been extremely strong candidates for inclusion in it. Their names were Robert Poley, Nicholas Skeres and thirdly Walsingham's private secretary, Ingram Frizer. They were all loyal to Walsingham and highly skilled in the art of deception.

Even the location of the 'murder' seems to have been carefully chosen also. It was in Deptford, Kent in the house and grounds of Dame Eleanor Bull who was a well-respected lady, a widow and the cousin of the queen's nanny, Blanche Parry. These very secluded grounds with no unwanted onlookers and just three plotters plus Marlowe, created a perfect environment for a 'set-up' of this kind. The only witnesses being the aforementioned threesome and these were almost certainly acting under the orders of Walsingham himself.

Deptford was also seemingly a well-chosen venue for the deception. Firstly it was a port with regular sailings to the European mainland which would have been perfect to facilitate Marlowe's swift getaway. Secondly, Marlowe was unknown there and so any inquest jury would not have been easily able to identify the corpse in those pre-photographic days and thirdly the most well-known and prominent inhabitant of the town was the Lord Admiral, who was the patron of Marlowe's own theatre company.

A.D. Wraight herself postulates that there may have been strong reasons for believing that the Queen herself may have been complicit in the plot. Walsingham was well known to her and importantly, highly regarded and trusted implicitly as a loyal subject to her. He also knew that her pet hate was being deceived and he may well have felt uneasy had he not confided in her. He also knew that she enjoyed a little subterfuge and intrigue herself. Indeed would the Queen have been happy to see England's foremost literary figure, tortured and executed, given her well-known love of literature and the theatre and the fact that she most certainly had no time for religious fanaticism in any form?

So, on the 30th May 1593, Marlowe and his three friends spent eight hours together at Dame Eleanor's house. The subjects under discussion may only be guessed at but it is certainly a rather unusual way to spend the day, alone with your three murderers-to-be. In the evening they were having supper together when (as the story goes) an argument erupted regarding the bill, 'ye reckonynge' and in the ensuing contretemps which continued, we are led to believe, back to the doorstep of their host, Marlowe was fatally stabbed by Frizer 'above the right eye', allegedly in self-defence. Of course this is a common occurrence is it not? Groups of friends often get into fatal arguments over something as trivial as a bill, especially affluent men such as these, to whom a bill of at most a few pennies would have been absolutely insignificant. It all seems more than a little suspicious to me, but anyway this was the story they recounted after the fatal event and indeed the one that has gone down in history as the reason for the untimely demise of Marlowe. Frizer himself received a small nick to his head – just serious enough to prove the alibi of 'self-defence' but not serious enough to cause any lasting damage.

Marlowe, by contrast, suffered a most strange wound. Forensic science would have us believe that it is impossible to push a knife through the skull just above the eye socket without using absolutely inordinate force. If a wound occurred in this region it would have to have been made by an axe or a pick or another heavy implement, to try and force a mere dagger through the skull bone at that point would have required immense strength. It would also be almost impossible to create a wound of that nature in what was in effect a short, hand-to-hand tussle. It seems more likely that the wound was designed to create a gory mess of the face and thus hinder identification rather than anything else.

In any event, two days later the inquest took place, presided over solely by Danby; the Queen's coroner who it turns out had no jurisdiction whatsoever to act alone but was legally bound to perform his duties alongside the local coroner, which of course was not the case. This act in effect, nullifies any decision made by this illegal inquest. The decision of the coroner based solely on the testimonies of the three 'stooges', Poley, Skeres and Frizer was that Frizer had acted in self-defence and was therefore not guilty of murder. The corpse was immediately and hastily buried in an unmarked grave in Deptford churchyard – a strange event in itself for the body of a very wealthy and famous young man.

In the immediate aftermath, two remarkable incidents took place. Firstly, Frizer was immediately pardoned by the Queen. Usually those involved in suspicious deaths had to wait many months, often languishing in jail before being officially pardoned by the monarch – even those deemed to be innocent and / or acting in self-defence. Secondly, the following day, Frizer and Skeres are on record as being involved in a business transaction with Walsingham. In fact Frizer continued in his role as Walsingham's servant without a break. This would in itself have been a highly unlikely turn of events had Frizer really been involved in the death of one of Walsingham's closest friends in a street brawl, whether or not he was considered to be acting in self-defence. I am in little doubt personally that Walsingham engineered the whole event in order to save the life of his esteemed friend, Kit Marlowe.

Perhaps a little more background to the relationship between Walsingham, Marlowe and his three protagonists may be of interest at this juncture. As stated earlier, Walsingham was a prominent member of the Elizabethan secret security services, overseen originally by John Dee, who incidentally was well known to be a practitioner of the dark arts of magick and Satanism and was suspected of being an adept exponent of early attempts at mind control. Indeed many researchers strongly believe that the writing of Shakespeare's works was in fact a form of mind control in itself and if so, this adds further credence to the case for Marlowe being the author of said works as it is beyond doubt that he was involved with the intelligence services in a major way.

In this same period, Francis Bacon, incidentally also one of the main suspects in the debate about the authorship of Shakespeare's work, wrote his treatise 'The New Atlantis' whilst hundreds of privateers, amongst whom the most prominent was Sir Francis Drake, were in the process of plundering the seas of all the loot they could obtain in order to swell the coffers of the Crown. In the meantime, Sir Walter Raleigh and his like were already preparing the colonies in Virginia for the mass immigration to come, thirty or so years later and through the pernicious methods of The British East India Company, corporatism and later, consumerism was beginning to establish a foothold in Britain and was soon to be emulated by the rest of the 'civilised' world.

So, these men, stalwarts of the Elizabethan establishment, were also the standard-bearers of Rosicrucianism, the mystery-teachings of Babylon, passed down through the bloodline families and soon to become what we today know as freemasonry. All of these men most certainly knew their 'real' history and were deeply ensconced in such subjects as ritual magick and esoteric ancient knowledge.

This group of people, this brotherhood, are the ancestors and architects of The New World Order we see developing today. They were instrumental in the establishing of London as the 'New Jerusalem' and also as the banking capital of the world for their masters, the ancient bloodlines whose origins as previously described can be traced back through all the preceding ancient civilisations into the mists of time.

However, back to the main thrust of the plot. Another interesting twist to this convoluted tale was that in 1601, the Queen seemed to be well aware of who was the real author of 'Shakespeare's' work. Prior to the Essex rebellion in that same year, the conspirators commissioned a performance of *Richard III* in the belief that this would incite the audience to support or at least condone a coup against Elizabeth I as had been the case in the play in question. This absolutely enraged her, not surprisingly and she was said to have exclaimed *"I am Richard III, know ye not that?"* She also directed the following tirade at the play's author... *"He that will forget God will also forget his benefactors. This tragedy was played forty times in open streets and houses."*

This comment could surely only have referred to Marlowe. 'He that would forget God'? Marlowe... the known atheist? '...would forget his benefactors'? The Queen, who helped expedite the plot and the subsequent cover-up, was the benefactor indeed! If she had believed that *Richard III* had been written by Shakespeare, he would at the very least have been arrested and warned, if not much worse.

Next we will examine the evidence presented to us, yet hidden in plain sight by Marlowe in the form of Shakespeare's plays and sonnets.

The sonnets in particular, paint a vivid picture of their author and this picture is most definitely not one of a struggling Stratfordian actor. They do however describe Christopher Marlowe, his life and alleged death, almost perfectly.

In sonnet no. 74 we discover the following lines...

"...my body being dead, the coward conquest of a wretches knife."

And also...

"But be contented when that fell arest,
With out all bayle shall carry me away,
My life hath in this line some interest."

Here 'Shakespeare' refers to his own arrest and bail! There is no record of Shakespeare ever having been arrested and bailed, but this is obviously not the case with Marlowe.

And in sonnet 72...
"My name be buried where my body is,
And live no more to shame, nor me nor you."

In sonnet 50 (below) we possibly have a vivid description of the author's journey into exile. Again how closely this would fit Marlowe's life and yet bear no resemblance to that of Shakespeare...

"How heavie doe I journey on the way,
When what I seeke (my wearie travels end)
Doth teach that ease and that repose to say
Thus farre the miles are measurde from thy friend.
The beast that beares me, tired with my woe,
Plods duly on, to beare that waight in me,
As if by some instinct the wretch did know
His rider lov'd not speed being made from thee:
The bloody spurre cannot provoke him on,
That some-times anger thrusts into his hide,
Which heavily he answers with a grone,
More sharpe to me then spurring to his side,
For that same grone doth put this in my mind,
My greefe lies onward and my joy behind."

Sonnets 25, 33, 34 and 36 also extensively refer to the author's name having fallen into great disgrace and strongly bemoan this fate. If Shakespeare's name had ever become embroiled in any kind of scandal or infamy then it would almost certainly have become public knowledge and have been recorded somewhere by someone. The fact that it was not would speak volumes on this subject.

On the other hand, Marlowe's life was blighted by infamy and disgrace and his contemporary rivals wasted no opportunity to express their schadenfreude at his expense. For example, the Welsh poet, William Vaughan would appear to take delight in Marlowe's death and the fact that he detected more than a little of the hand of God working behind the scenes...

"... he stabd this Marlowe into the eye, in such sort, that his brains
Coming out at the dagger's point, hee shortlie after dyed. Thus did
God, the true executioner of divine justice, worke the ende of
impious Atheists."

Nice man. He was however, far from alone in this. According to Marlowe's biographer, Charles Norman...

"The outburst of Puritan wrath against Marlowe is without parallel in literature. No vile epithet was too vile for his detractors to use, yet most of them wrote only from hearsay, or merely embroidered one another's accounts, hardly one able to contain his gloating."

This attitude is also fairly common today. Many present-day scholars regard Marlowe with contempt for his views and his rather colourful life as an occasional brawler and 'roaring boy' as well as being a homosexual predator.

In 'As You Like It', the character 'Touchstone' says...

*"When a man's verses cannot be understood, nor a man's good wit seconded by the forward child understanding, it **strikes a man more dead than a great reckoning in a little room.** Truly I wish the gods had made thee poetical."*

This is surely referring to Marlowe's alleged demise over the bill ('the reckoning' as it was called in Elizabethan times) and says that it was nothing compared to the continual agony of having to write in disguise and having someone else take all the credit for it.

I believe that this scenario is more than credible but the space available in a book such as this cannot do justice to the scores of examples of Shakespeare's texts where oblique references are made to Marlowe including anagrams of his name, and vain protestations of his suffering in exile and his innocence. It is clear that Marlowe was desperate to take credit for his own genius (who among us would not be?) and left as many obvious clues as he dare in his great works.

The Shakespeare story is a classical example of the distortion of history in terms of its background reasons. It is indeed just another small piece of the jigsaw puzzle that makes up the ongoing grand conspiracy against humanity. However, perhaps importantly it provides an example of how four or five prominent people working together in complicity can completely fool not just the literary establishment, but almost the whole of humanity for more than four centuries. It provides us with another case in point (should one be necessary) of how unbelievably 'simple' it is to falsify events to benefit the few.

The 'Gunpowder Plot'

Some of the 5th November 'gunpowder plotters'

The so-called 'Guy Fawkes plotters', Catesby, Percy and Tresham were in reality working for the English government and it was in fact King James I's spymaster, Robert Cecil, who blackmailed Robert Catesby into organising a plot to discredit Catholics.

Robert Cecil

As with the debunking of any of mainstream history's 'givens', we always need to ask the question 'why' and this can usually be answered by investigating as to who would most benefit from the deception, 'cui bono' in Latin. In this particular instance, the purpose was to expedite the smooth transition of King James VI of Scotland onto the throne of England as James I.

The previous reigns of James' 2nd cousins, Elizabeth and Mary had been greatly characterised by religious genocide, firstly by Mary against the Protestants and then by Elizabeth against the Catholics and these ongoing sectarian schisms of the previous half-century had created deep divisions and torn families and communities apart. So, placing a Catholic on the throne of a now thoroughly protestant nation required a large degree of what we would now refer to as political 'spin', in order to prevent insurrection!

James was thus engineered via the expedient of the gunpowder plot, to be seen as clamping-down hard on any Catholics who could have been perceived to be taking advantage of their presumed newly-found freedoms under a Catholic monarch.

So the scene was set for the deception. In 1604, Robert Catesby, in actuality an agent of the English government, was involved in the planning of the Gunpowder plot along with Sir Robert Cecil, ostensibly a scheme to blow-up the English parliament on the 5th November 1605 and kill King James and as many members of Parliament as possible.

On his death-bed, there were statements by Robert Catesby's servant that Robert Cecil and Catesby met on three separate occasions in the period leading up to the events of the night of 5th November 1605. At a meeting at the Duck and Drake Inn, Catesby explained the plan to Guy Fawkes, Thomas Percy who was another agent of the English government, John Wright and Thomas Winter and all of them agreed to join the plot.

In the following months Francis Tresham, another undercover government agent, Everard Digby, Robert Winter, Thomas Bates, and Christopher Wright also agreed to join the conspiracy. Immediately prior to the event, Thomas Percy was seen exiting the house of Robert Cecil and after the plot was 'discovered', Catesby, Percy, Christopher Wright and John Wright headed to Holbeche House in Staffordshire in the English midlands and on the 8th November 1605, government troops arrived at the house and shot dead the conspirators Robert Catesby, Thomas Percy, Christopher Wright and John Wright whilst Digby, Robert and Thomas Winter, Bates and Fawkes were executed by being hanged, drawn and quartered in January 1606 after suffering extreme torture in order to extract confessions.

It was also widely rumoured that Francis Tresham was poisoned while being held captive in the Tower of London.

In his book 'The Gunpowder Plot: The Narrative of Oswald Tessimond', Francis Edwards claimed that Francis Tresham escaped from the Tower of London, probably with the help of the Government, went abroad and changed his name to Matthew Bruninge.

"If Guy Fawkes case came up before the Court of Appeal today, the... judges would surely... acquit him...   ...no-one has ever seen the attempted tunnel.   Builders excavating the area in 1823 found neither a tunnel nor any rubble. Secondly, the gunpowder... In 1605, the Government had a monopoly on its manufacture... The Government did not display the gunpowder and nobody saw it in the cellars. Thirdly, these cellars were rented by the government to a known Catholic agitator... Fourthly, the Tresham letter... Graphologists [handwriting experts] agree that it was not written by Francis Tresham....Guy Fawkes was at a wedding of Cecil's niece, along with Cecil AND King James. ...Why didn't Fawkes kill the King there, and isn't it mysterious that all figures in the plot went to a wedding together?" R. Crampton, 'The Gunpowder Plot', 1990

So, the plot was just a charade, albeit one with a very serious purpose. It was all part of the Elite's ongoing grand conspiracy and this chapter of that conspiracy was the unification of England and Scotland to create a United Kingdom and thus the foundations of the future British Empire to-be. It was, at its roots, yet another False Flag operation this time using the protestant-catholic dialectic and it was this first stage of the unification of two hitherto completely distinct countries that was designed to facilitate the next 'Crown Empire' and the thrust towards globalisation.

I am also of the view that the King James Version of the bible, written in 1611 was another work of social engineering and is the script which, the hidden Elite and their not so hidden bloodlines are following as we approach the end of the age. The Pope declared some time ago that were are now in the time of Revelations, a point in our history that is also recognised in Freemasonry and of course 'apocalypse' is from the Greek, meaning the 'unveiling' – the 'reveal'.

When people talk about a conspiracy so large that it defies all belief and imagination, they really are not exaggerating.

The English Revolution and the Execution of King Charles I

There is of course no dispute that King Charles I of England was executed by being beheaded at the scaffold erected outside the Guildhall in the City of London in January 1649. However the events that led to his execution, as is often the case with many historical events have been twisted to fit the sanitised version of history that is always presented to the masses by our ruling Elite, in order to conceal the real truth.

"It was fated that England should be the first of a series of Revolutions, which is not yet finished." Isaac Disraeli, father of Benjamin Disraeli, former British Prime Minister, 1851

In London in the latter years of the decade of the 1630s, immediately prior to the English Revolution now more expediently known as the 'English Civil War', there were many minor, armed uprisings of the 'people', usually involving the same ringleaders and 'agents provocateurs', as is often the case today. These armed 'mobs' caused panic and fear in the streets wherever they went, including the sometimes violent intimidation they inflicted upon members of both houses of Parliament. This in fact was a very similar modus operandus as that employed by the 'Sacred Bands' and the 'Marseillaise' of the French revolution 150 years later. Indeed, the striking similarities between the two events are most noteworthy.

There were illegal print operations being instigated all around the city, producing inflammatory leaflets inciting the good citizens of London to revolt against the ruling powers that be. This period of unrest led directly to the conflict between 'the people' or in effect Parliament and the Monarchy, that was to be the defining attribute of the English Revolution or the Civil War as it is more commonly and yet misleadingly called. So who was behind this movement that was to culminate in the 'legalised' murder of the reigning British monarch and the abolition of the monarchy for a period of eleven years which came to be known as the 'Commonwealth' at the time and later, the 'Interregnum'?

Within the pages of works such as the 'Jewish Encyclopedia' and 'The Jews and Modern Capitalism', it is possible to discern that at this time, Oliver Cromwell, the prime-mover behind the conflict was in constant contact with and actually being financed by the powerful Jewish/Dutch banksters behind the Bank of Amsterdam scam that in effect usurped the control of currency issuance from the Dutch government in the early seventeenth century. Through such figures as Manasseh ben Israel and Fernandez Carvajal, both prominent Jews of the times, the whole of the English Revolution was funded. Carvajal himself was the paymaster of the entire 'New Model Army' or the 'Roundheads', as Cromwell's fighting forces were disparagingly named as a direct result of the round metal helmets they wore.

In the 12th century, some 500 years prior to the English Revolution, all Jews had been summarily expelled from England for various reasons but primarily because of their general propensity for usury, the lending of money at interest which at the time was totally contrary to the fundamental tenets of Christianity.

In the January of 1642, the attempted arrest of five Members of Parliament, had led to even more extreme mob violence and subsequently to the King and the royal family leaving their palace at Whitehall for security reasons. The five MPs backed by the mobs returned in triumph to Westminster and thus was the stage now set for the Jews to make their moves using none other than Cromwell himself to front their movement.

"1643 brought a large contingent of Jews to England; their rallying point was the house of the Portuguese Ambassador de Souza, a Marrano Jew. Prominent among them was Fernandez Carvajal, a great financier and army contractor." Excerpt from 'The Jews of England'

The actual bloodshed and open warfare between the two factions began in earnest at the Battle of Edgehill, Warwickshire later that year in 1642 where a contingent of Royalist troops commanded by Prince Rupert, a nephew of King Charles, fought against a Parliamentary army commanded by Cromwell. The outcome of this battle was totally inconclusive, both sides subsequently claiming victory and over the course of the next several years, a series of major battles and minor skirmishes took place at such locations as for example, Marston Moor, Oxford, Worcester, Newbury and finally Naseby amidst much bloodshed in an ongoing conflict that often pitted father against son and brother against brother in an attempt to gain ultimate supremacy by each of the respective 'sides'.

Eventually after years of attrition, it was Parliament who emerged as victor following the Battle of Naseby. Charles was taken prisoner and remained under house arrest at Holmby House in Oxfordshire awaiting a decision on his fate which at the time was fully expected to be no more serious than foreign exile, a fate befalling many a defeated 'royal' in the past. However in June 1647, things were about to take a major turn for the worse for Charles.

On 4th June 1647, Cornet Joyce, acting on secret orders from Cromwell himself and unknown even to General Fairfax, Cromwell's army chief of staff, descended upon Holmby House with 500 picked revolutionary troopers and seized the King.

According to Isaac Disraeli... *"The plan was arranged on May 30th at a secret meeting held at Cromwell's house, though later Cromwell pretended that it was without his concurrence."*

This move coincided with a sudden development in the army; the rise of the 'Levellers' and 'Rationalists' whose doctrines were identical in almost every facet to those of the French revolutionaries in the 1780s and 1790s. In fact, they were identical in most aspects to what is now known today as 'Communism'. These were the infamous regicides, the King-killers, who 'purged' Parliament until there were only 50 members remaining, all 'communist-like' themselves and who were ultimately responsible for Charles' execution around eighteen months subsequently. This was the Parliament that came to be known colloquially as the 'Rump Parliament'.

However, back to the main story; in constant collusion with his Jewish benefactors throughout the duration of the war, Cromwell wrote to them again at Mulheim Synagogue in Holland in a letter received by them on the 16th June 1647...

"In return for further financial support will advocate admission of Jews to England: This however impossible while Charles living. Charles cannot be executed without trial on adequate grounds which do not at present exist. Therefore advise that Charles be assassinated, but have nothing to do with arrangements for procuring an assassin, though willing to help in his escape."

To which the following reply was sent to Cromwell on the 12th July 1647...

"Will grant financial aid as soon as Charles removed and Jews admitted. Assassination too dangerous. Charles shall be given opportunity to escape. His recapture will make trial and execution possible. The support will be liberal, but useless to discuss terms until trial commences.".

The source of this dialogue was a weekly review, '*Plain English*' published by the '*North British Publishing Co.*' and edited by Lord Alfred Douglas, in 1921.

And so it duly came to pass that on 12th November 1647, Charles was 'allowed' an opportunity to escape in order to bring the plan to fruition and he duly absconded to the Isle of Wight, to where he was followed and quickly recaptured by Cromwell's men.

"Contemporary historians have decided that the King from the day of his deportation from Holmby to his escape to the Isle of Wight was throughout the dupe of Cromwell." Isaac Disraeli.

Now all that remained at this time to complete the blood-bargain was to stage the 'show trial' of Charles and sentence him to death and the Jews would have attained their goal of being allowed to officially set foot on English soil for the first time in almost 500 years.

It soon became apparent that even though the members of the 'Rump' who were allowed to remain in situ in Parliament, were broadly speaking anti-monarchists, most were still nevertheless in favour of a peaceful and amicable settlement with the king. On 5th December 1647, the house sat through the night in debate and finally carried the motion 'that the king's concessions were satisfactory to a settlement'. This of course was unacceptable to Cromwell and his plans for the Jews, not to mention his own bank balance and so he arranged for yet another 'purge' of the house, this time undertaken by one of his army officers, Colonel Pride in an action which has subsequently come to be known to history as 'Pride's Purge', on the 6th December 1647. And then on the 4th January 1648 the remaining 50 members of the house finally invested themselves with the supreme power required to usurp the role of the king.

However, Algernon Sidney warned Cromwell that...

"First, the King can be tried by no court. Second, no man can be tried by this court." And further added that... *"...no English lawyer could be found to draw up the charge, which was eventually entrusted to an accommodating alien, Isaac Dorislaus."*

It is probably superfluous to reason for me to report that Isaac Dorislaus was exactly the same 'type' of alien as Carvajal and Manasseh Ben Israel and the other financiers who paid Cromwell his blood-money. And so were the Jews thus permitted once again to live freely in England despite protests by the masses (who were of course ignorant of ll the background machinations) and by the sub-committee of the Council of State which declared them to be... *"...a grave menace to the State and the Christian religion".*

"The English Revolution under Charles I was unlike any preceding one ... From that time and event we contemplate in our history the phases of revolution." Isaac Disraeli

This was actually just the beginning. The English revolution was followed by the American, French and Russian versions of the same 'trick' all at the behest of and funded by the same group of people, albeit for differing reasons. In 1897 the Protocols of the Learned Elders of Zion surfaced and this document contains this noteworthy sentence... *"Remember the French Revolution, the secrets of its preparation are well known to us for it was entirely the work of our hands."* Protocol No.3 - 14 This statement could easily have referred to all of the above named events.

However, the real objective of the revolution was realised around half a century later with the formation of the Bank of England in 1694 and the instigating of the National Debt. The charter that provided for this, handed-over to an anonymous committee, the previously Royal prerogative of minting money and enabled the international banksters to secure their loans on the taxes of the country rather than simply upon a monarch's personal undertaking thus enslaving the people of Britain forever.

The Act of Union passed by Parliament shortly afterwards in 1706, was simply an expedient way of tying Scotland into the great scam in addition to England. Of course up until that point in time the two countries were distinctly separate, both politically and economically. This then had the effect of making redundant the Scottish Mint and also to bring it under the umbrella of the English national debt as a whole. Thus was the grip of the banksters extended over England's neighbours in one succinct move.

To safeguard against a possible negative reaction from Parliament, the party system was then brought into being, frustrating true national reaction and enabling the puppeteers to divide and rule using their newly-established financial power to ensure that their own henchmen and their own policies would predominate.

This was then the beginning of the bankers highly dubious practice of fractional reserve banking whereby gold became the basis of loans, ten times the size of the amount deposited. In other words, £100 pounds of gold would be legal security for a £1,000 loan. At 3% interest therefore, £100 pounds in gold could earn £30 pounds interest annually with no more trouble or inconvenience to the lender than the keeping of a few ledger entries. The owner of £100 worth of land however, still had to slave, often around the clock, in order to make a subsistence living.

The Founding of America – 'The New Atlantis'

Two thousand five hundred years ago, the Greek philosopher Plato wrote about the great city-state, Atlantis and described it as an ideal society that was unfortunately destroyed in some unknown cataclysmic event, several thousands of years previously. This event may have been a gigantic tsunami, an earthquake or the result of massive volcanic activity, but the real reason for its sudden demise is not known.

Ever since Plato's description of this 'utopian' world became widely known, there have been attempts to recreate it in all its glory and this indeed has been the aim and ambitions of the Elite since that time. The twentieth-century Freemasonic historian and philosopher, one of the foremost authorities on the occultist nature of the craft, Manly P. Hall recorded in his prolific writings that Atlantis had always been destined to be re-built and that indeed was the goal of the ancient secret societies such as Rosicrucianism which eventually became a forerunner of Freemasonry itself.

In the early 17th century, the prominent English secret society adept, Sir Francis Bacon, wrote his classic work 'The New Atlantis', citing America as the ideal location for the fulfilment of the long-held dreams of the Rosicrucians and the other forerunners of Freemasonry. Bacon in fact was the fundamental element in the concept of trying to create the New Atlantis on the American continent. He foresaw a 'new world' of technological and scientific achievements and believed passionately that this was the destiny of and the role earmarked for, the then 'virgin' territory of the American landmass. Bacon could quite legitimately be regarded as the very founder of America.

Bacon was the leader of the Rosicrucian movement and the fledgling organisation that would become the Freemasonry that we know today and it was these two movements that were to have a huge influence upon the development and progress of American society which would eventually lead to the institution of the 'United States' in the form we still see today. The Rosicrucians and Freemasons arrived in America in their great numbers during the mass immigrations of the first half of the seventeenth century, along with the Puritans and the repressed religious sects from England and eventually other nations. This huge movement of people was directly or indirectly encouraged by Bacon and his compadres as they sought to populate this new Atlantis for their own agenda, the eventually creation of the oft-quoted New World Order which I believe is a successor to the New Atlantis of Bacon's dream.

America or the USA as it is now is thus the promulgator of the New World Order, its short history having been hugely influenced by Freemasonry. Freemasons practised their art in much the same way as in Europe, embedding secret, esoteric designs in both individual buildings and indeed, entire cities and wider areas. For example, the original American major cities, Washington DC, Baltimore, Philadelphia, New York and Boston are all in *perfect* alignment along a 400 mile line, in effect connecting them together along the eastern seaboard of the US. This line, if continued eastwards also aligns perfectly with Stonehenge and then London. Can this be a coincidence? It is I believe extremely unlikely, but who knows what esoteric purpose this may serve?

In the 1920s an Englishman, Alfred Watkins discovered the concept of what he called, 'ley-lines' which connect many sites of ancient monuments throughout the world, again by the simple utilisation of straight lines drawn between them. It is believed by many that the constructors of these ancient sites, often thousands of miles apart, were aware of the 'energy' emitted from the Earth itself along these lines and meridians. Many of the great European cathedrals built in the medieval period, for example, are all connected by ley-lines to themselves as well as the Egyptian pyramids.

Washington DC itself stands on the 77th meridian which is also known as 'God's Longitude' for the esoteric properties it is said to possess. The first expedition of Sir Walter Raleigh to the American mainland in the 1580s was said to be a disaster and a failure, resulting in the deaths of many crew-members for what amounted to nothing, but could his voyage have had another purpose? Had he been sent by his Elite masters to seek-out the location of the 77th meridian in order to facilitate the future founding of the nation? In Washington DC there is an area known as Meridian Hill and this is likely the exact location of the famed 77th meridian itself. Raleigh was himself a member of Bacon's secret society, the Rosicrucians and like Bacon was committed to the establishment of a society wholly dedicated to the esoteric and the occult, the New Atlantis.

Despite what you may believe, the American Revolution was conceived and perpetrated by Freemasonry to further the financial interests of the North American Elite and create an impression of independence from British money interests and the 'Crown' and was not as we are told, the product of a popular uprising against British tyranny. Indeed most 'ordinary' Americans were not in favour of independence from Britain, most of them were of British ancestry, were fiercely loyal to King George III and in many cases still had family back in the 'old country'.

Benjamin Franklin, the American 'hero' was in reality an agent of British intelligence working towards the goal of transition of the American colonies from overt to covert control in a microcosm of what was taking place on a worldwide basis as openly monarchical dictatorships were replaced by a manufactured 'democracy' to create the false impression of 'government by the people, for the people'.

According to official history, the spark that ignited the conflict was when a band of men dressed as Mohawk Indians dumped all the tea from the British clipper, *Dartmouth* into Boston harbour in an event that has become known as 'The Boston Tea Party', as an alleged protest at excessive British taxation of imported foodstuffs and consumer goods. In reality, the 'Indians' were members of the St. Andrew's Freemasonic lodge in Boston, led by their junior warden, Paul Revere, he of the famous 'ride of Paul Revere' undertaken to warn the good American citizens that the

'British are coming'. The easy access to the ship was facilitated with 'insider' help from the colonial militia detailed to guard the waterfront at Boston harbour. The Captain of this militia was a certain Edward Proctor who by no small coincidence also happened to be a senior member of the St. Andrew's Lodge. Another lodge member also happened to be John Hancock, the first signatory of the Declaration of Independence and whose name has become synonymous with 'signature' as a result. All were also members of the 'Sons of Liberty' group that organised and perpetrated the 'Boston Tea Party'.

Of the fifty six signatories of the Declaration of Independence, at least fifty were known to be freemasons and only one was definitely known not to be. Is this significant in any way? I believe so. In addition, all the signatories were provably descended from British royalty as indeed most senior American politicians still are to this day. For example George W. Bush is a sixth cousin of Queen Elizabeth II.

So, on the 3rd September 1783, America was officially recognised by Britain as an independent country. Would this have been the case had the revolution really been to sever ties with Britain unilaterally? Highly unlikely, I would argue. The British establishment would have fought tooth and nail to retain the colony as their 'possession' had the War of Independence been lost against its will (instead of simply being 'handed over') and not meekly seceded to American local interests. The first President (although that was never his official title) George Washington, was from a British aristocratic background and was a 33rd degree freemason. His initiation ceremony was in effect a freemasonic ritual attended by all the freemasonic hierarchy of the country in full freemasonic regalia, aprons et al.

"The United States is still a colony of the Corporation known as 'The Crown', owned and managed by the Rothschilds and other Illuminati crime families. 'The Crown's' ownership of the United States Federal Reserve Bank guaranteed that the United States would be economically bled to death by foreign interests." Paul Drockton, 'Bankster Fraud and National Security', 7th January 2012

The new capital, Washington DC was designed and built on freemasonic principles with Babylonian and Romanesque architecture well to the fore including an abundance of esoteric symbolism in both its street-plan and its architecture. It is well known that occult and masonic ceremonies were common-place during the building of the city, when laying the foundation-stones of many of its original structures. As with the Egyptian pyramids, Washington DC is also in alignment with important star systems.

In actuality, the United States of America has never been a country in its own right, despite appearances to the contrary. It was established by British freemasonry, in conjunction with American freemasonry to perpetuate the deception of 'freedom of the people' and to enable covert control of the masses and facilitate huge, ongoing profits at the expense of those masses. In effect, the Virginia Company, established in the reign of Queen Elizabeth I, simply changed its name to The United States Corporation Inc. and this is the real power structure behind the scenes. The President is merely the president of a large corporation and so the 'war on terrorism' was launched by the president of a private corporation to further the geo-political interests and profits of that corporation. The privately owned 'United States' is in effect the holding company and the fifty states, its subsidiaries.

The French Revolution and the Napoleonic Wars

The French Revolution closely followed by the Napoleonic wars was the next instalment of the long-term Elite banksters plan to re-programme humanity to serve them and their god Lucifer.

"The Illuminati, operating in the guise of the Jacobins, forced the regime-change that historians now call the French Revolution." Andrew Smith, *henrymakow.com*

The value of history lies primarily in appreciating the current events of today. We have a sense that events are driven by the past and that history repeats itself. Why would this be? Perhaps, the hidden planners of historical events have an extremely limited repertoire of dirty tricks? They suppress the history of the deceptions practiced on our great-grandparents, so they can mislead and deceive us and later generations.

Only when we see that the French Revolution of 1789 was planned and financed from abroad (as was the English Revolution in the 17th century, the American Revolution in 1776 and the Russian Revolution of 1917) can we understand that the recent 'unrest' and 'revolutions' in Tunisia, Libya, Egypt, Bahrain, Thailand, Yemen, Syria and now Malaysia are not truly popular revolts but irregular warfare coups. Of course, in the case of Libya where Gadaffi came close to eradicating the rebels, the foreign coup has become a regular military operation supported by NATO air strikes. But they still call it a revolution.

There is no doubt that the French Revolution, which devastated the nation of France between 1787 and 1799, was inspired and instigated by Freemasonry and just as with the English Revolution, a century and a half earlier, things are not quite as portrayed by mainstream history. Although popularly believed to have begun due to a public uprising over lack of food and government representation, the real facts tell us that the revolution was instigated by cells of French Freemasonry and the German Illuminati.

Even the 'Encyclopedia Britannica' relates that in France there arose a political system and a philosophical outlook that no longer took Christianity for granted and indeed overtly and explicitly opposed it. The brotherhood taught by such groups as the Freemasons, members of secret fraternal societies, and the Illuminati, a rationalist secret society, provided a rival to the Catholic sense of community.

"The Masons... originated the [French] Revolution with the infamous Duke of Orleans at their head." Nesta Webster, secret society researcher, 1924

During the French Revolution, a key rebel leader was the Duke of Orleans, who was grand master of French Freemasonry before his resignation at the height of the Revolution. Marquis de Lafayette, the man who had been initiated into the Masonic fraternity by George Washington, also played an important role in the French revolutionary cause and the *Jacobin Club*, which was the radical nucleus of the French revolutionary movement, was founded by prominent Freemasons.

In 1789 the Duke of Orleans purportedly bought much of the grain in France and either sold it abroad, secreted it away or destroyed it thus engendering starvation amongst the French peasant classes. Galart de Montjoie, a contemporary, blamed the Revolution almost solely on the Duke of Orleans, writing that he *"was moved by that invisible hand which seems to have created all the events of our revolution in order to lead us towards a goal that we do not see at present..."*

"If, then, it is said that the [French] Revolution was prepared in the lodges of Freemasons – and many French Masons have boasted of the fact – let it always be added that it was Illuminised Freemasonry that made the Revolution and that the Masons who acclaim it are Illuminised Masons, inheritors of the same tradition introduced into the lodges of France in 1787 by the disciples of Weishaupt, patriarch of the Jacobins." Nesta Webster

Pro-revolutionary members of France's National Constituent Assembly had formed a group which became known as the Society of the Friends of the Constitution and after the Assembly moved to Paris, this group met there in a hall leased from the Jacobins' convent of Catholic Dominican Friars. These revolutionaries, sworn to protect the revolution from the aristocracy, became known as the 'Jacobin Club'. At least that is the official story of the Jacobins but the Jacobins are also tied to earlier secret societies, specifically regarding a plot to restore a kingship in Britain during the previous century...

In 1688, England's unpopular, Catholic Stuart king, James II, was deposed by his Dutch son-in-law, the Protestant William of Orange and James' daughter Mary. James, whose name in Latin was Jacobus, hence the name 'Jacobites', fled to France where he continued to be supported by Freemasons in Scotland and Wales who sought to restore him to the English throne. They were accused by French

Freemasons of subverting Masonic rituals and titles into political support for this restoration.

According to Masonic history, James was hidden from sight in the Chateau of Saint-Germain by his friend, the French King Louis XIV where he established a system of Freemasonry that became known as the 'Scottish Rite'.

After a series of failed rebellions, culminating at the Battle of Culloden in 1746, the Jacobite uprising in Scotland was finally crushed. Their leader, Charles Edward Stuart, 'Bonnie Prince Charlie, the young pretender', escaped back to France whence he came, taking with him Jacobite supporters imbued with 'Freemasonic ideals' and a year later in Arras, France, Charles chartered a Masonic Sovereign Primordial Chapter of Rose Croix (Rosicrucian order) known as the 'Scottish Jacobite Lodge'

All the revolutionaries of the Constituent Assembly were eventually initiated into the third degree of Illuminised Freemasonry, including revolutionary leaders such as the Duke of Orleans, Valance, Lafayette, Mirabeau, Marat, Robespierre, Danton and Desmoulins – all of whom were to have significant roles in the coming conflict.

Honre-Gabriel Riquetti, the Count of Mirabeau, a leading revolutionary, indeed espoused ideals which were all but identical with Adam Weishaupt, founder of Bavarian Illuminised Freemasonry. Mirabeau advocated the overthrow of all law and order and all power to 'leave the people in anarchy'. He said that the public must be promised 'power' and lower taxes but never given real power 'for the people as legislators are very dangerous as they only establish laws which coincide with their passions.' He also said that the clergy should be destroyed by 'ridiculing religion'. Mirabeau ended his tirade by proclaiming, 'What matter the means as long as one arrives at the end?' This of course is the same end-justifies-the-means philosophy espoused by Weishaupt, Lenin, Pike, Crowley ('do what thou wilt') and Hitler et al.

Contrary to popular belief and mainstream history, the storming of the Bastille was not the spontaneous action of the downtrodden masses, according to Nesta Webster... "That brigands from the South were deliberately enticed to Paris in 1789, employed and paid by the revolutionary leaders, is a fact confirmed by authorities too numerous to quote at length... In other words, the importation of the contingent of hired brigands conclusively refutes the theory that the Revolution was an irrepressible rising of the people."

It was during the French Revolution, that 'problem, reaction, solution', the Hegelian dialectic was put to good use whereby grievances were systematically created in order to exploit them. Such exploitation began with the Freemasons as early as 1772 when the Grand Orient Lodge was firmly established in France. At this time there were a total of 104 lodges and this number grew to 2,000 lodges by the time of the Revolution, with 447 lodge members participating in the 605 member Estates-General. One of their primary goals was the nationalisation of all Church property to help pay off the large debts revolutionary France incurred in assisting their Jacobite Masonic brethren's plans during the American revolution.

Meanwhile, buoyed by the situation in France, Freemasonic-based revolutionary clubs sprang up in other countries, including England, Ireland, the 'German' dukedoms, Austria, Belgium, Italy, and Switzerland and tensions between other nations and France rose until 1792 when France declared war on Austria and Prussia. Confronted with both a war and a revolution, France degenerated into the 'Reign of Terror', during which time King Louis XVI, Marie Antoinette, and many thousands of aristocrats, were executed by the Guillotine.

"Behind the Conventions, behind the clubs, behind the Revolutionary Tribunal, there existed... that most secret convention which directed everything... an occult and terrible power of which the other Convention became the slave and which was composed of the prime initiates of Illuminism." Nesta Webster

And so it was that the 'invisible hand' that guided the entire French Revolution was the Illuminati, still only 13 years in existence, yet powerful enough to cause a revolution in one of the major countries of the world. The wars, riots and coups d'états continued in France until a young General, Napoleon Bonaparte finally seized complete control in 1799. Although he carried on his own brand of terror in Europe for years, Napoleon proclaimed an end to the 'revolution'. France by this time was in absolute chaos. Hundreds of thousands had died of starvation, war, large-scale unrest, violence and by execution and the power of both the monarchy and the Catholic Church had been virtually destroyed.

The very same Elite forces that had directed and manipulated the French Revolution decided then to engage in another international plot and so they organised the 'Napoleonic Wars' to topple several more of the Crowned heads of Europe. One branch of the Elite financed Napoleon, whilst another branch financed Britain, the German states and other nations. Of course, both branches received their orders from the overall masterminds of the Elite, Illuminati organisation.

Immediately after the Napoleonic Wars, the Illuminati banksters headed by the Rothschilds assumed that all the nations would be so desperate and so weary of wars that they would be forced to accept almost any solution. So the stooges of the Illuminati set up what they called 'The Congress of Vienna.' At this meeting they tried to form the first 'league of nations', their very first attempt at 'one world government'. They espoused the theory that all the Crowned heads of the European countries were so deeply in debt to them that they would willingly or unwillingly serve as their stooges. But the Tsar of Russia somehow discovered the plot and completely foiled it. The absolutely livid Nathan Rothschild then vowed that someday they would destroy the Tsar and his entire family, a threat which was eventually fulfilled in 1917, one hundred years later. These people are nothing if not patient. They are prepared to wait generations to see their plans come to fruition and we should always keep in mind the fact that the Elite has never been geared to operate on a short-term basis.

The setback for the Elite at the congress of Vienna, as a result of exposure by the Tsar of Russia did not by any means destroy the conspiracy entirely; it merely forced them to adopt a new, longer-term strategy. Realising that their immediate plans for one world government was temporarily thwarted; the Elite decided that if they were to keep their power-base intact, they would have to tighten their control of the monetary system of the European nations.

'Revolution' may be defined as a *'sudden and violent change in government or in the political constitution of a country, mainly brought about by internal causes'*. But subversive elements in London working with French and European secret societies and not internal causes were responsible for the bloodbath that historians call The French Revolution.

Before 1919 when Nesta B. Webster published her history of the French tragedy, there was nothing in the English Language to inform the British and their Empire that all was not as it seemed, except Thomas Carlyle's *'The French Revolution'* (1837). In her preface to *'The French Revolution: A Study in Democracy'* (1919) Webster expressed the view that... *"So far, in England, the truth is not known; we have not even been told what really happened."*

Mainstream historians still claim that up until the French Revolution, the French aristocracy kept the peasants in a permanent state of hunger and desperation without any real hope or direction for the future. However, in her work, Webster comprehensively explodes these myths regarding peasant misery before 1789 with the letters of an Englishman Dr. Rigby who travelled through the French countryside in 1789 and who described 'its extraordinary fertility' and its 'state of the highest cultivation'. 'The crops are beyond any conception. I could have had of them ... tens of thousands of acres of wheat superior to any that can be produced in England...' He also described the ordinary French people as 'happy, prosperous and contented'.

Yet in the midst of this abundance there was suddenly an artificially-engineered famine and it was this that became the flashpoint that sparked the French Revolution. And we are also still taught that upon hearing of the starving French peasantry, Louis XVI's wife, Queen Marie Antoinette remarked, 'Let them eat cake'. This false quotation has been used to paint the French aristocracy as out of touch with reality. In truth, Marie Antoinette actually blamed England and she most definitely was well aware of what was really going on.

"What then, is the explanation of the belief in English co-operation with the revolutionary movement and of the English guineas found on the rioters? Of the Englishmen mingling in the mobs of Paris during popular agitations? Of the seditious pamphlets printed in London? Of the traffic in letters, messages, and money maintained

between England and the revolutionary leaders? Many of these leaders were constantly in England both before and during the Revolution... These facts admit of no denial". Nesta Webster.

A French historian and staunch Royalist, Felix Louis Montjoie, copiously documented the role of King Louis XVI's cousin the Freemason, the Duke of Orleans, who bought up large portions of the French grain in 1789. This action on his part turned out to be of no avail as he was despatched to Madame Guillotine in 1793.

Later historians documented the role of Prime Minister Pitt, the English Parliament and the British King's Privy Counsel in hoarding French grain with the aid of the Elite-controlled British East India Company in warehouses on the English Channel Islands of Guernsey and Jersey. However, England was merely a pawn in the Elite game of pseudo-revolutions that overturn governments and give credit to democratic/communist freedom-fighters (now re-branded as terrorists of course). These people eventually even propagandise and socially engineer the conquered population to celebrate the destruction of their own history, tradition and culture. So today, the French ironically celebrate the demise of their own culture on Bastille Day, the 14th July.

"The earlier revolutionary leaders were, as we have seen, the disciples of the German Illuminati and it was they who initiated them into the art of forming political committees to carry through the great plan of a general overturning of religion and government . . . . These committees arose from the Illuminati in Bavaria . . . and these committees produced the Jacobin Club." John Robison, 'Proofs of a Conspiracy', 1797

The chief lesson, Robison observed, that the revolutionary leaders acquired from the Illuminati, "... was the method of doing business, of managing their own correspondence and of procuring and training pupils."

So to conclude, the Elite operating in the guise of the Jacobins forced the regime change that historians now refer to as the 'French Revolution' and during the Russian Revolution it was the Bolsheviks that were used as the cover for their nefarious scheme.

Unelected Presidents of the USA

Whilst the recent, undemocratic seizure of the US presidency (on two occasions) by Bush the lesser was perhaps a most spectacular example of the uninhibited corruption abounding at high levels within western societies today, there are many other examples of this practice going back through the decades and centuries, all of which have either been air-brushed from official history or the facts have been distorted to protect the guilty.

Illegally disenfranchising voters and rigging the Diebold electronic voting machines, as happened in the Bush elections, are just two ways of achieving the ends of the unscrupulous Elite but there is another equally effective strategy that has been regularly employed. However, assassination is no bloodless coup, unlike the fixing of elections.

Almost from the beginning of the American republic, assassination has been used as an integral tool of control by those who enslave us, often resulting in the appointment of men who are in effect unelected leaders. It is a fact that Elite agents poisoned and killed William Henry Harrison on 4th April 1841 and Zachary Taylor on 9th July 1850. These two Presidents had opposed admitting Texas and California as slave-owning states and William Harrison was the first President ever to die in office, serving only 31 days and according to *Wikipedia* he died of 'pneumonia'. On the 3rd July 1850, Zachary Taylor threatened to hang those 'taken in rebellion against the Union' and the very next day, the President fell ill, vomited a 'blackish' substance and died within one week on the 9th July 1850. In fact Kentucky state authorities recently dug up Taylor's body in a search for evidence of arsenic poisoning, however none was found – or so they said. James Buchanan was also similarly poisoned in 1857 but he fortunately survived against the odds.

All three were obstructing on-going Elitist, Rothschild plans for the US Civil War (1861-1865). Later, Abraham Lincoln was famously assassinated by a single shot to the head at close range by John Wilkes Booth a 33rd degree freemason and Elite stooge at Ford's Theatre, Washington in 1865. Lincoln had recently introduced the debt-free currency 'greenbacks' thus bypassing the monopoly of the Bank of the United States (a forerunner of the Federal Reserve).

In fact, Booth was merely the front-man for a much wider conspiracy, a fact that was widely acknowledged at the time but has been conveniently ignored and/or deleted from history now. Four additional co-conspirators were hanged for the crime and two more received life sentences in jail. Lincoln's successor, Andrew Johnson, had just taken office as VP literally weeks before the assassination, replacing Hannibal Hamlin. Incidentally, Booth is commonly believed (according to official history) to have been silenced when he was killed whilst resisting arrest. According to a recent article by Mark Owen on the website *henrymakow.com*, Booth was actually killed by the 'outlaw' Jesse James a fellow high-ranking freemason, in 1903 for the heinous crime of breaking his masonic oath – a far worse transgression of course for freemasons, than assassinating the legally elected leader of a country.

According to Owen...

"*Booth's heavy drinking combined with his continual boasting of exploits within the KGC [masonic Knights of the Golden Circle] eventually brought him to the attention of Jesse James. It was also reported that Booth regularly partook of laudanum, an opium derivative. This is when he would become particularly verbose. Again we have to rewind... The outlaw Jesse James was not killed by Bob Ford in 1882. Jesse faked his death as an expedient way to throw off Pinkerton agents, assorted railroad barons, gun fighters and the bounty hunters scouring the country for him. He and Ford would become partners in many business ventures spanning decades. James operated under more than 50 aliases in his long life before dying at the advanced age of 107 under the alias 'J. Frank Dalton' in 1951 in Lawton, Oklahoma. Jesse James was a 33rd degree Freemason and a high-ranking Knight of the Golden Circle.*"

But, to get back to the main story... In every instance, the unelected Vice Presidents were swiftly drafted into office and duly 'played the game' as dictated to them by their Elite puppeteers. There is most definitely no room for independent thinkers in politics.

In 1901 Theodore (Teddy) Roosevelt was placed in office by 'default' by the assassination of President William McKinley. McKinley was shot and allegedly killed by an 'anarchist' Leon Csolgosz in Buffalo, New York. Two bullets struck the president, one in the abdomen and the other grazed his ribs, however neither was deemed to be fatal but regardless of this fact, McKinley surprisingly died eight days later, supposedly as a result of gangrene. Roosevelt at this time was just beginning his first term as vice-president, having recently replaced McKinley's previous VP, Garret Hobart but just six months later, Roosevelt assumed the presidency. Csolgosz the assassin, in the usual, standard tradition of American 'lone nut' gunmen, was rapidly dealt with. With seemingly indecent haste (within two months) he had been indicted, tried, convicted, sentenced and executed.

In 1923, Calvin Coolidge was similarly handed the office of President by virtue of the assassination of Warren G. Harding. Although the official cause of death was listed as an 'embolism' by his doctor, no autopsy was ever performed and so the correct diagnosis of the actual cause amounted to something akin to a remarkable feat of detection. Unsurprisingly, the good doctor suffered a similar fate less than a year later. According to a report in the *New York Times* at the time, the doctor's death '*was almost identical with the manner of death of the late Warren G. Harding when Doctor Sawyer was with the President in San Francisco*'.

Then in 1945, Harry S. Truman became the next unelected incumbent upon the death of President Franklin D. Roosevelt, which was also probably an assassination. Allegedly, Roosevelt suffered a headache, lost consciousness and then simply died. But whether this was from natural causes is highly debatable. Roosevelt had obviously felt well enough to begin an unprecedented fourth presidential term and did not appear overtly to be in failing health regardless of the fact that this is now exactly what history has been manipulated to state. In a similar vein to Teddy

Roosevelt, Truman had only just taken the office of VP, replacing Henry Wallace. Less than 3 months after becoming VP, Truman was holder of the ultimate office and in position to influence the final negotiations shaping the post-war world in the form demanded of him by the Elite.

Then in 1963, Lyndon B. Johnson assumed unelected executive office following the assassination of President J. F. Kennedy. There is obviously no doubt that Kennedy was assassinated, the only dispute being regarding by whom and why. Was it carried-out by the CIA, the FBI, the KGB, the Mafia, the Mossad, pro-Castro Cubans, anti-Castro Cubans, neo-Nazis, the Republican party or possibly even another 'lone-nut' by the name of Lee Harvey Oswald? Of course, Oswald was tried, convicted, sentenced and executed two days later by a another 'lone-nut' named Jack Ruby who just 'happened' to have been a colleague of Oswald in the same CIA section as well as having un-reported connections to the FBI, the KGB and the Mafia.

Five years later, the assassination of Robert Kennedy was an important factor in the presidential election victory of Richard Nixon. Kennedy was by far the strongest candidate and Johnson realising this fact had decided not to seek a second term of office. However, through Kennedy's untimely demise via the 'lone-nut' gunman strategy again (why change a successful formula?) Nixon was thus presented with almost a fait accompli.

However Nixon was soon playing the role of the victim himself as a result of an internal party power-struggle. Although it was dressed-up as an impeachment proceeding, evidence clearly suggests that what actually occurred was a CIA-directed coup, albeit bloodless, where Nixon was the victim of a set-up regarding the so-called Watergate affair. Watergate was without doubt a CIA/military intelligence operation, both the deliberately bungled burglary and the leaking of the fact afterwards. It is probable that Henry Kissinger was the driving force behind it in order to install his compliant stooge, Gerald Ford into office. It worked. As with the Bush coup in 2000, it resulted in yet another unelected president being sworn-in, namely Gerald Ford.

Ford was unique in that he was directly 'appointed' President without first becoming VP. He was just instantly elevated from Congress, where his primary duty had been to funnel covert, unaccountable funds to the CIA. In order to bypass the VP at that time, Spiro Agnew had to be disposed of by some means or another. Here is what Agnew himself had to say about it...

"...his remark sent a chill through my body. I interpreted it as an innuendo that anything could happen to me; I might have a 'convenient' accident. What had Haig meant when he said 'anything may be in the offing'? I was close enough to the presidency to know that the office could exert tremendous power. I was told... 'Go quietly, or else...' I feared for my life. If a decision had been made to eliminate me through an automobile accident or a fake suicide or whatever, the order would not have been traced back to the White House. The American people should know that in the last

hectic year or more of his residence in the White House, Richard Nixon did not actually administer all the powers of the presidency. As I have stated earlier, it was General Haig [a military officer of NATO – JH] who was the de facto President." Spiro Agnew, former US Vice President, in his book *'Go Quietly... Or Else'*.

Agnew eventually resigned as the result of a trumped-up financial scandal.

And then lo and behold in 1975 Gerald Ford himself was almost assassinated. He was shot at by another 'lone-nut', this time a woman, Lynnette Fromme who was part of the Charles Manson group of followers who as it happened, all turned out to have very shady, dubious backgrounds including covert links to the CIA, but she 'fortuitously' missed her target and Ford lived on to complete his presidential term and died in 2006 at the age of 93. He was one of the few lucky ones. Fromme is widely believed to have been a 'Manchurian Candidate', a product of MK Ultra, the mind-control branch of the US government implicated in many an assassination conspiracy. Had Fromme been successful, Nelson Rockefeller would have been raised from his position as the vice-president to become the second consecutive unelected president and the latest in a long, long list.

Moving on swiftly now to 1981 and the puppet-President Ronald Reagan and his controllers, the Bush crime-family. In that year, Reagan was the subject of an assassination attempt by another 'lone-nut' gunman, John Hinckley. Strange is it not how assassinations are never politically motivated? They are always carried-out by 'crazies', acting entirely alone and with 'crazy' motives. Anyway, Bush senior had, like Teddy Roosevelt and Truman before him, only just become vice-president at the time of the attack on Reagan and came extremely close to being the next in a long line of unelected presidents. The fact that the Hinckley and Bush families were known by many to be close friends and that this fact went unreported at the time and indeed ever since, is probably just a remarkable coincidence and nothing at all to be concerned about.

Covert coup d'états have always been a prominent part of the American political arena. Roosevelt, Coolidge, Truman, Johnson and Ford, achieved the highest office in this manner in the last 100 years alone and Nixon appears to have done so by violently eliminating his major competition (RFK) or by someone doing it on his behalf at least. There were also unsuccessful attempts at assassination such as for instance when two men allegedly attempted to assassinate President Truman in November 1951, as plans were being made for the 1952 presidential election campaign. The attempt failed, but Truman then, perhaps not unexpectedly, decided against running for a second term of office, effectively leaving the way clear for Eisenhower to become president.

In fact interestingly, every president who has taken office this past century as a direct result of assassination has inexplicably declined to seek another term of office at the subsequent elections. And this leads us neatly to the next phenomenon regarding the seemingly 'cursed' position of US President.   Commencing in 1840, every president prior to Reagan elected in a twenty-year cycle has 'died' in office. In chronological order:

William Harrison - elected in **1840**, assassinated in 1841
Abraham Lincoln - elected in **1860**, assassinated in 1865
James Garfield - elected in **1880**, assassinated in 1881
William McKinley - elected in **1900**, assassinated in 1901
Warren Harding - elected in **1920**, assassinated in 1923
Franklin Roosevelt - elected in **1940**, assassinated in 1945
John Kennedy - elected in **1960**, assassinated in 1963

Ronald Reagan – elected in **1980**, survived assassination attempt in 1981

Had Reagan succumbed to his wounds, he would have joined this list, proper.

What a shame it is now though that the cycle has been broken after 170 years, with the 2000 incumbent, 'Dubya' missing out. Could this be because the true rulers of the world have now *completely* gained control after two hundred plus years of chicanery and double-dealing in their attempts to bring the office of presidency under their influence? This would certainly appear to be the case, hence the lack of need for future assassinations barring rogue presidents usurping their authority.

Given the depth of corruption inherent within the US political system, there is strong reason to believe that the US (or indeed any Western government) can no longer be taken seriously as a democracy and there is a conspicuous pattern of Elite-Rothschild control throughout US history. To deny this fact would be ludicrous in the extreme. In fact the United States was actually created to advance the Elite's New World Order based on the Rothschild control of world finance. So-called 'American ideals' of freedom and democracy and the advent of the Constitution and the Bill of Rights were designed to con the masses into believing that they are 'free', not to be actually realised.

The founders, signatories of the Declaration of Independence and heroes of the US were mostly high-ranking freemasons including such luminaries as George Washington, John Hancock, Paul Revere, John Paul Jones and Benjamin Franklin as was Francis Scott Key who wrote the US national anthem, Stars and Stripes.

Jack the Ripper, Prince Eddy, Lord Randolph Spencer-Churchill and the Queen Mother

What do these seemingly unconnected people have in common? The answer may well surprise and shock you to the core.

The story begins in the late summer of 1888, the heyday of Queen Victoria's reign, in the gas-lit streets of London, when a young woman's horrifically mutilated body was discovered in a tawdry slum street in the run-down Whitechapel area of London....

On the evening of the 31st August 1888 the body of Mary Ann Nicholls, a common prostitute, was found prostrate on a pavement in the Whitechapel district in the East End of London. She had been brutally hacked to death, her throat having been slit and devastating cuts to her torso revealed her exposed internal organs. She was to be the first of a series of five victims of the now legendary killer who came to be known in popular folklore as 'Jack the Ripper'.

The so-called 'Ripper' murders came under the jurisdiction of the London Metropolitan Police Force and in particular an Inspector by the name of Frederick George Abberline who was tasked with the overseeing of the investigation. It is important to note that the diaries of Frederick Abberline did not see light of day until around 70 years after the unsolved murders, being in the possession during this time, firstly of Walter Sickert (1860-1942), the famous artist of the time and latterly of Joseph Sickert, his son. The full significance of this will become apparent later.

Walter Sickert had been employed by the royal family in the 1880s to provide private art lessons to their son and heir, Prince Albert Victor, the Duke of Clarence otherwise known by his colloquial name of 'Prince Eddy'. Eddy was in fact the eldest son of Albert Edward the Prince of Wales (later King Edward VII) and Princess Alexandra (later Queen Alexandra), the grandson of the reigning monarch, Queen Victoria and older brother of the future king of England, King George V and as such would eventually have been first in line to the throne. Unfortunately however, Eddy was not in the best of health. He had been born, mainly due to centuries of royal in-breeding, partially deaf and of well below average intelligence and was thus shunned by the majority of his cold-hearted family.

Queen Victoria, the reigning monarch at the time was a great supporter and patron of freemasonry as were all the Royal males of the age (and as they still are today). Indeed it was the Saxe-Coburg-Gotha family (the current British royals) that had sponsored the rise of Adam Weishaupt, the founder of the Illuminati, originally a freemasonry offshoot, in Bavaria in the 18th century. Weishaupt himself was born and raised in the Bavarian town of Gotha.

It is a little known or reported fact that there are several masonic lodges in the royal palaces of Britain, the most significant one perhaps being the Royal Alpha Lodge in Kensington Palace. In 1885 Prince Eddy was initiated into the Royal Alpha Lodge at the behest of his father.

Prince Eddy

As well as his membership of the lodge, Eddy was also a regular 'customer' at a homosexual-paedophile brothel in Cleveland Street, London and indiscreetly instigated a series of explicit love-letters with a young boy employed at these most vile of premises. The well-known Satanist, Aleister Crowley had these letters in his possession for many years but eventually they were lost or more likely destroyed and have never since seen the light of day. This incident alone had the potential to become a huge national scandal if made public, but events took a turn for the worse when it was discovered that Eddy had also made a young Catholic 'commoner' of Irish descent by the name of Annie Elizabeth Crook, pregnant with his child. Eddy also, as it turned out, had foolishly married her in a clandestine church service and this in effect barred him from ever becoming king as British royals are not permitted to marry Catholics, let alone one who is deemed to be a commoner and bearing a child conceived out of wedlock.

In 1883, Eddy's mother, Princess Alexandra, had asked the young painter Walter Sickert to introduce Eddy to the artistic and literary life of London. Sickert's studio, where he spent most of his time, was at 15 Cleveland Street near to Tottenham Court Road in north London. He duly introduced the teenage Prince to many of the area's 'bohemian types', including the theatrical friends he had made when, for four years, he had been a minor member of the Lyceum Theatre Company. Sickert also introduced Eddy to one of his models, a pretty Irish Catholic girl, the afore-mentioned Annie Crook who lived nearby at 6 Cleveland Street and who worked by day in a local confectioners or tobacconist's shop. They fell for each other and, according to Sickert, went through two clandestine marriage ceremonies, one Anglican and one Catholic. Soon afterwards, due to Annie's pregnancy, her employer needed someone to deputise for her during her confinement. Walter Sickert was asked if he knew anyone suitable and, after consulting friends, found a young girl by the name of Mary Jean (Marie Jeanette) Kelly, from the Providence Row Night Refuge for Women in Whitechapel. For some months, Mary worked alongside Annie Crook in the shop and the two became friends. In due course, on the 18th April 1885, Annie gave birth to Eddy's daughter, Alice Margaret and when she returned home, her new friend Mary Kelly moved-in as the child's nursemaid. Mary also worked as a prostitute in the evenings to supplement her meagre income.

Naturally, Eddy absolutely enraged the establishment with his 'illicit' marriage and this combined with the incident of the love-letters, threatened to tear apart the monarchy and spark a constitutional crisis of major proportions. So, as is always the case, the monarchy set in motion a huge cover-up operation as part of the damage limitation process. Annie was kidnapped from the small apartment in Cleveland Street in which she lived and in which Eddy spent time with her and at the same time Eddy was abducted into a carriage headed for Buckingham Palace where he was instructed, in no uncertain terms, to stay until further notice.

Fortunately, fearing the worst, Annie had already given the child, Alice to Walter Sickert for safekeeping shortly before she was forcefully taken to Guy's Hospital in London. She remained there for five months and whilst she was there, Sir William Gull, the Queen's personal physician performed a partial frontal lobotomy on her, in effect rendering her docile and compliant and thus easily controlled by these inhuman monsters. Subsequently certified insane by Gull, Annie lived for the rest of her life in institutions, spending her last days in the Lunacy Observation ward of St George's Union Workhouse, Chelsea and dying there in obscurity in early 1920 at the age of 57.

This was not the first time that Sir William Gull had been implicated in a scandalous royal cover-up operation. Around twenty years prior to this, the Prince of Wales (the future King Edward VII) the father of Prince Eddy, had been involved in a series of extra-marital affairs, one of which was with the young Lady Harriet Mordaunt. One day she foolishly confessed to her husband, Sir Charles Mordaunt, that she had been unfaithful with several men, one of whom was the Prince of Wales.

Sir Charles was absolutely incensed and he let it be known that he intended to sue for divorce, citing the Prince as a co-respondent. The Prince of Wales was rightly nervous about giving evidence in court as it would bring shame upon the entire royal family and cause an unacceptable scandal. So, at this point, Queen Victoria herself interceded on the Prince's behalf to protect the reputation of the family and instructed Sir William Gull to intervene.

Gull immediately, in consort with several other doctors conspired to have the young woman declared insane and locked away in a lunatic asylum, where she spent the last remaining 37 years of her life in abject misery, dying in 1906. Ultimately the case was dismissed, saving the Prince and the royals from acute embarrassment and no divorce was granted, not because adultery was unproven but simply because poor Harriet was declared insane.

However, to return to the main story, the matter might have ended there, but for Mary Kelly's greed. Back in Whitechapel, Mary had befriended three other local prostitutes to whom she boasted of her 'royal connections' and in the spring of 1888 the quartet, led by Mary, hatched a plan to demand money from Walter Sickert, threatening to otherwise make the story public. Being a simple girl, she had not fully comprehended the fact that was she in effect also holding-to-ransom a group of psychopathic murderers who would literally stop at nothing and had the means to kill with impunity whilst enjoying the 'protection' of people in high places.

Sickert immediately passed word to Eddy who informed his father and the Prince of Wales discussed the threat in the greatest secrecy with trusted fellow masons in the Royal Alpha Lodge. Subsequently, a special meeting was arranged at the Lodge by the royal masons known as the 'Princes of the Blood Royal' whereby they agreed to form a 'hunting party' to literally hunt-down and kill the hapless girls as punishment for their sheer audacity and significantly, as a masonic blood-sacrifice ritual.

The 'hunting party' was drawn exclusively from the Royal Alpha Masonic Lodge and included Sir William Gull, Eddy's former Cambridge University tutor J. K. (James Kenneth) Stephen and Sir Charles Warren, Commissioner of the Metropolitan Police (who took no active part in the killings but who helped facilitate the plot and expedite the cover-up). To drive them about their sordid business they recruited a coachman who had previously betrayed Prince Eddy's indiscretions to the royals, one John Netley.

Warren provided what information he could, on the girls' whereabouts using his privileged position in the police force and Sir William Gull prepared grapes injected with opium, which would be offered to the victims to subdue them so that the dastardly deed could take place with a minimum of fuss. It was arranged that John Netley, the coach driver and a particularly nasty character, was to be the 'getaway driver' and the 'lookout' would be J.K. Stephen, a cousin of Virginia Woolf and another freemason with royal links, whilst the murders were planned to occur within Gull's carriage – away from prying eyes.

It should be noted that Abberline's diaries confirmed that the modus operandus was not that of one person only and that the murders were planned and performed according to masonic ritual, similar to a fox-hunt. These are facts which were never allowed to come to light.

So, who was the ringleader of this murderous gang? None other than the prominent freemason, Secretary of State for India, the Leader of the House of Commons and the Chancellor of the Exchequer, Lord Randolph Spencer-Churchill, father of the future prime minister, Winston Churchill. Churchill was not only the 'brains' behind the entire operation, but he was also personally responsible for the cutting of masonic emblems and symbols into the bodies of the victims, whilst the skilled surgeon's hands of William Gull performed the organ removals.

The killings and mutilations were not observed by the police simply because four of them were not carried out in the streets where the bodies were found but in a moving coach, whilst the last was perpetrated *in situ*, in the victim Mary Kelly's own room. The police must have been aware that the bodies had been moved to their resting places due to the lack of blood as the whole pavement area would surely have been awash with blood had the rituals been performed there. Obviously though, this fact was never publicly disclosed by the police.

The assassins set about discovering the blackmailers' whereabouts with 'insider' help from Warren and then systematically plotted their executions. The ritualistic, murderous spree began on the 31st August 1888 with Mary Ann Nicholls as their first victim and continued with the killing of Annie Chapman on the 8th September. In turn each woman was lured inside the coach, then killed and mutilated in the ritualistic way that the three 'Juwes', Jubela, Jubelo and Jubelum, the murderers of Hiram Abiff, were executed in the old Masonic legend. Their throats were 'cut across', their bodies' torn open, their internal organs deftly removed and arranged around the corpses in their final resting places and their entrails 'thrown over' the left shoulder.

On the 30th September there were two further killings but on that night things did not go smoothly. As the murderers were dumping that night's first victim, Lizzie Stride, in Berner Street, they were interrupted and had to abandon her corpse before its ritual mutilation had been completed. More alarming still, the night's second victim, Catherine Eddowes, was, according to Sickert, almost immediately discovered to have been killed in error. It was learnt that poor Catherine had for some time lived with a man called John Kelly, had often used his surname and so had been wrongly identified by the gang's underworld informants as the blackmailer-in-chief, Mary Kelly.

That mistake nearly led to the group's undoing. In the mistaken belief that this was to be the climactic, final episode of their campaign, the group had already arranged Catherine's corpse, more completely mutilated than any of her predecessors, in Mitre Square (significantly masonic) opposite the masonic Temple and close to the Whitechapel Road. They had chalked on a nearby wall a masonic slogan to act as a postscript to the whole sordid affair. Abberline copied it down into his notebook and it said:

The Juwes are
the men that
will not
be blamed
for nothing.

Arriving on the scene suspiciously quickly, Sir Charles Warren, to the acute surprise of his underlings, ordered that the chalked epitaph, presumed by observers to be in the killer's hand, noted by Abberline to be that of an 'educated' man, should be immediately washed down and erased. The reason he gave was that he did not want anti-Jewish sentiment to be inflamed, but Sickert suggested the real reason was that too many insiders would recognise that the message referred not to the 'Jews' but to the 'Juwes' of Masonic legend, and would therefore identify the killers as freemasons.

After this setback there was a pause of more than a month, the longest interval between the killings, whilst the group redoubled their efforts to find the real Mary Kelly who was by this time lying low in fear of her life. Meanwhile, rumours of the killer's associations with freemasonry and with the royal family continued to grow. It was not until the 9th November that Mary Kelly was finally tracked down. To use the coach again was deemed to be too dangerous now, so she was dispatched in her own Dorset Street lodgings, more bloodily mutilated than any of her fellow-conspirators, her throat slashed, her body brutally cut apart and her intestines arranged ritually about the room.

There is in existence a police drawing of the last person to be seen with Mary whilst she was still alive and this bears an uncanny resemblance to no less a person than Lord Randolph Spencer-Churchill himself. Of course, this particular 'lead' was never followed-up by the masonic-controlled and run Metropolitan Police. J.K. Stephen, again according to Abberline's diaries, actually went to the police, made a full confession and surrendered himself in a fit of guilt but of course no arrests were made and Stephen was also released without charge whilst Abberline resigned his position with the force and retired forthwith as a direct result of his disgust at the inaction and cover-up on the part of the police. Indeed there are still files in existence in Scotland Yard that have been sealed forever to prevent the truth from ever being revealed. Stephen himself suffered a complete mental and physical breakdown shortly after the attacks and died a sad, lonely death in a lunatic asylum in Northampton, three years later at the age of only 33.

In the late 1970s, a researcher and author, Stephen Knight, managed to obtain limited access to the 'Ripper' files but discovered that there were many gaps in the records. Despite this, he still managed to unearth new leads and information based upon which he wrote a book 'Jack the Ripper – the final solution'. Unfortunately before publication, many of the more incriminating parts were 'stolen' and in those days, before personal computers were commonplace, he had no back-ups or copies as protection. After the book was eventually published, minus the more incriminating information, he published another book. 'The Brotherhood' which exposed the gross corruption and illegality prevalent in the freemasonic movement and shortly afterwards he was dead – allegedly poisoned, but of course no arrests were ever made. No change there then.

When Prince Eddy found out that his wife had been lobotomised he had a nervous breakdown as a result and when he learned the truth about the 'Ripper' murders, he withdrew within himself and was never the same again thereafter.

Sickert fled the country immediately, upon hearing the news of Annie Crook's abduction and took up residence in Dieppe, France in an attempt to protect the child, Alice. When Alice grew up, she and Walter became lovers and in turn had a child themselves who went by the name of Joseph Sickert – the very same man who held Inspector Abberline's diaries after inheriting them from his father.

In the meantime, Prince Eddy, his mental health by now completely shattered, was given into the care of the Earl of Strathmore who owned Glamis Castle in Scotland, until such a time as it had been decided by 'the firm' what was to be done with him. The royal family then blatantly lied to the world and announced that Eddy had sadly passed away at the age of only 28, on the 14th January 1892 due to influenza, but of course Eddy was still alive and being held in Balmoral Castle having not yet made the final move to Glamis.

Balmoral is approximately 1000 feet (300 metres) above sea-level and as such is partly surrounded by steep cliffs. This was the intended site for the planned murder of Eddy to be undertaken by Randolph Churchill and John Netley the coachman. The prince was pushed from the cliff-top but somehow managed to survive his fall and after the passage of two days had endeavoured to crawl all the way back to Balmoral where he was found at the door by his incredulous hosts. It was decided after this that the best option would be to just incarcerate him at Glamis for the rest of his life and the Earl of Strathmore agreed to undertake this task on behalf of the royals in return for one simple favour. The favour he stipulated was that **one of his daughters be allowed to marry a future king of England.**

Prince Eddy died in 1933, forty one years after his 'official' death date and during this time, his mother visited him only once, but took a photograph of him which she apparently sent to her cousin. This photograph is still in existence and shows a much older Eddy thoughtfully painting a picture which would sadly never be seen by anyone outside the walls of Glamis Castle.

The pact between Strathmore and the royal family was eventually fulfilled in 1923 when Lady Elizabeth Bowes-Lyon (his daughter, b. 1900) married the future King George VI of England after originally being promised to his brother, the heir to the throne and eventually the former King Edward VIII (he of abdication fame). In 1936 George ascended the throne upon his elder brother's abdication and Elizabeth became his queen consort. Elizabeth of course was more commonly known as the Queen Mother and the mother of the current incumbent of the family firm, Queen Elizabeth the second. She went to her grave in 2002 without ever revealing the secret and thus the world was never aware of this unholy pact.

In a further twist, as revealed in the Duke of Windsor's (the former King Edward VIII's) last known interview, shortly before he died, he revealed to Michael Thornton, the author of 'Royal Feud – The Queen Mother and the Duchess of Windsor' that the Queen Mother had been in love with him and not his brother Bertie (who eventually became King George VI). In fact it was the Queen Mother's treachery that was the reason why the Duke and Duchess of Windsor were banished from England and forced to live out the rest of their lives in France. Here is a transcript from the final interview of the Duke of Windsor (formerly King Edward VIII of England) with the author Michael Thornton:

"'So you're planning to write a book about the Queen Mother,' said the Duke, exchanging a conspiratorial smile with his wife.

'Well, we shall have to be extremely careful what we say on that subject, won't we darling?'

'Why is that, Sir?' I inquired innocently, although I was well aware of the reason.

The Duke, only months away from being diagnosed with inoperable throat cancer, was interrupted by a convulsive spasm of coughing.

He cleared his throat and added: 'I hope your book will tell the truth, instead of all that gush they dish out about her. Behind that great abundance of charm is a shrewd, scheming and extremely ruthless woman.'

He must have noticed my surprised reaction, for he quickly added, with his most charming smile, '... but, of course, you cannot quote that.'

The Duchess was less inhibited. 'The Duke would have loved to return to live in the land of his birth, but our way was blocked at every turn. We were never allowed to go back, and we never will be allowed. Not until the day we die. She will never permit it. When we are dead, perhaps she may at last forgive us'.

When I asked her the reason, the Duchess's right arm shot out as if she was taking aim with a gun and she said: 'Jealousy.'

'Jealousy of the Duke?' I wondered. 'No!' cried the Duchess, and for the first time her southern American origins were audible. 'Jealousy of me for having married him.'

The Duke, who appeared vaguely uncomfortable with this topic, murmured: 'Well, it's hard to explain. But, yes, Elizabeth (the Queen Mother) was rather fonder of me than she ought to have been. And after I married Wallis, her attitude towards me changed. 'My sister-in-law is an arch-intriguer, and she has dedicated herself to making life hell for both of us.'"

Was it intended then that they were introduced with the specific aim of a royal arranged marriage between the two in order to fulfil the promise to Strathmore, her father and then when she was rejected by him (he was a notorious playboy and rebel in his younger days so quite possibly he went against the wishes of his family in the matter) she/they decided she would have to settle for second best in his younger brother? After all it was she who fought tooth and nail to have them disinherited by the royals and banished to France.

And is it then also possible and most intriguingly of all, that Edward VIII was forced into abdication deliberately by denying him the right to marry Wallis Simpson whilst he was still King, in order that the decades-old promise would come to fruition and that Elizabeth Bowes-Lyon, the daughter of the Earl of Strathmore could become Queen? There was obviously no other way of fulfilling this promise if Edward was determined to marry Mrs Simpson. Had it been expedient for the powers that be, that Edward **was** to marry Mrs Simpson whilst still king, there is no doubt in my mind that this would have been allowed to happen. The rules are changed and manipulated to suit whatever is best for our controllers, after all.

And there is also much irony and even déja vu in the tragic story of the Queen Mother's nieces, Nerissa and Katherine Bowes-Lyon, both born mentally deficient and unable to speak. They were confined in the Royal Earlswood Mental Hospital at Redhill, Surrey in 1941, where they remained for the rest of their lives. Although the Queen Mother (incidentally, the patron of the charity 'Mencap') knew that the statement in *Burke's Peerage* that both women were dead (published after false information had been supplied by their mother) was untrue, she never visited or ever again acknowledged either of them.

In 1973, the BBC produced a truly bizarre investigation into the 'Ripper' story featuring, amongst other strange anomalies, fictional television detectives who all attempted to solve the enigma in their own styles. Several researchers were employed to extract all the information they possibly could about all the potential suspects and after speaking with a long-retired, un-named Scotland Yard detective, one researcher was advised to seek the help of a man by the name of Joseph Sickert who apparently knew about the clandestine marriage of Prince Eddy and a poor Catholic girl by the name of Annie Crook. The researchers could find no evidence of the marriage or the man Sickert and so puzzled by this, they went back to their Scotland Yard contact who revealed that the details he had given them were incorrect (apparently to test their intentions). He then gave them Sickert's real address and phone number no less and after being tracked down, Sickert willingly told his amazing story as it had been outlined to him by his mother and father many years previously.

Sickert explained that the monarchy had been very vulnerable and unpopular at that time and the news of a royal scandal was likely to cause a revolution. Queen Victoria supposedly handed the matter to Lord Salisbury, her Prime Minister, for resolution and Salisbury ordered a raid on the Cleveland Street apartment and Eddy and Annie were abducted in separate cabs. Her child, a girl by the name of Alice Margaret, had somehow escaped in the care of Walter Sickert who had been one step ahead of the royals all along.

Sir William Gull died shortly after the murders (early 1890) as did JK Stephen (early 1892) at the extremely early age of 33 and ironically both had been committed to insane asylums immediately prior to death. Randolph Churchill died in 1895 also rumoured to be insane, but it was claimed, as a result of syphilis. Annie Crook also died insane in a workhouse in 1920 as a direct result of a lobotomy and severe mental trauma. Netley was chased by an angry mob after he unsuccessfully tried to run over Alice Margaret with his cab shortly after the murders and he was believed to have been drowned in the Thames. There does appear to be an awful lot of insanity and strange deaths around at that time – nothing changes, really.

Sickert also said that his father was fascinated with the murders and bore great guilt over them. Walter Sickert, after all, had been the one who introduced Eddy to Annie and begun the grisly game. To attempt to alleviate his guilt, as he could say nothing safely, he painted clues as to the identity of the murderers into several of his most famous paintings and he later married Alice Margaret.

To say that the BBC researchers were stunned by these revelations would be a gross understatement. In checking the facts, they found that a woman named Annie Crook definitely lived in Cleveland Street at that time and that she did give birth to a daughter at the same time that Sickert said she did. They also believed strongly that this 'theory' was the most feasible one of all (as do I) and they incorporated it into the show.

When it was screened, the BBC production was confusing to many viewers. The ludicrous combination of facts with fictional detectives and what was to many, an outlandish theory involving people who in their beliefs could do no wrong, prompted much questioning of the programme's veracity at the time. Joseph Sickert appeared in the last episode and verified absolutely everything that had been said. As previously related, it was agreed by all that this version of events was the most likely solution to the mystery.

Stephen Knight, the late author, entered the story a little later. After watching the BBC programme, he asked Joseph Sickert for an interview and after some indecision, Sickert agreed. During the course of their interview, which took place over several meetings, Knight also became convinced that Joseph Sickert believed he was telling the truth. He said that the story had been told to him by his father to explain why his mother always looked so sad and why both she and Joseph were partially deaf (as was Eddy).

Once familiar with the basics of the plot, Knight then attempted to confirm the theory and eventually, he felt that the story warranted a book. Sickert was upset by this as he had only agreed to a short interview for an article and wanted no further publicity and exposure of his father's role in the story. Undaunted, Knight went ahead with his book anyway but amazingly and contrary to what he had been told by Sickert, attempted to implicate Walter Sickert as the murderer. As a direct result of this action, Joseph Sickert cut off all ties with Knight and immediately publicly denied the whole story – not just simply his father's alleged involvement in it all, saying that he had made it up for sensationalism.

This I find hard to believe. How could the detective, contacted by the BBC have known Sickert's whereabouts or even known who he was or somehow involved if the whole story was concocted? And also if Sickert did make it up for 'sensationalism', why did he retreat back into obscurity as soon as he realised that Knight was giving him the publicity he allegedly sought in the first place. No smoke without fire I strongly believe and knowing what I know about masonic operations and royal subterfuge down the ages, although there is no categorical proof that this version of events is the correct one, it does 'tick a lot of boxes' and contains more than a smattering of circumstantial evidence.

A further legacy of this sorry affair was that the payoff for the Spencers was two terms as prime minister for Lord Randolph's son and two generations later, Lady Diana Spencer became the wife of the future King Charles III and mother to the future King William V and his brother Harry, only to be famously discarded once she had fulfilled her wifely duties in providing her highly-desirable genes to produce a 'heir and a spare' and eventually being brutally and ritually murdered herself in 1997 in Paris.

This then is the **real** story of Jack the Ripper, straight from the 'horse's mouth' (ie. Joseph Sickert's mouth). These facts must be known by the current establishment but as always, they close ranks to prevent the real truth from becoming known. All of the multiplicity of theories that abound as to the identity of the killer and the many films, documentaries and TV programmes that portray an unending search for the 'truth' are nothing more than elaborate smokescreens, born from the deliberate confusion engendered by the Elite to protect the guilty, as is their usual modus operandus. Yet another tiny example of how easy it is for these psychopaths to provide us all with a completed distorted view of both history and our existing reality.

The Protocols of the Learned Elders of Zion

Whether it is an elaborate fake or an accurate depiction of the planned future for humanity, one thing is for sure and that is that this most controversial of documents depicts the society in which we live today almost perfectly, even more than a century after it first saw the light of day at the end of the 1800s. In one respect it is almost irrelevant as to whether it is a forgery as to argue the pros and cons of that premise merely detracts from the fact that it provides an almost perfect 'snapshot' of the absolute ugliness and debauchery to which our Western culture has descended in the past century or so.

If it is to be deemed a fake, then one would need to ask the question as to why it would appear that no other work has had more effort or money spent on its suppression than 'The Protocols of the Learned Elders of Zion', ever since it was first privately circulated in Russia in 1897. It has been attributed by some groups to the Tsar's secret police, who were alleged to have used as their model a book called 'Dialogues aux Enfers entre Machiavelli et Montesquieu' and another publication similarly named, 'Machiavelli, Montesquieu and Rousseau' written by Jacob Venedy, a Jewish Freemason.

Fake or not, it is certainly most remarkable that whoever wrote the Protocols (and someone must obviously have done so) had incredible prescience, for as stated, it mirrors almost exactly the events of the entire 20th Century and the first two decades of the 21st. However, it goes back in time much further than that. The 'Protocols' is not necessarily a modern work per se, but possibly the product of an ancient heritage, unbroken and unaltered for centuries and reflecting the long-term Elite plan in every minor detail.

The document itself is too lengthy to be reproduced in full here, but I would urge the reader to familiarise his/herself with it by searching on the Internet where the document is freely available as are many websites dedicated to the dissection of it and its contents.

In summary, the document is purported to be the game-plan of Zionism by which it intends to take-over the entire world. Even if it is a forgery as vehemently claimed by those who wish to enslave us, with the usual emotive cries of 'anti-Semitism', I believe that its accuracy in the way that it describes not just today's society, but the events of the past 100 years and more, gives it plenty of credence.

Please do not be deceived or deflected by the Zionist's attempts to divert you from the truth. As I say, even if this work was not produced by or at the behest of Zionism, its stunning accuracy can only mean that whoever produced and wrote it, clearly knew that the fate of mankind was being carefully planned and exactly what that fate was going to be.

The Federal Reserve and the Titanic

What was the real story behind the sinking of the RMS *Titanic* in 1912?

In 1910, seven men met on Jekyll Island just off the coast of Georgia, USA to plan the formation of a new central bank, the Federal Reserve Bank, in order to usurp the control of money creation from the US Government and place it into private hands. Nelson Aldrich and Frank Vanderlip represented the Rockefeller financial empire, Henry Davidson, Charles Norton and Benjamin Strong represented J.P. Morgan and Paul Warburg represented the Rothschilds banking dynasty of Europe. These men all took great pains to conceal their identities and their dastardly mission, all of them travelling incognito.

"Picture a party of the nation's greatest bankers stealing out of New York on a private railroad car under cover of darkness, stealthily riding hundreds of miles South, embarking on a mysterious launch, sneaking onto an island deserted by all but a few servants, living there a full week under such rigid secrecy that the names of not one of them was once mentioned, lest the servants learn the identity and disclose to the world this strangest, most secret expedition in the history of American finance. I am not romancing; I am giving to the world, for the first time, the real story of how the famous Aldrich currency report, the foundation of our new currency system, was written... The utmost secrecy was enjoined upon all. The public must not glean a hint of what was to be done. Senator Aldrich notified each one to go quietly into a private car of which the railroad had received orders to draw up on an unfrequented platform. Off, the party set. New York's ubiquitous reporters had been foiled... Nelson (Aldrich) had confided to Henry, Frank, Paul and Piatt that he was to keep them locked up at Jekyll Island, out of the rest of the world, until they had evolved and compiled a scientific currency system for the United States, the real birth of the present Federal Reserve System, the plan done on Jekyll Island in the conference with Paul, Frank and Henry... Warburg is the link that binds the Aldrich system and the present system together. He, more than any one man has made the system possible as a working reality." Bertie Charles Forbes, Forbes Magazine, 1928

The Morgans, the Warburgs, the Rothschilds and the Rockefellers are more often than not, fierce competitors for short-term profits, yet are prepared to commit to joint ventures whenever necessary to further the greater 'cause'. They established the US national banking cartel that is the Federal Reserve Bank in 1913. According to G. Edward Griffin in *'The Creature from Jekyll Island'* *"... it tells a story of how bankers have lured politicians with easy money and end up in control of most of the world."*

They are all part of and therefore controlled by the Elite hierarchy. These most powerful of families constantly strive to do whatever is necessary to destroy constitutional liberty in America (and worldwide). John Pierpoint (JP) Morgan was in control of the White Star shipping line as well as a significant portion of all American financial and manufacturing industry at the turn of the twentieth century. In 1908, he made the decision to build a brand new class of luxury liners to enable the wealthy to cross the Atlantic seaways in previously undreamed-of opulence. This class of ships was named the 'Olympic' class and construction of the giant vessels the 'Olympic', the 'Titanic' and the 'Britannic' began in 1909 at the Harland and Wolff shipyard in Belfast, Ireland.

Unfortunately for Morgan and his personal bank balance, this money-making venture went a little awry. The *Olympic*, the first one of the three sister-ships to be completed (followed by *Titanic* and then *Britannic*), was involved in a rather unfortunate accident caused by a heavy collision with the British Royal Navy cruiser, *HMS Hawke* in September 1911 in Southampton Water off the south coast of England, a few weeks after its maiden voyage and had to be extensively 'patched-up' before embarking on the return journey to Harland and Wolff's shipyard in Belfast in order to undergo full damage assessment and proper repair work.

Incidentally, does it not seem rather strange in hindsight that although the *Olympic* was the first of the (virtually) identical triplet 'sisters' to be completed and enter service, she was never given the publicity, nor enjoyed the huge public acclaim that her younger sister enjoyed, the following year? Why would that be? Surely the big fanfare and carnival-like atmosphere surrounding the maiden voyage of these 'floating wonders of the age' should have been reserved for the first one to enter service, *Olympic* not the second one, *Titanic*? Indeed, in comparison, the occasion of *Olympic*'s maiden voyage in 1911 passed relatively quietly. Could the huge accolades and publicity accorded to *Titanic*'s maiden voyage possibly have been part of a conspiracy to lure the rich and famous to her in great numbers for reasons that will become apparent shortly? Anyway, I digress somewhat....

In the meantime a Royal Navy enquiry into the accident, not unexpectedly, found the crew of the *Olympic* and thus the White Star Line culpable for the collision and this in effect meant that the White Star Line's insurance was null and void and the company would therefore be liable to pay all the costs of the repairs to both ships themselves. To cut quite a long story short, this meant that the White Star Line was out of pocket to the tune of at least £800,000 (around £60m today) for repairs and lost revenues whilst the ship was unable to ply its trade back and forth across the Atlantic. With the massive financial investment of the White Star company needing to be repaid sooner rather than later, this put severe pressure on the organisation and impacted upon the final completion of the *Titanic*, further contributing to the financial black hole in which White Star now found itself increasingly being consumed.

However, for JP Morgan and the White Star Line, even worse news was to come. The damage to the *Olympic* was far more severe than anyone had expected. It did not help matters at all when the *Olympic* was involved in a further collision, this time it was believed, with a partially submerged wreck. Although the damage inflicted in the *Hawke* incident had been shored-up as well as it could have been, there were rumours circulating amongst the Harland and Wolfe workforce and the White Star crews that all was not well with *Olympic* and this seemed to be confirmed when it lost a propeller blade in the above, second incident, causing further severe vibrational damage to the already damaged ship. It is believed that the keel of the ship was actually twisted and therefore damaged beyond economic repair, which would have effectively meant the scrapyard for her. If this had been the case, it is virtually certain that the White Star Line would have been bankrupted, given its now precarious financial situation.

'...it took a fortnight [two weeks] of emergency patching to Olympic's hull before she was in any fit state to attempt the journey from Southampton to Belfast for more complete repairs. Able to use only one main engine, the crippled liner made the voyage at an average speed of 10 knots, wasting the exhaust steam from the one usable engine. This steam would normally have driven the central turbine engine, which shows that this engine, its mountings or shafting had been damaged in the collision. As this engine sat on the centreline of the vessel, immediately above the keel, which the propeller shaft ran through, we can reasonably assume that the keel was damaged'. Robin Gardiner, 'Titanic, the Ship that Never Sank?'

If Gardiner's hypothesis is correct, then the seeds had been sown for a truly remarkable event – **the surreptitious switching of the identities of the two ships, Olympic and Titanic.**

In his well-researched work, Gardiner presents a long series of credible testimonies, indisputable facts and evidence, both written and photographic, that would seem to point to the fact that the two ships were indeed switched with a view to staging an iceberg collision or other unknown fatal event, with the *Titanic* (originally the *Olympic*) and many of its passengers and crew being sacrificed in an audacious insurance scam which would save the White Star Line from financial ruin.

According to Gardner, "Almost two months after the *Hawke/Olympic* collision, the reconverted *Titanic*, now superficially identical to her sister except for the C deck portholes, quietly left Belfast for Southampton to begin a very successful 25 year career as the *Olympic*. Back in the builders' yard, work progressed steadily on the battered hulk of *Olympic*. The decision to dispose of the damaged vessel would already have been taken. It must have been obvious from quite early on that the vessel was beyond economic repair, so these repairs need not have been quite as thorough as they otherwise might have been. Instead of replacing the damaged section of keel, **longitudinal bulkheads were installed to brace it**". [my emphasis – JH]

How significant then in the light of this statement, that when the wreck of the *Titanic* was first investigated by Robert Ballard and his crew after its discovery in 1986 that the first explorations of the wreckage revealed (completely undocumented in the ships original blueprints) iron support structures in place which appeared to be supporting and bracing the keel. This was never satisfactorily explained either at the time or subsequently but would certainly be significant if correct and there is absolutely no reason to believe that it is not correct, as it was reported by the puzzled Ballard himself who of course at that time knew nothing (and probably still does not even now) about the alleged switching of the two ships' identities.

Meanwhile, in the USA there were a number of powerful men who were not in favour of the proposed Federal Reserve Banking System. Benjamin Guggenheim, Isador Strauss and John Jacob Astor were most prominent among those who opposed the formation of this abomination. These men were some of the richest men in the world, but their money was accrued through industrial, retail and leisure interests, rather than through the financial sector and they stood firmly in the way of the banksters' plan. It is my view that either Morgan and the other co-conspirators hit upon a really neat 'kill two birds with one stone' solution, then not only would White Star have successfully solved the *Olympic* problem and thus its own financial worries, but J.P. Morgan would also have fulfilled his wishes to implement his plan to establish the Federal Reserve with little or no powerful opposition to thwart him. Perfect.

All three (along with many other prominent people of the day) were subtly enticed to board the by-now hyped-up to be, highly prestigious maiden voyage of the *Titanic* with a view to ending their opposition to the Federal Reserve plans and thus an additional reason for the ship's destruction was a stand-off between the mega-rich whereby Guggenheim, Strauss and Astor could be eliminated. They had to be destroyed by a means so outrageous and fantastic that no one would suspect they were murdered and also using a method that would completely obscure the real reason for their demise. Simply arranging for all three men to undergo separate 'accidents' would have appeared far too suspicious, so they had to be lured to the same place at the same time and *Titanic*'s pre-determined, ill-fated maiden voyage was the solution to the problem. Could this have been the real reason for all the hullabaloo and hype surrounding *Titanic*'s maiden voyage despite the fact that the *Olympic* was accorded a much less publicised or flamboyant 'send-off' on the 14th June 1911, even though she was after-all, the first one off the production line?

Morgan himself was supposed to be travelling on the ship, but as was always intended, he had a 'last minute change of plan' due to a 'bout of ill health' and significantly failed to show at Southampton at the appointed time and so his personal stateroom remained empty as the giant vessel pulled away from Southampton docks on the afternoon of the 10th April 1912, to the delight of the cheering multitudes on the quayside.

Is it possibly also significant that Morgan ordered that an expensive collection of bronzes that he had purchased in Paris, should be unloaded from the ship at the last minute, too?

The Captain of *Titanic*, Edward Smith had experience of the North Atlantic waters in abundance, indeed he had been crossing the North Atlantic for more than a quarter of a century. He was generally regarded as the *'world's most experienced captain'* in the North Atlantic seaways and it is my belief that Smith knew all along that *Titanic/Olympic* was destined to become the grave of the enemies of J.P. Morgan, his boss and its purpose, once the damage to *Olympic* was fully realised, was always that it would undergo a contrived accident on its 'first' voyage. He also had full and complete knowledge of exactly where the icebergs were. He guided *Titanic* full speed at around 22 knots on a moonless night into a huge ice field 80 square miles in area. Why would such an experienced captain undertake such a foolhardy course of action? The fact is that he had received his orders directly from his ultimate boss (JP Morgan) and therefore he was totally committed to leading his ship to disaster.

Captain Smith's actions immediately before the event and in its immediate aftermath were totally out of character for this experienced master mariner. Could he have been wrestling with his conscience perhaps? Should he become the heroic Captain, saving the day or against all his instincts, obey his master, sink the ship and in the process cold-bloodedly murder up to 3000 people? Significantly and conveniently (for the perpetrators) Smith in the age-old tradition, as Captain, went down with the ship we are told. Indeed, could Smith have even been 'allowed' to survive, knowing as he probably did, the real truth about the incident? One suspects not.

As is well known, there were not enough lifeboats for the full complement of passengers and crew and some of them left the ship as little as only one quarter full in any case and this fact could well have been used to its full advantage in the execution of the master plan. The Captain strangely ordered white flares to be launched, knowing full well that the international standard colour of distress flares was red. *Titanic* possessed a full complement of white, blue AND red flares. Other ships passing within sight of these flares were intentionally confused and thought that maybe those aboard *Titanic* were having a fireworks party. This of course was also all part of the master plan.

Even if my hypothesis could be criticised by some as mere conjecture, the true *Titanic* story is still very, very different to the official, ubiquitous one that we see depicted in books and numerous films and documentaries that have been spawned by this tragic incident. The book, published in the 1950s and the feature film of the same name, 'A Night to Remember' (Longmans, Green & Co, 1956) by Walter Lord is the source most responsible for the *Titanic* myths and legends still prevailing today. Lord was a 'former' member of the US intelligence services (OSS and CIA) but given the fact that it is well known that anyone who has *been* a member of these organisations always in effect remains a member, can we really rely on his accounts or are they just more subterfuge amongst a morass of contradictory stories surrounding the event? What would motivate a former member of one of the world's elite security services to write a book about an accident involving an ocean liner? As always seems to be the modus operandus in any suspected conspiracy, we are bombarded with these so-called 'facts' by the controlled media, to such an extent that we believe that they cannot possibly be untrue or deliberately misleading. However, many of the major *Titanic* 'facts' have subsequently been proven to be false but somehow the same version of the story still persists as the absolute de facto truth. Such is the power of propaganda on the human mind and symptomatic of the methodology by which most history is perverted.

Robin Gardiner further stated, *"As I delved deeper into the story, more and more inconsistencies became apparent. Inconsistencies that individually meant little but collectively pointed to a grimmer reality than that usually depicted in the heroic legend"*.

He continues, *"Officers who were later acclaimed as heroes were exposed as anything but. One in particular removed a little boy from a lifeboat at gunpoint, before escaping in that same boat himself"*.

"Descriptions of the collision and damage supposedly sustained by Titanic do not agree. The 'slight scrape' with the ice that was hardly noticed by most aboard contradicts solid evidence of structural damage at least 5½ feet (1.6 metres) within the outer hull of the vessel".

*"Then came evidence to show that the ice the ship encountered was seen first not 500 yards (480 metres) ahead but more like 11 miles (17km). I began to wonder if perhaps the sinking of the Titanic **might not have been an accident after all**"*. [my emphasis – JH]

Indeed, did *Titanic* actually strike an iceberg at all? We only have the eye-witness testimony of **four people** believe it or not, with which to confirm or deny this fact. First Officer Murdoch would have been the fifth witness but he did not live to tell his story. Gardiner himself offers no opinion on this theory, but the copious amounts of ice on the deck of *Titanic* reported by many survivors could easily have been the result of *any* collision dislodging the icy build-up on masts, funnels etc. or it could even have been easily shaken loose from the hundreds of yards of overhead rigging and wiring by the thrusting of the ships engines abruptly into reverse. It was after all, an extremely cold, still night with temperatures below freezing.

There have been many legends surrounding the incident but there is plenty of concrete evidence that *Titanic* was not the only ship at that precise location that night. For example, there is a photograph in existence of a drifting lifeboat that can be discounted totally as being from *Titanic* herself due to being of different colours and design to *Titanic's* lifeboats.

Then there is the gouge in the side of the ship itself – **1.6 metres deep** through the outer steel plates and into the inner skin! Compacted ice is known to be very strong, indeed stronger than steel under certain conditions, but there is no evidence that I am aware of that it is capable of doing such catastrophic damage to steel. In addition the relatively narrow, 15cm puncture line in the ship's hull in conjunction with a penetration of around 1.6m would indicate an almost impossibly-shaped ice outcrop colliding with the ship at exactly the most critical point.

Whatever the real truth, the point here is surely that there exist so many different possibilities that the official story is probably just an elaborate fabrication. Both the American and British official inquiries were even thought at the time to be pretty much a 'whitewash', with much evidence either ignored and eye-witness testimonies being twisted or indeed fabricated to fit the 'official' story. It is staggering also to report that of the 102 witnesses called to the British enquiry, only two were passengers (the influential Gordons of the famous London gin company) and it is even more surprising to learn that none of the witnesses (crew or passengers) were allowed to offer their own first-hand evidence of any kind and were strictly restricted to the simple answering of questions without elaboration. By any standards at all, this sounds very much like a 'whitewash' to me. The passage of time has also served to cloud the mystery still further.

We should also note that amongst all the myriad of (probably) deliberately conflicting information unearthed by the two inquiries, the most puzzling of all is the situation regarding the 'yellow-funnelled steamer' observed in the proximity of *Titanic* by the officers and crew of *Californian* at around the time of the incident and which has never been either identified or explained away at all. Significantly, this odd occurrence does not even warrant a mention in any surviving *Titanic* legends – very strange to say the least, despite its appearance in several contemporary newspapers.

The crew of this ship (who or whatever she was) must have been aware that they were in the approximate area of the *Titanic's* demise at the same time, so why did no-one from the ship come forward to volunteer any evidence or information or simply to state that they had seen nothing significant, instead of disappearing into the mists of history forever? It also begs the question as to why no attempts were made to discover the identity of this ship either by the inquiries or subsequently by independent investigators. Even if attempts were made at the time, as far as I am able to tell, they have been very successfully covered-up and no evidence remains today. Could this mysterious yellow-funnelled vessel have been responsible for the devastating damage to *Titanic* in any way? I personally believe it is a very strong possibility and that the 'iceberg collision' is just a cover story concocted to protect the guilty.

"...I saw another steamer approaching, and asked [the wireless operator] what vessels he had within reach; he replied: 'The Titanic', whereupon I replied, 'That is not the Titanic; she is too small and hasn't enough lights.' Shortly afterwards this steamer stopped and was bearing S.S.E. about five or six miles from our position. ...the chief officer was sweeping the southern horizon with his glasses, and finally reported he saw a four-mast steamer with a yellow funnel to the southward of us, and asked if we should try to get down to have a look at her." Captain Lord of *Californian* in an interview with an American newspaper, 1914

Lord became the official scapegoat for the disaster for his so-called 'negligence' in not rushing sooner to Titanic's aid as the Californian was probably only about 11 miles from her when she went down.

Furthermore, upon arriving back in England at Plymouth docks, from New York aboard the steamer *Lapland*, two weeks after the disaster, 173 of the surviving crew members both male and female were firstly, illegally denied their rights to speak with their trade union representatives. Then in addition they were also illegally detained overnight against their wishes (I believe the common terminology for this act is unlawful imprisonment or even kidnapping) in a containing area within the dockyard itself where they were forced to sign a document that they believed was the 'Official Secrets Act', promising to keep secret forever, the actual events of the night of 14th / 15th April. Otherwise, they were told, they would be prosecuted and 'never work again', not just for White Star but for any other employer. In those now long-gone days, the inability to procure gainful employment could be almost a death sentence to the crews *and* their families. So, make of that what you will, but I can personally think of no reason why this should happen if the official story was the truth. It is also worth noting that also in those now distant days it was far easier without mass and instantaneous communication devices, to invent or twist facts and bury individuals' own stories. Today of course, any of the survivors' personal experiences would be viral on the Internet within hours of the event.

The Red Star liner Lapland, which carried Titanic crew survivors home.

So did Captain Smith deliberately steer *Titanic* into a huge ice-field without reducing speed in order to create the cover-story of the iceberg collision knowing that he was setting-up *Titanic* to be rammed by the yellow-funnelled mystery ship, in fulfilment of the Elite's dastardly scheme? There were hardly any eye-witnesses to what actually happened after all, so the proposition would seem very plausible to me given all the circumstantial evidence. Along with the officer on duty on the Bridge at that time, First Officer William Murdoch and Quartermaster Hitchens plus Quartermaster George Rowe on the after-bridge, lookouts Frederick Fleet and Reginald Lee were the only other ones known to have personally witnessed the appalling events.

Of these five witnesses, only four survived, significantly all of them 'lower-class' people and placing undue pressure on four working-class people to keep quiet over a century ago, would have been a relatively simple task. First Officer Murdoch is perhaps significantly, said to have 'committed suicide' in the aftermath of the collision whilst the ship was being abandoned, however there is no solid evidence available with which to corroborate this fact. Why would he do this? He has also been accused of shooting passengers before turning a gun on himself, something that his family and descendants have disputed vehemently ever since and so could there be a more sinister explanation for his demise along with that of Captain Smith? Down the years, suicide has always been a very convenient cover-story for many a silencing murder and in addition it is perhaps significant that none of the 'three stooges', Guggenheim, Strauss and Astor survived to tell their stories either. How easy would it have been under the circumstances and in the post-collision mayhem and confusion, for a paid assassin to dispose of Messrs Smith, Murdoch, Guggenheim, Strauss and Astor to make absolutely certain that none of them escaped their planned fates against all the odds?

Thus, these wealthy men, who opposed the formation of the execrable Federal Reserve System (granted, due to their own conflicting financial interests and not out of any great concern for the plight of the masses) were disposed of, along with the 'collateral damage' of fifteen hundred other innocents. This effectively eliminated the major opposition, who due to their own large, personal fortunes amounting to hundreds of billions of dollars at today's values, and great influence could not have been 'bought' or unduly influenced in the same way that the politicians of Congress were.

"The Titanic was sunk deliberately to get rid of senior financiers who were opposed to the taking over of the Federal Reserve Board." Benjamin Fulford, October 2011

But would these people murder so many in cold-blood simply for financial gain? Unfortunately this is just one small example among many, many others too numerous to mention. As I state elsewhere in various chapters of this book, these multi-generational mass-murderers routinely kill and even commit genocide to maintain their own status, wealth and positions of power and promote their own agenda. Any person or persons capable of sacrificing billions of people's health, wealth and prosperity for generations to come, in a scheme to gain financial control of the world for themselves, would stop at nothing at all to achieve their own selfish ends. Murdering a ship-full of innocent passengers including women and children simply for financial gain in the form of a fraudulent insurance payout, would to my mind make them more than capable of sinking the same ship of people just to dispose of three powerful enemies who stand in the way of their nefarious ambitions. To them it is nothing personal, just 'business'. Where have we heard that before? The presence of both motives indeed, I believe, makes the scenario doubly plausible.

In December 1913, the Federal Reserve System thus came into being without serious opposition in the United States and very shortly afterwards, the Elite had accrued sufficient funding through the despicable methods of the Federal Reserve Bank to move to the next phase of their plan and start World War I...

World War I

"Wars are the best way of uniting slaves. They'll fight to the death to protect their slave master so that they can go back to being slaves." Aloysius James Fozdyke (probably a pseudonym), Elite, Illuminati insider, 20th January 2011

The Prelude

World War I was by no means an accident of history, a conflagration ignited by the spark of the assassination of Archduke Franz Ferdinand of Austria-Hungary, as we are all told and taught in our controlled educational establishments and peddled through the endless 'semi-factual' documentaries and false histories emanating from the hugely corrupt and controlled mainstream media. In fact WWI along with WWII was in the planning at least twenty years previously and possibly sooner.

World War I was originally contrived against Germany for one reason only; it stood guilty of being exceptionally economically successful, thus depriving British Royal and Elite commercial interests of profits they regarded as theirs alone. It had also built up a large, powerful army and navy and a strong economy with trade links worldwide. A mere 80 years previously, Germany consisted of around 300 small city-states, principalities and dukedoms and between the times of Napoleon and Bismarck, they were consolidated into one state, becoming in the span of 50 years, one of the world's great powers. Its naval strength equalled that of Britain and German commerce was conducting business world-wide and was gradually beginning to dominate commercial markets due to its extreme efficiency and therefore cost-effectiveness. Obviously this was not in the best interests of the long-established Western powers and the corporate interests of the British Empire, so a conspiracy was hatched between British, French and Russian Elites to eliminate Germany as a commercial competitor. Furthermore it could quite legitimately be argued that the war was a great opportunity for the Elite powers-that-be to destroy the existing status quo in order to re-shape the world to their own advantage. This is precisely what transpired.

In fact, I would challenge any contemporary, mainstream historian in the world to formulate a coherent, valid reason as to why at that time, those three countries would otherwise illegally decide to eradicate Germany from the political map.

On the 28th June 1914, Archduke Franz Ferdinand of Austro-Hungary and his wife were assassinated by four members of the *Black Hand*, led by an idealistic, but misguided youth by the name of Gavril Princip. The *Black Hand* was a Serbian secret society with strong links to the Elite via Freemasonry, in Sarajevo, Bosnia. The organisation was formed several years earlier as *'The Order of Death'* and in early 1914 some of its senior members had met with French Grand Orient Freemasons in Toulouse, France to plan the assassination, this having been calculated to be the most likely-to-succeed and practical method to bring about the 'Great War', as it was referred to at the time.

Franz Ferdinand's death duly set in motion a pre-planned chain of events as treaties were invoked and countries took their respective sides, resulting five weeks later in the world being thrown into turmoil as the Elite's largely conscripted armies prepared to face each other on the battlefields of Europe to act out yet another deadly game initiated by the Elite for their own devious ends.

After two years of indescribable carnage and bloodshed, by the end of the summer of 1916, Germany had won the war. Not in any metaphorical sense, but had *actually* won it. The German U-boats, which were a very potent weapon, ruthlessly 'ruled' the Atlantic Ocean and the Mediterranean Sea and Great Britain stood virtually alone with armaments almost exhausted and around one week's food supply and after that, just humiliating defeat and starvation to contemplate. The Battle of the Somme had ended in unmitigated disaster for Britain having lost more than one million men, either dead or injured and the French army had just mutinied having lost 600,000 men in the defence of Verdun on the Somme. The Russian army was retreating; they were out of the war and returning home as revolution was in the air and discipline among the troops had almost completely disintegrated. In addition to this, the Italian army had collapsed altogether and Britain was ready to capitulate, having no real choice in the matter any longer.

However, even though not a single enemy combatant had set one foot in its territory, Germany offered Britain and France peace terms. Britain was offered a generous negotiated peace on what is referred to in law as a 'status-quo-ante' basis, meaning 'everything reverts to exactly as it was before.' And so in the autumn (fall) of 1916 Britain was preparing to adopt this option as to be frank, it had no choice. It was in a situation where it had to either accept the negotiated peace that Germany was magnanimously offering or continue with the war and be annihilated.

In the meantime, the German Zionists who also represented the Zionists from Eastern Europe approached the British War Cabinet and to cut a very long story short, they offered their backing and support to Britain on the basis that they believed that is was possible, with their connivance, to contrive the entry of the United States into the fray as an ally of the British and French and this action would then be the decisive move that would almost certainly result in defeat for Germany.

The price required in return for this generous offer from the Zionists was a guarantee from Britain that they would be offered Palestine as the long-awaited Jewish 'homeland' after the war was won.

Obviously Britain had no right to promise Palestine to anyone and it is absolutely absurd that Great Britain, who never had any connection, any interest in or any rights to Palestine, should offer it as payment to the Zionists for bringing the United States into the war. However, make that promise they most certainly did, in October of 1916 (as confirmed by the Balfour Declaration of 1917) and shortly after that promise, the United States, which was ironically almost totally pro-German, entered the war as Britain's ally.

The 'Balfour Declaration':

"Foreign Office, November 2nd, 1917

Dear Lord Rothschild

I have much pleasure in conveying to you on behalf of His Majesty's government, the following declaration of sympathy with Jewish Zionist aspirations which has been submitted to, and approved, by the Cabinet:

His Majesty's Government view with favour the establishment in Palestine of a national home for the Jewish people, and will use their best endeavours to facilitate the achievement of this object, it being clearly understood that nothing shall be done which may prejudice the civil and religious rights of existing non-Jewish communities in Palestine or the rights and political status enjoyed by Jews in any other country.

I should be grateful if you would bring this declaration to the knowledge of the Zionist Federation.

Yours,
Arthur James Balfour"

This declaration in my view is comparable to Spain promising Ireland to China, but only using the values that we think we know to be true. In reality, all countries and their borders are entirely false constructs and the Elite world is entirely borderless. They do not regard themselves as belonging to any specific country, religion or belief system – except of course, their own and so making this strange promise is not as odd as it tends to appear at first sight.

At this time, the United States was almost totally pro-German and as is the case today, the newspapers were controlled by Zionists, the bankers were Zionists, all the media of mass communications were controlled by Zionists; and they, the Zionists, were pro-German. They were pro-German because many of them were ethnic German and also they, in line with the Rothschilds agenda emanating from the previous century and in retaliation for the Russian royal family's previous treachery, wanted Germany to destroy the Russian Czar, Nicholas II and the Romanov dynasty. The Rothschild Zionists also had other plans in store for Russia in the form of the coming 'communist' revolution. The German Zionist bankers, such as Kuhn Loeb and other big banking organisations in the United States refused to finance France or England as these two powers were allied with Russia, but they poured money into Germany and they fought beside Germany against Russia, trying to crush the Czarist regime that they saw as a barrier to their plans for the revolution to come.

Indeed these were the same Zionists, that when they saw the possibility of obtaining Palestine as a Jewish homeland, approached the British government and they made the aforementioned pact. Once the plan was agreed to, the world immediately changed, almost overnight in fact. Whereas previously most, if not all American newspapers had been pro-German, wildly exaggerating the difficulties that Germany was experiencing in fighting Great Britain commercially and in other respects, suddenly the Germans were depicted as the enemy. They were now 'criminals' and 'Huns'. They were raping and shooting Red Cross nurses and they were murdering pregnant women and babies, as is the manner in which all propaganda operates. Of course, very shortly after that, the Elite puppet President Woodrow Wilson declared war on Germany and joined the war on the side of Britain and France.

The Zionists in London had sent cables to the United States, to Justice Brandeis a presidential political advisor and friend, asking him to influence Wilson. The United States had absolutely no right or reasons to be involved in a European conflict other than those contrived. America was duped and subtly cajoled into taking-part simply so that the Zionists of the world could acquire Palestine and meanwhile the people of the United States were never told and never knew the real reasons that they entered World War I. President Wilson was directly involved in the deceptions and formally sanctioned the US participation in the war in a secret agreement with Britain on 9th March 1916. We are only aware of this agreement today because the agreement was leaked and confirmed by Sir Edward Grey, Ambassador Walter Hines Page, C. Hartley Grattan, and Colonel Edward Mandel House.

The rest of the story is well-known. America duly joined in the conflict and its superior numbers soon overwhelmed German resistance all along the 400 mile-long *Maginot* line, the line of fortifications running from the English Channel to the Alps, known to the Germans as the 'Western Front'. Apart from a brief, final rally in the autumn of 1918, the German forces were well beaten, surrendered unconditionally and the Armistice was duly signed which ended the war on the 11th November 1918 at 11.00am thus bringing to an end four years of horrific, unspeakable bloodshed. Now all that remained was the Treaty of Versailles, which the Germans believed would be a fair and just settlement of post-war reparations for a nation that had been absolutely shattered beyond the point of recognition, by the privations and horrors of the war. In this they were to be bitterly disappointed. In fact the terms of the treaty were so inordinately destructive to the German nation that it not only lost much of its territory but it did not actually make the final reparations payment until 2009! This in fact led directly to the economic conditions that set the scene for the rise of Hitler and ultimately to World War II. All as pre-planned, of course.

The Sinking of the Lusitania

One of the overt, primary catalysts for the entry of America into the 1914-18 war was also the sinking of the liner *Lusitania* by a German U-Boat off the southern coast of Ireland in 1915. The *Lusitania* was carrying hundreds of wealthy American passengers, but the significant load carried by the liner was not necessarily the passengers on this occasion. Deliberately, but unknown to most on board, *Lusitania* was illegally carrying a large cache of armaments bound for the battlefields of Europe.

It is now known for certain that Winston Churchill and Woodrow Wilson were complicit in an operation financed by the major Zionist banking houses, arranging for the shipment of weapons on board *Lusitania* in May of 1915. The *Lusitania* luxury ocean liner was owned by the Cunard Line Shipping Company and officially part of the British auxiliary navy. The ship's owners were paid £218,000 per year. As an auxiliary naval ship, *Lusitania* was under orders from the British Admiralty to ram any German ship seeking to inspect her cargo. Also, notably in 1915, it was against US law to place weapons on a passenger ship traveling to England or Germany.

Three German spies attempted to confirm that the so-called '90 tons of unrefrigerated butter' destined for a British naval base were weapons and ammunition. The spies were detained on the ship, but the weapons loaded onto *Lusitania* were seen by a group of German immigrant dock workers and reported to the German embassy. In order to warn Americans about the weapons shipment, the Imperial German Embassy attempted to place an advertisement in 50 East Coast newspapers. The ads were due to be printed on the 22nd April 1915, but the US State Department blocked all the ads except one which somehow escaped the net.

George Viereck, the man who placed the ads for the embassy, protested to the State Department on the 26th April 1915 that the ads were blocked. Viereck met with US Secretary of State, William Jennings Bryan and produced copies of *Lusitania*'s supplementary manifests. Bryan, impressed by the evidence that *Lusitania* had carried weapons, cleared publication of the warning but someone more powerful than the Secretary of State, most likely Colonel Mandel House or President Wilson, overruled Bryan.

Nonetheless, one ad slipped past the State Department censorship. The single advertisement that slipped past the government censors appeared in the Des Moines Register (below)

The warning read:

"NOTICE! Travellers intending to embark on the Atlantic voyage are reminded that a state of war exists between Germany and her allies and Great Britain and her allies; that the zone of war includes the waters adjacent to the British Isles; that, in accordance with formal notice given by the Imperial German Government, vessels flying the flag of Great Britain, or any of her allies, are liable to destruction in those waters and that travellers sailing in the war zone on ships of Great Britain or her allies do so at their own risk. IMPERIAL GERMAN EMBASSY WASHINGTON, D.C., APRIL 22, 1915."

Captain Dow, the *Lusitania's* captain immediately before the current incumbent, Captain Turner, resigned on the 8th March 1915 because he was no longer willing *'to carry the responsibility of mixing passengers with munitions or contraband.'* Captain Dow had a 'near miss' just two days earlier and was aware that the rules of naval warfare had changed in October 1914 when Churchill issued orders that British merchant ships with munitions or contraband must ram U-boats. Prior to this change by Churchill, both England and Germany adhered to Cruiser Rules. The Cruiser Rules enabled crews and passengers to escape in lifeboats before being fired on but the new Churchill ram rules meant that the German U-boats could no longer surface to issue a warning and fire while submerged. Churchill explained this ruthlessness thus:

"The first British countermove, made on my responsibility...was to deter the Germans from surface attack. The submerged U-boat had to rely increasingly on underwater attack and thus ran the greater risk of mistaking neutral for British ships and of drowning neutral crews and thus embroiling Germany with other Great Powers."

The above combined with the next Churchill quote speaks volumes about what really happened and why.

"There are many kinds of manoeuvres in war... There are manoeuvres in time, in diplomacy, in mechanics, in psychology; all of which are removed from the battlefield, but react often decisively upon it... The manoeuvre which brings an ally into the field is as serviceable as that which wins a great battle."

On the 7th May 1915, *Lusitania* slowed to 75% speed hoping the English escort vessel *Juno* would arrive. Unknown to Captain Turner, Winston Churchill had ordered *Juno* to return to port and so Churchill's order left *Lusitania* alone and unprotected in an area known to be swarming with U boats. To put this in perspective, Britain had deciphered the German communications code in December 1914 and therefore the level of detail known by the British Admiralty was so precise that even U boat numbers and general locations were known. For example, the British Admiralty knew U-30 left the area for Germany on the 4th May and the U-27 left the area because of jammed bow planes.

In a 1981 book, 'Seven Days to Disaster: The Sinking of the Lusitania', by Des Hickey and Gus Smith, they reported that one of the crewmen on the U-20 responsible for passing the order to fire to the torpedo room was Charles Voegele. Voegele refused to kill civilians of a neutral country, and upon returning to Germany was court-martialled and imprisoned for three years. One torpedo was fired on the 7th May and the warhead's 300 pounds of explosives detonated upon contact with *Lusitania*. The *Lusitania*'s Captain Turner reported the first explosion sounded 'like a heavy door being slammed shut' and was followed by a much larger explosion that rocked the ship. Turner wrote in the log 'an unusually heavy detonation'. *Lusitania* sank 15-18 minutes later with a huge loss of life.

On the 28th May 1915, Germany's official response to the U.S. government's protest states the German government has no intention of attacking US vessels which are not guilty of hostile acts. The Imperial German government wrote that *Lusitania*...

"...was one of the largest and fastest English commerce steamers, constructed with government funds as auxiliary cruisers, and is expressly included in the navy list published by the British Admiralty. It is, moreover, known to the Imperial government from reliable information furnished by its officials and neutral passengers that for some time practically all the more valuable English merchant vessels have been provided with guns, ammunition and other weapons, and reinforced with a crew specially practiced in manning guns. According to reports at hand here, the Lusitania when she left New York undoubtedly had guns on board which were mounted under decks and masked."

The official letter from the German government also spells out that *Lusitania* had 5,400 cases of ammunition that would be used to kill German soldiers. An exceptionally noteworthy section of the letter states that the British merchant marine ships received secret instruction in February by the British Admiralty to seek protection behind neutral flags and when so disguised, attack German submarines by ramming them. The German official response that war contraband was on board explains the second explosion.

The Elite banking families involved and Britain's leaders, even a century later, still fear the negative repercussions from Americans when they learn they were tricked into World War I.

For decades, the British and American governments have denied that there were weapons on *Lusitania* and the site was declared a protected wreck site, denying diver access. To further frustrate the ability to determine what *Lusitania* had really carried, since 1946 the Royal Navy has repeatedly dropped depth charges on top of *Lusitania*, using the site for target practice. In 1968, in further attempts to keep the truth hidden, the British Secret Service unsuccessfully attempted to buy the salvage rights to *Lusitania*.

In 2003 the then British Prime Minister Tony Blair, in a deliberate act of deceit and treachery designed to protect the version of history promoted by his puppet masters, ordered the destruction of government documents containing absolute proof that *Lusitania* was a covert munitions carrier. This is a classic example of one small attempt to re-write history or more accurately, to protect a false version of history.

While the British government aggressively worked to distort the truth, weapons were confirmed in July 2006 when Victor Quirke of the Cork Sub Aqua Club found 15,000 rounds of .303 bullets in the bow section of the ship. And on the 2nd April 2007, Cyber Diver News Network reported that the American owner of the *Lusitania* wreck, F. Gregg Bemis, Jr., had won the case to conduct salvage operations almost a century after the sinking. The British Arts and Heritage Ministry did not protest the use of the Lusitania as target practice for British depth charges but did help 'respect the sanctity of the site' by opposing salvage operations.

Authors have written for many years that 1,201 people were sacrificed on *Lusitania* to create a reason for the US to enter World War I. Historian Howard Zinn wrote in 'A People's History of the United States', that *Lusitania* carried 1,248 cases of 3-inch shells, 4,927 boxes of cartridges (1,000 rounds in each box), and 2,000 more cases of small-arms ammunition. Colin Simpson claims that 'Churchill conspired to put the Lusitania in danger with the hope of sparking an incident to bring America into World War I' and historian Patrick Beesley supports Simpson's assertion. Christopher Hitchens' book, 'Blood Class and Nostalgia', further implicates First Lord of the Admiralty, Winston Churchill in a deliberate action to pull America into World War I. History professor Ralph Raico and senior scholar of the Ludwig von Mises Institute notes that Churchill wrote the week prior to *Lusitania* sinking, that it was 'most important to attract neutral shipping to our shores, in the hopes especially of embroiling the United States with Germany'.

Winston Churchill did indeed say and do many things to drag America into World War I. He attempted to mislead both the British and American public that the sinking of *Lusitania* was premeditated. Churchill did this for several reasons including to distract people from the reports that the *Juno* destroyer protection had been deliberately removed. He attributed the lack of destroyer protection as being confused with internal disputes within the Admiralty about a bumbled Gallipoli campaign in the Ottoman Empire. His *Lusitania* war propaganda also included misinforming the public that multiple torpedoes were fired to explain how the ship sunk in 18 minutes and further fuel hatred for the German people.

Berlin announced on the 31st January, 1917 that its submarines would sink all ships aiding Britain. This announcement, combined with the *Lusitania* sinking and the British Intelligence service manufactured bombshell in the form of a telegram from German Foreign Minister Arthur Zimmerman to the German Minister to offering Mexico money to attack the U.S. ultimately proved successful and on 6th April 1917 the U.S. did finally declare war on Germany.

"If people really knew the truth, the war would be stopped tomorrow. But of course they don't know, and can't know." David Lloyd George, Britain's Prime Minister during the First World War, to C.P. Scott, editor of the Manchester Guardian, December 1917

The Treaty of Versailles

The treaty that officially ended WWI was the Treaty of Versailles in 1919. This is the reason why the dates of this war are sometimes recorded as 1914-19. Although it has to be said that it has now been recently surreptitiously announced (2009) that WWI has now 'officially' ended due to Germany's final reparation payment having been made, 90 years after the event.

Several interesting personalities attended these meetings. In the British delegation was the British economist John Maynard Keynes and representing the American banking interests was Paul Warburg, the Chairman of the Federal Reserve. His brother Max, the head of the German banking firm of M.M. Warburg and Company, of Hamburg, Germany and who was not only in charge of Germany's finances but was a leader of the German espionage network, was there as a representative of the German government. Do we need any more proof of collusion between the two sides to achieve maximum impact on the welfare of ordinary Germans?

The Treaty was written to end the war, but another delegate to the conference, Lord Curzon of England, the British Foreign Secretary, saw through what the actual intent was and said: *"This is no peace; this is only a truce for twenty years."* Lord Curzon felt that the terms of the Treaty were setting the stage for a second world war and what is even more interesting; he had correctly predicted the year it would start as 1939.

One of the major tenets of the Treaty specified swingeing war reparations to be paid to the victorious nations by the German government. It was this factor alone that precipitated three events.

The 'hyperinflation' of the German Mark between 1920 and 1923, causing untold suffering to the ordinary German people which also led to the virtual destruction of the middle classes and last but by no means least, facilitated the rise to power of someone who would rightly or wrongly be seen as a saviour, a messiah to the German people, Adolf Hitler.

Thus were deliberately sown the seeds of World War II, setting in motion an unstoppable chain of events that would eventually lead to the establishment of the Jewish homeland and to all the complex, inter-related actions that have shaped the world of the early twenty-first century, in which we all live today.

The extent of the war reparations were decided upon by the Elite stooge John Foster Dulles, one of the founders of the Council on Foreign Relations, and later the Secretary of State to President Dwight D. Eisenhower.

Even Keynes himself, not known for his liberal views, was so disturbed by the extent to which the Treaty had been slanted towards the impossibility of fulfilling the terms and therefore presaging the destruction of Germany (the object of the war in the first place) that he wrote, *"The peace is outrageous and impossible and can bring nothing but misfortune behind it"*.

In addition to penning the Treaty of Versailles, the victors also proposed and propounded the Charter of the League of Nations, ratified on the 10th January 1920, and signed by President Wilson for the American government. Wilson brought the treaty back to the United States and requested that the Senate ratify it. The Senate, for once remembering George Washington's advice to avoid foreign entanglements and reflecting the views of the American people who did not wish to enter the League, refused to ratify the treaty.

With the benefit of hindsight it has become apparent that Wilson intended to head the planned world government it was hoped to bring along by the imposition of the League of Nations upon the world. Unsurprisingly he was devastated when the Treaty was not ratified as he fully expected to become the first President of the World, only to have it taken away by the actions of the Senate of the United States. Of course, we are still to this day awaiting the dawn of world government but the Elite are nothing if not patient and they firmly believe that their efforts in this direction will be fully rewarded before much more time has elapsed, although they are not quite 'counting their chickens' just yet...

"As the World plummets into a contrived financial meltdown, those who believe themselves to be the rightful rulers of a planetary fiefdom are convinced that they have a very short window of opportunity to establish their One World Government. Their vision is for total control of all planetary resources including human resources, which will be reduced to the chosen 500,000,000. However, things are not going entirely to plan. Obama's mentor, Zbigniew Brzezinski recently identified 'the rapid political awakening amongst the masses' as the biggest obstacle to establishing a One World Government. In 1970 Brzezinski observed that the challenge for Western governments will be to keep their people locked into consumerist materialism ... preventing them from realising who they truly are!" Ian R Crane, geo-political researcher, February 2011*

One of the by-products of this devastating conflict was to provide an unparalleled opportunity for the Elite families to generate huge profits at the expense of governments and thus the public in the form of war supplies and armaments. These super-rich families, not only desired the war to be won, but they made sure that the victory was expensive to the common taxpayers and beneficial to their own finances. Indeed, one of the families who reaped the exorbitant profits were our old friends, the Rockefellers, who were for obvious reasons, very eager for the United States to enter World War I and who made more than $200m from the conflict which incidentally is $16bn in today's values.

However, support for the League of Nations continued. The Grand Orient Lodge of Freemasonry of France was one which advised all of its members, *"It is the duty of universal Freemasonry to give its full support to the League of Nations...."* Predictably, the League of Nations became a major issue during the Presidential election of 1920 when the Republican candidate Warren G. Harding was on record as opposing the League and further attempts to ratify the charter, saying, *"It will avail nothing to discuss in detail the League covenant, which was conceived for world super-government In the existing League of Nations, world governing with its super-powers, this Republic will have no part."*

He was opposed in the Republican primaries by General Leonard Wood, one of the Republican 'hawks', who was backed by a powerful group of rich men who hoped to install a military man in the White House. The American people, once again manifesting their disapproval of the League, voted for Harding as evidence of that distrust and concern and Harding beat the opposition by a greater margin than did President Wilson during the election of 1916. Wilson only managed to get fifty-two percent of the vote, whilst Harding achieved sixty-four percent.

Harding was a supporter of William Howard Taft, the President who opposed the bankers and their Federal Reserve Bill. After his election, he named Harry M. Daugherty, Taft's campaign manager, as his Attorney General. His other Cabinet appointments were not as wise however, as he 'inexplicably' surrounded himself with men representing the oil industry. His chosen Secretary of State was Charles Evans Hughes, an attorney of Standard Oil; his Secretary of the Treasury was Andrew

Mellon, owner of Gulf Oil; his Postmaster General was Will Hays, an attorney for Sinclair Oil; and his Secretary of the Interior was Albert Fall, a protégé of the oil men.

It was the aptly named Fall, who was indeed to be Harding's downfall as he later accepted a bribe from Harry Sinclair in exchange for a lease of the Navy's oil reserves in Teapot Dome, Wyoming. There are many who believe that the scandal was intended to discredit the Harding administration in an attempt to remove him from office for two very important reasons. Harding was consistently vocal against the League of Nations, and there was still a chance that its supporters could get the United States to join, as the League had survived the Senate's prior refusal to ratify the treaty and Attorney General Daugherty had been prosecuting the oil trusts under the Sherman anti-trust laws.

These activities did not please the oil interests who had created the Teapot Dome scandal. But Harding perhaps unsurprisingly as is often the case, unfortunately did not live to see the full repercussions of the artificial scandal, as he died on the 2nd August 1923, before the story completely surfaced. Indeed, there are many who believe that there were some who could not wait for the Teapot Dome scandal to remove President Harding and that he was poisoned as were several of his predecessors.

Nevertheless the oil barons allowed it to completely play its course as a warning to future Presidents of the United States not to oppose the oil interests or indeed any other powerful, vested, corporate interests and to date, with one or two notable exceptions, the warning has been generally heeded. Not many have chosen to contend with the true rulers of the United States – certainly not and lived to tell the tale anyway, eh Mr. Kennedy?

The League of Nations

The League, formed on the 28th June 1919, was a very early attempt to form a blueprint for 'One World Government', just as is its latter-day successor, the United Nations. Promoted under the banner of preventing future conflicts by virtue of the fact that all nations are part of the same 'club', both organisations have proved to be anything but benign.

The Elite gofer and 'fixer' Colonel Edward Mandell House planned the League as a ploy to coerce the United States into conceding its sovereignty to the organisation at the close of World War I. However, the US Senate refused to ratify America's entry into the League, resulting in Col. House's initiative towards world government being thwarted. Disappointed, but not beaten, House and his friends then formed the Council on Foreign Relations (CFR), whose purpose even from its inception was to destroy the freedom and independence of the United States and lead the nations into world government despite the failure of the attempt to achieve it through the

League of Nations. The control of that world government of course, was intended to be placed in the hands of House and his cohorts.

From its small beginnings in 1921, the CFR began to attract men of power and influence. In the late 1920s, important financing for the CFR came from the Rockefeller Foundation and the Carnegie Foundation and in 1940, at the invitation of President FD Roosevelt, members of the CFR gained domination over the State Department and much to the detriment of democracy in that erstwhile 'land of the free', they have maintained that domination ever since.

The Russian Revolution

So even before the outbreak of World War I, the Elite conspirators had a plan to carry-out Nathan Rothschild's vow of 1814 to destroy the Czar and also murder all possible royal heirs to the throne and it was planned to occur before the end of the war. The Bolsheviks were to be their chosen instruments in this particular plot.

The leaders of the Bolsheviks were Nicolai Lenin, Leon Trotsky and later Joseph Stalin but of course, those were not their true family names. Prior to the Revolution, their base was Switzerland and Trotsky's headquarters was on the lower East Side in New York, an area mainly inhabited by Russian-Jewish refugees. Both Lenin and Trotsky lived extremely well yet neither had a regular occupation and neither had any visible means of support, yet both always were well dressed and groomed, with plenty of cash at their disposal. From early in the year (1917), there were strange events taking place in New York. Night after night, Trotsky was at Jacob Schiff's palace-mansion and there were several gatherings of shady characters on the lower East Side, all of them Russian refugees, at Trotsky's headquarters and all were undertaking a comprehensive training-process that was completely shrouded in mystery. In fact, Schiff was discovered to be surreptitiously financing all of Trotsky's activities.

Eventually Trotsky disappeared with approximately 300 of his by now, well-trained thugs. Actually they were on a Schiff-chartered ship headed for a rendezvous with Lenin and his gang in Switzerland along with $20,000,000 in gold. This gold was provided by Schiff himself, to finance the Bolsheviks takeover of Russia. To celebrate Trotsky's arrival, Lenin gave a party at his Swiss hideaway which was attended by some of society's high flyers. Among them were the mysterious Colonel Edward Mandell House, Woodrow Wilson's mentor and more importantly, Schiff's special and confidential messenger. Other guests were the Warburg banksters of Germany, who were financing the Kaiser and in addition there were of course, the ubiquitous Rothschilds of London and Paris and also Josef Stalin who was at the time the head of a train and bank-robbing gang. He was even well-known as the 'Jesse James of the Urals'!

It is a matter of record that on the 3rd February 1917, US President Woodrow Wilson had broken off all diplomatic relations with Germany, therefore Warburg, Colonel House and the Rothschilds were strictly-speaking, enemies but of course Switzerland was a neutral country, as it always is in wars as it is the home of the financial backers of most conflicts. So it was natural that enemies could meet there, especially if they had some nefarious scheme in common.

However, Lenin's celebration was almost undone by an unforeseen incident when the Schiff-chartered ship on its way to Europe was intercepted and taken into custody by a British warship. But Schiff acted quickly and gave orders to President Wilson to demand that the British release the ship, with Trotsky, his thugs and the gold remaining intact. Wilson of course obeyed, as do all puppet politicians when given orders by the Elite who manoeuvred them into that position in the first place. In fact he threatened the British that if they refused to release the ship that the United States would not enter the war in April as he had faithfully promised a year earlier.

Fortunately for the whole sordid scheme, the British relented and allowed safe passage for the ship and Trotsky duly arrived in Switzerland and the Lenin party took place as scheduled, but they still faced what ordinarily would have been the insurmountable obstacle of getting the Lenin-Trotsky band of terrorists across the border into Russia. Fortuitously, Max Warburg, whom the Kaiser had made chief of the German Secret Police, was able through his position and contacts to ensure that all the perpetrators plus their loot were 'sealed' into railway freight-cars and made all the necessary arrangements for their secret entry into Russia. As they say, the rest is history. The revolution in Russia took place and all members of the royalty, the entire Romanov dynasty were murdered and the Bolsheviks had secured complete control of the country.

Can there be any further doubt that so-called communism, is an integral part of the Elite conspiracy for the enslavement of the entire world? Or even that communism is merely a weapon and fear-inducement to terrify the people of the whole world and that the conquest of Russia and the creation of communism was largely organised by Schiff and the other international banksters?

An almost incredible story perhaps, but in its support, many years later one of Randolph Hearst's newspapers published an interview with John Schiff, grandson of Jacob, in which Schiff confirmed the entire story and even named the figure that Jacob had contributed - $20,000,000. There is absolutely no dispute that communism was created by the Elite. In fact all records show that when Lenin and Trotsky engineered the subjugation of Russia, they operated as leaders of the 'Bolshevik' party. But 'Bolshevism' is a purely Russian word and the Elite knew that

'Bolshevism' could never be promulgated as an acceptable ideology to any but the Russian peoples. So in April 1918, Jacob Schiff sent Colonel House to Moscow with orders to Lenin, Trotsky and Stalin to change the name of their regime to the 'Communist Party' and to adopt the Karl Marx 'Communist Manifesto' as the constitution of the Communist Party. Lenin, Trotsky and Stalin concurred and so it came to pass that in 1918 the Communist party and the menace of communism was first brought to the attention of the world. This information is all confirmed in, and can be corroborated by 'Webster's Collegiate Dictionary, Fifth Edition'.

So, for the avoidance of doubt, communism was created by the Elite capitalists. Until 11th November 1918 and the end of World War I, the entire long-term plan of the conspirators had worked perfectly and all the major nations involved in the conflict, including the United States, were war-weary, devastated, and in mourning for their many dead. Peace was thus the great universal desire and so when it was proposed by Woodrow Wilson at the behest of his masters of course, to set-up a 'League of Nations' to ensure peace, all the great nations, with no Russian Czar to stand in their way this time, agreed instantly. All that is, but one, the United States. Ironically, the one country that Schiff and his co-conspirators least expected would be an obstacle and the fatal mistake made by the Elite was that when Schiff planted Wilson in the White House, it had naturally been assumed that they would have no problem with the United States.

However, Wilson had been 'sold' to the American people as a great humanitarian and there was every reason for the conspirators to have believed that he would have easily cajoled Congress into buying the 'League of Nations' hyperbole. But unfortunately for them, there was one man in the Senate in 1918 who 'saw through' the scheme, just as the Russian Czar did in 1814. He was a man of great political stature and very astute and was also highly-respected and trusted by all members of both houses of Congress and by the American people. His name was Henry Cabot Lodge and he completely exposed Wilson as the fraud that he most undoubtedly was and thus kept the United States out of the 'League of Nations'. As a result of this, the proposed stepping-stone to one world government was thwarted, for the time being and no further attempts were made to move the world down this route until after WWII and the advent of the 'United Nations'.

So, Communism facilitated by the Russian Revolution, was merely a fantasy to enable Capitalists to steal money from other Capitalists under the pretence of making a better world for the common man. How many millions of idealists have devoted their lives to this farce? And worse still, how many millions died in World War II when the same Elite banksters financed Hitler simply to keep Stalin in check? Then of course there are the literally trillions of dollars spent on weapons during the Cold War – all of which swelled the coffers of the Elite to bursting-point and yet still they were not satisfied. Also consider how little we in the West hear of Stalin's or Mao's atrocities in the name of 'Communism' compared to those of Hitler in supposedly opposing it.

The 1918 'Spanish Influenza' Pandemic

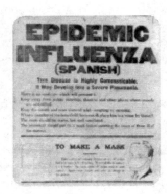

The so-called 'Spanish Flu' pandemic, responsible for the deaths of around 50 million people worldwide, in 1918/19, was not 'flu' at all, it was a simple, easily treatable chest infection. The fledgling 'wonder-drug' aspirin played a significant role in all those eminently preventable deaths, but the real question is this; was the pandemic a case of pharmaceutical genocide perpetrated by the Elite to further their stated population-reduction agenda or was it simply a case of misdiagnosis and/or prescription error, compounded by a huge corporation's desperation to put profits before people? I will let the reader decide for themselves. Here are the facts...

In 1899 aspirin was first produced and was patented by the German pharmaceutical company Farbenfabriken Bayer in 1900. Bayer is still one of the 'Big Pharma' companies (as Bayer AG) today. In the first decade of the 20th century its strenuous worldwide marketing efforts had left few places in the civilised world lacking aspirin. In the United States, Bayer's giant factory produced aspirin under American management and after Bayer executives were charged with violating the 'Trading with the Enemies' Act in August 1918, copious numbers of advertisements were produced that re-encouraged the lost confidence in aspirin.

The world has believed for almost a century that a new and virulent 'flu' virus appeared from nowhere and killed millions worldwide in 1918. However, two reports, one published in 2008 and the second in 2009, have now laid that particular myth to rest for good.

The first report came as a press release on 19th August 2008, from the American National Institute of Allergy and Infectious Diseases (NIAID)...

"Bacteriologic and histopathologic results from published autopsy series clearly and consistently implicated secondary bacterial pneumonia caused by common upper respiratory tract bacteria in most influenza fatalities. People were killed by common

bacteria found in the upper respiratory tract. The 20 to 40 million deaths worldwide from the great 1918 Influenza Pandemic were NOT due to 'flu' at all or even a virus, but to pneumonia caused by massive bacterial infection."

The NIAID press release did not however, address the actual cause of the bacterial infections, but further, follow-up research by Dr. Karen Starko certainly did. This research is quite categorical in its implication of aspirin as the real culprit, dovetailing with the NIAID research on pneumonia from massive bacterial infection and goes further in also explaining the extremely rapid deaths in young people.

Mortality was caused in this instance by two overlapping syndromes: an early, severe acute respiratory distress condition, which was estimated to have caused 10%-15% of deaths and a subsequent, aggressive bacterial pneumonia 'super-infection', which was present in the majority of deaths.

In examining reports of those who died, two distinct groups were discovered to be apparent, based on a very distinctive time-frame from health to death:

1. People who died of pneumonia from a bacterial infection became sick and deteriorated at varying rates from there to death, and...

2. People who died so astoundingly fast that those deaths became a classic part of the frightening legend of the 1918 'flu' – people perfectly well in the morning and dead before the afternoon was out.

It has subsequently been discovered that In both groups, ***aspirin was the likely cause.***

In the case of the first group, pneumonia, aspirin suppresses the immune system, allowing bacterial infections to take hold. Doctors at the time were relating pneumonias to the use of aspirin.

One contemporary doctor, Dudley Williams of Rhode Island, reported that he did not lose a single case of influenza and that the death-rate of his patients from pneumonia was 2.1%. The salicylates, including aspirin and quinine, were almost the sole treatments given by most doctors and it was quite common to hear them speaking of losing 60% of their pneumonia patients.

Aspirin directly or indirectly was the cause of the loss of more lives than was the influenza itself. Aspirin caused harm in two ways. Firstly, its indirect action derived from the fact that aspirin was taken until prostration resulted and the patient developed pneumonia. And for the second group which died so precipitously, their symptoms are consistent with aspirin overdose and with extraordinarily rapid deaths from it.

Another report noted that:

"The disease was a veritable plague. The extraordinary toxicity, the marked prostration, the extreme cyanosis and the rapidity of development stamp this disease as a distinct clinical entity heretofore not fully described. Salicylate toxicity is often overlooked because another condition is present, the dose is thought to be trivial and the symptoms (hyperventilation, vomiting, sweating, headache, drowsiness, confusion, dyspnoea, excitement, epistaxis, vertigo, pulmonary oedema and haemorrhage) are nonspecific. In 1918, differentiating progressive salicylate intoxication from infection pathologically or clinically, the dyspnoea lasts from a few hours to a day followed by respiratory failure, circulatory collapse, convulsions, and death."

To summarise, just before the 1918 death spike, the widespread use of aspirin was still in its infancy and was unfortunately being recommended in doses now known to be potentially toxic and to cause pulmonary oedema and may therefore have contributed to the overall pandemic mortality. Young adult mortality may be explained by their willingness to use the new, recommended therapy and the presence of youth in regimented treatment settings. The lower mortality of children may be a result of less aspirin use. The most influential source of paediatric medicine in 1918 recommended hydrotherapy for fever, not salicylate; however, its 1920 edition condemned the practice of giving 'coal tar products' ie. pharmaceuticals, in full doses for the reduction of fever. Varying aspirin use may also have contributed to the marked differences in mortality between cities and even between military bases.

In February 1917, Bayer lost its American patent on aspirin, opening-up a lucrative drug market to many manufacturers. Bayer fought back with a sustained advertising campaign, emphasising its own version of the brand's purity just as the epidemic was reaching its peak. The New York Times said;

"Aspirin packages were produced containing no warnings about toxicity and few instructions about use. In the fall [autumn] of 1918, facing a widespread deadly disease with no known cure, the surgeon general and the United States Navy recommended aspirin as a symptomatic treatment and the military bought large quantities of the drug. The Journal of the American Medical Association suggested a dose of 1,000 milligrams every three hours, the equivalent of almost 25 standard 325-milligram aspirin tablets in 24 hours. This is about twice the daily dosage generally considered safe today."

Dr. Karen Starko's research clearly demonstrated that... *"Aspirin advertisements in August 1918 and a series of official recommendations for aspirin in September and early October immediately preceded the death spike of October 1918. The number of deaths in the USA increased steeply, peaking first in the Navy in late September, then in the Army in early October and finally in the general population in late October."*

One single sentence in her work, stands-out as being extremely significant in my view: *"Homeopaths, who thought aspirin was a poison, claimed few deaths."*

That sentence alone speaks volumes about the millions of deaths caused by Bayer and the pharmaceutical industry of the day, as indeed it does today. Homeopathy threatened pharmaceutical industry profits (as it also does to this day – hence the massive propaganda campaign against natural remedies) and worse, the homeopathic doctors criticised coal-tar based synthetic drugs in general, the very basis of the pharmaceutical industry. Aspirin and the other coal-tar products are condemned as causing great numbers of unnecessary deaths and the omnipresent aspirin is the most pernicious drug of all. Its deceptive malignancy is partly concealed by its fast pain-relieving quality. In several instances, aspirin weakened the heart, depressed the vital forces, increased the mortality in mild cases and made convalescence slower. In all cases it masked the symptoms and rendered immeasurably more difficult the selection of the correct curative remedy. Apparently aspirin bears no curative relation to any disease and strictly speaking it ought to be removed from sale as unsafe. The alleged blood-thinning capability of aspirin, meaning that it is in widespread use for heart-attack patients, is also grossly over-stated. Whilst aspirin does not actually thin the blood, it does in fact inhibit the clotting process. However this truth is completely mis-represented by all producers of aspirin in order to maintain the huge annual profits engendered by this silent killer. Aspirin is widely thought to be directly responsible for at least 6000 deaths each year in the USA alone, not all through misuse or from incorrect dosages.

A disturbing side-effect of aspirin is also that it causes the lining of the stomach and intestinal walls to break-down after prolonged use, leading to irreparable tissue damage and the severe degradation and weakening of the digestive tract. Doctors today still advise angina and heart-attack sufferers to take an aspirin every day in complete and utter disregard of this fact. My own mother who recently passed-away had suffered with angina for twenty years and completely unknown to the rest of the family until shortly before her death from a ruptured colon, had been taking two aspirins a day for that entire time period – all under her 'ignorant' doctor's directives. Incidentally this is the same doctor that currently prescribes a never-ending regimen of sixteen different drugs for my father. My mother was sadly one of the hundreds of thousands of victims of doctor 'error', each year in the western world. But when one considers how dangerous most 'legal' drugs are, then these figures are actually rather unsurprising.

But back to the main thrust of the story. Perhaps the most shocking aspect of it however, is that using only natural (thus un-patentable) substances, homeopaths saved the lives of almost everyone who turned to them during the 1918 massacre of innocents, meaning in effect that millions died for no reason at all if corporate greed and criminal recklessness is excluded. This also threatened to expose the fact that the new coal-tar based synthetic drugs (derived of course from Big Oil), the basis for huge investment, were in fact disastrous medically – and that had to be prevented at all costs.

In 1918, The Rockefeller Foundation (shortly afterwards inextricably connected to Bayer) used the Spanish flu epidemic and the media (that it already controlled by this time) to start a witch-hunt on all forms of medicine that were not covered by its patents, the full force of which still continues and is being felt, to this day.

"The Rockefeller Foundation was the front organization for a new global business venture .... This new venture was called the pharmaceutical investment business. Donations from the Rockefeller Foundation went only to medical schools and hospitals, which had become missionaries of patented pharmaceutical drugs, developed by a new breed of companies that manufactured patented, synthetic drugs." From 'Rockefeller Medicine Men' by Richard Brown.

Also, from the same source; *"These newly discovered natural molecules had only one disadvantage: they were non-patentable. Thus, already in its first decades of existence, the pharmaceutical investment business faced a mortal threat. Vitamins and other micro-nutrients promoted as public health programmes would have prohibited the development of any sizable investment business based on patented synthetic drugs. The elimination of this unwanted competition from micronutrients and other natural therapies became a question of survival for the young pharmaceutical investment business.*

To promote public acceptance of his 'new medicine' as the philanthropic umbrella of the newly created pharmaceutical investment industry with patented drugs, the Rockefeller-controlled media used the Spanish flu epidemic of 1918, to start a campaign against all forms of non-patented medicine and discredit them as 'unscientific'. Within the next 15 years, essentially all medical schools in the US, all influential hospitals and, most significantly, the 'American Medical Association' became part of this strategy to align the entire health care sector under the control of the pharmaceutical investment business."

This witch-hunt, with Bayer in a leading role, has a long and violent history and continues today whereby Big Pharma is now resorting to draconian measures, with the banning of all herbal remedies across the EU, commencing April 2011, with the attempt to criminalise homeopaths and all natural practitioners including midwives, with the banning of IV vitamin C because it is a powerfully effective yet gentle treatment for cancer, in December 2010 and a plan in Australia to ban nature itself.

Given Big Pharma's epic battle against nature, suppressing the truth of what happened during 1918 and the pharmaceutical industry deliberately killing millions in the name of obscene profits, natural healing becomes even more important for them.

The *Centers for Disease Control* claims it has reconstructed the 'virulent' 1918 'flu' virus. *"CDC researchers and their colleagues have successfully reconstructed the influenza virus that caused the 1918-19 flu pandemic, which killed as many as 50 million people worldwide."*

Whatever the CDC 'reconstructed', it was certainly not what killed millions of people in 1918-19. The CDC appears unaware or more likely is totally ignoring the fact that the NIAID has proven beyond reasonable doubt that it was not a virus or flu but common upper respiratory bacteria and massive infection combined with an insidious and incorrectly-used drug that killed millions. Bayer was also, possibly unsurprisingly, responsible through its vaccine division, Baxter, for sending out to 18 countries, a seasonal flu vaccine in 2009 that contained live avian virus, a bioweapon, which could have killed millions itself. Had it not been for a single laboratory technician discovering that the vaccines were lethal through injecting ferrets which all died, Bayer's vaccines could have potentially initiated a pandemic such as nature has never seen. In 1918, the convergence of a toxic drug, massive corporate advertising and government, military and medical pressure to use the drug, led to millions of deaths. That combination of groups has joined forces again, this time behind vaccines.

Despite Bayer's 2009 seasonal vaccines containing a bio-weapon and there being no reasonable explanation, Bayer was never charged, not even with negligence, but instead was immediately selected by the WHO to produce the H1N1 vaccines. Those vaccines were promoted strongly by the government and the CDC, even as the CDC itself acknowledged that the H1N1 vaccines could be predicted to maim or kill 30,000 people in the USA alone.

So, why does the CDC persist in this myth, despite abundant evidence to the contrary? Disregarding motives, one might only suggest some effects of projecting the terrifying myth that millions of people could die from virus:

1. Distraction from the hard reality that natural treatments were the only effective treatments during 1918.
2. The hiding of Bayer, aspirin and the industry's role in the deaths.
3. The sales of billions in anti-viral drugs and vaccine development.
4. Increased financial power to the pharmaceutical industry to control media and influence governments.
5. Increased illnesses and deaths from chemical, pharmaceutical agents, one of the highest risk factors.
6. Fearful dependence on 'expert medical authority' and complex, expensive solutions to save people.
7. Surrender of unlimited authority to government regulatory agencies to 'protect' the public from natural products.
8. Use of the spectre of millions of deaths as the justification for the removal of human rights to 'protect' the public.
9. Enhancement of the pharmaceutical industry moves toward an uncontested global monopoly over health
10. The industrialisation, commercialisation and militarisation of disease.

11.   An open door to the use of 'pandemic emergency' to justify martial law.

The truth, that medical authorities using Bayer aspirin (and generic aspirin) killed so many millions of people that those deaths became one the most terrifying events in human history, fundamentally threatens a global multi-trillion dollar industry built around unassailable 'medical expertise' and their use of synthetic drugs.   But the fuller truth contains something even more dangerous to the pharmaceutical industry than simply the millions of deaths they caused, because something else of great significance occurred at that time too.   Non-industrial medicine ie. those using organic substances, actually **saved** further millions of people from death. The events of 1918 unknowingly instigated a world-wide trial, comparing millions of people who were treated by pharmaceutical medicine and those treated by organic medicine. The first group died in unimaginable numbers whilst of the second group, almost all of them survived.

More than anything else, this is the real, important lesson to be gleaned from this dark period in medical history. What stands-out is the spectacular failure and toxicity of one of the industry's oldest and purportedly most trusted products, aspirin. We can also add to that, Bayer's global advertising of its toxic product, government and media influence and the fact that it increased deaths to a level never seen before. Bayer's product, political and financial power and media influence, combined to produce so many millions of deaths that it actually merits comparison with the Black Death. 20 to 50 million deaths during 1918 and 1919 versus 25 to 75 million during the course of many years of the bubonic plague.

But that single, synthetic pharmaceutical product has by now far outstripped the number of deaths of the most infamous disease in history since the deaths have not ceased yet and are continuing to be of epidemic proportions. The numbers of those who have died from aspirin poisoning alone over the 90+ years since this huge tragedy are absolutely incalculable.

It was natural health practitioners who saved lives during 1918, while aspirin killed in vast numbers, but today the government is actively and vigorously suppressing access to natural health products which are perfectly safe and saved lives during 1918, in favour of predictably lethal vaccines and pharmaceutical products, the need for which is based on an immensely misdirecting myth. What does this tell us about the insidious methods of the Big Pharma companies, who operate with impunity, hand in glove with corrupt politicians of all affiliations, whilst carrying out their genocidal policies?

In light of the 1918 deaths from Bayer's pushing of aspirin onto an unsuspecting population and Bayer's and other manufacturers' vaccines (synthetic, even genetically engineered), an automatic reassessment of natural versus synthetic treatments is triggered.

"A confluence of events created a 'perfect storm' for widespread salicylate toxicity. The loss of Bayer's patent on aspirin in February 1917 allowed many manufacturers into the lucrative aspirin market. Official recommendations for aspirin therapy at toxic doses were preceded by ignorance of the unusual nonlinear kinetics of salicylate (unknown until the 1960s), which predispose to accumulation and toxicity; tins and bottles that contained no warnings and few instructions; and fear of 'Spanish' influenza, an illness that had been spreading like wildfire." Dr. Karen Starko

Given the role that it played in the millions of 1918 deaths, a further more in-depth assessment of aspirin is probably expedient. Bayer aspirin was one of the earliest of drugs from the pharmaceutical industry, dependent on the oil industry and has become the most commonly used and a staple, trusted drug. As such, it represents a good example of the displacement of natural treatments by synthetic drugs. But is it actually safe?

During 1918 repeatedly, first hand medical accounts point to aspirin as the source of pneumonias. *"I had a package handed to me containing 1,000 aspirin tablets, which was 994 too many. I think I gave about a half dozen. I could find no place for it. My remedies were few. I almost invariably gave Gelsemium and Bryonia. I hardly ever lost a case if I got there first, unless the patient had been sent to a drug store and bought aspirin, in which event I was likely to have a case of pneumonia on my hands."* Dr. J.P. Huff, Olive Branch, Kentucky

Upon reading the accounts of the epidemic it seems that most of the deaths were caused by a virulent pneumonia that was especially devastating to those who depressed their system with analgesics, the most common being aspirin.

Aspirin was the first of the non-steroidal anti-inflammatories, others not becoming available until 1955 when Tylenol was first marketed. They are the most commonly used drugs on the market, sold both with and without prescriptions. For Bayer and the entire pharmaceutical industry, they are the absolute foundation stones of their industry **and yet they all routinely kill.**

"Over 100,000 people are hospitalized for internal bleeding and of those, 16,500 die every year. And these values are considered 'conservative'. Also the figures only include prescription NSAIDs used to treat only arthritis and only in the United States. If prescription and over the counter NSAID-related hospitalizations and death rates were counted for not only arthritis, but for all conditions and throughout the world, the figures would no doubt be enormous. Taking those figures and applying them over the many years that this class of drug that has been available since the early 1970s and the numbers would be horrific. And yet, no study to date has attempted to quantify these figures." 'Toxic and Deadly NSAIDs', an investigative report by Roman Bystrianyk.

Another important observation is that most people receive no warning signs that these drugs are causing them internal damage before they end-up in hospital with a serious medical condition and approximately 10% of these hospitalisations end in death. Considering that aspirin is still being highly recommended by the vast majority of medical practitioners to reduce the incidence of heart disease we must also consider the catastrophic levels of gastro-intestinal damage being caused, as in the recent case of my own mother.

It has been discovered that that no particular dose of aspirin between 75 mg and 300 mg daily currently used in the treatment of heart ailments, is completely free of risk of causing intestinal bleeding. Even very low doses of aspirin reportedly caused gastric bleeding in volunteers. Some 10,000 episodes of bleeding occur in people aged 60 and over each year in England and Wales alone and it is estimated that around 90% of the 10,000 episodes could be associated with and directly ascribed to aspirin usage.

Unfortunately the risk of hospitalisation and death is not the only problem caused by taking these types of drugs. Other studies have also indicated that the risk of Congestive Heart Failure (CHF) while using NSAIDs is also quite substantial. One author suggested that the number of deaths could be similar to those that are evident with gastro-intestinal bleeding. If so, the numbers of deaths attributed to NSAIDs would increase dramatically from the already large figure of 16,500.

It was also discovered that recent use of NSAIDs by elderly patients doubles the odds of being admitted to hospital with an episode of Congestive Heart Failure. The estimated relative risk for first admission with heart failure and the risk of this outcome was increased substantially by NSAID use in those with a history of heart disease.

NSAIDs, particularly including generic aspirin are truly a silent epidemic that has caused a tremendous amount of pain and unnecessary, premature deaths. Public knowledge of this tragedy is virtually non-existent, with an enormous amount of critical information primarily existing within the sanctuary of medical libraries and thus being unavailable to the public in general. Big Pharma still markets and promotes worldwide sales of these toxic substances and governmental agencies have done nothing at all to alert the public or even medical practitioners, many of whom remain totally unaware of these facts.

The 20 to 50 million deaths during 1918 have long been attributed to a virulent new virus but the NIAID has now clearly stated that common upper respiratory bacteria was responsible, not a new virus. There was no new deadly virus but there was *something* new in 1918 and that was toxic aspirin, being used in totally inappropriate, dangerous dosages.

"... just before the 1918 death spike, aspirin was recommended in regimens now known to be potentially toxic and to cause pulmonary oedema and may therefore have contributed to overall pandemic mortality and several of its mysteries. Young adult

mortality may be explained by willingness to use the new, recommended therapy and the presence of youth in regimented treatment settings (military)." Dr. Karen Starko

Use of Bayer aspirin and other generic aspirin suppressed immunity, allowing the bacteria to develop into a massive bacterial infections and pneumonias. In addition to the deaths by pneumonia, the use of Bayer aspirin (and generic versions) at toxic doses can explain the lingering mysteries of extremely rapid deterioration from health to death as well as the death of young, apparently otherwise healthy people. Bayer's heavy advertising and government and medical recommendations fuelled use of both Bayer aspirin and generic versions.

Based on the primary role that aspirin played in the millions of 1918 deaths versus the survival of those who avoided it in favour of natural treatments, it would suggest that 1918 was not a plague caused by a virus, but a pharmaceutical industry issue. And given the scale of the deaths, it was without question, the greatest medical catastrophe in human history, exceeding even the 'Great Plague' of the Dark and Middle Ages.

Whilst the events of 1918 expose the extreme toxicity of Bayer's most staple of drugs, aspirin, it also reveals something even more profound; the continuing abject failure of the oil-based synthetic, pharmaceutical drug industry to treat disease and the persistent Elite propaganda directed at us, the masses, in order to cover up and obfuscate this fact.

The overall conclusion must therefore be that 'Spanish influenza' was not the cause of the 1918/19 deaths. Whilst I have focused on medical evidence indicating that aspirin overdose is the most reasonable explanation for the terrifying rapid deaths and aspirin use appears responsible for the massive bacterial infections that led to lethal pneumonias, there is an instigating factor prior to the use of aspirin itself and that is Bayer's desire for profits to the detriment of all else. As millions of people died in this reckless quest, how much money did Bayer make because of the 1918 'flu'?

This question is extremely pertinent and should be answered. However, I would not advise 'holding one's breath' on any answers being forthcoming any time very soon. As always, the Elite spider's web of deceit and chicanery will prevent anyone from investigating these issues too closely and anyone who does get too close... well I will leave that to reader's own imagination.

German Hyperinflation 1923

The true facts of this financial disaster do not appear in any history textbooks today. Today's history uses this inflation to twist the truth into its opposite. It cites the radical devaluation of the German mark as an example of what goes wrong when governments print their own money, rather than borrow it from private cartels run by the banksters. In reality the exact opposite is the truth as with so much of our accepted historical wisdom today.

The Weimar financial crisis actually began with the impossible reparations payments imposed at the Treaty of Versailles. Hjalmar Schacht (who was never a Nazi Party member and now it appears clear why that was the case), the Rothschild agent who was currency commissioner for the Republic, opposed letting the German government print its own money...

"The Treaty of Versailles is a model of ingenious measures for the economic destruction of Germany. Germany could not find any way of holding its head above the water, other than by the inflationary expedient of printing bank notes."

Schacht echoes the history books' deception that Weimar inflation was caused when the German government printed its own money; however, in his 1967 book 'The Magic of Money', Schacht revealed that it was the privately owned 'Reichsbank', not the German government that was injecting new money into the economy. Thus, it was that this Elite-owned and run private bank caused the Weimar hyperinflation.

Like the US Federal Reserve, the Reichsbank was overseen by appointed government officials, but was operated for private gain. What drove the wartime inflation into hyperinflation was speculation by foreign investors, who sold the German Mark short, betting on its decreasing value. In the manipulative device known as the 'short sell', speculators borrow something they do not own, sell it, and then 'cover' by buying it back at the lower price.

Speculation in the German Mark was made possible because the privately owned Reichsbank (not yet under Nazi control) made massive amounts of currency available for borrowing. This currency, like all first-world currency today, was created with accounting entries in the bank's books and then this 'magic' money was lent at compound interest. When the Reichsbank could not keep up with the voracious demand for Marks, other private banks were then allowed to also create Marks out of nothing and to lend them at interest. The result was runaway debt and inflation.

On the 24th June 1922, right-wing fanatics assassinated Walter Rathenau, the moderate German foreign minister. Rathenau was a charismatic figure and the idea that a popular, wealthy and glamorous government minister could be shot in a law-abiding society shattered the faith of the German people, who needed to believe that the country was in safe hands after the trauma of the previous decade. The wealthier, by now extremely nervous citizens were already taking their money out of banks and investing it into 'real goods' such as diamonds, works of art and safe real-estate, with true intrinsic values, unlike currency which the Elite will manipulate up or downwards to suit their own agendas. Eventually, the ordinary German citizens also began to trade their Marks for real commodities.

The British historian Adam Fergusson noted that pianos were being bought, even by non-musical families. Sellers held back because the Mark was worth less every day and as prices soared, the amounts of currency demanded became greater and greater and the German Central Bank responded to these demands through the printing of more, increasingly worthless paper. Yet still the ruling authorities did not acknowledge that there was anything amiss. A leading financial newspaper at the time, reported that the amounts of money in circulation were not excessively high but nevertheless Dr. Rudolf Havenstein, the president of the Reichsbank (German equivalent to the Federal Reserve / Bank of England) told an economics professor that he needed a new suit but wasn't going to buy one until prices came down.

Why did the German government not act sooner to halt the inflation? The problem was partly that it was a shaky, fragile government, especially after the assassination of Rathenau. The vengeful French sent their army into the Ruhr to enforce their demands for reparations due under the Versailles Treaty and the Germans were powerless to resist due to the virtual disbandment of their armed forces and they feared unemployment far more than inflation. In 1919, Communists had attempted a coup and severe unemployment may have given the Communists another opportunity to seize power. The great German industrial combines Krupp, Thyssen, IG Farben and Stinnes welcomed the inflation and survived it well by astute forward planning and possibly foreknowledge of what was to come. A cheaper Mark, they reasoned, would make German goods cheap and easy to export and they needed the export earnings to buy raw materials abroad. Inflation kept everyone working.

And so the printing presses continued producing the ever-decreasing in value Mark and once they began to run, they were impossible to stop. The price increases became unmanageable. Menus in cafes could not be revised quickly enough to keep up with the speed of the inflation. A student at Freiburg University ordered a cup of coffee at a café and the price on the menu was 5,000 Marks per cup. He had two cups but when the bill arrived, it was for 14,000 Marks. *'If you want to save money and you want two cups of coffee, you should order them both at the same time'*, he was told by the proprietor.

Things became so bad that people would not even bother to bend down to pick up a one hundred million Mark note carelessly discarded by a passer-by as by that time it had become worth less than the paper upon which it was printed. There was a famous case of a man walking along a street on a shopping trip to buy bread, carrying his money in a large wicker basket, such was the quantity and bulk of the notes he needed to carry. Upon unsuccessfully attempting to enter a particularly busy shop, he reasoned that he could quite safely leave most of his money outside in the basket as no-one would bother to risk stealing such a bulky yet paltry amount of money. He was absolutely correct. When he returned, he found his money was all still there but someone had stolen his basket!

The presses of the Reichsbank could not keep up to demand, even though they ran through the night. Individual cities and states began to issue their own money and Dr. Havenstein, the president of the Reichsbank, did not get his new suit. A factory worker described payday, which was every day at 11 am: *'At 11:00 in the morning a siren sounded, and everyone gathered in the factory forecourt, where a five-ton lorry was drawn up loaded to overflowing with paper money. The chief cashier and his assistants climbed up on top. They read out names and just threw out bundles of notes. As soon as you had caught one you made a dash for the nearest shop and bought just anything that was going.'* Teachers, paid at 10 am, brought their money to the playground, where relatives took the bundles and hurried off with them. Banks closed at 11am as by this time they had invariably run out of cash anyway.

The flight from currency that had begun with the buying of diamonds, gold, country houses and antiques now extended to minor and almost useless items, bric-a-brac, soap and hairpins to name but a few. This hitherto law-abiding country crumbled into petty thievery, petrol (gasoline) was siphoned from cars and people bought things they didn't need and used them to barter. A pair of shoes for a shirt or some crockery for coffee. Berlin had an unreal atmosphere, prostitutes of both sexes roamed the streets and cocaine was the fashionable drug. When the 1,000-billion Mark note was first issued in 1923, few bothered to collect the change when they spent it. By November 1923, with one dollar equal to one trillion Marks, the breakdown was complete and the German economy had become one of barter. The currency had completely lost its meaning.

Then, a new president took over the Reichsbank, Horace Greeley Hjalmar Schacht, who came by his first two names because of his father's admiration for an editor of the *New York Tribune*. The *Rentenmark* was not Schacht's idea, but he executed it and as the Reichsbank president, he got the credit for it. For decades afterward he was able to maintain a reputation for financial wizardry and he became the architect of the financial prosperity brought by the Nazi party.

Obviously, although the currency was worthless, Germany was still a rich country with mines, farms, factories, and natural resources aplenty. The backing for the Rentenmark was mortgages on the land and bonds on the factories, but that backing was a fiction; the factories and land could not be turned into cash or used abroad. Nine zeros were struck from the currency, that is, one Rentenmark was equal to one billion old Marks. The Germans wanted desperately to believe in the Rentenmark, and so they simply did.

But although the country slowly began to function almost normally again, the savings of the middle-classes were never restored, nor were the values of hard work and decency that had accompanied the savings. With the currency went many of the lifetime plans of average, ordinary citizens. It was the custom for the bride to bring some money to a marriage; so many marriages were called off and many widows dependent on insurance found themselves destitute. People who had worked for a lifetime and built up a sizeable pension fund, found that their pensions would not even buy a cup of coffee. Such are the ways that the ordinary citizens of the world are cheated out of the money by these vultures.

"The cities were still there, the houses not yet bombed and in ruins, but the victims were millions of people. They had lost their fortunes, their savings; they were dazed and inflation-shocked and did not understand how it had happened to them and who the foe was who had defeated them. Yet they had lost their self-assurance, their feeling that they themselves could be the masters of their own lives if only they worked hard enough; and lost, too, were the old values of morals, of ethics, of decency." Pearl Buck, American author

Thus, according to Schacht himself, the German government did not cause the Weimar hyperinflation. On the contrary, the government brought hyperinflation under control. It placed the Reichsbank under strict government regulation and took prompt corrective measures to eliminate foreign speculation. One of those measures was to eliminate easy access to loans from private banks and eventually Hitler regained Germany's financial stability through the issuance of Government Treasury Certificates.

Schacht, the Rothschild agent, disapproved of this government fiat money (obviously) and was consequently dismissed as head of the Reichsbank when he refused to issue it. Nevertheless, he acknowledged in his later memoirs that allowing the government to issue the money it needed did not produce the price inflation predicted by classical economic theory, which states (for obvious reasons) that currency must be borrowed from private cartels.

What really causes hyperinflation is uncontrolled speculation. When speculation is coupled with debt (owed to private banking cartels) the result is always disaster. On the other hand, when a government issues currency in carefully measured ways, it causes supply and demand to increase together, leaving prices unaffected. Hence there is no inflation, no debt, no unemployment, and no need for income taxes.

Naturally this terrifies the bankers, since it eliminates their powers and it also terrifies the Elite, since their control of banking allows them to buy the media, the government and everything else. Were the nations of the world to revert to Government-only money issuance, then the world financial crisis would be solved overnight, as would much of the ever-increasing poverty and suffering we are currently witnessing.

Significantly, it was in the midst of this financial carnage that further devastated an already prostrate nation, that an unobtrusive, former army corporal was thrust into the spotlight and promoted as a great 'leader of men'. The prevailing conditions of the time providing a perfect stage for anyone with any aspirations of greatness and the ability to 'mesmerise' his audiences with nationalist, patriotic rhetoric. And thus the world was introduced to the soon-to-be world public enemy number one, Adolf Hitler...

The Frankfurt School and the Tavistock Institute

I strongly suspect that the introduction and proliferation of psychometric testing for job applicants, especially in the public sector, has a hidden and nefarious agenda. Rather than being used to determine the candidates most suitable for specific jobs in a positive sense, this testing is being used to actually uncover and employ those with psychopathic and/or sociopathic tendencies.   This fact would neatly explain why there has been a huge paradigm shift in those we deal with in 'authority' and whose arrogance, intransigence, inflexibility and often sheer bloody-mindedness seems to have increased exponentially in the last few years.

This has led to a fundamental change in the relationship between the general populace and those wearing suits and uniforms and indeed any of those people who act as an interface between the public and an institution or corporation. Up until a short time ago, people undertaking these jobs still actually believed (and behaved as if) their role was to *serve* the public, but not any longer. Such old-fashioned values of courtesy and willingness to help have now been replaced increasingly by 'jobsworths' who waste no opportunity to flaunt and emphasise their 'authority' in any way possible, even on occasions going out of their way to be deliberately awkward or confrontational, resulting of course in extreme frustration which can often flare into anger and sometimes even violence.

How often do we now see notices in banks, local and central government offices and other institutions dealing directly with the public that state words to the effect of, 'this company/department has a zero-tolerance policy regarding verbal and physical assaults upon our staff'? All very commendable of course, but we should also question as to why these incidents would appear now to have become relatively commonplace. Could it be that their staff are actually selected and employed in the first place because in psychometric tests they exhibited the kind of intransigence that engenders such frustrations? I believe this to be a strong possibility. This has all been systematically planned and foisted upon us as we 'slept' in our apathetic states, in order to further destabilise society and cause maximum inconvenience and disruption with a long-term view to discouraging and making unacceptable any form of protest or dissent, even against gross injustice. We are meant to just simply 'accept our lot' and carry on with a 'stiff upper lip' and all that, even in the face of extreme provocation.

This was all planned many years ago by the Zionist 'Frankfurt School' established in 1932 in the German city from where it takes its name. It was subsequently relocated to California, which through no coincidence has now become the global epicentre of 'political correctness.'

The Tavistock Institute is merely the British branch of this insidious organisation. Its primary mission is to establish a global brainwashing and opinion-forming network. Tavistock is the originator of the Aquarian Conspiracy, designed to weaken the fabric of society by encouraging widespread drug use, promiscuity, homosexuality and lesbianism. It has been very successful in the United States as it works through many research institutes and think-tanks. The principal ones in the United States are the Stanford Research Institute, Rand Research and Development Corporation, the Institute for Policy Studies, the Aspen Institute, the Hudson Institute and the Brookings Institute. Tavistock in fact runs over 30 'research' institutions in the United States.

These were some of the stated aims of the Frankfurt School as long as *eighty years ago*:

- Create a culture of 'political correctness' thus disempowering free-thinking and individual opinions
- Promote continual change to create confusion and instability
- Expose very young children to sex and homosexuality
- Make homosexuality and lesbianism and other sexual deviancy the norm and 'positively discriminate' for it
- Undermine parents', schools' and teachers' authority
- Encourage mass immigration to destroy national identity and engender social unrest
- Create the crime of 'racism' to further facilitate a mass immigration policy in order to undermine individual nation states and build tension and resentment

- Promote a binge-drinking culture in order to destabilise society especially youth culture
- Undermine and discourage anything that brings people together socially
- Introduce a legal system biased against the victims rather than the perpetrators of crime
- Encourage a dependency on the state or state benefits
- Impose greater control of and facilitate the dumbing-down of the media
- Foster the breakdown of the nuclear family unit through the encouragement of promiscuity and 'free love'

Does any of that seem familiar, perchance? Does it possibly describe the society in which we all now live?

Political correctness has now become an obsession and a legitimate tool to deny us our rights and freedoms, wherever possible or practical.

Barely a day goes by where we do not read or hear of seemingly bizarre incidents that result from the above list of goals being fulfilled or from so-called politically incorrect attitudes. Here are a few from a list that would fill an entire book, let alone one chapter...

An employee at a police training centre related that they are not allowed to ask for 'black coffee' in the staff cafeteria, it must be 'coffee without milk' or refer to plastic bin bags as 'black bags' and also that they cannot refer to a 'blackboard' or a 'whiteboard', it has to be a 'pen board'.

A ten-year-old boy was left to drown in a pond in England by two Police Community Support Officers and the police spokesman subsequently justified their actions by stating that no rescue was attempted because the officers in question were *'not trained to deal with such an incident'*.

Paramedics in Somerset, England were prevented from treating a man with a broken back while he was lying in *six inches* of water. They were informed that this action would breach Health and Safety rules because they were *'not trained for water rescues'*. A spokesman for the South West Ambulance Service then said that *'the incident was managed in accordance with procedures.'*

Microsoft froze the account of a man who included the word 'gay' in his 'Xbox Live' profile. He did this because he lives in Fort Gay, West Virginia but this mattered not a jot to Microsoft even when the town mayor intervened on his behalf. They only reluctantly relented when the story was made public, probably in order to save face and not because they believed their policy was abjectly nonsensical or severely restrictive of personal freedoms.

Many British schools and nurseries (kindergartens) have changed the words of the previously popular nursery rhyme 'Baa, baa, black sheep' to 'Baa, baa, *rainbow* sheep.' Is there such a thing as a multi-coloured sheep, perhaps? The City of Birmingham in England actually wanted to ban the rhyme altogether until black parents vehemently protested.

This is the real point. Despite the pretence to the contrary, none of this utter stupidity is really about protecting peoples' feelings, freedoms, safety or preventing prejudice. It is in fact the polar opposite of this and all about control of the population as in the novel 1984 where 'newspeak' replaced 'oldspeak'. The language is being subtly modified and changed over time to eliminate words that allow us to express a strong opinion in order to dumb-down language to the point where people will eventually be unable to transmit ideas and concepts effectively. This of course is exactly as George Orwell himself predicted because he was an insider who knew what the agenda for the future was and is.

In fact, the systematic introduction of the 'jobsworth' and 'political correctness' mentality to all areas of our lives is part of the overall, long-term plan for the transformation of human society. We can accept this out of fear of being criticised or condemned or we can express our intelligence and consciousness and refuse to be told what we can and cannot say and in what context. In other words the choice between freedom and enslavement is in our own hands.

World War II

"History is subjective, though it was never meant to be. Real history has never been in [as much] danger as it is today. World War II wasn't the 'clean war' we purport it to be but as dirty as World War I, with its secret deals and payoffs. Everything in its aftermath has required a mythology, misrepresentation and disinformation, not only the war but it's after-shocks and how the conflicts continue, almost endlessly." Gordon Duff, historical researcher

"World War Two was the most egregious hoax in history. A cult of satanic Jews and Masons, financed by the Rothschild syndicate is responsible for destroying more than sixty million lives. Hitler proved by his actions that he was a traitor. He was installed by the Illuminati to destroy Germany so that it would slip neatly into the NWO." Henry Makow, researcher, 14th May 2011

The Prelude
World Wars I and II were planned as early as the latter part of the nineteenth century and promoted as a stepping-stone toward achieving the ultimate goals of the Elite in

the work known as 'The Protocols of the Learned Elders of Zion' which was written in the late nineteenth century and first came to light in the first decade of the twentieth century. The secondary intention was the establishment of a Jewish homeland in Palestine as a guaranteed future means of generating further conflicts as and when necessary with all the international protections afforded legitimate countries as opposed to 'rogue' states. How much more provocative could it be than to install an overtly aggressive and acquisitive Jewish 'state' in the centre of the Arab / Muslim world? However, as we will see, the events that transpired in the first half of the twentieth century were but a means toward both these ends.

Both World Wars were in actuality nothing less than cynically disguised attempts to totally subjugate Germany and its peoples and to destroy her growing influence in world affairs in order to remove her share of world trade markets which was ultimately depriving the British and more significantly, Elite industrialists of profit they regarded as their own and also, importantly to achieve the Zionist goal of a Jewish Homeland.

The cryptically-worded Balfour Declaration during WWI was merely Britain's promise to pay the Zionists what they had agreed upon as a consideration for enticing the United States into the war and was as a result described by one contemporary commentator as 'just as phony as a three dollar bill'. The rest, as they ironically say, is 'history'. The United States with a little help from its allies, Britain and France, crushed Germany as was expected and all parties attended the Paris Peace Conference in 1919 to determine the punitive reparations to be imposed in order to further decimate Germany. At this conference were 117 Zionist Jews, there as a delegation representing Zionist interests, headed by Bernard Baruch, the American bankster.

It was there at the conference where the Balfour declaration was made public. As the victorious nations were slicing up the map of Europe to share the spoils among the victors, the declaration was produced. At this point the Germans realised what the plan had been all along, but were powerless in the face of their unconditional surrender to do or say anything to affect the outcome of the talks and the resulting Treaty of Versailles. The Zionists coveted Palestine in order to further their secret agenda and were determined to get it at any cost, either monetarily or in the form of human suffering.

Germany, unsurprisingly regarded this as the ultimate treachery on the part of the Jews. To illustrate the point, a comparison would be to suppose that Britain was at war with Russia and was winning comfortably but in a humanitarian action, approached the Russians and offered them generous peace terms. Then suddenly China entered the war as an ally of Russia and their joining the war results in Britain's devastating defeat. Bear in mind also that this is not just an ordinary defeat; this is a crushing defeat, with post-war reparations demanded, the likes of which had never before or since been seen.

Further suppose then after that defeat, if it was then discovered that it was the ethnic Chinese in our own country, the Chinese-British citizens, whom we had previously thought were loyal citizens, were 'selling us out' to Russia and that it was through them that their mother country was brought into the war against us. How would we feel then, in the UK about our Chinese ethnic citizens? Would there be uncontained rage and bloodshed, countrywide? I submit that there would indeed. British indignation would know no limits at all and would be turned upon all far-easterners regardless of background and indeed anyone of even slight far-eastern appearance.

This then is exactly how the Germans felt towards the Jews. In 1905, when the first attempted Communist revolution in Russia failed and many Jews had to flee from Russia, almost all of them fled to Germany and Germany gave them unconditional refuge. They were treated with great respect and kindness and were for the most part made welcome. This then was how German generousity was repaid, for no reason at all other than the fact that the Jewish Zionists wanted Palestine as their so-called 'Jewish commonwealth.' Treachery is too mild a word to describe their actions accurately.

The Zionists themselves admitted that there were no racial or religious ill-feelings towards them from Germans; it was all political and economic. But the views that later manifested themselves in Germany were due to one thing only and that is that the German people held the Jews responsible for their crushing defeat and subsequent inhuman subjugation via the devastating reparations inflicted on them by the Treaty of Versailles. Once the pattern began to repeat itself in the early 1930s with the Jewish/Zionist declaration of war against Germany in 1933, then the situation began to escalate out of control.

When Germans first realised that the Zionist Jews were responsible for their defeat, they naturally resented it, but to their credit not a single Jew was physically harmed. Professor Tansill, of Georgetown University, who had access to all the secret papers of the US State Department, wrote in his book and quoted from a US State Department document written by Hugo Schoenfelt, regarding a Jew who went to Europe in 1933 to investigate the so-called camps of political prisoners and wrote back that he found them in very fine condition. Everyone was treated well despite the fact that the camps were filled with Communists. They were mainly Jewish Communists because about 98% of the Communists in Europe at that time were Jews. There were also some priests and ministers, labour-union leaders, Freemasons and others with internationalist affiliations.

Meanwhile, the Jews attempted to cover-up the fact that they had betrayed Germany and that the Germans naturally resented it. There is no question that the actions that the Germans took against the Jews were appropriate. They naturally discriminated against them wherever they could and shunned them, stopping short however of actually physically harming them in any way.

Naturally, the Germans questioned who these people thought they were to declare a boycott against them and cause their industries to come almost to a standstill. They naturally resented it and under the circumstances, one can almost sympathise with the fact that swastikas were painted on the doors of shops owned by Jews. In their view, why should a German give his money to a shopkeeper who was part of a boycott that was going to starve Germany into surrendering to the Zionists of the world? The boycott continued for some time and tensions escalated, until on the 7th November 1938 a young Jewish man, Herschel Grynszpan from Poland casually walked into the German embassy in Paris and shot Ernst vom Rath a German diplomat five times, leaving him for dead. He died sometime later in hospital. According to Hans-Jurgen Dosscher, a German historian, this was not a politically-motivated event as commonly believed, but the result of a homosexual love affair gone-awry between the diplomat and the young man. But I personally believe that it was a 'set-up', a 'false flag' operation to provide an excuse for a violent series of reprisals and if it was, it definitely worked.

This was most probably the 'straw that broke the camel's back' as far as Germany and her people were concerned and from that point on, the ethnic German people's relationship with the German Jews changed from one of grudging tolerance to overt hatred and open violence. This incident was the catalyst to 'Kristallnacht' on the 9th November 1938, a night of infamy which saw the violence escalate, Jewish shops burned and looted and Jews attacked, of whom 91 died. I do not attempt for one moment to pretend that the Jewish population deserved the violence directed at them or defend it in any way, but merely try to explain that there were underlying reasons for it, valid or not, which are hidden from general view in order to deliberately falsify history. However, violence of any kind and for whatever reason has no place in a civilised society.

Is it evil to persecute *all* the members of one particular race or religion for the sins and crimes of a few? Yes, of course it is. Any such actions should not be sanctioned at all, but unfortunately we humans are imperfect and emotions such as hate, thoughts of revenge, jealousy and anger will always exist in the psyche of mankind. However, all stories have two sides and relating these events of the 1930s as they actually happened, puts into perspective the fact that what you 'know' and have been taught as fact all your life about the sequence of events leading to the tragic war of 1939-45 is not necessarily the 'whole truth and nothing but the truth'.

Yes, the Nazis were an intrinsically evil organisation and Jews and other targeted groups were persecuted and many tragically died in the prelude to war, but these were not just the random acts and whims of an inherently racist regime and people with an irrational hatred of one small minority group, there were complex, underlying reasons for their actions. These reasons have been for the most part and still continue to be, deliberately hidden from you in an attempt to corrupt and distort history in order to benefit the Zionist minority by eliciting largely unwarranted sympathy for a small section of human society.

Who Was Adolf Hitler?

"All the world's a stage and all the men and women merely players. They have their exits and their entrances; and one man in his time plays many parts." William Shakespeare, 'As You Like It'

So exactly who was Adolf Hitler? Hitler (Heidler) was born at 6.30am on the 20th April 1889 in Braunau, Austria. He was the fourth child of his father Alois Heidler's third wife, Klara Pölzl, granddaughter of Johann Nepomuk Heidler, brother of Alois' deceased stepfather.

Alois' father was ostensibly a certain Johann Georg Heidler although many historians have now come to seriously doubt this fact. In the 1930s, Chancellor Engelbert Döllfuss of Austria conducted an investigation into Hitler's heritage, the result of which was a document that proved that Maria Anna Schicklgruber, Johann's wife and Hitler's grandmother was in fact living away from the family home in Spital at the time of her conception of Alois. She was employed as a live-in servant at the home of Baron Rothschild in Vienna and as soon as her pregnancy became known to the Rothschilds, she was immediately, conveniently dispatched back home to her husband in Spital, where Alois was eventually born.

If all this is true (and Döllfuss and many other researchers certainly believed it to be so) then this means that Hitler was not only *one quarter Jewish*, but also the *grandson of a Rothschild*. The significance of this fact should not be underestimated.

Hitler himself knew of the existence of this document and the incriminating evidence it contained and so in order to obtain it he initiated the assassination of Döllfuss on the 25th July 1934, an event which also ultimately precipitated the Anschlüss in Austria.

As I say, the fact that Hitler was a Rothschild is far from insignificant. The Rothschilds are a major Zionist-Jewish Elite family and **the** ultimate driving force of the world of banking (and indeed much of the Elite covert operations) today. It is at their behest (among others) that world events are stage-managed and manipulated and this has been the case for centuries. It would very succinctly explain how a lowly army lance-corporal could be groomed and manipulated into becoming a powerful world leader in the space of a little over ten years or so. Hitler's so-called master work *'Mein Kampf'* (my struggle) was in fact provably written on his behalf by a Jesuit priest named Father Bernhardt Staempfle who subsequently became a victim of the 'Night of the Long Knives' in June 1934 whereby as many as 400 of Hitler's black-listed enemies were disposed of in one night of bloody violence.
And interestingly, the word 'Nazi' was created by combining the National Socialist Party of Hitler (NA) with the Zionist International (ZI).

One of the most prevalent Elite strategies for maintaining power is by contriving to control both sides of any conflict. The banksters' control of Britain and America was without doubt an established fact and by placing, in effect 'one of their own' into power in Germany it enabled them to manipulate the world situation for their own ends.

According to detailed research carried out over the last few years, Wall Street bankers (amongst others) financed Hitler's rise to power whilst also making large profits in the process. What is yet still more deplorable, if unsurprising is the fact that direct ancestors and relatives of former US president George W. Bush were amongst this group of individuals.

"Germany issued debt-free and interest-free money from 1935 on, which accounts for Germany's startling rise from the depression to a world power in five years. The German government financed its entire operations from 1935 to 1945 without gold, and without debt. It took the entire Capitalist and Communist world to destroy the German revolution, and bring Europe back under the heel of the Bankers." Sheldon Emry, *'Billions for the Bankers, Debts for the People'* (1984)

Historians Webster G. Tarpley and Anton Chaitkin revealed in their recently published *'George Bush: The Unauthorized Biography'*, that Prescott Bush (George W. Bush's grandfather) and other directors of the Union Banking Corporation (UBC) were Nazi collaborators. The book relates how in 1922, when Nazism (National Socialism) was emerging, railways entrepreneur Averell Harriman travelled to Berlin and consulted the Thyssen family with a view to founding a German-US bank. The Thyssens were already behind-the-scenes owners of several financial institutions that allowed them to transfer their money from Germany to the Netherlands and from there on to the United States.

The banks in question were the August Thyssen Bank whose headquarters were located in Berlin; the Bank voor Handel in the Netherlands and the Union Banking Corporation in New York. In the early 1920s, one of the members of this family, Fritz Thyssen, author of *'I Paid Hitler'* contributed some $25,000 to the then newly formed German National Socialist Workers' Party, becoming the prime and most important financier of Hitler in his ascent to power.

According to the book's authors, Thyssen was fascinated by Hitler, citing his talent as a public speaker and his ability to lead the masses. However, what impressed him most was the order that prevailed at his rallies and the almost military discipline of his followers. And so, in 1931 Thyssen joined the Nazi party, becoming one of the most powerful members of the Nazi war machine.

At that time, Thyssen presided over the German Steel Trust, a steel industry consortium founded by Clarence Dillon, one of Wall Street's most influential people. One of Dillon's most trustworthy collaborators was Samuel Bush, Prescott's father, George Sr.'s grandfather and great-grandfather of George W. Bush.

In 1923, Harriman and Thyssen decided to form a new bank and appointed George Herbert Walker, Prescott Bush's father-in-law, as president and in 1926 they established the Union Banking Corporation (UBC) with Prescott Bush at the helm. That same year, he was also named vice-president and partner at Brown Brothers Harriman. Both organisations allowed the Thyssens to send money to the United States from Germany via the Netherlands.

US economist Victor Thorn observed that although a large number of other corporations aided the Nazis, such as Standard Oil and Rockefeller's Chase Bank, as well as several US automobile manufacturers and IBM, Prescott Bush's interests were much more profound and sinister. Thorn added that UBC became a secret channel to protect Nazi capital leaving Germany for the United States via the Netherlands. When the Nazis needed to retrieve their funds, Brown Brothers Harriman sent them directly to Germany.

In this way, UBC received money from the Netherlands and Brown Brothers Harriman returned it. Who was on the executive boards of both of these companies? Prescott Bush himself, the Nazis' money launderer-in-chief.

In their book, Tarpley and Chaitkin explain that in this way a significant part of the Bush family's financial base was related to supporting and aiding Adolf Hitler. Therefore, GW Bush the last US President prior to the current incumbent, Obama, just like his father (former CIA director, vice president and president) reached the peak of the US political hierarchy thanks to his great-grandfather and grandfather and generally his entire family, who made huge personal fortunes from financially aiding and encouraging the Nazis.

Years later, in October 1942, the US authorities confiscated Nazi bank funds from the New York UBC, whose then president was Prescott Bush. The bank was condemned as a financial and commercial collaborator with the enemy and all its assets were seized. Later, the US government also ordered the seizure of the assets of a further two leading financial companies directed by Prescott Bush through the accounts of the Harriman banking institution, the Holland-America Trading Corporation (a US-Dutch commercial firm) and the Seamless Steel Equipment Corporation.

Then on the 11th November 1942, an embargo was imposed on the Silesian-American Corporation another organisation headed by Bush and Walker, under the same 'Trading with the Enemy' Act. However, in 1951, the embargo was lifted and these most enterprising of businessmen recovered some $1.5 million, earmarked for new investments largely to swell the Bush family's personal fortunes. To this should be added a résumé of files belonging to Dutch and US information services confirming the direct links between Prescott Bush, the German Thyssen family and the blood money of a group of rich US families from the Second World War.

The Elite-engineered great financial crash of 1929 affected the United States, Germany and Britain, weakening their respective governments and at the same time, Prescott Bush became even more diligent, still more desirous of doing everything that was necessary to safeguard his own position of power and finances. It was during this crisis that some members of the Anglo-US Elite supported the installation of Hitler's regime in Germany. To sum up, the authors categorically state that the Bush family's fortune arose as a result of its unconditional support for Adolf Hitler's political project.

The UBC, under Prescott Bush's direction and with the long-term cooperation of Fritz Thyssen's German Steel Trust participated in the emergence, preparation and financing of the Nazi war machine through the manufacture of armoured vehicles, fighter planes, guns and explosives. And furthermore it can be shown that they continued these activities throughout the war.

But back to the main story; Hitler's rise to power as stated earlier was a minor miracle, given his lowly background. I would venture to suggest that had he not had 'friends in high places' via his Rothschild connections, this would have been next to impossible to achieve as *all* positions of power are filled strictly only by appointment from the unseen 'wizards behind the curtain'.

Official history would have us believe that his meteoric ascent was due to his ability to make passionate, patriotic speeches and a natural charisma that had the effect of influencing, mesmerising and galvanising people wherever he went. It is true that he certainly had the gift of influencing others through his stirring speeches, but is this factor alone enough to gain a position of absolute, unconditional power over a country and its peoples? I find that very difficult to believe. Other than that, his negative traits would seem to have far outweighed the positive. He was apparently of below average intelligence, vain and arrogant and also had to say the very least, dubious sexual preferences, not that that in itself is any bar to high-office as many a Royal, prime minister or president could testify.

Some researchers report that he had spent some time as a gay prostitute before WWI after leaving his home when his mother died and also reputedly had some distinctly aberrant relationships with women, being a copraphile, the scientific name for someone who derives sexual pleasure from human excrement and the excretory act itself.

His unhealthy, one-sided relationship with his niece Angelika (Geli) Raubal in fact led to her alleged 'suicide' at the age of 23, but whether it was suicide or murder at Hitler's behest is unclear. Indeed either alternative is plausible. She undoubtedly felt trapped by him as he would allow her no freedom to go wherever she might wish or meet whomsoever she may wish and all her requests so to do were met with his irrational, jealous rages. In 1931 she was found shot dead in her room in Hitler's apartments in Munich but whether this was her own solution to the problem or whether he had her killed in another paroxysm of jealous fury will almost certainly never be known.

Of course, Hitler was a tyrant, a 'monster' and the catalyst for one of the ugliest periods in human history. But please do not lose sight of the fact that above all he was a player, an actor, an Elite place-man acting out his designated role in the long term game-plan to subjugate humanity. He was a dupe, a 'patsy' who probably due to his own extreme vanity, believed that it was his destiny to be a world leader, a messiah even, come to lead his people to the 'promised land'. Oh, the irony. He must certainly have never known or even suspected until his latter days of power at least, that he had been set-up to be knocked-down again in the manner of all third-rate dictators.

Indeed, it is debatable as to whether or not he was any 'better' or 'worse' than many other so-called world leaders. I would suggest for example, that people of the ilk of Winston Churchill, both George Bushes, Bill Clinton, Tony Blair and even Barack Obama would give him a very good run for his money in any competition for the title of 'most evil person that ever lived' yet they are all feted in their own and various ways for their actions, despite the untold human misery and suffering for which they are all ultimately personally responsible. The difference obviously being that they are generally perceived to be and portrayed as being 'on our side', the 'good guys', whilst Hitler was most certainly not.

War is declared

The newspaper headline below depicts what really happened in March of 1933. World Jewry or Judea (actually Zionism and not the Jewish people) declared war on Germany – and not the other way around as is disingenuously portrayed to be the case. At this point in time, there had been no German pogroms against the Jews, no excessively anti-Jewish feelings manifest and no legislation discriminating against them; indeed the Jewish element of the German economy was regarded as being an essential component of the hoped-for wider economic recovery and prosperity of the country, its economy being as stagnant as it was, in this period prior to Hitler's mass re-armament of the German forces.

"The war against Germany will be waged by all Jewish communities, conferences, congresses... by every individual Jew. Thereby the war against Germany will ideologically enliven and promote our interests, which require that Germany be wholly destroyed. The danger for us Jews lies in the whole German people, in Germany as a whole as well as individually. It must be rendered harmless for all time.... In this war we Jews have to participate, and this with all the strength and might we have at our disposal." The Jewish newspaper, 'Natscha Retsch', 1933

This insidious campaign of lies and anti-German propaganda by the Zionist Elite in close conjunction and co-operation with its many tentacles in governments, banking and media was just the start of a long process to destroy Germany and simultaneously establish a Jewish state in Palestine. This latter intent was promised by Arthur Balfour, the British Foreign Secretary at the time of his 'declaration' of November 1917 in the form of a letter to Lord Rothschild.

However, the war declared by the international Jewish leadership on Germany not only sparked reprisals by the German government but also set the stage for a little-known economic and political alliance between the Hitler government and the leaders of the Zionist movement who hoped that the tension between the Germans and the Jews would lead to massive emigration to Palestine. The result was a tactical alliance between the Nazis and the Zionist founders of the modern-day state of Israel, a fact that many today would prefer to be forgotten.

The modern-day supporters of Zionist Israel and many complicit and/or ignorant historians have succeeded in keeping this Nazi-Zionist pact a secret to the general public for decades and while most people have no concept of the possibility that there could have been outright collaboration between the Nazi leadership and the founders of what became the state of Israel, the real truth has begun to emerge.

The British *Daily Express* urged Jews everywhere to boycott German goods and demonstrate against German economic interests. It said that Germany was *"now* confronted with an international boycott of its trade, its finances, and its industry....In London, New York, Paris and Warsaw, Jewish businessmen are united to go on an economic crusade."

The article continued, "Worldwide preparations are being made to organise protest demonstrations."

On 27th March 1933 the planned protest at Madison Square Garden, New York was attended by 40,000 protestors. The New York Daily News headlines proclaimed, "40,000 Roar Protest Here Against Hitler."

Similar rallies and protest marches were also held in other cities and the intensity of the Jewish campaign against Germany was such that the Hitler government vowed that if the campaign did not cease, there would be a one-day boycott in Germany of Jewish-owned stores. The propaganda campaign against Germany and its reciprocal action against Jews, elicited by this campaign had thus begun.

Hitler's 28th March 1933 speech ordering a boycott against Jewish stores and goods was in direct response to the declaration of war on Germany by the worldwide Jewish leadership. In the spring of 1933 there began a period of private co-operation between the German government and the Zionist movement in Germany and worldwide to increase the flow of German-Jewish immigrants and their available capital to Palestine.

Growing 'anti-Semitism' in Germany and by the German government in response to the boycott played right into the hands of the Elite Zionist leaders as indeed they had hoped it would. Prior to the escalation of anti-Semitism as a result of the boycott, the majority of German Jews had little sympathy for the Zionist cause of promoting the immigration of world Jewry to Palestine. Making the situation in Germany as uncomfortable for the Jews as possible, in cooperation with German National Socialism, was part of the Zionist plan to achieve their goal of populating Palestine with a Jewish majority.

"For all intents and purposes, the National Socialist government was the best thing to happen to Zionism in its history, for it 'proved' to many Jews that Europeans were irredeemably anti-Jewish and that Palestine was the only answer: Zionism came to represent the overwhelming majority of Jews solely by trickery and cooperation with Adolf Hitler." www.jewwatch.com

Furthermore, contrary to what you may have 'learned' in modern history lessons at school, college or University, read in articles or books or watched in fictional films and so-called 'factual documentaries' about the catalyst of the start of hostilities in 1939, the conflict was absolutely not initiated by Germany. In collusion with the Elite networks in Europe, primarily Britain, Poland did indeed attack Germany's borders without provocation.

"Germany is too strong. We must destroy her." Winston Churchill, November 1936

"The war was not just a matter of the elimination of Fascism in Germany, but rather of obtaining German sales markets." Winston Churchill, March 1946

"Britain was taking advantage of the situation to go to war against Germany because the Reich had become too strong and had upset the European economic balance." Ralph F. Keeling, Institute of American Economics

"I believe now that Hitler and the German people did not want war. But we declared war on Germany, intent on destroying it, in accordance with our principle of balance of power and we were encouraged by the Americans around Roosevelt. We ignored Hitler's pleadings not to enter into war. Now we are forced to realise that Hitler was right." Former UK Attorney General, Sir Hartley Shawcross, 16th March 1984

"The last thing Hitler wanted was to produce another great war." Sir Basil Liddell-Hart, historian

"I see no reason why this war must go on. I am grieved to think of the sacrifices which it will claim. I would like to avert them." Adolf Hitler, July 1940

"We entered the war of our own free will, without ourselves being directly assaulted." Winston Churchill in a Guild Hall speech, July 1943

"The state of German armament in 1939 gives the decisive proof that Hitler was not contemplating general war, and probably not intending war at all" (p.267) and *"Even in 1939 the German army was not equipped for a prolonged war; and in 1940 the German land forces were inferior to the French in everything except leadership."* British historian, Professor A.J.P. Taylor, 'The Origins of the Second World War' (p104-105)

In March 1939 Poland, already occupying German territory legally 'acquired' in 1919 at Versailles, invaded Czechoslovakia and during the months preceding the outbreak of war, Polish armed forces repeatedly violated German borders. On the 31st August 1939 Polish irregular armed forces launched a full scale attack on the German border town of Gleiwitz (significantly now Gliwice, in Poland).

Within hours Germany retaliated by launching an attack on Poland, resulting in Britain and France's declarations of war on the German nation on 3rd September 1939. In Britain's case this declaration of war was constitutionally illegal as it was never ratified by Parliament. Of course the allied propaganda machine churned out the untrue story that the attack on Germany's border had been carried-out by German soldiers dressed in Polish uniforms, in a bizarre double-bluff version of a false-flag operation. Indeed to this day, mainstream history holds this version of events to be true.

Despite her borders being constantly attacked by the numerically superior armies of France and England and economically strangled by Elite financial interests, Germany refused to be drawn into action against Britain, negotiated for peace and undertook no overt offensive strategies for around nine months. This period was known as the 'phony war'. Only when it accurately learned that England intended to broaden the western front by occupying the Benelux countries and Norway, thus threatening Germany's borders, did Germany carry out a full-blooded, pre-emptive strike, the Blitzkrieg (lightening war) on Northern Europe.

Germany's defensive counter-attack was launched on 10th May 1940. This resulted in the rout of 330,000 British and French troops by a significantly smaller German army. It was one of the worst debacles in military history, but the British press referred to it as a 'miracle'.

Russia had already invaded Finland on 30th November 1939 and Britain, not for the first time and France, invaded Norway's neutrality on 8th April 1940. To avoid attack via the Baltic Sea, Germany counter-attacked and in the battle that followed in Trondheim, 2,000 German troops routed a 13,000 strong British force. They were evacuated on 1st May and to save face Churchill disembarked 20,000 British troops at Narvik who were then subsequently ousted by 2,000 Austrian Alpine troops.

Canada declared war on Germany on the 10th September 1939 and in June 1940 Soviet Russia invaded Latvia, Estonia, Lithuania and Romania. In June 1940, Britain declared war on Finland, Romania and Hungary whilst having already occupied a virtually defenceless Iceland on the 10th May. All of these acts of aggression were in gross violation of international law and previously signed treaties.

In May 1940, the British expeditionary force found itself retreating through Belgium in the face of fierce German opposition and by the end of May, 330,000 British troops were surrounded at Dunkirk on the French coast, desperately seeking a way back across the English Channel to safety. Had Hitler chosen to do so, he could have annihilated the British at Dunkirk but when General Heinz Guderian and his troops began to destroy them, he was specifically forbidden by Hitler from doing so. Instead, Hitler deliberately allowed the British to 'escape' back home and re-group.

Months later, Hitler also 'inexplicably' abandoned his plans for a full scale invasion of Britain (Operation Sea-Lion) despite coming-off slightly, but not excessively worse than Britain in the famously 'heroic' Battle of Britain of summer 1940 which was hailed as a great British victory. The lack of a German invasion was of course attributed by mainstream history to 'bad weather' in the English Channel and subsequent, ongoing postponements, but if truth be told, Hitler never had the heart for it. He was, at this point in time, still working for and hopeful of a negotiated peace between the two nations and an invasion of the landmass belonging to one of his most powerful protagonists would have shattered that hope beyond redemption.

"Hitler wanted nothing from Britain or her empire, and all the German records uncovered in the last fifty years have confirmed this grim conclusion. Others now echo our view that Churchill knew from code-breaking that Hitler was only bluffing; but for reasons of domestic politics Churchill fostered the fiction in his public speeches ('We shall fight them on the beaches') and he did the same in his private telegrams to President Roosevelt." David Irving, 'Churchill's War'

"At the time we believed that the repulse of the Luftwaffe in the 'Battle of Britain' had saved her. That is only part of the explanation, the last part of it. The original cause, which goes much deeper, is that Hitler did not want to conquer England. He took little interest in the invasion preparations and for weeks did nothing to spur them on; then, after a brief impulse to invade, he veered around again and suspended the preparations. He was preparing, instead, to invade Russia." Sir Basil Liddell-Hart, British historian

Then on 7th December 1940, a British-backed coup overthrew the Yugoslav government and on 27th March 1941 British troops entered Greece. On 6th April 1941 Germany retaliated and Britain retreated again.

The United States, supposedly neutral, consistently attacked German shipping and arrested or otherwise kidnapped German citizens, even those living in South American countries until finally in August 1941, Germany retaliated against the US, leading ultimately to the entry of the US into the war against Japan and Germany immediately following the attack on Pearl Harbour on the 7th December 1941 by a squadron of Japanese torpedo bombers.

To backtrack a little, in April 1939, there was an exchange of documents and dialogue between US President Franklin Delano Roosevelt (FDR) and Adolf Hitler, as well as between the Polish and German governments. On 15th April, FDR sent a telegram to the Chancellor making claims about Germany as an antagonist and demanding assurances of non-aggression. Apparently, Hitler saw this as a last-minute chance to avoid open hostilities in Central Europe, thus avoiding a terrible global conflagration. He used this opportunity to openly and honestly address all nations, but especially those most directly involved. On 28th April he called a special session of the Reichstag and through German radio and relayed broadcasts, was heard by much of the world. Yet this important address, an honest and sincere effort to avoid war, is today ignored and air-brushed from history as it does not fit with the accepted view of what really happened. Upon reading the selections below, one may clearly see why the Elite chose to isolate and pay no heed to this document. Indeed, one may even notice parallels with current events.

"Adolf Hitler took a last minute opportunity to speak, not only to the USA, but to the whole world, just as dark war clouds were surely and certainly on the horizon. He not only addressed the topics in FDR's wire transmission, but spoke clearly on other problematic key issues of the day such as the Versailles debacle, the Anglo-German Naval Treaty, the Munich Agreements, etc. He told the truth about what had been and

what was going on in Europe, exhaustively responding to each point raised by the American leader. After a thorough reading, what did I conclude? For one thing, it is quite evident that Germany invited continuing dialogue, not war. Even the casual reader can see this. While the Chancellor speaks strongly and straightforwardly, there are no threats, no aggressive language or provocations. Interestingly, and contradicting the popular image of the 'anti-Semitic Jew baiter', he says little other than to assign them much of the blame for the financial failures of the post-war era and for the rise of Bolshevism; and this in just a few sentences. His talk logically progresses into a longer, more detailed examination of how the opportunities following WWI were squandered, hijacked and sabotaged. He asked that Woodrow Wilson's Fourteen Points be fully and equally implemented for all the nations, including Germany. And, he fully recognised Poland's right to the sea, but maintaining Danzig as a German ethnic area. Several sections recount the various efforts to secure fair and lasting agreements with Poland, but all were summarily rejected by the oppressive and recalcitrant military dictatorship that ruled the newly emerged state. And, there is more, but explore the selections below.

This fascinating manuscript is quietly suppressed by simply ignoring it. As said, the very limited partial translation does not do it justice, revealing very little of the real content of this timely foreign policy address by a major world leader. We cover sections which readers may, hopefully, find educational and enlightening. As said, almost all of the quotations herein seem to be unavailable anywhere else. The introductory headings are from those appearing in the margins of the booklet pages. Since the ill-fated Versailles Treaty was central to many of Europe's problems, we begin with that." Dr. Harrell Rhome

Hitler responded to Roosevelt... "But the millions were cheated of this peace; for not only did the German people or the other peoples fighting on our side suffer through the peace treaties, but these treaties had a devastating effect on the victor countries as well.

That politics should be controlled by men who had not fought in the war was recognised for the first time as a misfortune. Hatred was unknown to the soldiers, but not to those elderly politicians who had carefully preserved their own precious lives from the horrors of war and who now descended upon humanity as in the guise of insane spirits of revenge.

Hatred, malice and unreason were the intellectual forebears of the Treaty of Versailles. Territories and states with a history going back a thousand years were arbitrarily broken up and dissolved. Men who had belonged together since time immemorial were torn asunder.

No one knows this [the burdens of Versailles] better than the German people. For the Peace Treaty imposed burdens on the German people, which could not have been paid off in a hundred years, although it has been proved conclusively by American teachers of constitutional law, historians and professors of history that Germany was no more to blame for the outbreak of the war than any other nation. It is hard to imagine a clearer and more concise summary of the massive errors at the end of the war, setting the stage for the next one.

The resultant misery and continuous want [after the war] began to bring our nation to political despair. The decent and industrious people of Central Europe thought they could see the possibility of deliverance in the complete destruction of the old order, which to them represented a curse.

Jewish parasites, on the other hand, plundered the nation ruthlessly, and on the other hand, incited the people, reduced as it was to misery. As the misfortune of our nation became the only aim and object of this race, it was possible to breed among the growing army of unemployed suitable elements suitable elements for the Bolshevik revolution. The decay of political order and the confusion of public opinion by the irresponsible Jewish press led to ever stronger shocks to economic life and consequently to increasing misery and to greater readiness to absorb subversive Bolshevik ideas. The army of the Jewish world revolution as the army of the unemployed were called, finally rose to almost seven million. Germany had never known this state of affairs before.

As a matter of fact, these democratic peace dictators destroyed the whole world economy with their Versailles madness.

They [Western powers] declared at the time that Germany intended to establish herself in Spain, taking Spanish colonies. In a few weeks from now, the victorious hero of Nationalist Spain [Generalissimo Franco] will celebrate his festive entry into the capital of his country. The Spanish people will acclaim him as their deliverer from unspeakable horrors as the liberator from bands of incendiaries, of whom it is estimated that they have more than 775,000 human lives on their conscience, by executions and murders alone. The inhabitants of whole villages and towns were literally butchered, while their benevolent patrons, the humanitarian apostles of Western European and American democracy, remained silent."

Apparently all of this was too large a dose of the truth. As with most of the passages herein, this and the one before it are not found in the minimal translations available. He told the truth, not only about subversive Illuminati communists in Germany, but also about Spain, where the forces of Nationalism won a resounding victory over Bolshevism and world oppression.

Hitler stated.... *"Mr. Roosevelt declared that he had already appealed to me on a former occasion for a peaceful settlement of political, economic and social problems without force of arms. I myself have always been an exponent of this view and as history proves, have settled necessary political, economic and social problems without force of arms, without even resorting to arms.*

Unfortunately, however, this peaceful settlement has been made more difficult by the agitation of politicians, statesmen and newspaper representatives who were neither directly concerned nor even effected by the problems in question."

Does this sound like an unstable, power-mad dictator, ready to launch his legions on the world?   Or, is this the voice of a reasonable world leader, still ready to negotiate for real and lasting peace? Read on and decide for yourself.

"If the cry of 'Never another Munich' is raised in the world today, this simply confirms the fact that the peaceful solution of the problem appeared to be the most awkward thing that ever happened in the eyes of those warmongers. They are sorry no blood was shed, not their blood, to be sure for those agitators are, of course, never to be found where shots are being fired, but only where money is being made. No, it is the blood of many nameless soldiers!

They hate us Germans and would prefer to eradicate us completely. What do the Czechs mean to them? They are nothing but a means to an end. And what do they care for the fate of a small and valiant nation? Why should they worry about the lives of hundreds of thousands of brave soldiers who would have been sacrificed for their policy? These Western Peace-mongers were not concerned to work for peace but to cause bloodshed, so in this way to set the nations against one another and to thus cause still more blood to flow. For this reason, they invented the story of German mobilization.

Moreover, there would have been no necessity for the Munich Conference, for that conference was only made possibly by the fact that the countries which had at first incited those concerned to resist at all costs, were compelled later on, when the situation pressed for a solution on one way of another, to try to secure for themselves a more or less respectable retreat; for without Munich that is to say, without the interference of the countries of Western Europe, a solution of the entire problem if it had grown so acute at all would likely have been the easiest thing in the world."

Here, Hitler presents FDR with a necessary history lecture.....

"Mr. Roosevelt declared finally that three nations in Europe and one in Africa have seen their existence terminated. I do not know which three nations in Europe are meant. Should it be a question of the provinces reincorporated in the German Reich, I must draw the attention of Mr. Roosevelt to a mistake of history on his part.

It was not now that these nations sacrificed their independent existence in Europe, but rather in 1918. At that time, in violation of solemn promises, their logical ties were torn asunder and they were made into nations they never wished to be and never had been. They were forced into an independence which was no independence but at most could only mean dependence upon an international foreign world which they detested.

Moreover, as to the allegation that one nation in Africa has lost its freedom, that, too, is erroneous. On the contrary, practically all the original inhabitants of this continent have lost their freedom through being made subject to the sovereignty of other nations by bloodshed and force. Moroccans, Berbers, Arabs, Negroes, and the rest have all fallen victim to the swords of foreign might, which however, were not marked 'made in Germany' but 'made by Democracies'.

Ireland charges English, not German oppression. Palestine is occupied by English, not German troops. Arabs appeal against English, not German methods."

FDR made a sweeping, somewhat grandiose demand and it is clear that the Middle East, as it does today, occupied a crucial position; *"Are you willing to give assurance that your armed forces will not attack or invade the territory or possessions of the following independent nations: Finland, Estonia, Latvia, Lithuania, Sweden, Norway, Denmark, The Netherlands, Belgium, Great Britain and Ireland, France, Portugal, Spain, Switzerland, Liechtenstein, Luxemburg, Poland, Hungary, Romania, Yugoslavia, Russia, Bulgaria, Greece, Turkey, Iraq, the Arabias, Syria, Palestine, Egypt and Iran?"*

Hitler responded... "But I must also draw Mr. Roosevelt's attention to one or two mistakes in history. He mentions Ireland, for instance, and asks for a statement to the effect that we will not attack Ireland. Now, I have just read a speech by Mr. de Valera, the Irish Taoiseach (Prime Minister), in which he does not charge Germany with oppressing Ireland, but reproaches England with subjecting Ireland to continuous aggression. With all due respect to Mr. Roosevelt's insight into the needs and cares of other countries, it may nevertheless be assumed that the Irish Taoiseach would be more familiar with the dangers which threaten his country than would the President of the United States.

Similarly the fact has obviously escaped Mr. Roosevelt's notice that Palestine is at present occupied not by German troops but by the English; and that the country is undergoing restriction of its liberty by the most brutal resort to force, is being robbed of its independence and is suffering the cruellest maltreatment for the benefit of Jewish interlopers.

The Arabs living in that country would therefore certainly not have complained to Mr. Roosevelt of German aggression, but they are voicing a constant appeal to the world, deploring the barbarous methods with which England is attempting to suppress a people which loves its freedom and is merely defending it.

This, too, is perhaps a problem which in the American President's view should be solved at the conference table, that is, before a just judge, and not by physical force or military methods, by mass executions, burning down villages, blowing up houses and so on. For one fact is surely certain. In this case England is not defending herself against a threatened Arab attack, but as an uninvited interloper is endeavouring to establish her power in a foreign territory which does not belong to her."

Hitler then reminds America that it should not fear Germany as she did not have hidden intentions or motives. Besides, she did not have the natural or military resources to wage a world war across the Atlantic. Only the USA had the wherewithal to do that.

"And, I here solemnly declare all assertions which have in any way been circulated concerning an impending German attack or invasion on or in American territory are rank frauds and gross untruths, quite apart from the fact that such assertions, as far as military possibilities are concerned, could only be the product of the silliest imagination. Friendship and respect for the British Empire must be mutual.

During the whole of my political activity I have always propounded the idea of a close friendship and collaboration between Germany and England. In my movement I found others of like mind. Perhaps they joined me because of my attitude in this regard. This desire for Anglo-German friendship and co-operations conforms not merely to sentiments based on the racial origins of our two peoples but also to my realisation of the importance of the existence of the British Empire for the whole of mankind.

I have never left room for any doubt of my belief that they existence of this empire is an inestimable factor of value for the whole of human culture and economic life. By whatever means Great Britain has acquired her colonial territories and I know that they were those of force and often brutality, I know full well that no other empire has ever come into being in any other way, and that, in the final analysis, it is not so much the methods that are taken into account in history as success, and not the success of the methods as such, but rather the general good which those methods produce.

Now, there is no doubt that the Anglo-Saxon people have accomplished immense colonizing work in the world. For this work, I have sincere admiration.

I regard it as impossible to achieve a lasting friendship between the German and the Anglo-Saxon peoples if the other side does not recognize that there are German as well as British interests, that just as the preservation of the British Empire is the object and life-purpose of Britons, so also the freedom and preservation of the German Reich is the life-purpose of Germans.

A genuine lasting friendship between these two nations is only conceivable on a basis of mutual regard. The English people rule a great empire. They built up this empire at a time when the German people were internally weak.

Germany once had been a great empire. At one time she ruled the Occident. In bloody struggles and religious dissensions, and as a result of internal political disintegration, this empire declined in power and greatness and finally fell into a great sleep.

But as this old empire appeared to have reached its end, the seeds of its rebirth were springing up. From Brandenburg and Prussia there arose a new Germany, the Second Reich, and out of it has finally grown the Reich of the German people.

And I hope that all the English people understand that we do not possess the slightest feeling of inferiority to Britons.

The part we have played in history is far too important for that."

Then, he insisted on naval parity, renegotiating the Anglo-German Naval Treaty, and the return of all German colonies. It seems clear that Britain could have come to terms with the Reich, thus retaining her naval strength, her army and air power, and her colonies, therefore avoiding whatever hostilities there might have been on the continent. But largely due to the provocations of Churchill and the war party, this option was never considered. This is one of the great what-ifs of history.

Hitler continued;

"If however, President Roosevelt considers that he is entitled to address the problems of Europe, in particular to Germany or Italy, because America is so far removed from Europe, we on our side might by the same right, address to the President of the American Republic the question as to what aim American foreign policy in turn has in view, and on what intentions this policy is based, in the case of Central and South American states, for instance. In this event Mr. Roosevelt would, I must admit, every right to refer to the Monroe Doctrine and to decline to reply to such a request to interfere in the internal affairs of the American continent.

We Germans support a similar doctrine for Europe and above all, for the territory and interests of the Greater German Reich.

Moreover, I would obviously never presume to address such a request to the President of the United States of America, because I assume he would probably rightly consider such a presumption tactless."

A little later in the speech, more history lessons are offered by Hitler, especially with regard to the violent history of the USA, which remains pertinent to this day considering the actions of their current government.

"For not statesmen, including those of the United States, especially her greatest, made the outstanding part of their countries' history at the conference table. The freedom of the United States was not achieved at the conference table any more than the conflict between the North and the South was decided there. I will not mention the innumerable struggles which finally led to the subjugation of the North American continent as a whole. I recite all this only in order to show that your view, Mr.

Roosevelt, undoubtedly deserving of all respect, is not confirmed by the history either of your own country or of the rest of the world."

Hitler then openly declared his purposes and deeper allegiances...

"I took the leadership of a state which was faced by complete ruin thanks to the promises of the outside world and the evil of its democratic regime. Billions of German savings accumulated in gold or foreign exchange during many years of peace were extorted from us. We lost our colonies.   In 1933 I had in my country 7 million unemployed, a few million part-time workers, millions of impoverished peasants, trade destroyed, commerce ruined; in short, general chaos.

Since then, Mr. Roosevelt, I have only been able to fulfil one single task. I cannot feel myself responsible for a world, for this world took no interest in the pitiful fate of my people. I have regarded myself as called upon by Providence to serve my own people alone and to deliver them from their frightful misery. Thus, for the past six and one half years, I have lived day and night for the single task of awakening the powers of my people in face of our desertion by the rest of the world, and of developing these powers to the utmost and for utilising them for the salvation of our community.

I have conquered chaos in Germany, re-established order, immediately increased production of all branches of our national economy, by strenuous efforts produced substitutes for numerous materials which we lack, prepared the way for new inventions, developed transportation, caused magnificent roads to be built and canals to be dug, created gigantic new factories. I have striven no less to translate into practice the ideal behind the thought 'community', and to promote the education and culture of my people. To protect them against the threats of the outside world, I have not only united the German people politically, but also rearmed them, I have likewise endeavoured to rid them of that [Versailles] treaty page by page, which in its 448 articles contains the vilest oppression which has ever been inflicted on men and nations.

I have brought back to the Reich its provinces stolen from us in 1919; I have led back to their country millions of Germans who were torn away from us and were in abject misery; I have reunited the territories that have been German throughout a thousand years of history and, Mr. Roosevelt, I have endeavoured to accomplish this without bloodshed and without bringing to my people and so to others, the misery of war

For my world, Mr. President, is the one which Providence has assigned me and for which it is my duty to work. Its area is much smaller. It comprises my people alone. But I believe I can thus best serve that which is in the hearts of all of us, justice, well-being, progress and peace for the whole community of mankind."

This speech was not deemed worthy of a reply by the Allies, who of course predictably, totally ignored and buried it in the graveyard of unwanted history and thus the escalation of the war continued.

Pearl Harbour

It had already been planned that America would take part in World War II, the vast profits available for the military-industrial Elite corporations in an operation of this scale, being too good an opportunity to pass-up. However, the huge stumbling block to the US entering the conflict was Roosevelt's reticence to commit American forces as he had been re-elected on a 'no European war' ticket and at that time over 80% of the American population were not in favour of partaking in yet another European war which they felt (quite correctly) was 'none of their business'.

It is now also known that Roosevelt, under pressure from Elite industrial and financial interests and Churchill, desperate for the US to enter the war to aid a floundering British war effort, conspired together and with others to set in motion events to create a situation which would turn public opinion and generate the outcry that would make war inevitable.

Despite the fact that FDR had won a second term as President largely due to his oft-repeated promise that American soldiers would not become embroiled in the 'European war', he knew only too well that that is exactly what had been planned.

"But our boys are not going to be sent abroad says the President. Nonsense, Mr. Chairman; even now their berths are being built in our transport ships. Even now the tags for identification of the dead and wounded are being printed by the firm of William C. Ballantyne & Co, in Washington." Representative Philip Bennett, Missouri, 1939

Also in 1939, Senator Nye of North Dakota, quoted words in the Senate from a volume named 'The Next War', printed in London some years previously. In it was detailed the plan to drag America into WWII by whatever means it could muster and it said...

"To persuade the US to take our part will be much more difficult, so difficult as to be unlikely to succeed. It will need a definite threat to America, a threat moreover, which will have to be brought home by propaganda, to every citizen, before the Republic will again take arms in an external quarrel...

...The position will naturally be considerably eased if Japan was involved and this might and probably would bring America in without further ado. At any rate, it would be a natural and obvious effect of our propagandists to achieve this, just as in the Great War they succeeded in embroiling the United States against Germany."

Since the war it has been established without doubt that intercepted messages from Japan and warnings from other countries of the Japanese intent to attack Pearl Harbour, went deliberately unheeded in order to provide a justification to enter the war.

"We face the delicate question of diplomatic fencing to be done so as to be sure Japan is put in the wrong and makes the first overt move." Henry Stimson, US Secretary of War, 1941

In 1940 FDR ordered the fleet to be transferred from the West Coast of the US mainland, to its exposed position in Pearl Harbour, Hawaii and ordered that the fleet remain stationed there despite complaints by its commander Admiral Richardson that there was inadequate protection from air attack and no protection at all from torpedo attack. Richardson felt so strongly about this that he twice disobeyed orders to berth his fleet there. He raised the issue personally with FDR in October and he was unsurprisingly replaced soon after this. His successor, Admiral Kimmel, also brought up the same issues with FDR in June 1941 and was also ignored or forestalled.

Then on the 23rd June 1941, FDR's advisor Harold Ickes sent a memo to FDR the day after Germany invaded the Soviet Union, *"There might develop from the embargoing of oil to Japan such a situation as would make it not only possible but easy to get into this war in an effective way. And if we should thus indirectly be brought in, we would avoid the criticism that we had gone in as an ally of communist Russia."*

FDR was pleased too with Admiral Richmond Turner's report on 22nd July 1941 which read; *"It is generally believed that shutting off the American supply of petroleum will lead promptly to the invasion of Netherland East Indies [by Japan].....it seems certain she would also include military action against the Philippine Islands, which would immediately involve us in a Pacific war."*

On the 24th July, FDR told the Volunteer Participation Committee, *"If we had cut off the oil, they probably would have gone down to the Dutch East Indies a year ago, and you would have had war."* The very next day FDR froze all Japanese assets in the US cutting off their main supply of oil and forcing them into some kind of desperate action against the US. Intelligence information regarding the Japanese threat was deliberately withheld from the military command in Hawaii from this point forward.

After the Atlantic Conference on 14th August, Churchill noted the *"...astonishing depth of Roosevelt's intense desire for war."* Churchill cabled his cabinet *"FDR obviously was very determined that they should come in."*

"December 7th [the attack on Pearl Harbour] was... far from the shock it proved to the country in general. We had expected something of the sort for a long time." Eleanor Roosevelt, NY Times Magazine, October 8th, 1944.
"Yes, the Japanese attacked Pearl Harbour, but we [the US] pulled off an international sting operation to trick them into doing it. Roosevelt actually moved the shipping lanes so that the Japanese fleet would not be discovered and reported by some uninvolved ship's captain. Our own early attempts at radar picked up the incoming Zeros but that was explained as just a flock of birds, which given the unknown capabilities of radar at

the time was believable. The fact remains that Roosevelt knew that Pearl Harbour was to be attacked because we had broken the Japanese code. Pearl Harbour was not warned because we wanted to get rid of the WWI ships and be forced to buy new ones and because that war, like all the others was never about nation-states, it was always about the money that every nation needed just to fight in these contrived wars. It has ALWAYS been about the money. And those who died in the attack on Pearl Harbour were just the price of doing business". Jim Kirwan, Researcher November 2010

And so, by this elaborate deception and subterfuge, America joined the war, as had been planned all along. Among other horrors, this resulted in the deaths of more than one quarter of a million American servicemen and appalling injuries to many hundreds of thousands more.

Dresden – An appalling War Crime

On the night of 12/13th February 1945, over 1000 allied bombers attacked a non-military, civilian target in Germany, the town of Dresden. Dresden was (and is still) famous for its china pottery industry and at that time towards the end of the war, was the adopted home of several hundred thousand refugees from the far east of Germany, who were attempting to flee the marauding Russian hordes, rapidly advancing westwards towards Berlin.

There were no military installations in Dresden, no military headquarters or camps, no munitions factories and no heavy engineering of any kind that could have been linked to Germany's by this time seriously crippled, war efforts. In short, Dresden was a medium-large sized, rural, historical town with no strategic importance whatsoever.

What happened in the space of 12 terrifying hours in Dresden should live forever in the annals of the shame of the human race. It is thought by many credible commentators that as many as 4-500,000 innocent people died that night. Far more than double the two atomic explosions of Hiroshima and Nagasaki combined. In many cases, theirs was not a quick death but a slow agonising death through being 'eaten alive' by the phosphorus and subsequent firestorms generated by the half-million+ incendiary bombs dropped by the Allies.

More than 12,000 houses in the centre of the city were reduced to dust, not rubble, dust during the hellish firestorm. In view of the fact that, in addition to the 600,000 inhabitants of Dresden, another 5-600,000 people, all refugees, had found shelter in the overcrowded city, one can safely assume that each of these 12,000 houses contained no fewer than 20 people. But of these houses virtually nothing remained and the people who had been sheltering in them were transformed into ashes due to a heat of greater than 1600 degrees Celsius being generated by the fire-bombs.

The 'official' figure of 35,000 dead only represents the small part of the victims who could be fully identified. Erhard Mundra, a member of the 'Bautzen committee' wrote in the daily German newspaper 'Die Welt' on 12th February 1995...

"According to the former general staff officer of the military district of Dresden and retired lieutenant colonel of the Bundeswehr, D. Matthes, 35,000 victims were fully and another 50,000 partly identified, whereas a further 168,000 could not be identified at all."

It also goes without saying that the hapless children, women, invalids and old people whom the firestorm had transformed into nothing more or less than ashes, could not be identified either.

At the time of the attack, Dresden had no anti-aircraft guns and no military defence. It possessed no military industry at all and served as a shelter for refugees from the East, many of them ill, starving, emaciated and disabled. Indeed, many roofs of buildings where they were housed were marked with huge red crosses.

On that terrible night from 12th to 13th February 1945, one of the greatest war criminals of all time, Winston Churchill, was complicit, indeed instrumental in the senseless, pointless mass-murder of around half a million unarmed, helpless citizens, mostly women, children, the disabled and the aged.

"It cannot be disputed that the principles of international law forbade total carpeting bombing …..The historians considered the indiscriminate bombing as an abomination, but refused to lay the whole guilt on Air Marshall Sir Arthur Harris or the Bomber Command. According to them, the entire staff of the RAF, but even more the political leaders, especially Churchill and Roosevelt, plus the majority of their peoples shared the burden of guilt." The joint conclusions of military historians from five countries at a conference in Freiburg, 1988

On the 13th February 1990, exactly forty-five years after the destruction of Dresden, the British historian David Irving spoke in Dresden. In his speech, Irving quoted the war criminal, Churchill, thus… *"I don't want any suggestions how to destroy militarily important targets around Dresden. I want suggestions as to how we can roast the 600,000 refugees from Breslau in Dresden."*

But for Churchill, simply 'roasting' Germans was nothing like enough. On the morning after the firebombing of Dresden, he ordered low-flying planes to machine-gun the survivors on the banks of the river Elbe where they had dragged themselves to try and find shelter from the suffocating heat by water immersion.

However, to backtrack slightly, as the morning of the 12th February 1945 dawned in Dresden, the streets and squares were filled with refugees and the meadows and parks had been transformed into huge camps. When the fatal hour approached, about 1,130,000 people were living in Dresden. Here is an eyewitness account from a ten year old girl describing (many years later as an adult) what followed later that day…

"About 9.30pm the alarm was given. We children knew that sound and got up and dressed quickly, to hurry downstairs into our cellar which we used as an air raid shelter. My older sister and I carried my baby twin sisters; my mother carried a little suitcase and the bottles with milk for our babies. On the radio we heard with great horror the news: 'Attention, a great air raid will come over our town!' This news I will never forget.

Some minutes later we heard a horrible noise - the bombers. There were non-stop explosions. Our cellar was filled with fire and smoke and was damaged, the lights went out and wounded people shouted dreadfully. In great fear we struggled to leave this cellar. My mother and my older sister carried the big basket in which the twins were laid. With one hand I grasped my younger sister and with the other I grasped the coat of my mother.

We did not recognise our street any more. Fire, only fire wherever we looked. Our 4th floor did not exist anymore. The broken remains of our house were burning. On the streets there were burning vehicles and carts with refugees, people, horses, all of them screaming and shouting in fear of death. I saw hurt women, children, old people searching for a way through ruins and flames.

We fled into another cellar overcrowded with injured and distraught men women and children shouting, crying and praying. No light except some electric torches. And then suddenly the second raid began. This shelter was hit too, and so we fled through cellar after cellar. Many, so many, desperate people came in from the streets. It is not possible to describe! Explosion after explosion. It was beyond belief, worse than the blackest nightmare. So many people were horribly burnt and injured. It became more and more difficult to breathe. It was dark and all of us tried to leave this cellar with inconceivable panic. Dead and dying people were trampled upon and luggage was left or snatched up out of our hands by rescuers. The basket with our twins covered with wet cloths was snatched up out of my mother's hands and we were pushed upstairs by the people behind us. We saw the burning street, the falling ruins and the terrible firestorm. My mother covered us with wet blankets and coats she found in a water tub.

We saw terrible things: cremated adults shrunk to the size of small children, pieces of arms and legs, dead people, whole families burnt to death, burning people ran to and fro, burnt coaches filled with civilian refugees, dead rescuers and soldiers, many were calling and looking for their children and families, and fire everywhere, everywhere fire, and all the time the hot wind of the firestorm threw people back into the burning houses they were trying to escape from.

I cannot forget these terrible details. I can never forget them. Now my mother possessed only a little bag with our identity papers. The basket with the twins had disappeared and then suddenly my older sister vanished too. Although my mother looked for her immediately it was in vain. The last hours of this night we found shelter in the cellar of a hospital nearby surrounded by crying and dying people. In the next morning we looked for our sister and the twins but without success. The house where we lived was only a burning ruin. The house where our twins were left we could not go in. Soldiers said everyone was burnt to death and we never saw my two baby sisters again.

Totally exhausted, with burnt hair and badly burnt and wounded by the fire we walked to the Loschwitz Bridge where we found good people who allowed us to wash, to eat and to sleep. But only a short time because suddenly the second air raid began and this house too was bombed and my mother's last identity papers burnt. Completely exhausted we hurried over the bridge across the River Elbe with many other homeless survivors and found another family ready to help us, because somehow their home survived this horror.

In all this tragedy I had completely forgotten my 10th birthday, but the next day my mother surprised me with a piece of sausage she begged from the 'Red Cross'. This was my birthday present.
In the next days and weeks we looked for my older sister but in vain. We wrote our present address on the last walls of our damaged house. In the middle of March we were evacuated to a little village near Oschatz and on March 31st, we got a letter from my sister. She was alive! In that disastrous night she lost us and with other lost children she was taken to a nearby village. Later she found our address on the wall of our house and at the beginning of April my mother brought her to our new home.

You can be sure that the horrible experiences of this night in Dresden led to confused dreams, sleepless nights and disturbed our souls, me and the rest of my family. Years later I intensively thought the matter over, the causes, the political contexts of this night. This became very important for my whole life and my further decisions."

Dresden's citizens barely had time to reach their shelters. The first bomb fell at 10.09pm and the attack lasted 24 minutes, leaving the inner city a raging sea of fire. Precision saturation bombing had created the desired firestorm.

A firestorm is engendered when hundreds of smaller fires join together and become one vast conflagration. Huge volumes of oxygen are drawn-in to feed the inferno, causing an artificial tornado. Those persons unlucky enough to be caught in the rush of wind can be hurled down the entire length of a street into the flames. Those who seek refuge underground often suffocate as oxygen is extracted from the air to feed the blaze or they perish in a blast of white heat, intense enough to melt human flesh and bone, leaving no visible trace. Indeed, such was the power of the conflagration that night that air was sucked from basements and sewers where the populace hid in large numbers, suffocating many hundreds or even thousands, to death.

Another eyewitness who survived told of seeing *"young women carrying babies running up and down the streets, their dresses and hair on fire, screaming until they fell down, or the collapsing buildings fell on top of them."*

There was a three-hour pause between the first and second raids. The lull had been calculated to lure civilians from their shelters into the open again. To escape the flames, tens of thousands of civilians had crowded into the 'Grosser Garten', a beautiful area of parkland nearly one and a half miles square in area.

The second raid came at 1.22 am with no warning as the early warning sirens had been destroyed in the first attack, probably along with their operators. Twice as many bombers returned with another massive payload of incendiary bombs. The second wave was intended to spread the raging firestorm into the Grosser Garten and it was a complete success. Within a few minutes a sheet of flame ripped across the grass, uprooting trees and littering the branches of others with everything from bicycles to human limbs. For days afterward, they remained bizarrely strewn about as grim reminders of Allied sadism.

At the start of the second air assault, many were still huddled in tunnels and cellars, waiting for the fires of the first attack to die down. At 1.30 am an ominous rumble reached the ears of the commander of a Labour Service convoy sent into the city on a rescue mission. He described it this way...

"The detonation shook the cellar walls. The sound of the explosions mingled with a new, stranger sound which seemed to come closer and closer, the sound of a thundering waterfall; it was the sound of a mighty tornado howling in the inner city."

Others hiding below ground died, but they died painlessly - they simply glowed bright orange and blue in the darkness and as the heat intensified, they either disintegrated into ashes or melted into a thick liquid, three to four feet deep in places. Shortly after 10.30am on the morning of the 14th of February, the last raid swept over the city. American fighter-bombers pounded the rubble that had been Dresden for a full forty minutes, but this attack was not nearly as heavy as the first two.

However, what distinguished this raid was the cold-blooded ruthlessness with which it was carried out. US Mustangs appeared low over the city, strafing with machine gun fire, anything that moved, including a column of rescue vehicles rushing to the city to evacuate survivors. One assault was aimed at the banks of the Elbe River, where refugees had huddled together during this terrible night.

In the last year of the war, Dresden had become a hospital town. During the previous night's massacre, heroic uninjured individuals had dragged thousands of the devastatingly injured to the banks of the Elbe to escape the worst ravages of the firestorm. The low-flying American Mustangs machine-gunned those people and their helpless charges, as well as thousands of elderly and children who had escaped the city and when the last plane had departed, Dresden was a scorched ruin, its blackened streets filled with corpses. The city was not even spared further horror. A flock of vultures that had escaped from the ruins of the zoo fed on the carnage and rats also swarmed over the piles of corpses.

In Dresden, the Allied airmen under the orders of the Elite butchers fronted by the sadistic Churchill, murdered several hundreds of thousands people in one single, hellish night and destroyed countless cultural treasures. Women who were giving birth to children in the delivery rooms of the burning hospitals jumped out of the windows, but within minutes, these mothers and their children, who were still hanging at the umbilical cords, were reduced to ashes too. Thousands of people whom the incendiary bombs had transformed into living torches jumped into the ponds, lakes and rivers, but phosphorus continues to burn even in the water and is indeed 'fed' by water. Even the animals from the zoo, elephants, lions and others, desperately headed for the water, together with the humans. But all of them, the new-born children, the mothers, the old men, the wounded soldiers and the innocent animals from the zoo and the stables, horribly perished in the name of 'liberation'.

What justification is there for this utterly repugnant behaviour? Is it revenge, hatred, blood-lust or ritual sacrifice? I believe it is a mixture of all of these, but I do know one thing for sure and that is that no sane, balanced, rational human being behaves in this disgraceful, cowardly fashion. These people are undoubtedly clinical psychopaths with no empathy for the plight of their fellow man, whatsoever.

The Atomic Bomb

It is a popular, albeit cynically engendered misconception that credits the dropping of the two atomic devices on the Japanese cities of Hiroshima and Nagasaki on the 6th and 9th August 1945, respectively with ending the war months early and saving the lives of millions.

With World War Two rapidly coming to a close, the Elite needed an excuse to move into the next phase of their 'great work of ages', the 'Cold War'. The attack on Hiroshima and Nagasaki sent a clear message to the Soviets and indeed the rest of the world and it was known by the American branch of the Elite that the Soviets would not sit idly by and let American military technology intimidate them. The Soviets had already begun work on their own version of the terror weapon, subsequently helped enormously and probably intentionally by the wholesale leaking of atomic secrets by double agents. Within a year or so of the end of the war, the Russians had their own atomic devices and thus was born the 'Cold War' and the great 'Arms Race' of the second half of the twentieth century, designed solely to terrify and as an excuse to suppress the populations of the whole world in much the same way as the contemporary, bogus 'war on terror' works today.

The Americans and British blatantly and repeatedly ignored desperate Japanese attempts to unconditionally surrender because firstly they wanted to drag-out the war for as long as possible and also they needed to actually demonstrate to the world, the devastating effect of the atomic bomb, otherwise the planned, coming 'Cold War' could not have generated the same terror in people's minds.

"Our entire post-war programme depends on terrifying the world with the atomic bomb. We are hoping for a tally of a million dead in Japan. But if they surrender, we won't have anything." US Secretary of State, Edward Stettinius Jr., the son of a JP Morgan partner, early 1945

According to the historian Eustace Mullins, President Truman, whose only real job before Senator had been a Masonic 'organiser' in Missouri, did not make the fatal decision alone. A committee led by James F. Byrnes, Bernard Baruch's puppet, instructed him. Baruch was the Rothschild's principal agent in the USA and a Presidential 'advisor' spanning the era from Woodrow Wilson to John F Kennedy.

Baruch, who was chairman of the Atomic Energy Commission, spearheaded the 'Manhattan Project' named after Baruch's home town. He chose life-long Communist Robert Oppenheimer to be Research Director. It was very much the 'bankers' bomb'.

On August 6, 1945, a Uranium bomb (isotope U-235) of 20 kilotons was exploded 1850 feet in the air above Hiroshima, for maximum explosive effect. It devastated four square miles of the ancient, historical city and killed outright 140,000 of the 255,000 inhabitants. This figure does not account, however, for the many thousands seriously injured and the many thousands more that would die in agony from radiation in the succeeding months and years.

In the United States the news of the bombing of Hiroshima was greeted with a mixture of relief, pride and shock but mainly joy. Apparently it is reported that Oppenheimer himself walked around like a prize-fighter, clasping his hands together above his head in triumph when he heard the 'good' news.

American Concentration Camps 1945-47

We have been conditioned over the years to believe that during the Second World War the Germans and Japanese were the only ones capable of atrocities whilst 'our boys' were good, moral upstanding people who would never dream in a million years of committing immoral and repugnant acts or serious crimes against humanity and our illustrious leaders especially, even more so. The problem with this view is that it does not stand up to even cursory scrutiny. The number of Germans, civilian and military, murdered, starved and tortured to death in the two year period following VE day, far exceeded the worst excesses of Nazi brutality including the so-called 'holocaust'. War is horrific and the atrocities committed on both sides in every conflict are inexcusable but at the same time are inevitable consequences of the hatred engendered by propaganda from a country's Elite and its puppet leaders, fear of the enemy and also of misguided desire for retribution.

No, Germany's defeat in May 1945 and the end of World War II in Europe did not bring an end to death and suffering for the already vanquished German people. Instead the victorious Allies ushered in a terrible new era of destruction, looting, starvation, rape, 'ethnic cleansing' and mass killing.

A contemporary edition of *Time* magazine referred to this period as *"history's most terrifying peace."*

Even though this unknown holocaust is ignored in our motion pictures and classrooms and by our political leaders, the facts are well established. Historians are in basic agreement about the scale of the human catastrophe, which has been detailed in a number of other books. For example, American historian Alfred de Zayas, along with other scholars, has established that in the years 1945 to 1950, more than 14 million Germans were expelled or forced to flee from large regions of eastern and central Europe, of whom more than four million were deliberately or negligently killed or otherwise lost their lives.

British historian Giles MacDonough details in his book, *'After the Reich: The Brutal History of the Allied Occupation'*, how the ruined and prostrate German Reich (including Austria) was systematically raped and robbed and how many Germans who survived the war were either killed in cold blood or deliberately left to die of disease, cold, malnutrition or starvation. He explains how some three million Germans died unnecessarily after the official end of hostilities - about two million civilians, mostly women, children and elderly and about one million prisoners of war.

Some people take the view that, given the wartime record of the Nazis, some degree of vengeful violence against the defeated Germans was inevitable and perhaps justified. A common response to reports of Allied atrocities is to say that the Germans 'deserved it' but however valid or otherwise that argument may be, the appalling cruelties inflicted upon the totally helpless German people went far beyond any 'understandable' retribution.

It is also worth noting that they were not the only victims of post-war Allied brutality. Across central and eastern Europe, the brutality of Soviet suppression continued to take lives of Poles, Hungarians, Czechs, Ukrainians and many other nationalities in great numbers. As Soviet troops advanced into central and eastern Europe during the war's final months, they imposed a reign of terror, pillage, rape and killing without comparison in modern history. The horrors were summarised thus;

"The disaster that befell this area with the entry of the Soviet forces has no parallel in modern European experience. There were considerable sections of it where, to judge by all existing evidence, scarcely a man, woman or child of the indigenous population was

left alive after the initial passage of Soviet forces; and one cannot believe that they all succeeded in fleeing to the West ... The Russians ... swept the native population clean in a manner that had no parallel since the days of the Asiatic hordes." George F. Kennan, historian and former US ambassador to the Soviet Union

During the last months of the war, the ancient German city of Königsberg in eastern Germany held out as a strongly defended urban fortress. After repeated attack and siege by the Red Army, it finally surrendered in early April 1945. Soviet troops then ravished the civilian population. The people were beaten, robbed, killed and if female, raped first. The rape victims included nuns and even hospital patients were robbed of their possessions. Bunkers and shelters, packed with terrified people huddled inside, were torched with flame-throwers. In all, about 40,000 of the city's population were killed or took their own lives to escape the horrors and the remaining 73,000 German civilians were brutally deported.

In a report that appeared in August 1945 in the Washington DC *Times-Herald*, an American journalist wrote of what he described as *"...the state of terror in which women in Russian-occupied eastern Germany were living. All these women, Germans, Polish, Jewish and even Russian girls 'freed' from Nazi slave camps, were dominated by one desperate desire - to escape from the Red zone. In the district around our internment camp ... Red soldiers during the first weeks of their occupation raped every women and girl between the ages of 12 and 70. That sounds exaggerated, but it is the simple truth. The only exceptions were girls who managed to remain in hiding in the woods or who had the presence of mind to feign illness - typhoid, diphtheria or some other infectious disease ... Husbands and fathers who attempted to protect their women folk were shot down and girls offering extreme resistance were murdered."*

In accordance with policies set by the Allied leaders of the US, Britain and the Soviet Union, Roosevelt, Churchill and Stalin, millions of Germans were expunged from their ancient homelands in central and eastern Europe.

In October 1945, a New York *Daily News* report from occupied Berlin told readers;

"In the windswept courtyard of the Stettiner Bahnhof, a cohort of German refugees, part of 12 million to 19 million dispossessed in East Prussia and Silesia, sat in groups under a driving rain and told the story of their miserable pilgrimage, during which more than 25 percent died by the roadside and the remainder were so starved they scarcely had strength to walk.
A nurse from Stettin, a young, good-looking blonde, told how her father had been stabbed to death by Russian soldiers who, after raping her mother and sister, tried to break into her own room. She escaped and hid in a haystack with four other women for four days ... On the train to Berlin she was raped once by Russian troops and twice by Poles. Women who resisted were shot dead, she said and on one occasion she saw a guard take an infant by the legs and crush its skull against a post because the child cried while the guard was raping its mother. An old peasant from Silesia said ... victims were

robbed of everything they had, even their shoes. Infants were robbed of their swaddling clothes so that they froze to death. All the healthy girls and women, even those 65 years of age, were raped in the train and then robbed, the peasant said."
In November 1945 an item in the *Chicago Tribune* told readers;

"Nine hundred and nine men, women and children dragged themselves and their luggage from a Russian railway train at Lehrter station in Berlin today, after eleven days travelling in boxcars from Poland. Red Army soldiers lifted 91 corpses from the train, while relatives shrieked and sobbed as their bodies were piled in American lend-lease trucks and driven off for internment in a pit near a concentration camp. The refugee train was a like a macabre Noah's ark. Every car was packed with Germans ... the families carry all their earthly belongings in sacks, bags and tin trunks ... Nursing infants suffer the most, as their mothers are unable to feed them and frequently go insane as they watch offspring slowly die before their eyes. Today four screaming, violently insane mothers were bound with rope to prevent them from clawing other passengers."

Although most of the millions of German girls and women who were ravished by Allied soldiers were raped by Red Army troops, Soviet soldiers were not the only perpetrators. During the French occupation of Stuttgart, a large city in southwest Germany, police records show that 1,198 women and eight men were raped, mostly by French troops from Morocco, although the prelate of the Lutheran Evangelical church estimated the number at 5,000.
During World War II, the United States, Britain and Germany broadly complied with the international regulations on the treatment of prisoners of war, as required by the Geneva Convention of 1929 even though Germany did not formally recognise it. But at the end of the fighting in Europe, the US and British authorities scrapped the Geneva Convention. In violation of solemn international obligations and Red Cross rules, the American and British authorities stripped millions of captured German soldiers of their status and their rights as prisoners of war by strategically reclassifying them in true Orwellian fashion as so-called 'disarmed enemy forces' or 'surrendered enemy personnel.'

Accordingly, British and American authorities denied International Red Cross representatives access to camps holding German prisoners of war. Moreover, any attempt by German civilians to feed the prisoners was punishable by death. Many thousands of German POWs died in American custody, most infamously in the so-called 'Rhine meadow camps,' where prisoners were held under appalling conditions, with no shelter or sanitation and inadequate food.

In April 1946, the International Committee of the Red Cross (ICRC) protested that the United States, Britain and France, nearly a year after the end of fighting, were violating International Red Cross agreements they had solemnly pledged to uphold. The Red Cross pointed out for example, that the American transfer of German prisoners of war to French and British authorities for forced labour was contrary to International Red Cross statutes.

Another report by the International Committee of the Red Cross in August 1946 stated that the US government, through its military branch in the US zone of occupation in Germany, was exacting forced labour from 284,000 captives, of whom 140,000 were in the US occupation zone, 100,000 in France, 30,000 in Italy, and 14,000 in Belgium. Holdings of German prisoners or slave labourers by other countries, the Red Cross reported, included 80,000 in Yugoslavia, and 45,000 in Czechoslovakia.

Both during and after the war, the Allies extensively tortured German prisoners. In one British centre in England, 'the London Cage', German prisoners were subjected to systematic ill-treatment, including starvation and beatings. The brutality continued for several years after the end of the war and treatment of German prisoners by the British was even more harsh in the British occupation zone of Germany. At the US internment centre at Schwäbisch Hall in Southwest Germany, prisoners awaiting trial by American military courts were subjected to severe and systematic torture, including long stretches in solitary confinement, extremes of heat and cold, deprivation of sleep and food and severe beatings, including the crushing of testicles and kicks to the groin.

Most of the German prisoners of war who died in Allied captivity were held by the Soviets and a much higher proportion of German POWs died in Soviet custody than perished in British and American captivity. (For example, of the 90,000 Germans who surrendered at Stalingrad, only 5,000 ever returned to their homeland.) Up to ten years after the end of the war, hundreds of thousands of German prisoners were still being held in the Soviet Union. Other German prisoners perished after the end of the war in Yugoslavia, Poland and other countries. In Yugoslavia alone, authorities of the Communist regime killed as many as 80,000 Germans. German prisoners toiled as slave labourers in other Allied countries, often for many years. There is no doubt in my mind that all these acts were a not-so-subtle attempt to ethnically cleanse the German nation.

At the Yalta conference in early 1945, the Allied leaders agreed that the Soviets could take Germans as forced labourers, or 'slave labour', contrary to common human decency and morality. It is estimated that a further 874,000 German civilians were abducted to the Soviet Union. These were in addition to the millions of prisoners of war who were held by the Soviets as forced labourers. Of these so-called reparations deportees, 45% perished.

For two years after the end of the fighting, the Germans were victims of a cruel and vindictive occupation policy, one that meant slow starvation of the defeated population. To sustain healthy life, a normal adult needs a minimum of about 1800 calories per day. But in March and February 1946, the daily intake per person in the

British and American occupation zones of Germany was between one thousand and fifteen hundred calories.

In the winter of 1945-46, the Allies forbade anyone outside the country to send food parcels to the starving Germans. The Allied authorities also rejected requests by the International Red Cross to bring in provisions to alleviate the suffering.

Very few persons in Britain or the United States spoke out against the Allied policy. Victor Gollancz, an English-Jewish writer and publisher, toured the British occupation zone of northern Germany for six weeks in late 1946. He publicised the death and malnutrition he found there, which he said was a consequence of Allied policy. He wrote:

"The plain fact is ... we are starving the Germans and we are starving them, not deliberately in the sense that we definitely want them to die, but wilfully, in the sense that we prefer their death to our own inconvenience."

Another person who protested was Bertrand Russell, the noted philosopher and Nobel Prize recipient. In a letter published in a London newspaper in October 1945, he wrote:

"In eastern Europe now, mass deportations are being carried out by our allies on an unprecedented scale and an apparently deliberate attempt is being made to exterminate many millions of Germans by depriving them of their homes and of food, leaving them to die by slow and agonizing starvation. This is not done as an act of war, but as a part of a deliberate policy of `peace'."

As the war was ending in what is now the Czech Republic, hysterical mobs brutally assaulted ethnic Germans, members of a minority group whose ancestors had lived there for centuries. In Prague, German soldiers were rounded up, disarmed, tied to stakes, doused with petroleum, and set on fire as living torches. In some cities and towns in what is now the Czech Republic, every German over the age of six was forced to wear on his clothing, sewn on his left breast, a large white circle six inches in diameter with the black letter N, which is the first letter of the Czech word for German. Germans were also banned from all parks, places of public entertainment and public transportation and not allowed to leave their homes after eight in the evening. Later all these people were expelled, along with the entire ethnic German population of what is now the Czech Republic. In the Czech Republic alone, a quarter of a million ethnic Germans were killed.

In Poland, the so-called 'Office of State Security,' an agency of the country's new Soviet-controlled government, imposed its own brutal form of 'de-Nazification.' Its agents raided German homes, rounding up some 200,000 men, women, children and infants, 99% of them non-combatant, innocent civilians. They were incarcerated in cellars, prisons, and 1,255 concentration camps where typhus was rampant and torture was commonplace. Between 60,000 and 80,000 Germans perished at the hands of the 'Office of State Security.'

We are ceaselessly and unremittingly reminded, by the thousands of books and documentaries still being produced, of the Third Reich's wartime concentration camps, but few are aware that such infamous camps as Dachau, Buchenwald, Sachsenhausen and Auschwitz were kept in operation after the end of the war, only now packed with German citizens, many of whom also perished miserably.

For many years we have heard much about so-called Nazi art theft but however large the scale of 'confiscation' of art by Germans in World War II, it was dwarfed by the massive theft of art works and other objects of cultural value by the Allies. The Soviets alone looted some two and half million art objects, including 800,000 paintings. In addition, many paintings, statues, and other priceless art works were destroyed by the Allies.

In the war's aftermath, the victors put many German military and political leaders to death or sentenced them to lengthy prison terms after much-publicized trials in which the Allies were both prosecutor and judge. The best-known of these trials was before the so-called 'International Military Tribunal' at Nuremberg, where officials of the four Allied powers were both the prosecutors and the judges.

Justice, as opposed to vengeance, is a standard that is assumed to be applied impartially but in the aftermath of World War II, the victorious powers imposed standards of justice that applied only to the vanquished. The governments of the United States, Britain and the Soviet Union and other member states of the so-called 'United Nations', held Germans to a standard that they categorically refused to respect themselves.

Robert Jackson, the chief US prosecutor at the Nuremberg Tribunal of 1945-46, privately acknowledged in a letter to President Truman, that the Allies "...have done or are doing some of the very things we are prosecuting the Germans for. The French are so violating the Geneva Convention in the treatment of German prisoners of war that our command is taking back prisoners sent to them for forced labour in France. We are prosecuting plunder and our Allies are practicing it. We say aggressive war is a crime and one of our allies asserts sovereignty over the Baltic States based on no title except conquest."

Germans were executed or imprisoned for policies that the Allies themselves were carrying out, sometimes on a far greater scale. German military and political leaders were put to death on the basis of a hypocritical double standard, which meant that these executions were essentially acts of judicial murder dressed up with the trappings and forms of legality. If the standards of the Nuremberg Tribunal had been applied impartially, many American, Soviet and other Allied military and political leaders would also have been hanged.

An awareness of how the defeated Germans were treated by the victors helps in understanding why Germans continued to fight during the final months of the war with a determination, tenacity and willingness to sacrifice that has few parallels in history, even as their cities were being smashed into ruins under relentless bombing (Dresden for example) and even as defeat against numerically superior enemy forces seemed inevitable.

Two years after the end of the war, American and British policy toward the defeated Germans changed. The US and British governments began to treat the Germans as potential allies, rather than as vanquished enemy subjects and to appeal for their support. This shift in policy was not prompted by an awakening of humanitarian spirit. Instead, it was motivated by American and British fear of Soviet Russian expansion and by the realisation that the economic recovery of Europe as a whole required a prosperous and productive Germany.

Oswald Spenger, the German historian and philosopher, once observed that how a people learn history is via its form of political education. In every society, including our own, how people learn and understand history is determined by those who control political and cultural life, including the educational system and the mass media. How people understand the past and how they view the world and themselves as members of society, is set by the agenda of those who hold ultimate power, the Elite.

This is why, in our society, death and suffering during and after World War II of non-Jews, Poles, Russians and others, and especially Germans is all but ignored and why, instead, more than six decades after the end of the war, Jewish death and suffering above all, what is known as the 'Holocaust' is given such prominent attention, year after year, in our classrooms, documentaries and motion pictures and by our manipulated and controlled political leaders.

The 'unknown holocaust' of non-Jews is essentially ignored not because the facts are disputed or unknown, but rather because this reality does not fit well with the Judeocentric view of history that is all but obligatory in our society, a view of the past that reflects the Elite Jewish-Zionist hold on our cultural and educational life.

This means that it is not enough simply to 'establish the facts.' It is important to understand, identify and counter the power that controls what we see, hear and read in our classrooms, our periodicals and in our motion pictures and which determines how we view history, our world and ourselves, not just the history of what is called the 'Holocaust,' but the history and background of World War II, the Israel-Palestine conflict, the Middle East turmoil and much, much more.

History, as the old saying goes, is written by the victors. In our society, the victors, that is, the most important single group that sets our perspective on the past through its grip on the media, and on our cultural life, is the organised Elite community.

An awareness of 'real history' is in itself not enough. It is important to understand the how and why of the systematic falsification of history in our society and the power behind that distortion. Understanding and countering that power is a critically important task, not merely for the sake of historical truth in the abstract, but for the sake of and the future of all humankind.

What follows is a summary of an eye-witness testimony to the events leading up to and immediately following, the end of the war in Germany in 1945. These events are never mentioned in either contemporary or present-day literature and are not taught in schools or memorialised in countless films and documentaries ad nauseum, unlike the 'holocaust'. The question needs to be asked as to why this and many other similar events are conveniently air-brushed from history whilst others are continually alluded to, dramatised and sensationalised.

According to the testimony of a former American GI, in late March or early April 1945 he was sent to guard a camp full of German military and civilian prisoners near Andernach on the River Rhine, one of the infamous 'Rhine meadows' camps. He had studied German in high school for four years and so was able to talk to the prisoners, although this was actually strictly forbidden. Gradually however, he was used as an interpreter and asked to try to discover those who had been members of the SS. (He found none.)
In Andernach about 50,000 prisoners of all ages were held in an open field surrounded by barbed wire. The women were kept in a separate enclosure. The men had no shelter and no blankets and most had no coats. They slept in the mud, wet and cold, with inadequate slit trenches for use as toilets. It was a cold, wet spring and their misery from exposure alone was evident.

Even more shocking was to see the prisoners throwing grass and weeds into a tin can containing a thin soup. They did this to help ease their hunger pains but they soon grew very emaciated. Dysentery was rife and soon they were sleeping in their own excrement, too weak and crowded to reach the slit trenches. Many were begging for food, sickening and dying before the eyes of their captors who had ample food and supplies, but did nothing to help them, even refusing them medical assistance.

Outraged, he protested to the officers and was met with hostility or bland indifference. When pressed, they explained they were under strict orders from 'higher up.' No officer would dare do this to 50,000 men if he felt that it was 'out of line,' leaving himself open to charges. Realising that his protestations were useless, he asked a friend working in the kitchen if he could smuggle out any extra food for the prisoners. He too said they were under strict orders to severely ration the prisoners' food and that these orders came from 'above'. But he said they had more food than they knew what to do with and would see what he could do.

When he threw this food over the barbed wire to the prisoners, he was caught and threatened with imprisonment. After repeating the offence, one officer angrily threatened to shoot him but he assumed this was a bluff until he encountered a captain on a hill above the camp shooting down at a group of German civilian women with his .45 calibre handgun.

When asked why, he mumbled 'target practice' and fired until his pistol was empty. The women ran for cover, but at that distance it was not possible to see if any had been hit. He soon realised he was dealing with cold-blooded killers filled with moralistic hatred that considered the Germans subhuman and worthy only of extermination; another expression of the downward spiral of racism. Articles in the GI newspaper, *Stars and Stripes*, played up the German concentration camps, complete with photos of emaciated bodies. This amplified the Americans self-righteous cruelty and made it easier to imitate behaviour they were supposed to have been fighting to bring to an end.

These prisoners were mostly farmers and working men, as simple and ignorant as many of the US troops. As time went by, more of them lapsed into a zombie-like state of listlessness, while others tried to escape in a demented or suicidal fashion, running through open fields in broad daylight towards the Rhine to quench their thirst. They were mowed down by machine gun fire.

Some prisoners were as eager for cigarettes as for food, saying they took the edge off their hunger. Accordingly, enterprising GIs were acquiring hordes of watches and rings in exchange for handfuls of cigarettes or less. When he began throwing cartons of cigarettes to the prisoners to ruin this trade, he was threatened by rank-and-file GIs too.

The only bright spot in this gloomy picture came one night when he was on the 'graveyard shift' from two to four am. There was a cemetery on the uphill side of this enclosure, not many yards away. His superiors had omitted to give him a flashlight and he had not asked for one, disgusted as he was with the whole situation by that time. It was a fairly bright night and he soon became aware of a prisoner crawling under the wires towards the graveyard. They were supposed to shoot escapees on sight, so he started to get up from the ground to warn him to get back but suddenly noticed another prisoner crawling from the graveyard back to the enclosure. They were risking their lives to get to the graveyard for something.

Upon investigating in the gloom of this shrubby, tree-shaded cemetery, he felt overwhelmingly vulnerable, but somehow curiosity kept him moving. Despite his caution, he tripped over the legs of someone in a prone position. Whipping his rifle around while stumbling and trying to regain composure of mind and body, he was relieved that he had not reflexively fired a shot. The figure sat up and gradually, the beautiful but terror-stricken face of a woman with a picnic basket nearby became apparent. German civilians were not allowed to feed, nor even come near the prisoners, so he quickly assured her that he approved of what she was doing, not to be afraid and that he would leave the graveyard immediately.

Having departed the graveyard he sat down, leaning against a tree at the edge of the cemetery to be inconspicuous and not frighten the prisoners. Eventually, more prisoners crawled back to the enclosure and he saw that they were dragging food back to their comrades and he could only admire their courage and devotion in the face of such desperation.

On the 8th May 1945, VE Day, he decided to celebrate with some prisoners he was guarding who were baking the bread the other prisoners occasionally received. This group had all the bread they could eat and shared the jovial mood engendered by the cessation of hostilities. Everyone thought that they would be going home soon, which as it turned out was far from the truth. At this point in time however, they were in what was to become the French zone of occupation, where he soon would witness the brutality of the French soldiers when the prisoners were transferred to them for their slave labour camps. On this day, however, all were happy.

Shortly afterwards, some of the more weak and sickly prisoners were marched off by French soldiers to their camp and the GIs followed on a truck behind this column. On several occasions, temporarily it slowed down and almost stopped, possibly because the truck driver was shocked to see that whenever a German prisoner staggered or dropped back, he was hit on the head with a club and killed. The bodies were rolled to the side of the road to be picked up by another truck. For many, this quick death might have been preferable to the slow starvation that otherwise awaited them.

"...it is hard to escape the conclusion that Dwight Eisenhower was a war criminal of epic proportions. His policy killed more Germans in peace than were killed in the European Theatre." Peter Worthington, the 'Ottawa Sun', 12th September 1989

Eventually, famine began to spread among the German civilians also. It was a common sight to see German women up to their elbows in garbage cans looking for something edible. There were never any Red Cross personnel at the camp or helping civilians, although their coffee and doughnut stands were available everywhere else for the US troops. In the meantime, the Germans had to rely on the sharing of hidden stores until the next harvest.

Hunger made German women more 'available' but despite this, rape was prevalent and often accompanied by additional violence. In particular there was an eighteen-year old woman who had the side of her faced smashed with a rifle butt and was then raped by two GIs. Even the French complained that the rapes, looting and drunken destructiveness on the part of US troops was excessive. In Le Havre, the US forces were given booklets warning that the German soldiers had maintained a high standard of behaviour with French civilians who were peaceful and that they should do the same. In this they failed miserably.

'So what', some may say? The enemy's atrocities were worse than ours. It is true that he experienced only the end of the war, when the Allies were already the victors. The German opportunity for atrocities had ended, but two wrongs do not make a right. Rather than mimicking an enemy's crimes, should we not aim to break the cycle of hatred and vengeance that has always plagued and distorted human history?

We can reject government propaganda that depicts our enemies as subhuman and encourages the kind of outrages he witnessed. We can protest the bombing of civilian targets, which still goes on today in places like Iraq, Pakistan, Palestine, Afghanistan and Libya and we can refuse ever to condone our government's murder and torture of unarmed and defeated prisoners of war and helpless civilians.

Even GIs sympathetic to the victims were afraid to complain and get into trouble and the danger has not ceased. After this brave man spoke out many, many years later, he received threatening calls, was intimidated physically and had his mailbox smashed.

The abuses committed by the forces of the occupation in Germany reached such bestial extremes that various people in the Allied command structure opposed it, or tried to. Charles Lindbergh mentioned how the American soldiers burned the leftovers of their meals to keep them from being scavenged by the starving Germans who hung around the rubbish bins.

Lindbergh also wrote:

"In our homeland the public press publishes articles on how we 'liberated' the oppressed peoples. Here, our soldiers use the word 'liberate' to describe how they get their hands on loot. Everything they grab from a German house, everything they take off a German is 'liberated' in the lingo of our troops. Leica cameras are liberated, food, works of art, clothes are liberated. A soldier who rapes a German girl is 'liberating' her.

There are German children who gaze at us as we eat ... our cursed regulations forbid us to give them anything to eat. I remember the soldier Barnes, who was arrested for having given a chocolate bar to a tattered little girl. It's hard to look these children in the face. I feel ashamed. Ashamed of myself and my people as I eat and look at those children. How can we have gotten so inhumane?"

Colonel Charles Lindbergh was regarded as a national hero of the United States and was proposed as a candidate for the presidency of his country. He served in the USAF and was no Nazi or Nazi sympathiser, but simply recognised the injustices committed by man against his fellow man, supposed enemy or not.

The Fate of Adolf Hitler

The apocryphal story about Hitler and his wife Eva Braun's suicides and subsequent 'home-made cremations' with a can of petrol in the grounds adjoining the 'fuhrerbunker' at the end of April 1945 is simply Soviet Russian propaganda in collusion with British and American wartime High Command and nothing more.

Even the mainstream, politically correct, Elite-controlled *History Channel*'s own investigation in the early 2000s proved beyond reasonable doubt that the skull portion and dental fragments in the possession of the Russians, retrieved from the burial of the burnt corpse of 'Hitler' could not have belonged to him. And this was after an extensive forensic investigation lasting more than a year, during which his authenticated dental records were meticulously compared with the burnt tooth and bone fragments.

At the time, the Russians did not wish to admit that Hitler had evaded capture as was planned from the start. They believed it would have reflected extremely badly on them and so their propaganda machinery went into overdrive and concocted a credible story to deflect criticism from them, over the sorry affair. As time went on, the propaganda as always, came to be regarded as 'fact' and the real story died, along with the propaganda's perpetrators. In fact, the usual modus operandus.

It is well known that Hitler had more than one 'double', just as in more recent times there have been several Saddam Husseins and Osama bin Ladens and thus how easy would it have been to surreptitiously execute one of them and burn his body in a pit? I personally find it beyond incredible to seriously suggest that in the last months of the war when the Russians were rampaging through Eastern Germany towards Berlin that no arrangements had been made either through his own efforts or on his behalf by third parties, to evacuate him and Eva Braun to safety. Are we really supposed to believe that he just remained there in the bunker awaiting his ultimate and inevitable fate? All the other major Nazi figures (with the possible exception of Josef Goebbels and family – and even that is by no means certain) made good their escapes whilst there was still time enough to do so, albeit that several of them were 'captured' in the following weeks and months.

In accordance with my extensive research on the subject, I firmly believe that Hitler and Braun were secretly flown via Hamburg to Norway, where they were transported to South America (probably Argentina) by U-boat. According to contemporary *Pravda* (the Soviet newspaper) reports, at least five U-boats full of Nazi officials left Norway for Argentina during the period from the end of April to early May 1945. Furthermore I also believe that these people were not merely just allowed to escape, but were actively in effect 'rescued' in complicity with the British and the US Elite on the basis that in their eyes, they had committed no crimes but were merely acting out their intended roles in the stage play otherwise known as World War II and now that their performance was at an end, they were free to seek refuge with whomsoever would have them.

Hitler aged 90 in 1979

So, after the war the five German U-boats reached Argentina with no less than 50 high ranking Third Reich officials on board including Hitler and Braun. During the trip they even sank a US battleship and the Brazilian cruiser Bahia with a death toll of more than 400, including many US naval personnel. Both the US and the British Government have systematically covered up this operation. Why would this be? Did they actually arrange for Hitler to escape? I firmly believe so.

Operation *'Übersee Sud'* (Overseas South) was the code-name of the plan that helped certain high-ranking Nazi officials to escape from the Soviets, possibly in the safekeeping of, but certainly with the co-operation of the British and US Governments.

That same name that always seems to be lurking in the background in these clandestine affairs, Winston Churchill, was apparently the mastermind behind the escape. The Argentinian Navy established a 'freedom zone' to allow the Germans to disembark without being disturbed, in accordance with British Elite instructions. So, was Adolf Hitler definitely a passenger on one of these U-boats? It is believed by several respected researchers that Hitler, Eva Braun, her sister Gretel Braun and Martin Bormann escaped via this clandestine operation, however it does still remain unclear whether Hitler specifically landed in Argentina or not.

"We know for sure that Hitler fled either to Spain or to Argentina." Josef Stalin in conversation with the US Secretary of State, James Byrne in late 1945

"We have not been unable to unearth one bit of tangible evidence of Hitler's death. Many people believe that Hitler escaped from Berlin." General Dwight D. Eisenhower, 1946

"Russia must accept much of the blame that Hitler did not die in May 1945." Michael Mussmano, presiding judge at the Nuremburg trials, 1946

"We did not identify the body of Hitler. I can say nothing definite about his fate. He could have flown away from Berlin at the very last moment." Marshall Zhukov, Commander in Chief of the Soviet army, 1945

Do not these three quotations alone tell us everything that we need to know? If these people genuinely believed he had escaped, how does this reconcile with the popular myth of his death in the bunker? The simple answer is that it does not. These claims of suicide and cremation on waste land are provably false and were no doubt spread as deliberate disinformation to prevent the truth from reaching the masses. This of course is more compelling evidence of the systematic falsification of history at work.

Chicago Times 16th July 1945

Apparently, according to a Japanese source, Hitler flew to Norway at 4.14 pm on the 30th April 1945 in an unmarked aircraft together with Eva Braun and a small party of friends, then reached his final destination, Argentina by U-boat and went into seclusion after 'completing his duty'. He spent the rest of his long life in Mendoza in the northwest of Argentina, protected by the Nazi SS and the indigenous Jewish community (how ironic, but how appropriate). Hitler reportedly died in Mendoza, Argentina in December 1985 at the age of 96 and his remains were buried in a public cemetery in Palmero, thirty miles southeast of Mendoza. The fate of his wife, Eva Braun is unknown.

The murder of General George Patton

General Patton, perhaps the most popular of the WWII American generals had no qualms about killing enemy soldiers in combat but he 'drew a line' at the wholesale murder and starvation of helpless prisoners and civilians in his sector of occupation, as advocated by his superiors. However because of this, he came into serious conflict with another general of higher rank; General Eisenhower and from then on his fate was sealed. It is well-known that the two had on-going, extremely animated debates about how the civilian population of Germany was to be treated and Patton was in effect sentenced to death by the directors of this scenario.

One day Patton's car was in collision with a military truck in what was regarded as a very strange accident by witnesses. The General was taken by ambulance to a hospital, where he was observed to have serious, but not life-threatening injuries. However, despite this, just as he was recovering some days later, he died of a 'heart attack'.

Patton's death was extremely opportune. The General had announced that upon his return to the United States, he was going to denounce publicly what was taking place in Germany.

"I have a little black book in my pocket and when I get back home I'm going to blow the hell out of everything." General George Patton, August 1945
Unfortunately though, his views had conflicted with too many important people and so Eisenhower ordered that he be silenced, probably under orders from the very top of the tree. His 'black book' was never found.

At the Yalta conference earlier that year (1945) the Elite 'masters of the world' had agreed via their lackeys, Roosevelt, Churchill and Stalin that the Soviets would be the first to enter the German capital. They needed a strong Soviet presence in Eastern Europe after the war, to maintain the on-going conflict that is their life-blood, in the form of the Cold War and a Western Europe devoid of a Soviet presence would have severely weakened that strategy. Patton's troops could quite easily have entered both Berlin and Prague before the Russians, but were prevented from doing so by an order from Eisenhower.

Patton made no secret of his wish to prevent the entrance of the Red Army into Berlin and in so doing made an enemy of the 'controlled' Eisenhower. He was furious to be informed by his superiors that he was to refrain from taking Berlin. He, as did they, knew that it would have been simple for the Americans to reach Berlin before the Russians and thus gain control of the entire country but that would have been contrary to the Elite's plan for the instigation of the Cold War in the succeeding years which partly hinged upon the division of Germany into the two separate states of 'East' and 'West'. The American progress eastwards through Western Europe had been much swifter than the Russians westward march. In the main this was due to the Germans' readiness to surrender to the British and Americans as they knew that surrendering to the Russians was probably a death sentence. Hence many German units on the eastern front fought to the death of the last man in their futile bid to stop the advancing Russian juggernaut.

Patton's difficulties with the Elite 'powers that be' over the occupation of Germany were so great that Eisenhower stripped him of his position as Commander of the Third Army and gave him command of a secondary, lesser unit. Patton knew he was in danger of death and confided as much to his family and close friends. He was feared because of his prestige, popularity and influence on public opinion and was undoubtedly the most renowned American combat General, while Eisenhower was nothing more than a 'political soldier' and Patton's words could alert the public to the true reality of what was happening in Germany.

Thus the accident was arranged and set-up, but it was not by any means the first. On the 21st April 1945, the plane on which he was being transported to General Headquarters of the Third Army in England was attacked by what was assumed to be a German fighter, but it turned out to be a Spitfire piloted by a Polish RAF pilot. Patton's plane was shot at and badly hit, but was miraculously able to land safely. Then on the 3rd May, some days before the end of the war, the General's jeep was charged by an ox-drawn cart, leaving Patton with light injuries.

Then on the 13th October 1945 came the collision with the truck, but just as Patton appeared to be recovering after the accident, the 'heart attack' occurred. The fact is that after the 13th October only doctors were allowed to see Patton, with all other visitors forbidden.

From the hospital, Patton contacted his wife in America in a vain attempt to get her to have him moved from the hospital because, he said, *"They're going to kill me here."*

For many years it was only speculation that Patton had been assassinated. Now it is known for a fact to be the truth, for one very simple reason. An agent of the OSS (Office of Strategic Services – a forerunner of the CIA) an American military spy, Douglas Bazata, a Jew of Lebanese origin, announced it in front of 450 invited guests; high ranking, ex-members of the OSS and CIA, in the Hilton Hotel in Washington, USA on the 25th September, 1979. Bazata said, and I quote;

"For diverse political reasons, many extremely high-ranking persons hated Patton. I know who killed him because it was I. I am the one who was hired to do it. I was paid ten thousand dollars and General William Donovan himself, director of the OSS, entrusted me with the mission. I also set up the accident but since he didn't die in the accident, he was kept in isolation in the hospital, where he was killed by me with a cyanide injection."

The tragic fate of Patton convinced many others of his loyal colleagues and their honourable compatriots of the uselessness of fighting against the Elite-controlled war powers.

The Nuremburg Trials

The Nuremberg Trials were created by the Elite to prosecute the German general-staff and thereby eliminate anyone in authority that was aware of the pact signed between the Zionists and Hitler in 1923. The end of the German resistance in WWII was only the end of the first stage of the political ploy by the Zionists to illegally found the new home for themselves inside Palestine.

That they were a fair and impartial hearing seems very unlikely. That the evidence used against the defendants was very dubious and obtained by even more dubious methods is however, very clear. An example of the techniques employed is described by the distinguished English historian, David Irving in his book, 'Nuremberg: The Last Battle'...

"Garnering usable documentary evidence became a mounting nightmare for Jackson [the chief prosecuting attorney]. He had become disenchanted with the productivity and intelligence of General Donovan's OSS. They had promised much but delivered little. What Donovan regarded as evidence, he certainly would not. 'I never had any feeling that anybody had trapped me into the thing,' Jackson commented later. 'But I was in the trap!'"

It soon became clear that the OSS (the forerunner of the CIA) had intended all along to stage-manage the whole trial along the lines of an Soviet NKVD show trial, with Jackson engaged as little more than a professional actor. As part of the stage-management they proposed to run a pre-trial propaganda campaign in the United States with 'increasing emphasis on the publication of atrocity stories to keep the public in the proper frame of mind.' To this end the OSS devised and scripted for the education of the American public a two-reel film on war crimes, called 'Crime and Punishment'; it was designed to put the case against the leading Nazis. Jackson declined to participate. He refused even to read the speech that the OSS had scripted for him to read into the cameras. 'As you know,' he wrote to the OSS officer concerned, 'the British are particularly sensitive about lawyers trying their cases in the newspapers and other vehicles of communication.'

The film proposal was followed by an explicit OSS suggestion for launching 'black propaganda' during the course of the trial, with agents in selected foreign countries starting rumours designed to influence public opinion in favour of the trial and against the defendants. This would be far more effective, they pointed out, than mounting a straightforward public relations campaign which would obviously be seen as emanating from the powers conducting the trials. One of Jackson's staff secretly notified him that the suggestion was 'fantastic, if not entirely dangerous', and the justice himself pencilled a pithy comment on the letter: 'The scheme is cock-eyed. Give them no encouragement.'

Vestiges of the unsavoury methods of the OSS can still be seen among the earlier Nuremberg records. For instance, at the pre-trial interrogations the defendants were not accompanied by lawyers and were frequently persuaded by trickery or intimidation to subscribe to testimonies incriminating others which we now know to have been false. The files are full of curiosities, for instance anonymous typed extracts of documents instead of the originals and sworn statements by witnesses like Höss, commandant of Auschwitz, in which all the 'witnesses to his signature' have signed, but not Höss himself. Indeed it is well known that Höss's confessions were all obtained by torture. The Americans also submitted as exhibit 1553-PS a file of invoices for substantial consignments of Zyklon B (hydrogen cyanide pellets) supplied to the pest-control office at Auschwitz but they concealed the fact that the same file contained invoices for identical quantities of Zyklon B delivered to the camp at Oranienberg near Berlin, where it was never alleged there had been any 'gas chambers'.

These examples are of course only a very brief overview of the innumerable deficiencies of the 'evidence' at Nuremberg. The overwhelming Jewish presence behind the scenes as prosecutors, judges, interrogators, jailers and torturers is covered elsewhere in Irving's excellent, but far from complete, study. The sampling of techniques employed however, is more than sufficient to demonstrate that truth was never the objective of the orchestrators of the trial. The key point in evaluating Nuremberg is that all the evidence, real and faked at the trial, was evidence in pursuit of a pre-determined verdict. It was regarded desirable to demonstrate that the Germans were uniquely evil, that the Germans had waged aggressive, illegal war, that the Germans had committed great 'crimes against humanity' and that the greatest of these alleged crimes was the alleged systematic extermination of six million Jews. To reach these pre-determined verdicts, the court manipulated and distorted evidence on a massive scale. Therefore, any honest assessment of the German National Socialist government built on Nuremberg conclusions is inherently flawed. It is another supreme example of the art of writing history based on the propaganda of the victor.

The Diary of Anne Frank

The story contained within Anne Frank's diary, that world famous testimony to the sufferings of a Jewish family during World War II, may well be a true story as far as it goes, but it is one hundred percent certain that what was published and subsequently became a worldwide best seller was not written by Anne Frank herself.

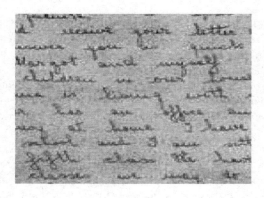

Anne's letter to an American pen-pal

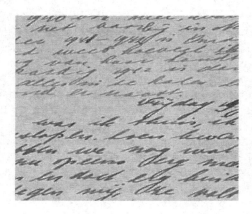

Anne's diary

Of the above examples of Anne's handwriting, the first example was written to an American pen friend who introduced the letter to the world after Anne had become posthumously famous and recognised the name – and the other is supposedly taken from the pages of Anne's diary, purportedly written shortly after the first sample.

Now, I would be the last to admit to being a handwriting analyst but there can surely be no doubt that those two samples were written by two completely different individuals. I do not believe it possible that one's handwriting could change that much over an entire lifetime let only in someone of poor Anne's tender years. And just to further prove the point, it is strange is it not that the latter example purporting to be her original diary is written in ballpoint pen? Ballpoint pens were invented by a Hungarian by the name of Laszlo Biro in the mid-1940s and most certainly did not become commercially available until well after Anne's death at Bergen-Belsen concentration camp from typhus at the age of fifteen in 1945.

'The Diary of Anne Frank' was first published in 1952 and immediately became a bestseller. It has been re-published in paperback, with over 40 printings and it is impossible to estimate how many people over the last 50-60 years have been touched and moved in some way by the subject matter.

An interesting question to consider is why the trial involving the father of Anne Frank, bearing directly on the authenticity of this book has never been officially reported by the overwhelmingly Zionist media? In royalties alone, Otto Frank profited greatly from the sale of this book, purporting to depict events in the tragic life of his family, but is it fact, fiction or propaganda or a combination of all of these? It certainly claims to be the truth but to what degree does it appeal to the emotions through misrepresentation? It was certainly convenient for Otto Frank that he was the only family member to survive the war – and I mean that in the sense of there being no-one left alive to corroborate or deny the story and in no way to diminish the anguish he must have suffered at the loss of his entire family.

School-book publishers have promoted this book for young people for many years, presenting it as the actual work of Anne Frank. Advertising in advance of the release of the movie certainly promoted the drama as being factual but do not writers of such editorials and promoters of such advertising in this way, keep alive the prejudices and hatred they profess to deplore and could this be the actual objective?

The Franks were upper-class German Jews, both parents emanating from wealthy families. As children, Otto and his siblings lived on the exclusive Meronstrasse in Frankfurt and Otto attended a private preparatory school and also the Lessing Gymnasium, the most expensive school in Frankfurt. Upon leaving school, Otto attended Heidelberg University from whence he eventually graduated.

In 1925 Anne's parents married and settled in Frankfurt, Germany where Anne was born in 1929. The Frank's family business included banking, management of the springs at Bad Soden a famous spa and the manufacture of cough sweets. Anne's mother, born Edith Holländer, was the daughter of a wealthy manufacturing family and in 1934 Otto and family moved to Amsterdam where he bought a spice business, Opekta, which manufactured pectin, a form of gelatine used in the making of household jellies.

In May 1940, after the Germans occupied Amsterdam, Otto remained in the city where his company did business with the German Wehrmacht, whilst his mother and brother moved to Switzerland to escape the German occupation. From 1939 to 1944, Otto sold pectin to the German army to be used as a food preservative, an anti-infectant balm for wounds, a thickener for increasing blood volume in blood transfusions and also as an emulsifier of petroleum to be used in the manufacture of fire bombs and flame-throwers. However, by supplying the Wehrmacht, Otto Frank became, in the eyes of many of his Dutch friends and neighbours, a Nazi collaborator. None of this aspect of the official story of course is ever mentioned or even alluded to.

On the 6th July 1942, Otto moved the entire Frank family along with two family friends into the so-called 'secret annex'. The annex was within a three storey townhouse that shared a garden park with fifty other apartments facing inwards to form an approximate square, but was not visible from the street. Whilst allegedly still in hiding, Otto Frank continued to manage his business, venturing downstairs to his office at night and at weekends. Anne and the others would also periodically go to Otto's office and listen to radio broadcasts from England.

The purported diary begins on 12th June, 1942 continuing through to the 5th December 1942. In addition to this first diary, Anne also supplemented it with personal letters. Otto said Anne heard Gerrit Bolkestein, a Dutch broadcaster, in a wireless programme ask his listeners to keep a diary and he would publish it after the war and that is why, Otto claimed, she rewrote her diaries for the second time in 1944. In this second edition, the new writer, Anne or whoever it was, changed, rearranged and occasionally combined entries of various dates.

When Anne allegedly rewrote the diaries, she apparently used a ball-point pen (confirmed in Otto Frank's court hearing) which was extremely enterprising of her since such a device did not exist in 1944 and also the diary was written with literary standards well surpassing those of which even the brightest of fourteen year old children would be capable, reading more like a professionally written documentary than a child's diary.

In 1944, the German authorities in occupied Holland determined that Otto Frank's company had been defrauding them via his extensive and very lucrative Wehrmacht contracts and subsequently the police then raided his offices where during a thorough search the annex was discovered and the eight occupants were sent initially to the *Westerbork* transit camp and forced to perform manual labour. Otto was later sent to Auschwitz and Anne, her sister Margo and her mother subsequently died in one of the frequent outbreaks of typhus in Bergen-Belsen two weeks before liberation by the Allies.

In 1945, after being liberated from German custody, Otto returned to Amsterdam, where he claimed he found Anne's diary cleverly hidden in the rafters of the annex. However, another version of the story tells of a Dutch friend, Meip Geis finding Anne's diary whilst caretaking the building in the Franks' enforced absence, which she then gave to Otto Frank upon his return. Otto took what he claimed were Anne's letters and notes, edited them into a book, which he then gave to his secretary, Isa Cauvern to review. Isa Cauvern and her husband Albert Cauvern, a writer, subsequently authored the first version of the diary.

Upon submitting the diary for publication, questions were raised by some potential publishers as to whether Isa and Albert Cauvern, who assisted Otto in typing out the work, used the original diaries or whether they took it directly from Mr. Frank's personal transcription, but it is known for certain now that the American author, Meyer Levin wrote the third and final edition which became the finished end-product.

Meyer Levin was a Jewish author and journalist, who lived for many years in France, where he met Otto Frank around 1949.

If ever file number 2241-1956 in the New York County Clerk's office is opened to public view and its contents widely publicised, then the true nature of this work will be exposed for all to witness. Misrepresentation, exaggeration and falsification has too often coloured the judgment of otherwise decent people and if Frank used the work of Meyer Levin to present to the world what we have been led to believe is the literary work of his daughter, wholly or in part, then the truth should be exposed. To label fiction as fact can never be justified nor should it be condoned.

Otto sued two Germans, Ernst Romer and Edgar Geiss in 1980 for distributing literature denouncing the diary as a forgery. The subsequent court case produced a study by official German handwriting experts that determined that everything in the diary was written by the same person but noted that this person (whoever it was) had used a ballpoint pen throughout! Unfortunately for Frank, as stated previously, the ballpoint pen was not available commercially until 1951 whereas Anne was known to have died of typhus in Bergen-Belsen in February 1945.

Because of this lawsuit in a German court, the German state forensic bureau, the Bundes Kriminal Amt (BKA) forensically examined the manuscript (which at that point in time consisted of three hardbound notebooks and 324 loose pages bound in a fourth notebook) with specialised forensic equipment. The results of these tests, performed at the BKA laboratories, showed that 'significant portions' of the work, including the entire fourth volume, were written with a ballpoint pen and since ballpoint pens were not available before 1951, the BKA concluded those sections must have been added subsequently and fraudulently.

More importantly perhaps, the BKA investigation *clearly* determined that none of the diary handwriting matched known examples of Anne's handwriting. The German magazine, '*Der Spiegel*' published an account of this report alleging that some editing post-dated 1951 and an earlier expert had determined that all the writing in the journal was by the same hand and thus that the entire diary was a post-war fake.

This BKA exposé, as a result of the frantic lobbying of Jewish/Zionist interests was immediately retracted but later 'inadvertently' released to researchers in the United States. I invite the reader to draw his / her own conclusions from this fact.

For what reasons could this fraud have been perpetrated? Were the reasons simply for financial gain or was there a more sinister motive underlying its execution? Could it be part of the overall conspiracy to gain sympathy for the Zionist cause by exaggerating Jewish suffering and casting further aspersions on Nazi activities or is this proposition too unrealistic to contemplate seriously? You decide, but whatever the reason for it, the end result is that the memory of an innocent child-victim has been sullied by being blatantly used either for personal, monetary gain or on behalf of a minority but widely influential group, Zionism in order to surreptitiously benefit certain vested interests. However, perhaps more importantly, this shameful episode further demonstrates how simple is the process by which it is possible to deceive huge numbers of people on virtually any subject one could choose by the simple expedient of powerful and persistent propaganda techniques and the constant, incessant repetition of statements designed to create a lasting impression.

Operation Paperclip

The systematic and secret expatriation to the US, the USSR and Great Britain of many Nazi scientists and experts in many diverse fields of study was known as Operation Paperclip. Operation Paperclip, in fact, has been de-classified for many years but has never managed to make its way into mainstream history or history textbooks in any way. Strange – or not? Please read on.

At the end of WWII in 1945, victorious British, Russian and American intelligence teams began searching throughout occupied Germany for military and scientific bounty. They were looking for items such as new rocket and aircraft designs, medicines and electronics. But they were also hunting down the most precious items of all, the scientists whose work had nearly won the war for Germany, in other words, the engineers, intelligentsia and intelligence-officers of the Nazi war machine.

The US and British military sought-out and brought to the UK and America many Nazi technicians in secret and in order to further the technical abilities of the military-industrial complex in its never-ending quests for the maximisation of profits. The original intent had been merely to debrief them and send them back to Germany, but when the extent of the scientists' knowledge and expertise was realised, it was decided it would be a waste to send them home. Following the discovery of Nazi flying discs and particle/laser beam weaponry in German military bases, the US War Department decided that the newly-formed CIA must gain control of both the technology and the Nazi engineers that had developed it.

There was only one problem regarding this scheme – it was highly illegal. US law explicitly prohibited Nazi officials from immigrating to America and around 75% of the scientists in question had been committed, ardent Nazis.

Convinced that German scientists could help America's post-war efforts, President Truman agreed in September 1946 to authorize Project Paperclip. However, Truman expressly excluded anyone found 'to have been a member of the Nazi party and more than a nominal participant in its activities, or an active supporter of Nazism or militarism.' The War Department's Joint Intelligence Objectives Agency (JIOA) was instructed to conduct background investigations of those scientists under consideration for the project. In February 1947, JIOA Director Bosquet Wev duly submitted the first set of scientists' dossiers to the State and Justice Departments for review.

The Dossiers were indeed damning. Samuel Klaus, the State Department's representative on the JIOA board, claimed that all the scientists in this first batch were 'ardent Nazis' and thus their visa requests were therefore denied. However, Wev was furious. He wrote a memo warning that *'the best interests of the United States have been subjugated to the efforts expended in beating a dead Nazi horse'*. He also declared that the return of these scientists to Germany, where they could be exploited by America's enemies, presented a *'far greater security threat to this country than any former Nazi affiliations which they may have had or even any Nazi sympathies that they may still have'*.

When the JIOA formed to investigate the backgrounds and collate dossiers on the Nazis, the Nazi Intelligence leader Reinhard Gehlen met with the CIA director Allen Dulles. Dulles and Gehlen become friends almost immediately. Gehlen was a master spy for the Nazis and had infiltrated Russia with his vast Nazi Intelligence network and Dulles promised Gehlen that his Intelligence unit was safe in the CIA. Subsequently, Wev decided to sidestep the problem. Dulles had the scientists' dossiers re-written to eliminate incriminating evidence and as promised, he delivered the Nazi Intelligence unit to the CIA, which later opened many umbrella projects stemming from Nazi research including such insidious secret programmes as MK Ultra (Mind Kontrolle) still in use as individual and mass mind control schemes.

Military Intelligence cleansed the files of all Nazi references and so by 1955, more than 760 German scientists had been granted US citizenship and given prominent positions in the American scientific community. Many of these individuals had been long-time members of the Nazi party and the Gestapo, had conducted experiments on humans at concentration camps, had condoned and used slave labour and had taken part in other war crimes.

In a 1985 expose in the *'Bulletin of the Atomic Scientists'*, Linda Hunt wrote that she had examined more than 130 reports on Project Paperclip subjects and every one *'had been changed to eliminate the security threat classification'*. President Truman, who had explicitly ordered no committed Nazis to be admitted under Project Paperclip, was supposedly never aware that his directive had been violated, but personally, I am not inclined to believe that particular fantasy despite State Department archives and the memoirs of officials from that era that would confirm this 'fact'.

One example of how these dossiers were changed is in the case of Wernher von Braun, the Nazi rocket scientist, the technical director of the Peenemunde research facility, responsible for the V1 and V2 'vengeance' weapons rained on London and South East England during the latter months of the war. A report on von Braun dated 18th September 1947 stated, *'Subject is regarded as a potential security threat by* the *Military Governor'*. And then subsequently, the following February, a new security evaluation of Von Braun read, '*No derogatory information is available on the subject... It is the opinion of the Military Governor that he may not constitute a security threat to the United States'*. Von Braun worked on guided missiles for the US Army and was later director of NASA's Marshall Space Flight Centre. He became a celebrity in the 1950s and early 1960s as one of Walt Disney's experts on the '*World of Tomorrow'* TV show. In 1970, he became NASA's associate administrator.

Here below is a small sample of the 700 or so, shady characters who were allowed to immigrate to the US via Project Paperclip.

Arthur Rudolph

During the war, Rudolph was operations director of the Mittelwerk factory at the Dora-Nordhausen concentration camp, where 20,000 workers died from beatings, hangings and starvation. Rudolph had been a member of the Nazi party since 1931; a 1945 military file on him said simply: '*100% Nazi, dangerous type, security threat..!! Suggest internment.'* But the JIOA's final dossier on him said there was '*nothing in his records indicating that he was a war criminal or an ardent Nazi or otherwise objectionable.'* Rudolph became a US citizen and later designed the Saturn 5 rocket used in the Apollo moon landings. In 1984, when his war record was finally investigated, he fled to West Germany.

Kurt Blome

A high-ranking Nazi scientist, Blome told US military interrogators in 1945 that he had been ordered in 1943 to experiment with plague vaccines on concentration camp prisoners. He was tried at Nuremberg in 1947 on charges of practicing euthanasia on sick prisoners and conducting illegal and immoral experiments on humans. Although acquitted, his earlier admissions were well known and it was generally accepted that he had indeed participated in the gruesome experiments. Two months after his Nuremberg acquittal, Blome was interviewed at Camp David, Maryland, about biological warfare. In 1951, he was hired by the US Army Chemical Corps to work on chemical warfare. His file of course neglected to mention the Nuremberg trials.

Major-General Walter Schreiber

The US military tribunal at Nuremberg heard evidence that '*Schreiber had assigned doctors to experiment on concentration camp prisoners and had made funds available for such experimentation.'* The assistant prosecutor said the evidence would have convicted Schreiber if the Soviets, who held him from 1945 to 1948, had made him available for trial. Again, Schreiber's 'Paperclip' file made no mention of this evidence and so the project found work for him at the Air Force School of Medicine at Randolph Field in Texas. When columnist Drew Pearson publicised the Nuremberg evidence in 1952, the negative publicity led the JIOA to arrange '*a visa and a job for*

Schreiber in Argentina, where his daughter was living.' On May 22, 1952, he was flown to Buenos Aires.

Hermann Becker-Freysing and Siegfried Ruff

These two, along with Blome, were among the 23 defendants in the Nuremberg War Trials 'Medical Case'. Becker-Freysing was convicted and sentenced to 20 years in prison for conducting experiments on Dachau inmates, such as starving them, then force-feeding them sea water that had been chemically altered to make it drinkable. Ruff was acquitted (in a close decision) on charges that he had killed as many as 80 Dachau inmates in a low-pressure chamber designed to simulate altitudes in excess of 60,000 feet. Before their trial, Becker-Freysing and Ruff were paid by the Army Air Force to write reports about their grotesque experiments.

Klaus Barbie

Known as the Nazi butcher of Lyons, France during World War II, Barbie was part of the SS which was responsible for the death of thousands of French people under the German occupation.

Licio Gelli

Head of a 2400 member secret Masonic Lodge, P2, (Propaganda due) a neo-fascist organisation in Italy that exists only for the Elite, Gelli had high connections in the Vatican even though he was not a Catholic. P2's membership is totally secret and not even available to its Mother Lodge in England. Gelli was responsible for providing Argentina with the Exocet missile. He was a double agent for the CIA and the KGB and assisted many former Nazi high officials in their escape from Europe to Central America. He also had close ties with the Italian Mafia. Gelli was a close associate of Benito Mussolini and was also closely affiliated with Roberto Calvi, head of the scandal-ridden Vatican Bank. Calvi was ritually murdered and his body was discovered hanging under Blackfriars Bridge in London, weighted down with bricks.

Gelli and his P2 lodge had staggering connections to banking, intelligence and diplomatic services. The CIA poured hundreds of millions of dollars into Italy in the form of secret subsidies for political parties, trades unions and communications all fronted by Gelli. Licio Gelli was an ardent Nazi and a perfect asset of the CIA. As part of Reinhard Gehlen's intelligence team he had excellent contacts and was also the go-between for the CIA and the Vatican through the P2 Lodge.

In Summary

World War II was the product of the collaboration between the Zionists and the Nazis who were created by the Elite as an 'enemy' to the Jewish interests specifically to fulfil that particular aspect of the on-going agenda; ie. the creation of the Jewish homeland in Palestine through the engendering of a huge outpouring of sympathy for Jewish suffering.

In addition, the vast, unimaginable profits generated for the Elite banking-military-industrial complex during the period 1939-45 at the expense of the lives of almost 75 million 'useless eaters', in the funding of all sides of the conflict, cannot be discounted as a key by-product.

As always, we are constantly drip-fed outright lies and propaganda about the causes of the war and even the individual elements of it are bent and distorted to fit the official story. Such distortions as:

Germany attacked itself to generate an excuse to provoke the outbreak of the war.

German brutality and genocide was endemic but the Allies always played by the rules. Hitler was hell-bent on conquering the world.

The Germans wished to totally eradicate the Jews from the face of the Earth.

The Japanese categorically refused to surrender and it was only the use of the atomic bombs that ended their resistance.

All these 'facts' have become embedded in our psyches as the absolute truth after decades of bombardment with them by the lapdogs of the media in all its forms.

WWII was no different to all other wars of the last five hundred years in that there was the same two-fold, underlying agenda. Firstly, the furtherance of the grand master plan, the great work of ages and secondly to further concentrate even more wealth and power into the hands of the Elite.

The deployment of the atomic bombs upon the Japanese civilian population further served to enable the next phase of the master plan; the atomic arms race, leading to the almost half-century long, stand-off now known as the 'cold war', designed to further subjugate and keep the world's helpless populace in a constant state of fear and dread.

Israel – the Land of the Rothschilds

"Central bankers start the majority, if not all of the wars so that they can enslave the combating nations and make huge profits on whatever is possible. Israel was founded by the most powerful central banker on the planet [Rothschild] in order to grant protections through dual nationality and other perks of having a sovereign nation, so that crime could be practiced without fear of the usual reprisals. It was a state founded on deception and historical revision which displaced 700,000 inhabitants, who were already living in Palestine and they have been practicing genocide on them ever since."
Les Visible, researcher, 2011

I would add to the above quoted reasons for the founding of Israel that the Rothschilds and their Zionist brethren also needed a strategically-placed 'base' in the epicentre of the Middle East from where they could wreak havoc on that region and wage their illegal wars on the multiplicity of Arab states that abound within short-range cruise missile launching distance, causing maximum disruption and unrest in their quest to subdue and conquer the entire world and ultimately to establish the 'New World Order' centred upon Israel.

This is the real reason that the Zionists were desperate to get their 'Jewish homeland' throughout the first half of the twentieth century and not, as they claimed' through any sense of loyalty to Jews. Israel was conceived and built by Zionism, a movement founded in the late nineteenth century by one Theodor Herzl, an Ashkenazi Jew, to facilitate this push for the 'Jewish homeland' in the Holy Land. This movement was subsequently hi-jacked by the Elite and used as a central plank of their plan for world government, the so-called 'New World Order'.

Have you ever wondered at the utter stupidity and crassness of creating a Muslim/Arab-hating enclave (I hesitate to call Israel a country in the truest sense of the word as it has no clear cut boundaries and is constantly expanding them, illegally) in the absolute centre of the Arab/Muslim world? Is it not almost guaranteed to cause conflict and mayhem in that region as 'God's chosen people' fight for supremacy and grab the land of their neighbours as has been the case for the entire six decades plus of Israel's existence?

Indeed, many people, myself included, can only conclude that this was the ultimate intention all along – to generate friction and instability in order that the Elite can make more dirty profits from promulgating many more of their seemingly endless wars and conflicts. Israel has been in a permanent state of war against one or more of its neighbours since its inception, not least the Palestinian peoples, whose land is continually stolen as Israel illegally, constantly expands its borders and wages a cruel and bloody war against Palestinian women and children, committing atrocity after atrocity against an innocent population including the illegal use of depleted uranium. The other purpose of the 'Jewish homeland' was to bring into existence a sovereign state that could operate a criminal banking cartel with the impunity of a nation.

"Of course, the unquestionable champ in this non-country category is Israel, which ignores all the laws of the civilized world but which writes laws for other countries (like the U.S.) that don't apply to itself. Israel, supposedly created as a refuge for oppressed Jews, is in reality the forward base for the never-ending white Western assault on the Islamic world, and a sanctuary for Jewish criminals from all over the world. But it is also a straw dog, too, as it takes the heat for homicidal Jewish behaviour around the planet whose architects may visit Israel from time to time but are really based in the posh suburbs of New York, London and other major metropolises, murderers of the planet hiding in plain sight and often seen on television." John Kaminski, geopolitical researcher, September 2011

"The 'state' of Israel was founded on pure lies; it was never about a homeland for the Jewish people. Israel was just the launching pad for the continuation of the Nazi State. The party that founded Israel is the same one that was formed when Hitler's National Socialist Party (NA) signed a pact with the Zionist International (ZI) and together these two entities created The NAZI Party, in 1923." Jim Kirwan, researcher 21st August 2011

After the Balfour declaration of 1917 effectively promised Palestine to the Zionists as the Jewish homeland in return for America entering WWI on the side of Britain, Russia and France, it needed another thirty years and a further World War to make the promise a reality. Despite Britain's generous offer of Palestine, the current 'rulers' of that country, Turkey, were unsurprisingly not too keen on this turn of events and so despite Britain's best effort at diplomatic negotiations, the Jews had to wait until 1948 to literally bomb and terrorise Israel into existence through such delightful, humanitarian-minded groups as Irgun and the Stern Gang led by David Ben Gurion who was to become the new state's first president.

"Israel has never had a government that so blatantly violates the core values of liberal democracy. Never has a Knesset passed laws that are as manifestly racist as the current one. Israel has had foreign ministers who were unworldly and didn't know English; but it has never had a foreign minister whose only goal is to pander to his right-wing constituency by flaunting his disdain for international law and the idea of human rights with such relish." Israeli Newspaper 'Haaretz', 24th June 2011

The totally racist, apartheid state of Israel today is comprised primarily of Ashkenazi Jews who occupy the top rung of the ladder of extreme racism currently prevalent in Israeli society. The Ashkenazis get the pick of the best available jobs, career opportunities and housing, closely followed by the Sephardic Jews. Some way behind these two groups are the Christians and last and certainly least, the Arab population of Israel is left with the metaphorical crumbs from the table. The 'official' view of the Israeli hierarchy on Jewish supremacy can be summed-up neatly by this quotation...

"Our race is the Master Race. We are divine gods on this planet. We are as different from the inferior races as they are from insects. In fact, compared to our race, other races are beasts and animals, cattle at best. Other races are considered as human excrement. Our destiny is to rule over the inferior races. Our earthly kingdom will be ruled by our leader with a rod of iron. The masses will lick our feet and serve us as our slaves." Former Israel Prime Minister and terrorist supreme, Menachem Begin

It is a fact that every single central bank throughout the Western world is Jewish/Zionist owned and also until very recently, every single member of the US Federal Reserve board was Jewish. Israel was founded by the most powerful bankers on the planet (the Rothschilds) in order to grant protections through dual nationality and benefit from other 'perks' of having a sovereign nation, so that international crime could be practiced without fear of the usual reprisals and under the protection of the assorted cowards and shills of the United Nations. It was a state founded on deception and historical revision which displaced 700,000 inhabitants, who were already living in Palestine and Israel has been practicing genocide on them ever since. Banksters start the majority of, if not all of the wars, so that they can enslave the combating nations and make huge profits on whatever is possible.

"Anti-Semitism is no longer the hatred of and discrimination against Jews as a religious or ethnic group; in the age of Zionism, we are told, anti-Semitism has metamorphosed into something that is more insidious. Today, Israel and its Western defenders insist genocidal anti-Semitism consists mainly of any attempt to take away and to refuse to uphold the absolute right of Israel to be a Jewish racist state." Professor Joseph Maddad, palestineremembered.com, 5th May 2007

Members of the US Congress are forced to sign a loyalty oath to Israel or they will be ruthlessly sabotaged in their political pursuits. Israel was behind 9/11 and all of the following wars/invasions that were justified as a result of this brutal, genocidal act. Osama bin Laden publicly said he had nothing to do with 9/11 and be assured that had he and the phony, invented Al Qaeda, a) existed in the first place and b) actually carried it out (a physical impossibility if ever I heard one) then they would have been falling over themselves to claim responsibility – as is the way of all so-called 'terrorist' groups.

Israel has been proven responsible for every war and conflict in which they have been involved and where provocation was needed to commence hostilities, practiced false-flag events and then used the Elite, Zionist-owned media to peddle its lies to the unsuspecting public. For example, Israel blatantly attacked an American ship, USS Liberty during the six-day war in 1967, killing and seriously injuring many Americans in an attempt to blame the attack on Egypt and thus engendering massive US support and sympathy for Israel's cause. Israel's attack on USS Liberty ought to have been a sensational, headline-grabbing news story, but beyond the fact that it was reported by the controlled media that an 'accident' had occurred and that Israel had apologised for the mistake, it did not receive any coverage by Western news organisations. Had it been an Arab or other Muslim country attacking an American ship, it is not unreasonable to assume that America would have resorted to a military strike, if not outright war, on the country it held responsible. So what did President Lyndon Johnson do instead? Out of fear of offending the Zionist lobby and its stooges in Congress, he ordered and led a cover-up which remains in force to this day. The mainstream media turned a 'blind-eye' to it at the time of course, as it still does.

"...every time we do something you tell me Americans will do this and will do that. I want to tell you something very clear, don't worry about American pressure on Israel, we, the Jewish people control America, and the Americans know it." Ariel Sharon, former President of Israel, October 2003

The significance of the cold-blooded attack on the Liberty is that there is nothing the Zionist state would not do, to its 'friends' as well as its enemies, in order to 'get its own way' and at the time of writing, Israel is presently lobbying internationally to have attacks launched on Pakistan and Iran in furtherance of it and the Elite's horrendous agenda.

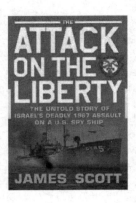

"Over the years, many of President Lyndon Johnson's former advisors-including the directors of the CIA, NSA, and State Department-acknowledged what many in the intelligence community secretly believed for years: the attack was no accident, but McGonagle would not live long enough to learn some of the darker secrets, including how senior American officials had contemplated sinking his ship at sea to block reporters from photographing the damage and sparking public outrage against Israel." 'The Attack on the USS Liberty', James Scott (page 5)

"More than two dozen lawmakers in the Senate and House – many from states with large Jewish populations, such as New York, New Jersey, and Connecticut – took the floor the day of the attack to applaud Israel for its stunning war effort. Others rallied for emergency economic aid, urged America to reinforce its commitment to the Jewish state, and argued that Israel should be allowed to keep the territories it captured in recent days. One senator even inserted Abba Eban's June 6 speech before the U.N. Security Council into the Congressional Record. But the laudatory speeches came even as American sailors aboard the Liberty struggled to put out fires, stop bleeding, and prevent the ship from sinking." 'The Attack on the USS Liberty', James Scott (pages 103-4)

"...Other sailors voiced the disbelief many felt about Israel's explanation that the attack had been a tragic accident. Sitting at the rectangular table in the wardroom where thirty-six hours earlier he had held down Seaman Gary Blanchard during surgery, Scott detailed his views in a five-page letter to his parents. 'I don't see how they made a mistake', the officer wrote. 'It was too well planned and co-ordinated. They knew exactly where to hit us and they did.'" 'The Attack on the USS Liberty', James Scott (pages 149-150)

More recently, Israel attacked the Gaza aid flotilla in 2009 and ruthlessly executed a number of unarmed, peaceful aid workers taking desperately needed supplies to Palestine, which is being blockaded by Israel in defiance of all international law and humanitarian principles. It was later reported that the soldiers of the IDF involved in these cold-blooded murders went on a spending spree in Tel Aviv with the stolen credit cards and pin numbers of many of the flotilla members. Compared with the original crime, this may seem a little 'tame' in comparison, but it speaks volumes to me of the utter unspeakable callousness and inhumanity of man to his fellow man exhibited by the Israeli 'Defence' Forces.

The 'nation' of Israel is indeed a satanic entity that worships and promotes extreme materialism in support of the corporations which in return offer their support and further its agenda. Even after peace was negotiated and agreed upon, Israel dropped over half a million cluster bombs on Lebanon in a war they started and 94% of all Israelis support the continual, genocidal, 'ethnic cleansing' in Gaza. Israel confines the original populations of the land they stole, with the complicity of the US and Britain, in a virtual concentration camp (Gaza) that has become the most highly concentrated, populous place on Earth, due to the constant eroding of the Palestinian lands and their illegal incorporation into 'Greater Israel'.

The Israeli security company ICTS was in charge of security at all the 9/11 airports, the London Tube stations and the Madrid train station during the 'false-flag' attacks. Indeed, it would be a massive surprise if ICTS was not one of the many Mossad fronts disguised as legitimate companies and waging covert war on almost every nation on Earth.

Israeli-backed Zionist bankers are constantly and systematically looting the economies of the somewhat euphemistically named, 'free world'. However, as the world continues its slow waking process, boycotts against Israel are mounting. The truth about Israel is manifesting itself, albeit slowly and Israel is becoming a pariah nation in the eyes of the world even while she is planning more massive false-flag events to distract the hearts and minds of the world's population from the truth of her outrageous, yet often unreported behaviour. Meanwhile, Israel and its adherents will continue to steal money from rich and poor alike through the usury and political arm-twisting practiced by these Zionist thugs and bullies.

Please do not ever lose sight of the fact that almost the entire world is under the boot-heel of these 'stormtrooper' banksters, whose religious books refer to 'Goyim', a disrespectful Hebrew name for non-Jews, as 'cattle' and even 'human excrement' and whose lives are unimportant, except as servants, profit centres or blood-sacrifices for the chosen ones. The cultural perception of what is acceptable or not is controlled by a 'political correctness' propaganda machine that purports to represent the rights of all downtrodden people but whose actual main function is enable the labelling and exposure of those committing so called 'anti-Semitic' acts for the purpose of sympathy and legislative changes on their behalf. The education system is in their hands and thus their progeny have first rights into all of the top-rated schools and Universities and the curriculum is bent to serve their agendas. They collect a 'kosher tax' on many foodstuffs worldwide and employ other hidden taxes and privileges, because they own the currency printing rights, which they have used to buy up all important agencies for the service of their elitist status.

"The Israeli government is actively engaged in military and industrial espionage in the United States."

That was the conclusion of a Pentagon administrative judge in 2006. One very good reason why Israel should not receive billions of dollars in military assistance annually is its espionage against the United States. Israel, a Fascist-Communitarian country where government and big business work hand in hand, has obtained significant advantage by systematically stealing American technology with both military and civilian applications. US-developed technology is then reverse-engineered and used by the Israelis to support their own exports with considerably reduced research and development costs, giving them a huge advantage against foreign competitors.

Most non-Jews are unaware that *all* food products marked with the 'K' or 'U' Symbols have been *taxed* by Jews. In every food cupboard and fridge in the Western World there are dozens of canned and packaged food products which have a tiny 'K' or 'U' printed on the label. This symbol informs Orthodox Jews that the items have been checked by a rabbi, to ensure that they have been prepared in accordance with 'Jewish dietary law', as set forth in the Jewish Talmud, the real bible of the Jews. Food companies are forced to pay multi-billions of dollars to several orthodox Jewish organizations, just so that orthodox Jewish people will buy their products. Please bear in mind that we are all forced to pay this kosher tax, just to appease considerably less than 1% of the population. Of course the food companies pass on these costs to the consumer so in effect this is a tax we are all paying every day on our basic needs ie. food.

This Elite group of evil psychopaths has been working towards its ultimate goal for centuries but now the time for their retribution is fast approaching. They know they are running out of time and the only solution, they think, is to plunge the world into another global conflict, the oft-prophesised World War III. In this venture, they are being assisted by their puppets that they have manipulated into the seats of power to serve their agenda.

With each passing day, around the world, people are being evicted from their homes for their inability to repay ever-more extortionate, immoral mortgage interest rates and jobs are being outsourced to the third world where people are being forced to live on the proverbial 'dollar a day' further exacerbating the problem. We are all being systematically forced and conditioned to live in abject fear of losing our homes, jobs and the non-existent terrorism threat in order to sap our wills to resist. We are being covertly poisoned and thrown into turmoil by the operations of those governing us, in cahoots with those governing our apparent rulers.

"They sold your country out from under you folks. And to get it back, they will need to be hunted down and removed… all of them who have worked with the Israelis. The numbers are huge and the names involved are big. So it's not going to be pretty. And if you haven't figured it out already, they have tons of money, their own private

intelligence resources, and they are not going out quietly. They have bet you will be the losers...and to date they have been correct." Jim W. Dean, editor, 'Veterans Today'

"The whole war against the Muslim people is being orchestrated by Israel and their ignorant slaves of the Christian fundamentalist movement, turned into Zio-clones, due to distortions in their holy book that twists scripture to the advantage of their deceivers. They literally control the American government and its economy through their central banks, which provided them the money to buy all of the media, publishing, entertainment and a host of other enterprises that grant them such an excessive control of the culture of the west. This is outrageously out of proportion to their numbers, which somehow increased from the beginning of WWII and into the aftermath. Explain that if you can. This is also easy to prove. Do so, if it interests you." Les Visible, smokingmirrors blog 21st October 2011

Most of the people who can see what is happening will not say anything and the rest are too dumbed-down, hypnotised by perverted mainstream religion and the lying media whores or in deep denial of what is going on, to even notice the 'elephant in the room'. Insane money-junkies aka the banksters, are gambling away our futures at no risk to themselves, whilst they quietly manipulate the eventual outcome to their own benefit. They are driving food and fuel prices to levels never seen before whilst we all await the arrival of global cataclysm, to reduce the population to their desired levels and thus free-up the entire world for further rape and plunder. The big players on both sides of the engineered conflict-to-come are already making their threats and shifting their game board pieces in readiness. They must be stopped somehow, before it is too late – for us all.

The Cold War

At the conclusion of World War II, the Elite needed to create the bogus 'Cold War' to justify the arms race and the national security state along with an ongoing fear factor affecting almost the whole population (just as the 'war on terror' replaces the Cold War today). The problem was that Communism could be traced back to the Elite Jewish bankers, most Communist spies were Jewish and Soviet Communism was Elite Jewish. They used McCarthy to fuel Cold War hysteria while de-emphasising the role Jews play as agent/dupes for the banksters. As soon as McCarthy outlived his usefulness they eliminated him at Bethesda Naval Medical Centre after earlier disgracing him.

The House of Rothschild are international bankers who made enormous profits during the nineteenth century and used their money to take over governments and infiltrate almost every powerful institution on Earth with a view to manipulating the world and events to their own unspeakable ends.

Bernard Baruch was the New York agent of the Rothschilds who at the turn of the century set-up the tobacco trust, the copper trust and other trusts for the Rothschilds. He became the grey eminence of the United States atomic bomb programme when his lackey, J. Robert Oppenheimer, became director of the Los Alamos bomb development team and when his Washington lackey, James F. Byrnes, advised President Truman to drop the atomic bombs on Hiroshima and Nagasaki.

Albert Einstein was a lifelong Zionist who initiated the United States' atomic bomb programme with a personal letter to President Franklin D. Roosevelt in 1939.

For many years, people have been concerned about the proliferation of atomic weapons. Even in their distress, no one seems to be interested in the historic or the psychological record of why these weapons were developed, and what 'special' breed of mankind devoted themselves to this diabolical goal.

Despite the lack of public interest, the record is clear and easily accessible to anyone who is interested and it took many weeks of research to uncover what turned out to be one of the most far-reaching conspiracies of all time, the programme of a few dedicated revolutionaries to seize control of the entire world, by developing the most powerful weapon ever seen.

The story begins in Germany. In the 1930s, Germany and Japan had a number of scientists researching the development of nuclear fission. In both of these countries, their leaders sternly forbade them to continue their research, indeed Adolf Hitler said he would never allow anyone in Germany to work on such an inhumane weapon.

The Emperor of Japan also informed scientists that he would never sanction such a devastating weapon. At that time the United States had no-one working on nuclear fission but disgruntled German scientists contacted friends in the United States and were told that there was a possibility of government support for their work there.

"Leo Szilard, together with his long-time friends and fellow Hungarian physicists, Eugene Wigner and Edward Teller, agreed that the President must be warned; fission bomb technology was not so farfetched. The Jewish émigrés, now living in America, had personal experience of fascism in Europe. In 1939, the three physicists enlisted the support of Albert Einstein. A letter dated August 2 signed by Einstein was delivered by Alexander Sachs to Franklin D. Roosevelt at the White House on 11th October 1939." Don Bayer

In Japan, at the Nagasaki Atomic Bomb Museum, photographs of two men are prominently displayed; Albert Einstein, and J. Robert Oppenheimer, who developed the atomic bomb at Los Alamos laboratories, New Mexico, USA. Also on display is a statement from General Eisenhower, who was then supreme Allied Military Commander.

"Secretary of War Henry L. Stimson first told Eisenhower of the bomb's existence. Eisenhower was engulfed by 'a feeling of depression'. When Stimson said the United States proposed to use the bomb against Japan, Eisenhower voiced 'my grave misgivings, first on the basis of my belief that Japan was already defeated and that dropping the bomb was completely unnecessary and secondly because I thought that our country should avoid shocking world opinion by the use (of atomic weapons)." 'Eisenhower' (p426) by Stephen E. Ambrose, 1983

Stimson was upset by Eisenhower's attitude *'almost angrily refuting the reasons I gave for my quick conclusion'*.   Three days later, Eisenhower flew to Berlin, where he met with Truman and his principal advisors and again Eisenhower recommended against using the bomb and yet again was ignored.

Other books about Eisenhower demonstrate that he endangered his career by his protests against the bomb, which the conspirators in the highest level of the United States government had already sworn to use against Japan, regardless of any military developments. Eisenhower could not have known that Stimson was a prominent member of Skull and Bones at Yale, the Brotherhood of Death, founded by the Russell Trust in 1848 as a branch of the German Illuminati, or that they had played prominent roles in organising wars and revolutions since that time. Nor could he have known that President Truman had only had one job in his entire career, as a masonic organiser for the State of Missouri and that the masonic lodges he built up later sent him to the United States Senate and then to the presidency.

The man who set all this in motion was Albert Einstein, who left Europe and came to the United States in October 1933. His wife said that he *'regarded human beings with detestation'*. He had previously corresponded with Sigmund Freud about his projects of 'peace' and 'disarmament', although Freud later said he did not believe that Einstein ever accepted any of his theories. Einstein had a personal interest in Freud's work because his son Eduard spent his life in mental institutions, undergoing both insulin therapy and electroshock treatment, none of which produced any change in his condition.

When Einstein arrived in the United States, he was feted as befits a famous scientist and was invited to the White House by President Roosevelt. He was soon deeply involved with Eleanor Roosevelt in her many left-wing causes, in which Einstein heartily concurred. Some of Einstein's biographers hail the modern era as 'the Einstein Revolution' and 'the Age of Einstein', possibly because he set in motion the programme of nuclear fission in the United States. His letter to Roosevelt requesting that the government inaugurate an atomic bomb programme was obviously stirred by his lifelong commitment to 'peace and disarmament'. His actual commitment was to Zionism. Ronald W. Clark mentions in *'Einstein; His Life And Times'*, Avon, 1971, p.377. *"He would campaign with the Zionists for a Jewish homeland in Palestine."* On p.460, Clark quotes Einstein, *"As a Jew I am from today a supporter of the Jewish Zionist efforts."*

Einstein's letter to Roosevelt, dated 2nd August 1939, was delivered personally to President Roosevelt by Alexander Sachs on 11th October. Why did Einstein enlist an intermediary to bring this letter to Roosevelt, with whom he was on friendly terms? The answer is because the atomic bomb programme could not be launched without the necessary Wall Street sponsorship. Sachs, a Russian Jew, listed his profession as 'economist' but he was actually in effect a 'gofer' for the Rothschilds, who regularly delivered large sums of cash to Roosevelt in the White House. Sachs was an advisor to Eugene Meyer of the Lazard Frères International Banking House, and also associated with Lehman Brothers, another well-known banker. Sachs' delivery of the Einstein letter to the White House informed Roosevelt that the Rothschilds approved of the project and wished him to go full speed ahead.

In May of 1945, the architects of post-war strategy, or, as they liked to call themselves, the 'Masters of the Universe', gathered in San Francisco at the plush Palace Hotel to write the Charter for the United Nations where several of the principals retired for a private meeting in the exclusive Garden Room. The head of the United States delegation had called this secret meeting with his top aide, Alger Hiss, representing the President of the United States and the Soviet KGB; John Foster Dulles, of the Wall Street law firm of Sullivan and Cromwell, whose mentor, William Nelson Cromwell, had been called a 'professional revolutionary' on the floor of Congress; and W. Averill Harriman, plenipotentiary extraordinaire, who had spent the last two years in Moscow directing Stalin's war for survival. These four men represented the awesome power of the American Republic in world affairs, yet of the four, only Secretary of State Edward Stettinius Jr., had a position authorised by the Constitution. Stettinius called the meeting to order to discuss an urgent matter; the Japanese were already privately suing for peace, which presented a grave crisis as the atomic bomb would not be ready for several more months. *"We have already lost Germany and if Japan bows out, we will not have a live population on which to test the bomb. ...Our entire post-war programme depends on terrifying the world with the atomic bomb."* said Stettinius.

"To accomplish that goal, you will need a very good tally. I should say a million." said John Foster Dulles.

"Yes" replied Stettinius, *"we are hoping for a million tally in Japan. But if they surrender, we won't have anything."*

"Then you have to keep them in the war until the bomb is ready" said John Foster Dulles.

"That is no problem. Unconditional surrender, they won't agree to that, they are sworn to protect the Emperor", said Stettinius.

"Exactly" said Dulles. *"Keep Japan in the war another three months and we can use the bomb on their cities. We will end this war with the naked fear of all the peoples of the world, who will then bow to our will."*

And that dear reader is the reality of what happened towards the end of World War II and not the sanitised version that has somehow become contrived to become our 'real' history. American Elite interests had to keep Japan from surrendering for a long enough period of time for the bomb to be ready. If the Japanese had capitulated too early then there would have been no Hiroshima and no Nagasaki and then the Cold War would have had to be engineered in another way, or not have come to pass at all.

Edward Stettinius Jr. was the son of a J.P. Morgan partner who had been the world's largest munitions dealer in the First World War. He had been named by J.P. Morgan to oversee all purchases of munitions by both France and England in the United States throughout the war. John Foster Dulles was also an accomplished warmonger. In 1933, he and his brother Allen had met with Adolf Hitler and guaranteed him the funds to maintain the Nazi regime. The Dulles brothers were representing their clients, Kuhn Loeb Co., and the Rothschilds. Alger Hiss was the head of the communist Elite in the United States and when he was chosen as head of the prestigious Carnegie Endowment for International Peace after World War II, his nomination was seconded by John Foster Dulles. Hiss was later imprisoned for perjury regarding his exploits as a Soviet espionage agent.

This secret meeting in the Garden Room was actually the first military strategy session of the United Nations, because it was dedicated to its mission of exploding the world's first atomic weapon on a living population. It also forecast the entire strategy of the Cold War, which lasted more than forty years, cost American taxpayers in excess of five trillion dollars and thus made the Elite powers behind the thrones the same amount and accomplished exactly nothing, other than the fear and trepidation in which most of the world was held, as was intended. Thus we see that the New World Order has based its entire strategy on the agony of the hundreds of thousands of civilians burned alive at Hiroshima and Nagasaki, including many thousands of children sitting in their schoolrooms. These leaders had learned from their master, Josef Stalin that no one can rule without mass-terrorism, which in turn requires mass-murder and where these two goals cannot be accomplished through an existing enemy, they have to invent them. *"We have got to scare the hell out of 'em."* Senator Vandenberg, leader of the Republican party, American Heritage magazine, August 1977

The atomic bomb was developed at the Los Alamos Laboratories in New Mexico. The top secret project was called the Manhattan Project, because its secret director, Bernard Baruch, lived in Manhattan, as did many of the other principals. Baruch had chosen Maj. General Leslie R. Groves to head the operation as he had previously built the Pentagon and had a good reputation among the Washington politicians, who usually asked 'how high' when Baruch asked them to 'jump'.

The scientific director at Los Alamos was J. Robert Oppenheimer, from a prosperous family of clothing merchants. In *'Oppenheimer; the Years Of Risk'*, James Kunetka, writes, *"Baruch was especially interested in Oppenheimer for the position of senior scientific adviser."* The project cost an estimated two billion dollars. No other nation in the world could have afforded to develop such a bomb and the first successful test occurred at the Trinity site, two hundred miles south of Los Alamos at 5.29:45 am on the 16th July 1945.

Oppenheimer's exultation at the success of the test derived from his realisation that now his masters had attained the ultimate power, through which they could implement their five-thousand-year desire to rule the entire world and thus set in motion the next critical phases of the plan.

There were still many anxious moments for the conspirators, who planned to launch a new reign of terror throughout the world. Japan had been attempting to surrender since early 1945 with its pleas being systematically ignored by the US administration. On the 9th and 10th of March 1945, 325 B-29 bombers had razed thirty-five square miles of Tokyo to the ground, leaving more than one hundred thousand Japanese civilians dead in the ensuing firestorm. Of Japan's 66 largest cities, 59 had been mostly destroyed, 178 square miles of urban dwellings had been burned, 500,000 died in the fires and now twenty million Japanese were homeless. Only four cities had not been destroyed; Hiroshima, Kokura, Niigata, and Nagasaki. Their inhabitants had no inkling at this time that they had been spared solely in order to be used as targets for the experimental atomic bomb. General Leslie Groves, at Baruch's insistence, had demanded that Kyoto be the initial target of the bomb. Secretary of War Stimson objected, saying that as the ancient capital of Japan, the city of Kyoto had hundreds of historic wooden temples, and no military targets but of course the Jewish influences wished to destroy it precisely because of its great cultural importance to the Japanese people.

While the residents of Hiroshima continued to watch the B-29s flying by without dropping bombs on them, they had no inkling of the terrible fate which the mass-murderers in Washington had reserved for them.

"There was another Japan, and MacArthur was one of the few Americans who suspected its existence. He kept urging the Pentagon and the State Department to be alert for conciliatory gestures. The General predicted that the break would come from Tokyo, not the Japanese army. The General was right. A dovish coalition was forming in the Japanese capital and it was headed by Hirohito himself, who had concluded in the spring of 1945 that a negotiated peace was the only way to end his nation's agony. Beginning in early May, a six-man council of Japanese diplomats explored ways to accommodate the Allies. The delegates informed top military officials that 'our resistance is finished'." William Manchester

"We brought them down to an abject surrender through the accelerated sinking of their merchant marine and hunger alone, and when we didn't need to do it, and knew we didn't need to do it, we used them as an experiment for two atomic bombs." Brigadier General Carter W. Clarke, US Army

So, it transpired that on the 6th August 1945, a uranium bomb isotope-235, 20 kilotons yield, was exploded 1850 feet in the air above Hiroshima, for maximum explosive effect. It utterly devastated four square miles and killed outright 140,000 of the 255,000 inhabitants and horrifically injured many more.

"It was strange to us that Hiroshima had never been bombed, despite the fact that B-29 bombers flew over the city every day. Only after the war did I come to know that Hiroshima, according to American archives, had been kept untouched in order to preserve it as a target for the use of nuclear weapons. Perhaps, if the American administration and its military authorities had paid sufficient regard to the terrible nature of the fiery demon which mankind had discovered and yet knew so little about its consequences, the American authorities might never have used such a weapon against the 750,000 Japanese who ultimately became its victims." Dr. Shuntaro Hida, doctor in Hiroshima at the time of the attack

"[Hiroshima was] the most ruthless and barbaric killing of non-combatants in all of history." General Bonner Fellers, an adviser to General MacArthur

One of the myths of Hiroshima is that the inhabitants were warned by leaflets that an atomic bomb would be dropped. These leaflets were dropped after the bombing because the President's Interim Committee on the Atomic Bomb decided on the 31st May 'that we could not give the Japanese any warning'. Furthermore, the decision to drop 'atomic' leaflets on Japanese cities was not made until the 7th August the day after the Hiroshima bombing. They were not dropped on Nagasaki until the 10th August, the day after Nagasaki had been atomic-bombed and therefore the residents of neither Hiroshima nor Nagasaki received advance warnings about the proposed use of the atomic bomb.   On 1st June 1945, a formal and official decision was taken during a meeting of the so-called Interim Committee not to warn the populations of the specific target cities. James Byrnes and Oppenheimer insisted that the bombs must be used 'without prior warning'.

Truman himself variously stated that the use of the use of the atomic bomb saved 'a quarter of a million American lives', a 'half-million American lives' and finally settled on the Groves figure of 'a million American lives saved'.

 "It is my opinion that the use of this barbarous weapon at Hiroshima and Nagasaki was of no material assistance in our war against Japan. The Japanese were already defeated and ready to surrender because of the effective sea blockade and the successful bombing with conventional weapons." Admiral Leahy, US Navy, from 'I Was There'

In fact Truman's wanton use of atomic weapons left the American people feeling dramatically less secure after winning World War II than they had ever felt before and these feelings of insecurity were subsequently exploited to the full by unscrupulous Cold War politicians ever since.

"The war would have been over in two weeks without the Russians entering and without the atomic bomb. The atomic bomb had nothing to do with the end of the war at all." General Curtis LeMay, chief of the USAF 29th September 1945

"In the councils of government we must guard against the acquisition of unwarranted influence, whether sought or unsought, by the military-industrial complex. The potential for the disastrous rise of misplaced power exists and will persist." President Dwight D Eisenhower's farewell address to the American nation on the 17th January 1961

The US Air Force had sole control of the atomic bomb and it became a billion-dollar 'game' for these scientists, with John von Neumann, their leading scientist, becoming world famous as the inventor of 'game theory', in which the United States and the Soviet Union engaged in a worldwide psychological skirmish to see which would be the first to attack the other with nuclear missiles.   In the United States, schools held daily bomb drills, with the children hiding under their desks. No one told them that thousands of school-children in Hiroshima had been incinerated in their classrooms; the desks offered no protection against nuclear weapons.   The moral and psychological effect on generations of children was devastating. If they were to be vapourised at any time, there seemed little reason to study, marry and have children, or prepare for a steady job. This demoralisation through the nuclear weapons programme is another one of the undisclosed reasons for the decline in public morality.

By failing to name the power behind the military-industrial complex, the international banksters, Eisenhower left the American people in the dark as to who he was actually warning them against. To this day the masses still do not understand that what he was trying to say was that the international bankers, the Zionists and the Freemasons had formed an unholy alliance whose money and power could not be overcome by the citizens of the United States or indeed the world and the sooner the populations of the world come to understand this fact, the sooner we can end this insidious attack on all humanity and construct a world where people matter more than the bank balances of the already obscenely wealthy.

The United Nations

Around 25 years after the failure of the proposed 'League of Nations', a second attempt was made to usher-in this early form of 'one world government', immediately upon cessation of hostilities in World War II. This time there was to be no dissenting voice and the UN was formed in line with the UN charter of 26th June 1945.

So, the USA encouraged and cajoled by Alger Hiss, a senior member of the Council on Foreign Relations (CFR) and a known-to-be communist sympathiser, enthusiastically joined the United Nations along with most of the rest of the world's nations as a first step down the rocky road to out and out communitarianism, as was in the planning all along.

The UN charter and constitution is a thinly veiled copy of the Soviet Union model which Hiss had co-authored some 30 years previously in preparation for the world's first communist state, Soviet Russia. In effect, this means that the UN constitution is therefore a Marxist-Socialist paradigm.

It was none other than the Rockefeller family themselves who donated the 18 acres of prime Manhattan real-estate, upon which its opulent headquarters sit and at the time of writing, the CFR chairman is David Rockefeller, leaving us in no doubt whatsoever as to the allegiances and goals of this truly execrable organisation.

"Some even believe we are part of a secret cabal working against the best interests of the United States, characterizing my family and me as 'internationalists' and of conspiring with others around the world to build a more integrated global political and economic structure - one world, if you will. If that is the charge, I stand guilty and I am proud of it." David Rockefeller

The Elite goals of 'World regionalism' are clearly defined in the UN charter, using such terms as 'regional arrangements', 'intergovernmental agreements', and 'metropolitan areas'. This organisation, replete as it is with covert communists and advocates of the planned 'New World Order' have already divided the world into 85 'regions' for policing and administration purposes and simply by adopting the UN Charter, the US Congress has established the Charter as the Supreme Law of the land (Fugi v. State of California, 1950-52) totally negating the current statutes of the United States.

The following are just some of the stated policies of the United Nations:

- Control of all zoning matters in the United States and the control of its national parks, rivers and historical sites.
- Control over whether women are allowed to have babies.
- Control over the economic and judicial policies of all nations.
- Programmes are currently being devised to create a tax on citizens of the United States as a permanent method of UN funding.
- The United Nations has its own Army and other nations' soldiers must swear allegiance to this foreign government.

By Executive Order #11647 on 10th Feb 1972, President Nixon announced the United States was divided into 10 Federal Regional Councils, each controlled by an appointed bureaucrat for the stated purpose of improving coordination of the activities of all levels of government. The 10 federal regions were to be empowered to control all forms of regionalism within the US Regional divisions supplementing the 10 federal regions include state sub-regions, federal reserve regions, population regions, and regions to control the land, water and natural resources of America. The goal of regional or metropolitan government is to eventually merge the US into the 'New World Order' ie. a one world Socialist state under the United Nations. Regional government is a plan to eventually control all facets of its citizens' lives. Executive Order #11490 assigns numerous emergency preparedness functions to federal departments.

Financing of regional governments is acquired through Federal Revenue sharing. Revenue sharing is a mechanism whereby state and local governments become financially dependent upon the federal government. Pressure can then be applied to any level of state government that refuses to comply with the dictates of the regional government rulers. All but one of the ten federal regional capitals is a Federal Reserve Bank city.

This is the 'One World Government' or 'New World Order' currently being promoted by all major world leaders and politicians who without exception are in the pockets of the Elite. Recently, the UN was wholly responsible for the destruction of two free sovereign nations, Rhodesia and South Africa, two nations which were not 'politically correct' and so, were systematically taken down. The Elite run-UN spread vicious lies about Rhodesia and crippled the nation economically, finally turning it over to the Communists led by the radical tyrant Robert Mugabe, who renamed it Zimbabwe and has done everything in his power to rape the country of all its money and resources and divert them into his own coffers. In South Africa, its capital, Johannesburg is now the most dangerous city in the world with one of the highest murder rates. Much the same policies are now being carried-out in North Africa with the recent regime changes and revolutions in Libya and Egypt and in the Middle East with Syria and Iran squarely in the gun sights as I write this.

We are also in the midst of a huge propaganda campaign desired to scare and encourage us to see things the way the NWO wishes us to see them. Their current tactic is... *'since another great depression and financial crisis is almost certain, nations should move now to organise themselves into a One World Economic Order to ensure that even though such a calamity may occur, there will be a reconstitution of a meaningful international monetary system'.*

I believe that this all proves beyond any reasonable doubt how the Elite have openly conspired to insidiously rule the world via the covert machinations of the CFR, the United Nations, the Trilateral Commission, and the Bilderberg group.

The United States of Europe (The European Union)

There is an Elite plan that has been in place for many decades if not centuries, to further the goal of the New World Order and one world government and that is for four global 'trading' blocs to be set-up and these were to be known as the European Union, The North American Free Trade Agreement (NAFTA), the African Union and the Pacific Union. These 'free trade' areas are a stepping stone to further draconian restrictions of freedom and a breaking-down of national identities in order to further destabilise societies, worldwide.

In fact the establishment of the 'United States of Europe' was one of the goals of the Knights Templar back in the 12th century. The Knights Templar, it is believed by many, were never destroyed but simply disappeared underground for a while, eventually emerging as the Scottish Rite of Freemasonry, which along with the York Rite makes up the two arms of this organisation.

The original architects of the European 'Common Market' as it was named originally, were Jean Monnet and Count Richard Coudenhove-Kalergi and Joseph Retinger all of whom were working on behalf of the Elite to further their insidious agenda. Indeed Retinger was also instrumental in founding the infamous Bilderberg Group which still flourishes and heavily influences, if not actually directs world political policy to this day.

Monnet was an influential character in the first half of the twentieth century, being instrumental in (amongst other nefarious activities) drawing-up the Treaty of Versailles which was coldly calculated to lead to the outbreak of World War II almost exactly twenty years after its imposition on the shattered German nation. He was also named as the Deputy Secretary General of the League of Nations before its swift demise, to the extreme chagrin of the Elite, shortly after its formation.

As for Coudenhove-Kalergi, he wrote a book in 1923, 'Pan Europa', calling for a 'United States of Europe' and a close friend of his father was Theodor Herzl, the founder of Zionism, no less. The rabbit hole goes very deep indeed and is extremely complex, to say the very least. Shortly after this he was involved in the founding of the Pan-European Union which had massive support within the Elite spider-web and was endorsed by Colonel Mandell House (whose name appears throughout this book in various guises) and also Herbert Hoover, the president of the US. Winston Churchill was also a fervent supporter and even wrote an article in 1930 entitled 'The United States of Europe'.

Post-war loans to Europe from America (The Marshall Plan) in the immediate aftermath of the war were, among other things, used to provide funds for the movement promoting a European Union and at the same time to attempt to undermine the sovereignty of the European nations in an attempt to destabilise the status quo and facilitate a smooth passage for their goal of European unity. The Marshall Plan, ostensibly an idea of General George Marshall, was in fact the work of none other than Jean Monnet and the Council on Foreign Relations.

The first practical step in the creation of the Common Market was taken in July 1952 and which under the banner of the 'European Coal and Steel Community', merged the coal and steel industries of France, West Germany, Italy, Belgium, The Netherlands and Luxembourg (the original six members) under central control. Once again the guiding hand behind the scenes was none other than a certain Jean Monnet. In addition to this, Monnet and his henchmen tried to introduce a European army under the same central control, but this failed to materialise when the French took exception to the plan. However on the 25th March 1957, the Treaty of Rome was ushered-in and signed by the 'six' marking the official birth of the Common Market or the European Economic Community (EEC) as it was to be come to be known shortly thereafter. This organisation began to bloom under the guidance and control of the CFR and well-away from the influence of the individual countries involved and thus neatly managing to bypass any kind of democratic control whatsoever.

In 1984 the Soviet defector Anatoly Golitsyn stated openly that there would shortly be a 'false liberalism' occurring in the Soviet Union and Eastern Europe and this would be welcomed heartily by the western powers. He also predicted that it would lead to a merger of the EEC with the countries of the Soviet Union with the pretence of peace breaking-out and the end of the Cold War, all of which happened exactly as predicted around six years later, but was in fact part of the Elite master plan and merely the next stepping-stone to all-out European 'unity' which continues apace to this day.

In the early days of the Common Market / EEC, the people of Britain and other non-member countries were constantly being fed the line that we had to join the 'club' or the economy would suffer badly or even collapse altogether and once most of Europe had fallen for this ruse and joined, then the next step was put in place. Softly, softly catchee monkey. The next step was to surreptitiously remove the word 'economic' from the title of the organisation, leaving us simply with the 'European Community' and then shortly thereafter, this was again subtly altered to 'European Union'. All seemingly insignificant changes but the implications are massively important for us all. What was sold as an 'economic alliance' benefitting the ordinary people of Europe, had now developed through a 'community' into a general 'union' of most of the countries of Europe. This is exactly what Hitler and the Third Reich had planned for Europe had they won the war (although them being victorious was never part of the script, unbeknown to Hitler). They even referred to it in captured documents as the 'European Economic Community'. Coincidence again? There are a lot of those around it would seem.

In 1988, the European leaders convened in Paris to celebrate the birth centenary of their mentor and 'hero', Jean Monnet and by implication his 'monster' the United States of Europe, whose plans are still to come to fruition, but not for the want of trying. The plans will no doubt continue, baby-step by baby-step until the complete integration of all Europe is finalised, destroying national identities and one step further down the road of making slaves of us all in the process. For the sake of all of us, we cannot and must not allow this to happen.

The Report from Iron Mountain

In 1966, a group of 15 environmental 'experts' assembled at a place called 'Iron Mountain', the site of a huge governmental semi-secret underground facility in upstate New York, to plan a strategy for controlling populations and centralising power without the need for war.

Since then, the contents of the resulting report have been leaked and although there are claims that the whole thing was an elaborate hoax, (the usual modus operandi in these circumstances is 'deny everything') if it is a hoax then it has been coincidentally, remarkably accurate in predicting the events of the next 40+ years.

The report describes one scenario for the overall control of humanity using environmental threats of Armageddon due to human activity - man-made global warming in other words.

However, the report begins by identifying war as the central organising principle of society. It states, *"War itself is the basic social system, within which other secondary modes of social organization conflict or conspire. It is the system which has governed most human societies of record, as it is today."*

The report goes on to say, *"The basic authority of a modern state over its people resides in its war powers."* It says that any failure of will by the ruling class could lead to *"actual disestablishment of military institutions."* The report says that the effect would be *'catastrophic'*.

The appearance of the report caused a sensation when it first came to light at the onset of the Vietnam War. This is because the report outlines the ways that the civilian population of a developed nation could be controlled even in the absence of a large-scale war that disrupted their daily lives. One of these ways is defined as follows: *"A possible surrogate for the control of potential enemies of society is the reintroduction, in some form consistent with modern technology and political process, of slavery. The development of a sophisticated form of slavery may be an absolute prerequisite for social control."*

We can see the development of such a 'sophisticated form of slavery' today. How else can a system be described that subjects the population to massive, growing personal and household debt, a widening gap between the rich and poor and constant warfare justified as necessary to fight 'terrorism'? And this as well as the ongoing erosion of personal freedoms, constantly expanding power allocated to the military and police, pervasive electronic eavesdropping, complete lack of accountability by politicians for their dishonesty and crimes and a mass media devoted solely to establishment propaganda.

War-making potential does not result from threats. In fact, *'threats against the national interest are usually created or accelerated to meet the changing needs of the war system'*.

"War's political importance is crucial. It defines and enforces relations with other nations. National sovereignty and the traditional nation-state depend on it. The war system is essential to internal political stability. "Without it, no government has ever been able to obtain acquiescence (to) its legitimacy, or right to rule its society."

A nation's authority over its people *"resides in its war powers,"* including local police to deal with *"internal enemies in a military manner."* Military service has a patriotic purpose *"that must be maintained for its own sake."*

Wars also serve an ecological purpose – *"to reduce the consuming population to a level consistent with the survival of the species,"* but mass destruction is inefficient, and nuclear weapons are indiscriminate, removing physically stronger members important to save. Because of medical and scientific advances, pestilence no longer can control populations effectively, balancing them with agriculture's potential. As a result, other measures are needed to control *"undesirable genetic traits."*

An effective political substitute for war requires *"alternate enemies....of credible quality and magnitude, if a transition to peace is ever to come about without social disintegration."* Most likely, *"such a threat will have to be invented."*

Other extreme ideas include; *"Poverty is necessary and desirable,* the same Orwellian social stability 1984 idea, about *"keeping the Low's in poverty and the High's in power, forever."* A modern, sophisticated form of slavery serves the same social control purpose.

Government must *"optimize the number of warfare deaths, never letting a good opportunity go to waste."*

"Intensified environment pollution," including air and water is acceptable, and, without war, a comprehensive eugenics program and *"universal test-tube procreation might have to substitute."*

The committee rejected individual freedom, opting for subservience to a ruling Elite, the system that governs world nations and America since inception, instituted by the Founders so the country's owners could run it, and wage wars to solidify control.

The Report concluded that:

"The permanent possibility of war is the foundation for stable government. It supplies the basis for general acceptance of political authority." It allows societies to maintain class distinctions and ensures the subordination of citizens to the state, run by elites with *"residual war powers."*

As for policy measures in a world at peace, members stated *"as strongly as we can, that the war system cannot responsibly be allowed to disappear, absent a credible alternative to ensure social stability and societal control."* Only then should transitional measures be considered.

However: *"Such solutions, if indeed they exist, will not be arrived at without a revolutionary revision of the modes of thought heretofore considered appropriate. Some observers....believe"* that the obstacles cannot be overcome *"in our time, that the price of peace is, simply, too high....It is uncertain....whether peace will ever be possible. It is far more questionable....that it would be desirable even if it were demonstrably attainable."*

Though repugnant to many, *"The war system....has demonstrated its effectiveness since the beginning of recorded history."* A viable peace alternative would constitute a giant leap *"into the unknown"* with its inevitable risks. Genuine peace will be destabilising until proved otherwise.

Recommendations included establishing a *"permanent WAR/PEACE Research Agency"* with unlimited funds to be used at its own discretion.

It would be organised on similar lines to the US National Security Council *"responsible solely to the President"* or officials he designates - then operate secretly for two purposes. First, to determine, from what's known and can be learned, the statistical probability for an eventual peace. Second, to conduct *"War Research"* to ensure *"the continuing viability of the war system"* as long as it's believed necessary and/or desirable for society's stability and survival.

Can there be any doubt that the Iron Mountain Report is indeed genuine and has and is being used as a blueprint for the present and future? Who would now dispute that we are all being callously manipulated by Elite interests and their associated profiteers that stand to benefit enormously both financially and socially from a strategy of perpetual war or at very least the ongoing threat of it?

None of this is accidental. As the Report from Iron Mountain made clear over four decades ago, it is what has been planned all along as part of the overall, ongoing master-plan for the total subjugation of humanity.

The Strange Story of our Moon

The Apollo moon landings 1969-1972

There is a growing band of people that absolutely, firmly believe and maintain that we humans have never set foot upon the surface of the moon and that the entire Apollo moon-landings programme was a well-produced hoax or to be more precise, a *not* very well-produced hoax by shills and apologists of the outright charlatans and liars of governmental agencies such as NASA in league with the mainstream media.

This section is not meant to follow the standard 'de-bunk' of the moon landings that is available on the Internet ad nauseum as much of this material, sad to say, is deliberate disinformation, carefully formulated and set-up using the 'straw-man' principle, to be deliberately 'shot down' by those who would deceive us and thus 'prove' that the conspiracists are way off-beam. Rather, I will try to provide an alternative view of the reasons why the whole scenario is highly unlikely, if not downright impossible. We need to understand, not only *how* this egregious hoax was carried-out but also, perhaps more importantly and significantly, why it was carried-out.

"[Why do] people cling so tenaciously, often even angrily, to what is essentially the adult version of Santa Claus, the Easter Bunny and the Tooth Fairy? What primarily motivates them is fear. But it is not the lie itself that scares people; it is what that lie says about the world around us and how it really functions. For if NASA was able to pull off such an outrageous hoax before the entire world and then keep that lie in place for four decades, what does that say about the control of the information we receive? What does that say about the media and the scientific community and the educational community and all the other institutions we depend on to tell us the truth? What does that say about the very nature of the world we live in? That is what scares the hell out of people and prevents them from even considering the possibility that they could have been so thoroughly duped. It's not being lied to about the Moon landings that people have a problem with, it is the realization that comes with that revelation: if they could lie about that, they could lie about anything." David McGowan, researcher

Had the very first transatlantic flight in 1919 not been followed-up for the next forty-odd years, would there not have been questions asked and would people not have found it strange or unusual to say the very least? If say, in the 1920s, had someone designed a jet airliner capable of speeds of 600mph or more and then after a short time that technology 'disappeared' and could not be re-created, would that not seem to be at odds with commonly accepted logic or reality at all? I submit that it most certainly would and yet this is exactly the case with the so-called moon landings of 1969-72.

Is it not also strange that almost up to the point in time when the alleged moon-landings took place, that the Soviet Union (USSR) had been leading the 'space race' by some considerable distance and yet to this day (early 2012) has never either bothered or managed to put a man on the moon. The Russians were the first to launch a vessel of any kind into space, the first to send a living creature into space, the first to perform a manned-space flight, the first to perform a space-walk, the first nation to have two spacecraft in orbit simultaneously and the first to perform a 'docking' manoeuvre in space. They also purportedly landed the first unmanned vehicle on the surface of the moon, achieved the first fly-by of the Moon, launched the first craft to impact the Moon, were the first to make a soft landing on the Moon, put the first object into lunar orbit and remain, to this day, the only nation to land and operate a robotic vehicle on the Moon. It should now make perfect sense to everyone then why the Soviets, who were ahead of the US in virtually all aspects of space exploration, in some cases by decades, never landed a man on the Moon or even sent a man to orbit the Moon. Up until the 'successful landings' by the Americans, they had been comprehensively beaten by the Russians in every important aspect of the space race. The Soviets had logged almost five times as many man-hours in space than the Americans and yet in the single-most important aspect, the landings themselves, the US had literally almost cruised to victory, totally unopposed. Very strange stuff indeed.

I also believe it significant that no other industrialised nation on Earth has managed to successfully visit the moon – or even attempted to do so, despite the fact that there have been massive, across-the-board technological advancements since the 1960s. I think that it is more than possible that the entire US space programme has largely been, from its first inception, little more than an elaborate cover-story for the research, development and deployment of space-based weaponry and surveillance systems. The compliant media never investigates or even mentions these things of course, but recently de-classified US government documents make clear that the goals being pursued through space research are largely military in nature.

"Control of space means control of the world. From space, the masters of infinity would have the power to control Earth's weather, to cause drought and flood, to change the tides and raise the levels of the sea, to divert the Gulf Stream and change the climates". Future US President, Lyndon Johnson, 1959

But if this hoax was perpetrated in almost total secrecy, how was it all kept from the thousands of people involved in the huge project, you may well ask? Please bear in mind that there were only around a hundred very senior people involved in the actual Moon landings hoax itself. Mission Control in Houston as well as most of the men and women who worked on this project over four decades ago, had no idea it was a fake. How was this possible to achieve? Very simply, the Elites who staged this fiasco never let anyone see more than a small fraction of the 'big picture'. The many thousands involved were only small cogs in a very large machine. Mission control was based in Houston, the launch site in Florida and the engineers, mechanics, computer programmers and assorted other technicians did not normally come into contact with each other, personally. So it would have been next to impossible to work out that the whole sordid enterprise amounted to nothing more than a sophisticated Hollywood production.

Why would the US not return again in the four decades that have elapsed since the last moon landings and why would other technologically advanced nations not attempt to emulate the feat? Could it be that the costs of such a venture would be totally prohibitive as some sources would have us believe? Even in those heady days of the late 1960s and early 1970s, the US was not exactly awash with money. Not only was it fighting an extremely costly, overt war in the Far East, but was also engaged in the covert, Cold War arms-race and yet still spending untold billions on the space-race, so I cannot see that money or lack of it would be a particular issue, especially not over a period of time as long as four decades – half a lifetime.

Also, consider this; the surface-to-surface distance from the Earth to the Moon is approximately 235,000 miles and since the last alleged, manned moon landing in 1972, not one human has been further out into space than 400 miles and very few have gone even that distance. Most space-shuttle orbits take place at around 200 miles from the Earth, the same distance away approximately, as the space-station. So, to put these facts into perspective, in the twenty first century, utilising the best technology that money can buy, NASA is only able to send humans around 200 miles into space, but in the 1960s it had the capabilities to reach an object 235,000 miles away, undertake several orbits of the Moon and then make the return trip – all on a single tank of fuel! Please pardon my scepticism here.

However, what about all the many hours of footage that NASA has of the moon landings and the astronauts on their moon-walks, transmitted back directly into our at the time, state-of-the-art TV sets that now with the benefit of hindsight, look like something out of the nineteenth rather than the twentieth century!? Even in the 1990s it was no simple task to transmit pictures directly from the Iraqi desert during the first Gulf War, so the transmission of pictures from a quarter of a million miles away almost a quarter of a century earlier was a really impressive technological feat, if it happened. Unfortunately, NASA has sadly 'lost' all the thousands of hours of tapes of the moon footage, 700 cartons in all.

"The U.S. government has 'misplaced' the original recording of the first moon landing, including astronaut Neil Armstrong's famous 'one small step for man, one giant leap for mankind' ... Armstrong's famous moonwalk, seen by millions of viewers on July 20, 1969, is among transmissions that NASA has failed to turn up in a year of searching, spokesman Grey Hautaluoma said. 'We haven't seen them for quite a while. We've been looking for over a year, and they haven't turned up,' Hautaluoma said ... In all, some 700 boxes of transmissions from the Apollo lunar missions are missing." Reuters, 15th August 2006

These tapes represented supposedly the greatest human achievement ever, both in technological and symbolic terms. How could such a thing happen? Surely these are historical records that should have been treated as one of the great human treasures – on a par with such priceless artefacts as the ceiling of the Sistine Chapel, the Mona Lisa and the Pyramids. Should such an irreplaceable treasure as these tapes, have not only been copied several times for security purposes, but also have been locked away securely in a fireproof, atomic bomb-proof, waterproof vault somewhere, just 'in case'? And also would not multiple copies have been made available for educational and/or scientific research and advancement purposes? Obviously NASA and the US government did not feel that they were important enough for any of that.

Surely this is all absolute and utter garbage? How could **700 cartons** of tapes be missing? Perhaps one or two boxes – possibly – but not the entire 700. For a start, they must fill several large rooms and it is therefore simply not credible in my opinion. Could it be that they do not want the tapes to be exposed to any kind of scientific analysis using today's technology? I believe that that is most likely the *real* reason and that in itself speaks volumes. This one factor alone carries far more weight than the somewhat trivial 'flag-waving-in-the-breeze' and 'shadows-at-the-wrong-angles' arguments that serve no purpose other than to distract the attention away from the real issues surrounding this huge non-event.

Reuters also commented that... *"Because NASA's equipment was not compatible with TV technology of the day, the original transmissions had to be displayed on a monitor and re-shot by a TV camera for broadcast."* So what we were actually seeing on our mediaeval TV screens were not 'live transmissions' as we were told, but was footage shot directly from a tiny black and white TV monitor and then re-transmitted second hand via the TV stations. All totally different of course to what we were led to believe at the time and subsequently. With this admission by NASA, surely it is not difficult to see how the entire footage could have been faked?

The next issue worth commenting upon is the absolutely bizarre movements of the astronauts in performing their many moonwalks as witnessed on the small portions of footage that still survive. As many sceptics have commented (and proved), if the tapes are played at approximately twice the speed, then these very odd skipping-type movements of the astronauts look extremely similar to normal speed movements on Earth.

So, the simple formula for creating Moonwalk footage is to take original footage of men in ridiculous costumes moving around awkwardly here on Earth, broadcast it over a tiny, low-resolution, black and white television monitor at about half-speed and then re-film it with a camera focused on that screen. The end result will be tapes that, in addition to having a grainy, ghostly, rather surreal 'broadcast from the Moon' look, also appear to show the astronauts moving about in entirely unnatural ways. But not, it should be noted, too unnatural. And does that not seem a little strange too? If we are being honest, the average male never stops being a little boy at heart and what red-blooded, macho-male, given the opportunity to spend some time in a greatly-reduced gravity environment, can resist seeing how high he can jump? Or how far he can jump? Or what dramatic somersaults he could perform? So what did the astronauts *actually* do? They hit golf balls. Yes that is correct, the only method by which they were prepared to demonstrate the lack of gravity on the moon, was to hit golf balls of which it was impossible to accurately judge the distance they actually travelled!

It seems more than a little odd to me that they failed to do *anything* that could not be faked simply by changing the tape speed? Some athletes here on Earth are able to perform a standing vertical jump of around four feet (1.3m) so I must also confess to finding it rather strange that the astronauts best efforts were only around 12 inches (0.3m). In one-sixth gravity, 10 feet (3m) at least should have been easily achievable, even for the most unfit among us, let alone for highly trained, super-fit professionals such as these young men allegedly were.

Indeed, should the astronauts' every movement not have been *quicker* than normal given the fact that there is virtually zero wind-resistance on the moon? If so then, why does all the available footage show only half-speed movement? It is almost as though it was the only way that NASA could think of attempting to represent anything that could be even remotely construed as resembling non-earthly movement. Maybe then it is completely unsurprising that all the original footage has mysteriously disappeared, as being submitted to modern-day technology would expose it as fake in around two seconds flat.

Somewhat worryingly also, it also transpires that it is not just simply the film footage that has disappeared in its entirety, but also the complete set of **13000+**, yes thirteen thousand plus reels of telemetry data including voice and biomedical data. All of that information, in fact the entire technical record of all the Apollo moon missions has gone, *plus* all the design blueprints for the lunar modules, the lunar rovers and the entire Saturn V multi-sectioned rockets. Worryingly that is for us but not for NASA of course as there is now no way at all that the contemporary scientific community could now ever have the opportunity of studying these documents in detail and thus prove them all impossibilities if not fakes of the most naïve kind.

For a short time there was a boost to the case of those who insist that Apollo project is not the almighty fiction that it most definitely is. This came in the form of a promise from NASA to send a probe (unmanned) 'back' to the moon to photograph the various bits of detritus left over from the Apollo missions which would prove conclusively that all the thousands of 'conspiracy theorists' out there, were all wrong. Sadly for the 'believers' though, no such images have ever been publicly forthcoming despite their wild claims to the contrary. Even the Hubble space-telescope was widely touted as being capable of homing-in on the lost Apollo artefacts allegedly spread liberally about the surface of the Sea of Tranquillity, but this too has proved a false dawn. Either the Hubble technology is capable of the feat or it is not, but whichever of these options is fact, there have been no images forthcoming from that source either.

In 2009, NASA announced that its 'Lunar Reconnaissance Orbiter' had returned the first images of the Apollo landing sites.

"The LROC team anxiously awaited each image. We were very interested in getting our first peek at the lunar module descent stages just for the thrill – and to see how well the cameras had come into focus. Indeed, the images are fantastic and so is the focus". LROC principle investigator, Mark Robinson of Arizona State University

Unfortunately that has proved not to be the case. The images are in fact not 'fantastic' by anyone's definition and neither is the focus. In actual fact the images are from such a distance that the tiny white dots they show – in shadow also, it must be noted – could be almost anything. Spot the Apollo debris (below).

Subsequent Japanese, Chinese and Indian unmanned lunar probes have also unsurprisingly perhaps, spectacularly failed to provide photographs of the Apollo landing sites.

"There's no reason to go back ... Quite frankly, the moon is a giant parking lot, there's just not much there." Val Germann, President of the Central Missouri Astronomical Association.

Strange then is it not that so many space agencies worldwide send unmanned probes there and focus enormously powerful telescopes on the Moon's surface? What could they possibly learn about this 'parking lot' from those distances that the Apollo astronauts did not already discover by actually being there?

NASA also claims that several of the Apollo missions left small laser beam 'targets' on the moon's surface that enable NASA scientists to bounce laser beams from them and which gives absolutely accurate readings of the distance from the Earth to the Moon. Now bearing in mind that these 'targets' were approximately the size of a small computer monitor screen, does anyone really believe that the technology existed in the 1960s and 1970s to accurately hit a target of that size with a laser beam from almost a quarter-million miles away? In fact is it even possible today? NASA states blithely and conveniently that there is no technology in existence that could accurately pinpoint the location of the Apollo detritus from the Earth, so how are they able to successfully locate a tiny laser target many times smaller than the artefacts supposedly left over from the moon landings? Nevertheless according to NASA and its many apologists, the fact that these signals are being bounced off these targets on a regular basis, 'proves' beyond doubt that Apollo astronauts went to the moon. I think not somehow.

The 'actual' Apollo lunar module

One could be forgiven for thinking that the above picture is of a model of a lunar landing module constructed by 10 year old school children in their arts and crafts classes, but nevertheless this is a 'real' lunar module allegedly sat on the surface of the moon, photograph courtesy of the Apollo astronauts and NASA. This incredible piece of technology, we are led to believe, actually not only landed on the surface of the moon, but 3 days subsequently, took-off again, flew 70 miles upwards, back into orbit around the moon and successfully re-docked with the command module, which was incidentally travelling at a speed of over 4000 mph at the time, in order that it could then navigate the quarter-million mile journey back across the empty nothingness of space to land precisely where and when it was programmed to do.

The most striking aspect of the photograph above though is not so much how a craft seemingly put together with duct tape, tarpaulin and bits of aluminium foil can perform such technologically advanced feats, but how did it manage to carry all the equipment and accessories that was necessary for it to carry in order to keep two human beings alive for three days in the most inhospitable environment man has allegedly ever visited?

According to NASA's own data, the lunar modules were only 12 feet in diameter. This being the case, how was it possible to accommodate all the navigational guidance equipment (in the 1960s of course, this would have been extremely bulky) and then there would have been the power supplies, the reverse thruster for landing and the powerful rocket motor required for take-off again? There would also need to be several other smaller rocket thrusters for stabilisation purposes, the massive amounts of fuel required to feed the rocket engines, especially upon take-off to accelerate enough to break-free of the moon's gravity despite the fact that it is only 1/6th that of Earth. There would in addition need to be plenty of equipment just to sustain life for two people for several days and provide some home comforts such as places to sleep, waste management facilities, food and water supplies, oxygen for three days for two people, the list just goes on and on. The oxygen tanks in the space suits would have also needed a recharge system to enable the surface-walks to take place over a concerted period of time. A back-up oxygen system may also be needed because no chances could have been taken.

The astronauts in addition to all of the above would also have desperately needed an air conditioning system, both in their suits and in the module itself, the capabilities of which would have to be seen to be believed. Consider this; the surface of the moon is subject to some incredible temperature swings. It can be +125°C in sunlight and -170°C in the shade with very little variation in-between these two extremes, so in the sunshine a human would be boiled alive and in the shade would be frozen solid in minutes. In order to cope with these extremes, the space-suits worn by the Apollo astronauts would have had to have technology light-years beyond what we have today, never mind in the 1960s. Also I think it quite pertinent to point out that air-conditioning systems in order to function correctly need a decent supply of air, the clue is in the name really and unfortunately air is a commodity which is apparently in fairly short supply on the moon, last time I checked. An air conditioner cannot possibly work in a vacuum. A space suit surrounded by a vacuum cannot transfer heat from the inside of the suit to anywhere else. A vacuum, as you may remember from school physics lessons, is a perfect insulator and therefore anyone would roast alive in his suit under such circumstances.

But we are not even finished there. The mission would also require equipment to maintain the 'ship' and to provide it with essential spares, for emergencies. And then there would be all the testing and portable lab kits that they used to conduct experiments on the moon's surface plus storage space for all the hundreds of pounds of moon rock that was allegedly brought back and which reportedly sits in hundreds of museums and scientific institutes around the world. The latter visits to the moon were also equipped with the 'moon rover'. This in itself was over ten feet long with four wheels larger than the standard car wheels of today – how did they get it in, I really do wonder? Well, according to NASA itself, this beast (below) actually folded-up to be the size of a large suitcase! Can anyone with even a semi-functioning brain really accept this abject nonsense?

The Lunar Rover – which, according to NASA folds neatly into a suitcase.

But last and definitely not least, the astronauts would have needed power – and lots of it. The only way that the ship and its vital functions could be powered whilst it was on the moon's surface would be with batteries, likewise anything else that needed a power supply, the life support system, the lights, the communications system, the television cameras and transmitters, the lunar rovers, the suits etc. etc. As it would also not be possible to recharge any of the batteries then they would have needed some pretty huge and powerful ones at that and these all have to be found a place in the severely restricted space on board that tiny module.

It is also important to acknowledge that, unlike the initial launch on Earth, which involved the collective, sustained efforts of thousands of technicians of all levels and the use of many types of peripheral computer and monitoring equipment, the astronauts leaving the Moon had only themselves and some completely untested-in-that-environment, assorted ironmongery, cables and plastic upon which to rely. I personally cannot imagine how uncomfortable and scary it must have felt to be on the surface of the moon for a few days performing experiments and hopping and skipping around the place in a seemingly carefree, happy-go-lucky manner, wondering that if or when the time came, whether that completely untested contraption would actually get me back home all the way from the Moon, or even back the 70 vertical miles to the rendezvous point with the command module. Fortunately though, the completely untested-in-the-conditions-prevailing-on-the-moon lunar module worked perfectly first time and with no need for modifications or last minute hitches, despite the literally, alien environment in which it was being utilised.

Today of course, NASA cannot even launch a highly technically-advanced space shuttle from Earth without occasional disasters, even though they have since modified their ambitions considerably. After all, sending spacecraft into low-Earth orbit (400 miles return) is infinitely more straightforward than sending spacecraft all the way to the distant Moon and back (470,000 miles). It would seem that although technology has advanced immeasurably since the Apollo Moon landings that tellingly, NASA has hugely downgraded its ambitions in space and now has a significantly worse safety record than in the 1960s, despite that downgrade.

In 2005, NASA made this incredible statement:

"NASA's vision for space exploration calls for a return to the Moon as preparation for even longer journeys to Mars and beyond, but there is a potential showstopper: radiation. Space beyond low-Earth orbit is awash with intense radiation from the Sun and from deep galactic sources such as supernovas. ...Finding a good shield is important". NASA spokesman, 24th June 2005

Do they really expect us to believe that it was possible to perform the Apollo missions in the 1960s and 1970s but now, more than forty years further down the line it has suddenly become impossible to leave the vicinity of the Earth because of space radiation? Did the technology to overcome this problem then exist in 1969-72 but has been somehow, inexplicably lost or forgotten or did the Apollo missions not actually take place as described? This statement narrows down the options somewhat, I am sure you would agree. If 'finding a good shield' is as indeed important as I believe it most certainly is, then why can they not just simply use the technology that was deployed on the Apollo craft? No-one died at the time and certainly none of the astronauts subsequently suffered from radiation-induced problems in any way that I am aware of.

Lead is the usual method of choice for radiation-shielding, but the issue is that lead is so heavy and impractical for use in anything but static situations on Earth. Attempting to build spaceships with a four feet thick lead encasement is far from practical as the Russians themselves discovered when they calculated that this was in fact the only way that they could penetrate the Van Allen Radiation Belts with a human cargo in the 1960s. Maybe this was why they simply 'gave-up' on the race to be first to the moon?

We will now turn our attention to the photographs asserted to have been taken on the moon by the intrepid Apollo astronauts. In actuality the very existence of the photographs is a technical impossibility. Unfortunately it would simply not have been possible to capture *any* of the images allegedly shot on the Moon in the manner that NASA describes them to have been obtained. In the 1960s, camera technology was very limited in comparison to today's and the cameras used by the astronauts, Hasselblads, although they were probably the best and most sophisticated on the market at that time, the simple fact is that they were incapable of generating the images claimed to have been taken on the moon, under the circumstances in which they were supposedly taken.

Cameras of those far-off times before micro-chip technology were not very 'intelligent', so every function had to be performed manually. The photographer had to manually focus each shot by squinting through the viewfinder and rotating the lens until the scene came into focus. The correct aperture and shutter speeds had to be manually selected for each shot also, in order to ensure the correct exposure time for the circumstances. This also required peering through the viewfinder, to meter the shot. Finally, each shot had to be properly composed and framed, which obviously also required looking through the viewfinder.

The problem for the astronauts was that the cameras were mounted on their chests, which made it completely and utterly impossible to see through the viewfinder to meter, frame and focus the shots. Everything, therefore, was total guesswork and focusing would have been entirely guesswork also, as would the framing of each shot. An experienced photographer can fairly accurately estimate the exposure settings, but the astronauts lacked this experience and they were also doubly handicapped by the fact that they were viewing the scenes through heavily tinted visors, which meant that what they were seeing was not what the camera was focusing upon.

To add to their not inconsiderable problems, they were wearing space helmets that seriously restricted their field of vision, along with enormously bulky, pressurised gloves that severely limited their hand and finger movements. The odds therefore of them getting even one of those three elements (exposure, focus and framing) correct under the prevailing conditions on any given shot would have been exceedingly low and yet, amazingly enough, on the overwhelming majority of the photos, they got all three right.

"For those who don't find that at all unusual, here is an experiment that you can try at home: grab the nearest 35MM SLR camera and strap it around your neck. It is probably an automatic camera so you will have to set it for manual focus and manual exposure. Now you will need to put on the thickest pair of winter gloves that you can find, as well as a motorcycle helmet with a visor. Once you have done all that, here is your assignment: walk around your neighborhood with the camera pressed firmly to your chest and snap a bunch of photos. You will need to fiddle with the focus and exposure settings, of course, which is going to be a real bitch since you won't be able to see or feel what you are doing. Also, needless to say, you'll just have to guess on the framing of all the shots. You should probably use a digital camera, by the way, so that you don't waste a lot of film, because you're not going to have a lot of 'keepers'. Of course, part of the fun of this challenge is changing the film with the gloves and helmet on, and you'll miss out on that by going digital. Anyway, after you fill up your memory card, head back home and download all your newly captured images. While looking through your collection of unimpressive photos, marvel at the incredible awesomeness of our Apollo

astronauts, who not only risked life and limb to expand man's frontiers, but who were also amazingly talented photographers. I'm more than a little surprised that none of them went on to lucrative careers as professional photographers." David McGowan, 2009

Despite all the acclaim he has received for his exploits as an astronaut, Neil Armstrong clearly has been unjustly denied recognition of his astounding abilities as a photographer. Some may argue that he clearly was not in the same league as say, David Bailey or Lord Lichfield, but I would disagree. Those two individuals created some stunning pictures throughout their careers, but could they have done so whilst wearing a spacesuit, gloves and helmet and with their cameras mounted on their chest and whilst working in an environment that featured no air, one-sixth gravity, and utterly stupefying extremes of heat and cold? I seriously doubt it.

Even more tellingly, the designer of the particular type of Hasselblad cameras 'used on the moon', has publicly stated to all who were prepared to listen that it would be impossible to use his cameras in the way described and under those circumstances, but of course this has not been widely reported and subsequently air-brushed from history. In addition, the film used must have been a hitherto unknown and since-forgotten variety of 'super-film' designed to withstand temperature fluctuations of over 300°C and also to withstand the lethal Van Allen radiation on the way home. Even relatively low-level radiation in airport X-ray machines has been known to totally 'wipe' conventional celluloid film.

Next, I would also like to ask the question; where are all the stars in the moon photographs? Not a single photograph allegedly taken from the surface of the moon shows even so much as one star in the background. Because of the prevailing circumstances and a single-light source only (the sun), there should have been a vista almost filled with tiny blazes of light, in any direction away from the sun. More stars then you could ever possibly see on even the clearest of nights on Earth because, the moon has no atmosphere to distort and dim the images. This phenomenon is explained away by NASA and its shills as being due to the fact that setting the exposure level to take account of the brightly glaring spacesuits would mean that the stars would be rendered invisible. However, this does not explain why in instances where the exposure was of a much lower level than when taking shots with the bright space suits, that stars still did not show, even on those photos.

For example, the scenes below which are obviously not very well lit, would have required a long enough exposure that would have been certain to capture every star in that part of the sky. So where are they all?

One could also legitimately question why there were no specific attempts to photograph the stars themselves? It would surely have made a beautiful visage, one never able to be seen from Earth and a change from all the pictures of the lander and the rover, moon rocks and mountains etc.

"It's as if someone went to Niagara Falls and the only photos they brought back were of the car they drove, sitting in a nondescript parking lot." David McGowan, 2009

In fact the astronauts were asked this very question about the stars at their press conference, post splash-down and the almost disinterested answer came back to the effect that they 'did not even notice' the stars in the sky! **Did not even notice them – excuse me?** It must have been the single-most wonderful sight they saw on the whole trip, the vast, unimaginable vista of all of creation stretched out before them to infinity. That is if they went in the first place, which of course they did not.

Amazing is it not how lying is so difficult to permanently maintain? And speaking of the press conference, if you have never seen the footage of this event, the DVD is available to buy at a very reasonable price on the Internet and I would strongly suggest that you track it down and do so. What is so striking and revealing about this is the absolute downbeat demeanour of the astronauts themselves throughout the entire session.

If someone had just completed the most wonderfully uplifting experience and had been on the most incredible adventure ever undertaken by the human race in its entire history, would I be wrong to suggest that they may have appeared happy, elated and exhilarated, flushed with success, even self-satisfied and have a feeling of great achievement that they would wish to share with the world? Obviously someone forgot to tell them this then in that case. I have never seen a more morose, sullen, disinterested, less co-operative bunch of people in my entire life. Anyone would have thought that they did not really go to the moon at all and were resentful of being 'put on the spot' and having to 'think on their feet' to answer all the awkward, unplanned-for questions they were being asked, including the one about the stars.

However, I think we may all have guessed the answer as to why NASA was so extremely coy about the star photography. Could it have possibly had anything to do with the fact that the moon is at a different angle to the stars in comparison with the Earth, albeit a barely detectable one, given the vast distances involved? And this would then have been guaranteed to constitute proof that the photographs had actually been taken on Earth as it would have only taken one vigilant, enthusiastic amateur astronomer somewhere in the world to find the nearest stars, take a few quick measurements and calculations and the whole thing would have been blown wide-open forever.

There are also issues with the shadows depicted in the photographs taken 'on the moon' as is pointed out by many a moon-landings sceptic. Indeed there are pictures that show the indisputable existence of **two** light sources, totally impossible of course in the case of the photographs in question. NASA itself states unequivocally that the only source of light utilised on the moon, was indeed the sun, so this all begs the question, how can these photographs be genuine?

Note the shadows at 90° to each other

The other contentious issue with the above photograph is the height from which it must have been taken if we are to accept NASA's implicit assertions, that it was a) taken on the moon and b) taken from a camera mounted on the astronaut's chest. Was he stood in a convenient nearby crater perchance? And another point about shadows concerns the fact the moon is a world of extremes. Extremes of both temperature and also of light and dark, black and white. Entirely due to its lack of atmosphere, the moon not only has extremely contrasting temperatures in and out of the sun, but this is also true of light and shade. In the sun, the light is utterly brilliant (in the sense of brightness and not in terms of quality!) and yet in the shadows it experiences an almost total inky blackness. However, in the majority of moon photos, the shady areas are anything but black, more of a watery grey colour, which is even more evidence of secondary light sources casting unintended illumination on the blackness. Here is allegedly the first ever photograph taken by human hand on the surface of the moon:

No problem there you may think? But you would be wrong. Leaving out the unlikely fact that it is once again almost perfectly 'composed', it shows clear evidence of secondary light sources evidenced by the top of the white bag and the 'United States' placard amongst several other examples. Below is probably the most iconic of all the moon photographs purporting to depict Buzz Aldrin as photographed by Neil Armstrong.

There are many issues with this photograph too. Again the composition is almost perfect, Buzz's spacesuit looks badly pressurised and the depth of field is also lacking, invalidating the reason that NASA tells us that stars are not visible in the darkness of the sky. Then there is the noticeable lack of any shadowing on Buzz's spacesuit. He is casting a shadow on the ground, but there is no corresponding shadowing of his body. Even here on Earth, that is only possible with a secondary light source.

Next, stars are by no means the only omission from the photographs. Also conspicuous by its absence is any evidence that the module actually landed on the lunar surface under its own power. Surely as a result of the reverse thrust from a 10,000lb rocket engine there would be some sort of sign in the surrounding dust in the form mainly of a massive displacement having taken place, perhaps a small crater or at the very least, evidence of dust being caked on the lander's legs? Even NASA's own artist depictions of the landings show these phenomena, so why do the photographs show no evidence of this fact?

As may be seen in the photograph below, not a single trace of any dust displacement whatsoever, exists directly below the rocket nozzle. Nor is there any evidence of scorching or displacement of any of the small moon rocks. The intense heat from the rocket motor should also have turned some of the dust to a glass-like substance and again no evidence of this is apparent.

Now let us turn our attention to the 'magic' space suits worn by all the Apollo astronauts. These suits were designed to provide all the elements needed to keep alive their human hosts in the most hostile place that human beings have allegedly ever visited. Not only were they able to protect the astronauts from the searing 125°c heat in the sunlit areas of the moon, but they were apparently also able to revert to the opposite extreme in an instant in order to protect the wearer from the numbingly cold -170°c upon stepping from sunlight into the shade. A supreme feat of technological prowess, I am sure you would agree. In addition to this, they were equipped with life-support systems in the guise of providing oxygen and eliminating CO_2 emissions as well as the ability to process both liquid and solid bodily wastes.

The suits would also have to be pressurised in order for the human body to survive and the evidence for this fact is most definitely absent from all the extant photographs of the astronauts in situ on the moon. Had the suits been at all pressurised, then their wearers would have in essence resembled the 'Michelin man' in the famous tyre advertisements, but of course that would not have created the same aesthetically pleasing effects for the TV cameras and the huge audience 'back home'.

In addition to all of the above, the suits also would have had to provide the astronauts with full body armour to protect them from the millions of meteoroids from which the moon is under almost constant, relentless attack.

"Meteoroids constantly bombard the Moon. Apollo moon rocks are peppered with tiny craters from meteoroid impacts. This could only happen on worlds with so little atmosphere, such as the Moon. Meteoroids are nearly-microscopic specks of space dust that fly through space at speeds often exceeding 50,000 mph – ten times faster than a speeding bullet. They pack a considerable punch ... the tiny space bullets can plow

directly into Moon rocks, forming miniature and unmistakable craters". David McKay, NASA spokesman

According to NASA itself then, every single piece of moon rock is covered with these minute craters and show evidence of multiple collisions from these tiny but deadly missiles. So in effect what NASA is saying is that the moon is not a safe place to be, with a constant hail of these minute 50,000 mph bullets raining-down on the surface of the moon and it would only need one, just one to penetrate the 'pressurised' suit of an astronaut and there is no way he would be making the return trip home again. Fortunately, none of the astronauts on any of the missions, nor the landing modules, nor the moon rovers were ever hit by any of these dangerous, ever-present 'space-bullets'.

In 2004 President George W Bush announced that the US planned to return to the moon, but that it would take at least fifteen years to achieve this feat. Pardon me? Fifteen years with 21st century technology and know-how to achieve what took only eight years with 1960s technology – amazing stuff indeed. Of course no-one from the mainstream bothered to ask the obvious question as to why it would take almost twice as long with 21st century technology than it did with technology from 40+ years previously, even with the distinct benefit of having 'done it before'!

However, US Republican senator, Sam Brownback did express a form of disdain at the President's statement by showing his disgust as follows... *"You've got the Chinese saying they're interested – we don't want them to beat us to the moon!"* Obviously someone else who in the heat and excitement of the moment forgot that of course, it had actually been done before.

"Conspiracy theories are always difficult to refute because of the impossibility of proving a negative." NASA spokesman, July 2009, in response to the so-called moon-landing deniers

This of course is a truly bizarre statement because of course it is not NASA that is being asked to 'prove a negative'. NASA is being asked to in effect prove that they DID land on the moon and not that they did not. This should be a comparatively easy task if it did happen. For starters they could make available all the allegedly missing data and film and all the blueprints of the hardware that they say they used to achieve this amazing feat and also provide a credible reason for the fact that most of the photographs they allege that were taken on the moon are provably fake.

One of the major problems that the Grumman, the company who designed and built the lunar landers, team faced was how to successfully insulate the entire vehicle from the intense heat of the unshielded sun not to mention the all-but ignored problem of intense space radiation. The spacecraft would have had to have been insulated almost perfectly because there were huge fuel tanks in there and the fuel would boil if not adequately protected. Also, the huge temperature variations on the Moon would cause the craft to buckle and warp which would be disastrous. It may also have been a tiny bit uncomfortable for the astronauts too. Since weight was a huge issue, heavy heat shields could not be used but as luck would have it, the DuPont Corporation had developed a new material, aluminised Mylar. It was gold in colour and supposedly if it was built-up to around twenty-five layers, it would prove to be an excellent insulator. DuPont's space-age material can be obtained very inexpensively today and is still a very lightweight material. I wonder why it should be then that we never see spaceships wrapped in it any longer?

Then in 1970, just as the whole world was getting complacent about how easy it was to get to the moon and back having now done it on two separate occasions, enter stage right, Apollo 13.

On the 13th April 1970, Apollo 13 was on its way to the moon for the next scheduled moon landing (the 3rd) when disaster struck. Apollo 13's command and service modules were allegedly rendered powerless by an explosion on the ship whilst around 200,000 miles from home on the outbound leg of the journey. This caused the three astronauts on board to have to retreat into the lunar landing module, whose functions were still operational, in order to survive. Not only did this allegedly keep the three astronauts alive but the lunar lander's engine also enabled them to 'sling-shot' around the moon using centrifugal force and plot a course back to Earth. However, the Apollo 13 astronauts were then faced with another life-threatening situation; carbon dioxide was rapidly building in the ship's confined airspace. Lithium hydroxide cartridges were supposed to be available to remove the carbon dioxide, but there was a limited supply of these cartridges in the lander. As luck would have it though, there were additional cartridges in the command module but unfortunately these were incompatible; the command module's cartridges were square while those in the lander module were round.

So what did the intrepid crew do to overcome this problem? They used duct tape and tubing from the spacesuits, plus an 'old sock' according to one of the trio, Gene Cernan, to rig-up a temporary fix and enable the incompatible cartridges to work as normal. It was indeed fortunate that next week's laundry was just lying around there on the floor. There were no seats in the lander as it had been decided that they would just add unnecessary weight. And also, there was just barely room for two people in the space allegedly now being occupied by three. All three, had this been a real life-and-death situation would have been wearing bulky spacesuits, boots, gloves and helmets. Somehow, they had to co-exist for four days and during that time all that separated them from the extreme hazards of outer space was a double layer of aluminum foil. One microscopic meteoroid or one misplaced foot would result in immediate destruction of the ship and instant death for the three 'heroes'.

I wonder why it is by the way, that the Apollo 13 astronauts were said to have been very cold throughout their return flight in their allegedly crippled ship? As recalled by Jim Lovell... *"The trip was marked by discomfort beyond the lack of food and water.*

Sleep was almost impossible because of the cold. When we turned off the electrical systems, we lost our source of heat and the sun streaming in the windows didn't much help ... It wasn't simply that the temperature dropped to 38°F, (4°c) the sight of perspiring walls and wet windows made it seem even colder. We considered putting on our spacesuits, but they would have been bulky and too sweaty ... We found the CM a cold, clammy tin can when we started to power up. The walls, ceiling, floor, wire harnesses and panels were all covered with droplets of water."

Where does one begin to analyse all that? For starters, why were they short of food and water at all? The trip had been curtailed by at least three days and as for the sun 'streaming in through the windows', how could the sun generating as it did, around 125°c of heat, not make a significant difference?

And what about the water droplets covering the interior of the command and lunar modules? Would not most of those droplets have become airborne in a zero-gravity environment? Would not the inside of the module have looked something akin to a child's snowstorm-globe? All utterly preposterous nonsense, I am afraid.

In 1929, the famous German film-maker, Fritz Lang, produced a film by the name of *Die Frau in Mond* which translates into English as *The Woman in the Moon*. Did this film provide the blueprint for the ritualistic procedures that were adopted for the Apollo programme? As can be seen in the still-shots below, all of the elements were present; the unnecessary vertical construction of the spaceship in a specially built hangar, the grand opening of the massive hangar doors, the excruciatingly slow roll-out of the upright rocketship from the hangar to the launch pad, the raucous crowds watching the spectacle live and even the now ubiquitous 'countdown' sequence. Even the shedding of two stages of the ship was there. In other words, the only elements of the performance that the public ever actually witnessed were all lifted directly from a forty-year-old (at the time) silent film.

Fritz Lang's technical adviser on the film was Herman Oberth, considered to be one of the three founding fathers of rocketry and assisting Oberth on the film project, according to the *Time-Life* book *To the Moon*, was one of his brightest students, nineteen-year-old Wernher von Braun. A decade-and-a-half later, both Oberth and von Braun would be recruited through *Project Paperclip* (see WWII chapter for more details) and brought to America to work on, among other things, the Apollo programme, whose modus operandi just happened to very closely match that of the very same fake moon-launch Oberth and von Braun had colluded upon forty years earlier.

In case you were wondering, the two screen-shots above were from the aforementioned 1929 silent film and not from footage of the Apollo 13 'near-disaster'. However one could be forgiven for thinking that, given the 'plot' similarities.

So, as always, we need to ask the pertinent question, why would they do it? Why would they go to all that trouble just to fake the moon landings and perpetuate this myth for more than four decades? And why and how could so many apparently intelligent people have been fooled by it all?

The most obvious answer and the one most frequently quoted by moon-landing sceptics, is that it was in order for the US to reclaim their national pride that had been stripped-away by the fact of America being solidly beaten in the space-race by the Soviets over a prolonged period of time. While this undoubtedly played a significant role, there are other factors also, factors that have not been explored as comprehensively as they might have been. However, before we analyse these other factors, we need to ask the question as to whether it would even have been possible to perpetrate a hoax on such a large scale.

Firstly, it is true to say that not everyone was deceived by the alleged Moon landings. Although it is not widely recognised today, a significant number of people were more than sceptical about NASA's television productions of the events. *Wired* magazine reported that, 'when *Knight Newspapers* polled 1,721 US residents one year after the first moon landing, it found that more than 30% of respondents were suspicious of NASA's 'trips to the moon.' And this is highly significant in itself, given that overall trust in government was considerably higher in the 1960s and 1970s, the fact that nearly a third of Americans doubted what they were 'witnessing' through their television sets is quite remarkable. But of course without the benefits of the Internet it was much more difficult to share information in those days, especially contentious information which would be filtered by the controlled mainstream media. Real information and statistics were thus not as widely distributed as today.

But of course, all the pro-Moon-landings websites conveniently omit to mention that of the people who experienced the events 'as they were happening' that almost 1-in-3 had doubts, a number considerably higher than one would imagine. And also, perhaps needless to say, the pro-NASA apologists fail to mention that 1-in-4 young Americans, still have doubts about the Moon landings today.

Returning then to the question of why such an egregious hoax would be perpetrated on an unsuspecting world, we need to travel back in time to the year 1969. Richard Nixon had just been inaugurated as the US President after the successful elimination of his strongest rival for the Presidency the previous year by the 'lone-nut gunman', Sirhan Sirhan (RFK) and his election to the highest office was based largely on his promises of winding-down the hugely unpopular war in Vietnam. However the truth was that the Elite had no intentions of ending the war at all and indeed, the exact opposite was true. His brief from his hidden masters was actually to escalate the conflict as widely as possible, but in order to do so, he needed to bring about a huge diversion, a means by which the patriotic fervour of the American people could be stimulated to undreamed-of new heights and so that they would blindly follow, wherever he may lead them.

Traditionally this tactic has often been facilitated by governments perpetrating short-term, low-risk military 'sabre-rattling' of one kind or another, but the huge problem for Nixon was that military entanglements are exactly what he was attempting to divert attention away *from*.

However, with not a moment to spare, Apollo 11 embarks upon its historic, heroic mission on the 16th July and with the entire American nation if not the world, in its thrall, five days later the lander allegedly sets-down on the Sea of Tranquility. Vietnam is all-but forgotten temporarily and American hearts burst with patriotic pride upon winning the race to the Moon. There is obviously no time to worry about hideous conflicts across the other side of the world whilst Neil Armstrong is taking his 'giant leap for mankind'.

However, the 'honeymoon period' is short-lived as just four months later, in early November 1969, the story of the brutal murder of over 500 civilians in the village of My Lai (The My Lai Massacre) breaks, bringing home to Americans the cold-blooded savagery of the Vietnam war once again. So then, time for another spectacular diversion and Apollo 12 duly departs on the 14th November, embarking upon another perfectly trouble-free lunar adventure before returning ten days later. America is once again mesmerised by its new heroes and suddenly the depressing old war news is off the front pages yet again.

Now let us fast forward slightly to March, 1970. A CIA-backed coup ousts Prince Sihanouk in Cambodia and Lon Nol is 'selected' by the US as his replacement. Cambodia then immediately joins the conflict and promises troops for the US war effort and the conflict is then even-further escalated in April when Nixon sanctions an invasion of Cambodia by US infantry forces, in yet another move engineered by the warmonger-in-chief, Henry Kissinger. Nixon has by this time been in office just over 12 months and the war, far from 'winding-down', has been substantially 'wound-up' by expanding into Cambodian territory.

Enter the knights in shining armour of NASA yet again. However, this next Moon mission was not to be just simply any old Moon mission as it turned-out. Having now had two successful missions go by with consummate ease and without the merest suggestion of a problem of any kind, the US population, not exactly renowned for their overly-long attention spans, had already begun to regard the moon adventures as a little too 'easy'. And so, what was needed to regain the public attention was a little injection of drama, not to mention extreme mortal danger.

On the 11th April 1970, the next instalment of the saga, Apollo 13, takes to the air. Unlike the first two missions however, the spacecraft fails to reach the Moon due to the unfortunate explosion of an oxygen tank as in the Fritz Lang film previously referred-to. The crew of Apollo 13 is by this time now in extreme danger of dying a horrific, lonely death in the vast emptiness of space. What better attention-grabber could there have been? Indeed, when three Vietnam veterans held concurrent press conferences in New York, San Francisco and Rome on the 14th April, attempting to draw the world's attention to the ongoing US government-condoned slaughter of the innocents in Vietnam and Cambodia, barely anyone notices. How could anyone be concerned about the fate of Vietnamese civilians, when their heroes are clearly in deep trouble? Fortunately it all ended in triumph yet again as the heroes defied all the odds, patched-up the crippled ship and returned home in a veritable blaze of glory. John Wayne, eat your heart out.

January 1971 saw the trial of Lt. William Calley, charged that he personally ordered and partook in the mass-murder of the inhabitants of the village of My Lai. But on the 31st of the month, Apollo 14 is launched before making, once again a flawless lunar landing. On the 9th February, the team returns, just a few weeks before Calley is finally convicted of murder. By the way, he served a ridiculously and inappropriately short sentence under 'house arrest' and none of his superiors were ever held accountable.

Then later in 1971, the New York Times began publication of the infamous Pentagon Papers, revealing American policy in Vietnam to be a complex tissue of lies. Further publication was vetoed by the US Justice Department but nevertheless resumed again in July. This was quickly followed, by the launch of Apollo 15 on the 26th of July. Five days later, yet another perfect-in-every-small-detail lunar landing clearly demonstrates American technological superiority over the rest of the world but the moon-landings were now becoming a little passé for the American people, so a new element was introduced and from then on, the astronauts were able to ride on the lunar surface in their moon rovers. The lunar modules were exactly the same dimensions as they had been all along, but apparently now they had enough space to transport unfeasibly bulky extra equipment to the Moon, with apparent ease.

The triumphant astronauts returned to Earth in early August and the rest of the year passed-by uneventfully. But then on the 30th March 1972, North Vietnamese troops mounted a massive offensive into Quang Tri Province, revealing as lies the statements by the mainstream media that after eight years of bloody conflict, horiffic brutality and massacre, victory was there for the taking. Nixon responded to this attack with deep penetration, carpet-bombing of North Vietnam and Cambodia and also with the illegal mining of North Vietnam's seaports. And NASA also responded by launching Apollo 16 on the 16th April and on the 27th April, the crew of Apollo 16 once again returned home to yet another hero's welcome.

Towards the end of 1972, a ceasefire and end to the hostilities in SE Asia looked fairly likely. In October, Kissinger and David Bruce, a member of the infamous Mellon family (of the 13 bloodlines) were secretly negotiating peace terms with the leader of North Vietnam, Le Duc Tho. In December however, the negotiations stalled, but not before Apollo 17 is launched on the 7th December. Whilst the latest group of super-heroes were far away in space however, the negotiations ceased abruptly without the courtesy of an explanation and Nixon through his controller, Kissinger unleashed one last ruthless carpet-bombing campaign against North Vietnam and Cambodia, costing countless thousands more innocent civilian lives.

Five weeks later in January 1973, upon the resumption of the negotiations, a peace agreement was finally announced and within a few days a ceasefire came into effect, thereby officially ending US military involvement in South-East Asia although of course the CIA remained to control and direct the remnants of the conflict, by proxy. All US troops returned home and the Apollo programme, despite three additional missions (Apollo 18, 19 and 20) having been planned and despite the additional funding that would have been available with the war drawing to a close, ends abruptly forever with barely a whimper. All a coincidence? Again, I will leave that to the discretion of the reader.

In addition to restoring national pride and providing a huge diversion from the savage colonial war being waged in South-East Asia, the Apollo programme undoubtedly served another useful function; covert funding of that war effort. Probably needless to point-out, fake Moon landings are by several magnitudes less expensive than actual Moon landings and the vast sums of money allocated to NASA during the Vietnam war-years to accomplish the *actual* landings was no doubt siphoned-off to covertly fund the war in the Far East, unnaturally prolonging the war as was the aim all along.

As a small postscript to this section it is also worth mentioning the three Apollo astronauts who died for the cause. Virgil 'Gus' Grissom, Ed White and Roger Chafee were burned alive during a test procedure in the command module of the Apollo 1 rocket. I believe it to be highly significant that all three were regarded by the NASA hierarchy as 'troublemakers' and there is considerable speculation that they did not agree to 'go along' with the Moon landings myths. On one occasion, shortly before the tragic fire that claimed their lives, Grissom hung a lemon on a wire coat hanger on the Apollo 1 rocket (picture below) during a publicity photo-shoot and in addition made an unauthorised statement to the press in early January 1967 to the effect that he believed that the 'Moon landings' were at least 'a decade away', for which he was severely reprimanded. That was probably his death sentence signed and sealed right there and then. Indeed less than a month later all three 'rebels' were dead. Shortly before his untimely death Gus Grissom had also said to his wife... *'If there is ever a serious accident in the space programme, it's likely to be me.'* How prophetic. Ed White's wife also died within two years of her husband, allegedly by suicide and Scott Grissom, Gus's son, a commercial airline pilot, adamantly maintains to this day that his father and the two others were murdered by NASA.

Grissom's lemon

Of the original astronauts recruited from the US Air Force at the beginning of the space programme, an inordinate number lost their lives in strange, never-to-be-explained circumstances and by such methods as car-crashes, air-crashes and 'suicides' among others. In addition to which a gentleman by the name of Thomas Baron who was a safety inspector for NASA and who delivered highly critical testimony and a 1,500 page report to Congress on the catastrophic safety failures of Apollo, only to then be killed along with his daughter less than a week later in an extremely suspicious car 'accident'. All the copies of his report were seemingly 'lost' at the same time too and the one he delivered to Congress was quietly buried with him. If not literally, then certainly metaphorically speaking.

The following are facts surrounding the Apollo missions courtesy of apollofake.bravehost.com

"Neil Armstrong is now reportedly suffering with mental illness as a direct result of him putting his name forward as the foundation stone for the biggest lie in history. OR it could be that he has become paranoid by the overwhelming number of web sites, exposing him as a liar.

Rumour has it that Apollo 12 astronaut Pete Conrad was going public about the fake Moon landings on the 30th anniversary back in July 1999. He was killed in a motorcycle accident one week before the 30th anniversary.

It takes the space shuttle 66 hours to reach the International Space Station which is a mere 185 miles above Earth. NASA claim Apollo 13 was 55 hours into its duration from lift off when it encountered a problem at a distance of 200,000 miles from Earth.

President Lyndon Johnson made certain Apollo files classified, with a declassification date of 2026. This is so that those involved in the Apollo scam would be long dead and gone, and no one alive to blame.

In the early 60s NASA officials, realising that a manned Moon landing was totally impossible before 1970, met in secret behind closed doors. It was at that meeting they agreed upon a decision to fake Apollo 11, in the hope they would get to the Moon later

on and then shroud the earlier faked pictures with genuine Moon pictures. The reality is they never succeeded with any mission.

Arthur C. Clarke referred to Apollo 11 as a 'Hole in History'. Historian A.J.P. Taylor referred to it as 'The biggest non-event of his lifetime'.

NASA had not perfected the lunar landing craft in time for Apollo 11. In 2011 they are still trying to get a rocket to land and take off again, 40 years after Apollo was supposed to have done just that.

Film footage taken inside the capsule of ALL Apollo missions, shows a light blue haze and curvature of Earth through capsule window, when they were supposedly half way to the Moon, and in the blackness of space. This proves that capsule was only in Earth orbit.

Moon pictures on NASA's web sites are fake, with backdrop scenes pasted. The pictures reveal a black line pencilled in where background meets daylight sky, which was blacked out completely.

The LM used on latter missions, was the same specification as the first mission, ie, no modifications. It would have therefore been impossible to carry the rover vehicle to the Moon in the same confined LM, even if it collapsed into a more compact form.

The lunar rover had inflatable tyres which would have exploded if pre-inflated, and there was no air on the Moon to inflate them. Pro-Apollo 'nutters' claim the rover had solid wire mesh tires. Yes, the rover in the museum had these fitted in the mid-70s when they realised pneumatic tyres could not have functioned on the Moon. NASA has had 40 years in which to clear up the plainly obvious mistakes within the Apollo programme. Each time someone brings up a query, NASA corrects it and says nothing, ie, they cannot say why the anomaly was there in the first place. Early close-up pictures of the rover on the Internet have CHANGED since the blunder was exposed on this web-site.

It would have been impossible to have a water-cooled space-suit on the Moon, when outside temperature was already at boiling point of water as there would be nowhere for the heat to dissipate.

The LM was suspended from a huge traverse crane based at Langley Research Center, Hampton, Virginia and was gently lowered at the same time it traversed over a mock Moon surface created beneath it. Check picture on REALITY site, and Channel 4 video 'As it Happened'.

Trainee astronauts were also suspended from this huge traverse crane in a horizontal position to simulate reduced gravity. Check picture on REALITY site with the NASA web site picture of Harrison Schmitt tripping up. The unusual high backward leg swing is identical in both pictures.

Film footage allegedly taken by Apollo 8 as it supposedly circled the Moon, is the SAME film used for the Apollo 11 mission, except that film is reversed and run backwards. Look for the 'tadpole like' mountain range. What NASA did was to film the mock lunar surface at LRC, traveling in one direction, then reverse camera and film surface travelling in opposite direction.

Film footage showing Apollo missions allegedly circling the Moon, was taken by a rail mounted camera which slowly moved toward a rotating plaster of Paris model of the Moon.

James Lovell was reading from a pre-written script in the simulator when he did the voice over for the above film and referred to the Moon as being 'essentially grey, no colour, looks like plaster of paris'. The recording was made long before the mission. Listen carefully on headphones, as he tries hard to suppress himself from laughing. Why otherwise would someone on such an important mission find it so comical? The answer is because it was indeed plaster of Paris he was referring to, hence the smirk on the face of Michael Collins after the remark.

The majority of NASA's fake Moon landing pictures were taken/composed in the mid-90s AND NOT in the late 60s as many are led to believe. This was because suspicion was aroused at the time regarding the limited number of photos available. NASA had to do something rapidly because of the onset of the Internet.

Earth is 235,000 miles from the Moon, yet reflected sunlight from its surface is strong enough to illuminate the darkness on planet Earth. Anyone hovering above the surface of the Moon would be blinded by the high intensity light reflected back.

In the mid-60s, Alan Sheppard was removed from ALL space missions due to vertigo and Meniere's disease. No one in such a poor state of health would be assigned to such a dangerous and complex mission. He was not even on the Apollo 14 mission, which in itself was only in Earth orbit.

The monitored radio/data signals were either transmitted from Earth and reflected back by bouncing signals off the Moon, or were transmitted via a leased channel. If a valuable source of monitoring equipment was left on Moon, then it would be used today, and not shut down in the 70s.

In a TV interview with journalist Sheena McDonald back in 1994, the NASA Administrator, Dan Golden, openly admitted that mankind cannot venture beyond Earth orbit until they can overcome the dangers of cosmic radiation. He managed to say this without any mention of the Apollo missions 25 years previously, which supposedly went 240,000 miles outside Earth orbit.

Neil Armstrong has NO mementos or photographs whatsoever from his alleged Moon mission; however he has plenty from his test pilot days. There are no photographs of Armstrong supposedly on the Moon, because Armstrong, knowing the saga was fake, refused NASA permission.

In 1969 computer chips had not been invented. The maximum computer memory was 256kb and this was housed in a large air conditioned building. In 2008 a top of the range computer requires at least 64Mb of memory to run a simulated Moon landing, and that does not include the memory required to take off again once landed. The computer on board Apollo 11 had 32kb of memory.

When Apollo astronauts were not in space, they were manning mission control communication for other Apollo missions, this was to limit the number of persons 'in the know'. There were in fact two communication links to every Apollo mission. First was launch control who dealt with communication at lift off and re-entry, however once in Earth orbit communication was handed over to the limited few astronauts manning mission control. Check it yourself on film coverage released at the time. Collins, Duke, Aldrin, Lovell, Shepherd, Schmitt, Cernan etc, are all there on various missions. Lovell himself admitted that there were two communication links to the astronauts.

It would have been impossible for the astronauts to get from the Lunar Module to the conical space capsule, as this section was occupied by the 3 large re-entry parachutes, which ejected from the conical end.

In 2011 NASA still does not have the technology to land a man on the Moon and return them safely. It may be possible in the future, but such a feat is still many, many years away.

Buzz Aldrin believes he has suffered brain damage as a result of his trip to the Moon. He knows very well that he never went anywhere near the Moon and so could not have suffered brain damage in the way he alleges. Aldrin was the only Apollo astronaut who went public and talked about the Moon landings during the 70s and 80s. The guilt, remorse, and stumbling over awkward questions put to him by the media, have put an intolerable strain on him. His psychological damage is the result of keeping it bottled up for 40 years, instead of getting it off his mind. In Aldrin's book 'Return to Earth', he makes a remark that all 6 of them have been made to look fools. Make of this what you will."

Finally, of course the above list of facts does not come anywhere close to providing a fully comprehensive list or breakdown of the anomalies surrounding NASA's claims of Moon missions. To do justice to the full list would be worthy in itself of a book of this size, alone. All I can do is provide a brief overview of some of the less well-known aspects and encourage the reader to undertake his/her own further research on the topic.

Stanley Kubrick - 2001, A Space Oddity

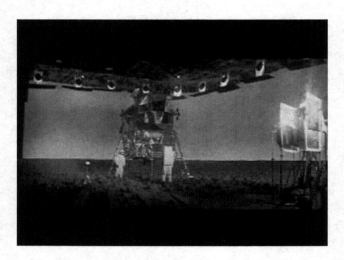

I am grateful for all the following information, to Jay Weidner, who amongst his many other talents is a highly skilled photographer.

It has now been 42 years (at the time of writing this) since the first Apollo moon landing. For as many years, there has also been a controversy between those who accept the landings as genuine and those who believe that they were faked. Could what we saw on TV of the alleged missions and landings possibly have been faked by none other than the late, great filmmaker Stanley Kubrick?

In early 1964, Stanley Kubrick had just finished his black satire *Dr. Strangelove* starring Peter Sellers and was looking to produce a science fiction film as his next big project. Whilst directing *Dr. Strangelove*, Kubrick had asked the US Air Force for permission to film one of their B52 bombers for the movie, but the Pentagon demurred. The movie, *Dr. Strangelove*, was about a flight squadron that had been ordered to fly to Russia and drop nuclear bombs on that country and the Pentagon read Kubrick's script and rejected his request to actually film the inside and outside, of a B52. The reason for this rejection was that Kubrick's film was clearly a satire on the military and US nuclear policy and the Pentagon did not wish to be held up to ridicule by Kubrick.

Undaunted by this rejection, Kubrick used various special effects to re-create the B52 in flight. When viewing *Dr. Strangelove* today, these special effects look dated and old fashioned, but in 1963 they seemed very plausible. Could it be at all possible that someone in high places saw these effects and admiring his creativity, decided to hire him to direct the moon landings charade?

After all, if he could do that well on such a limited budget, what could he achieve on a virtually unlimited budget? No one knows for sure how the powers-that-be convinced Kubrick to direct the Apollo landings footage but it is more than possible that he was compromised in some way. The fact that his brother, Raul Kubrick, was the head of the American Communist Party may have been one of the avenues pursued by the shadow government to get Kubrick to cooperate. But perhaps it was simply the payment of a huge sum of money into a numbered Swiss bank account that swung it for them.

Either way, it would appear that Stanley Kubrick faked the moon landings in return for two things. The first was a virtually unlimited budget to make his ultimate science fiction film: 2001: A Space Odyssey and the second was that he would be able to make any film he wanted, with no oversight from anyone, for the rest of his life. Except for his last film, Eyes Wide Shut, Kubrick got exactly what he demanded.

It is almost uncanny the way that the production of 2001: A Space Odyssey parallels the Apollo programme, in many respects. The film production commenced in 1964 and continued until the film was released in 1968. Meanwhile, the Apollo programme also began in 1964 and culminated with the first Moon landing on the 20th July 1969. Also, it is perhaps significant to note that the scientist Frederick Ordway was working both for NASA and the Apollo programme and was also Kubrick's main science advisor for 2001: A Space Odyssey. Once the deal was negotiated, the work began and the most pressing problem for Kubrick in 1964 was found to be how to work-out a way to make the shots on the ground, on the surface of the moon, look even close to being realistic. He had to make the scenes appear to be open and expansive, just as though the film really had been shot on the Moon and not, as it really was, in a film studio.

Eventually Kubrick settled on doing the entire project with a cinematic technique called Front Screen Projection. It is in the use of this cinematic technique that the 'trademark' of Kubrick can be seen all over the NASA Apollo photographic and video material. What is Front Screen Projection? Kubrick did not invent the process but there is no doubt that he played a huge role in perfecting it. Front Screen Projection is a cinematic device that allows scenes to be projected behind the actors so that it appears, in the camera, as if the actors are moving around on the set provided by the Front Screen Projection.

The process became possible when the company 3M invented a material by the name of Scotchlite. This was a screen material that was made up of hundreds of thousands of tiny glass beads each about 0.4 millimetres wide. These beads are highly reflective and in the Front Screen Projection process the Scotchlite screen would be placed at the back of the soundstage. The plane of the camera lens and the Scotchlite screen had to be exactly 90 degrees apart and then a projector would project the scene onto the Scotchlite screen through a mirror and the light would go through a beam splitter, which would pass the light into the camera. An actor would stand in front of the Scotchlite screen and he would appear to be 'inside' the projection. Today, Hollywood directors use green screens and computers for special effects, and so

Front Screen Projection has gone the way of all obsolete technology. But in its day, especially in the 1960s, nothing worked better than Front Screen Projection for the realistic look that would be needed both for the ape-men scenes in *2001: A Space Odyssey* and the faked Apollo landings.

If one watches *2001* on DVD today, it is possible to actually occasionally see the 'seams' of the screen behind the gyrating apes. Kubrick was performing Front Screen Projection in such a grandiose fashion that the technicians were forced to sew together many screens of Scotchlite so that Kubrick could create the vastness needed for the ape scenes to be believable.

While watching *2001*, with the scenes of the ape-men one can see the signatures of Front Screen Projection everywhere. It should be emphasised that the sets that surround the ape-men in the movie are real. There are 'real' rocks surrounding the ape-men albeit probably papier mache, but behind the fabricated rocks on the set, the desert scene is being projected via the Front Screen Projector. One of the ways in which one identify that the FSP system is being used is that the bottom horizon line between the actual set and the background Scotchlite screen has to be obscured so that the line remains unseen. Kubrick's tactic was to strategically locate rocks and other artefacts near the bottom of the scene in order to hide this 'joint' line.

Just as a stage magician needs the hidden pockets in his suit to hide the mechanisms of his tricks, so too Kubrick needed to hide the mechanism of *his* trick behind the carefully placed horizon line between the set and the screen. It is this signature that reveals, not only that NASA *did* fake the photographs of the Apollo missions but also *how* they faked them.

NASA photo clearly depicting the fake horizon line

One can see that there is a slight uprising behind the LEM, which is hiding the bottom of the screen. Also notice that even though everything is in focus in the background, there is a strange change in the landscape of the ground immediately above the 'horizon' line. This is because the photo of the mountains being used on the FP system has a slightly different ground texture than the set. Indeed, this 'fingerprint' is also consistent throughout many of the Apollo images.

However, not all lunar-surface shots use this process. Sometimes the astronauts are just standing on the set with a suspicious, completely black background. The early missions used the Front Screen Projection system only when they had to, but as the missions continued and they had to look more professional, Kubrick began to perfect the process.

Although it is possible to see the Front Screen Projection process on every mission, the seriously revealing images are in the later missions, namely Apollo 14, 15, 16 and 17.

Here are some images from Apollo 17:

That astronaut is driving the lunar rover parallel to the screen and the rover is only three or four feet away from the Scotchlite. Please note how the tyre treads just lead to nowhere. Actually, they are going to the edge of the set.

In the above photo, the astronaut is about six feet in front of the Scotchlite screen. Please also note how everything is in focus from the rocks and pebbles close to the camera all the way to the crystal clear 'mountain' behind the astronaut. Another huge impossibility among many impossibilities.

There is a stark difference in the ground texture between the set and what is being projected onto the screen. One can almost count the number of small rocks and the granularity of the ground is clearly seen on the set, but once we get to the screen on the other side of my line this granularity disappears.

This next image is interesting. When first viewed one is sure that they are looking across the vast unbroken lunar surface from beginning to end. With the Earth rising, it is truly a stunning shot.

But sure enough – a close examination reveals the set/screen line once again. Again, please note the change in the texture of the ground immediately on each side of the line. The little pebbles and dust seem to disappear behind the line.

What this means is that it is virtually impossible for two objects that are far apart in the lens of a 70mm camera to be in the same plane of focus. One of the two objects will always be out-of-focus. Filmmakers like to use depth of field because it creates soft out-of-focus backgrounds that are visually very pleasant to the human eye.

While watching the ape-men scenes at the beginning of 2001, one can see that everything is in focus. Whether it is the apes, or the far away desert background, they are all in focus. This is because the Front Projection Screen on which the background desert scenes are projected is actually not far away from the ape actor. In reality the Scotchlite screen containing the desert scene is right behind the actors just as the Scotchlite screen is right behind the astronauts in the Apollo images. So whatever is projected onto that screen will usually be in the same plane of focus as the actor-ape or the actor-astronaut.

This depth of field is impossible in real life using a large format film like 70 mm. Keeping everything in focus is only possible if everything is actually confined to a small place. It may look like the ape-men are somewhere in a huge desert landscape but in reality they are all on a small set in a studio. Similarly it may look like the astronauts are on a vast lunar landscape, but actually they are on a small confined set. Because of the vastness of the set and because he needed it to look like it was not done on a sound-stage, Kubrick had to sew several Scotchlite screens together. It was only when he had created a large enough Scotchlite screen, was he then was able to get a large enough background image that would look expansive enough to appear to be the surface of the moon or a desert four million years ago.

The process that created the desert backgrounds in 2001 is exactly the same process that created the lunar mountains backgrounds for the Apollo missions.

Maybe this is why NASA suddenly lost all of its lunar images. Maybe this is why NASA recently admitted that they 'accidentally' taped-over the original high-resolution tape of Apollo 11. Maybe this is why Neil Armstrong, 'the first man to walk on the moon', does not ever participate in the celebrations and anniversaries of the moon landings and maybe this is why we have never gone back to the moon.

As previously stated, many researchers have pointed out the different angles of light on the surface of the moon. Because there is only one light source (the sun) how can there be multiple shadow angles on the moon? If the shots were actually taken in the bright light of the sun, two individual shadows should be at the same exact angle. Yet they are not. Why? Simply because Kubrick used studio lighting, but why would Kubrick make a beginner's mistake like inconsistent shadow angles, being the supremely accomplished film-maker he indeed was? I believe that Kubrick did this intentionally.

One thing that we may be sure of is that some part of Stanley Kubrick wanted everyone to know what he had done and that is surely why he left behind clues that would explain who did it and how.

But also we can see that Kubrick used the faking of the Apollo moon missions as an opportunity to make one great film and because he had negotiated a deal where no-one would be given oversight on the film, Kubrick was allowed to make whatever movie he desired. Knowing as he did that no-one would object to his anti-Hollywood methods, he created the first abstract feature film, the first intellectual movie and the greatest esoteric work of art in the 20th century.

The president of MGM at the time in 1968 publicly admitted that he never even saw a rough cut of 2001: A Space Odyssey during the entire four years of production. Does that sound like the manner in which a head of a major studio would normally conduct his business? 2001: A Space Odyssey was one of the most expensive films ever made at that time so does it even seem remotely possible that no-one at MGM even cared to check-on the ongoing development of the film?

If so, it is a virtual certainty that 2001: A Space Odyssey is the only film in MGM history where the executives who funded the movie never oversaw the film's evolution. So why was there no interest in this very expensive endeavour?   Because MGM did not fund 2001, the US Government did. Outside of the Front Screen Projection evidence, which I believe conclusively proves the fraud of the Apollo landings, there is much circumstantial evidence that would lead us to draw the conclusion that Kubrick directed the filming of the Apollo missions. For instance, in the original release of 2001 there were many credits thanking NASA and many of the aerospace companies that worked with NASA on the moon landings but unsurprisingly, these credits have since been removed from all subsequent prints of 2001. For those old enough to remember, in the original credits Kubrick also thanks a vast array of military and space corporations for their help in the production and as these are the very same corporations that supposedly helped NASA get the astronauts to the moon – one has to wonder – what kind of help did they gave Kubrick? And for what price?

In Kubrick's film Wag the Dog; Dustin Hoffman plays a movie producer hired by the CIA to 'fake an event'. His name in the movie is Stanley and he mysteriously dies after telling everyone that he wants to take credit for the 'event' that he helped fake. Stanley Kubrick died soon after showing Eyes Wide Shut to the executives at Warner Brothers and it is strongly rumoured that they were very angry about the contents of the film. They wanted Kubrick to re-edit the film but he refused point-blank.

Warner Brothers subsequently admitted that they re-edited the film after Stanley's death and before release contrary to their agreement with Kubrick that he would have sole editorial discretion. To this day, WB still refuse to release a DVD of Stanley Kubrick's cut. Not only is this a direct violation of the agreement that Kubrick had with Warner Brothers, but it also means that there will probably never be an unedited version of this film. It really does beg the question as to what was actually removed from the original.

And finally, *Eyes Wide Shut* was released on the 16th July 1999. Stanley Kubrick insisted in his contract that this was to be the date of the release. The 16th July 1999 is exactly 30 years to the day that Apollo 11 was launched.

Natural or Artificial Satellite?

Ask yourself, what do you really know about our nearest neighbour?

Here are some stunning facts to start with:

The Moon's diameter is EXACTLY 1/400th of the diameter of the Sun and stands from Earth at EXACTLY 1/400th of the distance from the Earth to the Sun. Not 399.5, not 400.5 but EXACTLY 400. How improbable are both these facts when taken individually, let alone together?

This is the staggering fact that enables a total eclipse of the sun to occur – nothing else. If this ratio had varied even slightly then total eclipses would not occur.

And also, equally incredibly the Moon's 'day', is exactly equal to its 'year' ie. its period of rotation on its axis is EXACTLY equal to the time it takes for it to circumnavigate the Earth, hence we never see the far side, it is ALWAYS pointing away from the Earth. This time period on Earth is known as one month.

The staggering statistics continue...

The ancient human civilisations developed and utilised a unit of measurement which has today come to be known as the 'megalithic yard' or MY for short. It is based on 366° to a circle, sixty minutes to a degree and six seconds to a minute. This sequence generates a second of arc on the Earth's polar circumference that is 366 megalithic yards long.

Applying these principles of megalithic geometry to all of the planets and moons in the solar system, it was found that only the Sun and our Moon produced precise round-number results, a fact which is truly astounding and about as far from being the result of pure chance as it is possible to be.

The Sun is almost a perfect sphere. NASA quotes a best estimate of the circumference of the Sun as 4,373,096 km, which converted into megalithic geometry gives one second of arc as being 40,003.8 MY. This represents an accuracy of more than 99.99% to a round figure of 40,000 MY. Given that the NASA figure is based on a best estimate, it is not unreasonable to assume that 40,000 MY is yet another significant figure in the sequence.

Similarly, the moon is also close to being a perfect sphere and NASA's own figures specify a circumference of 10,914.5 km which converts to one second of arc, being 99.9MY. Given the irregular surface of the Moon and the small variation of the MY as +/- 0.061cm, again it is not unreasonable to conclude that we are dealing once more in significantly round numbers.

The Moon is also turning at a rate that is almost exactly 1% or 1/100th of that of the Earth and in addition, the Moon is also travelling around the Earth at a speed of exactly 1km per second which now brings into play the metric system itself. The metric system we know today was developed in France in the late 18th / early 19th century and has thus existed in its present form for around two centuries only. However, it is known to be based on an almost identical system of measurement developed by the Sumerian people several thousand years ago. In our modern metric system the circumference of the Earth at the poles is exactly 40,000 km. This is not a massive coincidence by any means, but simply a case of how the system was derived, the exact distance around at the poles being divided by 40,000 in order to determine the exact length of the kilometre and all the other sub-measurements being determined as direct derivatives of a kilometre.

There is another interesting correlation between the Moon and the kilometre. The distance from the Earth to the Sun measured in Sun diameters is precisely 109.2 at its farthest point and also the distance across the Sun's diameter is 109.2 Earth diameters. When we also add to this curious pattern that the circumference of the Moon is 109.2 x 100 km, a very strange co-incidence becomes apparent. Or does it? Can this extraordinarily unlikely series possibly be a co-incidence or is it something more than that?

Taken in isolation any one of the above relationships may be considered a co-incidence, but there reaches a point whereby when the co-incidences become too frequent that we realise that there simply must be something else going-on here.

The complete mathematical message in the Moon – Earth – Sun relationship is as follows:

366 – The no. of rotations of the Earth on its own axis in one Earth year.

366 – The no. of megalithic yards in one second of arc of the Earth.

366 – The percentage size Moon to Earth.

366 – The no. of lunar orbits in exactly 10,000 days.

400 – The ratio of the size of the Moon to that of the Sun.

400 – The no. of kilometres the Moon turns on its axis each day.

400 – The no. of times the Earth rotates faster than the Moon.

400 – The number of times further away from the Earth than the Moon, is the Sun.

40,000 – The no. of MY in 1 second of arc of the Sun.

40,000 – The no. of kilometres the Earth turns on its axis in one day.

40,000 – The no. of kilometres around the polar circumference of the Earth.

109.2 – The ratio of the size of the Earth to the Sun.

109.2 – The number of Earth diameters across the diameter of the Sun.

109.2 – The no. of Sun diameters across the Earth's orbit at it furthest point.

10,920 – The diameter of the Moon in kilometres.

27.322 – The sidereal days in 1 lunar orbit. (27.322 x 4 = 109.2)

27.322 – The percentage size Earth to Moon.

The chances of these numbers occurring randomly by chance are literally trillions to one against. So if my contention is that the precise relationships between the Sun, Earth and Moon are not purely chance then there must be a 'guiding hand' of some description behind it all.

It may be surprising to note that no matter how much technology develops in the next ten, one hundred or even 1000 years, the human race will never, ever be able to stand on an alien planet and watch something that over the millennia has in equal measures both fascinated and terrified the inhabitants of the Earth, a total eclipse of the sun. This is because Earth is most probably unique in experiencing total eclipses as they only occur because of a probably unparalleled, breathtaking, apparent co-incidence and that is that it has a moon at EXACTLY the right size and distance that EXACTLY obscures the light from its star, when conditions are exactly right.

However, this has not always been the case. Around 4.6 million years ago, give or take a few millennia, the Moon was much closer to the Earth than it is in its present position. And given the fact that the Moon is still receding from the Earth, then it can be logically argued that total eclipses are only going to be visible for a finite period of time. The Moon is a finite size as is the Sun, for now anyway and disregarding the fact that over the next several billion years it will swell to almost 10 times its current dimensions, swallowing all the nearest planets and rendering the Earth completely uninhabitable, long before that happens. So, given this fact, there is a fixed period only, whereby total eclipses can occur as the Moon will always be the same size but as it slowly but surely recedes, its visible size in relation to the Sun will be smaller and thus total eclipses will be gone forever.

There is also something else rather strange about the Moon. It is 1/3 of the size of the Earth, a huge ratio for a moon in relation to its host (in fact by magnitudes the largest such ratio in our Solar System) and yet it has only 1/81 of the Earth's mass. Had the Moon been composed entirely of Earth-type rocks, with the same gravitational pull it currently has then it would have had to have been much, much smaller, more on a par in fact with many other moons scattered liberally around the giant planets, Saturn, Neptune and Jupiter. And instead of being consistent, the gravity on the moon is subject to significant regional variations.

The fact that total eclipses are only able to occur now, at a time when the human race is sophisticated and technologically developed enough to recognise and study this fact is actually almost incredible. Some so-called experts will tell us that 'this is just the way it is' and that it is in effect 'no big deal' or a simple co-incidence, but I beg to differ somewhat. I believe strongly that it is more than significant when co-incidence is piled on top of co-incidence and numbers and sequences fit like the proverbial glove in instance after instance that does I believe point toward some kind of 'guiding hand' carefully leading us into the future. I am not invoking belief in a Christian or other mainstream religion's deity by that statement, simply speculating with what even mainstream science is now coming to regard as being more likely than not and that is that we and the Universe itself **must** be the product of some intelligent designer.

A recent, interesting discovery by astronomers is that in alien Solar Systems, the giant, gaseous planets such as our own Jupiter, Neptune and Saturn are all much, much closer to their parent star than is the case in any other example in our known 'neighbourhood'. It would therefore appear that the incidence of the larger planets being the furthermost planets from the sun is unique, as far as can be presently ascertained. It is also a fact that were Jupiter not more than five times distant from the sun than is the Earth, then intelligent life itself probably could not exist on Earth. This is due in no small measure to the fact that Jupiter fulfils the important role of protecting the inner planets from errant objects entering the Solar System from deep space and thus bombarding the smaller planets with deadly debris. Because of Jupiter's extreme size and thus its huge gravitational pull, any object entering its vicinity will be inextricably dragged-in towards the planet and effectively neutralised by collision with the giant body. For example in 1994, the comet Shoemaker-Levy was famously seen to be destroyed in exactly this manner causing a collision which created a fireball larger than the Earth itself. Had S-L managed to find its way past Jupiter and into the inner Solar System, it could have been absolutely disastrous for life on Earth.

All the above facts, I believe speak volumes. The chances of such random measurements, circumstances and facts occurring naturally are almost infinitesimally small and therefore it is not unreasonable to consider firstly, that the Moon is an artificial construct and secondly, that a guiding hand was present in designing our space-neighbourhood to offer maximum protection to our fledgling species aeons ago when life first began.

If the message contained within these measurements had been present in some electro-magnetic radio communication from outside the Solar System then the Search For Extra-terrestrial Intelligence group, otherwise known as SETI, would have wasted no time in claiming that they had at last found proof of other-worldly intelligence. So, if we accept that there has been an intelligent intervention in our past in order to facilitate our development into a technological society, could it have been an Alien race of beings planning our destiny, possibly the same ones who seeded the planet originally or indeed a spiritual presence that was responsible?

I cannot answer that question definitively, but merely present the above facts as worthy of further consideration and research or at the very least 'food for thought'. One thing of which I am certain however is that there is far more to know about the Earth, Sun and Moon's relationships than is ever given credence by those who control our thoughts and proscribe a 'reality' that is almost always at odds with the truth.

The Mysterious Georgia Guidestones

In 1979, an enigmatic stranger walked into the offices of the Elberton Granite Finishing Company in the town of Elberton in north-east Georgia USA, with a very strange request. He introduced himself as 'Mr. R. C. Christian' and stated that he wished to build a granite monument of such a scale and complexity, that he was immediately dismissed out of hand by Joe Fendley, the company owner as a crank or a practical joker. However, playing along, he sent him to visit a local banker Wyatt Martin in the hope that that would be the last he would see of the strange Mr. Christian.

Upon their meeting, Christian told Martin that he represented a group of individuals who had planned this project for more than 20 years and that each one of the group was a loyal American who believed in God and country. He said that the group of sponsors wished to remain anonymous and went on to say that his real name was not Robert C. Christian as he had introduced himself, but this was simply a name chosen because of his Christian faith.

"The group feels that by having our identity remain secret, it will not distract from the monument and its meaning," said Christian. *"The message to be inscribed on the stones, is to all mankind and is non-sectarian, nor nationalistic, nor in any sense political. The stones must speak for themselves to all who take note and should appeal to believers and non-believers, wherever and at all times,"* he continued.

To the absolute surprise of the Elberton Granite Company's owners, Christian made good his intentions and commissioned the company to construct the planned monument and it stands to this day in Elbert County, Georgia, almost like a modern-day Stonehenge. Christian's true identity has never been established but there has been much speculation in the intervening decades regarding his background and the identity of the group who sponsored this amazing, modern-day relic.

Let us now examine this strange work and attempt to establish its purpose and meaning, none of which was ever at the time disclosed to the constructors or indeed since and the mysterious character that was R. C. Christian has also long since disappeared into the mists of time, probably forever.

The monument is obviously built to stand the test of time, consisting of blue granite, one of the hardest rocks to be found, arranged as can be seen in the above illustration, with a central square pillar with four large rectangular slabs, placed diagonally at each corner of the central column, all topped with a square capstone.

The four major stones are arranged in a configuration oriented to the limits of the migration of the sun during the course of the year and also reflect the extreme positions of the rising and setting of the sun in its 18.6 year cycle. The centre stone has two interesting features; firstly, the North Star is always visible through a strategically placed hole drilled from the South to the North side of the centre stone and secondly, another slot aligns with the positions of the rising sun at the time of the summer and winter solstices and at the equinox. This in itself suggests esoteric intents in-line with the practices of the Elite.

I believe it is designed to communicate knowledge on many levels, philosophically, politically, and astronomically and the four large stone blocks contain ten guides for living, in eight languages: English, Spanish, Swahili, Hindi, Hebrew, Arabic, Chinese, and Russian. A shorter message is inscribed at the top of the structure in four ancient languages' scripts: Babylonian, Classical Greek, Sanskrit, and Egyptian hieroglyphs. It is important to note that those last four ancient languages are of great importance in the teachings of occult mystery schools, such as the Freemasons and the Rosicrucians and it is these facts that lead me to the conclusion that the monument was commissioned by present day descendants of the ancient bloodlines, the Illuminati, the Elite in other words.

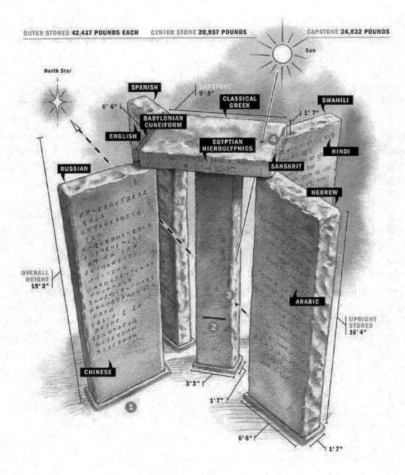

Astronomical features are of great significance in the design of the Guidestones. Monuments that are aligned with celestial bodies are often the work of secret societies, such as the Freemasons who garner their knowledge from the Mystery schools of Ancient Egypt, Greece or the Druidic Celts. They are well-known for embedding their sacred, ancient knowledge into monuments.

The 'ten commandments' literally set in stone, to be found on the Guidestones are:

1. Maintain humanity under 500,000,000 in perpetual balance with nature.
2. Guide reproduction wisely – improving fitness and diversity.
3. Unite humanity with a living new language.
4. Rule passion – faith – tradition – and all things with tempered reason.
5. Protect people and nations with fair laws and just courts.
6. Let all nations rule internally resolving external disputes in a world court.
7. Avoid petty laws and useless officials.

8. Balance personal rights with social duties.
9. Prize truth – beauty – love – seeking harmony with the infinite.
10. Be not a cancer on the earth – Leave room for nature – Leave room for nature.

I believe the first 'commandment' to be particularly significant, espousing at it does the elimination of 95% of the current world population. This is entirely in-step with Elite goals and plans and leaves no room for doubt that this whole exercise was their brainchild. This is without question part of the blueprint for the 'New World Order' promoted at every opportunity by the Elite and their 'gofers' and along with 'commandment' number 2, a central plank of the eugenics movement, promulgated by the very same 'Masters of the Universe'.

The last rule of the Guidestones, *'Be not a cancer on the earth – leave room for nature – leave room for nature'* is particularly disturbing as it compares human life to a cancer on earth. With this state of mind, it becomes easier to rationalise the extinction of nearly all of the world's population.

In 1988, Britain's Prince Philip expressed the wish that, should he be reincarnated, he would want to be 'a deadly virus' that would reduce world population and more recently, Bill Gates said, *"The world today has 6.8 billion people ... that's headed up to about 9 billion. Now if we do a really great job on new vaccines, health care, reproductive health services, we could lower that by perhaps 10 or 15 percent."* Along with tax-deductible donations of enormous amounts of money to help the depopulation cause, secret meetings of the world's Elite have been taking place for many years to discuss those very issues.

Most of the other rules of the *Guidestones* call for the creation of a world government, ruled by an 'enlightened few', who would regulate all aspects of human life, including faith, social duties, the economy, etc. etc.

Since the monument's completion on the 22nd March 1980, numerous authors and researchers have attempted to interpret the rationale behind the new 'ten commandments'. Do they really consist of a blueprint for the New World Order or are they simply rules applicable in the event of a major catastrophe? Obviously, the best way to obtain an accurate answer is to ask the authors of the rules themselves but as they have chosen to remain anonymous, it is impossible to do so. They did, however, leave an important clue to their intentions which has been overlooked by most researchers of the *Guidestones*. This astounding text, which describes their motives in great detail, can only be found in *The Georgia Guidestone Guidebook*, a pamphlet produced by the Granite Company, which manufactured and constructed the monument. It is obvious that the sponsors of the monument *do* indeed seek the creation of a New World Order and this is most definitely not a conspiracy theory or vague hypothesis, it is written in clear and unequivocal terms. So here it is, directly from the writings of its secret authors, the explanation of the 10 'commandments' of the *Guidestones*:

"It is very probable that humanity now possesses the knowledge needed to establish an effective world government. In some way that knowledge must he widely seeded in the consciousness of all mankind. Very soon the hearts of our human family must be touched and warmed so we will welcome a global rule of reason.

The group consciousness of our race is blind, perverse, and easily distracted by trivia when it should be focused on fundamentals. We are entering a critical era. Population pressures will soon create political and economic crisis throughout the world. These will make more difficult and at the same time more needed the building of a rational world society. A first step will be to convince a doubting world that such a society is now possible. Let us keep in view enduring appeals to the collective reason of humanity. Let us draw attention to the basic problems. Let us establish proper priorities. We must order our home here on earth before we reach for the stars. Human reason is now awakening to its strength. It is the most powerful agency yet released in the unfolding of life on our planet. We must make humanity aware that acceptance of compassionate, enlightened reason will let us control our destiny within the limits inherent in our nature.

It is difficult to seed wisdom in closed human minds. Cultural inertias are not easily overcome. Unfolding world events and the sad record of our race dramatize the shortcomings of traditional agencies in governing human affairs. The approaching crisis may make mankind willing to accept a system of world law which will stress the responsibility of individual nations in regulating internal affairs, and which will assist them in the peaceful management of international frictions. With such a system we could eliminate war. We could provide every person an opportunity to seek a life of purpose and fulfillment.

There are alternatives to Armageddon. They are attainable. But they will not happen without coordinated efforts by millions of dedicated people in all nations of the earth. We, the sponsors of The Georgia Guidestones, are a small group of Americans who wish to focus attention on problems central to the present quandary of humanity. We have a simple message for other human beings, now and in the future. We believe it contains self-evident truths, and we intend no bias for a particular creed or philosophy. Yet our message is in some areas controversial. We have chosen to remain anonymous in order to avoid debate and contention which might confuse our meaning, and which might delay a considered review of our thoughts. We believe that our precepts are sound. They must stand on their own merits.

Stonehenge and other vestiges of ancient human thoughts arouse our curiosity but carry no message for our guidance. To convey our ideas across time to other human beings, we erected a monument — a cluster of graven stones. These silent stones will display our ideas now and when we have gone. We hope that they will merit increasing acceptance and that through their silent persistence they will hasten in a small degree the coming age of reason.

We believe that each human being has purpose. Every one of us is a small but significant bit of the infinite. The celestial alignments of the stones symbolize the need for humanity to be square with External principles which are manifest in our own nature, and in the universe around us. We must live in harmony with the infinite.

Four large stones in the central cluster are inscribed with ten precepts, each stone carrying the same text in two languages. In the English version the message totals fewer than one hundred words. The languages have been selected for their historical significance and for their impact on people now living. Since there are three thousand living languages, not all could he chosen.

We envision a later phase in the development of the Georgia Guidestones. It is hoped that other stones can be erected in outer circles to mark the migrations of the sun and perhaps certain other celestial phenomena. These stones would carry our words in the languages of other individuals who share our beliefs and will raise similar stones at international boundaries in the languages of friendly neighbors. They would serve as reminders of the difficulties which all humanity must face together, and would encourage mutual efforts to deal with them rationally and with justice.

We profess no divine inspiration beyond that which can be found in all human minds. Our thoughts reflect our analysis of the problems confronting humanity in this dawning of the atomic age. They outline in general terms certain basic steps which must be taken to establish for humanity a benevolent and enduring equilibrium with the universe.

Human beings are special creatures. We are shepherds for all earthly life. In this world, we play a central role in an eternal struggle between good and evil – between the forces which build and those which would destroy. The Infinite envelops all that exists, even struggle, conflict and change, which may reflect turmoil in the very soul of God.

We humans have been gifted with a small capacity to know and to act– for good or for evil. We must strive to optimize our existence, not only for ourselves but for those who come after us. And we must not be unmindful of the welfare of all other living things whose destinies have been placed in our trust.

We are the major agency through which good and evil qualities of the spirit become actors in our world. Without us there is very little of love, mercy, or compassion. Yet we can also be agents of hate, and cruelty and cold indifference.   Only we can consciously work to improve this imperfect world. It is not enough for us to merely drift with the current. The rational world of tomorrow lies ever upstream.

In 1980, as these stones were being raised, the most pressing world problem was the need to control human numbers. In recent centuries technology and abundant fuels have made possible a multiplication of humanity far beyond what is prudent or long sustainable. Now we can foresee the impending exhaustion of those energy sources and the depletion of world reserves of many vital raw materials.

Controlling our reproduction is urgently needed. It will require major changes in our attitudes and customs. Unfortunately, the inertia of human custom can be extreme. This is especially true when those for whom custom is a dominant force are uninformed of the need for change.

Nearly every nation is now overpopulated in terms of a perpetual balance with nature. We are like a fleet of overcrowded lifeboats confronted with an approaching tempest. In the United States of America we are seriously overtaxing our resources to maintain our present population in the existing state of prosperity.   We are destroying our farmland and we have grown dangerously dependent upon external sources for oil, metals and other nonrenewable resources. Nations such as Japan, Holland and Haiti are even more seriously overpopulated and, therefore, in greater jeopardy.

In these circumstances, reproduction is no longer exclusively a personal matter. Society must have a voice and some power of direction in regulating this vital function. The wishes of human couples are important, but not paramount. The interests of present society and the welfare of future generations must be given increasing consideration as we develop mechanisms to bring rational control to our childbearing.

Irresponsible childbearing must be discouraged by legal and social pressures. Couples who cannot provide a decent income and support for a child should not produce children to be a burden for their neighbors. Bringing unneeded children into an overcrowded lifeboat is evil. It is unjust to those children. It is harmful for the other occupants and all living things. Society should not encourage or subsidize such behavior.

Knowledge and techniques for regulating human reproduction are now in existence. Moral and political leaders throughout the world have a grave responsibility to make this knowledge and these techniques generally available. This could be done with a fraction of the funds which the world now devotes to military purpose. In the long run, diverting funds into this channel could do more than anything else to reduce the tensions which lead to war.

A diverse and prosperous world population in perpetual balance with global resources will be the cornerstone for a rational world order. People of good will in all nations must work to establish that balance.

With the completion of the central cluster of The Georgia Guidestones our small sponsoring group has disbanded. We leave the monument in the safekeeping of the people of Elbert County, Georgia.

If our inscribed words are dimmed by the wear of wind and sun and time, we ask that you will cut them deeper. If the stones should fall, or if they be scattered by people of little understanding, we ask that you will raise them up again.

We invite our fellow human beings in all nations to reflect on our simple message. When these goals are some day sought by the generality of mankind, a rational world order can be achieved for all."

All very commendable you may think. Who could argue with such noble sentiments? However when one 'reads between the lines' of this message it is very simple to discern the fact that the message promotes a society that would fulfill the Elite goals, all of course dressed up in language that is designed to make this 'New World Order' sound like paradise and not as it would be, the world described by both Orwell and Huxley in their prophetic novels *1984* and *Brave New World*.

The Georgia Guidestones are a manifesto calling for a drastic change in the way the world is currently managed. The monument is of a great importance in the understanding of the forces covertly shaping today and tomorrow's world and it represents in stone the inextricable links between secret societies, the world Elite and the agenda for a New World Order. This agenda for one world government, population control and environmentalism are issues that are today discussed on a daily basis in current events; however this was not the case in 1980, when the Guidestones were erected.

The crude but nevertheless heartfelt sentiments of those who oppose all that these monsters represent

The Ritual Murder of Diana, Princess of Wales

Despite what the establishment and the Elite controlled, compliant media would like you to believe, there is absolutely no doubt that Diana was ritually and brutally murdered in line with Royal orders.

On the 31st August 1997, Princess Diana, the estranged wife of Prince Charles, and her lover, Dodi Fayed were killed in a car crash in the Pont de l'Alma road tunnel in the centre of Paris. They were on their way to Dodi's executive apartment just off the Champs Elysee after having had dinner together at the Ritz Hotel, owned by Dodi's father, Mohammed Fayed. (I will refer to him and his late son as 'Fayed' rather than 'Al Fayed' as this is the name with which he was born. The 'Al' prefix is merely a later affectation). The other occupants of the car were Henri Paul, head of security at the Ritz, the nominated driver for the evening and Trevor Rees-Jones another security man and the only survivor of the 'accident'.

We are, as is always the case, faced with the usual confusion and subterfuge surrounding the events of that night. Indeed there are so many conflicting versions of the story that it is extremely difficult for anyone to even come close to the actual truth without intensive, sustained research on the subject. However, what follows is substantially more than an educated guess about what actually happened that fateful night.

The story began in 1980, seventeen years earlier with a teenage girl from a privileged background, Lady Diana Spencer, meeting and falling in love with her Prince Charming (Charles) in a storybook romance that captured the imagination of almost the whole of our royalty-obsessed nation and most of the rest of the world too. The date was soon set for the wedding as the 29th July 1981 and little did poor Diana know that her troubles were only just about to begin.

She gave birth to William, the couple's first child, through an induced birth on 21st June 1982 (significantly, the summer solstice – an important occult date) and he was shortly afterwards followed by his younger brother, Harry, the two boys being jokingly referred to as the 'heir and the spare'. Once Diana had fulfilled her always-intended role as brood-mare (her term) for the future monarch and his 'back-up', all pretence of love was immediately dropped by Charles and he immediately resumed his long-term, ongoing affair with Camilla Parker-Bowles (if indeed it had ever ceased). Diana realised very quickly that the fairy-tale was over and she was basically shunned and treated as an interloper from that point onwards by the entire Royal family. Had she not been the strong character that she undoubtedly was, then she may not have even had the mental strength to assert herself where her boys were concerned. Ironically, that she did so, probably marked the beginning of the end for her. Anyone who crosses these people, for any reason at all had better beware.

The full force of the Royal propaganda machine was unleashed upon her as she had to endure all kinds of mental torture and accusations of unfaithfulness (most of her alleged indiscretions were probably more than understandable, but nevertheless true) whilst Charles' blame for the rapid disintegration of the marriage was deflected in her direction and for a considerable time she acquired a reputation as a 'mad woman' struggling with bulimia and mental illness.

In 1988, Diana was having a secret affair with her security guard, the detective Barry Mannakee which obviously became known to the Royals. Shortly afterwards, Mannakee was killed in a road traffic 'accident' and Charles cruelly and sarcastically broke the news to Diana by saying to her with a smirk, before she even knew of his death, 'Shame about poor Barry!' David Icke, the geo-political researcher, spoke to Christine Fitzgerald, an alternative healer and Diana's confidante at the time and she said to him..

"She was crying hysterically and I said 'What's the matter?' 'I can't believe it', she sobbed, 'They killed him, they killed him'. I said 'who did they kill' and she told me that he [Barry] had been decapitated on his motorbike and how she thought at first it was a terrible accident. But now she knows the Royal family killed him because Prince Charles' detective just told her that if she didn't cool it with Hewitt, the same would happen to him. **He told her that she should not think she was indispensible either."** [My emphasis – JH]

Diana in fact was absolutely convinced that she was going to be disposed of in a fake 'accident' scenario. She confided this fact to several friends and even wrote it in a letter.

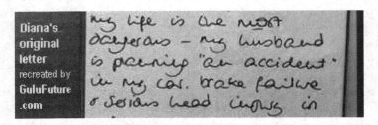

Diana's original letter recreated by GuluFuture.com

Diana's letter to her butler, Paul Burrell

This was later confirmed by James Hewitt himself in a TV documentary, 'Diana – secrets of the crash' in 1998. He also said that he too had been warned to stop seeing Diana or 'the consequences would not be pleasant'. He further said:

"The telephone calls were anonymous, but they left me in no doubt that they knew what the situation was. They were threatening. They said it was not conducive to my health to continue the relationship."

He also said that he had other warnings from Diana's personal protection unit, the Royal household itself and a specific 'senior' member of the Royal family whom he declined to identify. This person said:

"Your relationship is known about. It is not supported. We cannot be responsible for your safety and security and suggest that you curtail it forthwith."

However the clearest threat to him came when he was told outright that if he did not desist from seeing Diana, the same fate as befell Barry Mannakee would also befall him.

This latter statement alone, I believe tells anyone who was formerly in any doubt about the capabilities of these monsters, exactly what they are about and belies the 'cosy' homely image they love to project of their thoroughly evil-to-the-core family. Every time I hear anyone say anything along the lines of 'I am a staunch royalist' or 'I adore the Royal family' (and there are millions of these sheeple) it makes me thoroughly sick to my stomach. The time to wake up is long overdue.

But, back to the story…

After the end of her affair with James Hewitt, which had been duly 'curtailed' after the threats, which Hewitt obviously and understandably took fairly seriously, Diana's next 'public' amour was with Dodi Fayed and as we all know now, it was destined to be her last.

Mohammed Fayed, Dodi's overbearing father was instrumental in bringing the couple together. He had ingratiated himself with Diana in the past and always made a point of greeting her personally when she visited Harrods for her 'retail therapy'. They had built up quite a cosy relationship – she found him 'charming and funny' or so she said and when he invited her and the two teenage boys to join him and Dodi on his yacht *Jonikal* in the Mediterranean in the July of 1997, the relationship blossomed. At this point, it must be noted, Dodi was still engaged to his American fiancée, Kelly Fisher but father had spoken and Dodi had to obey.

Kelly was originally invited to be the guest on the yacht that summer but Dodi blanked her several times, would not answer her calls and she was told by the Fayed staff in no uncertain terms that they had been instructed not to connect her calls to either Fayed senior or Fayed junior. Eventually she did manage to speak with Dodi who cruelly cut her short and told her the engagement was off. They were never to speak again.

After a relaxing few days on the yacht, the boys were dispatched back home to Charles whilst Dodi and Diana flew to Paris to spend a couple more romantic nights together before the end of the holiday and their both going their separate ways again, albeit it was hoped, temporarily.

So, the 30th August, the last full day either of them would ever see, as it turned out, dawned and after a pleasant day spent together in Paris, Dodi had planned a romantic meal for two in an exclusive restaurant close to the Ritz Hotel. However, their plans were about to be thwarted. A huge posse of 'paparazzi' reporters had gathered outside the main doors of the hotel, making it almost impossible for the couple to pass through on their way to the restaurant and so they had a change of plan. Instead of going to the restaurant, they decided to eat in the hotel restaurant before making their way across Paris to Dodi's apartment in the Rue Arsene-Houssaye, where they intended to spend the night.

Just after midnight, they made their move. The paparazzi were still thronged outside the front door of the hotel in great numbers and would no doubt harass the couple all the way to the car and probably all the way to Dodi's apartment too. So, a plan was hatched by Mohammed Fayed whereby a decoy car would arrive at the front door, purportedly to take the couple to their destination and meanwhile the couple would sneak out of the rear door and into another car waiting to whisk them away before the reporters knew what was afoot. So far so good and the Mercedes sped away from the Ritz driven by Henri Paul, with Rees-Jones in the front passenger seat and Diana and Dodi in the rear seats.

None of the two cars or motorcycle chasing the Mercedes at this point contained any paparazzi; they all appeared in the first couple of minutes after the crash. As the Mercedes approached the tunnel it was being chased by the two cars and one motorcycle and one of the vehicles (a white Fiat Uno) rammed the Mercedes just before the crash. As the Mercedes got nearer the tunnel, another motorcycle prevented one car from taking the approach road that lead to the tunnel.

A remote-controlled device was likely used, causing an explosion (as initially reported by CNN and then mysteriously omitted from subsequent reports) which was heard by witnesses and which disabled the driving controls and electronics of the Mercedes. A laser strobe light was also seen by witnesses, which was used to blind the driver in the final seconds before it entered the tunnel - which incidentally, some witnesses claim was completely dark as the lights had been turned-off minutes earlier. A laser beam was being flashed into the eyes of the chauffeur, Henri Paul, causing the Mercedes to crash inside the Pont d'Alma tunnel. Witnesses told British detectives they saw a motorcyclist point a laser into the eyes of Paul. One witness said he saw 'an enormous radar-like flash of light.'

After hearing an explosion and then a bang, witnesses ran to the scene, only to be told to 'get back' by an unknown person who ran towards them out of the tunnel from the direction of the crashed car. A second person, whose identity is also still unknown, was seen in the Mercedes lifting the already dead driver's head from the blaring car horn. Witnesses also report that a helicopter was seen above just before the crash, presumably monitoring or even directing events on the ground. Since the electricity had been cut-off in the tunnel, the traffic cameras did not work, thus ensuring that there was no video evidence of the Mercedes final approach to the tunnel or of what vehicles may have been leaving it. One witness, Gary Hunter, saw two vehicles race out of the tunnel and others also saw a motorcycle tearing away at high speed.

Removing the evidence

MI6 certainly had the means to kill Princess Diana by faking a car crash. In 1992, for example, former MI6 agent Richard Tomlinson says they planned to kill President Slobodan Milosevic by using a fake car crash in Geneva. In 1996, according to the former MI5 agent David Shayler, they failed in their attempt to kill the Libyan leader Colonel Muammar Gaddafi, but the car bomb they used killed scores of Libyan civilians (thus, Gaddafi, who has survived at least three attempts made on his life by western intelligence services, was also the only leader of a country to openly speculate that MI6 had killed Diana).

It was indeed MI6 who had developed an assassination technique by the name of 'Boston brakes' so-named after the MI6 location where it had been successfully developed in Boston, Lincolnshire in the English east midlands. This technique simply put, is a method by which the target car can be remotely controlled from another nearby vehicle and which would explain why, in the case of Diana's car it was a fairly simple operation to smash it precisely into tunnel pillar 13 at very high speed. We will examine the significance of pillar 13 in more detail later.

French medics from the hospital where the princess died, claim she was pregnant at the time of the crash and this would tend to support the belief that Diana and her lover were killed to avoid the royal family's embarrassment at her having a child by a Muslim. The intelligence services in France, Britain and the USA have 'stonewalled' on this though we know that intelligence services had Diana under surveillance on the fateful night in Paris. And, as is always the case, there has been a concerted campaign to discredit any attempts to get at the truth.

Minutes before the crash, the couple head towards the car.

Every trick in the book and every tabloid technique known to man have been employed to fashion all the fiction that masquerades as the truth. Henri Paul was not drunk at all. Both Trevor Rees-Jones and Kez Wingfield (another Fayed security man) continue to insist that Paul gave no indication whatsoever of being drunk before he got behind the wheel. They had been with him for extended periods that evening and still maintain that there was nothing in his behaviour or general conduct to suggest that he had been drinking. If this is the case, how then do they account for the inquiry finding that, within three minutes of leaving the hotel, he was more than three times over the drink-drive limit? After three contradictory autopsies, Henri Paul was buried on the advice of his lawyers and not cremated, as they advised his body may have to be exhumed again. The Times published an article headlined 'Spy agencies listened in on Diana'. In this article, 'former intelligence officials' confirmed to the newspaper that spy agencies in Britain and America 'eavesdropped on Diana'. Given that Diana was mother to the future King and was often at odds with the Royal Family, it is frankly unbelievable that the security forces were taking no interest in her but the official line attempts to deny the obvious.

"... the late Princess of Wales had clearly been under some kind of surveillance, as evidenced by the 1,050 page dossier held by the US National Security Agency detailing private telephone conversations between Diana and American friends intercepted at MI6's request." From Stephen Dorril's best-selling history of Britain's overseas intelligence service, *'MI6: Fifty Years of Special Operations'* (p788).

By sheer co-incidence, Stephen Dorril is actually a neighbour of mine, living in the same small, Pennine village in rural Yorkshire. My wife was in fact his secretary for five years and he has verbally confirmed this fact to me, also.

The CIA and the National Security Agency (NSA) have confirmed that they hold 39 documents consisting of 1,056 pages of information relating to Diana and Dodi Fayed, but they refuse to reveal it on the grounds of 'national security'. Yeah, right.

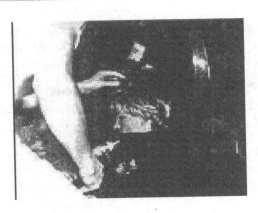

Last photo of Diana – receiving oxygen

There have been many theories about why the Elite wanted rid of Diana. One of the more popular ones is that Britain's establishment found her relationship with the Egyptian Muslim Dodi Fayed (and the possible pregnancy) utterly unacceptable and so conspired with the intelligence services to have them killed. Another theory has her death linked to Diana's campaigning against the use of landmines whilst another opinion is based on Occam's razor ie. the correct solution to a problem is usually the simplest one and that she was murdered to make way for Charles to marry the love of his life, Camilla Parker-Bowles plus possibly to remove her 'bad influence' from the two young princes. Maybe the truth is a blend of all these possible reasons.

It may or may not be true, but I have heard of a second-hand story from a friend of a friend (who incidentally absolutely swears it to be the truth) that she was in Paris on the night of the crash and got back to her hotel room after a late night out and switched on the TV in the room. The local 24-hour news channel was airing the first pictures to come-in of an appalling car accident in Paris and she was just in time to see images of a young blonde woman, obviously dazed and groggy, but who was nevertheless able to enter the ambulance on foot, albeit with assistance from paramedics on either side of her. She recognised this woman as Princess Diana and went to bed thinking that Diana had 'had a lucky escape'. She was obviously shocked and mystified next day when she awoke to all the reports of the princess's death in the car crash. Of course those images were never shown or referred-to ever again as is usual in these cases. As a footnote to this, I have recently seen confirmation that on that fateful night, the BBC newscaster Martyn Lewis in the BBC's first 'newsflash' announced that Dodi had been killed outright, but that Diana had been seen 'walking into an ambulance'.

Whatever the real truth regarding the above may be, this is certainly possible in my view. There was obviously no absolutely fool-proof way to ensure Diana's death, even in a staged crash and so there would have had to be a contingency plan in place in the event of her survival against the odds. If Diana had indeed survived the impact of the crash, then drastic steps would have needed to be undertaken to ensure that she did not survive and maybe this explains why it took the ambulance almost two hours to travel the 4km to the Pitie Salpetriere Hospital. I have not yet heard another credible reason as to why that should have been the case. At one point in the ambulance's journey it apparently parked at the kerb-side for over twenty minutes just 600 metres from the hospital. This has never been satisfactorily explained by those who control what we are meant to see, hear and believe.

Near the end of her life, Diana was increasingly becoming involved in politics and rattling more than a few cages on the way. She had criticised her own government and their policies and there were many in high places who resented her increasing involvement with politics combined with her extreme popularity – a dangerous mix in the eyes of the establishment. She was also viewed as a potential 'loose cannon' and was in a position, should she wish, to reveal some of the dark secrets of the Royal family. All of this, along with her relationship with Dodi Fayed probably sealed her fate. The same forces behind the murder of so many others, from heads of state such as JFK, Indira Gandhi and Olof Palme, to an ordinary civilian who knew too much, like Dr. David Kelly, were behind the murder of Princess Diana. MI6, the NSA, the CIA, the Bilderbergers, Trilateral Commission, CFR, Bohemian Grove, and other related secret agencies and societies that control the politics and media of supposedly 'free' nations all fall under the same umbrella and employ the same tactics in order to benefit the Elite few. Despite the lies dressed-up as truth in the popular press, many people believe Diana was murdered but we will never hear the truth of what really happened to her in the mainstream media, any more than we will with regards to countless others who have been and continue to be disposed-of at the hands of these murderous criminals. In the end, it is up to the people to decide if they can accept the truth about what kind of people control their own governments and if they can accept the truth about what really happened to Diana and so many others like her.

At this point of the story I feel it is worthwhile to mention the involvement of Mohammed Fayed in all of this intrigue. It is certainly true that his has been the loudest and most prominent individual voice of protest, but as with many other aspects of this sorry tale, I believe the truth of this to be not what it appears on the surface. Ask yourself who was the person who was controlling the couple's 'agenda' on that day? Who was the person who master-minded the logistical arrangements that evening? Who was the person who had slowly but surely ingratiated himself with Diana and acted as match-maker with his son those months previously? It was Fayed senior who indeed was pulling all the strings. Dodi was very much 'under the thumb' of his father and had no say in the events at all. Could Fayed's subsequent ravings about the 'murder' of his son and girlfriend and about senior Royalty involvement in the plot, have more than a little to do with the fact that Dodi's death had possibly not been part of the planned agenda and therefore the reason why Fayed's anger was unleashed? I firmly believe so. Moreover, I believe that Fayed had been cast in the role of 'Mr Fix-it', the facilitator of the entire operation but unfortunately he was not expecting Dodi to constitute part of the casualty list and therefore his extreme anger has been overtly apparent since the event.

Significantly, Diana is the name of the moon goddess worshipped in Rome and Greece and by the bloodline Merovingian dynasty in Paris. Pont de l'Alma means bridge or passage of the moon goddess.

The Illuminati torch symbol over the Pont de l'Alma tunnel where Diana was murdered

The princess was killed in a ritualistic sacrifice in Pont de l'Alma, Paris. This site is extremely ancient, dating back to the time of the Merovingian kings (c. 500-751 AD) and before and as we have seen in previous chapters, ritual and symbolism is a disproportionate obsession with the Elite. Once the decision had been taken to carry out the murder then it would have been planned in accordance with that ritual and symbolism, notwithstanding its being disguised as an accident.

The location chosen to murder Diana was a sacred site and an ancient Temple of the **Goddess Diana**, a Temple that was used for human sacrifice and ritual murder! In pre-Christian times, the Pont de l'Alma had been a pagan sacrificial site and in the time of the Merovingian kings, it was an underground chamber. So, was the choice of Pont de l'Alma as the site of her death deliberate? And if so, what message were her assassins sending and to whom were they sending it?

Did the men who murdered Diana know the occult history and significance of Pont de l'Alma? There is no doubt that the Mercedes was earlier stolen and rebuilt to respond to external radio controls. This is significant because the car crashed into the 13th pillar. Was the car responding to an outside radio signal as per MI6's 'Boston brakes' method? Was crashing the car into the 13th pillar done to **send** a signal? The Elite often use dates, places and rituals from the past in the present as symbolism, so this would seem to be a distinct possibility. In occult lore, this adds the esoteric 'power' of past events to the present and is also a way of communicating with each other through 'newspaper headlines.'

All of the royal families of Europe including also the Spencer 'clan' from which Diana emanated, can trace their lineage from the Merovingian kings (the so-called 13th bloodline). These kings are descended from Merovaeus the Young, king of the Franks of Yssel and Merovaeus was said to be born of 'two fathers', a Frankish king and a sea creature. According to tradition, Merovingian monarchs were occult adepts, initiates in arcane sciences, practitioners of esoteric art worthy of Merlin of Arthurian fame. Amazing is it not, that the mainstream sciences and media, controlled by these Elite groups, constantly tell us that all this information is 'legend' and 'myth' and not to be taken seriously, whilst the Elite themselves not only take it all extremely seriously, but they actually conduct their lives using these legends as a template for their very existences and a platform for their overall world-view?

Allegedly, by virtue of the miraculous property in their blood, they could heal by the laying on of hands and they were said to be capable of clairvoyant or telepathic communications with beasts and with the natural world around them.

They were regarded as the Priest-Kings, embodiments of the divine, in other words not unlike the ancient Egyptian pharaohs. They did not just simply rule by God's grace, on the contrary, they were apparently deemed the living embodiment and incarnation of God's grace, a status usually reserved exclusively for Jesus.

All Merovingians followed the Pagan cult of Diana, until Clovis (481-511). Badgered by his wife, Clotilde, Clovis converted to Christianity. In the Arthurian legends, Arthur was a Pagan who worshipped the Lady of the Lake and Princess Diana is now in a sense, also the Lady of the Lake because her tomb is symbolically placed on an island in the middle of a lake inhabited by specially imported black swans. Black swans are yet another occult / pagan symbol.

Also in the Arthurian legends, Arthur's wife, Queen Guinevere was a Christian. Her name means 'The white wave' and Christianity was a 'white wave' that swept over the pagan religions and drowned them.

As previously stated, all the royal families of the European continent and the majority of America's ruling class are descended from the Merovingians who believed that they could trace their lineage not only to Jesus and Mary Magdalene, but all the way back to King David, Noah and the 'visitors' from the star system of Sirius, the Annunaki. This belief not only confirms their superiority over other humans, it also gives them their belief in the 'divine right of kings' to rule over all other humans.
Why the Merovingian legend was created is unknown, but maybe it could be that it would have been easier to control people, when they believe that you are descended from Jesus and God. Merovingian legends also say that Pont de l'Alma was used by the Merovingian kings, to settle their blood feuds. If there was a dispute between

two Merovingian kings, they would go to Pont de l'Alma to settle their differences. The winner of the battle would contrarily be the one who was killed. He would go immediately to the throne of God, which they believed was in the star-system of Sirius. From there, he would become **the true ruler** of the Merovingians.

The survivor would rule the Earthly realms, subservient to the will of the one who ruled from Heaven. Supposedly, the survivor would be haunted and driven mad, until he acquiesced and followed the will of his slain rival.

Princess Diana was herself descended from a Merovingian king and if the legends are to be believed, then Princess Diana is now recognised by God, as the true ruler of the Merovingian bloodline. This bloodline includes not only her own sons, but Prince Charles, Prince Phillip, all the Hapsburgs, King Juan Carlos, King Constantine, King Michael, all the Esterhaszys of Hungary and every other European royal. If people with Merovingian blood believe the legend that they are descended from Jesus, then they must believe ALL Merovingian legends.

Diana Frances Spencer was born at Park House on the Royal Sandringham estate in Norfolk on the 1st July 1961, the third and youngest daughter of Viscount Althorp, later the 8th Earl Spencer and his first wife Frances Roche. Her parents separated when she was six which is significant considering the trauma that these blood-line families instil into a child up to the age of six as the heart chakra begins to activate in the natural growth of the human form. They eventually divorced in 1969. Diana's mother then married the wallpaper magnate, Peter Shand-Kydd.

Diana had a younger brother, Charles, the present Earl Spencer and two sisters, Jane and Sarah. There was a son born before Diana, but he died in infancy, a fact which given the 'rites' of the Elite could well have meant his being sacrificed as the first-born son. Shocking stuff, yes, but this really does happen within these families. It is a part of their heritage of which they are fiercely proud. Diana had always believed that her parents wished she had been a boy to give them a son and heir.

This is classic installation of underdog, unwanted feelings pushed into the mind of a chosen child which creates the lowered vibration for access by the negative energies into the being of the child. Diana had always maintained her childhood was very unhappy; this leads to a craving for love and affection and indeed as we know, she continued to crave love until the end of her short life. Living at Sandringham, she knew the Queen from being a small child and often played with the Royal children.

She always remembered with less than affection, being sent over to the Queen's residence during the holidays year after year to watch the film 'Chitty Chitty Bang Bang'. The significance of this is that from being a very small child, the fear created by such a satanic film, which it is, absolutely unquestionably, would form the patterns of her subconscious fears that could be manipulated as she grew older. The screenplay for the film was written by the 'former' intelligence agent Ian Fleming, friend to

Aleister Crowley, the well-known Satanist and also author of the James Bond stories. The film itself is blatant satanic symbolism. Briefly, it is a dark tale about a King and Queen who despise children and employ a child catcher to abduct them in a cage on wheels, take them to the castle and place them in a dungeon. Of course the final fate of these children, which is ultimately ritual sacrifice, is excluded from the film.

For what reason would the Windsors constantly show this film to a child who was a guest in their home? Diana told Andrew Morton, according to his book *'Diana Her True Story'*, *"...the atmosphere was always very strange when we went there and I used to kick and fight anyone who tried to make us go"*.

When Diana was thirteen years old, she moved from Norfolk to live at Althorp in Northamptonshire, the Spencer family's ancestral home after her father married Raine, the daughter of the novelist Barbara Cartland. Diana had a deep loathing for Raine and was quoted as saying in the book *'Diana: Her True Story'*, that in September 1989 she had unleashed her years of frustration on Raine: *"I told her what I thought about her and I've never known such anger in me. I remember really going for her gullet"*.

I said *"... if you only knew how much we all hated you for what you have done. You've ruined the house [Althorp], you spend all daddy's money and for what?"* This is a consequence of emotional distress and a result of the deep frustration she still felt from her childhood.

The Spencers are an Elite bloodline family. They are cousins of the Spencer-Churchills, related to the Marlborough family of Blenheim Palace in Oxfordshire, the birthplace of Winston Spencer-Churchill. Other forebears included the Duke of Marlborough and Sir Robert Walpole. The Spencer family inherited a considerable fortune from Sarah, Duchess of Marlborough and they also married into the Cavendish family, the Dukes of Devonshire at Chatsworth House in Derbyshire. This particular branch of the family became known as Spencer–Cavendish. Diana also shared common ancestors with Prince Charles through the third Duke of Devonshire and, most significantly, King James I, the first Stuart King of both England and Scotland and sponsor of Francis Bacon. Diana was also descended through several lines from the Stuart Kings, Charles II and James II, which connected her bloodline to the Carolingian bloodline in France, which regards itself as Merovingian.

Charles II had so many illegitimate children, that it is extremely difficult to guess how many 'offshoots' of the family exist today. However, one thing is for sure and that is that the Elite will know and monitor all of them. As Elite bloodlines go, the Spencer's line is extremely important; Diana was related to countless aristocratic lines, including the Earls of Lucan. Moving further afield, the Spencers have blood-ties with many leading American families and are distantly related to the Rockefellers. The bloodline has a long history of serving the monarch and the tradition continued with Diana's father. He was equerry to King George VI and to Queen Elizabeth II, herself.

Diana's sister, Jane, is married to Sir Robert Fellowes, the Queens private secretary at the time of Diana's death. Both Diana's grandmothers, the Countess Spencer and Ruth, Lady Fermoy, were inner circle members of the Queen Mothers Court, as were four of her great aunts.

The Spencers and the Queen Mother were extremely close and it was the Queen Mother and Lady Fermoy who manipulated Diana into her marriage with Prince Charles. The countdown to marriage began when Diana met Charles at Althorp whilst he was in a relationship with her sister Sarah, in 1977 and Diana was 16 and so it was not until three years later that the Windsors really made their move for her. Diana was invited to a party at Buckingham Palace to celebrate the 30th Birthday of Charles and then in July 1980, a friend of Charles, Philip de Pass, asked Diana to stay with them while the Prince was there. In Diana's own words, *"Charles was all over me and he leapt on me practically"*.

He asked her to accompany him to Buckingham Palace the next day and an invitation followed to join the Windsors in the September at Balmoral, their residence in Scotland. Eventually Charles asked her to marry him and she accepted. *"I love you so much"* Diana said to him, *"whatever love is"* replied Charles and this reply speaks volumes about the mental state of the man who is destined to be king, but also says even more about the royal family and their coldness and calculatingly callous behaviour.

The Elite bloodlines have no real idea what love is, none of them ever receive it and thus cannot express it. Unfortunately, this is the sad reality for their children and certainly puts into perspective these people's attitudes towards the rest of humanity.

During some of the interviews after the break-up of the marriage, Diana stated that on reflection, she could see that Charles had never been genuine in his affection towards her and even before the wedding she had realised she would also be having a relationship with his one true love Camilla Parker-Bowles the 'third person in the marriage', which of course became more apparent as time passed. During the marriage, Charles and Camilla communicated with the codenames 'Gladys and Fred'. Camilla like the Windsors, is close to the Rothschilds and on the first anniversary of Diana's death, she was on the Ionian island of Corfu enjoying the hospitality of Lord Jacob Rothschild, who just happened to have spent £16 million leasing and restoring the Spencer's 18th century mansion overlooking Green Park in London close to Buckingham Palace.

A week after her engagement to Charles, Diana's bulimia began in earnest. This is an eating disorder which results in vomiting every time food is eaten and Diana was suffering this three or four times a day and eventually became desperately thin. This condition could well be a direct result of the satanic upbringing experienced by Diana and in this case was triggered when Charles put his hand on her waist and said, *"Oh, a bit chubby here, aren't we?"* she stated. This may also be construed as yet another character assassination of Diana to ensure that by the time of her murder, she was seen as 'the crazy woman', to totally discredit her. Bulimia is of course a disease of the emotions, as most diseases are and Diana had been an emotional wreck since the break-up of her father and mother's marriage in-line with the standard upbringing of bloodline offspring.

She described the attitude of Charles thus:

"He found the virgin, the sacrificial lamb and in a way he was obsessed with me. But it was hot and cold, hot and cold. You never knew what mood it was going to be, up and down, up and down... He was in awe of his mama, intimidated by his father and I was always the third person in the room."

Just before the marriage to Charles, she met her sisters and told them she could not go through with the wedding, especially with Camilla still on the scene, but they said she had no choice because *"your face is on the tea towels and you're too late to chicken out"*. Immediately before the wedding, Diana stayed at Clarence House, the London residence of the Queen Mother but when she arrived, no-one was there to welcome her. It was, she said, like going to a hotel. How typical.

And so, Diana and Charles were married in St Paul's Cathedral on the 29th July 1981, the numbers here are very significant, but more importantly this just precedes the sacrificial ritual and feast of Lammas. That morning at Clarence House she said she felt calm, deathly calm: *"I felt I was a sacrificial lamb to the slaughter. I knew it but I couldn't do anything about it"*. How prophetic these words would turn out to be.

They spent their first night of their honeymoon at the Mountbatten (Battenberg) family estate at Broadlands in Hampshire, before sailing around the Greek Islands in the Royal Yacht Britannia. The Bulimia got worse and she considered suicide, such was the scale of her unhappiness and this was just the start of the marriage. She said at one point... *"My husband made me feel to inadequate in every possible way. Each time I came up for air he pushed me down again. I hated myself so much"*.

One of Diana's royal duties in 1982 was to represent the Queen at the funeral of Princess Grace of Monaco, herself a victim of murder by the Elite when the brakes on her car 'failed'. Princess Grace, formerly the actress Grace Kelly, ran the Monaco branch of the secret society, the *Order of the Solar Temple* with Jean Louis Marsan, the close friend of her husband, Prince Rainier.

And so, the Windsors achieved their first objective upon the arrival of Prince William. Diana was informed that the birth had to be induced to fit in with Charles' polo playing programme and William was duly born on the 21st June 1982, which just 'happens' to be the summer solstice. What kind of people, portrayed by the media as role models for us all, would induce a child's birth to fit in with the father's polo-playing programme? I think we know the answer to that question, well enough. Of course, in reality the inducement was to ensure the birth occurred on the solstice in accordance with occult ritual with which the Elite are so obsessed to the exclusion of all else, but the fact that they would regard birth inducement to fit-in with social activity as 'normal', speaks volumes about the mind-set of these people. The summer solstice esoterically represents the height of the sun's power in the northern hemisphere whilst it is at its highest point in the solar year and it is even possible to predict what colour outfits the Queen will wear each day such is their obsession with esoteric and occult principles.

So, the new-born was 'christened' William, for the bloodline of William the Conqueror, Arthur, for the sun god symbol, King Arthur, Philip, for the Duke of Edinburgh and Louis, for Lord Louis Mountbatten, Prince Charles' mentor. Two years later in 1984, Prince Harry was born and thus Diana's royal role was concluded, as she related to Andrew Morton:

"Then suddenly as Harry was born it just went bang, our marriage, the whole thing went down the drain".

Diana and Charles separated in 1992, divorced on the 28th August 1996 and then, just over one year later, she was dead. The cycle was complete.

The media onslaught against Diana commenced in earnest in 1992, shortly after the official separation. A tape of an intimate telephone conversation between Diana and the car dealer, James Gilbey, was released through the media at this time and in the tape Diana said that Charles was a real torturer. She told Gilbey:

"I'll go out and conquer the world, do my bit in the way I know how and leave him behind".

The irony of her character assassination by the Windsor's via the compliant press was that it actually worked in her favour and her popularity grew. Imagine the frustrations of the establishment as in their desperation they tried harder and harder to defame her and yet her star just seemed to continue rising. Of course this is a pertinent demonstration of the fact that the Elite have no idea what love is, as Charles himself stated and the fact that they find it difficult to combat what they cannot understand. The heady combination of Diana's enormous heart, her global public profile, her down-to-earth woman-of-the-people charisma and her intense desire to prove the Windsors to be the cold, heartless brutes they most certainly are, threatened the very survival of royalty in all its forms.

It is now, this gang of criminals and multi-generational genocidal murderers and their ancient practices and rituals, upon which we will focus. A necessary step, if we are to truly understand their motives and raisons d'etre.

Diana's natural compassion and empathy with people thoroughly exposed the

Windsors and their ilk as irrelevant in the eyes of the people. The shy and gullible child, whom the Windsors calculatingly enticed into their 'world of pain' to act as a 'brood-mare', became a woman of great mental strength who realised her true power and was not afraid to use it. This then was the beginning of her downfall. She brought the issue of landmines from obscurity into the open and thus to the minds of the masses and thus became a serious danger to the forces of evil and their profits. Diana also knew many intimate secrets within the establishment and was prepared to expose them to get what she wanted – her rights as a Princess and more importantly, a mother. Was there an element of vindictiveness behind it all? Probably, but who among us would blame her after the way she had been used and then discarded and had her life publicly devastated and torn apart?

In March 1997, a few months before she died, Diana made a phone call to someone who was amazed when she told him she was the Princess of Wales. Totally astounded, he first of all professed disbelief, especially when she told him she was calling from a 'supermarket phone' in England. Diana herself stated openly that she often made calls from public telephones, particularly from a certain department store in Kensington [Mohammed Fayed's *Harrods*], when she wanted to be certain the conversation would not be taped.

Diana admired the man she had called, who shall remain nameless, for his wisdom and knowledge and she told him she had something to reveal that would shake the world and asked for his advice on how best to go about it. He has never revealed exactly what she told him, yet one researcher called the man and asked him if it was her awareness of the Windsor's widespread connection to drug trafficking that was the issue. His reply was *"Oh no, it was much worse than that"*. So to lower initiates or outer-circle operatives, the fact that she was about to reveal something thoroughly incriminating, would be their understanding of why she was killed, but there is a yet more compelling reason for her untimely death – one which would have been planned long, long before.

Diana because of the 'quality of her soul' and into which bloodline she specifically chose to be born, was the reason she was chosen as the incubator and breeding partner for the House of Windsor to create a more acceptable genetic 'cloak'. With these genes, this ancient, royal bloodline could continue to thrive, thus rejuvenating the tired, old genes which had been re-cycled for generations resulting in in-breeding on an industrial scale and the health problems inherent with that particular philosophy (see the section on 'Jack the Ripper' regarding Prince Eddy, for example).

To the higher initiates or fully illuminated operatives of the Elite, this ritual was the killing of the moon Goddess in the middle earth, Diana in her highest form. As with John F. Kennedy, to the unaware masses, the deed appeared to be done because of the policies he was pursuing, but to the highest initiates it was an ancient Merovingian ritual known as the 'Killing of the King'.

The final sequence of events which led to her ritual murder involves as I state earlier in the chapter, at almost every turn, the man called Mohamed Fayed, the Egyptian former owner of Harrods. Many people in British high society see Fayed as an enemy of the establishment as proven by his long battle with the *Lonrho* tycoon and mass murderer in Africa, 'Tiny' Rowlands. This is a subtle ploy to 'control the opposition', a tactic used successfully in many covert Elite operations. The theory being that if you control both sides in a battle, you are bound to 'win the war'. And as time passed, sure enough, Fayed was ultimately 'defeated' in his so-called quest for justice which symbolically and psychologically implants itself in the minds of the masses who eventually will begin to believe that he was wrong after all.

Fayed has also lied extensively about his background, claiming to be from a wealthy family, when he patently was not. He is also well-known to be a sexual 'pervert' and has escaped prosecution for a growing number of sexual assaults on female staff working at Harrods. One girl, Samantha-Jane Ramsey, said that when she complained to her supervisor that she had been groped by Fayed, the supervisor sighed, 'not another one'. She was dismissed from her job for making the complaint which is the fate of all those who speak out about his molestation and 'style' of management. John Monks the general secretary of the Trades Union Congress, stated that; *"...there was a regime of fear and terror at Harrods".*

When Samantha-Jane took her complaint to the local Marylebone Police Station, she said that the officer told her; *"You are not the first to come to us. We have files inches high on Mr Fayed, but no proof. It would be your word against his".*

This is utter nonsense and garbage. If Fayed was as anti-establishment as he is portrayed to be, then this would have been used as an excuse to 'nail him' and silence him forever. Had the accused been a Harrods employee, such as a mere departmental supervisor or manager then his name would have been on the sex-offenders register faster than you can say 'police corruption'. This all sheds a completely different light on the man who was in total control of all security on the day and night of the 30th / 31st August 1997.

Fayed became close to the Spencer family through Diana's father, Earl 'Johnny' Spencer, and her stepmother Raine. He helped Johnny through financial difficulties and said he considered the Earl to be a brother and he had given Raine, whom Diana despised, a place on the *Harrods* board. Fayed sponsored prestigious royal events like the Royal Windsor Horse Show and polo competitions and he made absolutely sure that he always supported the charities and causes of the Princess.

Bob Loftus, the head of security at *Harrods* between 1987 and 1996, told the Channel 4 programme, 'Dispatches', in June 1998, that he was ordered to tell Fayed immediately if Diana came into the store. Fayed would then go to the department where she was shopping and 'accidentally' meet her. Every Christmas a green

Harrods van would call at Diana's home, Kensington Palace, with gifts for her and the boys from 'uncle Mohammed'.

When the evidence is examined thoroughly, it is plainly apparent that he made it his business to court the friendship of Diana in every way possible and at every opportunity. On the 3rd June 1997, he invited her to join him for a summer holiday at his beach-side villa in St. Tropez in the south of France and on the 11th June, he got the breakthrough for which he had worked so hard; she accepted. The following day he completed the purchase of a £15 million yacht, the *Jonikal*, through his (or rather the Sultan of Brunei's) Bermudan company, *Mohafa Shipping* and this was the boat upon which Diana and Dodi's relationship would blossom. On the 11th July Diana arrived in St. Tropez with her sons, William and Harry, to stay in the eight-bedroomed luxury apartment on the ten acre Fayed estate on the exclusive *Le Parc* development whilst Dodi at this time was still at his apartment in Paris with his fiancée Kelly Fisher, the American model.

Dodi was a 'gofer' for his father and lived on his father's wealth, although he had enjoyed some success in the movie industry at one time as the producer of the British film Chariots of Fire, again thanks to his father's money. He had a playboy reputation and was a very big spender, once running up a $100,000 bill in two months on his Amex card. He was dominated by his father and even in his film operation every decision had to be approved by his father – Dodi did whatever his father told him to do. He had been engaged to Kelly Fisher for eight months and she was expecting to spend her holiday on the *Jonikal*, but on the evening of the 14th July, Dodi took a phone call from his father who ordered him to go immediately to St. Tropez to be with Diana. Kelly Fisher described what happened next, in an interview with the *Dispatches* programme:

"Dodi said he was going to London and he'd be back and then we were going to St. Tropez. That evening he didn't call me and I finally got him on his portable phone. I said Dodi where are you? And he said he was in London. I said 'OK, I'll call you right back at your apartment'. He said 'No, no, don't call me back'. So I said 'Dodi where are you?' and he admitted he was in the South of France. His father had asked him to come down and not bring me, I know why, now."

Two days later Dodi sent a private plane to fly Kelly to St. Tropez. But while he stayed with Diana, Kelly was kept aboard another Al Fayed boat. *"I'm sitting here stuck"* she said. *"So he had me in my little boat-cage and he was, I know now, seducing Diana."* On the 31st July, Diana returned to St. Tropez for a second holiday with Dodi, this time alone. Meanwhile, Kelly Fisher was back in Los Angeles preparing for her marriage to Dodi which she said was due to take place on the 9th August. But two days before that, the story broke in the world's media of the romance between Diana and Dodi. Kelly heard from a friend who saw a picture in the paper and she recalls:

"I started calling him in London because at this time I was expecting his arrival in a day.

I called his private line, but there was no answer, so then I called the secretary and asked to speak to him and she wouldn't put me on. So Mohammed got on and in so many horrible words told me never to call back again. I said 'he's my fiancé, what are you talking about?' He hung up on me and I called back and the secretary said don't ever call here again, your calls are no longer to be put through. It was so horrible."

At this stage Diana had Kensington Palace swept constantly for bugging devices set by the intelligence operations, this on the advice of her body guards and now ironically, she placed herself in the hands of a man obsessed with bugging and video recording of everyone around him. The Fayed villa in San Tropez was bugged, as were all properties and vehicles within the clutches of Fayed and his personal army of security. Everything Diana said while in the hands of this man was heard. Bob Loftus, the former head of security at Harrods said the bugging at Harrods was 'a very extensive operation' and was always under the direction of Fayed.

Henry Porter, the London editor of the magazine *Vanity Fair*, had spent two years investigating Fayed and he said they discovered his obsessive use of eavesdropping devices to record telephone calls, bug rooms and covertly film people. Through mutual friends, Porter warned Diana about Fayed's background and activities *"...because we thought this was quite dangerous for her for obvious reasons"*. But Diana apparently felt she could handle it and although she knew Fayed could *"sometimes be a rogue"*, he was no threat to her, she thought. She apparently told friends, *"I know he's naughty, but that's all."* The *Dispatches* programme said they had written evidence that Fayed bugged the Ritz hotel and given his background and the deals that are hatched at the Ritz, it would be staggering if he did not. Kelly Fisher said that the whole time she was in Fayed property; she just assumed everything was bugged. It was known, she said and Dodi had told her everywhere was bugged. She went on, *"...as a matter of fact, when I confronted him about Diana, he said, 'I can't talk to you on the phone.' He said, "I'll talk to you in LA". I knew what that meant"*. Diana was under the 'protection' of the Fayed security machine and even her most private conversations were being monitored. Diana went with Dodi to Fayed's Elizabethan-style mansion, *Barrow Green Court* at Oxted in Surrey, formerly owned by fellow Satanist Lord McAlpine.

On the 21st August, despite Henry Porter's warning, Diana returned once again to St. Tropez for another holiday with Dodi. Fayed was milking the situation, briefing journalists and photographers and also enlisting the advice of the publicist Max Clifford.

After the announcement by ex-Metropolitan Police Commissioner Lord Stevens, on Thursday 14th December 2006, that the death of Diana was an accident, Fayed's 'front-man' Max Clifford appeared on TV to add more obfuscation to the issue by re-iterating Fayed's position.

The Fayed camp was constantly leaking the couple's whereabouts to the press to ensure maximum publicity for their relationship, yet Fayed had the sheer effrontery to complain after the crash that the photographers and journalists would not leave Diana alone and that action, given the circumstances, beggar's belief. Are we supposed to believe on the one hand that Fayed wanted to milk the publicity for all it was worth and yet when it suited him, to complain vehemently about the 'stalking' of Diana and Dodi by the paparazzi?

The Diana/Dodi romance by this time was in full-swing, with Fayed pressurising Dodi to intensify the relationship. What Fayed said, Dodi did and nothing at all was left to chance. Diana's favourite music, the theme from the film *The English Patient*, was played constantly as the couple cruised on the Jonikal. Diana and Dodi had much In common. Both were born into wealthy families and their fathers were distant figures. Both had experienced the breakdown of their parents' marriages as their mothers left home. They even attended finishing schools in close proximity to each other in Switzerland. Mind manipulation being used on both parties should not be ruled-out; indeed it is known to be a fairly simple task via mind-control techniques to cause two people to fall madly in love with each other.

The scientist Brian Desborough, states clearly that from his own research, the feeling of being in love is dependent upon the brain producing a chemical by the name of Phenylethylamine. This is also a chemical which seriously diminishes the ability to discriminate effectively – hence the saying, 'love is blind'. Production of this chemical is sustained by the release of endorphins, naturally occurring chemicals linked to memory, learning, pain suppression, sex drive and hormone regulation. If these chemicals can be stimulated in both parties simultaneously, they would instantly fall in love.

Personally, I believe that all the talk of engagements and rings was a blind to manipulate the masses into believing that this was the reason for the murder. This would in effect, play upon the fact that a Muslim would become the step-father of the future king, being supposedly abhorrent and unacceptable to the 'firm'.

Diana and Dodi left the South of France from Olbia airport at 1.30 pm on 30th August 1997 bound for Paris on Al Fayed's personal Gulfstream jet. They apparently intended to stay one night at Dodi's apartment, which overlooks the Arc de Triomphe, before going on to London where Diana was due to be reunited with her sons again. The plane touched down at Le Bourget airport in Paris at 3.20 pm and they were met by 20 or so paparazzi (the Italian word meaning buzzing insects). A Mercedes was waiting for the party and a green Range Rover was to follow on behind, this being normal security procedure and the very minimum one would expect to protect a Princess of the realm. Accompanying Diana and Dodi in the Mercedes was Dodi's bodyguard, Trevor Rees-Jones, the 29 year old former member of the elite Parachute Regiment of the British Army. Along with the SAS the 'Paras' are the most highly-trained regiment in the British forces. In the Range Rover was the driver Henry Paul,

Fayed's acting head of security at the Ritz and another bodyguard, Kes Wingfield. They drove from the airport to the villa Windsor on the Bois de Boulogne, the former home of the Duke and Duchess of Windsor (formerly King Edward VIII). Fayed stated that he was to give this villa to the couple as a wedding gift and that they were at the Villa discussing décor, but the bodyguard Kes Wingfield stated they were at the Villa Windsor no more than ten minutes. The whole idea of engagement and wedding was the fabrication of Mohammed Fayed, who in my opinion was the facilitator-in-chief for the whole operation. From the villa they were driven to the Ritz hotel where they arrived at 4.20pm.

The Ritz Hotel is in the Place Vendome and all around that square at the first floor level are the Illuminati / Babylonian symbols of the Sun and the cross, used by the ancients to symbolise the 'journey' of the sun through the year.

This symbolism is highly significant and is important to the entire ritual that would end in the couples' deaths. Exactly the same type of symbolism was present at the final journey of JFK, before his burial at Arlington under the esoteric symbol of the flaming torch. These symbols also relate to King Louis XIV, who was known as the Sun King. At his palace at Versailles in the 17th century he decorated rooms in honour of Apollo, the sun god, and Diana, the goddess of the moon. There was also a statue of the goddess Diana at Versailles.

In the centre of the Vendome Square is an immense pillar upon which stands a statue of Napoleon in effect mirroring the famous Nelson's column in Trafalgar Square in London. Pillars of this type represent masculine energy and phallic symbolism.

Surprisingly Diana at this stage had only a similar level of security to that which she had at the airport. Usually security for VIPs is increased beyond the confines of airports with a request to the French High Protection Police Security Service (SPHP) being usual, but in this case it was not requested. One wonders why? This of course then meant that the entire security operation around Diana in Paris was under the complete control of Fayed and his subordinates from start to finish. Had the SPHP been requested, they would probably both still be alive as the SPHP operate with a car in front and behind, together with two motorcycle police outriders on each side of the vehicle which the VIP occupies. The cars are driven by professional drivers carrying armed security men.

According to reports immediately after the crash, which as we have seen in many other instances, always provide a more accurate account of events, usually from both eye witnesses and footage, the SPHP made three possibly four, offers to protect Diana, each one refused by Fayed. An officer of the SPHP actually told Dodi, "..if you will not use our car, we recommend that two police cars accompany you on your excursions around the city."

This advice too was ignored and Diana and Dodi proceeded straight to the $6000 per night, 18th century Imperial Suite at the Ritz. The couple booked a table at the Chez Benoit restaurant for 8.45pm and they intended to spend the night at Dodi's apartment. At 6.30 pm Dodi went across the Place Vendome to a jeweller, *Repossi*, to buy a diamond ring for Diana which was later delivered to the Ritz. A little after 7 pm, the couple were driven in the Mercedes along the Champs Elysees to Dodi's apartment on Rue Arsene-Houssaye close to the Arc de Triomphe. Here they unpacked and prepared for dinner and again the back-up Range Rover was present as was another car carrying bodyguards for added protection. Why was this level of security thought necessary in the evening, but not in the early hours of the morning at the time of the crash?

Dodi's apartment was known as the 'Etoile flat', after the Place de l'Etoile, the Sun or the Star circle road around the Arc de Triomphe. The route taken to the apartment was out of the Place Vendome onto the Rue de Rivoli and half-way around the Place de la Concorde they turned right into the Champs Elysees and drove straight along that famous avenue to Dodi's apartment.

This is a straightforward journey; so why then in the early hours of the 31st August did they take the ludicrous detour to the Pont de l'Alma tunnel? If the idea, as has been suggested, was to avoid the paparazzi, surely the shortest and fastest route is the answer and not a journey that provided the paparazzi with a good, sporting chance of finding and catching-up to them?

This route is critically important. As the couple arrived at the apartment at 7.15 pm, bodyguards were seen to rush from their car to hold back six members of the paparazzi. Diana and Dodi became concerned about eating at the unprotected *Chez Benoit* restaurant and so took the decision to head back to the Ritz to eat. They took the same route back, down the Champs Elysees and around the Place de la Concorde. There is much more traffic in the early evening than in the early hours of the morning and so there were much better reasons to avoid this route at this point in time than in the early hours. The couple, along with bodyguards Wingfield and Rees-Jones, walked into the Ritz captured by the now famous video pictures, at 9.47pm and also at this time the paparazzi were gathering in large numbers outside, amid rumours of an engagement announcement.

We know for a fact that Fayed himself was manipulating the press all that day and evening and it is therefore obvious to me that the huge congregation of press was exactly what he wanted and had planned all along. Why? I believe it was to fabricate the story of impending marriage in order to enable the Elite to create a diversion from the truth. Did the Windsors actually believe that the nation loved them so much that it would seem reasonable to kill her to prevent a Muslim being ensconced in the heart of the establishment and therefore no big deal? This of course was before they were confronted with the huge outpouring of grief all over the world for Diana, after the event.

What a shock to their arrogant, pampered systems it must have been when they realised the truth in the days following the event. This more than anything else, terrified the Windsors and the Elite in general. The so-called 'Crown' represented by Queen Elizabeth at its head is without doubt the number one enemy of humankind.

The Ritz Hotel security video also identified a number of people who had been outside amongst the onlookers for most of the day and were still there on the edge of the crowd and here is where the plot seriously thickens. After speaking on the telephone with his father who was at home at his estate in Oxted, Surrey, Dodi Fayed announced a quite ludicrous plan. To avoid the paparazzi, 'he' decided that the Mercedes that had been transporting them all that day together with the back-up Range Rover were to be taken around the front of the hotel and used as a decoy in an attempt to deceive the paparazzi. At the same time another Mercedes would be brought around the back entrance of the hotel to whisk the couple away to the apartment on the Champs Elysees. Henry Paul, the 41 year old acting head of security at the Ritz, was called on his mobile phone by Dodi and told to report back to the hotel. Paul had gone off-duty at 7pm and by the time he returned it was 10pm yet no-one has established where he was in those missing three hours. Dodi said that his father, Mohamed Fayed, had personally authorised that Henri Paul should drive the Mercedes. There is little doubt that the whole of the new plan was passed-on to Dodi from his father and indeed those who know Fayed would be astonished if this was not the case. Dodi did not think or act for himself, ever – father was always the one in control. Now think upon this for a moment – Henry Paul was not a qualified chauffeur and had no authority to drive the hire car. Why would he be chosen to drive the Mercedes through such a ravening pack of wolves as the paparazzi had apparently become that night.

"No one has to direct an assassination – it happens. The active role is played secretly by permitting it to happen. This is the greatest single clue. Who has the power to call off or reduce the usual security precautions?" L. Fletcher Prouty.

If we apply Prouty's 'rule' to the ritual killing of Diana and ask who had the power and moreover actively used that power, to reduce the usual security precautions for Diana that night, we have a rather unsurprising answer: Mohamed Fayed. Given these circumstances he must answer the obvious question: Why was the security reduced?

When JFK was assassinated, there were no bodyguards standing on his car in contravention of the usual protocol, they were instead on the car immediately behind. There is a video in existence which clearly shows obviously mystified and protesting security agents being ordered to withdraw from the president's car as it turned into Deeley Plaza, seconds before Kennedy was shot. When Martin Luther King was assassinated, the police officer In charge of security for King was sent home under protest, shortly before the shooting.

In addition, when Robert Kennedy was assassinated, the security arrangements were again tampered-with. He was actually scheduled to walk-off the stage and exit through the crowd, but one of his aides ushered him away via the kitchen where he was met by Sirhan Sirhan, who had been on a 'Rosicrucian mind-expansion' course in the weeks before the murder (probably a euphemism for a mind-control course in which he was the victim). Frank Mankiewicz, the aide who guided RFK into the kitchen was a former public relations man for the Mossad front in America, the Anti-Defamation League (ADL). Interestingly this same character became head of publicity for the Oliver Stone movie *JFK*, which was supposed to be an exposé of the assassination of John F. Kennedy but was in reality just more obfuscation of the truth.

So we can see in these three examples how a similar modus operandus (Prouty's 'rule') was also used in Diana's case.

Regarding the way Diana's security was handled, there were last-minute changes to the arrangements, a change of cars and removal of the Range Rover with no back-up support whatever and then a change to the route, all on the orders of Mohamed Fayed, a man obsessed with security – at least for himself. Bob Loftus, the former head of security at Harrods, said *"Compared with the protection that Al Fayed affords himself, which is very professional, of a very high standard; that which was afforded to the mother of the future King of England was a 'Mickey Mouse' operation."*

He added that *"Fayed was absolutely paranoid about his personal protection."* Even whilst walking around his own store, there would be three or four plain-clothes members of his personal protection team who travelled with him all the time, plus another four uniformed security who would act as 'outriders' to create two rings of security around him and that is even in his own store! One could legitimately ask, is this paranoia or is it his involvement in the seedy cesspit of arms dealing and being part of the Elite in general, that prompts this security over-kill? Of course, Fayed's own delusions of grandeur must also be considered as a contributory factor.

Fayed always recruits former members of the SAS and the Parachute Regiment for his close security, which makes good sense apart from the fact that their loyalties are always to the Crown, even after retiring from the armed forces. He uses the elite operation, *Control Risks*, to make recommendations on security issues. Tom Bower tells in his book about Fayed of how armed guards at the Oxted estate hide behind bushes wearing full combat uniform and blacked out faces.

Whenever Fayed travelled in his chauffeur-driven Mercedes there was always a back-up Range Rover carrying emergency medical equipment and security staff, yet he strangely and significantly withdrew that protection from Diana and his son. Even more significantly, a 'new' car was introduced for their final journey, another Mercedes which was dispatched to the rear entrance to the Ritz, supplied by a car-hire company by the name of *Etoile Limousines*. *Etoile Limousines* is based at the Ritz and depends for its entire income on contracts with the hotel and its guests. In other words, it is controlled entirely by Mohamed Fayed or rather the Sultan of Brunei, that great friend to the House of Windsor and the Bush family.

This new Mercedes was an S280 model, much less robust and lighter in weight than the S600 series that Fayed usually used and also minus the dark-tinted windows. Other cars were available, but this one was chosen instead, for what are now obvious reasons. A director of *Etoile*, Nils Siegel, told the inquiry into Diana's death that he personally delivered the car to the rear entrance of the Ritz, but the *Dispatches* programme proved this to be a lie. It was delivered by a driver by the name of Frederic Lucard and he can be clearly seen in the act of doing so on the Hotel security video. Lucard said he found it was very strange that *Etoile* would allow Henry Paul, a man not qualified as a chauffeur, to drive one of their cars. So why did they do it? Brian Dodd, the former Head of Security for Fayed in the 1980s, gave his assessment of the situation to *Dispatches*:

"It's a new car that has come into the system. They wouldn't have had time to check that car out. It should have been checked out. There could have been a bomb on that car, for instance. It was a most stupid plan. It shouldn't have even been considered. The back-up vehicle is there, not just to avert the paparazzi, but for instance, a motor-cyclist with a pillion rider to pull up and shoot, or put a magnetised bomb on top of the car. God only knows why. [I think we all know why – JH] I had probably six or eight men I would consider professional bodyguards who I would have had on that job and Trevor Rees-Jones and Kes Wingfield, after what I have seen happened, would not have been in Paris that night."

The Mercedes S280 with Henry Paul at the wheel, sped-off from the rear entrance of the Ritz at 12.20 am with Paul telling the paparazzi not to bother following because they would never catch him. Diana and Dodi were in the back seat and in the front was Trevor Rees-Jones, who said he disagreed with the change of plan. He was not wearing a seat belt, which is normal practice in built-up areas because bodyguards need to be free to react quickly. The car was driven at speed along the Rue Cambon and turned right along the Rue de Rivoli into the Place de la Concorde where it stopped briefly at the traffic lights.

The paparazzi photographer, Romuald Rat, on the back of the motorcycle drew-up alongside them here, but he says that Henry Paul jumped the lights on red and headed onto the dual carriageway along-side the river Seine, the Cours la Reine. The car disappeared down one tunnel, came back to the surface and then almost immediately entered the short tunnel at the Pont de l'Alma. As the whole world knows, here it went out of control and struck the 13th of a whole sequence of concrete pillars in the centre of the tunnel which are completely unprotected by crash barriers. Henry Paul and Dodi Fayed died immediately.

According to the autopsy report, Diana was clinically dead within 20 minutes and this was long before she arrived at the hospital. Trevor Rees-Jones survived the crash because he was wearing his seat belt and Diana and Dodi were not. This could be highly significant. Rees-Jones was not wearing his seat belt when they left the Ritz in accordance with normal practice for bodyguards and when Romuald Rat took a photograph at the lights at the Place de la Concorde, Rees-Jones was still not wearing his seat belt. But a little more than a minute later when the car actually struck the pillar, he **was** wearing a seat belt. Why would this be? If he donned the belt because for some reason he sensed danger, why did he not scream at Diana and Dodi to put-on their seat belts too? After all it only takes a second to do so and the sole reason for his presence in the car, was to protect his two charges in the back seat. Rees-Jones should have had some serious questions to answer here but he has never been publicly quizzed about this and neither has he volunteered any information. He simply re-iterates that he did not know why he strapped himself in and that they were followed by two cars, one of them white and a motor cycle. These answers simply fit within the overall smokescreen.

Several independent people who watched the news reports just after the crash for the whole day, report that they definitely saw two people, a man and a woman who were together, state that the white car was parked in the tunnel and that from this car emanated a massive flash. These two people were shown on TV stating this fact several times and then suddenly this report was ceased and never shown again. I believe that this is the only reason that the white car was woven into the official story, yet slowly and subtly changed in its location in order to further the idea that it was the paparazzi to blame. After the crash, not even one single TV report nor one single newspaper report mentioned the detour from the route they had taken twice that day from the Ritz to Dodi's flat and back again. This detour was completely omitted from the first reports and it was only after independent researchers brought this to the world's attention that it was incorporated into the 'official version' of events. As already stated, the longer route would have given the paparazzi even more time to find the car and more time for them to arrive outside Dodi's flat before the arrival of the Mercedes there.

The one and only 'benefit' of taking this alternative route is that it took them via the Pont de l'Alma tunnel, the relevance of which will become apparent shortly.

As with Lee Harvey Oswald (John Kennedy), Sirhan Sirhan (Robert Kennedy) and James Earl Ray (Martin Luther King), Henry Paul became the scapegoat. Once the paparazzi card had been played and focused media and public attention to the story in the days after the crash, it was repeated ad nauseum in the media, the purpose of this tactic being to instil into the minds of the public that this could not possibly be untrue. Exactly the same scenario occurs over and over where cover-ups are being facilitated, the mainstream media bombard us 24/7 with outright disinformation in order to confuse and obfuscate the real facts.

It was soon afterwards, announced that Henry Paul was three to four times over the blood-alcohol limit and that his blood contained traces of anti-depressant drugs, including Fluoxetine, the active ingredient of Prozac. *"The cause of the crash was simple"* so we are told again and again, *"the driver was drunk"*. Tampering with blood samples or incorporating alcohol in the blood is ridiculously easy to achieve, especially when everything is being carried out in the strictest secrecy and was probably achieved by the insertion of tiny balloons which release alcohol into the blood stream in stages. There was certainly no sign of inebriation as he drove away from the Ritz. According to his blood tests, he drank the equivalent of eight scotches on an empty stomach and yet a behavioural psychologist on the TV documentary, *'Diana – Secrets of the Crash'*, could find no evidence that he was drunk after studying the Ritz videos of him that night.

Only two days earlier, Paul had undergone a rigorous medical for the renewal of his pilot's licence and there was no sign of the alcohol abuse the post-crash propaganda would have us all believe. One of Paul's close friends has also publicly stated he was not an excessive drinker. There was also another strange anomaly revealed by the TV documentary in 1998. The haemoglobin in Henry Paul's blood was found to contain 20.7% carbon monoxide and this would have been at a much higher level earlier because the carbon monoxide content halves every four to five hours once exposure to it has stopped. Haemoglobin carries the oxygen in the blood and Debbie Davis of the Carbon Monoxide Support Group said that at those levels, Paul would not have known his left hand from his right, because of the reduced oxygen reaching the brain and would have been unable to function at all let alone drive a car or even stand up. Dr Alistair Hay, an expert in carbon monoxide poisoning, agreed and could not explain why Paul showed no signs of the considerable symptoms that should have been evident.

"I find it difficult to rationalise everything. A blood-carbon monoxide level of 20% and a high blood-alcohol level suggests this would be someone with a much slower reaction time, certainly be someone who would be slowed up in the way he did things, would probably also be somebody who was in some pain, but none of those things appear to be evident from the pictures that we see of him. It's a bit of an enigma."

There is a lot more to know about Henry Paul. His best friend, Claude Garrec, told the ITV documentary that Paul had contacts with the French and foreign intelligence services and maintained them throughout his time at the Ritz. This is no surprise because the intelligence agencies recruit the security men for the top hotels and the Ritz, with its VIP clientele and reputation for espionage and arms dealing would have been a prime target. Paul certainly had unexplained sources of income. He earned only around £20-25,000 a year at the Ritz and yet he was a keen pilot with 605 hours of flying time at about £300 per hour. He had a string of bank accounts; there were two in a bank outside Paris and three further accounts, plus a safety-deposit box at the Banque Nationale de Paris near the Ritz. He had three accounts at the nearby branch of Barclays and one current and four deposit accounts at the Caisse d'Epargne de Paris. In the eight months before the crash, sums of £4000 were paid into an account here on five separate occasions. In total he had £122,000 deposited in his accounts (1.2 million Francs) and no one knows from whence it came. Then there is the question of where Paul was in the three hours between 7pm when he went off duty and 10pm when Dodi called him on his mobile phone and ordered him to return to the Ritz. His whereabouts in this period are a mystery, a very significant mystery at that.

To understand how the Elite operates requires detailed research over a vast array of interconnecting subjects, everything from ancient history, especially relating to satanic and occult symbolism and ritual. The Earth's magnetic grid, the power of the sun, the banking system and mind control are all elements that influence their beliefs and thinking and this needs to be borne in mind before one can begin to understand the ritual sacrifice of Diana. All the mainstream journalists that have produced articles and documentaries about the crash are operating under a disadvantage because of their lack of knowledge of the occult and thus it renders the whole story a mystery because of course they are of necessity dealing with only half of the picture and only with information within their own 'five sense' reality. This is true of all major events throughout history. They can only possibly be viewed and analysed using the reality thought and believed to be true and in working within this restrictive 'five-sense' reality are unable to comprehend that there are organisations operating within organisations which provide a methodology by which one single force may control apparently unconnected agencies such as British and French intelligence, the Paris Police, judiciary and medical services and most importantly of all, the inquiry investigating the cause of the crash.

In Britain there was an 'investigation' into the death crash by John Stalker, the former deputy-chief constable of Greater Manchester Police in which he dismissed all notions that Diana was murdered. Ironically, Stalker claimed, quite rightly, that he was the victim of a conspiracy to remove him from the police force after he identified a policy by the Northern Ireland police, the RUC, to shoot people they believed to be terrorists and ask questions later. This was the so-called 'shoot-to-kill' policy.

Pushing aside every suggestion of conspiracy to kill Diana, Stalker asked; "*Why would the French want to cover up the murder of an English woman?*" The answer to that is as stated earlier and that is that all seemingly unconnected agencies are intrinsically connected at the top levels. Operatives at Stalker's level do not understand anything bar the illusory outer-circle knowledge within Freemasonry, nor do they understand the true nature of the 'Crown'. However, to be fair, Stalker did ask some very pertinent questions about the crash and its aftermath; "*... why was the Fayed security around the princess reduced to one wholly inadequate man with no back up? Why did the police not appeal for help from the public? Why was there no post mortem-autopsy on Dodi Fayed's body?*" I would offer this answer to Mr. Stalker – simply because it is but a small part of an overall conspiracy of such magnitude that it absolutely and utterly dwarfs the conspiracy perpetrated against you when you were removed from office.

I have already broached the subject of mind control within this book, because understanding its widespread deployment is essential in order to understand the occult knowledge and the potential for it to be used in such operations by the subtle programming of its subjects' minds.

In the three hours Henry Paul went 'missing', this programming could have been instilled within him without his knowledge and it is therefore probably no coincidence that Henry Paul drove into the 13th pillar in the Pont de l'Alma tunnel in Paris. The elite networks (in which Fayed played a major role) were working through many seemingly disassociated yet co-operating agencies to ensure that Diana was in Paris that night, because at its foundation, the plan was to perform a specific satanic ritual for which the timing and circumstances and the place of death had to be arranged in intricate detail. Diana was under Fayed's security web for much of the time leading up to the crash and all of the time during the last few days.

All her conversations were heard and monitored throughout the Fayed bugging system, so if Fayed was, as he claims, himself a victim of the Elite, why does he not publish them? During those missing hours, Henry Paul, the asset of British and French intelligence would have had the final piece of his programming jigsaw inserted into place in addition to the programming already in place. Diana's ritual death was arranged from the very top of the Illuminati, via the Royal connections but Fayed for all his wealth and apparent power and influence is nothing more than a lowly minion, carrying out his role as dictated by the Illuminati and was probably never aware of the full consequences of his role, save possibly through hindsight after the event.

The Mercedes delivered to the rear of the Ritz Hotel had itself been 'stolen' some weeks earlier – before the Diana Dodi relationship began, stolen from *Etoile Limousines* and when it was recovered from this alleged theft it underwent extensive repairs. It had supposedly been standing outside the exclusive *Taillevent* restaurant when the driver's door was flung open and the chauffeur pulled out by three Arabic-speaking men with handguns. (Those awful Muslims again!) The vehicle was missing for two weeks and when it was found, the wheels were missing, the door ripped off and the electronic system and equipment controlling the braking system had gone. This car would have been written off by any insurance company, but of course this was the cover for the extensive Elite-controlled repairs which would install remote-control and much other electronic wizardry (Boston brakes technology?). Fayed controls the *Etoile Limousine* company which supplied the vehicle, is it surprising therefore that the French authorities refused the offer by experts at Mercedes to examine the car after the crash?

When Henry Paul reported back for duty that night, he seemed his normal self to most observers. The programming lies deep within the psyche until the arranged trigger is deployed which would have activated his excessively fast driving and route change. The 'Boston brakes' technology relating to remote control has already been described and it would certainly make sense that this was the real cause of the precision 13th pillar direct hit with the loss of brakes too. The white car, which was parked *in* the tunnel, and not travelling in the same direction through the tunnel, emitted a vivid white flash. This, I would strongly suggest is from where the remote control was being operated. The cover story for the white flash was simply that 'the paparazzi did it'. It was deemed necessary for the car to hit the 13th pillar because this marks the centre of the ancient spot of worship to the dark aspect of the goddess, Hecate. Diana even had a strong aversion to the number 13; she would not allow a thirteenth lot in her dress auction at Christies in the June immediately before she died.

It is also vital to understand that whenever an assassination occurs in a public place, two things of significance happen almost immediately. The first thing is to name the 'scapegoat' or 'patsy'. Then there are a multitude of diversions created, incorporating 'eye-witness' testimonies to back-up the version of events that has been pre-invented and made to seem like a reasonable story. Once the initial reports have aired they then have time to assess their impact and subsequently either remove the initial reports from the airwaves for good, or misuse true testimonies to create false leads for investigators, diverting them from the real truth.

In the first act of the play, they make an immediate arrest, or expose the person to blame, which cancels out further need for investigation, because now we all 'know' who is responsible.

The second act, diversion, ensures that those critical hours and days after the event are wasted as investigators and the lower ranks of the media chase a whole morass of false leads and stories.

The next stage is to wait for the 'official' investigation to begin. Once there has been enough time to incorporate all the information that was picked-up on, in the initial moments after the event and to add and merge it into the pre-planned version of events, the 'official' version is then propounded with vigour. This 'official' story is then played out across the full spectrum of the media as the evidence is manufactured and manipulated to match the official version. It is from that point onwards a relatively simple matter to control this process at editorial level and to filter-out all the evidence and facts that do not match the official version whilst strongly promoting those that do. .

In much the same way as the 9/11 debris and forensic evidence was cleared away with thoroughly indecent haste, this scene of a major accident involving arguably the most famous woman in the world, was destroyed in less time than it took to happen in the first place. Of course this makes perfect sense when we consider that, as with 9/11, the evidence has to disappear as quickly as possible to hide the truth and to prevent any real investigation into the incident. Indeed, everything relating to this murder is decidedly 'fishy', to say the least.

There were 17 security cameras on the route between the Ritz and the Pont de l'Alma tunnel, including those inside the tunnel itself. Do these perpetrators really expect anyone with an even semi-functioning brain to believe that on that particular night in **only** that particular part of Paris, the cameras were malfunctioning? On that single basis alone, anyone who declares themselves satisfied with the outcome of all the inquiries conducted so far and agrees with their findings, is either in league with them, or so incredibly stupid, as to beggar belief. However as most people are terminally 'asleep' these days, maybe the concept is not that badly thought-out.

The cameras are controlled by the police and are powered by an independent power supply, yet the Paris police refused categorically to explain why the cameras were out of action in that particular place and time on that particular night. Never before (or since) has this happened in Paris. In a letter to the UK *Daily Mail*, a correspondent said the cameras in the tunnel were pointing towards the wall on the morning after the crash. There is no doubt whatsoever that the police would not have failed to notice this situation.

Even more significantly, at exactly the same time as the fateful journey and subsequent crash, all the police communication frequencies in central Paris mysteriously went off-line. Simon Reagan in his book, *Who Killed Diana*, quotes a contact called Andre, who like many people enjoys listening-in to police radio messages. That night, Andre was sitting on a bench near the Eiffel Tower, a few minutes' walk from the tunnel, on the night Diana died. As was his usual practice, he was using a short-wave receiver to monitor the police communications, but suddenly and inexplicably at 12.20am, all the lines went down. There was a **total** police radio blackout which lasted for around 20 minutes and then, Andre said, the signal returned as quickly as it had disappeared and there was a sudden explosion of radio traffic as all police personnel realised it was active again.

12.20am was the exact time that Diana and her party was leaving the Ritz. Just a co-incidence though, I'm sure. By the time communication was restored, Diana was lying in the tunnel under the complete control of the Emergency team and according to the autopsy report, within a few minutes of clinical death. However, according to the Stevens report, there was not a shred of evidence that there was a conspiracy surrounding the death of Diana.

As previously alluded-to, causing the accident is easy for the powers involved to arrange, but of course it is not possible to guarantee that the target will be killed immediately. It is therefore essential to also be in control of the medical team, because although the target is not yet dead, there is now a credible reason for them to die, after the event as it were.

In this case, the job of the medical team is to ensure the target does not survive, no matter what condition they are in after the incident. Even those poor dupes who dismiss the idea that Diana was murdered, question the astonishing delay in transporting her to hospital, when according to the 'official' medical reports, she was suffering from an injury that required urgent surgery. The doctors said that the pulmonary vein had been ruptured near the heart and that this was filling her lungs with blood in effect meaning that Diana was lying in the tunnel bleeding to death. If that is indeed correct, then the only way to save her life would be with immediate surgery, so why was it more than an hour and a half before she arrived at hospital?

Doctor Frederic Mailliez, with an American 'friend' by the name of Mark Butt, just so happened to drive into the tunnel from the opposite direction in the immediate aftermath of the crash. The impact happened at 12.25am and by 12.26, Doctor Mailliez said he had seen the crushed Mercedes, stopped his car, turned on warning lights, run across to the Mercedes to establish there were two people dead and two alive, and had also phoned the emergency services. He is one of 160 Parisian doctors who are on constant call for emergencies in hospitals and private homes as part of a French insurance system, *SOS Medecins*. He had treated accident victims many times when he was a member of SAMU the French emergency ambulance service and yet a doctor on constant call for emergencies says all he had in his car to help Diana was an 'oxygen cylinder and mask'. Mailliez was in control of Diana and her condition for the crucial 15 to 20 minutes before his former employers, the SAMU emergency team arrived to take over.

He claimed initially that Diana did not say anything to him, contradicting his later comments to the UK *Times* newspaper, when he said she apparently repeatedly said that she 'hurt' as he put a resuscitation mask over her mouth. Trevor Rees-Jones, the bodyguard, also said that he has flashbacks of hearing a female voice calling out in the back of the car: *"... first it's a groan, then Dodi's name was called... and that can only be Princess Diana's voice"*, he told the UK *Daily Mirror*.

What does seem to be clear is that Diana was conscious when Mailliez arrived. He told the CNN chat show host, Larry King, that, *"... she looked pretty fine. But inside you know, the internal injury was already starting... its really funny. That's the only part, where she was sitting, that's the only part, which was still intact."* Eh?

Mailliez on the one hand told a French medical magazine that; *"I thought her life could be saved"*, and yet said on another occasion that *"it was hopeless there was nothing we could do to save her."* This is the big problem with lying – it is so difficult to get the story correct and consistent on every occasion it is told. He also told King that although Diana is the most photographed lady in the world, and that the paparazzi were taking shots of her while he was with her in the tunnel; he had no idea that she was the Princess Diana until he saw the news reports the following morning. Err, yeah right. What kind of an idiot is this man? And more to the point, how stupid does he think **we** all are? When the emergency team arrived, Mailliez said he then left the scene because there was nothing more he could do.

The official explanation for the incredible delay in taking Diana to hospital is that she was trapped in the wreckage. This is complete and utter nonsense. One of the ambulance crew told the French newspaper, La Parisien that when he arrived, Diana was lying with most of her body out of the car with her legs resting on the rear seat. "She was agitated, semi knocked-out, but conscious... she was groaning and struggling feebly. She murmured 'Oh my God' several times." The Scotsman newspaper, in an investigation published on the 11th September 1997, established that Diana was removed from the car shortly after the fire service arrived and the excuse of her being 'trapped' does not stand up to close scrutiny at all. Another excuse for the delay is that the emergency doctors had to give her a blood transfusion. This again is an utter lie. SAMU teams do not carry blood transfusion equipment because they would be unable to determine the victim's blood type and also to carry stocks of all the many different, available blood-types would be impractical. When the ambulance eventually did leave the tunnel, the driver was ordered to go no faster than 25 miles per hour and some reports say it took as long as 40 minutes to cover the 3.7 miles to the La Pitie-Salpetriere Hospital whilst four other hospitals quite capable of treating Diana were closer to the scene and the ambulance stopped twice on the way for 'delicate interventions', once whilst actually within sight of the hospital.

Diana arrived at La Pitie-Salpetriere Hospital at about 2.10am, an hour and 45 minutes after the crash happened. By any medical criteria whatsoever this delay is completely ludicrous. Of course it is only ludicrous unless it was meant to happen this way because they were performing horrendous occult practices. It doesn't take a genius to see why, despite such apparent incompetence, there has been NO inquiry into the medical response that night. According to Stevens report, they could not go at speed because of her injury but this is absolute nonsense. 1 hour and 45 minutes??

Waiting at the hospital was a surgical team headed by Professor Bruno Riou, the duty surgeon who we are told, first heard about the crash whilst on his routine rounds. Is that not a strange enough sentence in itself, a renowned, senior surgeon doing his rounds in the early hours of the morning? Waiting with him when Diana arrived was Professor Pierre Coriat, the head of anaesthetics, Professor Alain Pavie, a chest and heart specialist and Professor Pierre Benazet, another experienced surgeon. They had been in telephone communication with the emergency team in the tunnel throughout and we are told that they opened Diana's chest cavity, repaired the artery, and battled to save her for an hour and a half before admitting defeat. This is remarkable because the autopsy report shows that Diana was clinically dead at 12.45am whilst still lying in the tunnel. She was therefore clinically dead for an hour and 25 minutes before she even arrived at the hospital and for three hours before the professors walked out of the operating theatre to announce that she had died. Having the body examined at a location under the control of the perpetrators is vital in such assassinations. This is indeed a very similar game to the one that was played with JFK.

So who was behind Diana's assassination? Of course those who gave the order and those who actually carried out the deed would be rather different people. This is the spider's web of the Elite networks and whilst the order will no doubt have come from the spider in the centre, it would certainly have been carried out by one of the many 'flies'. It is highly unlikely that it would have been carried out by British intelligence directly, because of course that would be too obvious. Intelligence agencies subcontract the assassinations of their own citizens to distance themselves from the incident and allow them to plausibly deny that they were responsible. Not only that, the intelligence agency of the nationality of the victim is then 'free' to work on finding who was responsible.

For instance, there is considerable evidence to show that JFK was shot by members of an elite (small 'e') rifle team within the French intelligence called OAS, along with the Israeli Mossad. Olof Palme, the Bilderberger Prime Minister of Sweden, was murdered in Stockholm in 1986 on the orders of among others, George Bush senior. The killing itself was carried out by members of BOSS, the South African intelligence agency.

MI5 announced in 1998 that they do not assassinate people. No, instead they hire other branches of the intelligence family to do it. This rather weak denial was prompted by the revelations of the former MI5 agent, David Shayler, who stated that MI6 had organised a plot to assassinate Libya's Colonel Gaddafi. This attempt failed because the bomb had been placed under the wrong car. Shayler was head of the 'Libyan Desk' at MI5 and was in the perfect position to know. Robin Cook, the then UK Foreign Secretary, stated that he had been assured that no such event took place and the Attorney General banned David Shayler from appearing on the ITV programme, *Diana – Secrets of the Crash*.

So which organisation is most likely to have been involved in the death of Diana at operational level? A secret group by the name of the 'Pinay Circle' or 'Le Cercle' which has amongst its ranks a number of British establishment figures is a strong contender. Le Cercle is an offshoot of the even more elite 'Safari Club', which was set up by Count Alexander de Maranches, the director during the 1970s of the French 'Service for External Documentation and Espionage'. It was the Safari Club that arranged for the alliance between a French intelligence front-company called 'Group Bull' and the computer giant Honeywell which is, you may not be surprised to learn, the world's largest manufacturer of landmines.

The Le Cercle membership has included Nicholas Elliot, a department head at MI6; William Colby, a former director of the CIA; Colonel Botta of Swiss Military Intelligence; Stefano Della Chiaie, leading member of the Italian Secret Service; Giullo Andreotti, the former Italian Prime Minister from the notorious P2 Freemasonry

Lodge and the man who gave the Mafia 'Official Protection'; Silva Munoz, a former Minister for the fascist, Franco, in Spain and a member of the Elite secret society, Opus Dei; Franz Josef Strauss, the German Defence Minister; and Monsignor Brunello an agent of the Vatican. In America, one of the Le Cercle fronts is the CIA–backed Heritage Foundation in Washington. The potential for such an organisation to be the co-ordinating force between countless different agencies and countries, all aiming to a common operation is easy to see. The Safari Club / Le Cercle network provides the Arab-British-French connection necessary to arrange for Diana to be in Paris at the right time, the security for her to be withdrawn, the assassination to be carried out and most importantly, those involved to get away with it. So re-visiting the statement of outer initiate John Stalker, and his comment *"why would the French want to cover up the murder of an English woman?"* the answer is quite simple, because of Elite-level interconnection via organisations such as the Safari Club and Le Cercle. Simon Regan in his book, *'Who killed Diana?'*, says that it was Le Cercle that destabilised the Gough Whitlam government in Australia in 1975 and as already stated, the Queen of England was involved in this too, via her control of her Governor of Australia, Philip Kerr, who used his executive power to remove Whitlam. If the Crown, through the Windsors and Le Cercle worked together to bring down an elected Australian government, it is more than a distinct possibility that they would work together to eliminate Diana - the people's Princess?

Upon studying the history of assassinations, it becomes apparent that Paris is prominent as one of the major cities for this black art, going back many centuries. Amschel Rothschild from the English branch of the family was murdered there in 1996 in what many claim to have been part of another inter-Elite war, one of the many that litters the history of the this sect. For an organisation such as Le Cercle, or its many mirrors in London, it would have been very easy to place its people in the right places. Mohamed Fayed's security operation is composed primarily of ex-British elite military and police units, who know the consequences of saying 'no'. Remember that all these operatives belong to the Crown and certainly not to whichever individual company or organisation would be foolish enough to hire them. There will always be an odd exception, but for those who join the Field Lodges, the oath continues long after service terms are completed.

Fayed's personal investigation into Diana and Dodi's death was headed by Pierre Ottavoili, a former chief of the Criminal Brigade, the criminal investigation department of the French police. This is the same organisation that is also responsible for the 'official Investigation'. Fayed's chief lawyer in Paris is a former French Justice Minister and in overall charge in London at the time was John McNamara, his head of security and former Chief-Superintendent at the headquarters of London's Metropolitan police, at Scotland Yard. In the spring of 1998, McNamara was part of a sting operation involving the FBI, CIA and possibly the Israeli (Rothschild) intelligence Agency Mossad, to arrest a former CIA agent Oswald le Winter, a 67 year old American born in Austria. Le Winter contacted Fayed claiming to have documents for sale, proving the involvement of MI6 and the CIA in the murder of Diana. He was asking $10 million and after meeting with McNamara he was given an advance of $15.000. A further meeting was arranged in Vienna, Austria, for the key documents and for the rest of the money to be handed-over. In the meantime however, Fayed called a friend in the FBI, who contacted the CIA. Le Winter was followed, spied upon and lured to the Ambassador Hotel in Vienna on Wednesday the 22nd April, where with support from the Austrian police a combination of FBI, CIA and Mossad agents apprehended him.

If Al Fayed was indeed the grieving, wronged father, why would he ensure the man who could provide the proof he required, was offered up to his enemies? And if le Winter's offer was a hoax, why would so many agencies spend so much money, time and effort, to prevent him leaking information that was, as they put it, 'a lie' especially when if this was the case it would prove that MI6 was not involved? The whole thing is clearly a psy-op, a set-up to confuse and obfuscate.

This story incidentally, would have remained a secret, but for Peter Grolig, an Austrian journalist on the *Kurier* newspaper. He reported what happened and established that when le Winter's hotel room was searched, four documents, two of them in code were found and appeared to be genuine CIA documents. The CIA has since admitted tapping Diana's phone calls in and to America and passing the contents to British Intelligence. Le Winter was arrested and held in custody and Grolig's story forced Fayed to admit that it was true. Another intelligence insider also insists the crash was not an accident. Richard Tomlinson, a former agent of Britain's MI6, gave evidence to the French enquiry into Diana's death. In 1997 Tomlinson served a six month jail sentence under the official secrets act for trying to sell his memoirs and in 1998 he was arrested again, at gun point, in Paris at the request of the British government who were concerned at his association in that city with MI5 whistle-blower, David Shayler, (now a painted as a madman) who was also arrested and jailed in Paris. Tomlinson apparently told Herve Stephan, the judge in charge of the 'inquiry' that Diana was murdered and according to a report on the BBC's teletext news service, *Ceefax*, on 29th August 1998, he told the judge that Henry Paul was an asset of British Intelligence as was one of the bodyguards who remained un-named. However, despite all this information being freely given to the inquiry, Herve Stephan an obvious Elite placeman concluded, *'it was an accident'*.

In the words of the Roman writer Seneca; *"He who most benefits from the crime is the one most likely to have committed it"*.

The Windsors as a family certainly benefitted the most. No longer is there an inside threat to their secrets and actions. No longer is Diana there to continue her inevitable destruction of the Monarchy as a credible force able to own and influence the path of this nation and most of the rest of the world. No longer is she there to exert her own influence in the upbringing of her sons, William and Harry. The Windsors now have full and total control in the moulding of these two Princes, giving them the total ability to form them into their own sick image. Her death also cleared the way for Charles to marry Camilla.

Of course as we know, the House of Windsor is simply the public face of a much larger power structure, 'The Crown Temple.' which now no longer suffers from Diana publicly exposing its secret war against the populations of the world with landmines. She was almost certainly planning an escalation of that particular battle.

Susan Barrantes, the mother of Sarah 'Fergie' Ferguson, the Duchess of York and former wife of Prince Andrew, had been telling anyone who would listen that she thought Diana had been murdered. She however, was fatally injured herself in an extremely dubious car crash in Argentina on the 19th September 1998. Just a coincidence though, I'm sure. Confidential mail for Diana was delivered to Christine Fitzgerald and this included packages from a former member of the Elite-controlled SAS who was concerned for Diana's safety. He was warning her of what was going on behind her back. "Half of MI6 were on Diana's side too you know", Christine said. One day, a client who had involvement with the security agencies, saw some of these packages being delivered. Christine described what followed:

"She said I'm really worried for you, you don't know what you're getting involved in here. Diana's basically mad, she'll drop you in it, she will hang you out to dry, you'll end up dead, your kids will end up dead, your cats, and your business will be ruined. I couldn't believe how she was carrying on. She was so full of hate. Diana came in the next day and I gave her the mail. I said not everyone who bows to you has your best interests at heart. I told her what had happened and she went purple with rage. When she died, everybody came in and said 'they bumped her off didn't they'? But that client was the only one who was outraged at the suggestion. I was checked out by MI6, my phones were tapped, my house was burgled, the royal family kept a big check on me while I was dealing with Diana."

Christine and her contacts have no doubt about what happened in Paris: "She was bumped off; she was left to die at the roadside. Those responsible were above the elite of the army", she said. "It was not the secret squirrels (British intelligence) it was above that. Mohammed Fayed 'in his tortured little sense' wants to be part of the reptilian power because 'he likes all that'." Christine believes that Diana's romance with Dodi was engineered. She further said:

"Diana fell in love quite easily and he's a master of the smile. She was unfortunate in her love affairs because she rescued others in her own distress. So the men she went for were all emotional cripples because she was a healer, too. Most people who went with Diana used her and I think Dodi did also. He would have used her for his ego, the contacts and his dad. The Royal Family killed her for her light energy, especially when she was pregnant. I don't believe she was as badly injured as they say. If they checked her body they would see that the scar the surgeons made starts at her pubis and goes right up to her throat. They've even taken her thymus gland, the way we make *interstellar communication. I know from the best sources that she was pregnant and they took the baby. Pieces of that foetus will have been delivered everywhere. They can make babies from the cells. Parts of her body will have been used in their rituals as well. (Just to give insight, hope you are not eating! When children are sacrificed with their throat cut from left to right, the blood is drained and drank from their goblets, and specific body parts are eaten. The fat is scraped from the intestines and they rub it on their skin or scales. This is the mesa fat, or the anointing oil, this also is within the Jesus story the anointing of their Messiah. Sick aren't they). Diana was always having Kensington Palace swept for bugs, but they had Dodi bugged and they knew exactly what was going on. This was not the first time she thought she was pregnant and this nearly happened before, but she was not pregnant. That was with Hewitt."*

Christine Fitzgerald shared the most intimate details of Diana's life and knew her in ways and at levels that very few others did. The incredible revelations of the Windsor's treatment of Diana over many years, the threats made to her by Prince Charles' personal detective, the ritual sacrifices and the confirmation that they were responsible for the murder of Barry Mannakee, should not pass without note. There should be a campaign to press the Windsors to face these matters and for Al Fayed, Trevor Rees-Jones, Earl Spencer and the others I have named, to answer the questions that have to be addressed. Power must be stripped from the Windsors, their royal dynasty dismantled and their crimes against humanity publicly exposed. More than that, however, those in the political, security and medical professions, who are also involved, must be equally exposed. The Royal Family, Earl Spencer, and the Satanic, former British Prime Minister, Tony Blair, have all dismissed claims that Diana was murdered and called for such suggestions to cease 'for the sake of the boys'. These questions must not be allowed to be ignored or another Elite assassination will have been promulgated whilst those responsible go free.

Earl Spencer even went to the extent of issuing a statement on behalf of the Spencer family in February 1998 in which he asked: *"Is there any good in all this speculation? I ask that because there is clearly a lot of harm in it. All we, her family, ask is that Diana's memory be respected and the sensational speculation be left out of the public arena, where it undermines our aims to come to terms with her loss".*

Had Diana been your sister would you not be determined to find out what happened? If you were Prime Minister when such a famous and loved Princess had been killed, would you not insist that the truth be established? So why don't they? I think we all know the answer to that particular question,

Diana had a profound effect on millions of people as was apparent after her death and most people did not know the full extent of her suffering once the Windsors got hold of her. In many ways Diana was a mirror of Marilyn Monroe, used by the establishment and then cast aside and murdered when her usefulness was at an end. Marilyn had affairs with John Kennedy and also it seems, his brother, Bobby and when she became dangerous because of her inside knowledge she was killed because of what she knew. In another of those remarkable examples of synchronicity there are many 'coincidences' that connect her life and that of Diana's. They were both born on the first of the month and died at the age of 36 in August. They both married on the 29th of the month to men twelve years older. Marilyn called herself the Queen of Diamonds and Diana the Queen of Hearts and both were subjects of the Elton John song, *Candle in the Wind*, which he sang at Diana's funeral.

Since Christine Fitzgerald first spoke out about her relationship with Diana, the threat to destroy her business has been implemented. Suddenly the phone stopped ringing and she was seeing as many clients in a week as she had been in a day. This is unexplainable when you consider that she is one of Britain's most gifted and effective healers working in the centre of London. Unexplainable that is, unless one is aware of the story. But she is nevertheless determined that the truth shall be known, whatever the authorities seek to do to her: *"I don't want a war, I just want to end the bullshit"*, as she puts it. Looking back on Diana's life and their conversations together she reflects:

"Poor cow, she was in a house where no one gives a damn and it's a terrible state of affairs. She was all alone in a nest of vipers. I used to just patch her up. She just found me and came to me. I made her wait a fortnight until I checked it out. They used to say that I was giving her anger therapy. I didn't. I used to just listen to her, take it all in and think Jesus Christ! But I didn't think they would kill her. I can't believe that this information is so close to home and yet they are still managing to keep it at bay. My room is the truth room and it's a real place of safety and I don't judge anyone on their s**t and that's why I haven't spoken about any of this in the past. She was as screwed up as anyone you know and if you're going to tell the truth, you have to tell the whole truth. She wasn't crazy, she was mentally and physically abused, I feel, from a little girl. Her father was a nasty piece of work and her stepmother (Raine), too.

The Royal Family was very afraid. She would have taken the public away from them; she would have taken the world from them gradually. They recognised her worth and fed off her in a psychic vampire way for a long time. All she wanted was to get married and have children you know, bless her little heart. She wanted to live out what she had never had. The world would have come to rights with Diana because as f****d up as she was, she was a light being and wherever she went she manifested love. It was amazing. The sad thing was that she didn't know she was doing that and she needed proof of her worth and she was looking in the wrong quarters for that. But when she tried to break away, we went out and did normal things. She did Kung Fu with my husband for five years. She wanted to be normal, to link arms and walk down the street. She knew where her heart lay. She really and truly did amazing things."

Diana said she could not believe how cold the Windsors were and the public were shown a graphic example of this in the days after her death. They stayed out of sight in Balmoral in Scotland while the people mourned Diana in their tens of millions with an unprecedented explosion of grief. It was only the pressure from the public through the media that forced the Queen, kicking and screaming, to make a cold, emotionless and pathetic 'tribute' to Diana on TV the night before the funeral. Cold is a word constantly used about the Queen, Phillip and Charles and that's the mental and emotional profile of the Brotherhood and its networks. William (Bill) Cooper said that the Initiates that he met in his work for US Naval Intelligence had *"No conscience, no morals, no regrets, no feelings, and no emotion"*. This is precisely the same psychopathic character profile as the Windsors and indeed most of the Elite that control our lives.

We have all been hoodwinked for thousands of years. Hoodwinked about our history, hoodwinked about whom we really are and the true nature of life. Hoodwinked about the true background and agenda of those we have allowed to rule us. How apt, therefore, that this word should also derive from Freemasonry. Dr. Albert MacKey, the 33rd degree Freemason and foremost Freemason historian of the 19th century, defined the term 'hoodwinked' in his Encyclopaedia of Freemasonry as: *'A symbol of secrecy, silence and darkness, in which the mysteries of our art should be preserved from the unhallowed gaze of the profane'.*

Diana's tragic death is but one of a long, long line of others whose lives have been cut brutally short to serve the agenda of these monsters who rule us with an iron fist, encased in a velvet glove.

PART 3 – The World of Today – Our Distorted Reality

The distorted reality under which we all exist today is a direct result of the falsification of much of what we regard as our true historical heritage. In the first two sections of this book, I have attempted to provide evidence for and examples of the numerous ways in which we have been distracted and diverted from the real truth in order that a tiny minority of people may benefit from that lack of knowledge and thus maintain the status quo heavily in their favour. Maintaining this 'edited' view of the past is essential in their control of the vast majority of humanity and this is sustained by all the methods already covered, including but not exclusive to, the media, the entertainment industry, the medical profession, politics, law and the subtle utilisation of a group of people that have come to be known by the 'truth movement' as 'useful idiots'. However, more of this important group very shortly.

We have been lied to and deceived on a truly epic scale by those who rule over us, ever since human society first saw the light of day, regardless of whether, like mainstream history and archaeology you believe that to be ten thousand years ago – or even ten million years ago. As a timely reminder, here is a reprise of the quote from the first page of the introduction, by Dr. Henry Makow, who like myself has been researching these issues for many years and sums up this conspiracy succinctly, thus…

*"In fact, 'conspiracy' is very plausible. People who control a grossly disproportionate share of the world's wealth will take **extreme** measures to consolidate their position."* [My emphasis – JH]

This is the entire nub of the issue in two short sentences and summarises neatly the reason that humankind is now in the situation in which we find ourselves today. Everything else is just a means to this end, a method by which we can be controlled, indeed the 'extreme measures', to which Dr. Makow refers.

So, let us now move into the very recent past and from thence to the present day and examine the issues which confront us daily and which have as a result of the falsification of past events now become pertinent to our everyday struggle to survive. But firstly, let us examine the prominent role played by a group of people who are very important to the Elite's plans for keeping us all in a state of ignorance of the truth.

Useful Idiots

What do I mean by this term? 'Useful idiots', as distinct from 'shills' – people who are knowingly setting-out to deceive us, are those among us who are *unknowingly* furthering the agenda of the Elite by acting as unwitting purveyors of falsehoods and naysayers of the real truth.

For example, when confronted with the facts, they will ask lots of questions, but never wait to hear an answer. To their minds, questions are not a search for information, but rather a tool of disruption. In this way, the useful idiot never has to expose his ignorance because he never has to enter into a meaningful dialogue with anyone who has an opposing view. All he has to do is maintain an attacking stance and this perpetuates a useless, circular argument, usually ending in utter stalemate.

Another of the most common tactics used is the injection of 'humour'. He will turn everything into a joke, whether it is funny or not. Laughing at that which we do not understand often makes things appear less daunting, but it also makes us more passive and accepting.

The comedians that are most successful (and popular) are those that follow mainstream thinking and encourage us to laugh at anything that challenges these norms. A good example being the ridicule to which David Icke was subjected for many years in the early 1990s when he made the now self-acknowledged mistake of trying to bring his views to an unthinking majority by the very medium which would seek to destroy him (television). This made him an easy target for the 'comedians' of the day and even the mention of his name alone, would be guaranteed to raise a cheap laugh. In Medieval times, even the most tyrannical of rulers would allow a court jester to make jokes at his expense because the jester was an inconsequential figure, a powerless and non-threatening entity. A jokester can verbally undermine anyone to his heart's content, but will never really change the world because although he may make us laugh, ultimately no-one really cares what figures of fun have to say about anything of consequence. It is not too difficult to imagine a whole subsection of society emulating this dynamic; millions of people deluding themselves into thinking that being a slave is not all that bad, just as long as we are funny slaves.

Whenever the useful idiot is confronted with a truth that threatens his established world-view, he will do anything to distract or derail the argument. Making poor jokes, resorting to childish ridicule, ignoring cold hard logic and facts, making threats or denying that you are qualified to present the facts, even though the facts speak for themselves no matter who is relaying them. The list goes on and on and very seldom will he confront the truth presented on its own terms, instead, he will often make a point of making the 'messenger' the issue at hand and not the information being presented. For example, I have lost count of the times when in trying to present an argument that I have been cut-off in full flow by a mocking statement such as... 'You must have too much time on your hands'. As though 'having too much time' somehow is an actual impediment to seeking the truth and not the opposite ie. not having *enough* time on one's hands!

Is it so difficult to check information to confirm whether or not any premise is true? I have been asked many times when stating a fact to one of these people, to 'prove it' but when I offer to do so by pointing them in the right direction, they will often ostentatiously decline the offer on the basis that It cannot possibly be true. It obviously must be extremely difficult for some people to check information though because so many people believe absolutely everything they are told by the mainstream or figures of authority, or simply assume it must be true, without bothering to check it out for themselves.

If a so-called 'scientist' suddenly announced via the media that adding arsenic to coffee will increase one's desirability in the eyes of the opposite sex, would these people blindly ingest it or would a more sensible approach be to double-check the facts first? Obviously everyone *knows* that arsenic is poisonous, but how many other poisons do we westerners ingest daily because some petty official gave the all-clear to add it into our food supply. I am speaking of such horrors here as; mercury (thimerasol), aspartame, high fructose corn syrup (HFCS), fluoride, rBGH, Bisphenol-A, GMOs and others too numerous to mention and all of which appear with monotonous regularity on the ingredients list of popular foodstuffs. A few minutes of research via that invaluable tool, the Internet, which is available to virtually all now, would soon provide a mountain of evidence to demonstrate that these substances are far from the benign entities they are purported to be and indeed are in some cases, bordering on deadly. But are these people aware of this fact? Welcome to the world of the useful idiot.

However, having said all that, to be a truly useful idiot is not just simply a case of for example, taking part in the mass-ingestion of all this filth, but in order to qualify as a bona fide, paid-up member of the club, the really useful idiot is someone of the ilk of the official or the 'scientist' who vehemently propounds the purity of these substances. He may also be the dentist who mockingly laughs when questioned about the safety of fluoride in toothpastes or the nurse who threatens to call the Child Protection Service / Social Services if you refuse a vaccination for your newborn baby. It is often also the person who received his standard dose of academic propaganda without ever comprehending the fact that once upon a time, the first rule of 'good science' used to be to question everything and not just blindly accept anything laid down by someone claiming authority.

So, the useful idiot is not only conditioned himself, but is also a valuable distribution agent of that conditioning to others. When confronted with a viewpoint which falls outside of his dogmatic stance, his brain shuts down because he has lived most of his life with the ideas and propaganda inherent in a lifetime of brainwashing. To be confronted with the fact that everything he previously thought he knew and has based his entire life upon is false, is an extremely nasty medicine to have to swallow. This is an acknowledged condition known as 'cognitive dissonance'.

Of course, this all makes the useful idiot the prime target of Elite disinformation campaigns. Nearly all criminal actions by the Elite through their puppets in government, receive their primary support from this portion of the population exactly because they are so easily misled by authority. These people have been conditioned to automatically disbelieve and ridicule anything that comes with the engendered label of 'conspiracy theory' and instead of checking facts for themselves, firmly believe that there is no need to do that because if it is deemed to be a conspiracy theory, therefore by definition, it must be utter nonsense.

But why should we bother trying to communicate with these unquestioning robots at all? Surely they are the absolute definition of a lost cause? However, if we can demonstrate that beyond all doubt that just one of their misconceptions is totally without substance and unsupported by facts, it may just be that they are no longer able to assume that any of their other misguided views are of any real substance either. They may eventually be shamed or forced into doing the research, which may then lead to the world-shattering realisation that suddenly they know nothing. I have been in that position myself and believe me it is not a very pleasant place to be. It appears that the whole world has suddenly fallen apart and the question then becomes one of 'what is actually real and what is not?' and almost like a child, one has to start re-learning how to relate to this strange new reality, over again.

Eventually though, one accepts the loss of innocence. That dupe that was so convinced of what was right and wrong and certain of his place in the grand scheme of things suddenly finds himself in a scary place, a world he must now investigate alone to determine the truth, instead of being spoon-fed the reality proscribed by faceless others in the world of academia or the media. The empowerment and the sheer awe inherent in this process are almost unbelievable in their scope and have to be experienced to be understood. It is almost like a blind man who can suddenly see after forty years or so of blindness, never knowing what he was missing all that time because he had nothing with which to compare it. But, once the huge leap across this vast chasm has been made, it is not only impossible to go back to being the person we were before; it is absolutely unthinkable so to do.

Of course, no-one regards themselves as a useful idiot, blindly serving the interests of monsters in the cruel and heartless oppression of their fellow man, but the fact remains that many people are in just such a position. You may despise some of them or wish them ill, but please do not give-up on them all. There are some good, honest, well-meaning people amongst their ranks and confronting their unintentional ignorance is not simply just the duty of we who are better informed; it is also an act of compassion towards those who are not.

Corporations

"They decide who governs and how, who serves on courts, what laws are enacted, and whether or not wars are waged. Corporate dominance, especially financial power, and democratic values are incompatible. They operate ruthlessly as private tyrannies. They're predators, we're prey, and every day we're eaten alive. They do it because they can, and in America by mandate. Publicly owned US corporations, including financial ones, must serve shareholders by maximizing equity value through higher profits. They do it by exploiting nations, people and resources ruthlessly. Social responsibility doesn't matter, neither does being worker-friendly, a good citizen, or friend of the earth. Bottom-line priorities alone, matter. Failure to pursue fiduciary responsibilities means possible dismissal or shareholder lawsuits. Yet nothing in America's Constitution or statute laws endow corporations with their rights. They usurped them by co-opting Washington, the nation's courts, state capitals, and city halls. As a result, over half the world's largest economies are corporations. Financial ones controlling the power of money are most dominant. Corporate personhood enhanced their power, yet imagine. Although corporations aren't human, they can live forever, change their identity, reside in many places globally, can't be imprisoned for wrongdoing, and can transform themselves into new entities for any reason. They have the same rights and protections as people without the responsibilities. As a result, they operate freely unrestrained, especially financial giants controlling the power of money at the public's expense."
Stephen Lendman. *'The Network of Global Corporate Control'*, 16th December 2011

Let us begin with a brief comparison of Tanzania (the country) and Goldman Sachs (the corporation):

Tanzania – Annual GNP $2.2bn
25 million people

Goldman – Annual profit $2.2bn
160 partners

Spot the financial similarity and yet the discrepancy in the number of people who 'benefit'.

At present, giant corporations are becoming larger and larger, buying up their competitors, and bribing and lobbying local authority councillors, mayors and representatives of government to scrap legislation which curbs their insatiable appetite for growth to the detriment of all else. Already, the effect of this covert coup on free trade has left us with shopping malls which are almost exact copies of one another, offering little or no choice for the consumer and thus creating a virtual cartel. Parking restrictions are being placed by local authorities on roads where small businesses are desperately clinging on to what trade is left. Meanwhile, previously public spaces, even major roads, are being re-routed, driving traffic into giant shopping malls and supermarkets where the seemingly grandiose selection of shops is actually owned by just a handful of mega-corporations.

At present in the relatively small village where I live, opinion is divided on whether the supermarket giant, Tesco should be allowed to build a new store about one mile from the village centre. Those people who say 'yes' argue that it will lead to greater choice, more convenience (ie. not having to drive the whole 6 miles or so to the next nearest other supermarket) and best of all to lower prices than are currently available in the existing local shops. I can see the point to a certain extent but I firmly believe that it is far more important to our local community that we retain the existing, small, in many cases, one-man local businesses that have in some instances remained in the same families for a hundred years or more, rather than succumb to the might of the large corporations whose buying power and immoral treatment of suppliers and thus lower prices, will probably lead to the village centre becoming a ghost town in very short order.

In addition, should Tesco (or any other large corporate entity for that matter) decide say, two years hence that profits are not high enough after all, there not being a large enough local population to sustain their desired profit levels, then they will simply cut their losses and leave without so much as a thought to the local economy. The reality then will be that having destroyed all the small, local businesses, then there will be nowhere for the locals to shop and they will wind-up having to travel even further whilst leaving desolation in the village centre itself. It will also have a devastating effect on the local community in terms of job losses. The loss of say 30-40 jobs in a small area such as this would be critical. This scenario has been shown to happen in many, many examples throughout the Western world.

"One of the main problems that we have with our political system in the United States is that in many ways, corporations can literally buy seats in our Congress. We have the United States Supreme Court that recently upheld a decision to allow corporations to spend unlimited amounts on independent expenditures." Marcy Winograd, Congressional Candidate and co-chair of the Progressive Democrats of Los Angeles

Corporations play a huge role in our day-to-day activities and they are constantly making decisions that have a profound effect on our daily lives. For example, a corporation makes the decision to empty its chemical vats into a nearby river, the water supply is poisoned and residents of the adjacent town fall sick; or a corporation makes the decision to cut costs to increase profits and initiates a round of job losses and thus the community that was formed around the corporation is decimated. We have often been appalled, angry and go on rants about the evil of corporations but according to Professor Simon Baron Cohen, evil itself is not the issue.

Baron-Cohen, an expert in autism and developmental psychology, is also a psychology and psychiatry professor at Cambridge University. For many years he has spent considerable time researching the reasons why people commit vile and heinous acts. His theory is that the lack of empathy is the root cause of all evil deeds and that this lack of empathy can be measured and treated. He also defines empathy as the drive to identify another person's thoughts and feelings combined with the drive to respond appropriately to those thoughts or feelings.

He further asserts that the lack of empathy or failure to utilise it to its full potential is the driving force behind most of what ails our society on a global, domestic, community and family-unit scale. The abstract arenas of diplomatic, legal, and military channels are insufficient to appropriately deal with conflict because their involvement forgoes empathy from entering the picture on a true person-to-person level.

In his books Baron-Cohen describes an empathy bell-curve spectrum and quotient test that indicates where an individual will be placed along this curve. Most people naturally fall right in the middle but there is a zero degree empathy range and within this lie the psychopaths, narcissists, and individuals suffering with borderline personality disorders.

So what does all this information have to do with corporations? Simply that corporations are legislatively derived artificial 'individuals' that can sue and be sued, raise funds, make political decisions, etc. They are headed by a board of Directors that is by law duty-bound to make decisions in the best interests of the corporation and its shareholders and not necessarily in the best interests of mankind in general, nature et al.

Since corporations are businesses whose sole purpose is to make money whatever the consequences, overall best interests are almost always those that increase profit, to the detriment of all else and empathy be damned.

True, there are some organisations that whilst in the process of turning a profit, strive to do no harm to society. However embedded deep within Baron-Cohen's bell-curve are corporations that seem to have made human suffering into a profitable side-line. For example, that same name that has cropped-up in these pages many times, Monsanto Inc., creators of *Agent Orange*, *DDT*, *Roundup*, GMOs and a veritable plethora of other toxic substances that have caused horrific damage and injury to the world on a global scale.

Then there is Firestone and its rubber plantations in Liberia which poison the local and wider environment, pay slave-labour level wages and house workers in unsanitary conditions that most caring people would not see fit to keep an animal.

Likewise, Nestle and their cocoa plantations in the Cote d'Ivoire which employ young children and pay them less than subsistence wages and also keeps them living in substandard conditions. Also, Big Pharma and their concerted efforts to keep us purchasing medicines that either patently do not work or cause more harm than good.

Let us also not forget Coca Cola, that caring organisation that has probably justly been accused of murdering individuals seeking to form unions to gain fair wages and treatment, although no punishment or retribution of any kind was forthcoming from complicit, bought-and-paid-for governments.

Not one corporate executive involved in making any of the above decisions or 'giving the orders' for any of the above actions has served any jail time or indeed in effect committed a crime. By their very definition, corporations are able to forgo or bypass empathetic decision-making because they are abstract entities. When making decisions that directly affect humanity, empathy is a necessary ingredient. Take away the capacity for empathy and you are left with what we have today, psychopathic corporations spreading what we would deem to be evil all over the world, under normal circumstances. The corporate machine is a coldly calculating force that makes decisions that are solely driven by bottom-line figures with the wellbeing and basic needs of humanity in a distant second-place, if even considered at all.

In a fair and just society, corporations should be held to the same moral standards as individuals. Profits should not be allowed to be made to the detriment of the environment and equitable wages should be paid worldwide regardless of location.

Imagine a world where government leaders were not bribed and cajoled by corporations to make decisions directly against the best wishes of the people they were elected to represent in the first place and imagine a world where all corporate psychopaths did not exist. Is this really too much to ask? As long as all major corporations continue to be owned by the Elite few who we know literally stop at nothing in the garnering of their obscene profits, it would certainly appear so.

Bohemian Grove

The 40ft stone owl worshipped by 'Grovers'

Eighty miles north of San Francisco is a playground for the mega-rich known as Bohemian Grove and it is here where over 2000 members of the political, corporate, media, cultural and military elite of the world, gather every July for two weeks, for their annual Satanic rituals, possibly including human ritual sacrifice. They have been meeting here since the 1880s.

According to reliable sources, a ritual sacrifice, firstly of Mary Magdalene and then Jesus Christ takes place every year. A human body or an effigy of one is burned in front of the pictured, large owl symbolising Moloch, the pagan Canaanite God in a ceremony known as 'The Cremation of Care'. Indeed, there is very strong evidence that the Grove members are Satanists.

In 1978, the 'club' actually argued in court that it should not have to hire female staff because members at the Grove 'urinate in the open without even the use of rudimentary toilet facilities' and that the presence of females would 'alter club members' behaviour'.

"I was programmed and equipped to function in all rooms at Bohemian Grove in order to compromise specific government targets according to their personal perversions. Anything, anytime, anywhere with anyone was my mode of operation at the Grove. I do not purport to understand the full function of this political cesspool playground as my perception was limited to my own realm of experience. My perception is that Bohemian Grove serves those ushering in the New World Order through mind control and consists primarily of the highest Mafia and US Government officials.

I do not use the term 'highest' loosely, as copious quantities of drugs were consumed there. Project Monarch mind-control slaves were routinely abused there to fulfil the primary purpose of the club, purveying perversion. Bohemian Grove is reportedly intended to be used recreationally, providing a supposedly secure environment for politically affluent individuals to 'party' without restraint. The only business conducted there pertained to implementing the New World Order, through the proliferation of mind-control atrocities, giving the place an air of 'masonic secrecy'. The only room where business discussions were permitted was the small, dark lounge affectionately and appropriately referred to as 'the underground'.

My purpose at the Grove was sexual in nature and therefore my perceptions were limited to a sex slave's viewpoint. As an effective means of control to ensure undetected proliferation of their perverse indulgences, slaves such as myself were subjected to ritualistic trauma. I knew each breath I took could be my last, as the threat of death lurked in every shadow. Slaves of advancing age or with failing programming were sacrificially murdered 'at random' in the wooded grounds of Bohemian Grove and I felt it was 'simply a matter of time until it would be me'. Rituals were held at a giant, concrete owl monument on the banks of the Russian River. These occultist sex rituals stemmed from the scientific belief that mind-controlled slaves required severe trauma to ensure compartmentalisation of the memory and not from any spiritual motivation.

My own threat of death was instilled when I witnessed the sacrificial death of a young, dark-haired victim at which time I was instructed to perform sexually 'as though my life depended upon it'. I was told, '...the next sacrifice victim could be you. Anytime when you least expect it, the owl will consume you. Prepare yourself, and stay prepared.'

Being 'prepared' equated to being totally suggestible, ie. 'on my toes' awaiting their command." From Chapter 18, 'The Tranceformation of America' by Cathy O'Brien

Sonia Sotomayor is a member of the all-female 'Belizean Club' which is the lesser-known, female equivalent of Bohemian Grove. The evidence would appear to show that Elite 'gofers' are chosen by virtue of being sexually and morally compromised so that they will obey the dictates of Cabalist banksters who are attempting to establish the New World Order. She said that...

"I feel sorry for the innocent people who think Osama bin Laden was responsible for 9/11, that the media tells the truth and we live in a free country. We live in a world designed and controlled by Satanist central bankers according to the blueprint of The Protocols of the Elders of Zion. We are being harassed by terrorism, war, financial crises and viruses just as the Protocols promised. The purpose is to make us throw up our hands and accept world government, which is a euphemism for banker tyranny. Whether it is climate change, wars, bank bailouts or 'hate laws', there is less distinction everyday between the perversity of the Illuminati bankers and the actions of our government."

The very existence of Bohemian Grove is evidence that the leaders of the world have been seduced by or replaced by Satanists and perverts all of which is covered-up by the media, which is of course a part of the insidious plot, itself. The idea that the 'mock' sacrifices are the extent of the sinister events at Bohemian Grove is always open to speculation and there have been several official reports which include evidence of satanic ritual abuse, blood drinking and even child murder in the area. The 1993 murder of 12 year old Polly Klass has been linked to the area close to the Bohemian Grove.

Until we, as a species recognise that those who control our whole lives are not at all what they seem to be and act collectively to end their power over us all, then the future for our children is beginning to look very bleak indeed. Please, please do not allow the lackeys of the media to hoodwink you into thinking that all is well. It most certainly is not.

USA Incorporated

Surprisingly to many people, the United States of America actually exists in two distinctly separate forms. The original United States that was in operation until 1860 was a collection of sovereign republics (the individual States) in the overall Union and under the original Constitution the States controlled the Federal Government, the Federal Government did not control the States and had very little authority.

The original United States was however, usurped by a separate and different 'UNITED STATES' formed in 1871, which only controls the District of Columbia (Washington DC) and its territories and which is actually a corporation (the UNITED STATES Inc.) that acts as the current government. The US Corporation operates under Corporate/Commercial/Public Law rather than Common/Private Law.

Although the original Constitution was never removed or revoked, it has simply remained dormant since 1871, yet it is still intact to this day, despite its usurpation by the US Inc. This fact was made clear by Supreme Court Justice Marshall Harlan (Downes v. Bidwell, 182, U.S. 244 1901) by issuance of the following dissenting opinion: *"Two national governments exist, one to be maintained under the Constitution, with all its restrictions; the other to be maintained by Congress outside and independently of that instrument."*

The rewritten Constitution of the UNITED STATES CORPORATION bypasses the original Constitution of the United States of America, which explains why Congressmen and Senators do not abide by it and the fact that the President may issue Executive Orders at will, in order to basically do whatever he wishes, totally contrary to the supposed democratic process. They are following corporate laws that completely strip the citizens of the country of their unalienable rights and freedoms.

The US Government is therefore a Corporation actually functioning as the Federal Government and thus it does not need to abide by the Constitution. Also it does not actually matter whether or not Barrack Obama is not a natural born citizen (as has been argued by many commentators) since it is a corporation of which is in effect the CEO and not the president of a bona fide country.

The only way that a corporation can obtain the explicit permission of the people to rule them, is by deceit and this is achieved by subtle wording in Birth Certificates, Social Security Cards, driving licences, tax forms, marriage licences and many other 'legal' documents. In these documents, the 'person' is always referred to by all capital letters eg JOHN SMITH, meaning in law that the name represents a corporate entity and not a living being. This is how the corporate courts finagle jurisdiction over the people. These courts do not display the regular American flag; they actually use the military or admiralty flag. This flag is a standard 'stars and stripes', but with one important distinction and that it is that it bears a gold fringe around the edges. You may think that this is an unimportant, trivial issue, but you would be wrong. This flag is NOT the flag of the original US but that of the US Corporation, the US Inc. and its use is deliberately designed in order to deceive.

So in effect, when anyone enters a US Courtroom, there is a military or admiralty flag displayed. The US military does not have the protection of the Constitution and neither does it apply to admiralty laws with ships at sea. When anyone enters a court room and crosses the threshold, they are in effect symbolically boarding a 'ship' and in effect a foreign country as evidenced by the admiralty or military flag and thus the constitution is inapplicable and they are immediately under equity law and not common law. Ever wondered why in a court, the holding area for an accused person is called a 'dock'?!

Here is the sequence of events that led to the usurpation of the old by the current UNITED STATES...

On 1st January 1788, the United States was officially declared bankrupt.

On 4th August 1790, Article One of the US Statutes at Large, pages 138-178, abolished the States of the Republic and created Federal Districts. In the same year, the former States of the Republic reorganised as Corporations and their legislatures wrote new State Constitutions, absent defined boundaries, which they presented to the people of each state for a vote. The new State Constitutions fraudulently made the people 'citizens' of the new Corporate States. A Citizen is also defined as a 'corporate fiction'.

In 1845, Congress passed legislation that would ultimately allow Common Law to be usurped by Admiralty Law. The gold fringe around court flags proves that this is still the case. Before 1845, Americans were considered sovereign individuals who governed themselves under Common Law.

In 1860, Congress was adjourned Sine Die. Not even President Lincoln could legally reconvene Congress.

In 1861, President Lincoln declared a National Emergency and Martial Law, which gave the President unprecedented powers and removed it from the other branches. This has never, ever been reversed.

From 1864-1867, several Reconstruction Acts were passed forcing the states to ratify the 14th Amendment, which made everyone slaves.

In 1865, the capital was moved to Washington DC from Philadelphia, a separate country and NOT part of the United States of America.

In 1871, The United States became a Corporation with a new constitution and a new corporate government and the original constitutional government was vacated to become dormant, but it was never terminated. The new constitution had to be ratified by the people according to the original constitution, but it never was. The whole process occurred behind closed doors and the people were the source of financing for this new government.

In 1917, the Trading with the Enemy Act (TWEA) was passed. This act was implemented to deal with the countries with which the US was in conflict during World War I. It allowed the President and the Alien Property Custodian the right to seize the assets of 'the people'.

In 1921, the Federal Reserve Bank (the trustee for the Alien Property Custodian) held over $700,000,000 in trust. This trust was based on publicly held assets and not theirs. The 'Fed' is a private corporation.

In 1933, 48 Stat 1, of the TWEA was amended to include all United States citizens because they decided to remove gold from private ownership. Executive Order 6102 was issued which made it illegal for a US Citizen to own gold. In order for the Government to take the gold away from the people and violate their Constitutional rights, they were reclassified as ENEMY COMBATANTS.

In 1933, there was a second United States bankruptcy. In the first bankruptcy the United States collateralised all public lands and in the 1933 bankruptcy, the US government collateralised the private lands of the people (a lien). They borrowed money against all private lands which were then mortgaged. This is the source of and the reason for all property taxes.

"It is an established fact that the United States Federal Government has been dissolved by the Emergency Banking Act, March 9, 1933, 48 Stat. 1, Public Law 89-719; declared by President Roosevelt, being bankrupt and insolvent. H.J.R. 192, 73rd Congress m session June 5, 1933 – Joint Resolution To Suspend The Gold Standard and Abrogate The Gold Clause dissolved the Sovereign Authority of the United States and the official capacities of all United States Governmental Offices, Officers, and Departments and is further evidence that the United States Federal Government exists today in name only." Speaker Representative James Trafficant Jr., *'The Bankruptcy of the United States Congressional Record'*, 17th March 1993

The receivers of the United States Bankruptcy are our old friends the Elite international Banksters via the United Nations, the World Bank and the International Monetary Fund (IMF). All US Offices, Officials and Departments are now operating within a de facto status in name only under Emergency War Powers. With the Constitutional Republic form of Government now dissolved, the receivers of the bankruptcy have adopted a new form of government for the United States. This new form of government is known as a 'Democracy', it being an established Socialist/Communist order.

As any debtor would, the Federal United States government had to assign collateral and security to their creditors as a condition of the loan to resolve the bankruptcy. Since the Federal United States had no assets, they assigned the private property of their 'economic slaves', the US citizens, as collateral against the federal debt. They also pledged the unincorporated federal territories, national parks, forests, birth certificates, and nonprofit organizations as collateral against this debt. This has all now already been transferred as payment to the Elite international bankers.

Unwittingly, America has returned to its pre-Revolution feudal state whereby all land is held by a sovereign and the common people had no rights to hold titles to property. In 1944, Washington DC was deeded to the International Monetary Fund (IMF) by the Breton Woods Agreement. The IMF is made up of the wealthy Elite that own the banking industries of the world. It is an organised group of bankers that have taken control of most governments of the world which in effect allows them to surreptitiously run the world. The US Congress, the IRS, and the US President work for the IMF and not for the United States of America. The IRS is not a US government agency; it is an agency of the IMF.

The Elite-Controlled Mainstream Media

"We are grateful to the Washington Post, the NY Times, Time Magazine and other great publications whose directors have attended our meetings and respected their promises of discretion for almost 40 years. It would have been impossible for us to develop our plan for the world if we had been subjected to the lights of publicity during those years. But, the world is more sophisticated and prepared to march towards a world government. The supranational sovereignty of an intellectual elite and world bankers is surely preferable to the national auto-determination practiced in past centuries." David Rockefeller, speaking at the Bilderberger meeting in June 1991 in Baden Baden, Germany

"We are the tools and vassals of rich men behind the scenes. We are the jumping jacks, they pull the strings and we dance. Our talents, our possibilities and our lives are all the property of other men. We are intellectual prostitutes." John Swinton, editor New York Times, 1863

Being told or feeling that we can be and are being manipulated by an unseen or a hidden hand does not fit the world-view of most of the members of the human race. It is almost a matter of pride that we strongly believe that we are masters of our own destiny and would not be swayed by propaganda or subtle manipulation from a third party.

Let me say immediately that that view is absolutely, utterly wrong. It is a gross self-deceit to believe that we are able to resist the intentional programming, subtle social-engineering and psychological manipulation that is used upon us 24/7, all of our lives. Whether it be through the use of invasive advertising techniques or simply through subtle psycho-babble or even subliminal messaging, we are all subjected daily to a constant stream of data designed to shape our thinking and even influence our every action.

If any group, small or large intends to influence and therefore control the masses then it is a given that it will need to have absolute control over the information that they receive and by doing so exert a powerful, irresistible influence over them. This makes control of the media (of all kinds) absolutely essential to any tyranny, because please make no mistake, that is exactly what we have here.

It is not an exaggeration to state that 96% of the world's media, both written and audio/visual is owned and controlled by six Elite families. The two primary sources of the entire western world's news are Associated Press (AP) and Reuters and this is whence almost 100% of all newspaper and TV/radio news emanates. AP and Reuters are themselves owned by two related Elite families and may well now even be part of the same conglomerate at the very top. Newspaper editors, reporters, TV news presenters and roving reporters do not seek out for themselves they information they impart to us, they merely repeat information that is passed to them by what they assume to be reliable, trustworthy sources but are in actual fact, anything but.

Given these facts, are we surprised that it is so simple for such a tiny minority of people to control the vast majority with such ease? How many of us actually question whether the written media, BBC, SKY or ITV in the UK or Fox, CNN and CBS among several others in the US are telling us the truth when it is so easy for them to lie, not just about small events but about huge world and life-changing events also. All we hear/read unfortunately is nothing but Elite disinformation and propaganda and whilst the events being reported may well actually be happening, it is almost guaranteed that their causes and the parties involved are not as they are portrayed to us, but are twisted beyond recognition to fulfil the Elite agenda.

Why does this matter? Because influence via the adept packaging of information and images is extremely effective in creating a desired mind-set. The creator of the public relations industry, Edward Bernays, was the nephew of Sigmund Freud and he devised a methodology designed to use the subconscious to shape public opinion. His books included 'This Business of Propaganda' and 'Manipulating Public Opinion'. However, it absolutely does not fit our self-image of being the totally independent masters of our own views, to recognise that we are being artificially induced into self-denial of the fact that the truth is constantly being invented and manipulated to unduly influence our thinking.

In his classic work, 'Influence: The Art of Persuasion', Robert Cialdini describes how salesmen are now trained using basic sales techniques, to adroitly use social-conditioning and norms to elicit favourable responses. Cialdini, a social psychologist, notes that even though he is fully aware of these techniques, he is nevertheless unable to personally resist them. How simple then to use these very same techniques upon an entire, unsuspecting populace?

A major element of media manipulation is through the power of multi-national corporations. The media will never dare to report anything too negative about for example, banking, financial services, large corporations or government departments/individuals lest they lose access to the source of their information. This principle may also be applied to advertising revenues, which may well receive a fatal blow if the corporation/government in question decides to retaliate in return for unfavourable coverage. In many cases it may also be true that the media company has some deep-rooted connection to the corporation, if the pyramids are followed to the very top. The private sector has indeed learned the often effective lesson that the threat of freezing-out a reporter is an extremely powerful weapon in retaining control of its own versions of the 'truth'. This may well be the sorry state of affairs that one associates with communist/fascist dictatorships and banana republics from the twentieth century, but needless to say perhaps, unfortunately this has been the situation afflicting our society for many years now. Elite Corporate and governmental interests are now firmly in control of 'the message', whatever that may turn out to be.

So with what does this leave us? A mainstream media that predominantly bases its stories on what it is spoon-fed by third parties, because it has no choice in the matter. Ever-leaner staffing, compressed news cycles and access journalism all conspire to drive reporters to focus on the big stories of the day and which are to a large degree influenced by the parties that initiate the story in the first instance. This is all also similar to the effect achieved when reporters are seconded to military units on the 'front line' where they will naturally adopt the views of the people with whom they associate frequently and this only serves to help confirm that the media has fallen under the tight control of powerful interests.

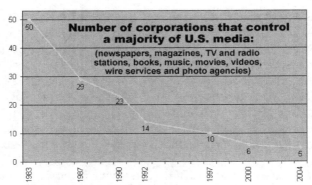

"The Media, which is almost exclusively owned by a tiny number of individuals who are loyal to the aims of the royal-political elite, promote the idea that via debate and elections, the People have some influence over the royal political elite. The media reinforces a view that the government exists in order to take on the responsibility of serving and protecting the People. The People have been sold the idea that because they have a government, then the responsibility of caring for their nation is being taken care of by the government. The People do not realise that by allowing a government of usually, wealthy individuals who play the role of politicians, to run a government 'for' the People, that this encumbers the People with a greater responsibility and that is to carefully scrutinise and monitor the activities of the government." Chris Everard, geopolitical researcher, author and film producer

The largest media conglomerate today is the Walt Disney Company Inc., whose chairman and CEO, Michael Eisner, is Jewish in line with the vast majority of the rest of the owners of the mainstream media and entertainment industry. There is of course nothing wrong per se with Jewish people owning media organisations, but when an entire industry is owned almost 100% by one group, representing a tiny minority of the overall population (less than 1%) then this should naturally lead to questions of impartiality regarding the overall message that we are being 'fed' 24/7. But of course it does not, as even that prerogative is denied us by dint of the fact that those in control of 'the message' also control who becomes privy to that fact itself.

The Disney Empire, headed by a man described by one media analyst as a 'control freak', includes several television production companies (Walt Disney Television, Touchstone Television, Buena Vista Television), its own cable network with 14 million subscribers and two video production companies. As for feature films, the Walt Disney Picture Group, headed by Joe Roth (also Jewish), includes Touchstone Pictures, Hollywood Pictures, and Caravan Pictures. Disney also owns Miramax Films, run by the Weinstein brothers (Jewish, too). When the Disney Company was run by the non-Jewish Disney family prior to its takeover by Eisner in 1984, it epitomised wholesome, family entertainment. While it still holds the rights to Snow White under Eisner, the company has now expanded into the production of works incorporating graphic sex and violence.

In addition, it also has 225 affiliated stations in the United States and is part owner of several European TV companies. ABC's cable subsidiary, ESPN, is headed by president and CEO Steven Bornstein, a Jew and this corporation also has a controlling share of Lifetime Television and the Arts and Entertainment Network cable companies. ABC Radio Network owns eleven AM and ten FM stations, again in major cities such as New York, Washington, Los Angeles and has over 3,400 affiliates. Although primarily a telecommunications company, Capital Cities/ABC earned over $1 billion in publishing in 1994 and it owns seven daily newspapers, Fairchild Publications, Chilton Publications and the Diversified Publishing Group.

Time Warner Inc., is the next largest of the international media giants. The chairman of the board and CEO, Gerald Levin, is also a Jew. Time Warner's subsidiary HBO is the country's largest pay-tv cable network. Warner Music is by far the largest record company in the world, with 50 labels, the biggest of which is Warner Brothers Records, headed by Danny Goldberg (Jewish). Stuart Hersch is president of Warnervision, Warner Music's video production unit and of course Goldberg and Hersch are Jewish. Warner Music was an early promoter of 'gangsta rap' through its involvement with Interscope Records and it therefore helped popularise a musical genre whose graphic lyrics explicitly urge black people to commit acts of violence against white people. In addition to cable and music, Time Warner is heavily involved in the production of feature films (Warner Brothers Studio) and publishing. Time Warner's publishing division (editor-in-chief Norman Pearlstine, a Jew) is the largest magazine publisher in the USA (Time, Sports Illustrated, People, Fortune). When Ted

Turner, a gentile (non-Jew) made a bid to buy CBS in 1985, there was panic in media boardrooms across the nation.

Although Turner employed a number of Jews in key executive positions in CNN and had never taken public positions contrary to Jewish interests, he is a man with a large ego and a strong personality and was regarded by Chairman William Paley (real name Palinsky, a Jew) and the other Jews at CBS as uncontrollable; a loose cannon who might at some time in the future turn against them. Furthermore, Jewish newsman Daniel Schorr, who had worked for Turner, publicly charged that his former boss held a personal dislike for Jews. And so to block Turner's bid, CBS executives invited billionaire Jewish theatre, hotel, insurance, and cigarette magnate Laurence Tisch to launch a 'friendly' takeover of the company and so from 1986 till 1995 Tisch was the chairman and CEO of CBS, removing any threat of non-Jewish influence there. Subsequent efforts by Turner to acquire a major network have been obstructed by Levin's Time Warner, which owns nearly 20 percent of CBS stock and has the power of veto over major deals.

Viacom Inc., run by Sumner Redstone (born Murray Rothstein) a Jew, is the third largest media corporation in the US, with revenues of over $10 billion a year. Viacom, which produces and distributes TV programmes for the three largest networks, owns 12 television stations and 12 radio stations. It produces feature films through Paramount Pictures, headed by Sherry Lansing (Jewish) and its publishing division includes Prentice Hall, Simon & Schuster, and Pocket Books. It distributes videos through over 4,000 Blockbuster stores. Viacom's chief claim to fame, however, is as the world's largest provider of cable programming, through its Showtime, MTV, Nickelodeon and other networks.

The most well-known of the 'smaller' media companies, DreamWorks SKG, is also Jewish owned and run. It was formed in 1994 amid great media hype by recording industry mogul David Geffen, former Disney Pictures chairman Jeffrey Katzenberg and film director Steven Spielberg, all three of whom are Jewish. The company produces movies, animated films, television programmes, and recorded music.

Two other large production companies, MCA and Universal Pictures, are both owned by Seagram Company Ltd. The president and CEO of Seagram, the brewing and distilling giant, is Edgar Bronfman Jr., who is also president of the World Jewish Congress. It is well known that Jews have controlled the production and distribution of films since the inception of the movie industry in the early decades of the 20th century. This, as can be witnessed in the previous paragraphs is still absolutely the case today. Films produced by just the five largest motion picture companies mentioned above; Disney, Warner Brothers, Sony, Paramount (Viacom), and Universal (Seagram) account for around 75% of the total box-office receipts for the entire industry.

The same story applies to TV and radio too with the entire market being corned by four at most five large conglomerates – all under the jurisdiction of Jews, mainly of American–Israeli dual nationality. Is there anyone who does not believe that this is not a dangerous state of affairs? To have a situation where an entire industry is controlled by a tiny minority interest group, whose motives in many areas of society have been seen and proven time after time to be not in the best interests of the overwhelming majority, surely cannot be regarded as healthy? Indeed, given the nature of that industry with its powerful capabilities of undue influence, should it collectively wish to bring those capabilities to bear, as it most certainly does, is not only an unhealthy situation, but I believe it no exaggeration to state that it is downright dangerous in the extreme.

After audio and visual news channels, daily newspapers are the most influential information medium in the western world. More than one quarter of a billion newspapers are sold each day in the US, South America and Europe alone. These millions are divided among some 4000 different publications. One might conclude that in the US, the sheer number of different newspapers would provide a safeguard against Jewish control and distortion. However, this is not the case as there is less independence, less competition, and much less representation of majority interests than a casual observer may give credit for. The days when most cities and even towns had several independently owned newspapers published by local people with close ties to the community are gone and unfortunately these days, most 'local' newspapers are owned by a much smaller number of large companies controlled by executives who live and work hundreds or even thousands of miles away. The fact is that only about 15 per cent of the country's 1,500 papers are independently owned; the rest belong to corporate chains. Only a few are large enough to maintain independent reporting staffs outside their own communities; the rest depend on these few for *all* of their national and international news.

In the newspaper industry, it is advertising revenue and not the relatively small retail cost price of the newspaper that pays the salaries and yields the owner his profits.

Whenever the large advertisers in a city choose to favour one newspaper over another with their business, the favoured paper will flourish while its competitor dies. Since the beginning of the 20th century, when Jewish mercantile power in America became a dominant economic force, there has been a inexorable rise in the number of newspapers entirely in Jewish ownership, accompanied by a steady decline in the number of competing non-Jewish-owned newspapers, primarily as a result of selective advertising policies by Jewish merchants. Furthermore, even those newspapers still under non-Jewish ownership and management are so thoroughly dependent upon Jewish advertising revenue that their editorial and news reporting policies are largely constrained by Jewish likes and dislikes. In the newspaper business as any other, the truth is that 'he who pays the piper calls the tune'.

The Wall Street Journal, which sells 1.8 million copies each weekday, is America's largest-circulation daily newspaper. It is owned by Dow Jones & Company, Inc., a New York corporation which also publishes 24 other daily newspapers and the weekly financial tabloid Barron's. The chairman and CEO of Dow Jones is Peter Kann, who is Jewish. Kann also holds the posts of chairman and publisher of the Wall Street Journal. Indeed most of New York's other major newspapers are also entirely owned by Jews. The New York Daily News is owned by Jewish real-estate developer Mortimer B. Zuckerman and The Village Voice is the personal property of Leonard Stern, the billionaire Jewish owner of the Hartz Mountain pet supply firm.

Three of the six largest book publishers in the U.S., according to Publisher's Weekly, are owned or controlled by Jews.

The three are; in 1st place Random House (with its many subsidiaries, including Crown Publishing Group), 3rd place Simon & Schuster, and 6th place Time Warner Trade Group (including Warner Books and Little, Brown). Another publisher of special significance is Western Publishing and although it ranks only 13th in size among all US publishers, it ranks first among publishers of children's books, with more than 50% of the entire market. Western Publishing is entirely Jewish owned and run.

I would urge you to check these facts for yourself and not simply take my word for it. The Internet is a very powerful tool so please do use it whilst we still can.

The questions here should be how can such a system exist in a supposed democracy such as in which we are supposed to live and also how can a tiny minority group such as this be allowed to get away with having such a hugely disproportionate influence over us all? For the avoidance of doubt and to sidestep any possible accusations of 'anti-Semitism' here, I should point out that I have no personal issue with the Jewish people of the world; they have probably been exploited more than most down the years, but it is a very dangerous state of affairs indeed to allow one tiny, vociferous group to exert such absolute control over us all, be they Jewish, Muslim, fundamental Christian or indeed any other narrowly-defined interest.

By permitting one tiny group to control our news and entertainment media, we are doing more than merely giving them a decisive influence on our political system and virtual control of our governments; we are also allowing them control of the minds and souls of our children, whose attitudes and ideas are shaped more by television and films than by their parents, their schools, or indeed any other influence.

Controlling the media does not mean controlling every single journalist, far from it in fact. All that is necessary to achieve this objective is to set the parameters through which the mainstream media filters everything. For example, five to six hundred years ago and earlier, the consensus passed-down from the hierarchy was that the world is flat and therefore this became the de facto 'truth' and anything that contradicted that premise was not even tolerated, let alone up for discussion. You may think that the days when this would be allowed to happen are long-gone, but you would be wrong. Take by way of an example, those old friends, the theory of evolution, the big bang theory and even global warming. Because these ideas are so deeply enmeshed into the belief systems of those who wish to deceive and thereby control us, anything that challenges these theories (for that is simply all they are) is either ignored, deliberately destroyed or mocked in order to maintain the status quo. Indeed such is the entrenchment of these false premises within our historical model that everything else, newly discovered 'facts' and theories alike, must either be ruthlessly suppressed or at best be 'bent' in order to fit the currently accepted paradigm.

Thus is it essential to maintain a media that conforms to these norms, these established 'truisms' and this is why the media themselves are wont to endlessly repeat these mantras in order to embed these falsehoods deep within our psyche and so when we hear challenges to these pre-conceived notions, we will experience a deep-seated urge to defend them unconditionally. Such is the programming to which we are subjected day after day, without any realisation of the fact that it is taking place at all. This is also true of the 'foot-soldiers' of the media, the TV reporters, the 'street-level' newspaper hacks and their ilk. All they do is repeat the 'party line' imbued in them by the society of which they are an integral part.

In addition, so many of these people are products of the Elite propaganda machine, euphemistically known as 'education'. The more education to which one has been subjected, the greater the resistance there will be to anything that contradicts its sacred edicts. It matters not whether these people are politically, right left or centre or even so-called radicals; they are all system-clones. They may well wish to change things politically and/or speak out against perceived injustices, but only strictly within the parameters of the system which they of course defend and support unconditionally and do not recognise as being a form of enslavement.

Once one is aware of what goes on daily in the media world, it becomes easy to see that journalists of all colours habitually misrepresent what is happening in the world today. They are of course bound by and unduly influenced by the laid-down 'norms' of society and so everything reported has to be twisted to fit within this fake architecture that has been in place for millennia, albeit incrementally adjusted over time. Not one serious mainstream journalist ever publicly questioned the official 9/11 story for example, despite the fact that it has more holes than a colander. Why? Because the official explanation has become the de facto truth and therefore anything that causes ripples or serious undercurrents to flow in that direction must be false by definition. This is how the whole process works.

In fact the official version of anything and everything is simply repeated ad nauseum by the media in all its forms and becomes the 'truth' by default even though the most cursory examination of the facts would reveal it all to be built on foundations of sand.

In conclusion to this section, the only 'real' journalism left on this planet is to be found via the Internet. The World Wide Web is full of alternative news sources, providing a more balanced view of the world and reporting facts without resort to lies and propaganda. Internet based researchers and journalists are often unafraid to go to places where their mainstream counterparts dare not venture. However, please beware of the 'shills' (paid agents of disinformation) that lurk there in huge numbers, purveying lies and distortions to throw the real truth-seekers 'off the scent' as it were.

The Elite families of course, control all the major Internet servers and search engines plus all the social media and networking sites and the Internet has aided their cause in several other important respects, not least of which is the area of covert surveillance. It is believed by many that the technology exists to read all emails sent from anywhere in the world, triggered by keywords and perhaps even more worryingly, to remotely read the contents of PC hard-drives via the Internet and also to detect keystrokes even as they are being made and thus spy on the author of any 'incriminating' writings, in effect.

However, the Elite is known to be terrified by the exponential growth of the 'truth movement', largely facilitated by the availability to all of the Internet and its power to inform and there is no doubt that there will continue to be efforts made to try to censor and restrict its availability in order to try to close-down this weakness in their defences.

It is up to us, the people to ensure that we do not allow this to happen by passively accepting whatever measures are used against us. Censorship and restriction of the internet may well be used as a tool disrupt the flow of valuable information to the masses. If the Elite succeed in cutting-off this lifeline, then the future could be very bleak indeed.

The Illusion of Democracy

In order to maintain absolute control of everything whilst maintaining pretence of the existence of freedom of choice for the people, the Elite must create the illusion of a fair and just system for all. This system is already in place and is what we now know as 'democracy' which effectively presents the illusion of giving precedence to the majority view, but which in reality does the exact opposite.

The only way that it is possible for a small few to control the majority of the world is through the utilisation of this illusion. As stated previously, the Elite learned long ago that attempting to control the masses using overt shows of force or by autocratic government, does not succeed because there will always be almost constant unrest and rebellion seething in the background which will occasionally erupt into violent confrontations and force them into battles they would not wish to fight, given the choice. So, how much better for them that the masses should be contented with a system that creates the impression that they are to all intents and purposes, free from tyranny and better yet, actually have a say and a stake-holding in their own lives and futures?

Politicians of all persuasions are mere puppets, slaves to the system controlled and run by a tiny minority in the shadows. These politicians will never be put forward for senior office within their parties unless they are willing and able to 'toe the party line' which is of course dictated from on high by the Elite. In this way they are able to control both sides of the illusory two-party state, with consummate ease. This creates an impression that it is the politicians themselves who control a country's purse strings and its domestic and foreign policies, but this is of course an illusion. How often do we see these glove-puppets in 'high-level' meetings and 'summits' issuing proclamations and decrees about this or that aspect of our lives or about events over which they have no control whatsoever?

This is the point at which our controlled media steps-in to the breach and perpetuates the illusion by grandiose statements about which politician has said what, about whichever subject is the 'hot' news of the moment.

In truth we all live in a one-party state in the western world, contrary to what we have been told and have believed all our lives. It is vital that we all cease believing that voting for one major party over another one will have any effect whatsoever upon our lives or our personal bank balances. Nothing can or will be changed by any politician, because they are all pawns, meaningless, powerless figureheads, marching to the tune of an unseen band. For example, in Britain, it is impossible to vote for a party which is not 100% committed to further and further centralisation of power in the EU, with a central currency and a central bank, simply because that is exactly what the Elite wishes to happen and therefore they would not permit any politician to come to power who is not prepared to follow that particular diktat to the letter.

And should anyone point-out that other, smaller party's policies may go against those of the mainstream, they are absolutely, completely missing the point altogether. Should political parties with any chance of winning, agree on the fundamentals, elections are instantly rendered an irrelevance, a farce if you will, because no matter who 'wins' the election, exactly the same policies will be promulgated.

What may be confusing to some is that politicians who are on different sides of the so-called divide appear publicly to be proscribing very different, often opposite viewpoints on party policies. This is simply because it allows them to appear to be in opposition when they are really on the same side.

"I will conclude by mentioning a factor which has unnecessarily puzzled some western commentators on my case. That was the liberal smokescreen behind which I concealed my real opinions. One writer who knew me in Beirut has stated that the liberal opinions I expressed in the Middle East were 'certainly' my true ones. Another comment from a personal friend was that I could not have maintained such a consistently liberal-intellectual framework unless I had really believed in it.   Both remarks are very flattering. The first duty of an underground worker is to perfect not only his cover story but his cover personality." Kim Philby, British-born Soviet spy

When assessing political views it is important to bear in mind that we are often observing a façade, a cover-up and a person concealing his real intentions and opinions to deliberately deceive us. Behind this thin veneer, lies the Elite and their insidious plans for mankind for which the covert one-party state is but a stepping-stone along the way.

9/11 – The 'Real' Background Story

"September 11, 2001 served as pretext to consolidate power, destroy civil liberties and human rights and wage permanent wars against invented enemies for global dominance over world markets, resources, and cheap labour - notably at home and throughout Eurasia, Europe, the Middle East, North Africa and Asia at the expense of democratic freedoms and social justice."   Stephen Lendman, 'The Business of America is War', June 2011

In mid-2000, the now sadly deceased film-maker Aaron Russo was invited to meet the Zionist Nicholas Rockefeller, an invitation which he accepted and they quickly became friends. After a few meetings, Rockefeller confided in Russo that 'next year there is going to be an event'. When Russo quizzed him about this 'event', Rockefeller told him that this event would give America and its allies an excuse to invade Iraq and Afghanistan in order that they could construct pipelines through to the Caspian Sea and also to take over the Iraqi oil fields and also that the 'bogeyman' Osama bin Laden would be blamed. This then he said, would lead to soldiers looking for non-existent enemies in caves in Afghanistan and Pakistan and that there would be an endless 'war on terror where there is no real enemy and the whole thing is a gigantic hoax'. It would also lead to further stringent restrictions and controls over the American people which they would accept for their own 'safety'.

On the 11th September 2001, the World Trade Centre complex in New York along with the Pentagon, the HQ of the US military in Washington DC was purportedly the victim of a concerted attack by Muslim terrorists, who according to George W. Bush, US president at the time, were 'resentful of American freedoms'.

Let us take a minute to re-acquaint ourselves with the official explanation, which is not generally regarded as a 'conspiracy theory' despite the fact that it comprises an amazing conspiracy. The official 'truth' is that a handful of young Muslim Arabs who could not fly planes, mainly Saudi Arabians who therefore came neither from Iraq nor from Afghanistan, outwitted not only the CIA and the FBI, but also all the other 16 US intelligence agencies and all intelligence agencies of US allies including Israel's Mossad, which is believed to have penetrated and/or be in control of or even have created, every terrorist organisation and which carries out assassinations with impunity, of those whom it deems to be terrorists.

In addition to outwitting every intelligence agency of the United States and its allies, this group of young Saudi Arabians defied all the odds, by four of their number learning to fly hugely complex, giant four-engined passenger jets by the simple expedient of undertaking a dozen or so flying lessons in single-engined, twin seater, turbo-prop planes and yet who were skilful enough flyers to perform high-speed, gravity-defying manoeuvres that even highly experienced airline pilots said were way beyond their own skills. They also outwitted the National Security Council, the US State Department, NORAD, airport security four times in the same hour on the same morning, air traffic control, caused the US Air Force to be unable to launch interceptor aircraft in time and also caused three well-built steel-structured buildings, including one not even hit by a plane, to fail suddenly in a few seconds as a result of extremely limited structural damage and small, short-lived, low-temperature fires that burned on a few floors.

These same 'terrorists' were even able to confound the laws of physics and cause WTC buildings 1, 2 and 7 to collapse at free-fall speed, a physical impossibility in the absence of explosives used in controlled demolition.

The story that the government and the media have told us amounts to a gigantic conspiracy, really a script almost too far-fetched for a film script. Yet, anyone who doubts this improbable conspiracy theory is either defined into irrelevance or consigned to lunacy by the world's compliant media.

Then we should consider the fact that the three WTC buildings all collapsed, we are meant to believe, due to the high temperatures generated by the burning jet fuel melting the steel supports and the so-called 'pancake-effect' of floor upon floor collapsing almost in free-fall and defying all known laws of physics. Surely it does not need a structural engineer to tell anyone that three gigantic steel and concrete buildings, two of 110 storeys and another of 47 storeys, plummeting to the ground at free-fall speed would require the assistance of strategically placed explosives in the form of demolition charges? All one needs is one working eye and even a partially-functioning brain to arrive at this most obvious of conclusions.

Should we then also disregard the plain, unambiguous scientific fact that jet fuels burns at less than 900⁰ F whilst steel will only begin to melt or even lose its strength at temperatures in excess of 1600⁰ F? In fact has anyone ever considered from what material jet engines are constructed? Hmm, yes let me see.... err steel is it not? Very strange then that there are no airliners constantly falling out of the sky all over the world if burning jet fuel is able to melt or even undermine the strength of steel.

However, this chapter is not meant to be a simple, standard 'de-bunk' of the official story as this approach is available from a vast multitude of other reliable sources. Rather it presents a possible, plausible alternative scenario, backed-up in the main by proven facts but with a little circumstantial evidence also thrown in for good measure.

"There is nothing wrong with circumstantial evidence. In criminal cases before a judge or jury, the verdict will depend on circumstantial evidence if there is an absence of direct or eyewitness evidence." Mary W. Maxwell PhD

So, who **could** have performed such an elaborate operation and why?

Firstly, let us turn back the clock to an unusual and eerie prediction that was made by a most sinister individual, many years ago. This prediction, in conjunction with the status of the person from whom it emanated, is extremely indicative and revealing in terms of who planned and executed 9/11.

Isser Harel was a spymaster of the Israeli Intelligence Services, director of Mossad and Shin Bet from 1952-1963. In 1979, twenty two years prior to 2001, Isser Harel predicted with uncanny accuracy the events of 9/11 to Michael D. Evans, an American Zionist.

On the 23rd September 1979, Evans visited Harel at his home in Israel and had dinner with him and Dr. Reuven Hecht, a senior adviser to the then prime minister, Menachem Begin. In an editorial entitled 'America the Target', published in the Jerusalem Post of 30th September 2001, Evans, an Ashkenazi Jew masquerading as a Christian, asked Harel about Muslim/Arab terrorism and if it would come to America. Harel told Evans that Arab terrorists would likely strike the 'tallest building in New York City' because it was a 'phallic symbol'. The fact that 9/11 was planned by the Mossad through the admittance of Isser Harel is well documented and appears in a book written by Michael Evans, 'The American Prophecy'.

The first step in the preparation of the 9/11 attacks was to secure the passing of the WTC complex into private hands. This was crucial to the success of 9/11 because without complete private control over the complex, there could be no opportunity or possibility of setting explosive demolition charges in place as the 'coup de grace' in razing the towers to the ground.

At this point, let us investigate in some detail, four key Jewish/Zionist crime-network assets:

Larry Silverstein. Silverstein is a Jewish Israeli-American dual nationality businessman from New York. He obtained a 99 year lease on the entire WTC complex on 24th July 2001, less than seven weeks before the fateful day. These buildings, at the time, were almost worthless due to the fact that they were riddled from basement to roof with tons of deadly asbestos that urgently needed removal on health and safety grounds; a process that would in cost-terms have been at least the equivalent of the cost of the lease itself, if not much more. Silverstein publicly explained his reason for purchasing the WTC twin towers as 'I felt a compelling urge to own them'. Is this really a believable reason coming from a supposedly hard-headed, successful businessman? He apparently took breakfast in the 'Windows on the World' restaurant (located in North Tower, 107th floor) every single morning apart from the fact that his routine was changed for the first time on the morning of 9/11 along with that of his two offspring, who also worked in the WTC and also conveniently decided to take the day off on that one particular day. Either the Silverstein family is clairvoyant, or they knew exactly what was planned that day. By all means, take your pick, but I know which scenario I feel is most plausible.

Silverstein obtained more than $4.5bn in insurance pay-outs as a result of the destruction of his 'past its sell-by date' complex. He also just so happened to be personal friends with that key player in the Zionist-controlled media, Rupert Murdoch and the former Israeli president and infamous Zionist war-criminal Ariel Sharon, as well as the Israeli PM, Benjamin Netanyahu. Silverstein was such good friends with Netanyahu that they spoke on the phone every week.

Frank Lowy. Lowy is a Czech-born Jew and was the owner of *Westfield America*, one of the biggest shopping-mall conglomerates in the world. Lowy leased the shopping concourse area 'The Mall' at the World Trade Centre, made up of approximately 427,000 square feet of retail floor space and he has quite an interesting history. He was a member of the Golani Brigade and fought in the Israeli 'war of independence'. Before this he was a member of Haganah, a Jewish terrorist organisation responsible for bringing about the founding of Israel and which incidentally was covertly funded by the Nazis during WWII. Frank Lowy spends three months of the year at his home in Israel and has been described by the Sydney Morning Herald as 'a self-made man with a strong interest in the Holocaust and Israeli politics'. He funded and launched the Israeli Institute for National Strategy and Policy, which 'operates within the framework of Tel Aviv University' in Israel. He is also close friends with many top Israeli officials such as Ehud Olmert, Ariel Sharon, Netanyahu (yes, him again), and Ehud Barak and was also implicated in an Israeli bank scandal with Olmert. Frank Lowy also 'fortunately' avoided the WTC carnage on 9/11, contrary to his normal habits.

Lewis Eisenberg. This Jewish 'criminal' was the head of the Port Authority of New York and authorised the lease being transferred to his Zionist brethren Silverstein and Lowy.   Eisenberg was a large financial contributor to the Bush-Cheney presidential campaign, as well as being a partner in the corrupt, Jewish/Zionist banking conglomerate Goldman-Sachs. Eisenberg has been both a member of the planning board of the United Jewish Appeal / United Jewish Federation pro-Israeli government pressure group in the US.

Ronald Lauder. This billionaire Estee Lauder cosmetics magnate was the chairman of New York Governor George Pataki's commission on privatisation. He is the key individual involved in lobbying for the privatisation of the WTC, but he was also instrumental in the transfer of the former Stewart US Air Force Base from public (military) to private ownership. Oddly and significantly enough, the flight paths of flight 175 and flight 11 converged directly over this very same base. Could both these flights have been diverted here and substituted for drones (radio controlled planes) mocked up to entirely resemble the originals?

Lauder is active in the following organisations: Conference of Presidents of Major American Jewish Organizations, Jewish National Fund, World Jewish Congress, American Jewish Joint Distribution Committee, the Anti-Defamation League (ADL) and the Jewish Theological Seminary. Ronald Lauder was elected president of the

World Jewish Congress on 10th June 2007. He also founded a school for the Mossad in Herzliya, Israel, the 'Lauder School of Government Diplomacy and Strategy'. He is the key player involved in the preparation of 9/11.

The second crucial aspect that needed to be established in order to perpetrate the 9/11 attacks was the necessity to gain control of the security of the WTC complex. This way, Mossad explosive experts that just 'fortuitously' happened to be in New York in the run-up to 9/11, could be readily allowed access to strategic areas of the buildings in order to prepare for the affixing of the demolition charges.

It is a little-known or reported fact that on the weekend immediately preceding 9/11, company owners and employees alike, were told that the twin towers would be closed from Friday night until Monday morning, for 'essential security maintenance' and therefore access to their offices would be temporarily unavailable at these times. Could 'essential security maintenance' perhaps be a euphemism for the emplacement of powerful explosive charges at strategic structural positions?

The contract to run security at the WTC was awarded to Kroll Associates after the 1993 WTC bombing. Kroll is sometimes referred to as 'Wall Street's CIA'. So, who awarded them the contract? The Port Authority of New York paid them $2.5 million to revamp security at the complex. The owners of Kroll were two Zionist Jews named Jules and Jeremy Kroll and the managing director of Kroll at the time was Jerome M. Hauer. Hauer was also the one chosen to run Mayor Rudy Giuliani's Office of Emergency Management (OEM) from 1996 to 2000. He is the key individual that lobbied for this office to be located in Silverstein's WTC building 7.

Jerome Hauer is also Jewish and a staunch Zionist. His mother, Rose Muscatine Hauer, is the retired Dean of the Beth Israel School of Nursing and the Honorary President of the New York Chapter of Hadassah, the Daughters of Zion movement that is one of the central Zionist organizations involved in the creation and maintenance of the State of Israel. Another barely known fact is that it was Jerome Hauer who advised the entire White House staff to take the antibiotic known to be most effective against Anthrax, 'Cipro', a week prior to the Anthrax mailings. How fortunate and convenient. How did he know?

Hauer is an 'expert' in bio-terrorism and was the one who was in charge of the response to the Anthrax attacks. His reactions to the Anthrax mailings were 'very slow' to say the least and he wasted no opportunity to invoke 'Osama Bin Laden' in his subsequent public rhetoric.

Former FBI special agent, John O'Neil, who was tasked with investigating Bin Laden coincidentally enough, was hired as head of security at the WTC by Jerome Hauer. Interestingly, O'Neil was killed on his very first day at work – 9/11.

It is important to note that O'Neil had resigned his post at the FBI after his investigation into the *USS Cole* attack in Yemen was obstructed and sabotaged by the US Ambassador to Yemen, the Zionist Barbara Bodine. This is because the *USS Cole* attack was not carried out by the non-existent 'Al Qaeda' as was widely reported by the mainstream, it was hit by an Israeli cruise missile and AQ was blamed (as usual) to sway public opinion against Arabs and Muslims in general as well as to demonise the Democrat party 'they did not take the terror threat seriously enough!', so that the Elite puppet George Bush the lesser, could be installed into office in time for 9/11. This was of course completely covered up, also as usual.

The third crucial aspect that had to be established was the gaining control of security at all of the airports from which the 'hijackings' would originate. Passenger screening needed to be handled by their operatives in order to allow certain people and certain items (i.e. weapons) onto the planes.

And who ran security at all three airports of the alleged hijackings?

None other than ICTS International and Huntsleigh USA (a wholly owned subsidiary) owned by Ezra Harel and Menachem Atzmon, both Israeli, Zionist-Jews. This organisation is run by 'experts' in the security and intelligence field. Israeli intelligence (Mossad) that is. Most employees are ex- Shin Bet agents.

Is this airport security company, who ran the security at Boston's Logan airport, as well as Newark, New Jersey airport, really so incompetent as to allow 19 Arab terrorists on board four different planes with box-cutters, mace and even guns, or is there something more sinister going on here? Menachem Atzmon, former Israeli Likud party treasurer in the 1980s, was involved in an Israeli political scandal involving Ehud Olmert and other Likud members in Israel. He was convicted of fraud, falsifying documents, as well as breaching Party Funding Law. However, back to the story;

ICTS was also in charge of airport security when the shoe bomber, Richard Reid, allegedly boarded a plane with a shoe bomb. If Reid was really a terrorist and not just an innocent man being used by the Mossad to incite more fear of terrorism, then why did ICTS let him board the plane knowing he could be dangerous?

Another point indicating ICTS's complicity is that a few hours before the Patriot Act was voted on, it was edited to make foreign companies in charge of security on 9/11 immune to lawsuits.   This would effectively prevent American courts from demanding that ICTS provide testimony or hand over the missing surveillance videos from the airports.

"Given the pervasiveness of Zionist influence in the US government and its intelligence and security agencies (including of course the Defence Department), two broad scenarios are possible. One is that the neo-cons and their cohorts were in the driver's seat with Israel in the passenger seat with a map and the baggage. The second sees Israel driving with the neo-cons and others handling the map and baggage. But they were both in the same car on the road to and from 9/11. Both were embedded in aspects of the planning and execution of the catastrophe, the wars it spawned and the wars its architects now want us to wage in Israel's name, linking treason and treachery in tandem no matter where the emphasis is placed." Dr. Alan Sabrosky, 'Israel and the Tactics of Mistake', 2011

To backtrack slightly, in October of 2000, approximately 11 months before 9/11, a retired Israeli Defence Force (IDF) officer and veteran of the Yom Kippur War (1973), was collecting ivy cuttings at the Gomel Chesed Jewish Cemetery located near the city boundaries of Elizabeth and Newark, New Jersey. He overheard two men having a conversation in Hebrew, which drew his attention. He remained behind an 8 foot wall and listened in to their conversation as they stood below. Shortly afterwards a car approached the two people, presumably Israelis and a man emerged to greet them. Normal pleasantries were exchanged, after which the third man said:

'The Americans will learn what it is to live with terrorism after the planes hit the twins in September.'

One of the men that had been leaning against the retaining wall expressed concerns regarding whether the upcoming presidential election (November 2000) could impact the plans but the man that arrived by car allayed their fears by saying:

'Don't worry, we have people in high places and no matter who gets elected, they will take care of everything.'

The observer who overheard this conversation related it to the FBI on numerous occasions only to be totally ignored each time. Nothing was done about it and no investigation into the incident has ever taken place.

The Israeli instant-messaging company, *Odigo*, later admitted that two of its employees received instant messages warning of an impending attack 2 hours prior to the first plane hitting. This warning, which could have saved thousands of lives, was not passed on to the authorities. I wonder why.

Odigo has a feature in its messaging service that allows the forwarding of messages through a search feature based on nationality, eg. Israeli. Knowing these two particular Israelis were forewarned, is it not very likely that they passed the message on to other Israelis considering that out of the 4000 Israelis believed to be working in and around the WTC and the Pentagon at the time of the attacks, only five were killed. Five out of 4000 Israelis? Mathematically (if Israelis were not forewarned), about 10% (400 of 4000) would have died; even as low as 200-300 of 4000 would not really indicate foreknowledge, yet only five Israelis died and two of the five were actually aboard the supposedly hijacked flights; therefore only three Israelis died at the WTC on 9/11. This is by any measure an utterly astonishing fact. To be clear, I am talking about 'Israelis' here and not simply 'American Jews'. Many innocent, decent Jewish people died in the WTC complex on 9/11.

Odigo has offices in New York and in Herzliya, Israel. Herzliya also happens to be the home of the Headquarters of Mossad. Not to worry – just a coincidence, I am sure. The company was later bought out by another Israeli company *Comverse*. The CEO of *Comverse* was Kobi Alexander, a dual Israeli-US citizen, with connections to Mossad. He has been charged on several counts of fraud.

It is now a matter of record that on 10th September 2001, the Tokyo branch of the Zionist-owned, Goldman Sachs organisation, formally warned its American employees to steer clear of American buildings.

ZIM, an Israeli company, vacated its offices (10,000 square feet) in the North WTC tower the week before 9/11, breaking its lease in the process. 49% of this company is owned by the Israeli government. The lease did not expire until the end of 2001, and the company lost around $50,000 for breaking the contract. Later, FBI agent Michael Dick who was investigating Israeli spy-rings before and after 9/11 and also enquiring into this suspicious move was removed from his duties by the head of the Justice Department's criminal division, the Zionist, Michael Chertoff.

According to a CIA source who worked closely with Dick, the Israeli movers moved in explosives when ZIM moved out. With ZIM Israel hastily exiting just in time, this left only one Israeli company, *Clearforest* with 19 employees, in the WTC on 9/11. Of their five employees in the building at the time, all managed to escape.

An elite US Army study centre had devised a strategy for enforcing a major Israeli-Palestinian peace accord that would require about 20,000 well-armed troops stationed throughout Israel and a newly created Palestinian state. The SAMS initiative attempts to predict events in the first year of a peace-enforcement operation and assesses possible dangers for US troops from both sides. Of the *Mossad*, the Israeli intelligence service, the SAMS officers said: *"Wildcard, ruthless and cunning. Has the capability to target US forces and make it look like a Palestinian/Arab act."*

Shortly before 9/11, over 140 Israelis had been arrested for suspected espionage. Some of them were posing as art students. These suspects targeted or penetrated military bases, DEA, FBI, Secret Service, BATF, US Customs, IRS, INS, EPA, the Interior Dept., US Marshal's Service, various US attorney's offices, secret government offices and unlisted private homes of law enforcement / intelligence officers. Most of the suspects served in military intelligence, electronic surveillance intercept and or explosive ordinance units.

Dozens of other Israelis were arrested in American malls selling toys, acting as a front for a spying operation. Sixty detained suspects worked for the Israeli company *AMDOCS* which provides most directory assistance calls and almost all call records and billings services for the US by virtue of its contracts with the 25 largest telephone companies in the US.

All the alleged 9/11 hijackers had fake IDs. During a joint FBI-CIA operation against the lead 'patsy' hijacker Mohammad Atta in Fort Lee, New Jersey in 2001, the operation was photographed by Israeli agents and thereby compromised. These Zionist Jews were providing cover for their future patsy hijacker teams.

Immediately following 9/11, over 60 Israelis were detained either under the Patriot anti-Terrorism Act or for immigrations violations. Some of them were active Israeli military personnel. A number of them failed polygraph (lie detector) interrogations when questioned for surveillance activities against the US and some of them were found to have been spying on Arabs.

Israelis caught up in terror sweep

■ Of the nearly 1,100 foreigners arrested after Sept. 11, 90 to 100 are Israeli citizens

By Jim Galloway
The Atlanta Journal-Constitution

NAZARETH, Israel — The day after the world changed, Roy Barak and his partner were in an empty rental truck, heading east on In-

are still in American jails are becoming increasingly impatient.
Local journalists now press the U.S. ambassador, Daniel Kurtzar, on the issue. Members of the Israeli parliament have handed him a petition. The parents of the five movers still being held in a federal prison in Brooklyn have enlisted the help of the mayor of Jerusalem. Ehud Olmert, relying on his close ties to New York City Mayor Rudolph Giuliani.
Olmert has called Giuliani twice, to no avail. Custody of the men is a

military — do the heavy lifting for the moving industry.
Barak, a former paratrooper, got a job with Urban Moving Systems of Weehawken, N.J., in summer 2000. Starting pay was $7 an hour plus tips. Mostly, Barak stayed east. He saw Miami, delivered furniture to Atlanta and drove by Graceland in Memphis.
Like other Israelis, he gave little thought to his expired visa — until Sept. 11.
At the police station, Barak allowed his

not smiling."
And even if they were smiling, he said, that the reactions of Israelis with fresh military experience are bound to seem peculiar to others. His friends had seen acts of brutality and terrorism nearly every day. Barak himself had spent six months in Lebanon.
"It's a little bit different how the Israeli thinks." Barak said.

Of the 90-100 or so detained Israelis there was a group of five individuals, now popularly known as the 'dancing Israelis' who were spotted in multiple locations filming and celebrating the WTC attacks.

The men were detained by the New York Police Department (NYPD). Both the police and FBI field agents alike became very suspicious when they found maps of the city with certain places highlighted, box-cutters, $4700 cash stuffed in a sock and foreign passports. Police also told the newspaper, the *Bergen Record* that bomb-sniffing dogs were brought to the van and that they reacted as if they had detected explosives.

The names of the five 'dancing' Israelis were Sivan Kurzberg, Paul Kurzberg, Yaron Schmuel, Oded Ellner and Omer Marmari and according to the TV programme *ABC News 20/20*, after this group were detained, the driver of the van, Sivan Kurzberg told the police officers:

"We are Israeli. We are not your problem. Your problems are our problems. The Palestinians are the problem."

They later appeared on an Israeli TV talk show and claimed to be there 'documenting the event'. Witnesses reported their cameras were all set-up and prepared to film and record prior to the first plane strike and were seen congratulating each another afterwards. The five jubilant Israelis were also seen photographing one another and dancing with joy. The FBI seized and developed their photographs, one of which shows Sivan Kurzberg flicking a cigarette lighter in front of the smouldering ruins in an apparently celebratory gesture.

The *Jerusalem Post* also reported that a white van with a bomb was stopped as it approached the George Washington Bridge, but the ethnicity of the suspects was not revealed. Here is exactly what the Jerusalem Post reported on 12th September 2001:

"American security services overnight stopped a car bomb on the George Washington Bridge. The van, packed with explosives, was stopped on an approach ramp to the bridge. Authorities suspect the terrorists intended to blow up the main crossing between New Jersey and New York, Army Radio reported."

Imagine the surprise of the officers involved in the arrests, when these terror suspects turned-out to be Israelis.

Another of the more bizarre events of the day was manifest in the form of a mysterious white van parked a few blocks away from the twin towers on 6th and King Street, that had a mural painted on the side that literally depicted a jetliner crashing into the twin towers and a wording of '9/11'. The sheer arrogance of this act defies belief. It also shows a blind indifference as to whether or not they would be considered suspects in the event – presumably being safe in the knowledge that they knew they would 'get away with murder' even in the event of their being arrested.

This photograph was taken 11th September 2001, New York City.
One heck of a fast paint job!

The two suspects sitting in the van ran away when the van was stopped and were apprehended shortly thereafter amidst a minor struggle. A police recording also indicates that the mural van subsequently 'exploded' following the detainment of the two suspects.

Further corroboration of this incident came in the form of a reference in the February 2006 Norman Y. Mineta International Institute for Surface Transportation Policy Studies (MTI) report entitled, *'Saving City Lifelines: Lessons Learned in the 9/11 Terrorist Attacks'*.

The relevant quote is as follows:

"There were continuing moments of alarm. A panel truck with a painting of a plane flying into the World Trade Centre was stopped near the temporary command post. It proved to be rented to a group of ethnic Middle Eastern people who did not speak English. Fearing that it might be a truck bomb, the NYPD immediately evacuated the area, called out the bomb squad and detained the occupants until a thorough search was made. The vehicle was found to be an innocent delivery truck."

Please pardon my extreme scepticism. Apparently the author of this quote would like us to believe that they did not find it odd that a delivery truck rented to 'ethnic middle-easterners' was professionally spray-painted with a mural depicting the exact events of the same day! The idiocy of their conclusion that this van was an 'innocent delivery truck' is totally beyond words. Also notice that there was no mention of it exploding as the police transmission confirmed. The 'ethnic middle-easterners' referenced in this quote were certainly not Arabic or Muslim individuals as there is not a single mention of this incident in the 9/11 commission report. If they were Arabs there would be no reason to cover this up and indeed a huge issue is likely to have been made of it. The fact that this incident was covered-up is also a strong indication that these 'ethnic middle-easterners', were in fact Israelis.

All of the white vans were working for the ostensible moving company, *Urban Moving Systems* under the direction of Dominic Suter, a known Israeli Spy who immediately fled (was allowed to escape?) back to Israel after the attacks. It was confirmed by two former CIA officers that this Israeli moving company was a front operation for the Mossad. The two CIA sources noted that movers vans are a common intelligence cover and the Israelis involved were held in custody for 71 days before being quietly released.

Most national security computerised systems responsible for the scrambling of jets in the event of national emergencies such as multiple hijackings were running on software developed by *Ptech Software*. The list of *Ptech* clients is a veritable 'Who's who' of governmental and associated organisations and includes the FAA, NATO, United States Armed Forces, Congress, the Dept. of Energy, Dept. of Justice, FBI, US Customs, the IRS, the Secret Service, most of the other US 'alphabet soup' agencies and even the White House.

The Zionist Jew Michael Goff was marketing manager at *Ptech* and also worked for an Israeli database company *Guardium* (Director, Amit Yoran). *Guardium* has been funded by *Cedar Fund*, *Veritas Venture Partners*, and *StageOne*, both of which are Mossad funding outfits. So, *Ptech*, was essentially a cover for an American 'Sayan' (i.e. a Jewish agent who works with the Mossad when necessary), Michael Goff, who had Mossad agents feeding him information and directing him while he worked with his Lebanese Muslim 'partners' in *Ptech*.

Now why would a young American lawyer working with a good law firm (Sedar & Chandler) in his home town suddenly abandon his practice of law and team-up with a start-up software company owned and financed by a Lebanese and a Saudi? Goff's family is a well-respected and well-known family in Worcester, Massachusetts. He was well set-up for life at a reputable, prosperous law firm after leaving law school, so why the sudden career change?

Because Mossad asked him to do it, presumably for the 'good of the Jewish people', etc, etc. Under Goff, *Ptech* software complete with 'trapdoors' and 'Trojan Horses' was sold and loaded onto the most sensitive computer systems that either failed miserably, or performed well (depending on your point of view), on the 11th September 2001. Goff's father and grandfather, Samuel, were accountants who belonged to Worcester's 'Commonwealth Lodge 600 of B'nai B'rith'. They were both 32nd Degree Freemasons.

Mitre is a major defence contracting organisation headed by former Director of Central Intelligence, James Schlesinger. It has been said that Schlesinger is a devout Lutheran, but Wikipedia states that he was born to Russian/Austrian Jewish parents. He is undoubtedly a Zionist. *Ptech* was with the *Mitre Corporation* in the basement of the Federal Aviation Agency (FAA) for two years immediately prior to 9/11. Their specific job was to investigate inter-operability issues the FAA had with NORAD and the US Air Force in the case of an emergency.

The first plane to hit the WTC (North Tower) directly hit the computer room of *Marsh & McLennan*, which had recently acquired Kroll Associates, which was jointly-owned by a son of AIG CEO, Maurice Greenberg and Jules Kroll. Was there precision guidance equipment in these offices, perchance? Many researchers have concluded that the planes which struck the twin towers were precision guided by remote control. Although sounding like science fiction upon first hearing, remote control technology of planes has been around for decades. *SPC Corporation* supplies the flight termination system and command transmitter system, the technology that allows planes to be remote-controlled should the pilots be incapacitated or the plane hijacked. Indeed, the remote flying of airliners uses almost exactly the same technologies as flying remote-controlled model planes (albeit on a much larger scale) and that activity is relatively commonplace and un-questioned.

Rabbi Dov Zakheim was the appointed Under-secretary of Defence and Comptroller from 2001 to 2004 under the George W. Bush administration. Zakheim is the man responsible for the disappearance of $2.6 trillion that went missing from the Pentagon books and which was announced by Donald Rumsfeld on the 10th September, 2001. This story was of course conveniently buried under the 9/11 rubble and never really questioned by the docile, subservient mainstream media stooges.

In fact, the specific section of the Pentagon that was hit by the 'plane' (it was almost certainly a cruise missile and not a Boeing 767) contained the years budgetary information as well as many obviously expendable clerks, accountants, bookkeepers and budget analysts of whom, many died on 9/11. Another bizarre coincidence, you will no doubt agree.

In May 2001, when Zakheim served at the Pentagon, it was an *SPS* (his firm's) subsidiary, *Tridata Corporation* that oversaw the investigation of the first 'terrorist' attack on the World Trade Centre in 1993. This would have provided intimate knowledge of the security systems and structural blueprints of the World Trade Centre. According to the SPS website, a recent customer at that time was Eglin AFB, located in Florida. Eglin is very near another Air Force base in Florida, MacDill AFB, where Dov Zakheim contracted to send at least 32 Boeing 767 aircraft, as part of the Boeing / Pentagon tanker lease agreement. Considering his access to Boeing 767 tankers, remote control flight systems and his published views in the Project for the New American Century (PNAC) document in 2000, it would appear more than likely that he is also in fact a key figure in the alleged terrorist attacks in New York City on 9/11.

Immediately following the attacks, the Jewish criminal network was methodically manoeuvring in unison behind the scenes to quash any legitimate investigation that world reveal what really happened that fateful day. They made it their goal to control any and all angles of the so-called 'investigation' so that they could quickly cover up any and all evidence that would unveil the unmistakable fingerprint of the Zionists.

In fact, all the appointed chief judges were Zionist Jews.

Alvin K. Hellerstein, a judge for the US District Court for the Southern District of New York has been involved in several high-profile 9/11 related cases including a consolidated master case against three airlines, ICTS International NV and Pinkerton's airport security firms, the World Trade Centre owners and Boeing Corporation, the aircraft manufacturer. Hellerstein is a dedicated Zionist and Israeli nationalist who has ties to the Jewish mafia dating back to 1956. Hellerstein's wife is a former senior officer and current treasurer of AMIT. AMIT's website states: 'Founded in 1925, AMIT is the world's leading supporter of religious Zionist education and social services for Israel's children and youth, nurturing and educating Israeli children to become productive, contributing members of society.'

Michael B. Mukasey an Orthodox Jewish judge oversaw the litigation between Larry Silverstein and insurance companies after 9/11. Silverstein was awarded billions and Mukasey actively prevented a full inquiry into the 'dancing Israelis' incident who were all arrested in the aftermath of 9/11. Indeed he played a major role in their release and was later appointed Attorney General by President Bush. He also defended the Patriot Act and openly supports US torture policies.

Michael Chertoff was In charge of the Criminal Division in the Justice Department on 9/11. Essentially responsible for the 9/11 non-investigation, he allowed hundreds of Israeli spies who were arrested prior to and on 9/11 return home to Israel without facing investigation. He was also a prosecuting judge in the first terrorist attack on the WTC in 1993. Chertoff purportedly holds dual citizenship with the US and Israel, his family is one of the founding families of the 'State' of Israel and his mother was one of the first ever agents of the Mossad, Israel's spy agency. His father and uncle are ordained rabbis and teachers of the Talmud.

Kenneth Feinberg (Zionist Jew) set up the victim's compensation fund ($7 billion) and this criminal cabal contrived to persuade 97% of the victims' families to agree to take the money in exchange for not demanding a legal investigation of 9/11.

Sheila Birnbaum was another key Zionist Jew involved in the cover-up of 9/11. Birnbaum was appointed 'special mediator' of the legal suits filed by the 3% of families who chose not to be bought off by the Zionists. Of course though, none of the suits were successful, thanks to her.
Benjamin Chertoff (cousin of Michael Chertoff) wrote the 9/11 'hit-piece' in Popular Mechanics debunking '9/11 conspiracies' using ridiculous strawmen. He claims his relationship to Michael Chertoff is 'distant' but this has since been proven otherwise.

Stephen Cauffman was the leader of the NIST cover-up of the destruction of WTC 7. These lowlifes to this day, continue to maintain the view that fire brought down WTC 7, a physical impossibility barring an extensive re-write of the laws of physics.

Philip Zelikow was appointed the executive director of the 9/11 commission, the most powerful position on the committee. This criminal Zionist Jew is responsible for concocting the utterly ludicrous, contrived fiction that was presented to us as the 9/11 Commission Report (i.e. the official story). This elaborately crafted fairy tale speaks of magical, explosion-proof paper passports being mysteriously expelled from the flames to the street below, building collapses violating all known laws of physics, careless Muslims leaving copies of the Koran and airliner flying instructional manuals wherever they went, planes performing 270° downward spiral turns at 500 mph whilst remaining under control of their hijackers, text and voice messages being sent from 15,000ft from planes with no in-flight phone capabilities and cave-dwelling, box-cutter wielding Arabs with super-human piloting skills. It also managed to completely omit blatantly anomalous events such as the self-demolition of WTC Building 7 at 5:20 pm and clairvoyant BBC and MSN reporters reporting live on air that WTC7 had also collapsed, 25 minutes before the actual event and the absence of any plane wreckage or bodies at other so-called 'crash-sites'.

Originally, Henry Kissinger was appointed as executive director of the 9/11 commission but surrendered the post after enormous protest. This cleared the way for Zionist operative Zelikow to take his place. However, Zelikow had numerous conflicts of interest that clearly inhibited his ability to tell the truth to the world about the 9/11 terror attacks.

Zelikow was a Bush 'insider', having been on the transition team in early 2000. In 1989-91 Zelikow worked with Condoleezza Rice on the National Security Council for the Bush Sr. Administration. In 1995, he and Rice co-authored a book together and from 1996-98 Zelikow was director of the Aspen Strategy Group which also included people such as Condoleezza Rice, Dick Cheney and Paul Wolfowitz as fellow members. After George W. Bush was 'elected', Zelikow was offered a position on the President's Foreign Intelligence Advisory Board (PFIAB) and worked on other task forces and commissions as well. In 2004 Zelikow manipulated the 9/11 investigation by deciding which topics would or would not be investigated. He was also secretly in contact with one of Bush's close advisors, Karl Rove.

Alan Ratner's *Metals Management* and the *SIMS group* were responsible for the indecent haste in which the WTC steel rubble was dispatched out of the country to Asian smelters without the opportunity to properly forensically investigate the crime-scene remains. Alan Ratner is also Jewish – *quel surprise*. He merged his company with the *SIMS group* and the *Hugo Neu Corporation*. Ratner sold over 50,000 tons of crime-scene evidence steel to a Chinese company at $120 per ton whilst Ratner had obtained them for $70 per ton. This criminal not only destroyed the evidence, but made a huge profit from it in the process. Nice work if you can get it.

Rabbi Dov Zakheim, co-author of the PNAC paper on rebuilding America's defences advocating the necessity of a Pearl Harbour-like incident in order to sway public opinion into supporting the 'war on terrorism', served as Pentagon Comptroller from 4th May 2001 to 10th March 2004. Two enormous sums of money disappeared from the Pentagon on his 'watch'. Initially $2.3 trillion was reported missing by Donald Rumsfeld (10th September 2001) and later Zakheim was unable to account for another trillion dollars. Well come on, it is easily done after all. Who among us would not admit to misplacing the odd trillion here and there, from time to time? Zakheim also arranged for still-operational squadrons of American F-15s and F-16s to be sold as 'surplus' to Israel at a fraction of their value.

Michael Chertoff's wife, Meryl, was a regional director of the ADL (the Zionist Anti-Defamation League, the organisation most responsible for the accusations of 'anti-Semitism' to anyone questioning Zionist motives). His mother was a flight attendant for El Al (the Israeli national airline) and thus by implication, had involvement with Mossad. His father and uncle are both Rabbis.

Richard Perle, Chairman of the Pentagon's Defence Policy Board was expelled from Senator Henry Jackson's office in the 1970s after the NSA caught him passing highly classified documents to Israel.

Paul Wolfowitz was Deputy Defence Secretary and a member of the Defence Policy Board in the Pentagon.

Douglas Feith headed reconstruction in Iraq. He was effectively in command, with Wolfowitz, of the War Department on 9-11 as undersecretary of War for Policy. He was fired from the National Security Council in 1976 due to suspicion of passing classified documents to Israel. Douglas Feith created the 'Office of Special Plans' shortly after 9/11 which was the source of all the fake intelligence accusing Iraq of developing WMDs and having ties to Al Qaeda.

Eliot Abrams was a key National Security Council Advisor. He was associated with the criminal, Zionist / pro-Israel think-tanks: AEI, PNAC, CSP, and JINSA. He is also closely associated with other criminal Jews, Perle, Feith, Wolfowitz and William Kristol. During the Iran/Contra Affair he was convicted of lying to Congress but was later given a pardon by Bush. How surprising.

Marc Grossman was Under-Secretary for Political Affairs on 9/11 and met with General Mahmoud Ahmad, head of Pakistan's ISI and erstwhile 9/11 financier, on the morning of 9-11. He is another dual citizen of the US and Israel.

Ari Fleischer was the White House spokesman for Bush on 9/11. Fleischer was responsible for peddling the Iraqi 'WMD' lies to the press and a dual citizen of the US and Israel and connected to the Jewish / Zionist extremist group 'Chabad Lubavitch Hasidics'.

Daniel Lewin, an Israeli Jew, was confirmed to be a member of the special Israeli commando unit, the 'Sayeret Matkal', which specialises in 'anti-hijack', takeovers and assassinations. Supposedly, Lewin became involved in a struggle with one of the alleged hijackers and ended up getting shot, which was later revised to being stabbed when it was belatedly realised that a gun on board would not be compatible with the pre-packaged 9/11 story line.

What are the odds that an Israeli 'Sayan' (part-time Mossad asset) would be on a plane hijacked by Arab terrorists? There is no suggestion that Lewin was on a suicide mission and flew into the towers, what is suggested is that he landed the plane at Stewart Airport and it was swapped for a remote-control drone. Stewart Airport was the 'privatised' former US Air Force base and interestingly, the exact point where the flight-paths of the alleged planes that hit the twin towers converged. This is all simply yet another co-incidence of course.

"We hold this truth to be self-evident that Israel attacked the United States on 9/11 and blamed it on the Muslim world. We hold it to be self-evident that Israel is not a nation but a collection of banker-gangsters who stole a land with people, for a people with no central criminal base, for the purpose of ritualized religious genocide, while seeking to economically enslave the entire world and then plunge it into a holocaust of war based on the recovered false memory of brain washed populations, who saw the movie and bought the t-shirt. If it is not self-evident then your self is in hiding from the fear of oppression, slander and loss, which are an inevitable certainty as a result. We hold it self-evident that when it is not self-evident it will, sooner or later, become evident in the most unpleasant possible way." Les Visible, musician and researcher, September 2011

On 20th September, 2001, in his address to the Joint Session of Congress following the 9/11 attacks, Bush grossly inflated the number of Israeli casualties in the attacks from 5 to 130. Obviously Bush did not write his own speeches (can he even write his own name?), so one cannot simply blame Bush for this blatant lie. Whosoever was his speechwriter at that time is the criminal culprit. So who was it?

David Frum, (yes you guessed, another Zionist-Jewish criminal) was Bush's speechwriter at this time and is the one responsible for inflating the number of Israeli dead by 2600% of the actual amount. Why would he do this? Because he is a Zionist of course and was attempting to garner sympathy for Israel and project them as the 'great ally' of the United States who are now 'partners' with them in this global fight against 'terrorism'. Incidentally, Frum was the man responsible for the coining of the 'Axis of Evil' epithet. He also co-authored a book with the Zionist warmonger Richard Perle, entitled *'An End to Evil: How to Win the War on Terror'*, which defended the illegal and fraudulent invasion of Iraq as well as calling for regime change in Iran, Syria and other Middle East states.

Less than one week before 9/11, several of the hijacker 'patsies', including Mohammed Atta, boarded a casino boat in Florida. No-one knows why and it has never been investigated. The boat was in fact owned by none other than Jack Abramoff yet another Zionist-Jewish criminal asset and he was the one who entertained the Arab patsies aboard his yacht. Abramoff is a Bush Administration insider having been part of the Transition Advisory team assigned to the Department of the Interior in 2001. Abramoff is also a convicted criminal lobbyist who is a central figure in a plethora of political scandals, fraud, and other scams. He is currently (2011) serving a five year prison term for fraud, conspiracy, and tax evasion. Abramoff also, according to Wikipedia, had foreknowledge of the Zionist-engineered War on Iraq.

Apparently the Israeli PM, Benjamin Netanyahu is so confident in Zionist control and domination and his own 'un-touchability' that he recently stated publicly that the 9/11 terrorist attacks were 'good' for US-Israeli relations and would generate 'immediate sympathy' for the Israeli 'cause' of ethnically cleansing the Palestinians. The Israeli newspaper 'Ma'ariv' reported that Likud leader Benjamin Netanyahu told this to an audience at Bar Ilan.

Of course Netanyahu's nonchalance about publicly making such controversial statements is not that surprising considering how much control Zionist Jews have over the American media. The aftermath of 9/11 saw the Zionist-media unveil a relentless demonisation campaign against Arabs, stereotyping them all as a bunch of fanatical plotting terrorists, no doubt a cause for huge celebration for Netanyahu and his criminal compadres who routinely look for any excuse to slaughter innocent Palestinians at a whim whilst confiscating their land in the process and vehemently protesting and issuing cries of 'anti-Semitism' at the merest sign of any criticism of their deranged actions.

"Anti-Semitism is a trick – we always use it when we are being criticised." Shulamit Aloni, former Israeli government minister

Indeed, Netanyahu is considered by many to be the likely architect of 9/11, directing the Mossad/Shin Bet. He was Israeli PM at the time as he is again now (June 2011) and has a long history of involvement in Israeli terrorism and politics (is there a difference?). He has been a prominent member of the Likud government since 1993. The Likud Party is the literal successor of the Jewish terrorist organisation known as the Irgun. Netanyahu wrote a book in the early 1980s called *'Terrorism: How the West can Win'* and he founded the *'Jonathan Institute'* in the late 1970s to study (and plan) terrorism. Egyptian Intellectual, Hassan Al Bana, has stated publicly that he thinks Netanyahu planned 9/11 with the Jews at the Jonathan Institute. Al Bana cites a book written by Netanyahu called *'Uprooting Terrorism'* which speaks of plans to attack the United Nations and the World Trade Centre with small nuclear bombs.

"I have had long conversations over the last two weeks with contacts at the Army War College and the headquarters, Marine Corps and I've made it absolutely clear in both cases that it is absolutely 100% certain that 9/11 was a Mossad operation. Period. The

Zionists are playing this as an all or nothing exercise. If they lose this one, they're done."
Alan Sabrosky, US Army War College, retired

On the 16th October 2001, a group of Israeli citizens were arrested in rural Pennsylvania for suspicious behaviour near a Pizza takeaway. The manager of the takeaway informed authorities that two 'middle-eastern-looking men' were dumping furniture from a truck with a 'Moving Systems Inc.' sign on the side, behind his establishment. Police quickly investigated the incident and confronted its occupant who identified himself as Ron Katar, an Israeli. Katar pointed across the street to his compatriot named Mosche Almakias who was approaching the detained suspect with a female named Ayelet Reisler. Reisler suspiciously began to quickly walk in a different direction once she spotted the police officer and when arrested, was found to have a German passport in one name and medication in another.

Almakias admitted being behind the Pizzeria and said his destination was New York, but he had to make a pick-up in Plymouth. However, the pathetic cover story began to fall apart when he could not provide a name or number for his supposed client.

The police searched the truck and discovered a Sony video camera containing a video film taken of Chicago with several suspicious zoom-in shots of the Sears (now Willis) Tower. Clearly these Mossad assets were planning some sort of false-flag attack but the Israelis were eventually taken in by the INS and neither they nor the incident itself was ever mentioned again.

A possibly significant fact is that the Sears (Willis) Tower was purchased by three men, two of whom are Jews, Lloyd Goldman, Joseph Cayre and Jeffrey Feil in 2004. These men belonged to the same group that backed Larry Silverstein's lease of the WTC complex providing $125 million to Silverstein for the purpose. It would seem that these criminal Jewish assets are all part of the same false-flag terror / real-estate insurance scams together.

In Mexico City as reported by the newspaper 'La Vox de Atzlan', two men posing as press photographers, but in reality Israeli Mossad agents, were arrested inside the Mexican congress on the 10th October 2001, armed with 9mm pistols, hand-grenades, explosives, three detonators and 58 bullets, but were immediately *released* from custody because of pressure from Israel.

The newspaper reported that.. *"We believe that the two Zionists terrorist were going to blow up the Mexican Congress. The second phase was to mobilize both the Mexican and US press to blame Osama bin Laden. Most likely then Mexico would declare war on Afghanistan as well, commit troops and all the oil it could spare to combat Islamic terrorism."*

The Jewish terrorists names were Salvador Guersson Smecke (retired Israeli IDF colonel), age 34 and Saur Ben Zvi, age 27. These Zionist terrorists were released as a consequence of a very high-level emergency meeting which took place between the Mexican Secretary of Foreign Relations, Jorge Gutman, General Macedo de la Concha and a top Ariel Sharon envoy who flew to Mexico City especially for that purpose. You may not be surprised to learn that Jorge Gutman is of Jewish descent.

On Monday 13th May 2002, Fox News reported that two Israeli nationals in a white van were pulled-over in Oak Harbour, Washington, near the Whidbey Island Naval Air Station with explosives in their truck. Federal Authorities brought in explosives-sniffing dogs which 'reacted' firstly to one of the Israelis and later to the van itself. High-tech equipment was later used and confirmed the presence of TNT and RDX plastic explosives. The Israelis claimed to be delivering furniture to California, but investigators unsurprisingly doubted the story. Authorities later stated that records for the Budget truck did not indicate any recent rental for the purposes of transporting explosives, which would require special permits; thus proving these explosives were illegal and obviously intended to be used for malicious purposes.

The Fox News article makes no mention to what became of these two Israeli terrorists but the lack of further media coverage probably points to the fact that it was taken no further and no charges were brought. They were probably quietly deported.

The former Italian President, Francesco Cossiga, who revealed the existence of Operation Gladio in the 1980s, told Italy's oldest and most widely read newspaper that the 9/11 terrorist attacks were run by the Mossad and that this was common knowledge among global intelligence agencies. In what translates awkwardly into English, Cossiga told the newspaper, 'Corriere della Sera':

"All the [intelligence services] of America and Europe know well that the disastrous attack has been planned and realized from the Mossad, with the aid of the Zionist world in order to put under accusation the Arabic countries and in order to induce the western powers to take part in Iraq [and] Afghanistan."

And in an interview shortly after 9/11, Hamid Gul, the former head of Pakistani intelligence (ISI) from 1987-1989, told United Press International his view as to who he believes was behind the attacks.

UPI: So who did Black Sept. 11?

Gul: Mossad and its accomplices. The U.S. spends $40 billion a year on its 11 intelligence agencies. That's $400 billion in ten years, yet the Bush Administration says it was taken by surprise. I don't believe it. Within ten minutes of the second twin tower being hit in the World Trade Center, CNN said Osama bin Laden had done it. That was a planned piece of disinformation by the real perpetrators. It created an instant mind-set and put public opinion into a trance, which prevented even intelligent people from thinking for themselves.

So, why is the focus of this chapter on the Israeli angle and the Zionist-Jewish conspiracy? I acknowledge that the CIA and MI6 were also likely involved in the attacks, but it is my considered opinion that Israel and its agents in the US Government played the primary role in the attacks and had the most to gain from them; therefore under the principle of *Occam's Razor*, it is correct, I believe, to focus more on the Israeli/Jewish/Zionist connection, whilst other explanations may focus more on the CIA or MI6 connection. There are hundreds of websites, documentaries, films and articles that concentrate on the Bush, Rumsfeld and Cheney angle etc. but not too many acknowledge the rock-solid evidence proving that 9/11 was most likely done by the Israeli Mossad in conjunction with the plethora of Zionist-American Jews whose duplicitous role in the attacks has been thoroughly documented. Could this be because of fear? Anyone who crosses these entities is very likely to be at best verbally attacked and have their writings suppressed, and at worst? Well, I will leave that to your imagination.

It is up to you, the reader, to decide whether this information has validity or not and whether you wish to believe it. Research is research and the truth is the truth, I have no preconceived ideas or prejudices of any kind. All I can do is present the facts as I see them. Nothing here is fabricated and it is all substantiated by myself. Indeed the evidence that 9/11 was an 'inside job', a 'false-flag' attack if you will, is absolutely overwhelming and beyond question. Indeed it is the 'official' story that is the fantastic 'conspiracy theory'.

Given all else we know about the Zionist / Israeli influence on anything of importance in the world, is it such a leap of faith to believe in their deep involvement in this issue. 'Cui bono?' Latin for 'who stands to benefit' is a test we should always apply to any situation which needs an in-depth analysis to determine a reason for it. I suggest that Israel and Zionism itself benefitted hugely in the furtherance of its deadly agenda, from the 9/11 attacks, far more in fact than any other entity.

However, let the last word on the subject be from Public Enemy number 1 himself, Osama bin Laden. This is the one and only statement that the real Osama made regarding 9/11, as officially verified by the CIA in a certified transcript. Osama bin Laden was dying when he made this statement on 24th September 2001 and provably passed away two months later in November 2001, despite all the lies and hype about his death occurring in an American raid on his HQ in 2011.

"The United States should try to trace the perpetrators of these attacks within itself; the people who are a part of the US system, but are dissenting against it. Or, those who are working for some other system; persons who want to make the present century a century of conflict between Islam and Christianity so that their own civilization, nation, country or ideology could survive. They can be anyone, from Russia to Israel and from India to Serbia. Then you cannot forget the American Jews, who are annoyed with President Bush ever since the elections in Florida and want to avenge him.

Then there are intelligence agencies in the US, which require billions of dollars' worth of funds from the Congress and the government every year. This [funding issue] was not a big problem till the existence of the former Soviet Union but after that the budget of these agencies has been in danger. They needed an enemy. So, they first started propaganda against me and Taliban and then this incident happened.

Drug smugglers from all over the world are in contact with the US secret agencies. These agencies do not want to eradicate narcotics cultivation and trafficking because their importance will be diminished. The people in the US Drug Enforcement Department are encouraging drug trade so that they could show performance and get millions of dollars' worth of budget. General Noriega was made a drug baron by the CIA and, indeed, he was made a scapegoat.

President Bush or any other US President, they cannot bring Israel to justice for its human rights abuses or to hold it accountable for such crimes. What is this? Is it not that there exists a government within the government in the United Sates? That secret government must be asked as to who made the attacks." Osama Bin Laden

The London Tube Bombings – 7th July 2005

On the 7th July 2005, one day after being surprisingly awarded the 2012 Olympic Games when Paris was the overwhelming favourite, London was rocked by a series of bomb blasts resulting in the deaths of more than fifty people. Not quite in the same league as 9/11 of course, well certainly not as regards loss of life, but more than sufficient to remind us all that we are extremely vulnerable and susceptible to attack by those who 'envy our freedoms', or so we are deceptively led to believe. Perhaps conveniently or even by explicit design, these incidents also coincided with the G8 summit of world 'leaders' which was in session in Scotland and which allowed a united front of condemnation to be forthcoming from the senior nations of the world all of whose presidents or prime ministers 'just happened' to be virtually 'on the doorstep' at the time.

Along with the 9/11 incident, the 7/7 attacks formed the second leg of a two-pronged attack on the freedoms of the people of the western world. Not at the hands of Muslim terrorists though, as they would have us all believe, but more at the hands of a local, home-grown variety of terrorist, better known as the British government in concert with MI5, the CIA and the Mossad (Israeli security services) and whom all have a much more credible vested interest in curbing our freedoms than do any so-called Muslim terrorist group.

The official story is that four disaffected British Muslim youths planned and carried out a sophisticated operation culminating in a simultaneous bombing attack on three London tube (subway) trains and a bus by virtue of the use of explosive devices carried in a backpack, killing themselves and fifty-plus others in the process.

As always in these cases, there are two directly competing and conflicting explanations for the 7/7 attacks. One is the 'official' version of events and the other is the 'conspiracy theory' version. Now let us examine all the facts and the evidence emanating from this day of infamy and let the reader decide for him or herself which is the more likely to be true and which the conspiracy.

In May 2004, an episode of the BBC 'Panorama' programme was aired during which a scenario was mooted whereby a bus and three tube trains would be attacked simultaneously by four suicide bombers during the morning rush hour. Is this starting to sound eerily familiar yet? The discussion panel included such notables as Michael Portillo, a former British government minister and a character by the name of Peter Power who just happens to be an ex-senior police officer (more of him shortly). The basis of the programme was a mock exercise in which the panel of experts discussed how a terrorist attack on London would be handled and this was revealed gradually through faux news reports as the show progressed.

"No terrorist attack would be complete without the advance airing of a scenario docu-drama to provide the population with a conceptual scheme to help them understand the coming events in the sense intended by the oligarchy." Webster Tarpley, historian and researcher, 2009

But for the moment, as promised, back to Peter Power. On the morning of 7/7, he and his training company were in the process of conducting an emergency terror drill that unbelievably almost exactly matched the real events unfolding around him in the city of London. The exact same three tube stations that were involved in the real world were the ones 'co-incidentally' being used by Power in his 'drill'! On the afternoon of 7/7 he was interviewed on the BBC Radio 5 'Drivetime' programme...

"...at half-past nine this morning we were actually running an exercise for, er, a company of over a thousand people in London based on simultaneous bombs going off precisely at the railway stations where it happened this morning, so I still have the hairs on the back of my neck standing upright!" Peter Power, CEO of Visor Consultants, a management training organisation

Yes we believe you, Peter. Of course we do – especially given your past background and your appearance in the 2004 docu-drama (above) and despite the odds against this scenario occurring by chance that have been independently calculated to be in the region of 14 billion to one. Was Power simply cleverly protecting himself by this announcement and thus ensuring that were he to become a statistic shortly afterwards, due to his 'insider knowledge' that there would almost certainly be questions asked regarding his death? If so, he would by no means be the first to use this tactic.

On the 5th-8th April 2005 a large scale terror-drill given the code name of 'Atlantic Blue' was undertaken involving the participation of many different facets of government. How interesting to note than that shortly after the 7th July 2005, the Independent newspaper reported that... "By an extraordinary coincidence, all the experts who formulate such plans are together in a meeting at the headquarters of the London Ambulance Service – and they are discussing an exercise they ran three months ago that involved simulating four terrorist bombs going off at once across London."

How the coincidences all pile up, all of course in close synergy with the story of 9/11. On the morning of 9/11, the security, emergency and rescue services were all hampered by the fact that there were several, not just one mind, but several simultaneous exercises taking place that almost exactly reflected the real world events occurring at that time.

In 2005, the Metropolitan Police exercise Operation Hanover just happened to be held on the 1st-2nd July and its theme was that of three simultaneous bomb attacks on three underground (tube) stations. The police have been extremely reluctant to discuss this amazing coincidence that occurred literally 5 days before the 'real' event. Why would this be? In fact this information only came to light in 2009, four years after the event.

Another virtually un-publicised fact that came to light during the 7/7 inquest was that no post-mortems were carried out on the bodies of the victims. This is most definitely against the law. All bodies believed to have suffered an un-natural death must by law undergo a post-mortem examination. In addition to this fact, would not a huge amount of information regarding the placement and composition of the bombs have been revealed by these examinations, had they taken place? Surely post-mortems would have revealed some definitive, incriminating information that would have provided clues to the many unexplained hows and whys of the tragedy. Indeed, what could possibly explain such a seemingly bizarre course of action other than of course the necessity of avoiding conflict with a completely fabricated narrative?

After the event, we were immediately informed that the explosives used were of military origin and as most people in the truth movement are well aware, the first reports are always the most revealing, but are often never heard again and suppressed once the powers that be realise that initial reports do not fit the concocted story at which they eventually arrive and which then becomes the de facto truth.

"The nature of the explosives appears to be military, which is very worrying....the material used was not homemade but sophisticated military explosives ..." Christophe

Chaboud, chief of the French anti-terrorism Coordination Unit who was in London assisting Scotland Yard with its investigation.

How, it is perhaps pertinent to ask, would four, to all intents and purposes, perfectly normal youths procure a substantial quantity of military grade explosive material? And also that being the case, why did the police several days later announce that they had found the homemade bomb 'factory' near the homes of three of the four alleged terrorists in Leeds, West Yorkshire? Surely an experienced, senior anti-terrorist officer such as M. Chaboud could not have made such a fundamental error could he?

"A bath filled with explosives has been found at a house in Leeds that was the 'operational base' for the London suicide bombers." 'The Independent' newspaper, 14th July 2005

The newspaper went on to blithely state that the explosives were made of black pepper and hydrogen peroxide. The notion of heating up hydrogen peroxide in their bathroom to the point where it would make an explosive mix with black pepper is simply laughable, to say the very least, let alone that a rucksack could hold enough of such a concoction that if and when exploding could supply enough energy to bend and even break steel bars. Also, how could they possibly test that their 'bombs' were actually going to explode on demand. Were they simply all going to go tramping across the city with this allegedly lethal mixture swilling around in their backpacks? Indeed, has anyone ever successfully managed to construct a bomb from a few such household ingredients, let alone one capable of such devastation as was created on 7/7?

Another perhaps obvious question is why would terrorists who wished to avenge themselves upon the British people for the UK's involvement in Iraq and Afghanistan, choose to kill themselves in the process? Surely on such crowded trains in rush-hour it would have been a simple task to set a timer to detonate the explosives and then quietly exit the trains, leaving their bags on the floor amongst the feet of hundreds of unsuspecting passengers. What would have been the risk involved there? Would not their cause have been better served by them living to 'fight' another day and possibly repeat the feat elsewhere? Suicide bombing is an expedient used only where smuggling explosives and leaving them in situ is impossible due to heavy security presence and not simply as a pointless statement of bravado, as the authors of this unlikely scenario would wish us to believe.

At the 7/7 Inquest in November 2010, Dr. Morgan Costello gave evidence that he was asked to attend two tube-stations, Edgware Road and Aldgate, for the *'purposes of certifying the extinction of life'*. He counted six bodies at Edgware Road and seven bodies at Aldgate and declared these as *'life extinct'*. The huge contradiction arising from this simple fact, completely unreported in the compliant media of course, was that the numbers should have been seven and eight respectively – that is of course if we count the bodies of the bombers. This is surely indicative of the fact that the alleged bombers were not on the trains at the time of the bombs exploding. No similar count seems to have been carried-out on the Russell Square train, but we do have certain information regarding the behaviour of the Russell Square bomber, Germaine Lindsay, immediately prior to his untimely death.

"*A New Zealander working for Reuters in London said two colleagues witnessed the unconfirmed shooting by police of two apparent suicide bombers outside the HSBC tower at Canary Wharf in London. The man who was not prepared to give his name said two English colleagues, whom he also refused to name 'witnessed the shooting from a building across the road from the tower'.*" 'The New Zealand Herald', July 2005

There is plenty of eye-witness evidence available proving beyond reasonable doubt that the 7/7 attacks were not 'suicide' bombings at all. For example, Bruce Lait who was in a tube train carriage near London's Aldgate East station when one of the bombs exploded described a scenario that absolutely confirms this fact without question.

According to Lait, as the survivors were being escorted from the wrecked train carriage by a police officer, he warned them... "*...mind that hole, that's where the bomb was*". The metal around the edge of the hole was pushed and twisted upwards exactly as though the bomb had been underneath the floor of the train. Surely if the bomb had exploded above floor level then the opposite effect should have been observed. Lait further commented that... "*They seem to think the bomb was left in a bag, but I don't remember anybody being where the bomb was, or any bag,*" he said. Very strange indeed.

On the 5th July 2005, one of the quartet, Mohammed Siddique Khan took his pregnant wife to Dewsbury Hospital in West Yorkshire with a suspected potential miscarriage. Upon returning home, Khan announced to her that he was 'going to see his friends' and this was the last time that his wife ever saw him. She miscarried on the 6th July. Would Khan or anyone for that matter, really have abandoned his ailing wife for a whole day while she was in such a precarious condition? He was a highly respected member of his community, not just by the Asian element, but by all races alike in what is an extremely multi-cultural environment. He was also highly respected by the headmistress (principal) of the special school in which he worked as a classroom assistant. In addition, the police had used him to mediate between rival gangs in local disputes because simply put, he was trusted by all sides. The MP, Hilary Benn had taken Khan on a tour of the House of Commons and he was specifically regarded as being politically neutral, by no means an extremist and an upstanding citizen, protective of the good name of his community and was always seen to be keen to maintain amiable relations with the local white community.

I believe that the most likely scenario for the four hapless young men being embroiled in this situation in the first place was that they had naively (as it turned out) agreed to take part in what they thought was going to be an anti-terrorism exercise. The plan was that they would pose as terrorists and to make the scenario absolutely realistic and plausible it would have to be planned exactly like a precision military operation. Of course there were no live bombs in the rucksacks, just dummies, but the four did not realise of course that the real bombs were planted under the exact seats in the exact carriages in which they had no doubt been instructed to sit and in the case of Hussain, the bus. The best laid plans of mice and men... All was probably going exactly to plan until the 6th July...

The most likely explanation for Khan's sudden disappearance on the 6th was that he informed his handler for the 7/7 exercise that he was not going to be able to meet his obligations due to his wife's extreme ill health. He may then have been told to ensure that the others could make it without him because it was certain that the bombings were not going to be called-off but unfortunately he had now presented his handlers with a problem that had only one possible outcome and I do not believe that I actually need to spell this out.

Could this possibly also neatly explain why the attendant at the filling station where Tanweer filled his car and argued about the change he was given, stated categorically that he only saw one other person in Tanweer's car, Hasib Hussain. Khan was almost certainly not there and probably unknown to Tanweer and Hussain, was already dead. This would also provide a reason that the now-suppressed BBC Radio 5 news reports from the morning of 7/7 reported that only two and not three 'suspected terrorists' had been shot at Canary Wharf and as seen by dozens of witnesses in the surrounding office buildings.

Anyway, on the morning of 7/7, Germaine Lindsay drove the relatively short distance from Aylesbury in nearby Buckinghamshire to meet the other so-called bombers at Luton railway station. He arrived too early and decided to take a short nap in his car before the others were due to rendezvous with him. Interestingly, he paid for a car park ticket for the full day but surely, had he been a real suicide bomber and not a patsy he would have known that he had only a few short hours left to live and this would then have rendered the purchase of a ticket totally unnecessary.

At the inquest, one of the station attendants, a Mr Patel, gave testimony to the Inquest to the effect that a man whom he identified from photographs as Germaine Lindsay, arrived on the concourse of King's Cross station and immediately asked to speak urgently with 'the Duty Manager' and stated that it was 'very important'. Mr Patel remembered Lindsay simply for the reason that it was extremely unusual for any member of the public to know the exact job title of the person in overall charge of the station. Usually people would ask for the 'supervisor' or simply the 'manager'. By this time there was utter chaos on the station concourse. The metal grilles on the outer doors to the station had been lowered and locked shut and passengers were not being allowed through the barriers. A sizeable crowd had gathered and were starting to abuse staff in their frustration at being unable to enter the station concourse and several police community support personnel were trying to keep order. However when Patel managed to finally locate the Duty Manager, Germaine Lindsay had disappeared, as it turned out – forever.

The primary cause of Lindsay's confusion was the fact that he was late for his date with destiny and events had already spiralled out of control for both the patsies and the real perpetrators, by this time. The train upon which the 'bombers' had been scheduled to travel from Luton to London King's Cross station, the 7.40am, had been cancelled. The train that they eventually caught was also delayed by 23 minutes and so by the time the hapless foursome arrived in London using their 'return' tickets, yes return tickets note, the master-plan was already underway without them as they had all already missed their respective trains.

According to many people who visited the Leeds area they had spoken with several local residents and all were adamant that all three of Khan, Hussain and Tanweer had shown no inclination whatsoever in their communities towards political or religious radicalism.

In much the same vein as other inside-jobs or false flag events, there are so few videos or even still photographs of the quartet together. Even those that do exist could easily have been 'photo-shopped' with only a basic knowledge of this technique. In reality there should be dozens if not hundreds of pictures of these men at various stages of the plot. London is the most CCTV-intensive environment on the planet and so the pertinent question must be, why are there only two extremely poor, grainy, still pictures of the four, one at Luton station and one at Kings Cross, Thameslink station, the date and time stamps on which could have easily been faked. In fact I could probably have done it myself! Is it possible perchance that the photos of Khan have been dubbed-in from the 'dummy run' that the foursome carried out on the 29th June 2005, a mere eight days earlier?

The mobile phone evidence places them all on the correct train at the correct time, the Luton to Kings Cross train that is. However, there are three issues here worthy of note. Firstly, this is relatively new evidence that was not released in the previous, 2006 hearing. Why should this be? Is it an invented afterthought maybe, to lend greater credence to the official conspiracy theory? Secondly, is it really likely that the four men would have been texting each other on a train upon which they were all travelling together? And thirdly and perhaps most significant, this type of evidence is ridiculously easy to fake. It is after all simply a series of printed characters on an official-looking piece of paper.

It is worth at this juncture mentioning the famous 'terror-warning' videos made by Khan and Tanweer and which have been submitted as 'proof' of their radical or terrorist tendencies. Khan and Tanweer could easily have been coerced into making the Jihad-inciting videos that have played such a large part in convincing the public to accept their guilt. They were employees of the government for at least two days (possibly more) after all and probably very well-paid employees for the dry-run on the 29th June and the day of 7/7 itself. They would no doubt have been told that the exercise had to be completely realistic and were probably told that the film would be used by the station staff and other authorities to aid them in intercepting the four suspected 'terrorists'. The 'threats' from Khan and Tanweer on the videos are totally vague and unspecific and unconvincing in the extreme. When Khan's wife first saw the video it was reported that she said, *"That's not my husband."* Her brother however, said he believed it was Khan. I would surmise that it is most likely that her words were taken completely out of context and that she actually meant 'that is not the husband I know as he would never say those things'.

Daniel Obachike is the most famous of the survivors of the bus blast in Tavistock Square, the '4th bomb' as it has come to be known. Daniel's experiences, terrible as they were on the day were also matched subsequently by the sheer terror he experienced by being subjected to several years of overt threats and surveillance by MI5. All he is guilty of is telling the truth as he saw it that day.

"I'm just a regular guy, I was born and bred and work in London and that day I was on my way to work in Old Street and there was some kind of disruption going on. We were told that it was a power surge on the underground and that's how I came to be on the bus." Daniel Obachike

He described in detail how he boarded the bus at Euston along with several dozen others who had all been denied access to the tube station as he thought that the bus was going in the direction he required. Shortly after the bus had started its journey, Daniel looked out of the window and saw two cars, a black Mercedes and a blue BMW blocking the road and their drivers directing the bus away from its normal route, towards Tavistock Square. It was in Tavistock Square where the bus exploded and this is where events took a distinctly sinister turn.

After the explosion, instinct took over and he just ran as fast as possible off the bus and away down the street in the direction the bus had just travelled in order to escape the scene. A few yards down the street, Daniel noticed that a man was actually filming him running away at which point he became confused and stopped. He looked around him and back in the direction of the bus which he could now see had the entire top-deck blown away by the blast

The 7/7 bus explosion

At this point his demeanour abruptly changed from fear to curiosity as he became aware that something strange was going on.

"I was looking at the people moving into the actual space on the square. There were guys who were hanging around. There was a row of policemen who were just standing there in yellow fluorescent jackets, they weren't doing anything, they were just watching. There was this guy filming and I'm saying 'what is going on here'. It didn't feel right."

Contrary to other witness' statements, Daniel says he did not see any Asian-looking man on the lower deck of the bus, nor did he see an Asian man get on the bus at any time. The Metropolitan Police later changed their initial reports that the bomber was on the lower deck and instead placed him on the upper deck of the bus.

Daniel then described a man who he noticed after the blast, as he appeared to be injured but was acting very strangely. He (Daniel) went to help an injured woman and was assisting her down the street ahead of the bus towards a hotel where she could at least sit whilst waiting for medical attention and in doing so he passed a man who seemed to be injured himself as he was swathed in bandages. However, he was extremely confused by this because the man was forty or fifty metres ahead of the bus and the bomb blast had actually travelled backwards and had even killed a passer-by behind the bus. This person was making a lot of noise and generally creating a fuss by rolling around in the road which Daniel thought at the time was extremely strange behaviour, not to mention poor acting.

Do not forget that all this took place within perhaps a minute of the explosion and so how on earth had this man managed to gain medical assistance let alone be already sporting bandages?

In addition to this strange scenario, Daniel noticed that...

"Some people were running forward, the medical staff and the medical professionals, you could tell who they were because they were seeing what they could try and do for people. But then there were these other people who were just watching, taking notes, organising people, moving things around."

Daniel then went on to say that he believed that this person whoever he was, had prior knowledge and prior intelligence and was placed at the scene for some ulterior purpose. He actually conducted his own search on the Internet after the event, because a few days after the event, his picture 'was everywhere' and yet has now been removed from Internet. The face of this man complete with bandaged head was all over the BBC and British news websites as well as most of the international ones too.

There were also four men in a blue uniform and who had rucksacks and also two or three people who were just standing in doorways watching the scene and there was another person who was controlling everything. He was in plain-clothes and was co-ordinating police activity once they had started to actually do something other than simply standing around.

Following the day of the attacks, Daniel made several attempts to contact the police to give his statement, but they simply did not want to talk to him. Eventually he gave up trying in frustration but soon noticed that he was under supposed covert surveillance. He also received several intimidating phone calls warning him to stop trying to make public his suspicions and knows that he was being followed for almost a year after the event.

Interestingly, it was later discovered that the day prior to the incident, this bus had been off the road all day for 'maintenance' work to be carried out. It is also noteworthy that both security cameras on the bus were 'inoperative' that day, despite the fact that the bus had just undergone a full maintenance check the previous day. How convenient this is, but of course why would we expect them to change a successful cover-up strategy when it is proven to be effective in incident after incident, with never a query or even a passing comment from the lapdogs of the media, let alone the general public.

Daniel is absolutely 100% certain to this day that Hasib Hussain was not on the bus and did not carry out the bombing.

The four alleged terrorists all had four or more mobile phones each; one of their own private phones and at least three other 'operational' phones that they are supposed to have used to confound anyone who might attempt to track their communications and obstruct their diabolical plan. However, I believe it much more likely that these phones were supplied by their handlers and that their possession of them facilitated the tracking of their every movement. For example Tanweer and Lindsay were easily traced to Canary Wharf after they had panicked and gone on the run. They were presumably, naively hoping to tell their story to the British press before the security services caught up with them, an endeavour which to their great personal cost, ultimately failed miserably.

Anthony John Hill aka 'Muad'Dib' (named for a character in Frank Herbert's sci-fi story 'Dune') produced an excellent video-film '7/7 Ripple Effect' bringing much hitherto unknown information to the attention of the public and when in 2008 a group of 'Islamic terrorists', allegedly associates of Khan, were arraigned for trial at Kingston Crown Court, Hill mailed two copies of his DVD to the court. One envelope was addressed to the judge and the other to the foreman of the jury. Neither DVD reached its intended recipient but shortly afterwards a request for Hill to be extradited from Ireland (he lived in Kells, County Meath at the time) was sent to the Irish Ministry of Justice. The request was successful and Hill was arrested on a charge of attempting to pervert the course of justice by a British policeman, accompanied back to Britain and incarcerated in Wandsworth prison shortly before the start of the 7/7 Inquest. After much legal argument and a completely farcical and biased court case, Hill was eventually acquitted by a sympathetic jury much to the great chagrin of the presiding judge who had instructed them to find him guilty regardless of the fact that there was no evidence to support the Crown's claims against him. Justice? What justice?

A tragic but nevertheless interesting postscript to this whole sorry incident was the shooting of the Brazilian man, Jean Charles de Menezes two weeks following 7/7. The official version of events was that he was thought by a group of armed policeman to be a terrorist as he was (according to them) wearing a large overcoat on a warm sunny day and appeared to be hiding something underneath it as well as having a 'foreign' appearance. According to the police account, he was spotted and chased, at which point he fled in panic, vaulted the barrier at Stockwell tube station and boarded a train in his futile attempts to avoid arrest. At this point the police caught him and held him down and simply shot him seven times in the head. Not once, but *seven* times.

Why would they do this when he was already under restraint? Again the official version stated that it was because they thought he had a bomb and was going to detonate it at any moment. Do they really think we are all so stupid? What purpose would shooting someone in the head seven times when already under restraint, serve? Why would simply handcuffing him not fulfil much the same purpose? There is no doubt in my mind that this action was taken in order to ensure that there was no way that de Menezes could survive and as with many aspects of this whole sorry story, there is far more to this particular incident than meets the eye.

For a start, it was subsequently proven that de Menezes was not wearing a large overcoat as the police had falsely claimed; he was wearing a t-shirt, lightweight jeans and a short, light denim jacket.   He had no bag with him and nor was he carrying anything else that could have been mistaken for a bomb or explosive device. In fact the whole story about him fleeing and the police giving chase into Stockwell tube station was a complete fabrication. Jean actually sauntered into the station, used his 'Oyster' pre-paid travel card in the normal fashion and headed for a train bound for his destination of North West London where he happened to be working at the time. Having disembarked from the escalator at the appropriate platform, a train was just arriving and so he jogged leisurely along the platform and boarded the train carriage. He sat down at a convenient seat and took out the newspaper he had with him, to read on the journey.   At this point an undercover, plain-clothed police officer standing in the tube carriage identified Jean to nearby (similarly plain-clothed) officers at which point they raced onto the tube-train carriage, dragged him out of his seat, held him down and shot him as described previously, killing him instantly. Incidentally, the bullets used were known as 'dum dum' bullets which are particularly vicious, causing maximum possible damage to human flesh and bone. These bullets are 'illegal' in international warfare so it really does beg the question as to why the Metropolitan police were issued with them – or indeed was this a 'special' case that warranted their use?

Jean's family were not informed about his killing until more than 24 hours after it happened despite the officers on the scene finding Jean's wallet with his Brazilian driving licence inside it. The Metropolitan Police immediately began briefing the press with 'off the record' statements saying that Jean was a terrorist, that he was acting suspiciously, that he was wearing a bulky coat and that he was challenged but refused to co-operate. All of these statements have of course subsequently proven to be absolutely, totally false.

Usually in the event of a death at the hands of the police, an immediate investigation is begun by the Independent Police Complaints Commission (IPCC). However, one hour after Jean was killed; the head of the Metropolitan Police, Sir Iain Blair contacted the Home Office asking for the immediate suspension of any investigation by the IPCC. He ordered his officers to close Stockwell tube to any investigations and as a result of this it was six days before the IPCC could begin their investigations. This of course was six days during which vital evidence could have been fabricated or destroyed and a cover-up could have been instigated.

Five hours after de Menezes was murdered, Sir Iain Blair appeared on national television stating that the 'incident' at Stockwell tube was related to the anti-terrorism operations and that Jean was challenged and resisted (a blatant lie). He also claimed that he was not told until the next day that Jean had been an innocent man but this must be a blatant lie, I feel. Do they seriously expect us to believe that a man was shot to death in this brutal, illegal manner and yet the head of the force was not told about it until the next day? In any event it was subsequently discovered that Blair had contacted the Home Office regarding the matter, one hour after the incident.

The family of de Menezes firmly believe that the actions of police officers and of Sir Iain Blair constitute an attempted 'cover-up' operation. The disappearance of the CCTV from Stockwell tube (that old trick again), the attempt to block the IPCC from commencing their investigations, the tampering of the police records on the day, the police briefings suggesting Jean was acting suspiciously, all suggest that the police knew far more than they were admitting. To this day, no officer has yet been prosecuted or disciplined for the de Menezes killing, thus confirming the impression that the police in the UK are free to act with impunity and without consequence to their actions.

So, was this really all a huge mistake or could it have been something more sinister? The undercover police officers obviously knew where to find de Menezes on that day, unless we believe that they just happened to be loitering at Stockwell tube station, armed to the teeth, at that precise moment with nothing particularly better to do with their time. If this was not the case, then what was the reason for the elaborate cover-up and frantic attempts to cover their tracks? The primary justification from the police for de Menezes' shooting was that they suspected him of being a terrorist simply because he was wearing a large coat which they 'believed' was concealing a bomb but as this has since been proved to be a gross lie, it also negates the excuse given for shooting him seven times in the head, which even assuming the police were telling the truth, was extremely flimsy at best. So what could the real motivation have been?

Jean Charles de Menezes was an electrician by trade, a fact never disclosed by the police at the time. In fact at one point in the aftermath of the event they actually point-blank refused to name his occupation. This I believe to be highly significant in the light of subsequent information I received.

Several years ago whilst in London at a conference, I happened to sit next to a local man who claimed that he had known him vaguely. He told me that de Menezes' occupation was electrical engineer and that he had been working as a contractor on the London tube immediately prior to 7/7. This person then told me that he strongly believed that de Menezes was brutally murdered not because he was mistaken as a terror suspect at all, but simply because he had been privy to aspects of the plot, in particular relating to the planting of the explosives under the floors of the trains which were detonated by means of 'power surges' and afterwards, despite serious threats against him and his family, he could not resist telling what really happened, to anyone who would listen.

This is complete speculation as I have no proof whatsoever that it is true but it does have a certain 'ring of truth' to it and would neatly explain the mystery.

However, no matter what the real truth, the fact remains that the illegal shooting of Jean Charles de Menezes was certainly no mistake and was, I am convinced, part of the cover-up operation of the 7/7 tragedy.

The fake 'War on Terrorism' and the real 'War on Islam'

Despite the fact that you may not believe it to be possible, terrorism was actually created by Western governments to justify perpetual war. It is not an expression of dissent from a suppressed minority as we are constantly led to believe (except in rare, minor cases). For example, the **Taliban** is not a terrorist organisation as we are always told by the compliant media, but a movement attempting to unify Afghanistan under Muslim law and the only westerners threatened by the Taliban are the ones sent to Afghanistan by their 'governments' to kill Taliban and to impose a puppet state on the Afghan people in order to facilitate the expansion of corporate profits and interests, currently denied them by the actions of said Taliban. One man's terrorist is indeed another man's freedom fighter.

In George Orwell's 1984, the fake terrorist threat is very effectively used as a tool to spread fear and compliance among the population of 'Airstrip One', the new name for Great Britain. Whenever the government wishes to impose a new law or further restrict freedoms in any way, they wheel out their utterly invented, fake nemesis, 'Emmanuel Goldstein' who is then, along with his band of terrorists, said to have committed such and such an atrocity, effectively smoothing the way for further draconian restrictions of freedoms by invoking the Hegelian Dialectic (problem, reaction, solution). Does this sound at all familiar? For 'Emmanuel Goldstein' simply read 'Osama bin Laden', 'Colonel Gaddafi' or 'Saddam Hussein' and all may become clearer.

The utterly ridiculous assertion that Iran is supplying sophisticated arms to the Palestinians is like the similarly false assertion that Saddam Hussein had weapons of mass destruction in Iraq. These assertions are propagandistic justifications for killing Arab civilians and destroying civilian infrastructure in order to further US, British and Israeli hegemony in the Middle East.

The current perceived threat posed by Islam is the main barrier to the widespread expansion of Elite Zionism and therefore this makes it necessary for the Zionists to totally eliminate this threat. They do this by painting all Muslims as potential terrorists and then infiltrating Muslim dissident groups and by the use of coercion and the funding of their activities, these groups are subtly enticed to carry out minor acts of terror that can be inflated beyond all belief by the lackeys of the press and then used as examples of 'the horrors of Islamic extremism'.

It may thus be seen therefore, that the 'war on terror' is a gigantic hoax among many others that combine to make-up and sustain our fake reality.

Consider these numbers for a moment; the reason will soon become apparent...

In the USA in 2008, heart disease killed 870,000 people, doctor and hospital errors 200,000, road deaths were 43,000, salmonella poisoning 600 and terrorism 6 (and even that low figure is being extremely generous!)

In 2009 the heart disease prevention budget was $2.9 bn whilst the anti-terrorism budget was $160 bn.

What is wrong with this picture? Where is the war on heart disease, the war on medical inadequacy, road deaths and salmonella?

Unfortunately, heart disease does not generate profits for the Elite military-industrial complex on the same scale as terrorism or indeed further the Elite agenda in any significant way. 'Fighting terrorism' is a wonderfully expedient way of continuing a war economy without end against an enemy that cannot even be adequately defined let alone conquered, has no discernible borders and no national identity to destroy. It is in fact the perfect 'enemy' for those who wish to deceive and enslave us and keep us in a permanent state of poverty and disenfranchisement by waging perpetual, unwinnable war, exactly as described in glorious detail by George Orwell in 1984.

"According to US government propaganda, terrorist cells are spread throughout America, making it necessary for the government to spy on all Americans and violate most other constitutional protections. Among President Bush's last words as he left office was the warning that America would soon be struck again by Muslim terrorists. If America were infected with terrorists, we would not need the government to tell us. We would know it from events. As there are no events, the US government substitutes warnings in order to keep alive the fear that causes the public to accept pointless wars, the infringement of civil liberty, national ID cards, and inconveniences and harassments when they fly. The most obvious indication that there are no terrorist cells is that not a single neocon has been assassinated." Paul Craig Roberts, The War on Terror is a Hoax, 2009

The evolution of western societies as genuine democracies with the ability to unify mankind on a broad basis, has been derailed consistently and perhaps irreversibly, by corporate cartels that have taken these countries down the path of global conquest and total exploitation of many poor but resource-rich countries, committing genocide in the process.

"The world does not hate the freedoms of Americans. They hate the assumptive power and presumptive freedoms of the US government that thinks it can tell any lie, fabricate any war, kill entire villages and destroy entire nations to terminate one alleged 'terrorist.' After one egregious act after another, and with no disregard for life whatsoever, they have the gall to pass yet another law to defend them from having to face the truth and be held accountable for their actions that have besmirched and

defamed the name of America and all of its citizens." Karl W. B. Schwarz, 16th December 2011

The Elite corporations involved in this insidious plan, operate secretly, often illegally, sometimes within utterly immoral 'laws' lobbied-for by themselves and without regard for the wider interests of humanity in general. Thus, the exploited countries see the western democracies, in particular, the US, the UK and Israel as a power of unprecedented and unmatched ruthlessness. The US is not only the greatest super-power in history, but it is also the greatest subversive power ever to inflict itself upon humanity.

"Every 10 years or so [even more frequently than that recently – JH] the US needs to pick up some crappy little country and throw it against the wall, just to show we mean business." Michael Ledeen

This 'business' is corporate business. Corporations have infiltrated the White House, the US legislative bodies and judiciary, as well as the US 'alphabet soup' agencies, some of which, such as the CIA, were created at the behest of Wall Street financial interests anyway in order to further their own agendas on foreign soil. And this is also true of America's allies' secret services. Indeed, not one of the so-called 'western democracies' have escaped corporate infiltration and in effect a secret takeover by Elite, corporate interests. This corporate ascendancy in the western power structure is now a constant and deeply-embedded feature of international politics. The people of the world are now almost 'out of the loop' completely as democracy has been totally hijacked. This is in fact the **real** danger to the future of mankind, not so-called 'terrorism'.

How often are we warned of the extreme dangers posed to our 'democracy' and 'way of life', by the 'terrorist' group *Al Qaeda* that according to the Elite, has cells everywhere in the world simultaneously, all in possession of unlimited funding? The popular translation attributed to 'Al-Qaeda' is 'the database,' which is said to refer to the CIA records of supposed Muslim extremists. However, the correct translation of the Arabic term Al-Qaeda is 'the toilet'. The Arabic verb 'Qa'ada' means 'to sit on the toilet'. Arab homes have one or more of three kinds of toilets: 'Hamam Franji' or 'Al-Qaeda' or foreign toilet, 'Hamam Arabi' or Arab toilet, and a potty used by children called 'Ma Qa'adia' or 'Little Qaeda'. 'Ana raicha al Qaeda' is a colloquial expression for 'I am going to the toilet'. Why would a terrorist group call itself 'the toilet'? Simply because Al-Qaeda is CIA/MI6/Mossad-Zionist fiction and a pathetic, humourless attempt at an 'insider' joke. These entities love nothing better than a good old laugh at our 'ignorance'.

"Al Qaeda has never existed; there are no magic worldwide terror conspiracies other than those run by governments. There are several of those and I have written extensively on these. Google will help you with this if you are curious." Gordon Duff, *Veterans Today*, August 2011

Azzam Yahiye Gadahn also known as 'Azzam the American' and the 'new Bin Laden' is the so called Al-Qaeda spokesperson who releases videos tormenting the world with his anti-American rants. The FBI even has him on their 'most wanted terrorist' lists. However, in reality he is an American Jew named Adam Pearlman, from California. Pearlman's grandfather, Carl Pearlman, was a prominent surgeon and on the board of directors of the Zionist Anti-Defamation League. This is another sick joke which could almost be funny were it not so serious a matter. They are taunting us and laughing at us all whilst we all slumber in our blind apathy.

"International terrorism is a fantasy that has been exaggerated and distorted by politicians. It is a dark illusion that has spread unquestioned through governments around the world, the security services and the international media." British author, Adam Curtis

"It is the policy of the United States government to provoke violent extremist groups into action. Once they are in play, their responses can then be used in whatever way the government that provoked them sees fit. And we also know that these provocations are being used, as a matter of deliberate policy, to rouse violent groups on the 'Af-Pak' front to launch terrorist attacks." Chris Floyd 'Darkness Renewed: Terror as a Tool of Empire' 2009

Some highly-paid intellectual prostitutes-cum-guardians of the Elite-approved 'truth' allege that Islam breeds terrorism. The western mass-media then complements this theoretically convenient notion to poison the public perceptions against Arabs and all Muslims in general. And thus the perception of 'radical Islam' was manufactured and enhanced by the 'fear' of terrorism as if Arabs and Muslims in general are all evil personified and terrorism was an exclusive domain of the Islamic religious tenets.

"Terrorism is a political technique, not an ideology and any group willing to use violence in pursuit of its political goals may resort to it. There are left-wing terrorists and right-wing terrorists; national terrorist and international terrorists; Christian, Muslim, Jewish, Hindu, Buddhist and atheist terrorists. In theory, you could have a 'war against terrorism', but it would involve trying to kill everybody who uses this technique anywhere in the world. The United States is not trying to do that, so it is not fighting a 'war against terror'. In reality, what the United States leadership is doing is fighting its own articulated war against the people and nations who had no animosity, nor did any perceive a capability to threaten the US as a global power". Gwynne Dyer, 'The International Terrorist Conspiracy.' June 2006

Bush's famously emotive rhetoric 'you are either with us or you are with the terrorists' is perfectly worded to emotionally influence the masses. Emotional appeals to fear and to patriotism have led most of the population to accept unaccountable government in the name of 'the war on terror'. What supreme irony it is that so many people have been convinced that their 'personal safety' depends upon the sacrifice of their civil liberties and truly accountable government.

There is absolutely no 'terrorism' in the thoughts and in the words of Islamic prayers and no Arabic-Islamic vocabulary exists of 'extremism' or 'terrorism' to reciprocate the western accusations and Elite media propaganda campaigns. In a rational context, the 'War on Terrorism' has nothing to do with the alleged terrorists; it is a war to help Halliburton, Bectal, Blackwater, Wackenhut, Exxon, BP, Shell and other mega-corporations to capitalise their holds on the oil supplies and gas pipelines. US Defence Secretary Donald Rumsfeld (Mr. Aspartame) contracted Halliburton, run by Dick Cheney for $7 billion works to be done in Iraq before the invasion of March 2003. President Bush passed Executive Order #13303, providing complete immunity from criminal prosecution to the American oil companies dealing with the Iraqi oil management. Is history going to wait for the cessation of the unilateral hostilities? Will the American-led war achieve its agenda priorities or meet the same fate as the Roman, Nazi and the Soviet Empires? Hopefully, history will judge the nations involved by their actions, not by the false claims of their leaders.

"The United States government is planning to use 'cover and deception' and secret military operations to provoke murderous terrorist attacks on innocent people. Let's say it again: Donald Rumsfeld, Dick Cheney, George W. Bush and the other members of the unelected regime in Washington plan to deliberately foment the murder of innocent people – your family, your friends, your lovers, you – in order to further their geopolitical ambitions". Chris Floyd 'Darkness Renewed: Terror as a Tool of Empire' 2009

So, in summary, I would make this plea to anyone who cannot see how fear and 'terror' is being used as a tool to subjugate the world and its gullible peoples... Please wake up and look beyond the mainstream news media. Look a little deeper into both current and past events. By doing so, you will help prevent your children and your children's children from becoming the slaves and pawns of the super-rich, forever.

HAARP - the High Frequency Active Auroral Research Program

Weather and Geological Manipulation

HAARP is possibly the most dangerous and sinister weapon known to man as well as being probably the least well known to the general public. I would place it ahead of even the Atomic and Hydrogen bombs in this respect.

It consists of a huge installation of antennae, in Alaska USA and is the largest ionospheric heater in the world (see picture above) capable of heating a 1000 square kilometre area of the ionosphere to over 50,000 degrees. It is also a phased array, meaning that it is steerable, despite widespread claims to the contrary by its apologists and its waves can be directed to a selected target area. By transmitting radio frequency energy up into the skies above us and focusing, it causes the ionosphere to heat considerably. This heating literally lifts the ionosphere within a 30 mile diameter area thereby changing localised pressure systems or perhaps the route of jet streams. Moving a jet stream is in itself a phenomenal event. The problem being that it is not possible to model the system accurately. Long term consequences of atmospheric heating are unknown. Changing weather in one place can have a devastating downstream effect and HAARP has already been accused of modifying weather for geopolitical as well as other possibly even more sinister functions.

Manipulating the weather and the environment for the purposes of US government sponsored terrorism is definitely not within the discussion remit of the mainstream news. But it would appear that that is exactly what is happening.

HAARP is part of the weapons arsenal of the New World Order under the Strategic Defence Initiative (SDI). From military command points in the US, entire national economies could potentially be destabilised through climatic manipulations. More importantly, the latter can be implemented without the knowledge of the enemy, at minimal cost and without engaging military personnel and equipment as in a conventional war. The use of HAARP, if it were to be applied, could have potentially devastating impacts on the World's climate.

HAARP is based in Alaska, where not only are we witnessing an increased incidence of earthquakes, but the prolonged eruption of volcanoes. In 1958, then chief White House adviser on weather modification, Captain Howard T. Orville said that the US Defence Department was looking for ways to *manipulate the charges of the earth and sky and so affect the weather by using an electronic beam to ionize or de- ionize the atmosphere over a specific area.* Recently, an ice bridge in the Antarctic collapsed and the Wilkins Ice Shelf could be on the brink of breaking away. Is HAARP melting ice? Is HAARP mapping weather patterns, agricultural seasons and crop cycles, or actually influencing them?

Responding to US economic, strategic and geo-political interests, it could easily be used and indeed has been used to selectively modify climate in different parts of the World resulting in the destabilisation of agricultural and ecological systems. It is also worth noting that the US Department of Defence has allocated substantial resources to the development of intelligence and monitoring systems on weather changes. NASA and the Department of Defence's National Imagery and Mapping Agency (NIMA) are working on 'imagery for studies of flooding, erosion, land-slide hazards, earthquakes, ecological zones, weather forecasts, and climate change' with data relayed from satellites.

2004 Asian Earthquake /Tsunami

On 26th December 2004, the Indian Ocean earthquake that generated the subsequent tsunami that killed over one quarter of a million people was unleashed on an unsuspecting world. The magnitude of this earthquake was 9.3 on the Richter scale, making it one of the most deadly and destructive in all known history. Wikipedia states that the earthquake itself lasted almost ten minutes when most major earthquakes last no more than a few seconds. It caused the entire planet to vibrate several centimetres and it also triggered earthquakes elsewhere, even as far away as Alaska. The section in Wikipedia, 'Tectonic Plates' provides more shocking pieces of information.

"Seismographic and acoustic data indicate that the first phase involved the formation of a rupture about . . . 250 miles . . . long and . . . 60 miles wide, located . . . 19 miles . . . beneath the sea bed - the longest known rupture ever known to have been caused by an earthquake.

As well as the sideways movement between the plates, the sea bed is estimated to have risen by several metres, displacing an estimated . . . 7 cubic miles . . . of water and triggering devastating tsunami waves. The waves did not originate from a point source, as mistakenly depicted in some illustrations of their spread, but radiated outwards along the entire . . . 750 miles . . . length of the rupture. This greatly increased the geographical area over which the waves were observed, reaching as far as Mexico, Chile and the Arctic. The raising of the seabed significantly reduced the capacity of the Indian Ocean, producing a permanent rise in the global sea level by an estimated 0.1 mm."

These facts are truly astounding. There has obviously been a massive impact, including the raising of the seabed, causing the sea level worldwide to rise by 0.1 mm.

In the section entitled 'Power of the earthquake', there are even more disturbing statistics.

"The total energy released by the earthquake in the Indian Ocean . . . is equivalent to 100 gigatons of TNT, or about as much energy as is used in the United States in 6 months. It is estimated to have resulted in an oscillation of the Earth's surface of about 20–30 cm (8 to 12 in), equivalent to the effect of the tidal forces caused by the Sun and Moon. The shock waves of the earthquake were felt across the planet; as far away as Oklahoma, vertical movements of 3 mm (0.12 in) were recorded. The entire Earth's surface is estimated to have moved vertically by up to 1 cm. . . . It also caused the Earth to minutely 'wobble' on its axis by up to 2.5 cm (1 in) . . . or perhaps by up to 5 or 6 cm (2.0 to 2.4 in)."

So, here is an event that expends so much energy it literally shortens the day, causes the earth to wobble and its surface to raise significantly.

Why would the Elite-controlled, US military-industrial complex want to turn the Indian Ocean area into a huge disaster area? It seems inconceivable and pointlessly destructive – at first glance. However, consider this; the Aceh area of Indonesia, the geographical location most badly hit by the earthquake/tsunami is known to be extremely rich in untapped oil resources. Once this fact is understood it all becomes much clearer. At this time, probably significantly, Aceh was in the grip of a devastating civil war, largely unreported in the Western, controlled media and seriously hampering the extraction and distribution of the oil reserves.

It would seem that on the morning of 26 December 2004, despite subsequent denials, the US authorities had foreknowledge of the earthquake (via the extensive early warning system in place) and the probable course of and the effects of the resulting tsunami. As was the case on 9-11, the automatic warning system stood down, to allow a terrorist act to occur using the HAARP technology, to justify upcoming militarisation of the area with US troops in an area rich with oil. Whether HAARP-induced or not, the critical issue would be the stand-down of the automatic earthquake warning system among its subscribing member nations. This is at best criminal negligence and at worst a deliberate act of genocide for monetary and geopolitical gain.

The provable fact that an advance warning was given to Australia and the US military base in Indonesia only, demonstrates conclusively that there was criminal intent involved. The third-world areas affected were left to suffer horrendously whilst oil-rich Aceh was invaded by over 2000 heavily armed US marines and two aircraft carriers equipped with dozens of 'state of the art' Cobra attack helicopters. Strange also that the US military base in Indonesia also knew in advance about the planned attack / Tsunami. The critical point of fore-knowledge, whilst not comprising conclusive proof of the use of HAARP technology, at least makes this possibility realistic. We know that the technology has the capability to create the Asian tsunami so it is a fairly simple step of logic to deduce that the end-goal, ie. the US invasion of Aceh province would have justified the action in the twisted minds of those self-styled masters of the Universe. Why would it be left to chance and the hope that a purely-by-chance incident of geological devastation would occur to facilitate a planned invasion?

"Others (terrorists) are engaging even in an eco-type of terrorism whereby they can alter the climate, set off earthquakes and volcanoes remotely through the use of electromagnetic waves... So there are plenty of ingenious minds out there that are at work finding ways in which they can wreak terror upon other nations... It's real, and that's the reason why we have to intensify our (counterterrorism) efforts." US Secretary of Defence, William Cohen, April 1997 at a 'counter-terrorism conference'

Am I alone in finding the irony in this statement?

Cohen confirmed that there are in existence, electromagnetic weapons of this nature and there have been for many years, which have been and are being used to initiate earthquakes, engineer the weather and climate and also initiate the eruption of volcanoes. Several nations now indeed have these weapons.

Following on shortly after the tsunami, on 28th March 2005, there was another earthquake in Northern Sumatra and Indonesia, measuring an almost equally gigantic 8.7 on the Richter scale, according to the National Earthquake Information Centre, US Geological Survey. In addition, there were to be a total of six giant earthquakes around the World in 2005, all with a magnitude greater than 7.0.

Woods Hole Oceanographic Institution issued a news release entitled "*Major Caribbean Earthquakes and Tsunamis a Real Risk — Events rare, but scientists call for public awareness, warning system.*"

Paragraph 2 states that, "*In a new study published December 24, 2004 in the Journal of Geophysical Research from the American Geophysical Union, geologists Uri ten Brink of the U.S. Geological Survey in Woods Hole and Jian Lin of the Woods Hole Oceanographic Institution (WHOI) report a heightened earthquake risk of the Septentrional fault zone, which cuts through the highly populated region of the Cibao Valley in the Dominican Republic. In addition, they caution, the geologically active offshore Puerto Rico and Hispaniola trenches are capable of producing earthquakes of magnitude 7.5 and higher. The Indonesian earthquake on December 26, which generated a tsunami that killed (to date), an estimated 250,000 people, came from a fault of similar structure, but was a magnitude 9.0, much larger than the recorded quakes near the Puerto Rico Trench.*"

There appeared to be a sudden spate of major earthquakes in 2005. On 8th October 2005, yet another massive quake killed over 25,000 people and injured and displaced many thousands more in the Hindu Kush mountain region of southern Pakistan. Estimates of the quake's magnitude varied from 6.8 to 7.8, with the United States Geological Survey putting the number at 7.6. Its epicentre was roughly 60 miles north of the Pakistani capital, Islamabad, where 20 'significant aftershocks' measuring between 5 and 6.2 magnitude were felt throughout the day, said Dr. Qamar-uz-Zaman Chaudhry, director general of the Meteorological Department in Islamabad.

The earthquake, which sent tremors as far east as New Delhi, the Indian capital, and west to Kabul, the capital of Afghanistan, the 'biggest shock to strike the country in a century', besides of course the US and allied Military forces.

Two other major, more recent earthquakes are worthy of further mention in this context.

2008 China earthquake, Sichuan Province

China actually seriously considered going to war with the USA in retaliation for what was seen as deliberate act of terrorism in instigating the 2008 earthquake.

Photographs proved that 90 million watt, pulsed long-wave radio waves from the HAARP array in Alaska, combined with pulsed microwaves from a US Military Satellite in orbit, caused Chinese land to 'resonate'.

As the land began resonating, its movement tore itself apart, causing the massive earthquake.

Photos from Tianshui city, Gansu province, China the city nearest the epicentre of the quake, show strange cloud patterns a full two days before the quake hit. The cloud formations can be seen breaking apart in patterns indicating they were being hit systematically with something from above.

The clouds were being affected by the two sets of waves. As the waves beamed down from the sky, the clouds broke apart in very orderly fashion; proving that something from above, other than the wind was affecting this region of China. Some clouds even had their own rainbow signatures. At the time of writing, these images may still be seen here:
http://www.youtube.com/watch?v=KKMTSDzU1Z4

In this video it is actually possible to see that as the clouds move into the area being pounded by high-powered radio and micro waves, the clouds develop the internal rainbow motif. As they drift out of the high-powered radio and microwaves, the rainbows disappear.

The 'long wave' attack originated from the HAARP array in Alaska. These extremely long radio waves were pulsed slowly and travelled deep underground when they hit. The much smaller, pulsed microwaves emitted from a US military satellite, pulsed at a faster rate and, because the wavelength is so much smaller, they did not penetrate deeply into the ground. The deep rock began to resonate at one frequency and the surface rock/soil began to resonate at a different, faster rate.

The two separate rates of resonation caused literally billions of tons of dirt and rock to begin subtly, almost imperceptibly grinding against each other within the ground. With all that movement it did not take long for a key geological lock to be crushed, allowing a sudden movement of a large land area underground, which was felt as a massive earthquake at the surface.

If you think that electromagnetic waves cannot cause anything to move, consider your microwave oven. Using as little as 500 watts, microwaves travelling through food 'excite' the molecules within the food. The molecules begin rubbing together and the friction generated by the molecules bouncing off each other causes heat and the heat cooks the food. Now, take that same proven technique and multiply it to ninety million watts, pounding on a particular area for at least two full days. Would it not be possible for that amount of energy, bearing down relentlessly for at least two days, to cause the molecules inside the rocks to start moving? As the first rock molecules start to move, they move against other molecules causing not only heat but also tiny vibrations. As the vibrations spread to other rocks underground, they too start to vibrate.

When several billion tons of earth and rock start to vibrate, even imperceptibly to humans, the enormous weight of that small vibration has a truly devastating impact. All it takes is for that impact to act upon a weak point in the earth's rock structure, crushing it, which then allows a tectonic plate to move a distance possibly as small as one inch. When billions of tons of rock and earth suddenly move one inch, the resulting shockwave is felt as a huge earthquake.

Humans, surrounded by a buffer of air and subjected to local noise from traffic, aircraft and all other everyday sounds, would not hear or feel the subtle vibration underground, although Chinese seismic sensors had detected the movement.

Initially, even meteorologists in China thought this was a natural phenomenon - until the earthquake struck in the exact same area. Then by the simple process of putting two and two together, they deduced that China had been subtly attacked.

At least 90,000 innocent people lost their lives whilst many hundreds of thousands were injured and left homeless. More than half a million buildings collapsed and the full scale of the disaster is unimaginable and its effects will be felt for decades to come.

While the human cost was steep, the financial impact of this attack total in the hundreds of billions, perhaps even trillions of dollars.

I believe that this attack was deliberate and it was done to show the Chinese who were the masters. Obey us (the Western Elite, 'New World Order') or China will be destroyed with a weapon that cannot be defended against and which leaves no forensic evidence to prove the quake was deliberate. The long-term ramifications of this are yet to fully unfold, but rest assured that China has not forgotten and will not just stand by and allow itself to be attacked in this manner. There have already been suspected moves on the part of the Chinese to use their massive financial capabilities to attack the US economy in retaliation and possibly de-stabilise the dollar and we are just now beginning to see the effects of this policy coming to fruition.

2010 Haiti earthquake

The 7.0 Earthquake striking Haiti destroyed much of The Haitian National Palace and most of Haiti as well. With most living well below the poverty threshold on £1 per day and one in four people living with mud floors, one can only imagine the devastation to a country that was barely surviving after being hit with four hurricanes in quick succession. The better-off in their concrete homes were crushed to death while the poor survived in tents.

Haiti is an independent black nation, a long time threat to American hegemony and imperialism and has defied the US government control structure for years. It is relatively close to a HAARP array in Puerto Rico, just a few hundred miles away and is a 3rd world country sat in the middle of 'Western civilisation'. Its citizens are little better off than peasants and ripe for exploitation without the rest of the world asking too many questions.

A street camera at the time of the earthquake clearly showed the ground moving up and down only, as if roiling, percolating or boiling. There was very little sway in the telephone poles. This very salient fact indicates super-heated ground water, not crust breaking or crust slippage which always goes sideways. This has to be the most telling evidence uncovered so far.

A video, taken above the city http://www.youtube.com/watch?v=tB_XXqu6pmk shows dust and what appears to be steam rising all across the quake zone. There also appear to be some HAARP clouds, but this could possibly be just the sunset catching the bottoms of clouds as the quake occurred at 5.00pm.

A strange anomaly is that the earthquake was not actually on a fault line, but far south of the North American and Caribbean plates. Earthquakes are a particularly rare occurrence there, much less huge ones like this one. HAARP is able to create earthquakes anywhere there is water or trapped moisture and our planet is obviously riddled with underground water and pockets of gas. There were an excessive number of 5.0 aftershocks. This is highly unusual and may indicate the superheated ground could not cool off quickly enough, causing a recurrence of the problem. Scalar waves which are generated from electromagnetic waves can accomplish this and so this is crucial circumstantial evidence pointing to HAARP as the culprit.

Mainstream news blatantly lied about the earthquake being on the North American and Caribbean fault lines. If they tell lies about this issue, the question that remains in my mind is 'why is the media peddling disinformation about the issue?' When unnecessary lies are being propagated, one can only conclude that something is being covered-up.

Actually, Haiti is prime real estate once all the locals are disposed of or marginalised. The US military is now in control, without firing a shot and they seem to be doing a pretty good job of bringing about the destruction of the country's infrastructure having been given a good head start by its clandestine technology. The speed with which the 20,000 US troops arrived on the island, proves that plans were already in place before the event. And subsequent delays in the provision of vital supplies of food and medical aid, created the desperation and violence by the frustrated masses of survivors that provided a perfect excuse or justification for the imposition of heavy security measures.

Respect to the Elite is due. They are indeed very, very clever and audacious. Using HAARP technology, they have now perfected the science of taking over a country, murdering thousands of its citizens in cold blood and then being thanked by their victims.

Leaving aside the Earthquake situation for the moment, we can also investigate and scrutinise the recent spate of hurricanes, especially the two most disastrous in American history, Andrew in 1992 which devastated a large area of Florida and

Katrina in 2005, which drowned an entire American city, New Orleans and made it resemble a third world disaster zone.

Hurricane Andrew 1992

Hurricane Andrew made landfall in the early hours of 24th August 1992 in South Dade County, Florida. According to the eye witness report of K T Frankovich, reported in Nexus magazine;

"Contrary to what the American news media broadcast across the United States and throughout Europe, the first outer wall of the hurricane unexpectedly slammed into South Dade, packing 214+ mph winds which quickly escalated to 350+ mph. Most of the 414,151 residents living in the danger zone were asleep when the outer wall struck. Thousands of them lost their lives, for no one in South Dade had been evacuated or even advised to evacuate. Instead, residents had been repeatedly informed by local news media that South Dade should expect to experience "50 mph winds".

By 11.00 am the following morning, 8,230 mobile homes along with 9,140 apartments had vanished off the face of the Earth. The Hiroshima-like horror was beyond catastrophic. Entire families perished in ways too horrifying to describe. The stench of death had already begun to saturate miles and miles of the massive devastation; the hot humid air was reeking with foul, rotting flesh.

How do I know? Because I was in the midst of it all!

Never will I forget the frantic, last-minute "emergency alert" broadcast that was aired on television just before all hell broke loose. My son and I had the TV on, hoping to catch an updated report on the hurricane, when the screen suddenly went blank with a loud warning signal. Before we knew it, a panic-stricken voice began the announcement:

We interrupt this program to bring you an emergency alert from the National Broadcast Emergency Centre. This is an emergency alert! I repeat, this is an emergency alert! The outer winds of hurricane Andrew have just reached the Florida coast. Hurricane Andrew has unexpectedly shifted five degrees south. I repeat, Hurricane Andrew has shifted five degrees south. Andrew is expected to strike South Dade within minutes. I repeat, Andrew is expected to strike South Dade within minutes. All South Dade residents should take immediate cover! I repeat, all South Dade residents should take immediate cover! This is an emergency alert!

Our tiny pre-fab apartment, which was nothing more than a glorified mobile home, had been constructed to withstand maximum wind speeds of 90 mph. The blood-curdling announcement gripped us both. Paralyzed by sheer terror, our bulging eyes stayed glued to the television as the voice continued.

All South Dade residents are advised to stay put! Do not attempt to leave the area!

Within seconds, we actually heard hurricane Andrew bearing down on us, slamming into us with all the force of a speeding locomotive. The horrendous wall of winds crashed against our tiny apartment like an exploding bomb! Glasses flew off the kitchen counter, shattering onto the quaking floor. Hanging pictures plunged straight down the walls towards the ground. The huge hanging mirror crashed on top of the television set, spraying the living room with shattered glass. The entire apartment resembled a rickety old train, shaking fiercely out of control while rumbling down a railroad track. The screeching winds quickly transformed into the piercing, monotone hum of a jet engine, sounding as if it had sucked us inside! It was so deafening, all other noises ceased to exist. It felt like a monstrous earthquake-and-tornado hitting at the same time!

Before either one of us could react, the metal front door of our apartment began to peel steadily downward towards the floor, like a piece of wet, limp paper. Then the voracious jaws of Andrew attacked for the final kill. A mega-giant, two-storey-tall, solid concrete transformer pole with electrical cables attached, torpedoed right through our living room wall and roof, exploding the entire building on impact! And that was just the beginning.

There isn't a person on the face of this Earth who will ever convince me that hurricane Andrew was a "hurricane" by any sense of the definition. Just ask any survivor of Andrew what the six-and-a-half-hour siege was like and the answer will always be the same.

"We didn't have any prior warning. We heard hurricane Andrew suddenly bearing down on us like a speeding locomotive."

This is the same description given by survivors of monstrous F-5 tornadoes (packing winds of 350+ mph) the only difference being that tornadoes strike for just seconds, whereas hurricane Andrew struck and stayed for hours on end.

The injuries of those who survived were mind-boggling. I had a broken jaw with eight teeth knocked out. Huge shards of glass impaled my body so deeply, they were impossible to remove without the aid of a scalpel. My head injuries were so severe that they permanently affected my eyesight.

But I was only one amongst thousands of severely injured victims who struggled to survive the aftermath. For ten long days we were roped off from the outside world by United States military forces, leaving us stranded with no food, no water, no medical supplies, no shelter. Suffering from severe shell-shock, we waited and waited for rescue teams to arrive, but that just never happened. None of the injured in the roped-off areas was ever rescued from the devastation. It was the worst gut-wrenching betrayal I have ever experienced. I saw grown men lying on the ground in the foetal position, moaning and groaning pathetically as they tried to hug and rock themselves. My son was amongst them.

Don't get me wrong. United States military forces were indeed present in the roped-off areas within hours of Andrew ending. But they were not there to help survivors. The National Guard along with the Coast Guard, the Army, FEMA (the Federal Emergency Management Agency), Metro Dade Police, state police and local police removed dead bodies and body parts as quickly as possible during those first ten days of the aftermath. Horrified survivors watched as both uniformed and civilian- clothed men searched the rubble and filled body bags, which they then stacked in military vehicles or huge refrigerator trucks normally used to transport food, only to drive off and leave the stranded injured to fend for themselves.

Not until I managed to escape the aftermath did I discover that the 'thermo-king' sections of these same refrigerator trucks, jam-packed with wall-to-wall body bags, ended up being stored at Card Sound Navy Base, located in an isolated area just above the Florida Keys. The inside temperature was kept cool by portable generators until the bodies were either incinerated or just plain dumped into huge open grave-pits.

Those working on the body pick-up operation were forced to take what is known as the Oath of Sworn Secrecy, which is strictly enforced by the government. Many of them plunged into shock, once exposed to the ghastly devastation and countless mutilated bodies.

The horrors were way beyond human comprehension. I can vouch for this, as I accidentally stepped on the severed hand of a young child when I initially crawled out of the debris, only to witness shortly thereafter two dead teenagers and the decapitated body of a baby girl.

Fighting mental shock became such a big problem for the body pick-up teams that a special group of psychiatrists had to be brought in to help them cope with it. I believe this in itself is the reason why many who worked on the body collection didn't comprehend the tragic consequences this would inevitably lead to in the future.

The survivors of hurricane Andrew and the rest of the American people were betrayed by their own government. But the betrayal also extended to foreign nationals. At the time Andrew struck, South Dade was inhabited by a large population of Mexican illegal immigrants. The United States Department of Immigration was fully aware of their presence but quietly turned its back on the situation, knowing full well that South Dade farmers couldn't afford to harvest their crops without the help of the Mexican illegals. The heavily populated migrant camps were situated at the edge of the Florida Everglades. The people who lived there vanished without a trace during that fated night. Many bodies were found way out in the Everglades.

When I lectured at the Clearwater Convention in Florida in 1999, a man in the audience stood up and introduced himself as Chief Petty Officer Roy Howard. He proceeded to address the audience with this exact statement, which is now a matter of public record:

'Just for your information, I was called up to active duty after hurricane Andrew went through South Dade County. I spent nine weeks down there. Now I will certify for the benefit of our audience here that the death figures that were officially published are totally inaccurate. According to the information which I received from my own sources within the National Guard, the figure I was quoted when I was down there was 5,280-something. And they were quietly disposed of in incinerators that were hurriedly put together by both the National Guard and FEMA..'.

As the Chief Petty Officer stated, '5,280-something' bodies were confiscated by the United States National Guard. In addition to this, the Coast Guard independently confiscated 1,500 bodies from the lakes and surrounding waters. Neither one of these figures embraces the number of dead bodies confiscated by other branches of federal and state government directly involved in the body pick-up operation. This leaves the number of dead confiscated by various US authorities in South Dade still unknown.

The total number who died during hurricane Andrew is obviously staggering, yet whenever the 'official death toll' is mentioned in the media, a figure of anywhere between 15 and 59 is quoted. The population of the 21 communities annihilated by Andrew's eye-wall had been officially recorded by the Dade County Census Bureau as 415,151 before Andrew struck.

Bodies of human beings confiscated and disposed-of like rubbish, as if their lives had no more worth or meaning than a piece of discarded litter - it's horrifying to be suddenly confronted by the same kind of atrocities as perpetrated by the Nazis. Once again repeating history, a master-minded cover-up was dutifully carried out by armed military forces, right smack in the midst of horrendous human suffering.

To complete this historical comparison, in the same way that many residents who lived near Nazi concentration camps were unaware or in denial of the atrocities close by, so too were many residents who were located just outside the catastrophic devastation left behind by Andrew's eye-wall.

So what actually did take place when Andrew survivors tried to get help from those collecting dead bodies in the aftermath? Well, I for one can give a first-hand account.

About the third day into the aftermath, a long line of police cars cautiously drove into my area during the late afternoon. We had not had contact with any other people from outside the devastation up until this point. There were approximately 12 to 15 police cars comprising this caravan, each marked from different locations throughout the state. Each car was driven by a man dressed in a dark police uniform and had three other plain-clothed men riding as passengers, making a total of four men in each vehicle.

Someone from our group spotted the caravan and ran to get me, knowing that I had been badly injured and urgently needed emergency medical help. My twenty-five-year-old son and one other adult male survivor helped escort me to the caravan. We hurried towards the lead car. It stopped moving when we approached the driver's side. The officer sitting behind the wheel rolled down the window. For a few moments he rudely ignored us, at one point giving us an impatient look of disgust.

This is the exact conversation and course of events that took place....

"Please, sir, I need medical help," I begged, barely able to speak. The officer sitting behind the wheel sighed heavily. He turned his head away from me and gazed out his windshield. The other three men in the car quietly looked at me.

"Sir, please, I need to get to a hospital...," I begged frantically.

The officer took his time about reaching over to turn off the engine. With another sigh, he slowly opened the door and climbed out. He then proceeded to close the door and stood there with his legs spread astride. "Lady, do me a favour," he answered. "Find yourself a piece of paper and a pencil. Write down your name and social security number next to the telephone number of your nearest living relative. Tuck the piece of paper in your pocket so tomorrow, when I find your body, I'll know who to contact."

"No! No!" I cried out. "You don't understand. I need to get to a hospital. I've been badly injured."

"No! You're the one who doesn't understand," he hissed back. With that, he reached over to his holster and took out his gun. He grabbed me, forcing me up against the side of the car, and proceeded to put the barrel of the gun against my temple. I heard the hammer cock.

From the position he had pushed me into, I could see directly into the car. The man sitting in the front passenger seat looked away from me immediately, glancing down at the floor. The two passengers in the back seat turned their heads quickly, staring out the window on the opposite side of the car.

My son and the other survivor watched as the officer had pulled back the hammer on the gun. So shocked out of their minds by what they were witnessing, neither one could move!

"You don't belong here!" the officer growled, pressing the barrel into the side of my head. "Now you get the hell outta here before I blow away your ass!"

He shoved my face into the car window and then released me. Someone grabbed me from behind and whirled me around so fast, I didn't have time to think! Before I knew it, I was being thrown over a shoulder. My rescuer took off running as fast as he could! I caught a brief glimpse of my son running next to me. With one gigantic leap, he and the survivor who carried me, dove behind a pile of debris. All three of us crashed on top of each other in one tangled-up heap.

"I'll shoot your damn asses!" the officer's voice rang out.

When hurricane Andrew slammed into South Dade, the State Attorney of Florida was none other than Janet Reno. Her office was located at the Dade County Court House in the City of Miami. The President of the United States was President George H.W. Bush, and the Vice-President was Dan Quayle. Bill Clinton was running for President, and Al Gore for Vice-President. Senator Bob Graham held office, and the late Lawton Chiles was Governor of Florida. His successor turned out to be Jeb Bush, still the Governor of Florida and, ironically enough, the son of former President Bush whose other son, George W. Bush, the then Governor of Texas, has since become the "self-selected" President of the United States...

Curious how the United States Government evacuated Homestead Air Force Base just before hurricane Andrew struck, yet never released the information to the civilians of South Dade.

"This is worse than anything we saw in Saudi," said Master Sgt Lester Richardson (who had spent six months in the Middle East during Operation Desert Storm) one week into the aftermath. "These people need a miracle" The survivors did need "a miracle", but what we got instead didn't resemble anything near it.

While we remained roped off from the outside world by Metro Dade Police and the military, the news media reported grossly understated information from the first day onward.

On August 24, 1992, the morning hurricane Andrew ended, the Miami Herald broke with:

Andrew Hits Hardest in South Dade. Five thousand people were left homeless by the storm, Metro Dade Police Director announced. They'll be moved into shelters in North Dade. Over subsequent days, the Miami Herald read as follows:

August 25, 1992:

Destruction at Dawn. Among worst hit in the Country Walk area of South Dade, few homes escaped at least minor damage and many were utterly destroyed. 10 killed in Dade.

August 27, 1992:

The Toll Rises. 22 dead as the search continues. 63,000 homes destroyed. 175,000 homeless. 1 million without power.

August 28, 1992:

WE NEED HELP. Relief effort collapsing due to United States inaction, Metro charges. Aid us now or more will die, Feds told. As Dade County's hurricane relief effort neared collapse Thursday, more than 1,500 airborne US soldiers were ordered into the county to cope with what is now being called the worst natural disaster in United States history.   The move came after a day of bitter sniping among agencies that share responsibility for the relief effort.

United States aid official Wallace Stickler stated:

"Andrew has caused more destruction and affected more people than any disaster America has ever had." Dade County's Emergency Director pleaded for federal help, one angry voice among many that spoke in dire terms of needs unmet. Frustrated to the point of tears, Kate Hale said that the relief project was on the brink of collapse, a victim of incompetence and political games:

"Where the hell is the cavalry on this one? We need food! We need water! We need people! If we do not get more food into the south end [South Dade] in a very short period of time, we are going to have more casualties!

"We have a catastrophic disaster. We are hours away from more casualties. We are essentially the walking wounded. We have appealed through the State to the Federal Government. We've had a lot of people down here for press conferences but Dade County is on its own. Dade County is being caught in the middle of something and we are being victimized.

"Quit playing like a bunch of kids and get us aid! Sort out your political games afterward!"

On the same day Hale made the desperate plea, Miami Herald staff writers Martin Merzer and Tom Fiedler wrote: "The question echoed through the debris Thursday: If we can do it for Bangladesh, for the Philippines, for the Kurds of northern Iraq, why in God's name can't we deliver basic necessities of life to the ravaged population of our own Gold Coast?"

The short answer: because no single person or agency is in charge. The result: a planeload of food and equipment is still a rarity. Instead of delivering goods, helicopter pilots shuttle government officials who just sit idle. Metro police turn away individuals trying to bring in food or water to a barren South Dade.

On August 29, 1992, six days into the aftermath, the Miami Herald reported:

Problems Plague Red Cross.
The man on the phone wanted to donate 100 electric generators, extension cords and enough tools to build a small subdivision. But the operator who took his call at the Red Cross Command Centre in Miami had no idea what to do with the offer.

"We get a call, we take a message, we give it to somebody who signs it to somebody else," said the operator, Melitta de Liefd.

"We have no idea what happens to it. The whole place is being run by senior citizens and college kids."

Welcome to Red Cross headquarters - where the brains of Dade County rescue effort have been knocked almost unconscious most of the week.

Callers offering services and supplies are put on hold. Others can't get through at all. The hurt and suffering plead for help over ham radio. On August 29, 1992, one week after hurricane Andrew struck, the Fort Lauderdale Sun Sentinel reported 250,000 people homeless in South Dade.

A NUCLEAR INCIDENT

Of course, the rather 'insignificant' incident resulting from Andrew's winds bombarding the Turkey Point Nuclear Power Plant was not aired by the news media either nationally or abroad.

Tom Dubocq reported in the Miami Herald of September 5, 1992:

Demolition crews toppled a 400-foot smokestack at Turkey Point [Nuclear] Power Plant [owned by Florida Power and Light Company], Friday [September 4]. The stack, which had a gaping 200-foot crack, was dropped without a hitch, a Florida Power and Light [FPL] spokesman said. The other smokestack at the plant will be salvaged. Turkey Point *will be shut down for several months while repairs are made. The cost will exceed $90 million, according to an initial damage report.*

When Turkey Point was built in the 1960s, its main structures were designed to withstand 235 mph winds. Hurricane Andrew was clocked at 164 mph at the plant. FPL officials don't know why the smokestack didn't hold up...

One hundred million dollars' worth of damage resulted from the nuclear power plant's smokestack having been cracked wide open. The plant is situated approximately 15 miles northeast of where I lived. How well I recall the leaflets circulated several months before Andrew struck, advising all residents within a "thirty-five mile radius" of Turkey Point nuclear plant to be aware of the potential hazards involved if an event such as a natural disaster or unexpected catastrophe happened. Such a grim reminder of the Chernobyl tragedy.

Could it be more than coincidence that within 24 hours of hurricane Andrew ending, all 12 survivors in my little group, including our animals, broke out in big, raw, oozing sores which itched and burned at the same time? We suffered horrible headaches which made us so nauseous we had the dry heaves, and our stomachs cramped badly from sudden onsets of diarrhoea. These symptoms lasted well over three months. Within a relatively short period of time, each one of our surviving animals died from cancer.

HURRICANE BUREAU'S FAILURE TO WARN

Speaking of coincidence, I often wonder what kind of a coincidence it is that the National Hurricane Bureau is responsible for reporting to the US Department of Commerce - especially considering that during 1992 South Florida did $31 billion worth of trade in tourism.

Hurricane Andrew had barely left Florida, heading for Louisiana, when the Division of Tourism placed a $47,000 advertisement in USA Today, reading 'Florida, we're still open.'

"Most people have very short memories. We're all sort of banking on that," said Donal Dermody, Director of the Nova University Centre for Hospitality Management.

Kind of puts a big damper on belief in the human race: hide the truth, ignore the suffering, do it for a dollar!

What upsets me most is the incident that happened during the late afternoon hours just prior to Andrew striking. I had just walked out to the garbage dumpsters, located by the parking lot, to throw away some garbage. I turned to head back to the apartment when the horn of an oncoming car began blasting away. I looked up to see a familiar resident, whom I had spoken to on many different occasions, heading directly towards me. This particular individual worked at Metro zoo. Being affiliated with wild animals, he frequently stopped by to ask me questions about the behaviour of certain species. He sped right up to me and then slammed on the brakes.

"Come here!" he whispered excitedly. I leaned down close to him. "What's the matter?"

"Listen!" he paused to look around nervously. "You've got to get the hell outta here now!"

"Why?" I asked, puzzled by his behaviour. "I haven't got time to explain," he whispered. "But I just came from the National Hurricane Bureau in the Gables. Gotta friend of mine who works over there; bigwig - know what I mean?"

"Yeah..." I nodded.

"Well, this isn't for public information, if you get my drift," he went on rapidly. "But the National Hurricane Bureau has known all along that hurricane Andrew is going to slam into South Dade! They're telling the public it's going to come in at Palm Beach because they want Miami Beach evacuated, and there aren't enough shelters for South Dade residents to evacuate to. They don't wanna cause panic, so they're keeping quiet. We're all a bunch of god-damn sitting ducks! You got to get the hell outta here! This is a killer hurricane! Nobody's ever seen anything like this before!"

"Holy shit!" I exclaimed, shocked out of my mind. "You mean Andrew's coming over South Dade?"

"Damn straight! That's exactly what I mean! They figure the eye of the storm is coming right in over us! Those fellas at the National Hurricane Bureau have known it all along! I'm gettin' the hell outta here now! Shit, man, this thing is a killer hurricane! Listen, I gotta run! Get your son and get the hell out now! You ain't gonna have a shot in hell once it hits!"

I ran into the apartment and called my son at work, begging him to come home so we could get out. I had no reason to disbelieve anything I had just heard. I knew my neighbour well enough to know he wouldn't fabricate anything like this. So I related the entire conversation to my son, Eric. He was stunned! Eric said he would leave work within a few minutes, but as the minutes ticked on they dragged into hours.

Another immediate course of action I took after hearing the terrifying warning from my neighbour was to phone the local CBS television station located in Miami. I called three separate times. Each time, my call went directly into the local news broadcast room of meteorologist Bryan Norcross. Although I never spoke to Norcross directly, I did manage to speak to three separate individuals working in the broadcast room.

I specifically stated: "I live in South Dade, adjacent to Metro zoo and within walking distance of Country Walk, in a pre-fab apartment that is constructed to withstand up to 90 mph winds. Should I evacuate?"

All three individuals advised and reassured me that I was situated in a safe area. There definitely wasn't need for me to take any evacuation measures.

Meanwhile, one work catastrophe after another seemed to crash down on my son, until finally it was just too late for us to evacuate. By the time he got home it was almost midnight. Within minutes of his arrival, Andrew slammed into us with full force.

ONGOING TRAGEDIES FROM THE COVER-UPS

It's not easy dealing with the anguish I feel because of all the perpetrated lies. So much suffering resulted. It took three-and-a-half weeks before my son and I managed to escape the devastation on our own. Homeless and penniless, with no insurance to cover our losses, we slowly made our way north towards Broward County, our only possessions being the clothes on our backs and a demolished van. The long, agonizing journey turned out to be another nightmare from hell.

Over 4,000 people were officially listed as 'missing' in Andrew when we parted South Dade. I had lost 23 pounds during those wretched weeks of being trapped in the devastation and still had not received any medical attention. Little did I realize it would take another three weeks before a doctor would even agree to see me without any money or identification. By then, six weeks had passed since I had been injured. Most of my teeth had turned a putrid grey colour because the nerves had died as a result of fierce blows to my head, complicated by my broken jaw. The final heartbreak came when doctors discovered the optic nerve in both my eyes had begun to die off - which meant, because of the head injuries, I was going blind.

This may sound strange but, regardless, it is the truth. Today, in the year 2001, there still remain three ongoing tragedies created by hurricane Andrew cover-up - -tragedies which remain unbearable for the survivors to live with.

The first tragedy is the horrifying fact that the bodies of our loved ones were intentionally confiscated from us by our own government and then so inhumanely disposed of. Without graves, or some kind of memorial erected in their memory, we have no hope of reaching closure.
The second tragedy is the impact the cover-ups had in downplaying, dismissing and ignoring our horrendous suffering.

And the third tragedy is the great number of Andrew survivors who were inevitably forced to join the ranks of approximately 10 million other homeless Americans struggling to stay alive on the streets. With 10 million Americans homeless, and another

32 million Americans going to sleep hungry each night, the United States Government can't truthfully claim to be a government for all the people.

Maybe it's just me, but I honestly thought the world learned a lesson from the Nuremberg trials in Germany: 'Evil can only be defined as absence of empathy...'

It is not so much the disaster that was Hurricane Andrew that marks out this incident as a deliberate act. It is more the fact that people were deliberately deceived into staying within the potential disaster area and then once the main tragedy was over, *deliberately* and blatantly denied food and medical aid in the aftermath. Notice that it was mainly the trailer-park dwellers and lower-class housing residents who bore the brunt of the storm system. Something says to me very strongly that Andrew was purposely steered in this particular direction. After all who was going to miss a few thousand 'trailer trash'? Indeed, in the minds of the perpetrators it was probably a 'good thing'. Whilst it is probably true to say that Andrew was not specifically engineered via HAARP as it was possibly not operational in 1992, I include it here in this section as I believe it was more than likely engineered in some other 'connected' way. A few less 'useless eaters' and the blood lust satisfied into the bargain, all in all, a good days work really.

Hurricane Katrina

Thirteen years later and the similarities are all too evident. Katrina was the eleventh named tropical storm, fourth hurricane, third major hurricane, and first Category 5 hurricane of the 2005 Atlantic hurricane season. It first made landfall as a Category 1 hurricane just north of Miami, Florida on August 25, 2005, then again on August 29, then travelled along the Central Gulf Coast near New Orleans, Louisiana, as a Category 4 storm. Katrina resulted in breaches of the levee system that protected New Orleans from Lake Pontchartrain, and most of the city was subsequently flooded by the lake's waters. This and other major damage to the coastal regions of Louisiana, Mississippi, and Alabama made Katrina the most destructive and costliest natural disaster in the history of the United States.

In 2001, FEMA (Federal Emergency Management Agency) warned that a hurricane striking New Orleans was one of the three most likely disasters in the U.S. But the Bush administration cut New Orleans flood control funding by 44 percent to pay for the Iraq war. A year prior to Katrina, the U.S. Army Corps of Engineers proposed to study how New Orleans could be protected from a catastrophic hurricane, but the Bush administration ordered that the research not be undertaken.

One could conclude that Katrina was a matter of criminal negligence or an extreme example of apathy on the part of the establishment. Yet I include it in this larger picture of world environmental terror because terror is exactly what resulted, especially given the human, physical and economic destruction.

Here is an eyewitness report at the time;

"Following Hurricane Katrina and the levee that failed, people are now dying due to the lack of aid relief, some by drowning; others by starvation, dehydration, from the heat or from lack of medical attention, old and young alike, babies, grandmothers and the infirm are forced to endure this. Some are even dying from sharks that made it through the broken levee but most of all; people are dying from central government's planned denial of care.

Central government is the major hindrance to people getting what they desperately require, there are even check points set up on the escape routes to prevent people from leaving this quagmire and going to places where there is food, water, electricity and shelter! Likewise, those wishing to assist, ordinary professional folk, coming with food, water, aid etc are turned back and thus the situation is perpetuated.

It is quite possible that further major problems will result, much due to the 'deliberately inept' handling of the crisis by FEMA / Central Government. Loss of life will be far greater and damage to properties due to sustained water exposure will also be at a higher level. Resultant diseases from allowing the situation to fester will be more widespread. Various unpredictables and unknowns such as the impact of placing Level 3 & 4 Bio Labs into such unsuitable surroundings may well take their toll, with the escape of some seriously dangerous biological / chemical toxins into the environment. A similar case will apply to industrial operations, eg from stored chemicals."

Could the levees in New Orleans have been intentionally blown? Many local eye-witnesses stated that they heard loud explosions immediately before the water began pouring through the breached flood defences.

So the locals certainly seem to think so, yet as usual, the mainstream media totally ignored this theory. When Katrina hit, it drifted 15 miles to the east of where forecasters said it would strike. Therefore it wasn't quite the monster described. The storm passed through with relatively minor damage, it was the storm surge from the Gulf that caused Lake Pontchartrain to rise three feet and the subsequent flooding.

This scenario is not as crazy as it sounds. In fact this exact thing has happened before in the same city.   In 1927, the Mississippi River broke its banks in 145 places, depositing water at depths of up to 30ft over 27,000 square miles of land.

The disaster changed American society, shifting hundreds of thousands of delta-dwelling blacks into northern cities and cementing the divisions and suspicions that benign neglect has ensured remain today.   New Orleans' (mainly white) business class pressurized the state to dynamite levees upstream, releasing water into mainly black occupied areas of the delta. Black workers were forced to work on flood relief at gunpoint, like slaves.

Two parishes, St. Bernard and Plaquemines, which had a combined population of 10,000, were destroyed. Just before Katrina, these parishes had about 10 times the 1927 population. Both parishes were totally inundated and uninhabitable in 2005 in the aftermath.

It is a known fact that New Orleans has some very valuable real estate and also that plans have been in the pipeline by Elite moneyed interests, for quite a while, to turn New Orleans into the 'entertainment capital of the south', with hundreds of casinos, theatres, hotels and entertainment complexes to rival Las Vegas itself.   Could this have been the first step along the road to achieving this goal? It is significant that the worst devastated areas of New Orleans were occupied by poor, black families, regarded largely as expendable and at best as collateral damage by the perpetrators of this evil plot. Those 'fortunates' that were not killed or badly injured in the floods, were mainly shipped, not just out of the City, but out of the state, to various temporary shelters and refugee camps set up by FEMA in the aftermath (or possibly even before the event). As I write this in October 2010, there are still hundreds, if not thousands of still displaced New Orleans families who will probably, due to their prevailing conditions of poverty, never manage to get back home to New Orleans. How convenient for some.

There are countless other instances of 'suspicious' natural disaster-type events and it is not my intention to bore the reader with a dissection of every single one. Suffice it to say that since the turn of the 21st century and just before, the number of 'natural disasters' has increased exponentially, with a new one appearing what seems to be on an almost monthly basis. See chart below.

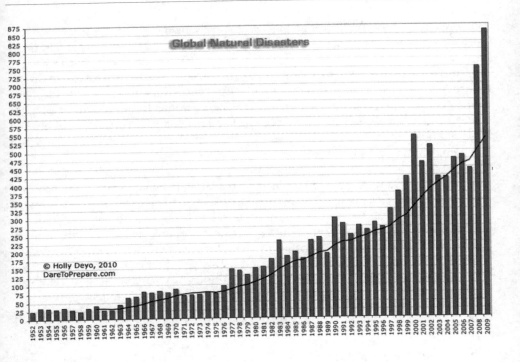

© Holly Deyo, 2010
DareToPrepare.com

What is the significance of this chart? The trend would appear to be very worrying, whether or not one blames nefarious activity on the part of a small section of humanity.

If there are new attacks against the United States, Great Britain or any other country, what we witnessed in New Orleans, Dade County, Florida, China, Haiti and many others, may have been but a fleeting glimpse into the future of global communitarianism, the Elite's so-called New World Order.

HAARP Mind Control

The ionosphere is being manipulated by US government and black ops scientists using HAARP. Of that there is not much doubt. HAARP emits focused, radiated power heating up sections of the ionosphere, which reflects ELF (extremely low frequency) waves back down to Earth. This then can then be used surreptitiously to create mood changes affecting millions of people and focussed on specific geographical regions.

The earth's natural rhythm is set at 7.83 Hz and is in perfect harmony with that of the human brain, also 7.83 Hz.

Our brains are extremely vulnerable to any technology which emits ELF waves, because we immediately start resonating to this signal as in the 'tuning-fork' effect. In the 1950s, Dr. Andrija Puharich's experiments discovered that 7.83 Hz transmissions made a person 'feel good', producing an altered-state. 10.80 Hz transmissions cause riotous behaviour and 6.60 Hz causes depression. Puharich also made ELF waves change RNA and DNA, breaking hydrogen bonds to induce a higher vibratory rate. James Hurtak, who once worked for Puharich, wrote in his book 'The Keys of Enoch' that ultra-violet caused hydrogen bonds to break and this also raised the human brain's vibratory rate.

Eventually, upon the completion of his research Dr. Puharich presented the proof of the physical and psychological effects of ELF waves on the human brain to the US government and military leaders but his research was discredited and ridiculed. He then offered this information to other Western nations and in return, the US government burned down his home in New York to shut him up and he fled to Mexico. However, the Russians discovered the ELF frequencies that negatively affected the human brain and began zapping the US Embassy in Moscow on 4 July 1976 with electromagnetic-waves, varying the signal as the experiment progressed. Indeed the Russians and North Koreans still use the 10 Hz transmissions in portable mind-control machines to extract confessions.

"Think about this for a moment - a system which can manipulate emotions, control behaviour, put you to sleep, create false memories and wipe old memories clean. Realizing this was a forecast and not necessarily the current state of technology should not cause one to believe that it is not a current issue. These systems are far from speculative. In fact, a great deal of work has already been done in this area with many systems being developed. The forecast went on to say:

'It would also appear possible to create high fidelity speech in the human body, raising the possibility of covert suggestion and psychological direction. When a high power microwave pulse in the gigahertz range strikes the human body, a very small temperature perturbation occurs. This is associated with a sudden expansion of the slightly heated tissue. This expansion is fast enough to produce an acoustic wave. If a pulse stream is used, it should be possible to create an internal acoustic field in the 5-15 kilohertz range, which is audible. Thus, it may be possible to "talk" to selected adversaries in a fashion that would be most disturbing to them.'

Is it possible to talk to a person remotely by projecting a voice into his head? The forecaster suggests that this would be "disturbing" to the victim - what an understatement, it would be pure terror. A weapon could intrude into the brain of an individual represents a gross invasion of his private life. The idea that these new systems could be created in the next several years should be cause for significant discussion and public debate." Dr. Nick Begich, 'Star Wars, Star Trek and Killing Politely'

And the mportant point of all this? It proves beyond a shadow of a doubt that HAARP's capabilities extend to exerting an influence over the human psyche. Who knows to what past and possible future, diabolical use these capabilities will be put?

In conjunction with the absorption of metals into our bodies via the high quantities of barium and aluminium present in the air (see section on chemtrails), it would appear that we are, if not already under severe attack from HAARP at present, certainly being prepared for some sort of future, sinister purpose. Whether or not this plan actually comes to fruition, only time will tell, by that time however, it will be far too late to prevent it.

We will leave this particular chapter with some further very apposite words of Dr. Nick Begich in his essay, 'Star Wars, Star Trek and Killing Politely'.

"This essay is about some of the science being developed and contemplated by military planners and others which could profoundly affect our lives. The intent of this essay is to focus discussion on these new systems by bringing them into the light of day.

Is it possible to trigger earthquakes, volcanic eruptions or weather changes by man-made activities? Is it possible to create and direct balls of energy at lightning speeds, to destroy an enemy? Is it possible to manipulate the behaviour, and even the memories, of people using specialized technologies? The United States military and others believe that this is the case. Many of these systems are well on their way to being used in the battlefield.

If you believe, as I and others do, that we've gone past the realm of probability into the realm of a dangerous reality, especially given the frequency of catastrophic events, isn't it time to send our own beam of energy to the US government, and demand a full investigation into the activities of HAARP, in particular the manipulation of hurricanes and earthquakes? This kind of activity is another form of terror we live with, because it seems like it can strike anywhere, anytime, in the guise of natural event.

Perhaps it is just Mother Nature kicking up her heels, perhaps not. In either case, a return to reality is called for in these surreal days. The simple presence of HAARP is a form of psychological terror, threatening not just the weather, but the well-being of man and survival of the planet. And that's something you'll never hear from your media weatherman."

Fukushima and the Japanese Tsunami 2011

Former NSA (US National Security Agency) analyst, Jim Stone, argues with some conviction and with solid evidence to back up his hypothesis, that there was no earthquake either on the land or in the sea either. The tsunami that devastated the Fukushima area and in particular the nuclear facility there, according to Stone, was caused by nuclear bombs in the sea and the Fukushima meltdown and explosion was a direct consequence of 'mini-nukes' concealed in cameras installed by an Israeli security firm.

What could possibly have been the motive for the such apparently senseless, deliberate destruction of a nuclear plant, which to this day is still leaking radiation and has been described (outside the mainstream of course) as being of a magnitude of seventy (70) times greater than Chernobyl? Could it have been to punish Japan for offering to enrich Iranian uranium and thereby defying the wishes of the Elite in their build up to the coming attack on Iran? I firmly believe this to be a distinct possibility given the track record. In any event, it would certainly not be a precedent. The Chinese earthquake of 2009 that caused untold destruction and the deaths of several hundred thousand people was also believed by many commentators to have been a HAARP-induced 'punishment' attack and designed specifically to show China 'who is boss'.

In comparison to the 6.8 magnitude earthquake which devastated Kobe, Japan on the 17th January 1995 the evidence speaks volumes. In Kobe there was widespread, unprecedented destruction of buildings, bridges, elevated road systems and other infrastructure. Whereas the 2011 earthquake with a magnitude of 9.0 (incidentally more than 100 times the intensity of a 6.8 mag quake) allegedly struck about 70km off the North East coast of Japan on the 11th March. It resulted in a 30 metre tsunami swamping totally undamaged bridges, houses, roads and vehicles of all kinds. In addition there had been no advance warning because there was no earthquake, yet helicopter news teams were waiting, cameras rolling and the ensuing devastation was watched by millions on live TV.

A 9.0 magnitude earthquake, which incidentally is the largest EVER recorded, should have devastated everything within a 1,000km radius. There should have been widespread urban carnage, far worse than that inflicted upon Kobe in 1995 and yet the 2011 quake did not cause a single structure to collapse.

Please check this out for yourselves. There is plenty of tsunami footage available on the Internet and if you closely examine the infrastructure the tsunami was relentlessly crashing through in several different towns and cities, there is not the slightest bit of damage to be seen to any building prior to the wave hitting. This is simply not logical at all.

Jim Stone acquired and analysed the Japanese seismographic data and proved that there was no 9.0 quake and no epicentre out at sea. However, there were three simultaneous tremors of much lesser magnitudes, all of them inland, which are to-date unexplained. In fact, the authorities blatantly lied about the 9.0 quake and as it was no natural earthquake that caused the tsunami, it therefore follows that there must have been another cause.

The official explanation for the Fukushima reactor explosions was blatant deception too. Nuclear power containment walls are extremely thick and strong and hydrogen explosions could never have destroyed them. As a historical reference point, hydrogen explosions occurred at Three Mile Island in the US in the 1970s and caused neither structural damage, nor even any injuries to plant personnel.

In a similar vein to the 'smoking gun' evidence of building 7 at the World Trade Centre on 9/11, reactor #4 at Fukushima contained no fuel on the 11th March and was therefore non-operational. And yet it exploded and was destroyed as completely as were the other reactors on that day of infamy. Reactor #4 exploding of its own accord is an utter impossibility as a reactor containing no fuel whatsoever cannot function and a non-operational reactor cannot explode unless deliberately destroyed. The destruction of reactor #4 therefore can **only** have been the result of sabotage.

Enter our old friends, the Israelis. In February 2010, Japan offered to enrich Uranium for Iran and shortly thereafter an Israeli company by the name of Magna BSP secured the contract to run security at the Fukushima Daiichi plant. They installed oversized cameras strongly resembling gun-type nuclear weapons and there is also strong evidence that they also planted Stuxnet, an Israeli computer virus that attacks Siemens power plant control systems and which Israel had previously employed to damage Iran's nuclear programme. Magna BSP also established internet data links in the reactor cores, in blatant violation of international nuclear regulations.

In the days immediately preceding the 11th March, all twelve on-site members of Magna BSP returned to Israel (shades of 9/11 again?) and in the aftermath of the disaster the Israelis publicly monitored the reactor cores via their illegal internet data-links, yet no one confronted them over this. 'Twas ever thus!

Using the skills acquired as a former NSA analyst with an engineering background, Jim Stone concluded that Israel was behind the destruction of Fukushima Daiichi. Stone proved that there was no 9.0 magnitude quake to cause the tsunami and that the tsunami must have been artificially induced, probably by a strategic nuclear device placed in the Japan Trench. The tsunami was blamed for flooding the reactors and causing the explosions, but Stone presents compelling evidence that Israel destroyed the Fukushima Daiichi plant by installing gun-type nuclear weapons in the guise of security cameras and then triggering them in the tsunami's aftermath.

Even more significantly, Stone has demonstrated that the Stuxnet virus continues to distort sensor readings at the disaster site to this day and unlike many others in the world of whistle-blowers, Stone bases his conclusions on hard evidence and unassailable logic. In fact he openly encourages and invites anyone to review and challenge his work, indeed he actively encourages it.

However, since releasing his report and making several radio appearances to support it, Jim Stone has been harassed, threatened, accused of anti-Semitism (that old chestnut again) unlawfully detained against his will and is currently facing prison on completely manufactured charges. In short, the Zionist Elite are employing the usual MO used to deal with persistent, credible dissenters to their lies and fictions.

Some slander Stone mercilessly whilst others attempt to destroy his work and yet significantly, no one has managed to successfully counter his arguments but his conclusions have ramifications that make 9/11 pale in significance. Some people have expressed suspicion that Stone might not be all he claims to be, especially given his former background, however, facts are facts and the truth stands or falls on facts.

In conclusion, it seems clear to me that Jim Stone's research is not to be taken lightly. A 9.0 magnitude earthquake never happened either in Japan or off its coastline on the 11th March 2011 and so the tsunami *must* have been artificially induced. Nor did hydrogen explosions obliterate containment walls of concrete and reinforced steel several feet thick in the Fukushima reactors. As is the case with many other incidents described in this book, the 'official' story is an outright impossibility. Israel/USA was punishing Japan for its blatant defiance and Zionist agents are currently attempting to destroy Jim Stone, the man who exposed the truth.

Meanwhile, more importantly, the Fukushima disaster continues to spew radiation at an horrific rate, wreaking absolute havoc on world ecosystems and the populations, not just of Japan but also the whole world. Strong rumours abound that the Japanese government as well as undertaking a huge cover-up operation regarding the sheer size of the problem, is desperately seeking to de-camp from Tokyo to somewhere relatively much safer, India being the favoured location.

Chemtrails – Our Toxic Skies

Have you ever heard it said that there are two types of aircraft condensation trails (contrails) that appear in the sky? Well, 'officially' there *are* two; persistent and non-persistent contrails. Let me just say right away, that this is absolute dis-information and nonsense. Unfortunately, it is yet another example of how we are being lied-to and treated like idiots again.

How often have you seen skies that look like this? Would you believe me if I told you that prior to around 1996, you would never have seen this sight. It is totally a modern phenomenon and we have become so accustomed now to this sight that we believe it has always been like this.

Often on a beautiful summer morning, the sky is a lovely clear, deep blue with no clouds in sight at all. However this will then over the course of the next few hours become criss-crossed with jet 'vapour trails' which instead of dissipating quickly, as they should (it is only crystalline water vapour after all), remain in the sky several hours after the plane has passed over, slowly spreading until often they obliterate the sun completely and turn the entire sky a watery grey colour.

There is nothing 'normal' about these contrails despite what the controlled mainstream media and government sources would have you believe in their ceaseless and relentless efforts to deflect you from the truth with their blatant disinformation. One needs only to watch the skies intermittently for a few hours to soon notice the bizarre patterns emerging as these planes track back and forth creating deliberate grid-type, x-shaped or even sometimes circular patterns on many occasions, to ensure maximum coverage. If this were a natural event, then it would happen every day in line with regular plane flight schedules, but keen observers will soon notice that there are days when we get none at all, days when we get isolated batches of trails and other days when the entire skyscape is totally obliterated.

Normal contrails are composed of tiny, fragile ice crystals formed by aircraft flying at altitudes of 33,000 feet (10km) or greater. At altitudes below 33,000 feet, normal vapour condensation trails are unable to form behind an aircraft, regardless of its type or design. Whereas above 33,000 feet, normal contrails are formed and these will appear to an observer on the ground as narrow streaks of white cloud-like material which totally dissipates in seconds, rarely extending for any appreciable distance behind the aircraft.

Chemtrails, in complete contrast to this, may be observed at any height. They have been seen emitting from aircraft flying at altitudes as low as 8,000 feet, but may be seen at all altitudes above this also. Since normal contrails cannot form at these low altitudes, any contrail formation that is observed at these elevations is probably not a contrail at all, but a genuine 'chemtrail'.

Chemtrails usually appear as normal contrails for the first few seconds, but unlike standard contrails do not evaporate almost immediately, but slowly become broader and denser over time. Over periods of several hours, parallel and ninety-degree chemtrail grid formations will eventually spread and merge to form a continuous, cirrus-like cloud formation in the sky.

Shortly after this merging, what just hours earlier was a perfectly clear blue sky will appear as a kind of insipid milky-haze, totally unnatural in all respects. Another distinguishing factor between contrails and chemtrails concerns their relative location or position in the local sky, as well as their directional characteristics.

Aircraft emitting normal contrails are constrained by FAA regulations to operate only over designated air routes; therefore, the contrails that they generate will be found consistently only within local flight-corridors, which are easily discerned by an observer at any given geographic location on the ground. In addition, air traffic along these designated routes is always unidirectional. Aircraft flying in opposing compass directions are never permitted to use the same air-routes, at the same altitudes, for obvious reasons. Therefore, only those contrails that are formed within these restricted air corridors and consistently with the same vector or direction should be considered normal contrails resulting from normal commercial airline traffic.

Another phenomenon observed to be associated with chemtrail formation is the significance of the local surface wind speed over the dispersion area. Chemtrail flights are invariably suspended whenever the ground wind speed reaches or exceeds 20 miles per hour (28 kph). This has been a consistent limiting factor throughout the range of areas where chemtrail activity has been observed and obviously normal contrail activity is never subject to this restriction, and can be seen over a wide range of measured surface wind velocities.

So of what exactly *are* these Chemtrails composed? Laboratory analysis of their contents that fall to Earth reveal the presence of several biological agents, Pseudomonas Fluorescens, Streptomyces and a restriction enzyme used to create viruses. A chemtrail researcher who had been travelling around the country for several years had a medical test which discovered dangerous pathogens in his body, the extremely rare V2 Grippe virus among them, that should only be found in laboratories. In addition many samples analysed after falling to the ground as sticky spider-web type substance have been found to contain unusually high traces of metals, and in far higher concentrations than could be expected naturally, particularly aluminium and barium.

Strange cloud patterns are not the only by-product of the chemtrail campaign. There is another, far more sinister side to this phenomenon. Whether this is a by-product or the objective of these attacks is yet to be determined. In either case however, the side effects associated with these chemtrails should be the primary focus of our attention, as this ancillary effect could very well pose a particularly serious threat to every human being living on Earth today.

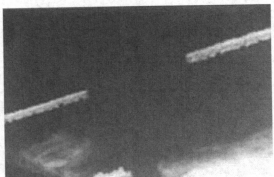

What a giveaway! Short of switching off the engines for a second, how else would this effect be achieved?

There are no known health or environmental issues associated with normal contrail emissions. They appear at this time to be completely harmless and benign. This same statement however, cannot be made in the case of authentic chemtrails. It has been shown by many dedicated researchers and posted extensively on the Internet, that the formation of chemtrails has a direct correlation to the localised, time-synchronised, outbreak of a broad range of primarily, respiratory-related or flu-like illnesses. In light of this apparent relationship, chemtrails should not be considered inherently benign, but should be treated with caution and indeed concern by those who are either studying them or simply observing them.

Since the regular spraying of our skies commenced in the late 1990s, another disturbing phenomenon has been noted and that is its correlation to the outbreak of a flu-like disease, which has been named, 'Respiratory Distress Syndrome'. Disturbingly, the components of this illness, namely the chemical, bacterial and fungal elements have been strongly linked to the bio-chemical footprint of Chemtrails.

Once again we see the same pattern unfolding, the denials by government and military agencies and as usual, total and complete avoidance by the media. Radio, television, and the press alike have all either ignored it completely or in instances where it has been brought to their attention, dismissed it as mass-paranoia or our old favourite, a *'conspiracy theory'!*

Literally thousands of eyewitnesses, with not only photographic proof, but with the entire evidence manifest in the skies above them, have been either totally ignored or dismissed by *all* the mainstream media organisations. Up to the current time, no individual researcher has as yet been successful in attracting as much as the passing attention of even the smallest of these media organisations. What is even more interesting and disconcerting is the fact that, with all of the widespread discussion surrounding this phenomenon, its link to a near-epidemic outbreak of a serious and debilitating range of illnesses, and the evidence in the skies right above their offices and studios, not one member of the mainstream media has come forward with a story to discredit the data, contradict the evidence, or calm the growing concerns and justified suspicions of the public. Is this not the very minimum response that we have a right to expect from any news organisation that claims to serve 'the people'? The silence speaks volumes, to my mind.

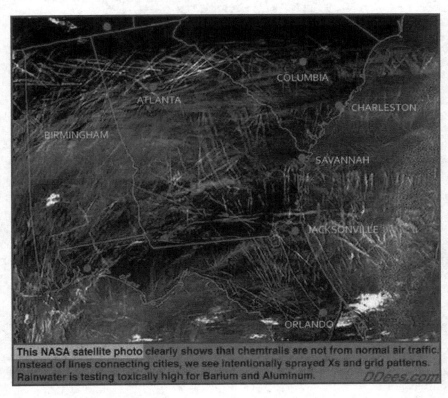

This NASA satellite photo clearly shows that chemtrails are not from normal air traffic. Instead of lines connecting cities, we see intentionally sprayed Xs and grid patterns. Rainwater is testing toxically high for Barium and Aluminum. *DDees.com*

Here is an interesting statement from an American aviation technician. I have no reason to doubt the veracity of this testimony.

"For reasons you will understand as you read this, I cannot divulge my identity. I am an aircraft mechanic for a major airline. I work at one of our maintenance bases located at a large airport and I have discovered some information that I think you will find important. Firstly I should tell you something about the 'pecking order' among mechanics. It is important to my story and to the cause to which you have dedicated yourself.

Mechanics want to work on three things. The avionics, the engines, or the flight controls. The mechanics that work on these systems are considered at the top of the 'pecking order'. Next come the mechanics that work on the hydraulics and air conditioning systems. Then come the ones who work on the galley and other non-essential systems. But at the very bottom of the list are the mechanics that work on the waste disposal systems. No mechanic wants to work on the pumps, tanks, and pipes that are used to store the waste from the lavatories, but at every airport where I have worked there are always 2 or 3 mechanics that volunteer to work on the lavatory systems.

The other mechanics are happy to let them do it. Because of this you will have only 2 or 3 mechanics that work on these systems at any one airport. No one pays much attention to these guys and no mechanic socialises with another mechanic who only works on the waste systems. In fact I had never thought much about this situation until last month.

Like most airlines we have reciprocal agreements with the other airlines that fly into this airport. If they have a problem with a plane, one of our mechanics will take care of it. Likewise if one of our planes has a problem at an airport where the other airline has a maintenance base, they will fix our plane. One day last month I was called out from our base to work on a plane for another airline. When I got the call, the dispatcher did not know what the problem was. When I got to the plane I found out that the problem was in the waste disposal system. There was nothing for me to do but to crawl in and fix the problem. When I got into the bay I realized that something was not right. There were more tanks, pumps, and pipes then should have been there. At first I assumed that the system had been changed. It had been 10 years since I had worked on one. As I tried to find the problem I quickly realized the extra piping and tanks were not connected to the waste disposal system. I had just discovered this when another mechanic from my company showed up. It was one of the mechanics who usually works on these systems. I happily turned the job over to him. As I was leaving I asked him about the extra equipment. He told me to 'worry about my end of the plane and let him worry about his!'

The next day I was on the company computer to look up a wiring schematic. While I was there I decided to look up the extra equipment I had found. To my amazement the manuals did not show any of the extra equipment I had seen with my own eyes the day before. I even tied in to the manufacturer files and still found nothing. Now I was really determined to find out what that equipment did.

The next week we had three of our planes in our main hanger for periodic inspection. There are mechanics crawling all over a plane during these inspections. I had just finished my shift and I decided to have a look at the waste system on one of our planes. With all the mechanics around I figured that no one would notice an extra one on the plane. Sure enough, the plane I chose had the extra equipment!

I began to trace the system of pipes, pumps, and tanks. I found what appeared to be the control unit for the system. It was a standard looking avionics control box but it had no markings of any kind. I could trace the control wires from the box to the pumps and valves but there were no control circuits coming into the unit. The only wires coming into the unit was a power connection to the aircraft's main power bus.

The system had one large and two smaller tanks. It was hard to tell in the cramped compartment but it looked like the large tank could hold 50 gallons. The tanks were connected to a fill and drain valve that passed through the fuselage just behind the drain valve for the waste system. When I had a chance to look for this connection under the plane I found it cunningly hidden behind a panel under the panel used to access the waste drain. I began to trace the piping from the pumps. These pipes led to a network of small pipes that ended in the trailing edges of the wings and horizontal stabilizers. If you look closely at the wings of a large airplane you will see a set of wires, about the size of your finger, extending from the trailing edge of the wing surfaces. These are the static discharge wicks. They are used to dissipate the static electric charge that builds up on a plane in flight. I discovered that the pipes from this mystery system lead to every 1 out of 3 of these static discharge wicks. These wicks had been "hollowed out" to allow whatever flows through these pipes to be discharged through these fake wicks.

It was while I was on the wing that one of the managers spotted me. He ordered me out of the hanger telling me that my shift was over and I had not been authorized any overtime. The next couple of days were very busy and I had no time to continue my investigation. Late one afternoon, two days after my discovery, I was called to replace an engine temperature sensor on a plane due to take off in two hours. I finished the job and turned in the paperwork.

About 30 minutes later I was paged to see the General Manager. When I went in his office I found that our union rep and two others who I did not know were waiting on me. He told me that a serious problem had been discovered. He said that I was being written up and suspended for turning in false paperwork. He handed me a disciplinary form stating that I had turned in false paperwork on the engine temperature sensor I had installed a few hours before. I was floored and began to protest. I told them that this was ridiculous and that I had done this work. The union rep spoke up then and recommended that we take a look at the plane and see if we could straighten it all out.

It was at this time that I asked who the other two men were. The GM told me that they were airline safety inspectors but would not give me their name.

We proceeded to the plane, which should have been in the air but was parked on our maintenance ramp. We opened the engine cowling and the union rep pulled the sensor. He checked the serial number and told everyone that it was the old instrument. We then went to the parts bay and went back into the racks. The union rep checked my report and pulled from the rack a sealed box. He opened the box and pulled out the engine temperature sensor with the serial number of the one I had installed. I was told that I was suspended for a week without pay and to leave immediately.

I sat at home the first day of my suspension wondering what the hell had happened to me. That evening I received a phone call. The voice told me 'Now you know what happens to mechanics who poke around in things they shouldn't. The next time you start working on systems that are no concern of yours you will lose your job! As it is I'm feeling generous, I believe that you'll be able to go back to work soon' CLICK. Again I had to pick myself from off the floor. I made the connection that what had happened was directly connected to my tracing the mysterious piping. The next morning the General Manager called me. He said that due to my past excellent employment record that the suspension had been reduced to one day and that I should report back to work immediately. The only thing I could think of was what are they trying to hide and who are THEY!

That day at work went by as if nothing had happened. None of the other mechanics mentioned the suspension and my union rep told me not to talk about it. That night I logged onto the Internet to try to find some answers. I don't remember now how I got there but I came across a site dealing with chemtrails. That's when it all came together. But the next morning at work I found a note inside my locked locker. It said, 'Curiosity killed the cat. Don't be looking at Internet sites that are no concern of yours.'

Well that's it. THEY are watching me. Well you already know what they are doing. I don't know what they are spraying but I can tell you how they are doing it. I figure they are using the 'honey trucks'. These are the trucks that empty the waste from the lavatory waste tanks. The airports usually contract out this job and nobody goes near these trucks. Who wants to stand next a truck full of shit? While these guys are emptying the waste tanks they are filling the tanks of the spray system. They know the plane's flight path so they probably program the control unit to start spraying some amount of time after the plane reaches a certain altitude. The spray nozzles in the fake static wicks are so small that no one in the plane would see a thing."

Reported at Cosmic Conspiracies cosmic-conspiracies.com and reproduced here with their kind permission.

Satellite photo of chemtrails over the Great Lakes (These days, photos of chemtrails are airbrushed out before release).

Although this statement is not personally verified by me, I feel that it definitely has a ring of truth about it. The modus operandus of the way the mechanic's 'indiscretions' are dealt with is entirely consistent with other examples of the way these situations are handled by the Elite. Once you are identified as a problem to their agenda, either directly or via their paid lackeys, they will spare no expense to intimidate, threaten or even kill should the pressure not be heeded. This person was possibly lucky to live to tell his story. History is awash with others in many different scenarios, who did not.

So why are they doing it? Why would they be spraying harmful chemicals from planes onto an unsuspecting population, on a huge scale, worldwide at what must be an astronomical cost? What could the motivation possibly be?

There are several possible reasons. Maybe they are all partly true or maybe there is just one reason alone. No-one is 100% sure, but here are some possibilities:

Initially it was thought that the real reason for Chemtrails was the de-population agenda because of the bio-chemical and metal content found in the substances and the link to the stated Elite agenda of population reduction. Over the years however, it has become apparent that it has not had a large effect in reducing population sizes. Although it probably has had some negative impact on health and more than likely has been the cause of deaths, especially in the already sick or elderly, it is probably not actually genocidal. There have certainly been reports of hospitals experiencing a large intake of patients with lung issues after exposure to chemtrails, but this was usually in the early days. However, this does not appear to be the primary function of chemtrails.

Another use for chemtrails has been suggested as weather control. This may or may not be wholly or partly true. There is some evidence to suggest that this may be happening in conjunction with the HAARP project (see relevant sections) and whilst this theory has some possibilities, I believe that if true, it is a secondary objective only.

There has also been much disinformation spread on the Internet as with all these issues, regarding the 'real reason' for chemtrails. Another supposed theory is that it is done to counter the effects of 'so-called' global warming, but I think this one is easy to dismiss. Firstly, global warming is a complete fabrication in any case and the Elite know this only too well. Indeed it is they that invented the myth, for other reasons which we cover in more detail in the relevant section of the book. However, the most important negative here is that chemtrails have been around since the mid-nineties and the nonsensical pseudo-science of global warming did not actually come to prominence until around ten years later.

The Hollywood movie 'Toxic Skies' (2006) that purports to be a dramatised exposé of the chemtrail conspiracy is actually easily dismissed as another example of disinformation. Disinformation is a very successful tool used by the Elite, whereby so-called conspiracy theories are exposed as nonsense by distorting the real facts by the presenting of a false paradigm. Any future discussions about the subject can then be side-tracked or dismissed easily as a conspiracy by referral to the false premise, despite the fact that it can easily be proven untrue. In the film, the conspiracy is revealed as being perpetrated by a lone, rogue element in the pharmaceutical industry whose primary motivation is money in the form of sales of the cure of the ailments caused by the chemtrails. But as in all good fiction, he is finally stopped by the 'good guys' at the end of the movie and we all get to live happily ever after.

However, could the *real* reason behind chemtrails be related in some way to *living* people, not de-population, weather control or genocide?

In the observing of people's behaviour over the past several years, some researchers, myself included, feel that it is now very apparent that there is a general 'dumbing-down', of people taking place. This is achieved mainly through education, planned distractions such as 24/7 mass entertainment, blanket sports coverage and the preponderance of 'popular' music and computer games (see appropriate chapters for more detail). But, could there be another, more subtle method of bringing about changes to the way we think and the working of our minds? It is now even more of a struggle with certain sections of the populace, to invoke an interest in anything other than the latest football scores or which celebrity is in a relationship with which other, let alone about even such simple, yet more pertinent issues as improving one's diet or political awareness. Could it be that we are deliberately being programmed not to think coherently about what is really happening in the world?

Here is a section of dialogue from the film, *They Live* (1985) which is particularly relevant to what I believe is happening today:

"...our impulses are being redirected. We are living in an artificially induced state of consciousness that resembles sleep... ...the movement was begun eight months ago by a small group of scientists who discovered, quite by accident, these signals are being sent through television... ...the poor and the underclass are growing. Racial justice and human rights are nonexistent. They have created a repressive society and we are their unwitting accomplices... ...their intention to rule rests with the annihilation of consciousness. We have been lulled into a trance. They have made us indifferent, to ourselves, to others and we are focused only on our own gain. ...please understand, they are safe as long as they are not discovered. That is their primary method of survival. Keep us asleep, keep us selfish, keep us sedated... ...they are dismantling the sleeping

middle class. *More and more people are becoming poor. We are their cattle. We are being bred for slavery. The revolution... ...we cannot break their signal, our transmitter is not powerful enough. The signal must be shut off at the source."*

One common element that seems to be present in all analyses of chemtrails is barium. In Phoenix, Arizona, USA, a group of people had their hair spectrographically analysed as part of the investigation into the effects of chemtrails and their hair was found to contain dangerously high levels of barium. If barium is present at those levels in our hair, then it must also be present at similar levels in our bodies too. What could this mean and what is its significance?

Mind control is not something from a cheap science fiction 'B movie'. It goes on all the time, surreptitiously. From Project MK Ultra (see relevant section) to simple subliminal advertising techniques to persuasive propaganda, we have all been subjected to a form of mind control no matter how minor, at one time or other in our lives.

Human bodies are electrical in nature, as are all our individual living cells. In addition to our complex electrical makeup, we have an *energetic* side as well. Our meridians and chakras are only the most basic component of this hidden side. This energetic element is very sensitive to electromagnetic and scalar magnetic signals reaching into the terahertz band. Saturating human cells with metallic compounds makes them more sensitive to man-made signals in these ranges. Much research has been conducted and many patents have been awarded relating to remote influence, electromagnetic telepathy and mind control. I do not believe that anyone would go the trouble and considerable expense of applying for patents for processes and devices that are not intended to be used actively.

Introducing the **H**igh frequency **A**ctive **A**uroral **R**esearch **P**rogram (HAARP). (for fuller details, please see the relevant section), but very briefly;

HAARP is a semi-secret American government project located in Alaska. It is widely believed that the reasons stated by the government for its existence are a major cover-up.

"HAARP will zap the upper atmosphere with a focused and steerable electromagnetic beam. It is an advanced model of an 'ionospheric heater.' (The ionosphere is the electrically-charged sphere surrounding Earth's upper atmosphere. It ranges between 40 to 60 miles above the surface of the Earth.)

Put simply, the apparatus for HAARP is a reversal of a radio telescope; antennas send out signals instead of receiving. HAARP is the test run for a super-powerful radio wave-beaming technology that lifts areas of the ionosphere by focusing a beam and heating those areas. Electromagnetic waves then bounce back onto earth and penetrate everything -- living and dead.

HAARP publicity gives the impression that the High-frequency Active Auroral Research Program is mainly an academic project with the goal of changing the ionosphere to improve communications for our own good. However, other U.S. military documents put it more clearly -- HAARP aims to learn how to "exploit the ionosphere for Department of Defense purposes." Communicating with submarines is only one of those purposes.

Press releases and other information from the military on HAARP continually downplay what it could do. Publicity documents insist that the HAARP project is no different than other ionospheric heaters operating safely throughout the world in places such as Arecibo, Puerto Rico, Tromso, Norway, and the former Soviet Union. However, a 1990 government document indicates that the radio-frequency (RF) power zap will drive the ionosphere to unnatural activities.

At the highest HF powers available in the West, the instabilities commonly studied are approaching their maximum RF energy dissipative capability, beyond which the plasma processes will 'runaway' until the next limiting factor is reached. If the military, in cooperation with the University of Alaska Fairbanks, can show that this new ground-based "Star Wars" technology is sound, they both win. The military has a relatively-inexpensive defence shield and the University can brag about the most dramatic geophysical manipulation since atmospheric explosions of nuclear bombs. After successful testing, they would have the military megaprojects of the future and huge markets for Alaska's North Slope natural gas.

Looking at the other patents which built on the work of a Texas' physicist named Bernard Eastlund, it becomes clearer how the military intends to use the HAARP transmitter. It also makes governmental denials less believable. The military knows how it intends to use this technology, and has made it clear in their documents. The military has deliberately misled the public, through sophisticated word games, deceit and outright disinformation. The military says the HAARP system could:

* give the military a tool to replace the electromagnetic pulse effect of atmospheric thermonuclear devices (still considered a viable option by the military through at least 1986);
* replace the huge Extremely Low Frequency (ELF) submarine communication system operating in Michigan and Wisconsin with a new and more compact technology;
* be used to replace the over-the-horizon radar system that was once planned for the current location of HAARP, with a more flexible and accurate system;
* provide a way to wipe out communications over an extremely large area, while keeping the military's own communications systems working;
* provide a wide-area Earth-penetrating tomography which, if combined with the computing abilities of EMASS and Cray computers, would make it possible to verify many parts of nuclear non-proliferation and peace agreements;
* be a tool for geophysical probing to find oil, gas and mineral deposits over a large area;

* *be used to detect incoming low-level planes and cruise missiles, making other technologies obsolete."* Dr. Nick Begich. Haarp.net

If HAARP can perform all these electromagnetic feats, then I firmly believe that it is more than possible that HAARP in conjunction with chemtrails could easily be used (among other nefarious possibilities) to manipulate the individual and collective mind-sets of the human race.

Dr. Begich explains that HAARP uses a frequency range that is the same as the human brain. By sending specific frequencies, the populace can be made to feel different emotions/manipulations: fear, ecstasy... influencing elections... etc. The military-industrial complex undoubtedly has some of this mind control equipment in their black ops arsenal.

The website haarp.net also states:

"The military's Pandora's Box

The mental-disruption possibilities for HAARP are the most disturbing. More than 40 pages ... with dozens of footnotes, chronicle the work of Harvard professors, military planners and scientists as they plan and test this use of the electromagnetic technology. For example, one of the papers describing this use was from the International Red Cross in Geneva. It even gave the frequency ranges where these effects could occur — the same ranges over which HAARP is capable of broadcasting."

The following statement was made more than twenty-five years ago in a book by Zbigniew Brzezinski (the mentor and puppet-master of Barack Obama) which he wrote whilst still a professor at Columbia University.

"Political strategists are tempted to exploit research on the brain and human behavior. Geophysicist Gordon J.F. MacDonald, a specialist in problems of warfare, says accurately-timed, artificially-excited electronic strokes could lead to a pattern of oscillations that produce relatively high power levels over certain regions of the earth ... in this way one could develop a system that would seriously impair the brain performance of very large populations in selected regions over an extended period. ... no matter how deeply disturbing the thought of using the environment to manipulate behavior for national advantages, the technology permitting such use will very probably develop within the next few decades."

Also, *"Unhindered by the restraints of traditional liberal values, this elite would not hesitate to achieve its political ends by using the latest modern techniques for influencing public behavior and keeping society under close surveillance and control. Technical and scientific momentum would then feed on the situation it exploits,"* Brzezinski predicted, in the same source.

"If one questions why THEY would initiate this 'mass murder' – across the entire planet and still expect to survive it should be noted that in the past 20 years these Illuminati elitists have built huge underground facilities throughout the world. The fact is that they have developed massive underground facilities to avoid the Holocaust that they are creating. The fact is they have literally launched an all-out attack on the Earth's Atmosphere. These Malthusian Minded Maniacs have the Minds of Monsters. No one who is not either Satanic or insane would order millions of tons of deadly toxins containing aerosol compounds composed of Aluminum Oxide, Strontium, Barium, and Sulfur Hexafluoride to be dumped upon the population of the world. Just look to the skies. This is not a Conspiracy Theory – This is Frightening – This is a Fact." Aircrap.org

The abundant circumstantial and actual evidence here points firmly to the fact that we are being manipulated against our knowledge or will, in an attempt to control us all. We are being electronically influenced to focus inwardly and in consequence of this, turn a blind eye to what is going on in the world today right under our noses. The 'elephant in the room' is the construction of the Elite's 'New World Order' which is designed to suppress and subjugate us all, before we even realise what is happening.

This is but one more small piece in the overall jigsaw puzzle that leads me to conclude that the human race is under severe attack by a Satanically motivated cabal and our freedoms of thought and movement are being eroded as quickly as is possible. Unless we stand up very soon and say 'no more', our time will soon have run out and our last opportunity to counter this threat will be gone forever.

FEMA – The Federal Emergency Management Agency

FEMA's role in any disaster scenario in the US has to be seriously questioned. Indeed they seem to specialise in aggravating the disaster by being deliberately obstructive, preventing medical and other aid reaching the victims and generally creating an atmosphere of fear and truth suppression among those they are supposedly trying to help.

I believe that the mission of FEMA has never in reality been to bring people food and water and help in times of crisis. Alex Jones of 'Infowars' relates that he has attended numerous FEMA drills where the whole point of the exercise is to round people up, break up families and institute a brutal police state crackdown.
For example, FEMA needed to create a chaotic atmosphere in New Orleans after the artificially induced Hurricane Katrina so they could legitimise what they were doing. Immediately following the disaster, there were multiple reports of police being ordered to guard key infrastructures in order to defend them from FEMA federal

agents. Sheriffs in several different counties were guarding highways to keep FEMA out.

They were treated as the enemy because they were known to be sabotaging key facilities in an effort to intentionally worsen the already desperate scenes of horror in New Orleans. They were known to also be sabotaging lines of communication so that their activities could not be exposed to the wider relief authorities and the media.

Commenting on the sabotage by FEMA of communication lines, Washington insider Wayne Madsen stated that;

"Jamming radio and other communications such as television signals is part of a Pentagon tactic called 'information blockade' or 'technology blockade'. This tactic is one of a number of such operations that are part of the doctrine of 'information warfare' and is one of the psychological operations (PSYOPS) methods used by the US Special Operations Command."

Radio host Carol Baker who was tracking the FEMA sabotage stated that Plaquemines Parish Sheriff Jeff Hingle had his deputies patrol the county line under orders not to let FEMA in. As was discussed in the 'Meet the Press' interview, Jefferson Parish Sheriff Harry Lee also has armed guards patrolling the county line in order to prevent the FEMA sabotage. FEMA has a number of Presidential executive orders to fall back upon that allow for the total federal takeover of any US city.

FEMA was clearly using this human catastrophe as a means of executing its long-term plans and providing the pretext for future takeover scenarios of all major American cities. Amongst a litany of government inaction and outright dereliction, this is the most alarming evidence to emerge yet that clearly indicates an agenda for the federal government to profit and expand its power from exploiting the aftermath of disasters.

*"FEMA is not an elected body, it does not involve itself in public disclosures and it even has a quasi-secret budget in the billions of dollars. It has more power than the President of the United States or the Congress, it has the power to suspend laws, move entire populations, arrest and detain citizens without a warrant and hold them without trial, it can seize property, food supplies, transportation systems, and can suspend the Constitution. Not only is it the most powerful entity in the United States, but it was not even created under Constitutional law by Congress. A Series of Executive Orders dating from the 1960s onwards underlines the history of FEMA. **The plan for total control of every aspect of our lives has been under construction for a long time"**. [my emphasis – JH] Steve Watson, Infowars.com, 6 September 2005*

"A trained National Police Force, formally referred to by the name of Multi-Jurisdictional Task Force (MJTF), wearing black uniforms and composed of:

1. *Specially selected US military personnel*
2. *Foreign military units carrying United Nations ID cards, and*
3. *Specially trained existing police groups from larger metropolitan American cities.*

These members of the MJTF will implement and enforce martial law under the direction and control of FEMA. The President and Congress are out of the loop. FEMA is the Trojan Horse by which the New World Order will implement overt, police-state control over the American populace". Ken Adachi, educate-yourself.org

So what does all this mean? It was clear from the start that the goal of FEMA and Homeland Security was, not to rescue people, but to *control* them. Their directive was to relocate families and businesses, confiscate property, commandeer goods, direct labour and services, and establish martial law. This is what they have been trained to do. The reason they failed to carry out an effective rescue operation is that this was not their primary mission and the reason they blocked others from doing so is that any operations not controlled by the central authority are contrary to their directives. Their objective was to bring the entire area under the control of the federal government - and this they succeeded in doing very well.

William Anderson, in an article posted to the website of the von Mises Institute, came to the same conclusion but from a slightly different perspective. He calls attention to the need for politicians and government agencies to be in the spotlight during emergencies so they can look good to the voters and claim credit for all positive results. They are not interested in sharing the praise.

Anderson writes: *"While the world is preoccupied with trying to fix the blame for the government's failure in New Orleans, the reality is that it did not fail at all. It was a huge success in promoting its own agenda. Unfortunately, that agenda was not to rescue American citizens. Once this simple fact is understood, everything that happened in the wake of Katrina becomes understandable and logical."*

The Man-made 'Global Warming' Hoax

Have you perhaps noticed that 'global warming' has lately disingenuously been re-branded as 'climate change' by most commentators and reporters? This is because it has now been shown beyond all doubt that the Earth is currently entering a period of cooling which is expected to continue for the next several decades. Indeed this is all part of a natural cycle of warming and cooling that has been going-on for millions of years.

The utterly ridiculous and easily disproved fantasy of human-caused global warming by CO_2 emissions is nothing but a gigantic hoax, a confidence-trick designed to extract even more money from we, the people in taxation, to further line the pockets of the already super-wealthy.

There are also other powerful factors at work here. 'Climate change' as we must now refer to it, is also being used to justify the ongoing centralisation of power, de-industrialisation, the passing of global laws and an expansion of the surveillance of the world population, all as part of the inexorable march towards the much-vaunted 'New World Order'. This is also another major example of the Hegelian dialectic; problem, reaction, solution technique. Create a problem, wait for a demand for action and then provide the solution you wanted to see implemented in the first place. By that method is the agenda advanced step by step by step.

Enter Mr Al Gore, fresh from his (planned) defeat at the hands of Bush the lesser in the 2000 presidential election campaign. I can just imagine the scenario right now...

Rothschild: Sorry Al, but Georgie-boy is our choice this time around, but don't worry, we have something even more important lined-up for you. We want you to front this massive con... er, campaign that we have thought of to make us all even more billions. Basically we are going to employ a whole bunch of scientists, corporations and politicians to falsely promote the fact that the Earth is suffering from some kind of runaway warming and that the only solution that will save mankind will be draconian measures that will ahem, stop it all. Of course this will cost every single person on Earth an absolute 'arm and a leg', but never mind eh? What do you say Al? Will you do it Al? You know it makes sense, Al.

Gore: Yes of course, Mr. Rothschild, sir. Of course I will, sir – only too delighted Mr. Rothschild. When can I start?

So, Gore embarked upon his quest to convince the entire world that the Earth is warming dangerously as a result of excessive CO_2 emissions, all of course funded by the Rothschild millions. One of his first actions was to produce the horrendously scientifically inaccurate film, *An Inconvenient Truth* which became the third most successful documentary in history and unsurprisingly won the 'Oscar' for best documentary. Gore's book of the same name also reached the top of the best-sellers list in America as the public fell for his scam 'hook, line and sinker' and furthermore, as if this was all not enough, Gore subsequently 'won' the Nobel Peace Prize for this great work of fiction.

Please bear in mind that this is the same Al Gore that Phillip Eugene de Rothschild, referred to thus:

"President Clinton has 'full-blown' multiple personality disorder and is an active sorcerer in the Satanic mystery religions. This is also true of Al Gore, as well; I have known Clinton and Gore from our childhoods as active and effective Satanists."

Incidentally, the *Inconvenient Truth* documentary has been distributed to all schools in Britain to be shown to teenagers, by the government *despite* a High Court judge ruling that it was too full of unscientific inaccuracies as well as gross distortions of the truth to be shown to impressionable youths. But the law matters not a jot to these people of course. Laws are only there to be obeyed when expedient for their agenda to do so; otherwise they may be ignored by them at will. And perhaps even more tellingly, the psychological damage has now been done and the purpose of the film has been served. No matter how much proof of its distortions and inaccuracies may now be forthcoming, the falsehoods it portrays are now firmly established in millions if not billions of human psyches all around the world. This then of course renders the refuting of its false information, much, much more difficult.

Of course any concerned person realises that protection of the environment is vital to long-term human and indeed all life's survival on the Earth, but that is not the real issue here, despite the fact that it is disingenuously portrayed as being so. Climate change 'theory' is based on the complete myth or even downright lie, that global temperatures are inexorably increasing solely due to the levels of CO_2 emitted by human-caused activities, whilst the real truth is that from the 1970s to the early 2000s, the Earth was actually undergoing a short period of naturally induced warming as part of a normal cycle of sun-spot activity. This trend is now rapidly being reversed as we are now entering a sun-spot induced period of cooling, but of course this fact does not figure too prominently in the 'warmists' agenda and they therefore deny, but mainly ignore this particular inconvenient (for them) truth.

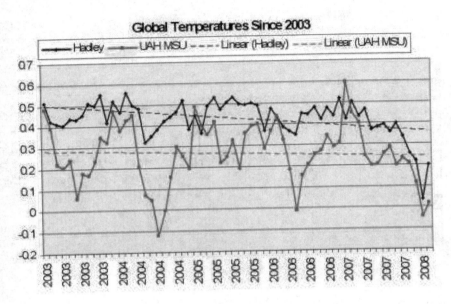

All their 'warming' predictions are based on totally unscientific premises and selective data derived mainly on the old computer principle of 'garbage-in, garbage-out' which roughly translated means that if the initial data input is incorrect then the resultant computer predictions based on that data will also be incorrect.

It is falsely claimed by these grand-scale con-artists that it is the excessive amounts of the 'greenhouse gas', CO_2 emanating from vehicle exhausts and industrial processes, especially those of the third world that is the root of the problem. According to their shills, 'useful idiots' and downright professional liars, this excessive CO_2 is collecting in the atmosphere and preventing the natural escape of heat into space and thus causing a build-up of warm air all around us that is the issue.

Of course we are now being extolled to become 'carbon neutral' and partake in the 'carbon offset' scam just as many companies that wish to cause pollution are now able to 'buy' 'carbon credits' from those who do not exceed their stated carbon emission limits. What a farce it really is. So essentially what is being said then is that is OK to cause pollution as long as you pay for it. And where does this money go, you may well ask? Well, luckily for us all, Gore has set up a company to facilitate it all, *Generation Investment Management*, based in London.

"So Al can buy his carbon offsets from himself. Better yet, he can buy them with the money he gets from his long-term relationship with Occidental Petroleum. See how easy it is to be carbon-neutral. All you have to do is own a gazillion stocks in 'big oil', start an eco-stockbroking firm to make eco-friendly investments, use a small portion of your oil company's profits to buy some tax-deductible carbon-offsets from your own investment firm and you too can save the planet whilst making money and leaving a

carbon footprint roughly the size of Godzilla's at the start of the movie when they're all standing around in the little toe wondering what the strange depression in the landscape is." An Internet commentator

So please, please never, ever submit to the blatant con now being perpetrated by some airline companies that generously invite you to buy your carbon credits when paying for a ticket. This is all nothing but a highly lucrative fraud being perpetrated against us all through the emotional blackmail of 'saving the planet'. At the time of writing, these airline carbon credits are voluntary, but in line with the 'totalitarian-tiptoe' it is simply the prelude to more and more taxation, even more Orwellian controls and perhaps most importantly to prevent the developing nations (third world) from gaining a share of the profit gravy-train currently being enjoyed almost exclusively by the first world and the likes of Gore and his cronies.

"In searching for a new enemy to unite us, we came up with the idea that pollution, threat of global warming, water shortages, famine and the like would fit the bill. All of these are caused by human intervention. The real enemy then is humanity itself." Aurelio Pecci, The Club of Rome, a part of the Round Table network, 1991

In 2006 an offshoot of the United Nations, *The International Panel on Climate Change* (IPCC) began to inform the world that global warming is the direct result of human-caused carbon emissions. It has since become the de facto truth (along with many other lies exposed in this book) that carbon emissions are warming the planet at an unsustainable rate despite the now proven fact that the Earth is now in an intensive period of 'cooling'. However, please note that the IPCC is not a scientific body at all, despite some of its apologist's claims; it is a purely political institution with its own agenda and replete with all the bias inherent in such organisations.

"The IPCC is not a scientific institution; it's a political body, a sort of non-government organisation of green flavour. It's neither a forum of neutral scientists nor a balanced group of scientists. These people are politicised scientists who arrive there with a one-sided opinion and a one-sided assignment." Vaclav Klaus, President of the Czech Republic

The IPCC's claim that it represents 2000+ of the world's foremost scientists is an unadulterated lie. Its report purportedly had the backing of all these scientists, most of whom are blatantly and deceptively, named within its covers. However since the publication of this huge fairy-tale masquerading as truth, at least 60% of these named scientists have formally protested at the inclusion of their names within its pages, all of which were used without their express permission and indeed many have demanded that their names be specifically excluded from it – all of which has fallen of course upon 'deaf ears' and as usual remained unreported by the compliant media.

As an example (among many) Professor Paul Reiter one of the world's foremost authorities on tropical diseases, whose name was included without his express permission, gave an example of the blatant untruths within the report when he said that it states within its pages that tropical diseases such as malaria were more likely with the advent of global warming, to spread to formerly 'colder' parts of the world than before. This he pointed out is in fact, nonsense. Mosquitos actually thrive better in colder temperatures and are abundant within the Arctic Circle in such places as Siberia for example where there are 13 million cases a year reported on average. In fact, he said, he was horrified by the entire report as it was he said... '...so much misinformation... virtually without mention of scientific literature by specialists in those fields'.

The IPCC report is simply put, a document compiled to support a pre-arranged outcome and designed to fool the public into believing that which is not true. In this it has been a raging success.

"The IPCC like any other UN body is political. The final conclusions are politically driven." Professor Phillip Scott, the department of Geography, University of London

We are constantly being fed the line that the Earth is now 'warmer than at any time since records began'. Sounds impressive yet foreboding does it not? However, upon hearing statements such as these it is worth remembering that records only began in fact as recently as 1914, less than 100 years ago, at the time of writing. Yet another example of the depths of deceit to which the warmists do not hesitate to stoop in their constant battering of our senses to drive home their messages of doom and gloom. As I stated previously, the Earth is subject to constant and ongoing fluctuations in the warming and cooling cycle that has been in evidence for hundreds of millennia and a mere one hundred year period taken in isolation, forms no statistical basis whatsoever upon which to base proper scientific data.

In fact it is quite simple to demonstrate using such methods as tree rings and ice cores that temperatures in what scientists refer to as the 'medieval warm period', were considerably higher on average than those of today. And there is also much socio-historical evidence to suggest that life in this period was far more comfortable than today despite their being an approximately two-degree higher average temperature than at present and absolutely no evidence of polar ice-cap melt or of coastlines being inundated worldwide. Indeed, were the temperatures to rise by as much as two or even five degrees in the next few years, then far from it being cataclysmic, most true scientists believe that it would be highly beneficial to life on Earth, especially the human variety.

"What has been forgotten in all the discussions about global warming is a proper sense of history. We have this view today that warming is going to have apocalyptic outcomes. In fact, during the 'medieval warm period', the world was even warmer than today and history shows that it was a wonderful period of plenty for everyone. When the temperatures began to drop, harvests failed and England's vine industry died. It *makes one wonder why there is such a fear of warmth."* Professor Phillip Scott, the department of Geography, University of London

"Warming fears are the worst scientific scandal in scientific history… When people come to know what the truth is, they will feel deceived by science and scientists." Dr. Kiminori Itoh, environmental physical chemist

A small point maybe, but a valid illustration of how we are all being conned by these people and their extravagant lies and distortions, is the myth of imminent polar bear extinction. According to Dr. Mitchell Taylor who has been involved for decades in the research of polar bears in northern Canada, this is absolutely untrue. They are in fact experiencing their highest numbers for almost sixty years. The famous photograph of the two polar bears standing on an ice floe and used by Gore for his infamous *An Inconvenient Truth* was in fact taken by Amanda Byrd who publicly stated to no avail that the bears were in no danger whatsoever. In fact polar bears far from being in danger of drowning in these situations are well-known to be capable of swimming for up to 200 miles at a stretch when seeking-out new food sources.

Then in late 2009, we suddenly saw the final nail in the 'warmists' coffin with the exposure of the 'climategate emails'. Upon reading the 1000+ emails and 72 leaked documents it becomes immediately apparent why the East Anglia Climate Research Unit would have wished to keep them under lock and key. Here are just a few snippets below as examples of how the warmists have faked and manipulated data to further their own ends as have been revealed in these highly incriminating emails:

"I've just completed Mike's Nature trick of adding in the real temps to each series for the last 20 years (ie from 1981 onwards) and from 1961 for Keith's to hide the decline."

"The fact is that we can't account for the lack of warming at the moment and it is a travesty that we can't. The CERES data published in the August BAMS 09 supplement on 2008 shows there should be even more warming: but the data are surely wrong. Our observing system is inadequate."

"Can you delete any emails you may have had with Keith re AR4? Keith will do likewise. He's not in at the moment – minor family crisis. Can you also email Gene and get him to do the same? I don't have his new email address. We will be getting Caspar to do likewise."

"… … Phil and I have recently submitted a paper using about a dozen NH records that fit this category, and many of which are available nearly 2K back–I think that trying to adopt a timeframe of 2K, rather than the usual 1K, addresses a good earlier point that Peck made w/ regard to the memo, that it would be nice to try to 'contain' the putative 'MWP', even if we don't yet have a hemispheric mean reconstruction available that far back…."

"This was the danger of always criticising the skeptics for not publishing in the 'peer-reviewed literature'. Obviously, they found a solution to that–take over a journal! So what do we do about this? I think we have to stop considering 'Climate Research' as a legitimate peer-reviewed journal. Perhaps we should encourage our colleagues in the climate research community to no longer submit to, or cite papers in, this journal. We would also need to consider what we tell or request of our more reasonable colleagues who currently sit on the editorial board... What do others think?"

"I will be emailing the journal to tell them I'm having nothing more to do with it until they rid themselves of this troublesome editor. It results from this journal having a number of editors. The responsible one for this is a well-known skeptic in NZ. He has let a few papers through by Michaels and Gray in the past. I've had words with Hans von Storch about this, but got nowhere. Another thing to discuss in Nice!"

Although replete with in-jokes and in-house references, I think this gives an overall flavour of what is going on here. And despite the reluctance of the mainstream media to cover it in full, with a few noteworthy exceptions, I believe it demonstrates pretty conclusively the institutional deception taking place in order to perpetuate the hoax. How much more evidence do we need to realise that the whole concept of global warming by human-caused CO_2 emissions is a monumental fraud?

And so to conclude, yes, I am afraid it is all a huge hoax, a game to convince us that we are in danger of imminent disaster from the slightest warming of the planet and the only way to prevent this will be to give even more money to an already wealthy Elite group who care nothing whatsoever for you and your families, despite maintaining a thoroughly deceptive pretence to the contrary.

The Elite controlled and run Music & Entertainment Industry

If you believe that the music and entertainment industry is there simply to entertain us and make money in the process for its artists, promoters and producers, please think again.

Popular music especially and its highly-paid exponents are merely pawns of the Elite and are there in order to further manipulate our minds – especially those of impressionable youth and now even young children.

There is a long history of manipulation in the music industry, going back many, many years. The music 'business' itself has actually been around since medieval times, but can only be referred to as a true 'industry' since the early nineteenth century with the simultaneous developments of the orchestra, the employment of conductors and certain publishing and printing innovations that allowed music to be easily transcribed, passed-on from person to person and to be sold as sheet music.

In the early eighteenth century, there is recorded to have been around 8500 composers of music in Europe alone and yet around 8400 of them, despite the fact that their music may have been brilliant or innovative, have never had their music extensively published or played, other than in small, localised concert halls and much of it is today now long-forgotten, lost or deliberately buried. Why should this be? Mainly because, as today, the music industry then had its favourites and certain personalities including the likes of Mozart, who whilst feted as a celebrity of his time, probably did not compose much of the music attributed to him then and since.

Mozart was simply a manufactured 'focal point' in effect, upon which the money-interests of the music business of the time could focus and from whom it could derive its profits, as was Beethoven. This may well sound cynical and possibly unbelievable, but I can assure you that it is true. How similar to today then? Today's music industry is rife with such characters, people who have been chosen and indeed 'created' to be focal points and the personalities, celebrities if you will, who carry the burden of providing profits for an intensely money-focussed industry, ultimately regardless of the degree of talent they may or may not possess.

Musical history does not wish us to be aware of this fact; it just wishes to continue to promote the popular icons of the day, focussing on an artificially generated, elite group of composers who with the passage of time have been placed on pedestals and thus made immortal, just as many famous rock stars have been made the 'saints' of the new religion that is music, today.

The involvement of occultists in the creation of the 'superstars' of their day, such as Mozart, Beethoven and Haydn, cannot be ignored. Indeed the occult influence in music has always been a factor and today is absolutely rife throughout the whole of the music industry.

There is also a long history of connectivity from music to mind control going back to the 1950s when 'pop music' in its present form was first pushed upon an unsuspecting world by the mass-manipulators of the Frankfurt School and the Tavistock Institute and many performers, singers and members of bands are manipulated into promoting a satanic agenda by recording labels and producers who are also 'up to their eyes' in the deadly scheme. Is it at all artistic for people to sing about pain, suffering, death, sadness and despair in such quantities and who would want to taint the formerly beautiful art of music with such things? It is actually an essential aspect of the latter-day degeneration of music and the lowering of consciousness. This works in the same vein as film and television programmes that seem to have now evolved into excessively depressing and/or violent experiences for the viewer, even for very young children who are being increasingly exposed to overt sex and violence and when those few who still actually care about such things complain or point it out they are often labelled as a 'prude' or 'old-fashioned'. Often today music is excessively depressing, replete with songs contain lyrics extolling the virtues of extreme selfishness, greed, violence, death, suicide and murder. And this is not just in heavy metal (the previous chief culprit) any longer but has now been expanded to all forms of modern music even the 'middle of the road' ballads aimed at the younger, more impressionable generation. Even fun 'children's' pop music, the likes of which our children and grandchildren listen to all the time, is not immune and is often riddled with overt, sexually explicit and satanic and occult lyrics.

Interestingly, a huge number of artists have commented publicly and even composed songs about literally 'selling their souls' to the devil to further their musical careers. Many well-known rock artists are well-versed in the occult and are aware that spiritual entities and multidimensional 'demons' can manifest themself through music of a lower vibrational nature. They have admitted that they use rock music and the rhythms, the lower guttural tones, and their insidious lyrics to lower the vibrational levels of concerts and thus their attendees. They have also even admitted countless times that they are possessed by their own music and have little control over where these vibrations lead them. This is typical of almost any satanic 'ritual' or practice; the lowering of consciousness and allowing lower vibrational entities to control a person. These practices often lead to complete loss of control and it was well known to the people at the last Woodstock anniversary concert that a form of 'bad energy' had manifested itself throughout the huge audience following many hours and days of extremely heavy, depressive and violent songs.

This information emanates from many sources; there have been many books written and several films made on the subject and many well-known artists have been exposed and even admitted themselves that this is taking place. However, the idea that rock music is a tool of the 'devil' has been pushed so relentlessly by religious leaders and evangelists that people are now more often likely to laugh at or mock the idea, rather than take it seriously. Nevertheless, well-known musicians are often reported as admitting to the practice of Satanism and their friends or colleagues will often mention that they have multiple personalities and that 'what you see on the stage is not really that person'.

Unfortunately, rock and pop music has become mostly a grossly degenerative art form. Some musicians are exempt from this tag, but the music industry contributes to this view generally by actually enhancing and promoting the popularity of the 'heaviest' bands or the most emotionally depressing artists. The rock music of today is several magnitudes darker and more depressing than Led Zeppelin, Black Sabbath and other well-known 'devil-rockers' of past decades and at the time these bands were considered the very epitome of evil by the deeply religious. Heavy metal music has now become almost completely demonic per se and many performers revel in this fact, openly flaunting it. It is devolution of society and the art of music for the purpose of lowering the vibration of the consciousness in order to manipulate the youth of today into fulfilling the purposes of the Elite. It is, in short the next baby-step on the road to the complete undermining of human society and the human psyche in order to exert control over minds.

As I say, many artists are aware of this and some became aware of the fact that they have been manipulated by the music industry or began to recollect memories of their brainwashing, either through the military or through 'handlers' who often happen to be their manager. These are often the artists we know to have so famously died by 'drug overdose' or have suffered other strange deaths. Many of these artists have either confided before their deaths in individuals who would later relay this information to those behind the scenes in the music industry or indeed may even 'go public' with their knowledge as did Michael Jackson shortly before his untimely demise at the hands of his 'doctor'. Jackson had been telling anyone and everyone during the period prior to his death that the CEO of Sony, Tommy Mottola (who by the way virtually owned Jackson body and soul, if not actually literally) was 'the devil incarnate'. A metaphor or figure of speech? Maybe, maybe not.

The deeper that one delves into this murky pit, the more one realises that the 'musical greats' are often occultists with exceptional talent and who are intentionally using that talent to manipulate the consciousness of listeners. However, I also believe that many of the 'household-name' musicians early in their careers are lured into a subtle trap baited with money and fame but then once their handlers in the recording companies completely sink their claws and teeth into them, they realise that they are caught, with no possible escape route and thus are condemned to continue with their charade for the rest of their careers, which often ends prematurely for one reason or another. The premature end to musical careers can and does occur for several reasons. Obviously, there are some genuine cases of accidental drug overdoses, but I am equally sure that some of these are murders and some suicides. But we need to ask the question as to why drug overdose and suicide (murder?) is so prevalent among this group of people?

There is so much information on this topic that could be included, that to do it justice would really justify a book in its own right. The number of examples of the satanic nature of the entertainment business is truly staggering and so we will concentrate on a few specific examples and events, but please bear in mind that this is only the tiniest sliver of ice on top of the very tip of an extremely large iceberg.

Premature death seems to be an occupational hazard amongst so-called celebrities in all fields. Again there are many reasons for this, some of them even genuine ones, but there are also many suspicious ones, some of them extremely suspicious bordering on the blatantly obvious. As stated above, Michael Jackson would fall neatly into that particular category, as would Whitney Houston who died shortly before my writing of this chapter in early 2012 and as the most recent incidents tend to be the ones that are freshest in the mind, let us concentrate on that particular one.

"It's a very predictable pattern that happens with all famous artists. They become valuable commodities. If they were shares, you would see Bay Street buying them up and fundamentally, it's the realisation that it's the end of the artist's productivity, that they won't produce anything more that sparks the buying frenzy." Theo Peridis, professor of strategic management at York University

Regarding Whitney Houston's recent sad demise (11th February 2012) and as with any other recently deceased 'megastar', it is a fact that the record company stood to gain massively in terms of vastly increased sales, albeit short-term. However how much better for them to have a short, one-off major boost than a long, lingering virtually profit-less demise to any artist's career?

The 2012 Grammy Awards took place shortly after the sudden, mysterious death of Whitney Houston. As the old tradition would have it, the show went on nevertheless, but not without an abundance of strange symbolism and ritualism that made it extremely clear that there is a definite 'dark side' to the entertainment business.

Upon the analysis of the facts surrounding Whitney Houston's death coupled with the symbolic elements of the 2012 Grammy awards, the entire event has the look and feel of an occult ritual, complete with a blood sacrifice, a celebration and even a 're-birth'. Some of the things described below were pre-planned, while others were possibly just odd coincidences. Let us now examine the most significant events that happened during the fateful weekend of Houston's death.

The highly symbolic 2012 Grammy awards ceremony

Whitney Houston's untimely death is strikingly similar to many other celebrity 'sacrifices'. Accounts of strange events before the death, the bizarre behaviour of the so-called authorities when the death was discovered, conflicting reports, the vagueness surrounding the cause of the death and last but not least, a typical response from the music industry via the Grammys 'ceremony'. Her case indeed followed the same pattern as several other celebrity deaths that were blamed on drugs excesses, despite much conflicting, albeit circumstantial evidence to the contrary. As was the case for other celebrities, the controlled media almost immediately began a campaign depicting Whitney as a hopeless drug addict. Maybe she was a drug addict, but if so, that is probably just a convenient side-issue, a symptom of the true killer of Whitney, ie. the much vaunted entertainment industry itself.

As with the recent cases of Michael Jackson, Amy Winehouse, Heath Ledger, Brittany Murphy and many others too numerous to mention, going back through the years, bizarre events both preceded and followed the death of Whitney Houston and after even a cursory examination of those events, it is impossible not to ponder as to whether her death (and the others) was truly an accident or a deliberate 'sacrifice' planned and undertaken by hidden hands? The majority of mainstream media sources have emphasised the drugs connection ad nauseum but several, more reliable sources have revealed other details that may provide evidence for an alternative view of the situation.

At the Beverley Hilton where Whitney Houston died, in the ballroom several floors below her suite of rooms at the time of her death, there was a 'pre-Grammys' party in full-swing. As the news broke regarding her death, Whitney was still lying there in her room in her fourth floor suite. She had been discovered dead in her bath, but it is unclear exactly by whom as there were several people in her suite at that time (3.50pm local time). Her body was not moved out until shortly before the party ended around midnight.

What has not been made public (at least in the mainstream) is that at around 11pm, paramedics were called again and security services and police also rushed to the scene and a medical-type wheelchair with restraints was also wheeled-in as Whitney's daughter Bobbi Kristina had become hysterical and paramedics were on the point of removing her to the hospital. Why should this happen, at least seven hours after Whitney's death? Very strange indeed.

Also, at 2.30am during the night immediately preceding Whitney's death, a man in a 3rd floor room immediately beneath her suite complained that water was cascading into his room from above. This was no mere trickle this was a full-blown gushing of water. He called security and accompanied them upstairs to see for himself what on earth was going-on. According to this man, it was the bathtub that was overflowing but he noticed that a large-screen television had also been smashed.

Significant or not, neither of these incidents were reported by the mainstream media at the time or as far as I know, since the event and from an organisation that usually picks-up on the most trivial of incidents and blows them out of all proportion, I have to say I find that fact more than a little strange, to say the least.

So as it turned-out then, there was a party in full-swing going on three floors below Whitney's body whilst it just lay there for hours on end. Is this not more than a little distasteful especially given the fact that many of the attendees were Whitney's close colleagues and friends and acquaintances in the music business? Why was it not simply cancelled out of respect for her death or was there some kind of warped thrill to be had in partying-on below the dead body? Could it even have been part of some sick ritual or ceremony? It would not surprise me in the least, given the track record of these people.

Immediately before Whitney's death, in another strange occurrence, she had been seen fraternising with a person who had also been hanging around Michael Jackson through his last few months alive and in the hours leading up to his death. This man goes by the name of Raffles van Exel (a pseudonym if ever I heard one). He apparently is from Amsterdam in Holland and has also been known to use the aliases of Raffles Dawson and Raffles Benson. He was present in WH's suite of rooms at the time of her demise and apparently appeared downstairs in the hotel lobby shortly thereafter wearing aviator-type sunglasses and ostentatiously weeping and wailing. His usual entourage was there with him, including Quinton Aaron, a Hollywood B-grade movie actor and despite his terrible shock at Whitney's death he still managed to force himself to attend the party in the ballroom. He was bearing Whitney's entry ticket in his hand when he entered the room to what was apparently an outpouring of sympathy, but obviously not enough sympathy to actually halt the party.

A security guard confirmed that Exel had been hanging around Whitney for a few days and was actually pictured standing behind her as she emerged from a nightclub earlier that week, looking confused and disorientated. So who really is this Exel character? He apparently was to be seen hanging around Michael Jackson and his family and friends during Jackson's child molestation trial also. No-one really seems to know who he is for sure, but he is often seen and pictured around celebrities.

Exel claims to own several companies including Raffles Entertainment and also claims to be the manager of Chaka Khan. There are a multitude of photos of him on the Internet posing with almost everyone who is anyone. He apparently does not respond to any emails or phone messages to his published contact points and thus very much remains the archetypal 'mystery man'.

So, was Exel an instrumental part in Whitney's death in any way and had she become persona non gratis to the Elite's music industry in some way? Was she becoming 'out of control' or 'losing' her programming perhaps? It has been reported that she had had premonitions about her own demise (where have we heard this before?) and shortly before her death she allegedly passed a note to her friend, the singer, Brandy who flatly refused to reveal its contents, other than to ambiguously state that 'Whitney meant everything to me. She's the reason that I sing'.

There is also an occult/numerology connection to Houston's death, in this case a connection with the number 11. In occult rites the number 11 is a master number as it cannot be reduced and because it exceeds the number 10 (regarded as perfection) by 1, it is also linked to black magic and 'bad vibrations'. Kabbalists tend to associate this number with transgression of the law, sorcery and possibly significantly, martyrdom.

It is also linked to sacrifice. For example, 9/11, the twin towers looked like a large number 11 and Remembrance/Veterans Day the 11/11 at the 11th hour. There is yet another link to consider and that is concerning Lady Gaga (another mind-controlled MK Ultra slave) and previous Grammy awards ceremonies. Gaga had close links to the fashion designer, Alexander MacQueen who was strongly involved with the occult and mind control and who himself died on the 11th February 2010, exactly two years to the day before Houston. Could it also be significant that Whitney Houston's room number the day that she died, was 434 which in numerology equates to 4+3+4 =11. Again, certainly food for thought.

At the Grammy awards ceremony in 2011, Lady Gaga said, *"I need to thank Whitney Houston. I wanted to thank Whitney, because when I wrote 'Born this Way', I imagined she was singing it because I wasn't secure enough in myself to imagine I was a superstar. So, Whitney, I imagined you were singing 'Born This Way' when I wrote it."*

'Born this Way', surprise of surprises was released on the 11th February 2011, exactly one year to the day before Whitney's death. Significant? Most certainly, I would venture to suggest. It is highly likely that Gaga (or more likely her controllers) in conjunction with Houston's, planned it all very carefully. Gaga's outfit for the 2012 awards was all-black, possibly symbolically signifying death?

Celine Dion was extraordinarily quick in apportioning the blame for Whitney's death. During a TV interview shortly after the event, she blamed the bad influence of the industry and even stated the need to be 'afraid' of it and its over-reaching influence.

"It's just really unfortunate that drugs, bad people or bad influence took over. It took over her dreams. It took over her love and motherhood. When you think about Elvis Presley and Marilyn Monroe and Michael Jackson and Amy Winehouse, to get into drugs like that, for whatever reason, is it because of the stress and bad influence? What happens when you have everything? What happens when you have love, support, the family, motherhood? You have responsibilities of a mother and then something happens and it destroys everything. That's why I don't do parties and I don't hang out. That's why I'm not part of show business. We have to be afraid. I've always said you have to have fun and do music and you can never be part of show business because you don't know what it's going to get you into. You have to do your work and get out of there." Celine Dion

"I think we all, as artists, because we're highly sensitive people and this machine around us, this so-called 'music industry,' is such a demonic thing. It sacrifices people's lives and

their essences at the drop of a dime ... I had a manager once say to me, 'You know you're worth more money dead than alive'." Chaka Khan

Are Chaka Khan's references to 'demonic' and 'sacrifices', to be taken literally? Judging by the symbolism at the Grammy awards and the strangeness surrounding Whitney Houston's death and that of many others down the years, it would certainly appear so.

Please understand however that the above events are just one example and one tiny pinprick on the finger-tip of the very large body of evidence linking show business to the satanic arts. Many, many artistes are said to be involved in this whole charade, many knowingly but nevertheless unable to escape its clutches for fear of the Michael Jackson / Whitney Houston experience befalling them and many unknowingly through subtle mind-control techniques as described previously in this book.

The presence of occult, satanic and Illuminati/freemasonic symbolism throughout the whole entertainment industry is rife, to say the very least.

During the 1950s and 60s, occult practices were slowly but surely absorbed into popular music and today the industry literally thrives by using an outward spectacle of occult and satanic rituals and symbolism. The entire music and entertainment industry is an important indoctrination tool used by and for the Elite and many musicians are introduced to Satanism and occultism. Today, the most popular musicians, such as for example, Lady Gaga and Britney Spears are totally controlled by the occult and the music industry and Hollywood are fixated by Black Magic and Witchcraft. Music has always been associated with the occult and can be effectively used as a tool for programming minds.

Satanism and the occult are also known to specifically extract energy from humans who are manipulated into trances. Throughout the twentieth century and now into the twenty-first, music has been manipulated from its initial state of innocence, goodness and wholesomeness to become in many cases, downright vile and nasty. Throughout the world many people, especially the 10-30 age range are listening to vacuous, emotionally-numbing and trance-inducing negatively-vibrational music and demonic lyrics, which at one time were uniquely present within heavy metal rock, but now seem to emanate from and be present in all genres.

'Rock and Roll' originally emerged as a defined musical style in the United States in the early to mid-1950s. It is descended directly from the rhythm and blues music of the 1940s, which itself developed from earlier blues, jazz and swing music and was also influenced by gospel, country and western and traditional folk music. Rock and Roll in turn gave birth to 'rock music' in general and over the last fifty years the individual musical genres have expanded greatly, presumably in order to cater for everyone's individual tastes and ensure that no-one escapes the net.

It is extremely important to identify which types of music are harmful to the human psyche and which are negative. The vast majority of pre-1950s music calibrates in our consciousness as positive and positive consciousness in turn creates high levels of confidence and a healthy self-esteem.   This cannot be said however of a vast majority of post 1950s music, especially from the 1980s onwards.   Its insidious influence on our psyches has no doubt left its mark on us all to a greater or lesser degree and there is no doubt that certain songs, artists and lyrics contribute in some way, however large or small, to the huge increase in suicide among the under 25 age groups, which stands at record levels and is no doubt welcomed enthusiastically by the Elite in line with their stated policy of huge population reduction.

Indeed, music has a very strong, very definite physiological and psychological effect on people, especially the more impressionable among us. Disharmonic, discordant and cacophonic music engenders a number of negative behaviours, although those affected are often unaware of the extreme effect it is having upon them.

When Mick Jagger of The Rolling Stones wrote the song 'Sympathy for the Devil', in the 1960s, this was one of the first examples of Satanism in rock music. To many observers, the occult and Satanism began to expand its influence through such bands as Led Zeppelin and even the Eagles a band which is generally regarded as being 'soft' rock oriented. And so the Elite now performs its satanic rituals upon us all, via our favourite musicians and through all the dozens of pop music TV channels that exist today and also their contrived, highly ritualistic awards ceremonies in front of millions of deluded viewers.

The American researcher and author, David McGowan in his serialised Internet story, 'The Strange Story of Laurel Canyon', relates how most of the popular musicians and entertainers in the 1960s had some connection to the American military and thus to the myriad of intelligence networks. He tells the totally credible story of how these artists were 'artificially' brought to prominence at this time and describes the strange goings-on around the music scene in those days and the insidious influence that these people and their suspect connections had on the music of that period and henceforward from that time.

In 1985, the *New Solidarity* newspaper, which has since been closed-down by the US federal government, conducted an interview with Hezekiah Ben Aaron, who at the time was the third-ranking member of the Church of Satan. In this interview, Aaron revealed that it was his 'Church' that started such heavy-metal genre rock groups as Black Sabbath, The Blue Oyster Cult and many others. The Church of Satan was then headed by its high priest, Anton LaVey but many people believe that LaVey, was just a front man for the real high priest, Kenneth Anger, the man who had been responsible for introducing the Rolling Stones to the occult.

It is a fact that the human brain thinks at a rate of approximately eight thoughts per second and that the eyes see 20 to 30 separate actions per second, but the brain only uses eight of these to send to the conscious mind. The subconscious absorbs the rest, subliminally and indiscriminately.

However, most live musical performances incorporate video screens with their music at 30 frames per second at the standard American television resolution but they colour eight of the 30 frames differently. They choose which ones we think consciously about and which are just subconsciously absorbed as programming. Hollywood has used this trick, invented originally by Disney, for many years. It is now illegal in television commercials and regarded as subliminal advertising, which, as most people know is an extremely powerful conditioning tool.

The 'eight per second' frequency is also used by bass tones or bass drums or lights or all together, in a concert or live-show setting and this has the same effect upon the brain as does hypnosis. That is it fragments analytical thoughts so that certain mispronounced or difficult to understand lyrics are immediately absorbed by the subconscious mind. If we then add in a mix of illegal drugs and fake (or even real) sacrificial blood, create a circle with a pentagram using the stage lights and positions of the musicians within it, place large speakers in strategic positions for 13 separate points of origin of musical sound, altogether this constitutes a bona fide 'Black Mass' replete with 'sacred geometry'.

So we have now seen how pop culture is filled with occult and masonic symbolism. The Illuminati symbolism apparent in Gaga's stage and TV appearances is utterly blatant and is becoming so transparent that analyses almost become a simple statement of the obvious. Her whole persona, whether it is an act or not, is a tribute to mind control, freemasonry and the occult where being vacuous, compliant, incoherent and simply absent-minded is manipulated into being a 'fashionable' state.

The 'lady' herself – in action

Incorporated in the videos, photos and shows of Lady Gaga and many other pop icons, is symbolism that refers explicitly to the Elite and to mind control. This symbolism is deep, esoteric and even pseudo-spiritual and whilst millions of young people imitate Gaga's gestures, her act is part of a much bigger picture that includes many other 'stars' displaying and promoting the same overt symbolism. 'Lady Gaga' is in fact a fake persona, a manufactured Illuminati puppet, created to unduly influence the impressionable youth of today and to indoctrinate them in the insidious ways of the Elite. In this she is not alone, the majority of the mainstream music industry is also under their deceptive spell.

Eugenics and the Great Myth of World Overpopulation

"Depopulation should be the highest priority of US foreign policy towards the Third World." Dr. Henry Kissinger.

According to Wikipedia... *"Eugenics is the applied science or the biosocial movement which advocates the use of practices aimed at improving the genetic composition of a population."*

My definition would be... *"Eugenics is the pseudo-science used as a cover by the Elite to facilitate the mass de-population of humanity in accordance with their stated goals."*

"What most Americans don't realize is that the upper echelons of the United States government is no longer a government 'of, by and for' the people. The United States government as with all other major governments of the world is under the total domination and control of the Illuminati (architects of the so-called New World Order). The Illuminati's plan to reduce the global population by 4 billion people before the year 2050 was laid out in the Global 2000 report assembled by the Carter administration in the late 70's." Ken Adachi, researcher, educate-yourself.org

How often do we hear the oft-repeated mantra of reduction of population being essential if we are to save the planet? The Global Warmists are forever telling us that man-made CO_2 emissions are the cause of Global Warming (now euphemistically re-named Climate Change as it has become obvious that the Earth is actually cooling) and thus population needs to be reduced to eliminate this effect. This is all absolutely blatant eugenicist propaganda on behalf of the Elite I am afraid and eugenics is just a racist tool to justify genocide.

Consider this; the world population at the time of writing is approximately 6.8 billion – expected to grow to 9 billion by 2050 *if* current trends continue. It sounds huge and unsustainable does it not?

However, would you be surprised if I told you that the entire current population of the world (June 2011) could fit quite comfortably into an area the size of the US State of Texas at a density of less than 40 people per acre? Most modern housing developments can comfortably fit housing for around 100 people into a one acre development providing larger than average plots and without excessive overcrowding and an apartment tower block can contain as many as one thousand people in a ground area considerably smaller than one acre. Approximately 16,000 people live and work in the Willis (formerly Sears) Tower in Chicago, the tallest building on the American continent, which has a 'footprint' of just over one acre, at 225 by 225 feet. However this fact is simply by way of an illustration of the point. I am certainly not advocating tower blocks, let alone one the size of the Willis Tower as an answer to the so-called, non-existent over-population 'problem'.

If the Elite wished to do so, they could easily divert some tiny percentage of the vast amounts of money spent on their constant conflicts and wars to further their corporate ambitions and a miniscule amount of the obscene profits from their usury and solve the world housing and food shortages virtually overnight, thus eliminating poverty forever. That they choose not to, speaks volumes about their motives and motivations to me. 'Overpopulation' of certain areas of the world is a *symptom* of poverty, ignorance and want and not the cause. If all people were treated as valuable human beings instead of as 'useless eaters' by the tiny minority pulling the world's strings then we would *all* be educated by society, our parents and peers from birth to understand co-operation and working together as a species and thus overpopulation and poverty would instantly become an non-issue.

I have to tell you that the world food and water shortage we are constantly reminded of by the compliant media is entirely engineered and managed, to further our rulers' stated goal of population reduction and secondarily to inflate food prices even further as a means of control. Food production and distribution is slowly being concentrated into the remit of fewer and fewer organisations through such devices as Codex Alimentarius and the recent US Food Safety legislation S510, in order to facilitate its scarcity and thus control the size, spread and composition of human populations worldwide.

Through corrupt, evil corporations such as Monsanto, we are seeing the introduction of Genetically Modified (GM) foods, calculated to contaminate and disrupt the food chain as well as maximise their profits by in effect 'cornering the market' on certain foodstuffs that have in effect become Monsanto's own genetic property, contrary maybe not to *their* laws but certainly to human morality and ethics.

In the late 18th century an Anglican priest named Thomas Malthus demonstrated with '*mathematical certainty*' that the world was heading toward demographic disaster. After all, human population increases exponentially while food supply increases arithmetically, does it not? From this it logically follows that it is only a matter of time before the world population outstrips our ability to feed ourselves. Or does it?

Using the same logic, a parent might well view his child's first year of growth and extrapolate that he will be 25 feet tall by the time he is 40 years old, but more than 200 years of the expected population crisis failing to arrive has demonstrated that there are fundamental flaws in Malthus' reasoning. The earth is not a zero-sum game and human ingenuity has always and in every generation somehow managed to expand the available resources even as we take larger and larger portions of our seemingly finite resources. Now even the despicable United Nations' most alarmist predictions admit that global population will level-out and even begin declining by 2050. Malthus is now well understood to have been a complete fraudster propounding his fairy tales for the benefit of the corrupt, Elite-run British East India Company that employed him.

Incredibly though, despite every one of the doomsday predictions of Malthus and his adherents proving to be false, decade after decade for more than two centuries, Malthus' ideas are still being taken seriously or at least we are told that they are taken seriously and are still being hyped and promoted by the Elite oligarchs who benefit from the idea that there are too many 'useless eaters' using up the world's resources.

Malthus himself, an Anglican minister, wrote that *"We are bound in justice and honour formally to disdain the right of the poor to support,"* arguing for a law making it illegal for the Anglican Church to give any food, clothing or support to any children. How very Christian in its sentiment. Not content with consigning thousands of children to death for the misfortune of being born poor however, Malthus also advocated actively contributing to the deaths of more of the poor through social-engineering.

"Instead of recommending cleanliness to the poor, we should encourage contrary habits. In our towns we should make the streets narrower, crowd more people into the houses and court the return of the plague. In the country, we should build our villages near stagnant pools, and particularly encourage settlement in all marshy and unwholesome situations. But above all we should reprobate specific remedies for ravaging diseases and restrain those benevolent, but much mistaken men, who have thought they are doing a service to mankind by protecting schemes for the total extirpation of particular disorders." Thomas Malthus, Anglican Priest

This in itself, succinctly tells us all we need to know about the motives of the hierarchy of mainstream religion, in my view. The horrific nature of this idea is made all the more preposterous by the fact that Malthus was encouraging the spread of disease and plague in order to 'save' humanity from the diseases and plagues that overpopulation fosters. But this self-contradiction is completely lost on those whose bloodlust drives them to support such drastic population reduction schemes in their vile scheming to exterminate the poor and downtrodden of society.

As repulsive as Malthus' ideas are in our more 'enlightened times', they have provided an ideological framework for those with a psychopathic urge to dominate others for the past two hundred years.

In his infamous 1968 book, 'The Population Bomb', Paul Ehrlich and his wife Anne wrote...

"A cancer is an uncontrolled multiplication of cells; the population explosion is an uncontrolled multiplication of people... We must shift our efforts from the treatment of the symptoms to the cutting out of the cancer. The operation will demand many apparently brutal and heartless decisions."

Ehrlich felt that the blight of new-born babies was so potentially devastating to humanity that in 1969 he actually advocated adding sterilisers to the food and water supply. Lest there were any doubt about his remarks, he further elaborated on them in '*Ecoscience*', a 1977 book that he co-authored with Barack Obama's current science Czar, John Holdren, in which they once again advocated adding sterilising agents to the water supply.

In 1972, ex-World Bank advisor and UN functionary Maurice Strong advocated government licencing for a woman's right to have children and in 1988, Prince Philip uttered his deplorable comment *"In the event I am reborn, I would like to return as a deadly virus, in order to contribute something to solve overpopulation."* However Prince Philip knows very well that one day he will be re-born as are we all, fortunately for him not as a deadly virus, but one would sincerely hope as a poor, starving peasant in a remote village somewhere in the third world. That would really be karma in action.

In the 1990s, Ted Turner told '*Audubon*' magazine that *"A total world population of 250-300 million people, a 95 percent decline from present levels, would be ideal."*

Of course, the overpopulation myth itself crumbles under the slightest scrutiny. No one, not even the UN, is projecting limitless growth of the human population. Even the most alarmist projections show the world population levelling off within 40 years. Significantly, the birth rate in every major industrialised nation in the world is now below the replacement level of 2.01, meaning that they are all in fact dying nations of aging populations that require an ever-increasing influx of immigrants just to maintain their population levels. In addition to the well-known phenomenon of industrialisation reducing the sizes of families, there are now indications that chemicals called endocrine disruptors which are mysteriously (or perhaps not so mysteriously) ending up in our foods, plastics and drinking water are limiting our biological ability to reproduce, with sperm rates among Western men declining by a staggering 50% in the last 50 years with 85% of the remaining sperm being abnormal.

But still, even if we were to take the hysteria about population size at face value, the 'solutions' suggested by the Malthusians – forced sterilisation programmes, de-industrialisation, and even genocide – represent the biggest fraud of all; the idea that merely reducing the size of a population will somehow reduce the inequalities and iniquities within that society.

But therein lies the secret. The people who are seen to 'worry' the most over the overpopulation non-problem cannot be reasoned-with because their concern for humanity is only pretence. The way they approach the problem itself clearly exhibits their bias in the matter. Most reasonable people see an increase in the number of people on the planet not as a scourge, but as an opportunity to increase our understanding of the human species and its capabilities. In the twisted vision of the overpopulation fearmongers however, new-born babies are not a joy to behold, not a gift, not the living, breathing potential of the future of the human race, but a cancer on the Earth that must be destroyed at all costs.

The Elite are not interested in increasing food production, lifting the poor out of poverty or developing technology to increase our ability to share in the abundant wealth of the world. Instead they wish for the forcible sterilisation of the poor, the consignment of billions around the world to grinding poverty and the elimination of vast swathes of the population. They do not wish to reduce the pain and suffering in the world, but to increase it. In short, the overpopulation hysteria is a convenient lie for the ruthless Elite who stand to benefit from the panic they themselves cause.

Bill Gates (of Microsoft fame – or should that be infamy) and Warren Buffett are major funders of global population reduction programmes, as is Ted Turner, whose UN Foundation was created to funnel $1 billion of his tax-free stock option earnings in AOL-Time-Warner into various birth reduction programmes in the developing world. The programmes in Africa and elsewhere are masked as philanthropy and providing health services for poor Africans. In reality they involve involuntary population sterilisation via vaccination and other medicines that make women of child-bearing age infertile, without their express consent.

The Gates Foundation, where Buffett deposited the bulk of his wealth several years ago, is also backing the introduction of GMO seeds into Africa under the cloak of the Kofi Annan-led 'Second Green Revolution' in Africa. The introduction of GMO patented seeds in Africa to date has met with enormous indigenous resistance. The introduction of this abomination into India over a decade ago has resulted in the suicide, so far, of over 250,000 farmers at a conservative estimate (see Health section for full details).

Health experts point out that were the intent of Gates really to improve the health and well-being of black Africans, the same hundreds of millions of dollars the Gates Foundation has invested in untested and unsafe vaccines could be used in providing minimal sanitary water and sewage systems. Vaccinating a child who then drinks sewage-polluted river water is hardly healthy in any respect. But of course cleaning-up the water and sewage systems of Africa would revolutionise the health conditions of that continent and save thousands of lives. How undesirable would that be to these monsters masquerading as human?

Gates' comments in 2010 about devising new vaccines to *reduce global population* were obviously not a simple off-the-cuff remark or error. For those who doubt this fact, the presentation Gates made at the TED2009 annual gathering said almost exactly the same thing about reducing population to cut global warming.

"The world today has 6.8 billion people. That's headed up to about 9 billion. Now if we do a really great job on new vaccines, health care, reproductive health services, we could lower that by perhaps 10 or 15 percent." Bill Gates, founder of Microsoft and avid Eugenicist, 2010

This statement, when examined, says two things to me. Firstly it says that he strongly advocates population reduction, but perhaps even more chillingly it openly admits that vaccinations really do kill people! How much more proof do we need than this that we are not just under physical attack by these people, but also under psychological attack in the form of pro-vaccination propaganda.

Education

"The aim of public education is not to spread enlightenment at all; it is simply to reduce as many individuals as possible to the same safe level, to breed a standard citizenry, to suppress dissent and originality." H.L. Mencken

The western educational system is a sham, a disgrace, an international embarrassment. But please do not worry; your government has a brilliant idea as to how to mend our 'broken' model and that is the introduction of extensive, all-pervasive, mind-numbing, time-consuming testing of our schools, culminating in league tables which effectively expose those schools that are 'failing' our children. The result of this overall policy has been a natural tendency for schools to concentrate their resources into ensuring that 'standards' are met, to the detriment of the actual education of children. Notice how it is always the individual schools that are the problem and not the education system in its whole, sorry entirety? They never actually propose providing any extra funds or resources to improve our schools, because of course *'we cannot just keep throwing money at the problem'*, although in truth, little money has been thrown in that particular direction for many years now.

It is abundantly clear that 'they', the Elite do not want children to think, know or understand anything of consequence, rather it is all really about what your children can contribute to the corporations and the global economy once they are spit-out at the far end of the educational 'sausage machine'.

There is not the slightest intent on the part of those who would enslave us, to educate us in the truest sense of the word. The only reason that state education is compulsory is not through benevolence or societal responsibility as they would have us all believe, but put simply it is the most convenient and effective expedient by which we may be controlled and indoctrinated into the insidious philosophies of the corporate mind-set from an early age. We are not taught at school how to think logically, independently or even how to survive independently outside the system and what the 'big wide-world' is really all about, rather we are treated as and nurtured to be future corporate employees or other system-servers such as the armed forces, the police, the civil service and the law. This is simply and efficiently achieved by forcibly 'teaching' and conditioning us to conform and be utterly submissive to, and compliant with authority and also by having largely useless, pure 'facts', rather than practical subjects forced down our throats for 14 or 15 years before we enter University and the beginning of our indebtedness to the banking cartels through the student loan scam.

In all that time we are never, ever taught how to think 'outside the box' or even simply how to think critically at all. We are never taught how to become self-sufficient, should we choose to go down that route or any practical skills, to help us survive outside the system that enslaves us. We are simply taught facts and how to regurgitate them at will and this is what passes as our so-called 'education'. I would go even further and say that this extreme emphasis on the teaching of facts rather than the actual understanding and in-depth comprehension of topics is a huge factor in the deliberate 'dumbing-down' of society that is undoubtedly taking place.

Who really *cares* what the value of 'y' is if $2x+3y=21$, that the coefficient of linear expansion of brass is 0.0000187 or what Boyle's Law has to say about the pressure and volume of gases? These facts in themselves bear no relation to the lives of 99.9999% of the population of the world and are only of limited value in themselves, even to those whose profession it is to actually put them to any practical use. If this knowledge was being used as a stepping-stone for the furtherance of human knowledge to the greater benefit of all, then fine, but unfortunately that is not the case. This knowledge is placed in our heads for one reason only and that is so that ultimately a miniscule proportion of those that learn it in the first place can take their places in the corporate world and help to swell the coffers of the parasites at the top by using their 'education' to dream up new money-making schemes or at least help participate in expediting them or the administration of them. For me, our current educational model can be likened to a huge game of *Trivial Pursuit* – art for art's sake and education for education's sake.

Think about the subjects that could be taught in a different, more benevolent society where people co-existed through co-operation and caring for each other rather than having to fight and struggle on a daily basis simply to survive as is the case for most people. Children and young adults could be taught how to co-exist in peace, how to manage their lives in the most efficient yet caring way, how to run a household and its finances successfully and how to rear children properly as well as the spiritual side of life and how to look after one's own physical and mental health using natural products. But of course, we are not allowed to learn these subjects, because they do not fit into the agenda of first and foremost, keeping us in our 'little boxes' and nor are they profitable to the Elite corporations earmarked as our future masters, slave-drivers and 'benefactors'.

Also, what better way of developing the next generation of system-servers than by forcibly removing them from their homes and parents in their tender, formative years and have them spend the next fifteen years becoming embedded inextricably into the warp and weft of the corrupted society in which we all now exist? Think about it for a moment...   What were we taught at school that has any real relevance to the lives we now live, apart from basic reading and writing skills which could both easily have been taught at home? I concede there may be a few people who can possibly name something worthwhile, but I guarantee that this will only be in order to enable them to perform their corporate 'roles' for the most part and not life-enriching per se and I am certainly not in that category, personally speaking. This is also the reason that 'home-schooling' is under severe attack and is even being legislated against now in some areas. It just simply does not benefit our masters for anyone to be brought up to question the world and become a free-thinker in the way that home-schooling encourages its adherents to become. It is a much better solution for the Elite, that their 'education' be under the direction of the state, so that what is learned, or more accurately what is **not** learned can be controlled much more efficiently.

The teaching of life skills and values to children by the majority of parents at home is now long-gone; thanks to incessant Elite distractions of various kinds and so the public education system is the sole arbiter of that today. Most of us work five or six days a week for corporations to earn money to pay our debts to those same corporations and our children go to school where they are taught the way of the state and learn to become cogs in the great machine (like us and our parents and grandparents before us) and expand the profitability of their masters. We must submit and obey but above all else, not ask questions, just depend on the system to instruct us as what to do, what to think and most importantly, what people think of us and what we need to do to gain acceptance in 'society'. This is an anathema to our survival as a species. We must teach our children how to survive independently of the 'system' and we must pass on our own knowledge to them at every feasible opportunity.   Once multi-generational knowledge is gone, this expedites and facilitates the re-writing of history and once that is achieved, people can be easily deluded into living a fantasy orchestrated by forces of which they know or understand nothing – exactly as is the case today.

This is another reason why home-schooling is now frowned-upon and indeed is being legislated against in many areas. As far as our masters are concerned, it is far too dangerous for any child to be given a 'real' education whereby they might eventually see-through the current sham and actually start to think and act for themselves, instead of in the way proscribed by the state.

"Education should aim at destroying free will so that pupils thus schooled, will be incapable throughout the rest of their lives of thinking or acting otherwise than as their schoolmasters would have wished. Influences of the home are obstructive; and in order to condition students, verses set to music and repeatedly intoned are very effective. It is for a future scientist to make these maxims precise and to discover exactly how much it costs per head to make children believe that snow is black. When the technique has been perfected, every government that has been in charge of education for more than one generation will be able to control its subjects securely without the need of armies or policemen." Bertrand Russell, 'The Impact of Science on Society', Columbia United Press, 1951

So, what is really needed, according to the diktats of the Elite, is to test schools in their currently grossly under-funded conditions, apparently to verify what is already known – that many of them are 'under-performing'. Once they are identified, they are targeted as underperformers and the ultimate solution is to shut them down.

In reality, do you honestly believe that your so-called elected leaders care anything at all about the education of your children? They could not even care less about your local school's test ratings either. The truth, unpalatable as it may be to some, is that they never did care. Public education has never been about learning the curriculum offered and gaining an informed view of the world or an insight into the things that really matter in this world. Unsurprisingly, nothing in fact, could pose a greater threat to the Elite than an informed, free-thinking, logical and well-educated population. How fortunate it is then that free, state (or even private) education has never been about imparting real knowledge and truly educating children. It has always been about *how* that knowledge is delivered, the 'process' being the all-important factor.

"Give me four years to teach the children and the seeds I have sown will never be uprooted." Vladimir Ilyich Lenin

Public schooling does not emanate from state 'benevolence' as they would deceptively lead you to believe. No, it arose as a necessary by-product of the Industrial Revolution, which was, in essence a process whereby archaic concepts such as 'skilled labour' and 'craftsmanship' were increasingly discarded in favour of mass-production by largely unskilled assembly-line workers, to facilitate efficiency and thus greater profits.

Of course this then required a fundamental change in the make-up of the labour pool. What was thenceforth needed were masses of interchangeable labourers willing to perform mindless, unfulfilling, regimented and repetitive tasks day in and day out, year in and year out as well as a mindless obedience to authority, an ingrained awareness of the importance of punctuality, the 'Christian work-ethic' and a thorough socialisation of the values of the corporate state.

The route to achieve the Elite aim of producing endless numbers of mindless, robotic workers, was thus through state education and the real truth is that state schools have never been 'failing', they have performed exactly as planned at the task for which they were originally designed. Naturally, they have failed to 'educate' children in the truest sense of the word, to produce students capable of independent thought and logical reasoning, but they were never, ever designed to do that. Now the concept of public education appears to be rapidly going downhill which is no real surprise. The 'industrial age' is more or less gone and we are now entering what is being branded as the 'information age' and the western workforces are once again being transformed as all those industrial jobs that once needed to be filled with a steady influx of bodies, slowly but inexorably disappear.

In other words, in the eyes of our corporate masters, state schooling has now lost its purpose and what this means for future generations is, to put it bluntly, they are no longer needed to generate Elite profits. The state no longer has a reason to condition our children for jobs that no longer exist and are no longer required in the modern, technological age and therefore the desire to impart 'knowledge' to them has disappeared as a consequence. Any still remaining jobs requiring repetitive, manual processes have now been farmed-out at starvation-level wages to slave labourers in China, Taiwan and India, to name but a few countries where this practice is the norm.

The good news for our children is that they no longer need worry about becoming some random, insignificant cog in a huge wheel but conversely, the bad news is that the corporate-controlled state has no other use for them, either. We have all become or are about to become, to paraphrase the immortal words of the Elite stooge, Henry Kissinger, a generation of 'useless eaters'.

Children *want* to learn; in fact they are eager to feast on knowledge but by the end of fifteen or sixteen years of state education only the most dedicated and brainwashed still derive enjoyment from learning. The government education system will literally destroy a child's interest in learning as it is indeed designed to do. In fact, many students, now used to such modern educational devices as the Internet and computers, are classified by the dinosaurs of the education system in conjunction with Big Pharma (the pharmaceutical cartel) as having ADHD 'Attention Deficit Hyperactivity Disorder'. These 'abnormal children', for some strange reason just cannot seem to handle out-dated, centuries-old educational systems since they already have access to much more interesting methods of self-learning. So, what do the authorities do with these 'misfits'? They drug them to dumb them down and make them compliant and unresponsive whilst labelling them as a 'problem child' so that they can handle sitting in an uncomfortable wooden chair and reading uninteresting facts out of dingy old books all day long.

If you are a young person wondering about your future, one of the last things you should consider doing is paying to go to a college or University. If your main intention is to learn however, there is no excuse for not doing so completely outside of any organised school system. Thanks to the internet the world is at your fingertips so take advantage of it before the governments begin to shut it down.   And, of course, no school education can compete with real life experiences; travel is one of the best educations anyone can ever have.

The Student Loan Scam

However, education or more specifically further education or tertiary education is now being used as a cash-cow both for governments and for the banksters who enslave us, alike. Here is the gist of the plan:

Step 1. Ensure that the benefits of a University or college education are aggressively 'sold' to the public by the expedient of substantially increasing the criteria by which candidates qualify for jobs in the first place. ie. Ensure that more and more jobs can only be performed by 'graduates' thus dramatically increasing the uptake of University and college places.

Step 2. Lower the standard of examinations to ensure that more and more students pass them and thus qualify for tertiary education.

Step 3. Gradually, in a series of small steps, increase tuition fees and thus by default the amount of money that needs to be borrowed by students in order to complete their courses. Significantly in Britain in 2011, tuition fees tripled literally overnight, thus ensuring that student debt to the bankers becomes an almost intolerable burden. Indeed, in the future, some students will never be able to pay back these manufactured debts.

The effect of this is that many students, whether or not they actually graduate, will have debt burdens exceeding £100,000, before they start in employment and attempt to obtain mortgages. If repaid over 30 years, this debt represents a £500,000 windfall for the banks and in the event of default, even more. As a result, once entrapped in this way, escape will be nigh on impossible, the bondage will become permanent and future lives and careers will be impaired or ruined, before they even start in many cases.

In Britain at least, there is currently a moratorium on repayments before a certain age and/or income level is attained, but not so in the US where Congress ended bankruptcy protections, refinancing rights, statutes of limitations, truth-in-lending requirements, fair debt collection and state usury laws when applied to federally guaranteed student loans. As a result of this abomination, lenders may freely deduct from salaries, income tax refunds, earned income tax credits, as well as Social Security and disability income to assure defaulted loan payments. In addition, defaulting may cause loss of professional licenses and status, making repayment even harder or impossible. How long before this insidious state of affairs comes to pass elsewhere, do you suppose? My guess would be 'fairly imminently', to be frank.

As a result of this, for many people, permanent debt bondage is assured. In addition, no appeals process allows determinations of default challenges under a process letting lenders rip-off borrowers, often in perpetuity. The truth is that there now exists a conspiratorial alliance of lenders, guarantors, servicers, and collection companies enriching themselves hugely at the borrowers' expense, thriving on extortionate fees and related schemes. It is essentially a government-sanctioned racket, scamming millions of indebted victims. Lenders thrive on bad debts, deriving income from inflated service-charges, default and collection fees. Today we have created a paradise for the unscrupulous lenders as default rates soar and people begin to drown in debt and student loans have become a dramatically increasing percentage of that overall debt.

The end product of all this is that several education policy experts have predicted serious implications for future graduates...

"If you have a lot of people finishing or leaving school [entrapped in] debt, their choices may be very different than the generation before them. Things like buying a home, starting a family, starting a business, saving for their own kids' education may not be an option if they're trying to repay student debt. There's much more awareness about student borrowing than there was 10 years ago. People either are in debt or know someone in debt." Lauren Asher, President of the Institute for College Access and Success

Many of them have their own personal horror stories about how predatory lenders, servicers, guarantors, and collection companies rip them off under a totally escape-proof system. In fact the entire scheme amounts to nothing more or less than legalised theft and enslavement, in fact in much the same way as the banksters treat their investors and steal from them with impunity.

"About two-thirds of the people I see attended Universities. Most did not complete their programme, and no one I have worked with has ever gotten a job in the field they were supposedly trained for. For them, the negative (debt default) mark on their credit report is the number one barrier to moving ahead in their lives. It doesn't just delay their ability to buy a house; it gets in the way of their employment prospects, finding an apartment, almost anything they try to do." Deanne Loonin, National Consumer Law Centre attorney

Western society today is characterised by a combination of rising prices, rising poverty, unemployment, mortgage foreclosures, homelessness, hunger, student debt entrapment and despair, completely mocking the notion of a fair and equitable society. Instead we have a corrupt political duopoly, sucking public wealth into the already-bulging coffers of the super-rich, neglecting public want and needs, waging permanent war and driving other nations down the road of permanent war leading to tyranny and ultimately, ruin. Anyone attending a college or University in an attempt to 'get ahead' of the rest in the labour market will unfortunately be several years behind those who go directly into a job from school and what is much, much worse, will no doubt be in debt for the rest of their life.

Charities

So-called 'charities' for the most part are nothing more or less than a means of extracting even more money from the masses to swell the already overflowing coffers of the mega-rich. We need to collectively realise that we are being scammed on a massive scale and every time we respond to the emotional blackmail emanating from these highly dubious institutions 24/7, we are no more contributing to a 'good cause' than we are in buying the corporate rubbish masquerading as 'consumer goods', which largely originate from the same sources, as the large charities are more often than not, simply a thinly-disguised front for propounding corporate policy and interests.

It very much goes against 'the grain' to actually even attempt to write this section, such is the power of the propaganda directed at us, but write it and fight the internal conflict I must, if we are to put an end to this hoax. But firstly let me state for the avoidance of doubt, that I have nothing but admiration, except maybe tinged with a little sadness, for the millions that freely give what little spare time they have as voluntary workers for many of these utterly unscrupulous organisations. These people are some of the most selfless on the planet and yet they are being deceived on a monstrous scale by the Elite bloodsuckers who perpetuate this state of affairs without even so much as a mild attack of conscience.

Whether we are being almost literally accosted in the street by someone thrusting a collecting box at us, or subjected to massive multi-million pound advertising campaigns in the media, the name of the game is indeed emotional blackmail of the most insidious yet persuasive kind. There is something innate in the human psyche (apart from those psychopaths who prey upon us) which engenders in us a need to show others that we are essentially, 'good' and 'caring' people and it is this desire that is subtly turned against us to perpetrate the hoax of charitable donations.

I do not include within this category, small local charities, run by and for victims of various kinds of suffering or injustice, but all those world-wide and nationwide, household-name type charities, whose names with whom we are all so familiar.
We should also consider the more basic issue of why these grand-scale charities are needed in our supposed enlightened times, anyway. Are we not supposed to be civilised beings? Or are we so un-civilised that we cannot or will not adequately feed

and otherwise generally care for every under-privileged member of our species? Have you even ever asked yourself the question as to why this may be the case? If the mega-rich really wanted poverty and hardship to end, they could do so almost overnight by expending a small amount of the daily interest from their enormous fortunes. The very fact that they do not, speaks volumes to me. Put another way, why should we, those of us who are strictly speaking just above the poverty line, contribute from our meagre disposable incomes, whilst the rich sit back and happily allow this state of affairs to continue? The answer is, because they can.

Then there is the question of the patronage of charities. The patron of a charity is usually a high-profile personality, whose names are highly sought-after for patronage in the full knowledge that as this is a so-called 'well-respected' person, ensuring that the charities will be more high-profile and thus attract even more of the public's money. For example, the Queen of England is patron to over 600 charities. Yes, that is correct – over 600! Do you really believe that this woman, head of the most ruthless family on the planet and personally responsible, directly and indirectly (along with the rest of her genocidal brood) for millions of deaths worldwide in her own lifetime, actually cares a damn about starving children or victims of the wars that her and her ilk are responsible for causing in the first place? I think not somehow.

Indeed some charities have been with us for centuries and so it is blatantly obvious to me that the reasons for the charity's founding in the first place have not been solved. So realistically speaking, that charity has failed in its objectives to exacerbate or end the problems it was set-up to counteract. If a charity did succeed in solving the problems it was created to fight, then it would in effect be responsible for its own demise, logically, would it not? Of course this is a paradox that will never be reconciled whilst charities continue to so successfully deprive the masses of their hard-earned funds.

Here are some examples from many instances.

Live Aid / Live8

Whenever funds need to be raised to feed the starving millions, to bring clean water to those without, to build homes and habitats for those in need and to help rescue the victims of natural disasters or famine, one person always seems to be prominent – none other than 'Sir' Robert Geldof himself, the original 1970s 'teenage rebel'.

"I think Band Aid was diabolical... Bob Geldof is a nauseating character. Many people find that very unsettling, but I'll say it as loud as anyone wants me to. In the first instance, the record itself was absolutely tuneless. One can have great concern for the people of Ethiopia, but it's another thing to inflict daily torture on the people of England. It was an awful record considering the mass of talent involved. And it wasn't done shyly; it was the most self-righteous platform ever in the history of popular

music." Morrissey of the British band 'The Smiths', referring to the hit song, 'Do They Know its Christmas'

Since then, Geldof and others such as Bono of the rock band U2 have almost made new careers of being figureheads of poverty relief whilst reaping the benefits these events provide them, that is name and face recognition. For instance, in November 2008, Geldof was paid $100,000 in Australia for a brief speech addressing Third World poverty whilst Bono was recently implicated in a scandal relating to his own charity and its total lack of actual monetary contributions to the causes it is said to support, despite its £12m per annum turnover.

Brian Johnson, lead singer of AC/DC, said that people like Geldof and Bono should dip into their own bank accounts, as do the members of AC/DC and give without publicity, rather than being *'pop impresarios of poverty'*.

Michael Chussodovsky scathingly dissected Geldof's role in this financial charade, thus...

"Most casual observers might assume that the money generated by corporate sponsors, DVD sales, performance royalties and direct contributions would be funnelled into various charitable organizations aiding the poorest people of developing nations around the world. They would be wrong."

Instead, as Chussodovsky illustrates, the money raised in almost every instance, is used to pay off the corporate creditors of indebted countries. In effect, the **entire** focus of the money generated by *Live8* was to provide direct funds to corporations that were 'owed money' by these impoverished nations.

As if that were not sufficiently outrageous, the reality is actually much worse than that. Those same monetary amounts contributed by *Live8* to these private corporations to provide more relief to them for the money they had lent to these impoverished nations was then deducted from the direct aid packages and social service programmes formerly contributed by the G8 to these countries.

As Chussodovsky also clearly states, *"For each dollar of 'debt cancellation' to the international financial institutions, the G8 will reduce the flow of foreign aid to these countries. In other words, the foreign aid earmarked to finance much needed social programs will now go directly into the coffers of the IMF and the World Bank."*

Moreover, the International Monetary Fund and The World Bank and The African Development Bank never write-off their debts. So what was being promoted and touted around the world as a way to help some of the poorest countries on the planet was actually a covert exercise in paying off international financial institutions for aid they had previously lent these nations, whilst guaranteeing the reduction of the same amount in future funding for these very programmes.

In effect, Live Aid and Live8 were nothing more or less than gigantic propaganda pieces and financial con tricks to repay private institutions and their criminal friends at the IMF and World Bank. Live8 acted as a direct reimbursement process for the creditors of the poorest countries on the planet, while further binding these countries, their industries and exports, to the future predations of the World Bank and IMF.

This allowed them to impose even more social control on their political processes by insisting on 'democratic reforms' commensurate with the same sort the West has imposed on Iraq, Afghanistan and now Egypt and Libya, thereby allowing Western governments to control the election process and the officials who will come to power in these countries while insisting on 'free market reforms', all of which does nothing more than to diminish their sovereignty while transferring ever more overt socio-political control to nations outside these countries and the corporate predators that lurk there ever-ready to exploit new markets. This arrangement also makes it impossible for these countries to default on their debt, perpetually keeping them in the cycle of debt-repayment and financial servitude.

Frauds like Geldof have promoted this Elite, globalist charade, enjoying the fame and royalty income which their appearance on world-wide television provides, whilst at the same time turning a cynically blind eye to the financial sleight of hand going on behind the scenes which does nothing more than to keep these countries and peoples steeped in poverty whilst reducing the social services these countries so desperately need.

Geldof supposedly organised all of the Live8 concerts (the 20th anniversary of Live Aid) in 2005, on his mobile phone. This is a very interesting concept considering the fact that he is supposed to be 'Mr. Anti-establishment' and a 'champion of the poor and hungry'. If that is indeed the case then the question needs to be asked as to how he managed to get several governments to co-operate with him and endorse his plans so easily? Why did these governments not just tell him politely to 'go away' or indeed any other two-word phrase with the same implication? Actually, I can almost guarantee that if Bob Geldof really was assisting starving Africans to the detriment of the money-interests in the ways popularly described, then he would almost certainly have ended the same way as John Lennon, JFK, RFK and MLK and others whose motivations were against the best interests of the Elite, let alone being fêted as a saintly figure.

Ever wondered why 'Sir' Bob was given an honorary knighthood (as an Irishman he is not entitled to a 'regular' knighthood)? Was it for helping the world's poor and oppressed perchance? Or was it more likely to be for his contribution to the financial bottom-lines of the World Bank, the IMF and the Bank of International Settlements – all run and owned by our Royal and Elite masters? Geldof was used by them as the 'good guy' to promote their greed as a charitable event and good old Bob, for his part was only too willing to comply. Did he do it knowingly or unknowingly? Was he paid for his services or did he give all his free time willingly and without thought of remuneration? I know where my vote would be cast on that particular issue.

The picture below tells us all we need to know about 'Sir' Bob's real affiliations...

The sheeple, as usual were fooled yet again because they had already been indoctrinated and conditioned into accepting that Geldof possesses saintly qualities and that Live8 was another blow for the poor against their heartless oppressors. There is only one way to prevent a repetition of this scam, for scam is exactly what it is and that is to make sure that we never, ever contribute a penny to these 'charities' as doing so I am afraid, will only exacerbate the situation and further contribute to the utter misery being deliberately inflicted on the helpless peoples of the Third World.

The Red Cross

The International Red Cross, like the International Monetary Fund (IMF) and the World Bank, is an Elite-controlled front organisation whose true purpose is the complete opposite from their stated purpose.

The IMF tells the world that they are there to 'help' countries recover from economic difficulties (which incidentally the IMF and World Bank blatantly created in the first place) but in reality, the IMF breaks countries and ruins their economies. The same could be said of the Red Cross.

The moment a 'natural' disaster such as for example Hurricane Katrina, the Haitian earthquake or the Japanese Tsunami occurs; radio and TV ads flood the airwaves seeking monetary donations to be sent to the Red Cross. With music full of pathos playing in the background, the announcer tells us that the Red Cross is 'always there in time of need' and now that the poor victims are suffering terribly with this appalling tragedy, 'won't you please open your heart' and make a 'generous donation' to this 'worthy cause'?

These people, who in my humble estimation are thoroughly beneath contempt, have totally mastered the science of extracting money from the unthinking masses. For example, the dust from the World Trade Centre collapses had not even settled (literally) before the Red Cross were appealing to us all to give blood and money to help the victims and the families of the 'terrorist' attack. Thousands of people gave blood and even more gave millions upon millions of pounds to the Red Cross. It would maybe have been pertinent to ask 'blood for whom'? Everyone was dead (there were few injuries, relatively speaking) so why was the Red Cross asking for blood donations day and night for a week or longer?

The answer is reflective of the true purpose of the Red Cross. Sad to say the Red Cross is a disaster 'racket' which is in the business of making money from people's misery, especially with totally engineered disasters such as 9/11. They sell the blood on, of course, but they apparently also use the blood for other things to which the public is generally not privy and one could legitimately ask where does all the money go and to whom? For the most part, they keep it for themselves as do the vast majority of major, household-name charities. The families of the victims of 9/11 had to badger, harrass and threaten the Red Cross in an attempt to obtain $11 million that they would not release to the families, as long as one year after the event – and that is just what we were told in the media, so my guess would be that it will be a pretty safe bet that the actual figure was much, much higher than this.

The CEO of the Red Cross and other senior administrators receive obscene salaries and other massive perks, all of which are paid directly from the man/woman in the street's direct contributions to these supposed 'good causes'. At the time of writing, the salary of the current president, Marsha Evans is $651,957 per annum and the total revenue of the Red Cross is well in excess of $3bn per annum (three billion dollars!).

"As the aftermath of hurricane Katrina continues to wreak mayhem and havoc amid reports of mass looting, shooting at rescue helicopters, rapes and murders, establishment media organs are promoting the Red Cross as a worthy organization to give donations to. The biggest website in the world, Yahoo.com, displays a Red Cross donation link prominently on its front page. Every time there is a major catastrophe the Red Cross and similar organizations like United Way are given all the media attention

while other charities are left in the shadows. This is not to say that the vast majority of Red Cross workers are not decent people who simply want to help those in need". Paul Joseph Watson and Alex Jones, 1st September 2005

In fact, the Red Cross has been caught 'red-handed' many times in withholding money in the wake of terrible disasters that require immediate release of funds. In the name of the 'Liberty Fund' for 9/11 family relief, the Red Cross collected $564 million in donations from around the world and yet only actually distributed around $150 million. Its explanation for keeping the majority of the money was that it would be used to help 'fight the war on terror'. In other words, this means that the money was spent bombing third world countries like Afghanistan and setting up surveillance cameras and expanding the police state in US cities and not put towards helping the families of victims to rebuild their shattered lives.

The then Red Cross President Dr. Bernadine Healy arrogantly responded when accused of withholding of funds by stating, *"The Liberty Fund is a war fund. It has evolved into a war fund. We must have blood readiness. We must have the ability to help our troops if we go into a ground war. We must have the ability to help the victims of tomorrow."*

At whose behest or say-so may I humbly enquire? Does the official mandate of the Red Cross now extend to collecting donations under false pretences and in lieu of possible future wars instigated by the Elite? Evidently it does, with nary a word of condemnation from those who either contribute their hard-earned cash or those who are supposedly its intended recipients, let alone government, in whose best interests this sorry state of affairs appears to be perpetuated.

However, the scandalous activities of the Red Cross extend way back, long before 9/11 in fact. Following the disastrous San Francisco earthquake in 1989, the Red Cross donated only $10 million of the $50 million that had been raised, and kept the rest. Similarly, following the Oklahoma City bombing in 1995 and the Red River flooding in 1997 many donations were also withheld. In fact the Red Cross has a long, long sordid history of stealing cash donations intended for disaster relief. Even as far back as the Korean War the Red Cross was plundering soldiers' relief packages, the famous 'Red Cross Parcels' from home. The Red Cross is very adept at stealing money and looting mail and has been exposed in this respect many times but it has been allowed to escape sanctions, punishment or exposure because the organisation is so closely allied with and indeed is inextricably linked with the Elite establishment. It is without doubt an organisation run by Elite insiders whose purpose is to gather intelligence and steal from the poor, underprivileged and needy to further line the pockets of the rich.

And these are just a few examples of its ongoing highly deceptive and fraudulent activity. Several minor charities that were involved with the 2004 Tsunami relief project expressed outrage in public to say that large charities like Red Cross and

Oxfam were engaged in secret negotiations that resulted in a large amount of the public-donated money being withheld from those most affected by the disaster.

It is abundantly clear that the Red Cross and other large so-called charities are in actual fact merely fronts for collecting funds on behalf of the Elite military-industrial complex. Some respected historians have even alleged that the Red Cross was used as a *Skull and Bones* cover to overthrow the Russian royals and pave the way for the rise of the Communism and to be frank my research would tend to lead me to believe that to be the truth.

The message here should be clear to all. Under no circumstances donate money to major charitable organisations unless you would like your money to go to benefit the Elite's expansion of their empires and the fast-developing police state in your own backyards. Find smaller independent charitable organisations that you know to be reliable and make your donations to them.

"Charities swung into action after the September 11 terrorist attacks, raising more than $1 billion. But questions are being raised about where and how and how much of that money is being distributed. Bearing the brunt Tuesday during a hearing of the House Energy and Commerce Committee's oversight panel was outgoing Red Cross President Dr. Bernadine Healy. The Red Cross has raised more than $564 million for the Liberty Fund, which was set up in response to the attacks on the World Trade Center and the Pentagon. While the agency states on its Web site that it is spending more than any other relief agency responding to the terrorist attacks, it has distributed only $154 million. Healy was hammered by one New York official for the Red Cross' decision to put aside nearly half of the money raised for future needs that may include terrorist attacks. 'I see the Red Cross, which has raised hundreds of millions of dollars that was intended by the donating public to be used for the victims of September 11 -- I see those funds being sequestered into long-term plans for an organization', testified New York Attorney General Eliot Spitzer." CNN, 3rd January 2005

WWF (The Worldwide Fund for Nature – formerly the World Wildlife Fund)

This organisation is another complete and utter sham. Purporting to be active in protecting all flora and fauna throughout the world, it is merely another Elite front for extracting our money under false pretences and for furthering the aims of the multi-national corporations in the rape and exploitation of the natural resources of the third world.

All around the world, in under-developed countries, children are being kidnapped and forced into schools and churches against their will and that of their tribes. Poor people in such diverse regions as South East Asia, South America and throughout Africa are being forcibly removed from their ancestral homelands into shoddy, crumbling shanty towns with poor sanitation and little food. These people ask for nothing more than to be able to stay in their own homelands where they have existed for many generations, living as they choose, in peace and with no so-called 'civilised' nations and their malignant gangs of corporate thieves and their mercenaries dictating to them how they should conduct their lives.

Unfortunately for them, in many instances, the land where they happen to live is rich in minerals and trees coveted and therefore ripe for theft by the mega-corporations. Would it surprise you to learn that the WWF is often the facilitator of these crimes – all over the world? Behind their cosy, homely, defenders-of-all-things-natural image and their cute little panda logo (above), lies an evil organisation that would give Attila the Hun and his marauding hordes a good run for their money.

The WWF was created 50 years ago when serious wildlife trophy hunters such as the former Nazi and one of the original Bilderbergers, Prince Bernhard of the Netherlands, the Elite place-man Julian Huxley, senior industrialists, bankers and top politicians realised that one of their most beloved all trophies, the tiger, had been hunted to the edge of extinction. It was funded originally by the Rockefeller foundation via the World Bank. What more proof of it being a complete and utter sham does anyone need than that? Prince Bernhard became the first WWF President, since followed by that great defender of all wildlife, the royal trophy hunter himself, Prince Phillip the Duke of Edinburgh, prince consort to the head of the family 'firm'.

From the very beginning, the WWF has received much appreciation from all governments on earth and even substitutes in many nations as a de facto ministry for the environment, for some if not all of the following reasons...

 WWF serves to enhance a governments' 'respecter of the environment' image.

It helps to protect very small, hugely restricted areas as nature reserves and therefore creates space for the indiscriminate destruction of the huge remaining areas of land, by industrial and commercial/corporate interests.

Their stand on 'illegal' logging is merely a distraction to cover up the 95% of logging that is legal.

WWF helps to develop remote places with large areas of unspoilt environments and obtain control over it. As these remote areas are generally tribal lands of nonassimilated peoples, WWF assists governments to assume control of them and to assimilate them into the mainstream – almost always against their will.

As a result of all this, the losers are indigenous, tribal peoples and as paradoxical as it may seem at first glance, Mother Nature in general due to the sacrifice of most of the land to the corporatocracy. As usual, the ultimate beneficiaries are the Elite and their bedfellows.

The oppression of traditional, tribal people by nature conservationists has never been a subject for mainstream debate and the results of nature conservation activities have always been 'spun' to imply that the damages done to the native tribes were properly redressed. In much the same way as the native American Indians were confined to their oppressive 'reservations' following the theft of their traditional homelands and hunting grounds, shanty towns and modern consumerism are by no means a replacement for thousands of years of local tradition and culture. The main point here is that compensation is highly irrelevant anyway, since these people should not have been forcibly removed from their own lands in the first place and no amount of cash can compensate for the loss of an entire way of life. The argument about compensation is in fact a 'red herring' to divert attention from the ongoing genocide being conducted upon them by non-governmental organisations that pretend to support human rights.

For example...

In Namibia the Hai'om Bushmen have been driven out of their ancestral lands, the Etosha Pan, which WWF was involved with securing as a conservation area. Conservation of what you may be entitled to ask, when 'conservation' involves so much complementary, wanton destruction.

In consultation with the WWF, the government of Botswana declared in February 1996, that the 3000 last remaining Bushmen, in their traditional hunting and gathering lifestyles, had to leave their ancestral land and their traditional lives. The reason given being that their ancestral land is now proposed as a new 'game reserve'.

In South Africa the 40 last remaining Bushmen have been forced out of their ancestral land which is now largely used as the Kalahari Gemsbock National Park. The WWF has been and still is involved in this criminal activity in cahoots with the corrupt South African government.

Whilst in India the Gujjar nomads in Uttar Pradesh, are victims of a 'nature conservation' project, where the WWF is also directly involved and the last few aboriginal people belonging to the Negrito race, have been victimised by National Park projects in the Nilgiri mountains where the WWF was and still is active in promoting 'wildlife projects'.

There are many, many more cases, too numerous to mention here of small groups of traditional, native peoples victimised by joint governmental and WWF 'nature conservation' activities and policies and as with most other conservation programmes, this is a simply a front for corporate expansion and destruction of the environment in the name of obscene profiteering. These downtrodden groups have very few friends left and virtually no-one to champion their just causes. If the process of 'civilisation' and globalisation is allowed to destroy the last remaining non-western cultures, we will be left with a human monoculture and if biodiversity is important, then human diversity is also. We must make alliances with and give support to these last bastions of hope for the future of humanity.

Cancer Research

Cancer research charities throughout the world today, only ever undertake research that involves chemotherapy, radiotherapy and invasive surgery. If their 'treatments' don't involve butchery, poisoning or radiating your body to such an extent that your immune system becomes shattered and healthy cells will be destroyed along with the cancerous ones, then they are not interested. Sometimes this destructive course will lead to an apparent 'cure' but this is often very short-lived as the disease returns to destroy what little is left of a devastated immune system, killing the patient long-term anyway but without that person's death appearing in the statistics of 'cancer victims'.

The myriad of charities and research institutions that make up the 'cancer Industry' exist only to support the profits of the criminal, Elite-controlled pharmaceutical industries. In fact billions of pounds worldwide are siphoned from us, the poor deluded masses, into the coffers of the already mega-rich through highly persuasive, guilt-enhancing and fear-mongering advertising techniques as the controlled global media report one false breakthrough after another with monotonous regularity. The simple truth is that there *are* cures for cancer but we are not allowed to know about them – as discussed in the health section of this book.

Indeed there is very impressive, certifiable evidence from former cancer patients who, having exclusively used 'outlawed' treatments, have won their battles against cancer successfully with no side-effects whatsoever. The question we must therefore ask ourselves is, why do the cancer research charities not spend our donations testing the efficacy of all possible cures and not just ones that fulfil their own twisted agendas?

The answer to this question is fairly obvious really. There are no mega-profits to be made out of ill health by promoting so-called 'alternative' or natural medicine and therefore it follows that in conventional medical research, there is no 'level playing-field' for those who wish to explore the efficacy and effectiveness of these apparently safe and proven treatments. Unfortunately the Elite are completely in control of our medical profession, from medical education through to the highest-paid consultants, meaning in effect that even the majority, well-meaning, decent doctors and scientists are dictated-to by a system they do not fully understand and which they blindly serve without realising how they are being deceived on a massive scale. Cancer research charities are in effect a complete and utter sham and means by which huge sums of money are stolen every year from the people that they purport to be there to serve. A strong case could easily be made against them for causing appalling and unnecessary harm to people's, health, wealth and happiness.

Their experts in cancer care may only advise patients to look at alternative therapies in order to help mitigate the dangerous and unpleasant side-effects of chemotherapy and radiotherapy and on no account are they allowed to view them as a way of curing and beating the cancer itself.

Poppy Day / Remembrance Day / Veterans Day

Poppy Day, (sometimes Remembrance Day) 11th November or to those across the Ocean, 'Veteran's Day', is nothing more than a complete and utter farce.

Every time we switch on the TV in Britain around that time of year, we see presenters and guests alike, bedecked in poppies, sometimes from as early as late October. This is allegedly to honour those who died and were maimed 'fighting for our freedoms' but the real reason for this charade is completely different to the one promoted by the Elite powers that be.

In the week leading up to Remembrance Day 2011, the world governing body of football (soccer) FIFA, decreed that the English football team could not wear poppies embroidered onto its shirts in the upcoming game against Spain. Of course there was absolute mayhem and uproar as a result – all instigated of course at the behest of the controlled mainstream media in all its forms. Apparently FIFA has a strict policy against the wearing of political emblems or insignia of any kind on the shirts of those taking part in games under its jurisdiction – quite rightly in my view. A very sensible, fair and equitable policy one would think.

For the previous two weeks all English league games (they are not under the jurisdiction of FIFA) featured teams sporting the poppy emblem on their shirts and this bear in mind is despite the fact that approximately 50% of the players involved in these matches are not even British. They include Germans, Japanese, Italians and many other nationalities against whom the British have fought in the past century. Of course this is defended by saying that the poppy is to honour ALL war dead and not just those 'on our side'. In that case I would ask how much money the British Legion, the supposed recipient of all the money raised through the sale of poppies, contributes to its foreign counterparts in lieu of this fact? There would be no point in doing so of course, because I already know the answer to that question and it is a very round number.

However, the ensuing venomous outcry against FIFA regarding this decree from both media sources and public alike had to be seen to be believed. Why should this be?

I submit that it is because the general public, the sheeple, those whose lives are unknowingly controlled by those who deceive us on a daily basis, are programmed by the use of institutions such as 'poppy day' to behave in this way. We are all led to believe that by buying and wearing a poppy we are somehow 'honouring' those who died fighting futile wars in distant foreign hell holes in the name of expansion of the corporate interests that control and run the world. It is merely an expedient (and a very powerful one) by which the masses are conditioned to believe that fighting these bloody, tragic wars is done for the purpose of saving us all from some deadly enemy who would soon be on our shores breaking down our doors, raping our women and killing our children or at least committing terrorist atrocities by the thousand, if we did not halt them in their tracks 'over there'.

This is all absolute, abject nonsense of course, but a wonderfully simple, expedient way of propagandising and promoting their wars of capitalist expansion in furtherance of British and American imperialism and corporate/banking interests. It also keeps these wars in the forefront of everyone's minds whilst continuing to morally justify them by way of labelling their victims as 'heroes' and glorifying their 'sacrifices' for their 'country'. The BBC have a thoroughly despicable track record in this respect, producing programmes and documentaries by the hundred, that maintain this illusion and keep all the wars of the last century or more constantly in the public eye. Even such programmes such as 'Antiques Roadshow' are not spared in this respect. The edition of AR on Sunday 13th November 2011 was a blatant example of the glorification of war by the BBC, every item examined by the experts having some connection to war and the tragic yet glorious sacrifice of the subject's relatives. Words fail me really.

But back to the FIFA issue. After being thoroughly vilified for its stance and even the heir to the throne, Prince William being involved in writing a letter to the Secretary General, Sepp Blatter, FIFA eventually compromised and decided to allow poppies to be worn by the England team on its armbands. The power of falsely engendered public opinion never ceases to amaze.

I believe that in the weeks leading up to the event, mainstream TV stations are told that everyone who appears on screen MUST be seen to be wearing a poppy, as no-one ever is shown without one – and even more tellingly, the poppies are all of exactly the same design across most of the main stations. This would say to me that those people appearing on screen, for the most part, do not turn up to the studios wearing their own poppy and are provided with the 'standard issue' poppy upon arrival and are coerced into wearing it on camera whether or not they agree with the principle underlying it all. In one extreme instance during the 'remembrance weekend' in 2011, the BBC programme 'Countryfile' even interviewed a man who was constructing a roof and yet still sported his obligatory 'same design' poppy whilst doing so. Of course who among us has not felt that same overwhelming need to show our allegiance to the heroes of our brave armed forces, whilst 20 feet up a ladder working on a roof in a force 9 gale? Propaganda and mind control in its most ugly form, in my view.

Of course most will not understand the issue and blindly agree to wear it, but I would love to be a 'fly on the wall' in that situation and hear a conversation between anyone with broadly similar views to my own arguing their case in the countdown to going 'on air'. However I strongly suspect that they would not 'win' and would not be allowed to appear without the poppy. In contrast, on the 8th November 2011, three days before Remembrance Day, I appeared on the independent TV station, Edge Media Television, to discuss my chapter on Jack the Ripper from this book and refreshingly, there were no poppies to be seen anywhere, either on the presenter, Theo Chalmers or any of the technicians and staff.

Would not a better way to honour the dead and wounded be to end the raping and oppressing of poor nations and stealing their resources and call a halt to the exploitation and murder of their peoples in the name of corporate hegemony, thereby saving the lives of thousands of our 'heroes'? I strongly believe it would.

The above, scant examples are by no means a definitive list of the great charity deception that blights our life daily and until we collectively resist contributing to these evil monsters and instead where we are able, give directly to those in need, no doubt this disgraceful state of affairs will continue unabated and unreported by the unspeakable, craven cowards and shills of our controlled media.

Harry Potter

Who among us could not fail to enjoy the harmless fun and yet enjoyably scary tales about Harry Potter, the heroic boy-wizard and his epic fight against the forces of evil, along with his plucky chums, Hermione and Ron Weasly?

What wonderful entertainment we have all had from the vivid imaginings of Joanna K. Rowling, that 'single-mother made good' who somehow against all the odds, managed to drag herself almost from the gutter singlehandedly, to become a multi-billionaire and a role-model to which we can all aspire.

If only all was as it seems...

Joanna Rowling is a mind controlled Monarch slave, selected to be the author of the stories because she is a single parent and as part of the Tavistock Institute/Frankfurt School controlled plot to subvert society by promoting its extreme (homo)sexualisation, feminism and the 'positives' of single parent status. She is a member of the Fabian Society and the Church of Scientology. The Church of Scientology is of course a CIA-run front for the Royals, Rockefellers and Rothschilds, in other words the Elite.

Around Christmas 2011, I corresponded with and spoke to someone who claimed to be the father of JK Rowling's child, born in 1995. I believed him to be telling the truth because of the detailed story he related to me. He said that in the early 1990s, he, Jessica Mitford and her husband Bob Treuhaft (who was apparently JK Rowling's 'handler') in a long-delayed train journey 'brainstormed' the entire Harry Potter story whilst JKR took copious notes. This story was then written by someone whom he referred to as a 'pen and ink stand', a term used to describe someone who is hired to write a story that is not their own idea, with the decision subsequently being made to use JKR as the 'front' for it in-line with the Tavistock plan for the aggressive promotion of anything that undermines family values (ie. her single-mother status).

He also said that it was based loosely on the CS Lewis 'Narnia' stories but qualified that further by saying that he had no idea at the time that all the references to paedophilia, witchcraft, Satanism etc. were going to be incorporated and nor that he would subsequently be subjected to multiple attempts on his life orchestrated by orders from Prince Phillip himself and who he believed was meant to be represented in the stories by Lord Voldemort.

He also told me that the scar on Harry Potter's head is a representation of the symbol of the British Union of Fascists. Jessica Mitford's sister was married to Oswald Mosley who fronted the BUF during WWII and he also told me that Jessica Mitford told him bluntly that his grandparents were Unity Valkyrie Mitford, her sister and a certain Adolf Jacobus Hitler!

Following on from these discussions I undertook some research of my own on the Mitford / Treuhaft connection and found that Bob Treuhaft's business partner in his legal firm for almost 20 years was someone who went by the name of 'Dobby' Walker. This was just her nickname but even so her Wikipedia obituary refers to her as 'Dobby Walker' and not 'Doris Walker', her real name. For those of you unaware, 'Dobby' was an elf-like character in the HP stories who was employed as a 'manservant'. Maybe this is how Treuhaft and Mitford regarded Walker? In delving even further into Walker's background it appears that she was an active member of the Communist party in the 1940s and 1950s as were Mitford and Treuhaft. As related in a previous section, despite what the Elite what like us all to believe, there is virtually no difference between Communism and Fascism, in practice. They are 'sold' to the masses as being at the opposite ends of the political spectrum to one another but perhaps a more accurate depiction of the linear political spectrum would be to think of it as a complete circle with Fascism at 1 minute before twelve o'clock and Communism at one minute past. For the record, Dobby Walker died in 2009.

Also, interestingly enough, an intern by the name of Hillary Rodham began work for the law firm of Treuhaft and Walker in the early 1970s, now better known of course as the lovely Hillary Clinton herself. Just a coincidence? Maybe, who knows?

Whatever the truth really is, and it may never be known for sure, there is far more to all this than meets the eye, as always and the rabbit-hole goes very deep indeed.

Crop Circles

Please do not be taken-in by many false mainstream media reports that abounded in the 1990s in a vain attempt to shift the blame for every single crop circle event on two semi-drunken Englishmen going by the names of Doug and Dave. As with all other disinformation this was meant to confuse and distract us from the real truth.

And what is the real truth, you may well ask? To be frank, no-one knows for sure, but I can assure you that it is 100% certain that those two inebriated Englishmen, although they may have had the odd expedition in a few crop fields with a wooden board and two pieces of string, most certainly are NOT responsible for 99%+ of the mysterious phenomenon we will discuss here.

For example, could Doug and Dave after a drunken night at the pub, have been responsible for this...

Or this...?

What about this one...?

I think you understand my point here. Whatever the source of crop circles, and I do admit that they could well be an Elite-inspired, governmental hoax of some kind, one thing is for certain and that is that the sophistication of many of them, definitely do not steer us in the direction of amateur pranksters when searching for a solution to the mystery.

So what are the possibilities? There have been as many theories abounding as those covering the possibly-related UFO phenomenon. Are they for example, a communication from extra-terrestrials as evidence of other dimensions or a catalyst to advancing our way of thinking?

Governments have discussed them and then sought to confuse and mis-inform the populace through their control and manipulation of the popular media. The military have endangered life and safety in order to investigate and monitor crop formations, yet they deny involvement and Hollywood, that great propaganda machine itself, has sought to manipulate the truth and credibility of scientific evidence and facts, yet film-goers become ever more intrigued.

Hoaxers have sought to deceive, confuse and muddy research waters, in the same way that computer virus writers seek attention and attempt to contaminate data but the truth still remains that some crop circles are hoaxes and some are not. It is obviously undeniable that crop circles exist. Their beautiful and often very complex patterns have been photographed, filmed and witnessed by countless numbers of people but the big question is, who or what put them there and why?

Let us briefly examine the prosaic and the more esoteric explanations. Leonie Starr is a founding member of the Centre for Crop Circle Studies in the UK and she explained that crop circles are formed when vegetation is flattened in a particular pattern. She even concedes that by the late 1990s the majority of crop circles, as much as 80%, were *possibly* deceptively created by teams of people, but that does not necessarily mean that many of the rest were not created in some other way.

Starr further commented... *"There is a huge body of people who actually reckon that a lot of them were done by UFOs and part of me likes to think that may be the case, but not all of them."*

If it is possible to gain access to the crop circles soon enough after they have been discovered, it is apparently easy to tell whether they have been created by people, according to Starr. One clue to this is to determine whether or not the plants have been bent or broken in the flattening process. If they are bent, we have to look at something other than people stamping them down, she said. There are changes in the molecular structure of the crop itself and that happens within the circle and some of these crop circles, where the stalks were bent but not broken, demonstrated very interesting changes that had happened to the crops themselves.

Leonie Starr's own belief is that the patterns are a manifestation of collective human thought and however crazy you may believe this hypothesis to be, there is no denying that it is certainly one possibility, given what we know about the very strange nature of reality.

The genuine crop circles range in diameter from as small as 3 metres (10 feet) to over 100 metres (315 feet), usually appear overnight and no tracks leading up to them are found, suggesting some external force from above is responsible. Visually, the stems are partially flattened, and entangled or intertwined and the plants themselves are all bent and face the same direction, clockwise or anti-clockwise. The crops are never damaged, broken, or show signs of unduly forced bending and the plants continue to grow normally throughout the rest of their growing cycle. UFO sightings, moving orange lights and/or strange 'whooshing' or warbling sounds have often been observed to precede the formation of circles.

For the UFO enthusiasts, the circles are signatures left behind by visiting spaceships, for Gaia mystics and so-called 'tree-huggers', they are the manifestations of deep waves of natural energy, whilst for psychics, they are the conscious results of remote-viewing experiments. As far as armchair physicists are concerned, they are the tracks of ionised plasma whirlwinds, but perhaps needless to say, as yet no conclusive evidence has been found for any of these theories.

One of the earliest reports was in Lyon, France in 815AD and a late 16th century woodcut depicts the devil mowing a field into circular patterns. They began to appear in significant numbers in the fields of southern England in the mid-1970s and early circles were quite simple, appearing overnight, in fields of wheat, oilseed rape, oats and barley but as the crop circle phenomenon gained momentum, formations have also been reported in Australia, South Africa, China, Russia, and many other countries, frequently in close proximity to ancient sacred sites. For the thousands reported every year, the vast majority go completely undetected. However, by far the majority of the complex formations occur in the United Kingdom and these are more likely to be detected because of the country's relatively smaller land mass and compact geography compared to the wide open, extensive prairies of North America, for example.

During the last 25 years, the formations have evolved from simple, relatively small circles to huge designs with multiple circles, elaborate pictograms and shapes that invoke complex non-linear mathematical principles. Since the early 1990s however, the phenomenon has enjoyed world attention as the formations evolved into enormous, increasingly mathematically complex and perfectly executed shapes appearing in fields, often near the ancient sites of Wiltshire in southern England. The largest to date, a perfectly formed spiral formation 244 metres in diameter, composed of 409 circles covering almost the entire field, appeared overnight on a rainy night at Milk Hill in Wiltshire in August 2001.

The movie 'Signs', starring Mel Gibson, whilst universally scorned by serious crop circle researchers, nevertheless renewed interest in crop circles after years of the phenomenon being dismissed in the media as a sophisticated hoax, following the announcement of Doug Bower and Dave Chorley who 'confessed' in 1991 that they had been creating crop circles in English fields since the 1970s after reading about the Tully, Australia Saucer Nest of 1966. The real truth of Doug and Dave's involvement is that they were both unable, when challenged, to create a credible crop circle in daytime and also to remember the exact locations of their alleged exploits.

Each year more than 100 formations appear in the fields of southern England. About 10,000 crop circles have been documented worldwide since records were first kept in the 1970s and England tops the list with around 1,800, followed by the US with 230, Canada with 135, Germany with 105, Australia with 70, the Netherlands with 62, Hungary with 23 and Japan with 19, most of which appeared in rice paddy-fields. Several other countries on every continent have also reported small numbers of simple formations but the county of Wiltshire in England is the acknowledged epicentre of the phenomenon and is widely known as being home to some of the most sacred Neolithic sites in Europe, many having been built as far back as 4,600 years ago, including Stonehenge, Avebury, Silbury Hill and burial grounds such as West Kennet Long Barrow.

Is the crop-circle phenomenon related in some way to these ancient human artefacts? We may never know for sure but one thing is for certain and that is that although many crop circles are easily proven as hoaxes, there are huge numbers of completely unknown origin. Many of these may well be sophisticated governmental or other hoaxes designed to deflect us from the truth, but certainly, for now anyway, there is one thing for sure and that is that the speculation and intrigue will not be going away anytime very soon.

Agenda 21

Let me now introduce you to the United Nations' 'Agenda 21', the 'Blueprint to Advance Sustainable Development'. How forward-thinking and environmentally responsible, you may think. Who could possibly be against advancing 'sustainable development' and who does not care deeply about mother Earth, Gaia if you will? Let's save the planet and all that.

Unfortunately there is rather a large catch, several actually and one of them is our old friend population reduction, rearing its head again, preferably by 90-95% of the current total.

This Elite plan dressed up as the strategy that will save the world, has been around, for those who do not walk around with their eyes wide shut, since 1992. However in the last 4 to 5 years the agenda and timescales have been really cranked-up and we are now starting to see some of these deadly plans beginning to be put into place. Those indispensable allies of the New World Order are taking shape around us as I write. Mass-distractions, the dumbing down of future generations and the poisoning of the planet and its indigenous animal and plant life are all gathering pace. And this is despite the lip service being paid to allegedly saving the planet through such initiatives such as *Agenda 21* which purports to save the planet, whilst actually covertly bringing about destruction of human society as we know it.

The Georgia Guidestones as we have discussed in a previous section, are in effect the 'ten commandments' of the Elite. Whilst creating an impression of being green, eco-friendly and superficially people-friendly, their overt message hides a covert agenda that is far from benevolent, advocating huge population culls and the mass-relocation to what in effect would be akin to reservations, of the remaining few 'slaves-to-be'.   Indeed, *Agenda 21* is dressed-up in such cosy euphemisms that few people seem even remotely concerned about its far-reaching, draconian proposals. *Agenda 21* actually promulgates the total, centralised, global control over human life absolutely in line with the New World Order agenda. It advocates, no rights of property ownership, indeed no rights at all, for anyone other than of course, the ruling Elite and the methodology by which the planet will be 'sanitised' of its surplus 95% of the population is not made explicit, only that it must happen.

However, there are enough ongoing policies of the Elite currently that demonstrate that indeed a pretty good start has already been made on this particular task. I refer here to such delights as the pharmaceutical and medical industries, vaccinations and genetically modified foods and their ilk, a comprehensive list of which, I have compiled below:

Vaccination programmes
Bogus healthcare programmes
Failing healthcare systems
Pharmaceuticals
Contrived epidemics
        Swine Flu
        Bird Flu
        AIDS/HIV
        Ebola
        Legionnaire's disease (flu)
Sperm count reductions through...
        Radiation
        Poisons in plastic packaging
        Chemicals in food
Food additives
        Aspartame
        MSG
        Soya Bean Extract
        Refined Sugar
        HFCS
Food restrictive practices
Codex Alimentarius
Food Safety Bill S510
Contrived food shortages
Fluoride in water (tap and bottled) and many other drinks
Chemtrails
Ecological weapons (eg. HAARP) causing man-made...
        Hurricanes
        Tornados
        Earthquakes
        Volcanic activity
        Tsunamis
        Floods
        Famine
        Crop failures
Nuclear power
Radiation
Microwave radiation
Electromagnetic radiation (wireless networks)

Wars - Illegal and contrived
Western-backed political coups
Mass species die-offs / extinctions
Pollution of eco-systems
Pollution of oceans and waterways
Mass deforestation
Economic sanctions

It is a fact that there are tens of millions of plastic coffins stacked-up in huge storage facilities in Georgia, USA and this fact has led to much speculation as to their actual purpose. Could they be there just waiting for the 'great cull of humanity' to commence or is there a more benign reason? Personally I cannot imagine an innocent reason for the considerable expense to which whoever stockpiled these coffins must have gone and believe that they must be the precursor to some kind of entirely expected, cataclysmic event.

It would also appear to be the case that these coffins are air-tight and are capacious enough to comfortably 'lay to rest' an entire family of four people. It has also been reported that no-one in the US government is prepared to comment on this phenomenon, leaving the obvious conclusion to be that they must have something to hide.

Some researchers and commentators believe that this is all simply preparation for the Elite to launch their oft-vaunted disease epidemic, which we have all been conditioned to expect over the years with the various bird and swine flu epidemics, perhaps being used as 'dry runs' and to establish public reaction and also to prepare the ground for forcible mass-vaccination programmes.

Apparently the US Government has also just completed the building of several hundred concentration camps, under the auspices of FEMA (see relevant section), which are, at the moment, standing empty yet fully equipped. These camps are not dissimilar to the Nazi concentration camps in Germany and Eastern Europe during WWII, with barbed wire fences and railway tracks leading to their gates and each are designed to house thousands of families in what are in effect highly-secured units and now it appears that the government is ready to push forward with the bidding for contracts for these camps. Services up for bid include catering, temporary fencing and barricades, laundry and medical services, power generation, refuse collection and other services required for temporary 'emergency environment' camps located in five regions of the United States. (See document reproduced below).

The government contracting organisation, Kellogg, Brown, Root (KBR)'s tender for FEMA camp service bids came soon after the US Senate passed the National Defence Authorisation Act (NDAA) which expressly permits the military to detain and interrogate supposed domestic terror suspects and which is in direct violation of the Fourth Amendment and Posse Comitatus.

Section 1031 of the NDAA bill declares the whole of the United States as a 'battlefield' environment and allows American citizens to be arrested on US soil and incarcerated at the camps at Guantanamo Bay. This is indeed the stuff of Orwellian nightmares.

From: **Carlton, Bobbi (CED)** <Bobbi.Carlton@ky.gov>
Date: Wed, Nov 16, 2011 at 10:44 AM
Subject: FW: Potential Subcontracting Opportunity
To: "Carlton, Bobbi (CED)" <Bobbi.Carlton@ky.gov>

Below is an opportunity for potential contracting.

If interested, please submit a brief description of your services/capabilities to the following: Bob Siefert at bob.siefert@kbr.com. This is all the information that was given to me. Please contact Bob Seifert with any questions.

Kellogg, Brown & Root Services (KBR) is seeking subcontractors on a national basis to provide temporary camp services and facilities as part of its current and future emergency services contracts for the Federal Emergency Management Agency (FEMA), U.S. Army Corps of Engineers (USACE), and state/local government agencies - http://www.aptac-us.org/new/upload/File/RFI%20for%20KBR%2011-16-11.pdf.

Government, Defense & Infrastructure

Project Overview and Anticipated Project Requirements
KBR is establishing a National Quick Response Team for our current Federal Emergency Management Agency (FEMA) and U.S. Army Corps of Engineers (USACE) work, and for anticipated future contracts. Upon completion of evaluation, certain subcontractors may be invited to establish a Master Services Agreement (MSA) with pre-established lease rates and terms and conditions.

The Continental US will be broken up into five regions - Services will be required in each State within each region. See map in link above.

Anticipated Project Requirements:
Establish services listed below within 72 hours for initial set-up and respond within 24 hours for incremental services. This is a CONTINGENCY PROJECT and it should be stressed that lead times will be short with critical requirements due to the nature of emergency responses. Subcontractors must be flexible and able to handle multiple, shifting priorities in an emergency environment. Supply lines needed must be short but not necessarily pre-positioned.

The personnel on site to be covered by these services will depend on the size and scope of the recovery effort, but for estimating purposes the camp will range in size from 301 to 2,000 persons for up to 30 days in length.

· The offeror will not have to submit a proposal for each service in each state.

· Please identify which state and/or region your company can perform the requested services.

The descriptions of the services are for reference only. Any and all specific requirements will be forthcoming with a detailed Statement(s) of Work in an RFP solicitation.

Catering Services
This service is open to companies that wish to provide food preparation services only, and to companies that wish to provide the food supplies in addition to food preparation services. Subcontractor shall provide food and food preparation services capable of providing meals per feeding sufficient to meet the prime contractor occupancy levels. All meals may be prepared in accordance with the Army 14 Day Menu program (or equivalent like NIFC Mobile Food Services contract (http://fs.fed.us/fire/contracting/index.htm) and may be enhanced based on individual chef specialties and skills.

Temporary Fencing and Barricades
Subcontractor will mobilize, transport, erect, install and demobilize temporary fencing, barricades, and associated equipment according to federal, state and local laws, codes and manufacturer installation instructions. The Subcontractor shall be able to mobilize and deploy key personnel(s) within four (4) hours of NTP to meet with KBR Site Manager at the Responder Support Camp (RSC) site in order to finalize the site design plan and acquire site specific design requirements and layout.
Number of linear footage:
Approximately 2,300LF for a 301 person camp after 36 hours of NTP
Approximately 3,600LF for 1,000 person camp after 72 hours of NTP

Next time you hear anyone say 'it's just not possible' or 'they would never do that' please show them the above email. The extreme gravity of Agenda 21 renders it difficult to write about without sounding alarmist, but these Elite psychopaths are obsessed with power and the centralised control over all aspects of human life and innocent-sounding euphemisms such as 'sustainable development', 'saving the planet' and the 'green cause' are often used to mask their true intent. Agenda 21 is indeed worthy of far more public scrutiny than that to which it is currently being subjected.

In fact the whole concept of Agenda 21, when one delves beneath its thin outside veneer, would appear to be as far from true environmentalism as it is possible to get, but as with all things Elite and New World Order oriented, nothing is ever as it would seem. And what is more, it is these very same psychopathic Elite that are actually destroying the very planet about which they pretend concern, in their endless quest for obscene profits.

Indeed, the same power-mad psychopaths most responsible for the self-defeating fossil fuel economy are the very drivers of Agenda 21. The perpetual, colossal consumption of earthly resources, especially energy, cannot be maintained with so many people on *their* planet competing for *their* resources and this is the primary reason that only a deliberately engineered cull of 95% of humanity can safely preserve those Elite 'comfort zones' such as their 'gated communities' liberally sprinkled with sprawling mansions, golf courses, country clubs and helipads. It of course, takes obscene amounts of starvation, polluted water, death and disease to support even one billionaire.

So, as the old saying goes, 'something's gotta give' and one thing we can count on for sure is that it most certainly will not be any of the Elite's own home-comforts. Psychopaths have no conscience, no empathy and very little humanity, however, the one thing that really scares them is that we 99%, to use a current idiom, outnumber them by almost a million to one and the ultimate power belongs to us. Is it that much of a leap to actually organise ourselves to do something about it and stop them in their tracks? Apparently so, judging by the disbelief and apathy I encounter whenever the subject is raised.

But, we digress slightly. To wake up the masses to nefarious, crackpot schemes such as Agenda 21, how many more ringing alarm-bells do we need? This scheme-from-hell claims to be a *'comprehensive blueprint of action to be taken globally, nationally and locally by organisations of the UN, governments and major groups in every area in which humans directly affect the environment'*. However, it is really about depopulation, purloining much of the Earth's surface in the name of protecting it and imposing a rigid control structure that would bring back the Dark Ages for humanity as a whole.

If none of the above makes any kind of sense, perhaps we should ask ourselves this somewhat obvious question...

Why would the very people responsible for all the pollution, destruction, radiation, poisoning and devastation of the environment suddenly turn out to be eco-friendly?

Obviously this is not the case as Agenda 21 is the work of the bloodline-created and controlled United Nations. It propounds a programme to hijack the world on behalf of its devotees and the ultimate goals include, among many other disturbing facets... (by the way I have not stolen this list from the Communist Manifesto, although you could be forgiven for thinking so):

- An end to national sovereignty
- State control of all land resources, ecosystems, deserts, forests, mountains, oceans, fresh-water lakes and rivers, agriculture, rural development, biotechnology and ensuring equity. (In other words we will all be equally enslaved)
- State defined roles of business and financial resources
- Abolition of private property
- 'Restructuring' the family unit
- Children raised by the State
- People allocated their jobs
- Major restrictions on movement
- Creation of 'human settlement zones'
- Mass resettlement as people are forced to vacate land where they live
- Dumbing down education (see relevant section)
- Mass depopulation

This is the plan for the entire world and not just for the USA, but below is a plan of how the proposed new order will look in North America, if the Elite manage to get their evil way.

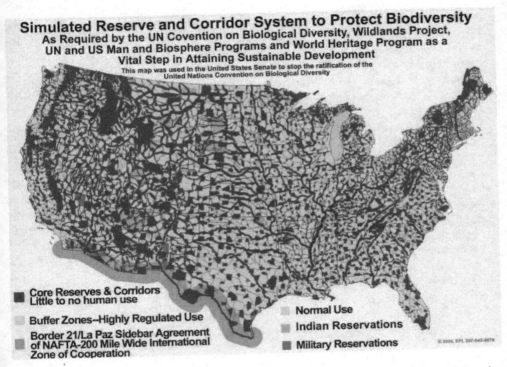

Simulated Reserve and Corridor System to Protect Biodiversity
As Required by the UN Covention on Biological Diversity, Wildlands Project,
UN and US Man and Biosphere Programs and World Heritage Program as a
Vital Step in Attaining Sustainable Development
This map was used in the United States Senate to stop the ratification of the
United Nations Convention on Biological Diversity

Core Reserves & Corridors
Little to no human use

Buffer Zones--Highly Regulated Use

Border 21/La Paz Sidebar Agreement
of NAFTA-200 Mile Wide International
Zone of Cooperation

Normal Use

Indian Reservations

Military Reservations

Harvey Rubin, vice-chairman of the Agenda 21 front operation, the International Local Governments for Sustainability was asked how all this would affect liberties with regard to the US Constitution and Bill of Rights, private property and freedom of speech. His reply was short but not very sweet. *"Individual rights must take a back-seat to the collective".* Spoken like a true Stalinist!

One of the reasons for the planned systematic dumbing-down of education is encapsulated in this comment in another 'sustainability' document:

"Generally more highly educated people who have higher incomes can consume more resources, than poorly educated people who tend to have lower incomes. In this case more education increases the threat to sustainability."

This of course is utterly terrifying stuff that could have been lifted verbatim, from the pages of 'Brave New World' or '1984'. Have these people no shame at all? That, by the way, is a rhetorical question.

As mentioned elsewhere in this book, the late Aaron Russo, the award-winning film producer who produced 'Trading Places' with Eddie Murphy, began to alert people to this conspiracy shortly before he died. He said publicly in 2007 that a member of the Rockefeller family, Nick Rockefeller, had told him that the population was going to be reduced by 'at least half'.

John P Holdren, the 'Science Czar' appointed to the Obama administration, is another advocate of 'human culling'. He says that the optimum human population is one billion and he co-wrote the 1977 book, 'Ecoscience', which proposes mass-sterilisation by medicating food and the water supply and imposing a regime of forced abortion, government seizure of children born outside of marriage and mandatory bodily implants to prevent pregnancies.

Indeed, there has been nothing of significance omitted from their plan; it guarantees both birth-control and death-control, not by the individual but by the 'State'. It promises the basic necessities of life in return for total and absolute submission to the 'State'. It guarantees the substitution of critical analysis for re-education and brainwashing by the 'State'. It destroys the very fabric of society, culture and the family unit, proscribing only one way to live, that of the 'State's' making. It herds the population into small, easily managed areas in order that we may be more effectively controlled by the 'State' and it creates an environment where we will all be more easily managed by the promise of being taken care of by the 'State'.

Karl Marx, Leon Trotsky and Josef Stalin would be very proud indeed of their twenty-first century protégés.

World War III

Towards the end of the nineteenth century, Albert Pike the Sovereign Grand Commander of the Scottish Rite of Freemasonry in America reportedly wrote in a letter, an outline of the Elite plans for the twentieth century which included three World Wars leading to total Elite domination of the world. We have had the first two already as everyone knows but not yet the third, which has obviously been delayed by circumstances beyond the control of the perpetrators, for the moment anyway.

Pike wrote that the first war would be a war to overthrow the Russian Czars, as related in a previous chapter and to destroy the Russian monarchy through a contrived conflict with the British and Germanic empires. The second war would be instigated through the Zionist struggle and would establish a Zionist-Jewish 'homeland' in Palestine (again, see the chapters on WWI and WWII).

Regarding the possible third war, Pike wrote:

"The Third World War must be fomented by taking advantage of the differences caused by the agents of the Illuminati, between the political Zionists and the leaders of the Islamic world. The war must be conducted in such a way that Islam [the Arab nations of the Middle East] and political Zionism [Israel] will mutually destroy each other. Meanwhile, the other nations, once more divided on this issue, will be constrained to fight to the point of complete physical, moral, spiritual and economic exhaustion... We shall unleash the nihilists and the atheists and we shall provoke a formidable social cataclysm which in all its horror will show clearly to the nations the effect of absolute atheism, origin of savagery and of the most bloody turmoil." Albert Pike, 1871

Pike was certainly a distinguished prophet, unless of course he had foreknowledge of the grand master-plan to enslave the world. Even the phrase 'World War' was not in common usage at that time and indeed only came to prominence several years after the first war, which for many years, even after the event itself, had been commonly referred to as the 'Great War'. But is this not what we are seeing today, the sabre-rattling and aggressive rhetoric currently aimed at Syria and especially Iran, by and on behalf of the Israeli Zionists? The world could explode into WWIII at any moment given the current fragile state of the peace in the Middle East area. In fact I would go as far as to say that the world has never been nearer to world war since the last one ended, even throughout the dark days of the 'cold war' in the second half of the last century.

Since the terrorist attacks of 9/11 and 7/7, world events in particular in the Middle East, demonstrate the growing unrest and instability between Zionists and the Arabic world. This is completely in line with the call for a third world war to be fought between the two and their allies on both sides. This third world war is still to come and recent events would tend to create the impression that it is imminent.

In July 2009, the President of China openly warned the US that in the event of an Israeli attack upon Iran, *"World War will be our response."*

The above information also demonstrates clearly to me, that historical and political events do not happen by accident. We are being led by a group of people and their stooges in governments throughout the world, who are following a script that has been laid down many years previously and whilst the minor details may be subject to the occasional tweak, the major premise remains unchanged throughout and that ultimate goal is of course the total subjugation of humankind and the establishment of their New World Order.

Big Brother is Watching You

Surveillance

As I describe throughout this book, the world is becoming more like the dystopian nightmare portrayed by George Orwell in his extremely prescient work *1984*, almost by the day. Indeed the above chapter title is taken from that very book and for the benefit of those have not yet read it, the phrase refers to the fact that a supposed benevolent entity, known by the cosy, friendly name of 'Big Brother' is constantly watching over the citizens of 'Airstrip One', the new name for the United Kingdom, in order to 'protect them from harm'.

However 'Big Brother', in reality, is far from a cosy, friendly entity. He is a euphemism for the fascist/communitarian state in which all Airstrip One's citizens live. He is not simply watching his citizens either, in anything resembling a caring, parent-like manner; he is actually spying on them and their every move through a comprehensive network of one-way only 'tele-screens' that are installed not just on every street, highway and in every building, but in every *room* in every building, including those of the repressed citizens' own homes. How similar then to our own society? Although we do not *yet* have spy-cameras in our own homes, it is virtually impossible now in any town in Britain, to escape the gaze of the ubiquitous 'security camera' wherever we may wander, down its streets and alleyways and in its shops, banks and public buildings.

It is also common knowledge among the 'truth' community, that we are also now being watched covertly from space. Yes, that is absolutely true. There are literally hundreds of spy satellites circling above us, watching us whenever expedient for our controllers so to do. It is also known that they have amazing capabilities, for example the ability to 'listen-in' on conversations we may be having in our own sitting rooms at home and to be able to zoom-in on individual buildings and individual people at a resolution to which most regular camera manufacturers could only dream to aspire.

"Every now and then I like to lean out of the window and smile for a satellite picture." Steven Wright, American comedian.

Tongue-in-cheek, the above statement may be, but nevertheless accurate with regards to the capability of satellite spy cameras.

We often hear the claim that 'if you have got nothing to hide, than you have nothing to fear', but as I have covered in detail in another section of the book, there is so much wrong with that statement that I barely know where to start, to refute it. Suffice to say at this juncture, that this statement is a gross distortion of the truth and one which is easy to prove as inaccurate.

The amount of public money spent on 'security' especially here in Britain is truly staggering and that is just the sums that the authorities admit to spending and for all those millions and billions worldwide spent on security cameras, I should very much like to ask the question, where are they when we *really* need them? I am thinking here for example of 9/11, 7/7, the Madrid train station bombing, the Pont de l'Alma tunnel when Diana died and the list goes on and on. All the security cameras that could have prevented conspiracy theories from springing-up around these incidents seemed to have either failed or have been switched-off in error for the duration of these and many other incidents. So it would seem that they are absolutely perfect for spotting and recording crimes committed by the 99% but not too efficient at detecting those of the 1%. This is obviously another rather large co-incidence of course and nothing at all to concern us in any way.

In Britain the total amount of public money spent on installing and operating CCTV cameras alone during the 2007 to 2010 period, was £321,331,453.18. When broken down this figure would equate to the employment of more than 13,500 extra police officers over a three year period. There are currently five million CCTV cameras in the UK to cover a population of 60 million, so this equates to one camera for every 12 people and there is absolutely no sign of this ratio decreasing. On the contrary, it is expected to increase proportionately as time goes by. The UK Home Office has spent a mind-boggling 78% of its crime prevention budget since the 1990s on surveillance cameras and the numbers are still increasing month on month and year on year.

Cameras are now being installed that can lip-read and recognise 'suspicious' body language – in other words pre-crime and there are now many cameras in London streets and maybe elsewhere too by the time you read this, that possess speakers whereby the operator can give orders to unsuspecting pedestrians passing-by. 'Pick up that litter' or 'no loitering in this area' or 'keep off this grass'. It saves money on signs I suppose.

A recent 'freedom of information' request revealed that CCTV cameras solve less than one in 1000 crimes and yet surveillance cameras account for 75% of the spending on 'crime prevention' overall. What is wrong with this picture? This amply demonstrates to me that these cameras are not there for our protection or to prevent or solve crimes, they are there to spy on us in much the same way as the tele-screens in 1984. In fact I would say that the Elite, far from wishing to prevent crime, indeed encourage it. It is in their best interests to engender a crime-ridden society as this leads to fear and thus ultimately more control through the very surveillance that purports to protect us all.

Another reason for all this overt and covert surveillance is to track resistance to the step-by-step imposition of the Orwellian state and not the 99.9% of the general public who are no threat to the system at all.

Not only is our every movement as pedestrians tracked, but so also are our movements when travelling. There are speed cameras along most of our streets and highways, many containing sophisticated licence plate recognition systems and security cameras in buses, trains, ships and airplanes. The licence plate recognition system is intelligently linked to various databases of information, enabling, for example, insurance details to be checked, where deemed to be appropriate. The 'speed' cameras are obviously not there to prevent accidents as the police disingenuously claim, as it has now been proven beyond reasonable doubt that the presence of traffic and speed cameras actually causes more accidents than it prevents, probably through the fear factor of people slowing down dangerously quickly, once a camera is spotted, causing skids, swerves, rear-end collisions and often complete loss of control of the car. In fact a recent independent report concluded that 85% of traffic accidents are not caused by excess speed, contrary to what they would have us all believe.

We are also under covert surveillance through our computers and cell-phones. Social networking sites such as Twitter and Facebook and search engines such as Google are known to have connections to the security services and every transaction (and there are billions each day) is individually tracked and monitored for any small clue that that person may be plotting against authority. Every email, every telephone conversation and every text message is similarly monitored and filed using keyword detection technologies and all the details of this intrusion into what should be our private lives is stored in a monster database that also links with other governmental databases and allows 'public institutions' to access everything that is stored against our names. Local councils and state bodies made one request every second on average in 2009 for access to this information to check-up on our movements and private information.

'The Guardian' newspaper recently reported that photographs and intimate personal details relating to tens of thousands of individuals who have attended protests and rallies are being stored in secret national databases and labeled as 'domestic extremists'.

So, this is but a small snapshot of how the world really works in these 'enlightened' times and please, please do not be fooled by anyone who may tell you that we are in effect being spied-upon for our own safety and protection, as frankly that concept is utterly laughable.

The Police – To Protect and Serve the Elite

The recent, ongoing spate of police brutality is no accident and no coincidence; it is exactly the way that society is deliberately being steered and the increasing militarisation of the police is a carefully contrived phenomenon designed to slowly ensnare us all in a spiders-web of oppression and fear.

There are many, many examples of the police taking the law into their own hands and remaining unpunished for doing so. Some of these are listed in the introduction and here for good measure are a couple more.

In 2010 a student was tasered by police for persistently asking questions of the politician John Kerry at a public meeting. To be unscrupulously fair, Andrew Meyer, the student in question was behaving a little too disruptively for his own good and was eventually tasered several times when he mentioned 'Skull and Bones', the secret society of which Kerry is a fully-paid-up member along with the entire Bush family. However, his behaviour certainly did not warrant his being subjected to 50,000 volts and surely, simply 'poor behaviour' does not give licence to the police to use ultra-excessive force. The fact that the police actually tasered someone who was already subdued and lying on the ground under arrest is utterly reprehensible and inexcusable by any standards, let alone those of they who are supposed to 'serve and protect' us. When there are six officers surrounding a suspect who should have simply been ejected peacefully, there is absolutely no need to taser him, at least not in my view.

And then there was the case of the wheelchair-bound schizophrenic. Police officers said they arrived to find Ms Delafield in a wheelchair, armed with two knives and a hammer and that she was swinging the weapons at family members and police. Within an hour of the 911 call, Ms Delafield, a wheelchair-bound woman certified with mental illness, was dead. Her family attorney, Rick Alexander said that her death could have been prevented and that there were four things that stood-out to him about the case. *"One, she's in a wheelchair. Two, she's schizophrenic. Three, they're using a taser on a person that's in a wheelchair and then four is that they tasered her 10 times for a period of two minutes."* Alexander said.

According to the police report, one of the officers used her taser gun nine times for a total of 160 seconds and the other officer discharged his taser gun once for a total of no more than five seconds. Obviously this was no doubt a difficult situation, but was it absolutely necessary to taser an elderly woman in a wheelchair? Surely a person unable to walk can be restrained fairly easily by other less deadly methods?

In my considered view this all points to a larger problem in our society and this is that the police are almost completely out of control and more significantly, this is exactly the state of affairs planned for us by the Elite.

There is a common misconception about police, throughout the world at large. Some people, it has to be said, mostly white, middle-class people, think that the police are here to 'protect and serve' everyone, but it is worth pointing-out that nowhere does this motto say anything about protecting *everyone*, or even treating everyone equally. This small point is totally conspicuous by its absence, in fact and the simple truth is that the police are paid to protect and serve the Elite and only the Elite, and the group from which the Elite mostly need protection is the 99%, we the 'underclasses', the useless eaters.

The western world, especially Britain and America are societies that are riven in two by a huge 'class-divide' despite all the false claims by some, that America is the ultimate classless society and this class division is as stark as the difference between black and white. Poor and dispossessed people naturally get angry and sometimes even violent when they realise that their own situation is completely hopeless. No amount of hard work will make them rich or powerful when their only skills are street-sweeping or toilet-cleaning. So, sometimes the poor take matters into their own hands and steal from the rich and that is when the police intervene. If they steal from a house or steal a car they will obviously be arrested, but, what happens when the rich steal from the poor as we have seen with all the recent bank bail-outs, banker-bonuses and white collar crime such as the MPs' expenses scandal in the UK in 2009?
Usually, the answer is 'nothing at all'. The Elite can almost literally write their own laws with a few well-placed political campaign contributions or some intensive lobbying of politicians. They ghetto-ise our inner cities, outsource our jobs to the third-world, make beneficial medicines and drugs illegal, send our children to die in pointless wars, kill anyone who stands in their way of their obscene profiteering and terrorise the world with their wars and there is virtually nothing that any of us 99% can do about it.

Aside from occasional high-profile cases such as the Enron scandal in the 1990s, the Elite are completely free to do as they will and mould society to their own designs in whatever ways they may choose. In other words, the rich are free to do whatever they want, when they want but the poor and middle classes must be monitored constantly and harassed or arrested instantly, often violently if they step out of line in any way at all.

The police are obviously aware of this, maybe not overtly however. They do know that becoming a police officer grants them immense power over others, but they know not to abuse this power where the Elite are concerned. We rarely see people in Aston Martins, Bentleys and Rolls Royces being detained by the police and that is not simply because they never break the law, but the police know better than to bother with the rich. After all, the rich are no easy target unlike the poor. They tend to have expensive lawyers, they have friends in high-places, they often have unlimited resources and most importantly, they often know politicians who will put pressure on their superiors to get them reassigned to plodding 'the beat' again, should an officer fall foul of them. Of course, poor people have none of these connections or resources and so by default become 'fair game'.

It is not a problem with the Elite if the police wish to oppress the poor; in fact it is actually actively encouraged. The rich know that by granting the police special privileges they can help secure their loyalty to their cause and so the police are permitted to act more or less as they please just so long as they do not step on the toes of the Elite, who are after all the only people who 'out-rank' the police in the 'power games' being played-out in our twisted society.

So, the real role of the police in society is to protect the Elite from the underclasses, which also includes the middle class. However, the middle classes tend to be less disruptive as they are usually pacified by the plentiful distractions on offer from today's society, such as 24/7 entertainment, sports and other leisure activities that are well-within their economic grasp, unlike the lower classes and dispossessed. The police are thus free to amuse themselves by harassing the poor to their hearts' content, just so long as they do not harrass the powerful. The Elite have manufactured a situation whereby the police are hated and feared by the poor and respected and feared by the middle class. This in effect gives them a free reign since the police only fear and respect the upper class; the one social group more powerful than they, themselves.

The militarisation of the police

Street-gang members regard the police as just another gang; a more powerful one, but a gang nevertheless, but the people who actually control the police, the Elite, are increasingly arming them in much the same way as a military force. The full-scale militarisation of the police has been slowly imposed upon us over the last 50 years and this situation is encouraged and enhanced by two fake ideological wars, the 'war on drugs' and the 'war on terror'.

In fact, the police services in most major first-world cities now (even in England where the standard arming of police is still not quite with us yet) have sufficient firepower and armaments to invade and occupy a small country. They could probably have been sent to Afghanistan and Iraq and probably would have done a better job at subduing the populace there since they are more thoroughly trained in those tactics than are the military. This is no accident, the police *are* an army of sorts, the private army and mercenaries of the Elite and their enemy, lest there be any lingering doubt about it, is you and I, our families, friends and acquaintances.

This is all actually an integral part of the plan for the New World Order; ie. to transform the entire world into a fascist/communitarian state. The momentum is now very much increasing and as they have both gained and been given strength by draconian new laws, both in a physical and psychological sense, should this trend continue, then the end result is inevitable; a police state.

Yes, I am afraid that the Elite control and run society as though it is their personal fiefdom, which in many ways it is of course, because they hold the purse strings and thus the power. When there are demonstrations, labour disputes or strikes, even if peaceful, they simply call in the police the police will, if necessary and often even if not, use extreme violence against the ranks of the demonstrators and/or striking workers and either force them to disperse or force them to return to work for their pitiful wages. I am sure many British readers can remember the miners' strike of the mid-1980s where police brutality was rife and an everyday occurrence. Of course the controlled media always dressed it up as if it was the miners themselves who instigated the violence, but most people could see the real truth.

In many, many demonstrations the police will use undercover agitators to incite the demonstrators to violence and this then provides the excuse for them to use brute force in order to quell the 'riot' as it often becomes. The idea that the police can act as an arm of the Oligarchy is unfortunately not a new one. The situation had become slightly better throughout the early decades of the twentieth century, but now we seem to be right back to where we were a hundred years ago and earlier, when police and militia brutality was often the norm.

But the accompanying propaganda is many magnitudes more powerful today. Most people believe that the police are there to protect everyone, but that is quite simply not the case. In many poorer neighbourhoods, if the police are called, they *may* arrive four hours later *if* the caller is lucky, *if at all*. The 'better' the neighbourhood, the quicker the response and indeed many poorer people sadly do not even bother calling the police at all and this, again, is not a new phenomenon. In fact, this is how the Mafia came to prominence in America. The Italian and Irish gangs were formed simply because a person of Italian or Irish descent could not expect to be treated fairly under the law and they knew that they had to take care of each other because no-one else would. Indeed, the police were more likely to arrest them than to listen to their tale of woe. The growth of the Mafia was also made possible by the staggering profits made through prohibition, with the sale of 'bootleg' liquor. When such a popular product as alcohol is made illegal, it can be extremely lucrative for those on the wrong side of the law; so much so that they will 'buy' influence on the other side of the law and corrupt the entire system in the process.

The weapons a police officer are allocated are paramount to his power over others. Everyday citizens are obviously not allowed to openly carry dangerous weapons around and an officer's gun identifies him as a member of a powerful group and symbolises his social superiority over the masses.

The police now use Tasers almost indiscriminately because it easy to do so. Much easier than for example trying to subdue a miscreant by the use of a baton and it should be noted that Tasers are most definitely not 'non-lethal'; they are 'less-lethal' maybe, but for that matter so is a knife compared to a gun. In no way are Tasers harmless despite propaganda to the contrary, they have been and continue to be, responsible for many hundreds of deaths in the last few years. Between Tasers, pepper-spray and batons, the police now have several 'less lethal' devices to ensure our submission. Add in handguns, shotguns, sniper rifles and the heavy artillery used by SWAT teams this constitutes enough firepower to subdue a major rebellion, which of course may well be the plan.

The Elite seem to be expecting trouble from us, the unruly populace. Unsurprisingly really as they know only too well how oppressive their policies are. If so, they can no longer plead ignorance to our plight and they are in fact responsible for it. They have no love for democracy and clearly prefer fascism as it is so much more convenient for their purposes and the police see their badge as a license to take the law into their own hands and even to kill if that suits their purposes. In other words, if you do not like someone for whatever reason or even simply feel like it, taser them, there will be no comeback or consequences, no investigation or inquiry. It is all made too easy for them, but if any of us did the same things (even to each other) we would quickly end up in jail and for a very long time. This is the justice that we have today, justice Elite-style.

The Free-man Principle

Another of the many ways in which we are covertly imprisoned as human beings is via the completely false paradigm of what is loosely referred to as the 'law'. To be clear, there is a huge difference between 'lawful' and 'legal' and this difference is deceptively used to enslave us in so many different ways.

Let me explain...

The Elite bloodlines have in effect 'hijacked' the law, not just in Britain, but also in North America and even world-wide, especially in the countries comprising the former British Empire. The plan for the total global enslavement of populations is almost impossible to expedite under the real law known as 'Common Law' and so over time they have imposed their own system by deception.

We are all living human beings with a soul and not legal entities as our corrupt legal systems attempt to treat us. This is the fundamental principle which differentiates between our freedom and our enslavement to the Elite.

There is in existence a language of which some people may be vaguely aware and that is for the want of a better term, 'legal-ese', otherwise known as the language of the law as used by solicitors, lawyers, magistrates and judges. It is quite similar to English in many ways, but also, as we will see, in many aspects, completely different.

Over the years it has been written and developed, just as any other language, by its users and that is of course in this case, the legal profession. Proposed new legislation is discussed by committees, voted in or out by members of Parliament or Congress and becomes 'law' once it has been approved at the final stage by royal or Presidential assent. It is at this point now regarded as a statute; albeit a statute written in its entirety in what is in effect a foreign language, legal-ese.
Despite the fact that these statutes are written in a language unfamiliar to the vast majority, we are nevertheless still expected to abide by them and obey their diktats. However, when people talk about the 'law' they are referring, mostly without realising it, to Statutory Law and not Common Law. This has been developed over centuries in a deceitful attempt to impose control over us all.

"Back in the Celtic times the British Isles were populated by tribes. They had traditions and customs. Nothing was permanently written down, but they lived by rules that everyone knew. This entirely mirrors the situation world-wide. There was a time when everything was tribal, and each member knew the rules that governed their lives. If anyone broke these rules there would be some kind of Tribal Meeting, and the Chief or Holy Man would preside. A judgment was made on the basis of arguments put forward by both sides, and that judgment was executed." Veronica: of the Chapman family (so-called)

Common Law was first laid down in the original Magna Carta which King John was forced to sign by the Barons in 1215 at Runnymede, near London, England. Simply speaking, if we do not breach the peace, nor cause harm or loss to another nor employ mischief in our agreements, the tenets of Common Law will not be breached. The use of Common Law is the use of common sense in that each situation can be judged on its merits without 'statutory' laws or statutes that are all essentially 'modern' laws that tell the judge what he or she must do in given circumstances. One modern definition is this:

"Common law is the system of deciding cases that originated in England and which were latterly adopted in the USA. Common law is based on precedent (legal principles developed in earlier case law) instead of statutory laws. It is the traditional law of an area or region created by judges when deciding individual disputes or cases. Common law changes over time."

However, this change is so slow a process that Common Law was of little use to the Elite families. Because they wished to create a 'closed' society they needed laws that can be introduced quickly and be changed at will to suit their agenda, whenever it was expedient. One thing that they certainly did not want was for people to be able to create their own laws.

So, in a nutshell, the Elite usurped Common Law which is the law of the land, as the prime arbiter of human affairs, with Statute Law which is in effect the law of the sea. This is also referred to as Maritime Law or Admiralty Law, Commercial Law and Civil Law, among other terms. Thus, the Elite bloodlines took the laws of shipping and trade by sea and brought them to dry land and named them 'Statute Law', which by its nature is *commercial* law or the law of contracts.

These then are the 'laws' introduced by governments and parliaments and they can often do this overnight, literally, if it suits their agenda – and it often does and of course this is absolutely perfect for the imposition of onerous, draconian laws that create a virtual slave state. When the Queen signs an Act of Parliament or the US president signs a bill into law they are simply signing a 'contract' to make a 'contractual' agreement and this is not actually 'lawful' under Common Law.

During the last Labour government in Britain (1997-2010) they created 3,800 new criminal offences almost one new crime for every day they were in office. This is possible using Statute Law, the law of the sea, but not with Common Law, the law of the land. The other important aspect to Common Law is that it refers to a living, breathing human being whilst Statute Law is the law of contracts and so the instigators of Statutory Law had to invent fake 'personas' ie corporations, to which the contrived new 'laws' could apply.

This is the 'straw-man' principle, a 'legal' (but not lawful) fiction, which is in effect activated by writing names in all-capitals. So peter smith and its other variations, such as peter: smith and peter: of the smith family are, under Common Law, the living, breathing, human being with a soul and PETER SMITH is the legalised fictional corporation, created to fall under the jurisdiction of Statute Law.

Whenever governments, law enforcement, corporations, legal and financial agencies etc, communicate with us they almost always write our names in all capital letters and this is because they are not writing to us, the living, breathing being, but to the fake 'straw-man' that is created when your birth is 'registered'. What they would like us to believe is that peter smith and PETER SMITH is exactly the same, whereas in truth it most certainly is not. We all need to understand that countries, governments, local councils, courts and the police force etc. are actually *private companies and corporations* and this can easily and simply be confirmed by checking this information with Dun and Bradstreet, which provides credit information on businesses and corporations worldwide.

Actually, THE UNITED STATES OF AMERICA INCORPORATED and THE UNITED KINGDOM CORPORATION plc are at this moment in a state of what is referred to as 'Chapter 11 bankruptcy' which... *"... allows businesses to reorganise themselves, giving them an opportunity to restructure debt and get out from under certain burdensome leases and contracts. Typically a business is allowed to continue to operate while it is in Chapter 11, although it does so under the supervision of the Bankruptcy Court and its appointees."*

So who controls the 'Bankruptcy Court and its appointees' that are currently 'supervising' the 'government' corporations of the United States and United Kingdom? None other than our old friends, the House of Rothschild banksters and their international banking conglomerate. So in truth, governments are corporations and the Presidents, Prime Ministers, Royalty and cabinets are the CEOs and the boards of directors. Only insiders of course, will know this, but most of them will be unaware of how the very system they are briefly administering, really works. The shareholders in these corporations are the general population and citizens of the country, but of course we are never told this plain fact.

Each and every time a new-born baby is registered, a single share in the corporation is issued in its name in all-capital letters of course, but because this fact is systematically kept from us we never ask for either the share or the money it is worth. Instead, the share is held in trust by the government as are all dividends due and the corporate voting rights that go along with it. The trustee, the government corporation, uses these 'votes' to decide the future of the corporation and whether for example, it will agree to a 'corporate merger' in the creation of the European Union or North American Union.

So by keeping their true lawful status from the people, they turn the shareholders into employees of the corporation, or actually slaves to be more accurate and one of the principle ways this is achieved is by the utilisation of words that have one meaning to the population and another in law. As alluded to already, the term 'legal' is not the same as lawful. This is why banking is sometimes derided by being referred to as 'legalised robbery'. It is certainly 'legal' under Statute Law, but it is also in effect robbery which is under Common Law, an unlawful offence. So, Common Law is that which is lawful and Statue Law is that defined as 'legal'.

We may believe that a 'person' is a living human being, but under the 'legal' definition of Statute Law a 'person' is a *corporation* and, to meet the criteria of Maritime Law, the 'person' represents a ship in effect and so that is why when a 'person' attends court, which in reality is a *maritime* court, the 'person' stands in the *dock*. We see this symbolic language also in other areas of the law, for example, all the maritime language in everyday use, especially with reference to governments and legal terms such as ownership and citizenship. We also indulge in courtship before agreeing a corporate merger, more commonly referred to as marriage in which we contract with the other government subsidiary corporation (the spouse) by means of a marriage certificate. And of course when that merger subsequently results in the patter of tiny subsidiaries, the new corporation's registration is confirmed by the issuance of a birth / berth certificate.

The 'Stars and Stripes' flags displayed in every federal building, court, school etc, in the USA are all framed with a gold/yellow fringe for this reason. And whenever the President makes an address or speaks officially there is always the flag behind him, complete with its gold/yellow fringe, signifying that all those institutions/corporations operate under maritime law and not the 'law of the land'.

Under the International Law of the Flags, the type of flag displayed by a ship decrees the law that applies aboard that vessel and by boarding the ship you are automatically accepting the jurisdiction of the law that applies to that flag. Exactly the same is true with regards to foreign embassies. The flag they display/fly ensures that the law of the country it represents applies within the confines of the embassy. A flag with a gold fringe always indicates Admiralty Law and so if we are summoned to appear in a court displaying this version of the flag, we are in effect agreeing to be tried under Statute Law, the law of the sea that applies to a legalised fiction and not to the person.

"When you enter a courtroom displaying a gold or yellow fringed flag, you have just entered into a foreign country, and you better have your passport with you, because you may not be coming back to the land of the free for a long time. The judge sitting under a gold or yellow fringe flag becomes the 'captain' or 'master' of that ship or enclave and he has absolute power to make the rules as he goes. The gold or yellow fringe flag is your warning that you are leaving your constitutionally secured rights on the floor outside the door to that courtroom." usa-therepublic.com

Even the US troops fighting abroad in such places as Afghanistan, have the gold-fringed flag clearly displayed on their uniforms, indicating in fact, that they are the army of the corporation of the United States and not of the people or the country for which they believe they are fighting. Many lawyers, solicitors and court officials genuinely have no idea of what Statute Law really consists, but this certainly cannot be said of those in the upper echelons of the global legal profession including the judges and senior government administrators, whom I suppose must be appraised of the real facts as they reach a certain stage on the career ladder.

However the tangled mess is slowly beginning to be unravelled by those brave pioneers and champions of Common Law who are now challenging magistrates and judges in their own domains throughout the country and demanding evidence of the proof of the lawfulness of courts and their deceptive practices. It is absolutely possible, as these fearless men and women have shown, to permanently disconnect from statute slavery if you have a basic awareness of Common Law and have the fortitude to stand-up for your rights as a citizen.

In addition, the wording of all communications with the State and 'authority' should be carefully constructed, not least of which is the way in which our names are denoted on documents. We should never forget that we are peter: smith and not PETER SMITH. Indeed should we respond to communications referring to us as PETER SMITH, then we have lost the war before the first battle has begun as Statute Law will then prevail. But use peter: smith and we will no longer be subject to Statute Law, only Common Law.

There will of course be no anarchy when Statute Law is eventually overturned and Common Law is returned to its rightful place in human affairs. If the peace is breached or should we cause harm or loss to another or employ mischief in our agreements, then we are still subject to the penalties of Common Law, no matter what.

Social-engineering

What is social-engineering? Social-engineering may be defined as the art or science of psychologically manipulating people into acting or thinking in way that may not be their natural, normal mode of behaviour, usually without their express permission or knowledge.

It may take the form of one of the two extremes of a one-off, simple confidence trick such as making someone believe something untrue in order to deceive them. Or it can be used against an entire population by the ruling Elite in order to modify their beliefs about society and the world around them into thinking that they are entirely different constructs to that which they assume to be the truth.

It is this latter circumstance upon which we will concentrate for the purposes of this section.

Before governments can engage in social-engineering, they must have reliable information about the society that is to be engineered and also must have effective tools with which to carry out the engineering. Both of these elements only became available relatively recently, roughly within the past century. The development of social science made it possible to gather and analyse information about social attitudes and trends, which is necessary in order to judge the initial state of society before an engineering strategy is undertaken and the success or failure of that attempt after it has been implemented. At the same time, the development of modern mass-communications technology and the media also provided the tools through which social-engineering may be performed.

Whilst social-engineering may be, and often is, carried out by any organisation whatsoever, whether large or small, public or private, the most comprehensive (and therefore the most effective) campaigns of social-engineering are those initiated by powerful central governments controlled by our Elite masters.

Extremely intensive social-engineering campaigns have always occurred in countries with authoritarian governments. In the 1920s for example, the revolutionary government of the Soviet Union embarked on a campaign to fundamentally modify the behaviour and ideals of Soviet citizens, to replace the old social mores of the Czarist government with a new 'Soviet' culture, to create the modern Russian citizen. They used newspapers, books, film, mass relocations and even architectural design tactics to serve as social modification techniques in order to change personal values and private relationships into those which benefitted the state.

Similar examples would be the Chinese 'Great Leap Forward' under Chairman Mao Tse Tung and the 'Cultural Revolution' programme and also the Khmer Rouge's plan of de-urbanisation of Cambodia under Pol Pot in the 1970s.

More recently, sustained social-engineering campaigns that create more gradual, but ultimately far-reaching, changes would include initiatives such as the 'war on drugs' and the 'war on terror', both fake constructs which have seriously changed the hearts and minds of western populations towards a multitude of issues, such as Islam itself and primarily the attitudes to the ongoing foreign wars being fought in the name of British, US and Israeli hegemony and empire-building.

Other examples would include such as the ever-increasing encroachment of intellectual property rights on behalf of the Elite-run corporations and the copyrighting of anything remotely profitable including the human genome, which in my view is an absolutely scandalous act that should never have been allowed in a fair and equitable society. We may also include here, the promotion of faux elections as a political tool, a tactic that has now been in place for over two centuries.

Social theorists of the Frankfurt School (see relevant section) such as Theodor Adorno also commentated upon the new phenomenon in the 1920s and 30s of mass culture and remarked on its manipulative power. When the rise of the Nazis in Germany drove him out of the country around 1930, he and many others of his ilk became involved with the 'Institute for Social Research' in the United States. The Nazis themselves of course, were no strangers to the idea of influencing political attitudes and re-defining personal and social relationships. The Nazi propaganda machine under Josef Goebbels was a sophisticated and effective tool for creating and manipulating public opinion to the benefit of the regime.

Social-engineering can and is being used constantly by the Elite, as a means to achieve a wide variety of different results, as illustrated by the many different governments and other organisations that have employed it as an effective tool to retain the balance of power in their favour.   The possibilities for large-scale manipulation became more realistic immediately following WWII, with the widespread, exponential growth of television and ongoing social-engineering, particularly with regard to advertising techniques is still pertinent in the abhorrent western model of consumer capitalism that enslaves us all.

In his classic political science work, 'The Open Society and Its Enemies, The Spell of Plato', Karl Popper examined the application of the critical and rational methods of science to the problems of the open society. In this respect, he made an important distinction between the principles of what he referred to as 'piecemeal social-engineering' and 'Utopian social-engineering'.

"The piecemeal [social] engineer will adopt the method of searching for and fighting against, the greatest and most urgent evil of society, rather than searching for, and fighting for, its greatest ultimate good." For him, the difference between 'piecemeal social-engineering' and 'Utopian social-engineering' is "…the difference between a reasonable method of improving the lot of man, and a method which, if really tried, may easily lead to an intolerable increase in human suffering. It is the difference between a method which can be applied at any moment, and a method whose advocacy may easily become a means of continually postponing action until a later date, when conditions are more favourable. And it is also the difference between the only method of improving matters which has so far been really successful, at any time, and in any place, and a method which, wherever it has been tried, has led only to the use of violence in place of reason, and if not to its own abandonment, at any rate to that of its original blueprint."
Karl Popper, Austrian philosopher, 1902-1994

We are all subjected to and affected by social-engineering whether we like it or not but as Popper rightly points-out, there is a world of difference between benign social-engineering and its hugely more malignant cousin. Unfortunately the insidious, covert use of social-engineering techniques upon the whole of mankind is a valuable tool in the armoury of those who seek to deceive us and thus enslave us. Social-engineering could also be said to be a less-intrusive version of that other popular Elite tool, mind-control techniques.

Mind Control

MK Ultra (short for the Germanic form, Mind Kontrolle) was introduced shortly after WWII using Nazi scientists and hypnotists procured via Project Paperclip (see section on WWII). Its aim was to research into hypnotic techniques for interrogation, secure courier duties and reducing fatigue for the armed forces and also to research the effects of primitive drugs like barbiturates and cannabis for drug-assisted interrogation.

A man by the name of George Estabrooks was the leading proponent of hypnosis as the ultimate method of manipulation of the human mind. His book, *Hypnotism*, published in the early 1940s, has been decried as too fantastic and improbable in terms of describing the capabilities of hypnosis with certain very suggestible subjects, but his arguments and examples remain valid to this day. Estabrooks admitted in 1971 to creating hypnotic couriers and programmed multiple personalities for Military Intelligence purposes.

The commencement of the Cold War and the Korean War in particular saw an upsurge in mind control research and also the emergence of the term 'brainwashing'. Supposedly a development of the Chinese communists, the term was actually coined by a magazine writer later found to be on the CIA payroll as an agent of influence. In postulating a 'brainwashing gap', the CIA were given permission to undertake research into countering communist mind-control efforts and developing their own as an aid in the espionage wars that were a prominent feature of the second half of the twentieth century.

Hypnosis and drugs were the primary tools of this search for the ultimate truth-serum and also regarded as an extremely desirable goal was the capability to create an agent who would never reveal his mission even under extreme torture, or even be aware that they were carrying secret information given to them in an altered state of consciousness. Sophisticated 'designer' drugs were also developed and tested, such as LSD, Ketamine, and Psilocybin whilst partial lobotomy and the implantation of electrodes were considered as methods for creating a fully-compliant, 'non-tamperable', secure field agent. Electro-convulsive shock treatment, combined with LSD, semi-permanent sedation and constantly replaying the subject's own voice through headphones were also experimental techniques in this field.

One of the most notable cases of mind control at this time involved a famous model of the late 1940s and 50s named Candy Jones. In the book, *'The Control of Candy Jones'* the author reviewed hours of tapes made by Candy Jones and her husband which revealed a systematic programme to create and manipulate alternate personalities (known as 'alters') as the basis of programmed couriers resistant to torture, where the primary personality would not even be aware of the secret information being carried by the alter. In this state, the information carried could be extracted via either a post-hypnotic command or response to a pre-programmed cue.

Research continued into early 1970s by the CIA's own admission and John Marks, author of the best study of CIA mind control experiments, makes the subtle differentiation that the CIA congressional witnesses might truthfully say that all research done by the TSS Directorate had ended, since the programmes were moved into other areas once operational techniques had been developed. Many of the names mentioned in reference to mind-control research occur in the references to supposed dead-end research in extra-sensory perception (ESP).

As the years and decades wore on, these techniques began to be used more and more for clandestine civilian purposes as opposed to the initial, almost exclusively military use.

In the 1980s and early 1990s more than 30 scientists working on top secret British projects, mostly computer technicians, died in very strange and unexplained circumstances. Several defence contractor companies such as Marconi, Plessey and British Aerospace, among others were involved in what can only be described as a bizarre series of events.

In 1986, Vimal Dajibhai, who was working for Marconi Underwater Systems, drove from London to Bristol, a city with which he had no connection and threw himself off the famous Clifton Suspension Bridge located there. A few months previously, Arshad Sharif, a computer programmer with Marconi Defence Systems, also drove from London to Bristol and hanged himself. Why Bristol of all places? Bristol is a former Knights Templar port and before that a Phoenician port. Its name has evolved from Barati, the Phoenician goddess. It just so happens that an elite unit of British intelligence called the Committee of 26 is based there and they use the runway of the British Aerospace complex to clandestinely fly British and foreign agents in and out of the country. In that period of the 1980s there was a multiplicity of strange deaths of people at the cutting edge of development in the defence industries.

What possesses a man to get into his car, drive more than two hours to the Clifton Suspension Bridge and jump off?

A CIA scientist once told a researcher he was put through forms of mind control to prevent him from recalling his knowledge once a project was completed. By way of another example; David Sands was a highly skilled scientist working on a very sensitive area of defence, but at 37 he was talking about leaving the industry and changing his lifestyle. (Moral of the story: never tell anyone what you propose to do, just do it). He was happily married with two small children, a son aged six and a three year old daughter. Sands and his wife had just returned from an enjoyable holiday in Venice when he died in mysterious circumstances, although they are not so mysterious once mind-control is understood to be the cause. He worked for Easams who were fulfilling contracts for the Ministry of Defence and it appears that whilst Sands and his wife were in Venice, the company was visited by members of the elite British police unit, the Special Branch.

Then, on Saturday 28th March 1987, David Sands told his wife he was going out to refuel the car, but he didn't return for six hours. No one, least of all himself had any idea where he was. His wife Anna called the police and Constable John Hiscock was at the house when Sands returned at 10.20pm. When questioned about his whereabouts he said he had been 'driving and thinking'. His wife said it was out of character for him to be away for so long and she did not think he realised how long he had been out. He seemed confused, but happy, she said. Two days later, on Monday, 30th March, he climbed into his excellently maintained Austin Maestro car and began his regular journey from his home in Itchen Abbas, near Winchester, Hampshire to Easams at Camberley in Surrey. His wife said there was nothing unusual about his demeanour or behaviour and driving conditions were good but about 30 minutes into his journey when he was driving along the A33 at Popham, near Basingstoke, he suddenly did a U-turn across the dual carriageway and headed at high speed in the opposite direction to his destination. Turning onto a slip road at about 80 miles an hour, Sands then drove his car straight into a disused café building, killing himself in an explosion of flame. There were no skid marks and he had not even tried to brake.

It is fairly obvious to anyone who has knowledge of the way mind-controllers operate, that in the time he was missing, he had his mind programmed to act in a certain way with some kind of trigger, which could be a word by phone, a particular sign or symbol on the road, a particular sound, a light or some kind of action outside of his vehicle. Whatever was programmed into his mind would be activated via one of these methods and at that point he would have switched from his normal self to a man focused only on driving into the café building being unaware of the consequences. In effect the subconscious programming overpowers the conscious mind and the programme takes over to replace the consciousness of the victim. This is exactly how the armed and Special Forces turn humans into 'killing machines'. And there are plenty more examples of this phenomenon...

Roger Hill, a designer at Marconi Defense Systems, allegedly committed suicide with a shotgun in March 1985.

Jonathan Walsh, a digital communications expert employed by GEC, Marconi's parent firm, 'fell' from his hotel room window in November 1985, shortly after expressing fear for his life.

Ashad Sharif, another Marconi scientist, tied a rope around his neck and then to a tree in October 1986, sat behind the wheel of his car and stepped on the accelerator pedal – with predictable results.

In March 1988, Trevor Knight, also employed or contracted with Marconi, died of carbon monoxide poisoning in his car.

Peter Ferry, marketing director of GEC Marconi, was found electrocuted with electrical leads in his mouth in August 1988.

Also in August 1988, Alistair Beckham was also found electrocuted with electric leads attached to his body and his mouth stuffed with a handkerchief. He was an engineer with the associated company Plessey Defense Systems.

And finally, but by no means the sole remaining death in this cluster, Andrew Hall was found dead in September 1988 of carbon monoxide poisoning. Altogether it was estimated that there were more than 30 similar deaths at defence contractors between 1985 and 1990

Learning of these incidents has stimulated eerie echoes in my own experiences. In the early 1990s, around 1991/2, I worked in the computer industry for a medium-sized software company based in the north east of England and obviously worked alongside many programmers and software technicians who were often seconded to work at the computer installations of client companies on a temporary basis. One of our clients was the defence contractor Vickers who just happened (at the time) to build nuclear submarines and was (and indeed still is) located in the English north-western seaport of Barrow-in-Furness.

One of my colleagues spent some considerable time there working on their top-secret computer installations until one day the news came through to the office where I was located that this person had been killed in a 'tragic accident'. The official, police explanation was that he had been working 'long hours' and the previous evening he had set-out on his journey home and at some point had inexplicably, nowhere near his home, left the motorway (freeway) at an exit ramp, rounded the roundabout (traffic circle) at the top of the ramp, proceeded back down the same ramp from which he had exited and ended-up travelling south on the northbound lanes at great speed. Of course he had not gone very far when he was inevitably involved in a high-speed, head-on collision with a car travelling in the opposite direction and both drivers were apparently killed instantly.

It was only upon relating the above, previous, similar examples to this that it stirred-up distant, dormant memories and then suddenly, realisation hit me like a brick. Of course, at the time I thought it was nothing more than a tragic accident caused by over-tiredness, as portrayed by the official version of events, but thinking about this with the benefit of 20/20 hindsight, why would tiredness make anyone exit the motorway early (less than halfway home) and then in effect make a 'U-turn' back down the same stretch of road just negotiated? It does not really make any logical sense upon closer examination and to my mind constitutes a good example of how easy it is to make people believe anything with a few well-chosen 'official' words.

In October 2011, the British illusionist, hypnotist and entertainer Derren Brown devoted a whole one hour TV programme on British mainstream television to a demonstration of how relatively simple it is to 'programme' someone to kill using simple hypnosis and mind control techniques. In this elaborate demonstration he selected a young man from an invited audience (who by the way had no idea why they were *really* there until after the event) and over the course of the next few days and weeks programmed him to 'kill' a British celebrity, Stephen Fry. All throughout the programming, the man was told and believed that he was simply being used as a 'guinea pig' to prove that it was possible to improve someone's marksmanship with a gun by the use of hypnosis, and not to be become a 'mind-controlled' assassin. Sure enough, at the appropriate time and place, the man was given the subliminal signal (a woman in a polka dot dress walked by – significantly the exact same trigger used to activate Sirhan Sirhan's assassination of RFK). He then simply took the gun from its case and coolly and clinically 'shot' Fry three times in the chest from a distance of about 30 feet before casually returning the gun to its case. He had never even held a gun in his hands prior to his meeting with Brown. Obviously for the purposes of the demonstration, the bullets were blanks, but the subject had no idea of this. Indeed he had no idea at all of what he had even done until he was 'released' from his programming by Brown and was able to watch unbelievingly, with jaw-dropped, the TV footage of the event.

This is proof conclusive in my view, of the ability of our unseen masters to use such techniques for their own nefarious purposes and goes a long way towards explaining why many assassinations are undertaken by the 'lone-nut' gunman. This is an extremely convenient and believable expedient by which the Elite can dispose of people who stand in the way of their agenda without garnering the suspicions of the majority of sheeple, who continue to be unknowingly duped in this way.

Project Bluebeam

The infamous NASA controlled 'Project Blue Beam' exists in order to implement the Elite's new age religion with the Antichrist at its head. Please note that this so-called new age religion is the very foundation for the New World Order government, without which religion the proposed Elite dictatorship cannot be sustained and this is the primary reason why the Blue Beam Project is so important to them, but has been so well concealed until relatively recently.

Significantly, the Canadian, Serge Monast and another journalist, both of whom were researching Project Blue Beam, died of 'heart attacks' literally within weeks of each other although neither had a history of heart disease. Monast was actually in Canada and the other Canadian journalist was visiting Ireland at the time of his death. Prior to his untimely death at the age of 46, the Canadian government illegally abducted Monast's daughter, under the pretence of her being 'in danger' from him, in an attempt to persuade him from discontinuing his ongoing research into Project Blue Beam. His daughter was never seen again. As related in a previous chapter, artificially-induced heart attacks are a favourite method of silencing people who manage to get too close to the truth and probably not coincidentally, one of the alleged methods of death that can be induced by Project Blue Beam.

Monast's contributions to humanity are immense and should never be forgotten. As is the unbelievable courage he demonstrated in making public these incredible revelations which were secretly or anonymously given to him by contrite politicians, military personnel and intelligence people who still possess a conscience and a sense of humanity.

"Serge Monast has died of a 'heart attack'. This man has faithfully exposed the New World Order for the last decade. His children were home-schooled, so the authorities took his eight year old daughter away, then his seven year old son was taken, as they said the parents were abusing them emotionally by stopping the children going to a State school. The father was then arrested and spent the night in jail. Next day at home, he had a 'heart attack'. He was 46 years old. This brave man has left a wife, who now has no family. Pray that she can get her little ones back. Our source said that the Canadian investigator, Serge Monast, wrote to her in Australia not long ago, saying he had been threatened many times, and did not except to survive." An unknown Canadian investigator into New Age globalism

Serge Monast's investigative work revealed that the first step in the NASA Blue Beam Project concerns the re-evaluation of all current archaeological knowledge. It reveals the initial set-up of the false paradigms, by the expedient of artificially-created earthquakes at certain precise locations on the planet, of supposedly new discoveries which will finally explain to all people the 'error' of all fundamental, current mainstream religious doctrines. The falsification of this information will be used to make all the nations of the world believe that their religious beliefs have been misunderstood and misrepresented for centuries. Psychological preparations for that first step have already been implemented with a myriad of 'sci-fi' films emanating from Hollywood, including, '2001: A Space Odyssey', 'Independence Day', and the 'Star Trek' series, all of which deal with alien entities from space and the coming together of all nations to repel the invaders. The 'coming-together' of nations is of course a pre-cursor to one-world government. The popular film 'Jurassic Park' subtly promotes the theory of evolution (again, see relevant section) amid claims that God's words are lies.

What is important to understand is that the earthquakes, triggered during the first stage, will hit many different parts of the world where scientific and archaeological teachings have indicated that arcane mysteries have been buried. As a direct consequence of those earthquakes, it will be possible for scientists to 'rediscover' those arcane mysteries which will be used to discredit all current and fundamental religious doctrines. This is the preparation for the plan for humanity because what the Elite wish to do is to destroy the beliefs of all Christians, Jews, Hindus, Buddhists and Muslims on the planet as well as all the less popular religious beliefs. To achieve this, they need some false 'proof' from the far past that will demonstrate to all nations that their religions have all been misinterpreted and misunderstood.

The second step in the NASA Blue Beam Project plan involves a gigantic 'space-light-show' complete with three-dimensional optical holograms and sounds and laser projections of multiple holographic images simultaneously to all the different countries of the world, each receiving a different image according to the predominant regional or national religious faith. This new 'god's' voice will be speaking in language relevant to that particular region. Computer scientists have now perfected an advanced computer and input to it the minute physio-psychological particulars based on studies of the anatomy and electromechanical composition of the human body and the studies of the electrical, chemical and biological properties of the human brain. This computer was also subjected to the input of the languages of all human cultures including all known dialects. It was then programmed to electronically project holographic images and sounds of the proposed new 'messiah'.

This space-show's holographic images will be used as a simulation of the fulfilment of each religion/country's desires in order to verify the prophecies and events of their own religious beliefs and these images will be projected from satellites onto the sodium layer about 60 miles above the earth. (We occasionally see tests of this technology, but they are passed-off as UFOs and 'flying saucer' sightings). Then these deliberately staged events will introduce the world its new 'messiah', Maitreya, as a prelude to the immediate implementation of the new world religion. Enough truth will be foisted upon an unsuspecting world to hook them into the lie and even the most intelligent will be deceived.

The Blue Beam Project will thus purport to be the universal fulfilment of the prophecies of old, as major an event as that which allegedly occurred 2,000 years ago. In principle, it will make use of the skies as a movie screen as space-based laser-generating satellites project simultaneous images to the four corners of the planet in every language and dialect known to man. It will effectively deal with the religious aspect of the New World Order using deception and obfuscation on a massive scale.

The projected images of Jesus, Mohammed, Buddha, Krishna, etc., will merge into one after the answers to the mysteries and the revelations have been disclosed. This one, composite god will, in fact be the Antichrist, who will explain that the various scriptures have been misunderstood and misinterpreted and that the religions of old are responsible for turning brother against brother and nation against nation, therefore these old religions must be abolished to make way for the new age, new world religion, representing the one true god, the Antichrist they see before them.

Naturally, this superbly staged falsification will result in worldwide social and religious disorder with nation blaming nation for the deception. In addition, this event will occur at a time of profound worldwide political anarchy and general tumult created by some manufactured worldwide catastrophe. The United Nations is planning to use Beethoven's 'Song of Joy' as the anthem for this event.

It is strongly suspected that the government of the United States has already developed secret communications equipment which can make the blind see, the deaf hear and the lame walk. It can relieve the terminally ill from pain without the use of drugs or surgery in order that someone may retain the use of all his faculties right up to the moment of his death. This communications equipment depends upon a newly discovered concept regarding the way that the human brain and neuromuscular systems and radiation pulses at ultra-low frequencies. This equipment is now operational within the Central Intelligence Agency (CIA), and the Federal Bureau of Investigation (FBI) although it is extremely doubtful that it will ever be used for benevolent purposes because it is central to the domestic political agenda and foreign policy of the Elite and their puppets of the NWO.

Elite, government agencies and the corporations that are actively working with them towards a New World Order are prepared to promote anything that will help them achieve their objective of total social control. The reason for this has already been covered in much detail throughout this book and is simply because, by terrifying the public and causing them to fear for their safety, the masses will then allow the authorities to implement draconian laws, disarm them and maintain extensive and intrusive records on them, all for their own 'protection' of course. Secondly, it also promotes the decay of the present 'democratic' form of politics and leads societies to search for alternative methods of political ideology. Of course, the alternative has already been planned and is commonly known as the 'New World Order' and it absolutely will not have the safety or interests of the 99% at heart.

The old maxim, 'divide and conquer', is being used to the maximum worldwide to ensure that everyone is frightened for their own personal safety and encouraged to be suspicious of everyone else. This, too, is a form of social-engineering or mind-control.

"The day has come when we can combine sensory deprivation with drug hypnosis and astute manipulation of reward and punishment to gain almost absolute control over an individual's behaviour. It should then be possible to achieve a very rapid and highly effective type of positive brainwashing that would allow us to make dramatic changes in a person's behaviour and personality." Psychologist James V McConnell in a 1970s issue of 'Psychology Today'

The next step in the process would be, electronic telepathy involving ELF, VLF, and LF waves, which will penetrate the brain, interweaving with our natural thinking to form diffused artificial thought and making everyone believe that God is speaking to them from within their own souls. This will then be followed by an electronic universal 'supernatural' manifestation designed to deceive humankind into believing that an alien invasion is imminent, make Christians believe a rapture is imminent and that the aliens have come to rescue them and generally convince us all that global, satanic, supernatural forces and manifestations penetrating worldwide and travelling through optical fibre, coaxial cable, electric and phone lines are everywhere and inescapable.

The former Nazi rocketry engineer and father of the NASA space programme, Dr. Wernher von Braun predicted as early as 1974 that the hoaxed alien invasion would be the first threat the world would face after the threat from the Middle East war to-come. Dr. Carol Rosin first met von Braun in the February of 1974 and it was at this time, three years before his death in 1977, that von Braun stunned Dr. Rosin by describing this plan, point by point, as well as describing in fine detail exactly where it was all leading; planetary control under an oppressive One World Government.

According to Dr. Rosin, von Braun then gave her one supreme challenge that would above all others, thwart this plan and that was to try to prevent the weaponisation of space by all possible means. He explained that failure to do so would lead to disaster for the entire human species as a secretive transnational power, already in existence, would move to permanently take control of this planet 'through a hoaxed alien invasion from outer space'.

Werner von Braun

In 2008 the young, independent researcher Rik Clay, whom I met in 2009, shortly before his extremely premature, suspicious death, also went public with his whistle-blowing investigations connecting the 2012 London Olympic Games with Zionism and the false UFO invasions as well as their relationship to the coming 'New Jerusalem' to be ushered in via Bluebeam.

As outlined previously, the 2012 Olympic symbol clearly spells out the word 'Zion', even including the minor detail of the dot above the letter 'i'.

The highly suspicious Olympic logo

So, what are we to conclude from all this? There is so much evidence in support of the 'Bluebeam' premise and if my research has taught me one thing; that would be that there is never 'smoke without fire' where these entities are concerned. There is obviously no 100% proof that all this subterfuge is happening whilst we collectively 'look away', but given the track record of our lords and masters, it does not take a huge leap of faith to believe that it is all eminently possible.

The NASA Blue Beam Project is the prime directive for the NWO's absolute control over the populations of the entire earth. I would strongly encourage the reader to investigate this for themselves before dismissing it as the absolute lunacy it would appear to be upon first reading.

Suppressed Technologies

As early as the late 1880s, trade journals in the electrical sciences sphere, were predicting free electricity and free energy in the near future. Incredible discoveries about the nature of electricity were becoming common place and Nikola Tesla was demonstrating 'wireless-lighting' and other wonders associated with high frequency currents. There was indeed much excitement about the future such as had never been seen before.

Within 20 years, there would be cars, planes, movies, recorded music, telephones, radio and easily portable cameras and the Victorian Age was giving way to a truly technologically-based future. For the first time in history, the masses were being encouraged to envision a utopian future filled with abundant modern aids and communication, as well as plenty of jobs, housing and food for everyone. Disease would be conquered as would poverty, life was improving exponentially for the previously dispossessed and everyone was going to benefit from this 'brave new world' of science. So, what happened to shatter this optimistic illusion? Where did all the promises of 'free' energy breakthroughs go? Was it all simply wishful thinking that science eventually disproved?

Actually, the answer to that question is 'no'. In fact, the opposite is true. Many free energy technologies were developed with all the other breakthroughs and even since that time, multiple methods for producing vast amounts of energy, free or at worst, extremely low cost have been developed. None of these technologies have ever managed to find their way to the bulk of the world's consumers however. Exactly why this is the case, I will discuss shortly. But first, here is a short list of free energy technologies that are currently inexistence and that are proven beyond all reasonable doubt to be effective. The common feature connecting all of these discoveries is that they use a small amount of one form of energy to control or release a large amount of a different kind of energy. Some of them tap into the underlying ether field in some way; a source of energy which is conveniently ignored by 'modern science' and technology.

Wireless Electricity

The Serbian inventor Nikola Tesla, whose contribution to subsequently suppressed technologies cannot be underestimated, was the undisputed 'father' of many of the inventions that define the modern electronic era and was the first person to demonstrate this principle, in 1890.

Tesla based his wireless electricity idea on a concept known as electromagnetic induction, which was discovered by Michael Faraday in 1831 and purports that electric current flowing through one wire can induce current to flow in another wire, nearby. To illustrate that principle, Tesla built two huge 'world power' towers that would broadcast current into the air, to be received remotely by electrical devices around the globe.

Few believed it could work and to be fair to the doubters, it did not work that well. When Tesla first switched on his 200 foot-tall, 1,000,000-volt Colorado Springs tower, 130-foot-long bolts of electricity shot out of it, sparks played around the toes of passers-by and the grass around the laboratory glowed blue. Despite this initial failure, there is little doubt that Tesla eventually succeeded in his quest to produce wireless electricity, but it has remained commercially un-used and dormant for more than one hundred years, largely due to the energy cartel's suppression of the technology to protect their own profit-streams.

However, after a gap of greater than a century, several companies are now coming to market with technologies that can safely transmit power through the air, a breakthrough that portends the literal 'un-tethering' of our abundant electronic devices. Until this development, the phrase 'mobile electronics' has been somewhat of a deception. How 'portable' is your laptop if it has to feed every four hours, like an embryo, through a cord? How 'mobile' is your phone if it shuts down after too long away from a power-source?

The technology about to arrive upon the electronics market is an inductive device, much like the one Tesla designed, but much smaller. It looks like a mouse pad and can send power through the air, over a distance of up to a few inches. A powered coil inside that pad creates a magnetic field, which as Faraday predicted, induces current to flow through a small secondary coil that's built into any portable device, such as a flashlight, a phone, or a portable computer. The electrical current that then flows in that secondary coil charges the device's integral rechargeable battery.

Radiant Energy

Nikola Tesla's magnifying transmitter, T. Henry Moray's radiant energy device, Edwin Gray's EMA motor and Paul Baumann's Testatika machine all run on radiant energy. This natural energy form can be gathered directly from the environment via 'static' electricity or extracted from standard electricity by a method known as fractionation.

Radiant energy can perform exactly the same functions as ordinary electricity, at less than 1% of the cost. It does not behave exactly like electricity, however, which to be fair, has contributed to the scientific community's misunderstanding of it. The Methernitha Community in Switzerland currently has 5 or 6 working models of fuel-less, self-running devices that tap this energy.

Permanent Magnets

Dr. Robert Adams of New Zealand has developed several electric motors, generators and heaters that run via the use of 'permanent magnets'. One such device extracts 100 watts of electricity from the source, generates 100 watts to recharge the source and in addition produces over 140 BTUs of heat in two minutes. An American scientist, Dr Tom Bearden has constructed two working models of a permanent magnet-powered electrical transformer. It uses a 6 watt electrical input to control the path of a magnetic field coming out of a permanent magnet and then by channelling this magnetic field, first to one output coil and then to a second output coil and by repeating this rapidly, the device can produce a 96 watt electrical output with no moving parts. Bearden calls this device a Motionless Electromagnetic Generator, or MEG. Jean-Louis Naudin has duplicated Bearden's device in France. The principles for this type of device were first discovered by Frank Richardson in the US in 1978. Troy Reed also in the US has developed working models of a special magnetised fan that heats-up as it spins. It takes exactly the same amount of energy to spin the fan whether it is generating heat or not. In addition to these developments, many inventors have identified working mechanisms that produce motor torque from permanent magnets alone.

Mechanical Heaters

There are two classes of machines that transform a small amount of mechanical energy into a large amount of heat. The best of these purely mechanical designs are the rotating cylinder systems designed by Frenette in the US and Perkins, also in the US. Within these machines, one cylinder is rotated within another cylinder with about one eighth of an inch of clearance between them. The space between the cylinders is filled with a liquid such as water or oil, and it is this fluid that heats-up as the inner cylinder spins. Another method uses magnets mounted on a wheel to produce large currents in a plate of aluminium, causing the aluminium to heat rapidly. These magnetic heaters have been demonstrated by several scientists from various countries. All of these systems can produce ten times more heat than standard methods using the same energy input.

Super-Efficient Electrolysis (The Water-Powered Car)

Water can be broken down into its constituent parts of hydrogen and oxygen using electricity. Mainstream science however, claims that this process requires more energy than can be recovered when the gases are recombined. This is true only in the worst case scenario. When water is bombarded with its own molecular resonant frequency, using a system developed by Stan Meyers also by others, it collapses into hydrogen and oxygen gas with very little electrical input. Also, using different electrolytes (additives that make the water conduct electricity better) changes the efficiency of the process dramatically. It is also known that certain geometric structures and surface textures are more effective than others. The implication of this is that unlimited amounts of hydrogen fuel can be made to drive engines eg. in cars for simply the cost of water. Even more amazing is the fact that a special metal alloy was patented by Freedman in 1957 that spontaneously breaks water into hydrogen and oxygen with no outside electrical input and without causing any chemical changes in the metal itself. This in effect means that this special metal alloy can make hydrogen from water free of cost, forever.

Stan Meyers, the American inventor of a working, patented vehicle that ran only on normal, household water, was allegedly murdered by poisoning in the late 1990s after successfully demonstrating his prototype which was capable of 100mph+. He had been the subject of harassment and threats by Elite 'Big Oil' interests and his death was perhaps the not too surprising culmination of his refusal to cease the project.

So what is happening today regarding Meyers' great invention? Absolutely nothing. The patent still exists and is available to view on the Internet, so therefore the technology or at least the wherewithal to recreate the technology, still exists, so why is this invention not being manufactured today? Simply because it would solve all the world's energy problems instantly and almost literally overnight, eliminate oil as an essential fuel and as we now know, that is not how politics and commerce works. It is always money that rules and common sense is not the determining factor.

Implosion Engine

All current, major industrial engines use the release of heat to cause expansion and pressure to produce energy, as in a standard internal combustion engine. Nature uses the opposite process of cooling to cause suction and vacuum to produce energy as in a tornado. Viktor Schauberger of Austria was the first to build working models of implosion engines in the 1930s and 1940s. Since that time, Callum Coats has published extensively on Schauberger's work in his book 'Living Energies' and subsequently, a number of researchers have built working models of implosion turbine engines. These are fuel-less engines that produce mechanical work from energy accessed from a vacuum. There are also much simpler designs in existence that use vortex motions to tap a combination of gravity and centrifugal force to produce a continuous, perpetual motion in fluids.

Cold Fusion

In March 1989, two chemists from the University of Utah announced that they had produced atomic-fusion reactions in a simple table-top device. The claims were forcefully 'debunked' within six months and the public subsequently lost interest. Nevertheless, cold fusion is a very real phenomenon and not only has excess heat production been repeatedly documented, but also low-energy atomic element transmutation has been catalogued, involving many different reactions.   This technology definitely could produce low-cost energy and prove beneficial in many, many other important industrial processes.

Anti-Gravity Propulsion

Perhaps the most fanciful of all the alternate technologies, anti-gravity propulsion is today regarded by science as impossible. However, there are reports from several sources that state that captured 'flying saucers' have been back-engineered in order to produce and take advantage of this supposed 'sci-fi' technology.

Bob Lazar worked at Area 51 in the late 1980s on a back-engineering programme that he claims began there in 1979. He says that an 'exchange' program with ETs occurred in the 1970s, which resulted in the acquisition of nine UFOs so that their technologies could be researched. That there were indeed strange craft at Area 51 seems to be corroborated by several other sources spanning several decades.

Here is Bob Lazar's own take on what he discovered...

"Assuming they're in space, they will focus the three gravity generators on the point they want to go to. Now, to give an analogy: If you take a thin rubber sheet, say, lay it on a table and put thumbtacks in each corner, then take a big stone and set it on one end of the rubber sheet and say that's your spacecraft, you pick out a point that you want to go to - which could be anywhere on the rubber sheet, pinch that point with your fingers and pull it all the way up to the craft. That's how it focuses and pulls that point to it. When you then shut off the gravity generators, the stone (or spacecraft) follows that stretched rubber back to its point. There's no linear travel through space; it actually bends space and time and follows space as it retracts. In the first mode of travel, around the surface of a planet, they essentially balance on the gravitational field that the gravity generators put out, and they can ride a 'wave', like a cork does in the ocean. In that mode they're very unstable and are affected by the weather. In the other mode of travel, where they can travel vast distances, they can't really do that in a strong

gravitational field like Earth, because to do that, first of all, they need to tilt on their side, usually out in space, then they can focus on the point they need to with the gravity generators and move on. If you can picture space as a fabric, and the speed of light is your limit, it'll take you so long, even at the speed of light, to get from point A to point B. You can't exceed it, not in this universe anyway. Should there be other parallel universes, maybe the laws are different, but anyone that's here has to abide by those rules."

Interestingly, recent research into Bose-Einstein condensate has found that by slowing down a body of atoms, to within a fraction of one degree Kelvin (near absolute zero), they coalesce into a 'super-atom' and when suitably excited by an oscillating field this BEC super-atom propagates matter waves. It is at a very early stage of development at present but it is hoped that one day this technology will produce a tightly focused 'matter wave beam' (much like that of the laser light beam) and what is so interesting, is that elements of the gravity generators described and drawn by Lazar, look exactly like the rings of optical lasers and magnetic traps used in BEC technology to slow down the atoms and that these generators emit a beam, one of which is enough for the craft to ride upon, it could mean that the ETs use a system closely related to the propagation of such matter waves.

All highly speculative, granted, but nevertheless strong rumours that this technology exists and is being suppressed by the US government, do not seem to want to go away.

In addition to the above list of examples, there are dozens of other inventions that have been omitted due to space constraints. Many of them are just as viable and well tested as the ones listed, but this short list is sufficient to prove the point; free energy technology is here, now. It offers the world pollution-free, energy abundance for everyone, everywhere for next to nothing at all.

It is now possible to halt the production of greenhouse gases and shut down all of the nuclear power plants. We can now desalinate unlimited amounts of seawater at an affordable cost and bring adequate fresh water to even the most remote habitats. Transportation costs and the production costs for just about everything could decrease dramatically and food can even be grown in heated greenhouses in the winter, anywhere at virtually zero cost. All these possibilities provide wonderful benefits that could make life on this planet so much easier and better for everyone, yet have been suppressed and covered-up for many decades. Why should this be? Whose purposes are served by this action and what forces are impeding the availability of free-energy?

In the western world and as discussed in a previous section, there is a money-monopoly in place. This money-monopoly is solely in the hands of a small number of privately-owned banks, and these banks are owned by the wealthiest families in the world, Elite bloodlines. Their future plan is to eventually control 100% of all of the capital resources of the world, and thereby control everyone's life through the availability (or non-availability) of all goods and services. Therefore an independent source of wealth (free energy device) within the reach of every person in the world ruins this plan for world domination of the money supply, permanently.

Currently, a nation's economy can be either slowed-down or speeded-up by the raising or lowering of interest rates, but if an independent source of capital via free energy were present in the economy and any business or person could raise more capital without borrowing it from a bank, this centralised strangulation of interest rates would simply not have the same effect. Free energy technology changes the value of money, simply put. The Elite do not want any competition, they understandably wish to maintain their current monopoly control of the money supply and so for them, free energy technology is not just something to suppress, it must be permanently deleted from history if at all possible.

Their motivations, as we discuss throughout this book are their imagined divine right to rule us all, greed and their insatiable need to control everything except themselves. The weapons they have used to enforce the permanent suppression of technology beneficial to mankind include intimidation, 'expert' debunkers, the covert buying-up and shelving of competitive technology, and often murder or attempted murder of the inventors, character assassination, arson and a wide variety of financial incentives and disincentives to manipulate possible supporters. They have also promoted and supported the general acceptance of a scientific principle that states that free energy is impossible, via Newton's laws of thermodynamics.

The second force in operation against free energy technology is national governments. The problem is not so much related to competition in the printing of currency, but in the maintenance of national security. The fact is, the world out there is a dog-eat-dog world and humans can be counted upon to be very cruel, dishonest, devious and sneaky and it is government's job to provide for the common defence. For this, police powers are delegated by the executive branch of government to enforce the rule of law. Most of us who consent to the rule of law do so because we believe it is the right thing to do, for our own benefit. There are always a few individuals, however, that believe that their own benefit is best served by behaviour that does not voluntarily conform to the generally agreed-upon social order. These people choose to operate outside of the rule of law and are considered outlaws, criminals, subversives, traitors, revolutionaries and often now, terrorists.

Most national governments have discovered, by trial and error that the only foreign policy that really works, over time, is a policy of 'tit for tat'. What this really means to us all is that governments treat each other the way they are being treated. There is a constant jockeying for position and influence in world affairs and the strongest party wins. In economics, the golden rule states: 'The one with the gold makes the rules'. So it is with politics also, but its appearance is more Darwinian. It is simply the survival of the fittest. However, in politics the fittest has come to mean the strongest party who is also willing to fight the dirtiest. Absolutely every means available is used o maintain an advantage over the adversary and everyone else is the adversary egardless of whether they are considered friend or foe. This includes outrageous sychological posturing, lying, cheating, spying, stealing, the assassination of world eaders, proxy wars, alliances and shifting alliances, treaties, foreign aid and the resence of military forces wherever possible.

ike it or not, this is the psychological and actual arena national governments operate vithin. No national government will do anything that simply gives an adversary an dvantage for free, it is national suicide. An activity by any individual, inside or utside the country that is interpreted as giving an adversary an edge or advantage vill be deemed a threat to 'national security'.

o therefore, free energy technology is a national government's worst nightmare.)penly acknowledged, free energy technology sparks an unlimited 'arms race' by all overnments in a final attempt to gain absolute advantage and domination. For xample would Japan not feel intimidated if China gets free energy? And would srael sit by quietly as Iran acquires free energy?
Inlimited energy available in the current state of affairs on this planet would lead to n inevitable reshuffling of the balance of power. This could become an all-out war o prevent the 'other' from having the advantage of unlimited wealth and power. verybody will covet it and at the same time, want to prevent everyone else from etting it.

here is also the credible argument that governments will suppress alternate echnology for the reason of preserving income streams derived from *taxing* energy ources currently in use. Their weapons include the preventing of the issuance of atents based on national security grounds, the legal and illegal harassment of nventors with criminal charges, tax audits, threats, phone-taps, arrest, arson, theft f property during shipment and a host of other intimidations which make the usiness of building and marketing a free energy technology practically impossible.

he third force operating in an attempt to postpone the public availability of free nergy technology consists of a group of deluded inventors and outright charlatans nd con-men. On the periphery of the extraordinary scientific breakthroughs that onstitute the real free energy technologies, lies a shadow-world of unexplained nomalies, marginalised inventions and unscrupulous promoters. The first two orces have constantly used the media to promote the worst examples of this group, o distract the public's attention and to discredit the real breakthroughs by ssociating them with the obvious frauds.

)ver the last hundred years, dozens of stories have surfaced about unusual nventions. Some of these ideas have so captivated the public's imagination that a nythology about these systems continues to this day. There may possibly be real echnologies behind these names, but there simply isn't enough technical data vailable in the public domain to make a determination. These ideas remain associated with free-energy mythology however and are cited by debunkers as examples of fraud.   .

So, the third force postponing the public availability of free energy technology is delusion and dishonesty within the movement itself.   The motivations are self-aggrandisement, greed, desire for power over others and a false sense of self importance.   The weapons used are lying, cheating, the 'bait and switch' con, self-delusion and arrogance combined with fake science.

The fourth force operating to postpone the public availability of free energy technology is 'all of the rest of us'. It may be easy to see how narrow and selfish the motivations of the other forces are, but actually, these motivations are still very much alive in each of us as well. As with the Elite, don't we each secretly harbour illusions of false superiority and the desire to control others instead of ourselves? Also, would anyone of us not 'sell out' if the price was right, say, a million pounds cash, today, in our hands? Or like governments, do we not all wish to ensure our own survival? If caught in the middle of a full, burning theatre, would we panic and push all of the weaker people out of the way in a mad, scramble for the door? Or like the deluded inventor, would we not trade a comfortable illusion once in a while for an uncomfortable fact and do we not still fear the unknown, even if it promises a great reward?

All four forces are just different aspects of the same process, operating at different levels in our society. There is really only one force preventing the public availability of free energy technology, and that is the non-spiritually motivations of we humans, but in the final analysis, free energy technology is an outward manifestation of divine abundance. It is the engine of the economy of an enlightened society, where people voluntarily behave in a respectful and civil manner toward each other, where each member of society has everything they need and does not covet his neighbour's possessions, where war and physical violence has become socially unacceptable behaviour and people's differences are at least tolerated, if not enjoyed.

The appearance of free energy technology in the public domain represents the dawning of a truly civilised age. It is an epochal event in human history and no one individual can take credit for it. No-one can become rich on it, no-one can rule the world with it, it is simply a gift from the 'gods'. It forces us all to take responsibility for our own actions and for our own self-discipline and self-restraint when needed The world as it is currently ordered cannot have free energy technology without being totally transformed by it into something else and this civilisation, imperfect though it undoubtedly is, has reached the pinnacle of its development because it has birthed the seeds of its own transformation.   Un-spiritualised humans cannot be trusted with free energy, they will only do what they have always done, which is to take merciless advantage of each other or kill each other and themselves in the process.

Upon reading Ayn Rand's work, 'Atlas Shrugged' or the Club of Rome Report, it becomes obvious that the Elite families have understood this for decades. Their plan is to live in a world of free energy, but permanently freeze-out everyone else. However this is not new, for example, royalty has always considered the general population to be its subjects. However, what is new is that we can communicate with each other now better than at any time in the past. The Internet offers us all an opportunity to overcome the combined efforts of the other three forces preventing free energy technology from spreading.

Health and Nutrition and the false medical paradigm in which we all live

Health

"Our current system of drugs-and-surgery conventional medicine will bankrupt any state or nation foolish enough to depend on it. No nation that bets its future on pharmaceuticals and chemotherapy is going to win that bet. They will all collapse in the end because you can't create a healthy nation by drugging your population into a state of health. As long as Big Pharma dominates health care and it currently runs the medical journals, medical schools, hospitals, and even the FDA so you will never have a health care system that has any interest whatsoever in teaching people how to be healthy. When profits come from sickness, the corporations always find new ways to keep people sick." Mike Adams

Medical fascism is undoubtedly with us and has permeated our entire mainstream health regime.

Probably one of the most callous and insidious ways by which we are being covertly attacked as a species is not only via the food we eat, but also through our totally corrupt healthcare system which has been infiltrated and is largely controlled by 'Big Pharma' the large pharmaceutical cartels and to a lesser but nevertheless significant extent, 'Big Food' the giant food conglomerates.

To say that our healthcare system has failed us in the past, continues to fail us in the present and is constantly being manipulated to fail us in the future, is a contender for understatement of the millennium. Make no mistake about it, general human health is not improving one iota, despite the so-called 'medical advances' of the last century or more. It is an undisputable fact that the incidence of all the newer, major destructive diseases is increasing exponentially as time goes by, despite the near-eradication of certain formerly 'killer' diseases.

Fifty years ago, one person in 50 would have been expected to contract cancer during their lifetimes and now that situation has deteriorated to the point where we are lucky if it is as low as 1 in 3 and decreasing yearly. This is also true of many diseases such as Diabetes types 1 and 2, Alzheimer's, Multiple Sclerosis, AIDS / HIV and the many invented 'mental' syndromes that have only been prevalent for a decade or so, ADHD, Bipolar Disorder and the like.

Why should this be? Does anyone ever really try to answer that question? I believe that this question is side-stepped and avoided at all costs by the Elite-run medical establishment because they know the answer to the question already, but would very much rather that you did not, if at all possible.

For example, consider this for a moment; a typical medical doctorate takes about 4 to 6 years of study to achieve, depending on the exact course undertaken, at any Western medical education establishment or University. One would naturally expect that any education or teaching programme about the workings of the human body should include a rather finely detailed study of human nutrition, its effects on all the bodily organs and functions and how to help *prevent* disease and other ailments by way of a balanced diet and vitamin consumption. Is it not more than a little strange then that our standard medical education *does not include one single lecture in six whole years of study, on the subject of nutrition or disease prevention?*

'Surely not', you may say. 'How can that be possible?' I was absolutely stunned when I first investigated this issue myself and actually made a spurious visit to my GP (General Medical Practitioner) just to find an excuse to ask him the question myself. 'Can you recommend any good nutrition programmes that will help me recover from the bad bout of general tiredness and lethargy I have been experiencing?' I asked him. His reply did not surprise me knowing what I now know about the issue. Without embarrassment or even hesitation, he actually replied that nutrition was not the answer. He mumbled something along the lines of as long as my diet was reasonably OK then it is not a problem. Instead he began without asking whether or not I wanted it, to write out a prescription for some drug or other, which I politely declined. 'It's quite harmless' he said and 'it will make you feel better and more energetic'. After again declining his kind offer, I then asked why he did not believe that good healthy natural nutrition was the answer. Again without any embarrassment he simply stated that nutrition was not an area of his expertise and therefore he could not suggest anything to help. I thanked him and left (without the prescription).

Do you not find it absolutely amazing that someone who is paid a very substantial salary from the public purse to look after human healthcare, firstly did not know or understand anything about the effect that good or bad nutrition has on our bodies and secondly was prepared to 'push' a pharmaceutical drug on to me without a second thought or to consider the implications of introducing an unnatural, artificial substance into my body? He knew nothing of course about nutrition and so was unable to help in that respect, but the question remains, how much does he really know about that drug other than what the local pharmaceutical rep had told him or what the accompanying leaflet or DVD had said and how reliable is that information likely to be? 'Not very', is the answer to both questions I strongly suspect.

I also strongly believe that we are conditioned and encouraged to pay a visit to our doctor for the slightest ailment to which we are subjected. An itch on your leg? Go to the doctor, he or she will give you some patented product or other to 'cure' it. Severe headache? Go today and get some industrial-strength painkillers.

I am sure you get the picture. However, I am absolutely convinced that this is a huge mistake. Our bodies possess a remarkable ability to heal themselves given a little time and encouragement and many small (or even large in some cases) ailments can be 'cured' by allowing the body a little breathing space to work its own magic. The problem is that once we embark on a course of pharmaceutical treatment, this then interferes with and interrupts our bodies own natural curative abilities, prolonging and even exacerbating the issue. This of course is exactly what Big Pharma wants, because their profits are greatly enhanced by this state of affairs. Instead of allowing ailments to be naturally soothed away, how much better for their 'bottom-line', that we undertake a course of treatment which will in many cases make the problem worse and require further drugs to counteract the sometimes catastrophic side effects of the first one and so it goes on.

There has recently been much new independent research into the efficacy of pharmaceuticals in general, leading to the inescapable conclusion that most of them work only in the same way as do placebos and that is because the recipient actually expects them to work and not because they have any beneficial chemical effect on the body. For example, when controlled test subjects were told that they were not receiving pain-killing medication, even though they were, the medication proved to be completely ineffective.

In other words it is the mind of the patient that controls the effectiveness of the treatment and not the medication itself.

"These findings call into question the scientific validity of many trials. It completely blows cold randomised clinical trials, which don't take into account expectation." George Lewith, Professor of Health Research, University of Southampton, 2011

"But it all brings up a question: If many pharmaceuticals only work because the mind makes them real, then why do some drugs appear to out-perform placebos in clinical trials?

The answer to that will probably surprise you: It's because when people are in randomized, placebo-controlled studies, they're usually hoping to get the real drugs, not the placebo. And how do they determine whether they're getting the 'real' drugs? By the presence of negative side effects! As those side effects begin to appear -

constipation, sexual disorders, nausea, headaches, etc - then those participants convince themselves that they received the 'real' drugs! And from that point, their mind makes it real! So the blood pressure actually then starts to go down, or their cholesterol numbers drop, and so on.
The patients make real whatever expectation they were given when they were recruited for the drug trial in the first place. Even the act of recruiting people for drug trials sets an expectation in their minds. Patients, after all, are recruited for a 'cancer drug trial' or a 'blood pressure drug trial' or some other trial in which the expected outcome is made evident during the recruitment phase." Mike Adams, Natural News, 22nd February 2011

Please indulge me once again whilst I relate another story from my own experience. In 1999 and before my subsequent research led me to become aware of what was really happening in the world today, I was diagnosed with Benign Prostatic Hyperplasia (BPH) commonly known as a swelling of the prostate gland and very common in males over the age of 40. The main symptoms were an increased frequency plus a greater urgency in passing urine and a severely reduced ability to 'shut off the flow' as it were. For those of you who have not experienced this condition personally or are of the female persuasion, I will describe its effects. Although not at all painful, it is extremely disruptive to one's life due to the need to be a maximum of 30 seconds from a toilet and even worse, being awoken five or six times each night with the urge to 'go'. This has a quite a serious effect on both one's physical and mental welfare due to lack of sleep and frustration at being unable to live life fully.

So, to begin the story, I visited my local doctor's surgery in early 1999 and after a short examination, he diagnosed the problem as BPH. He prescribed a drug to cure the problem, but after several weeks it became obvious that the problem was getting worse not better. His response to this was to increase the dosage and this he did progressively until the manufacturer's 'maximum recommended dosage' figure was reached about six months later. By this time, I was in a bad state both physically and psychologically, my life quality had markedly deteriorated due to problems with my job (it is virtually impossible to hold down a job in this condition) and this had a knock-on effect on my family and thus my general mental state. In short, I was desperate. About six months later still, in the midst of my despair and searching for possible solutions on the Internet, I came across a 'natural health' website that was to change my life. I now know that it is just one of many thousands on similar themes, but at the time it was truly 'ground-breaking' for me.

To cut this long story short, I decided that I would visit my doctor again and ask him to wean me off the drug I was on. How much worse could things be, I reasoned with myself. Of course, he was not happy with this idea. I suppose when you are conditioned all your life to believe that the whole premise upon which your career is built, that pharmaceutical cures are the only answer to health problems; then understanding that there is sometimes possibly a different, better way is not going to be easy to even consider as a possibility, let alone accept. At first he tried to talk me out of it and gave me plenty of 'reasons' why I should stay on the drugs, but I persisted and he reluctantly agreed. And so, in the space of the next three months I was drug-free.

The one thing I noticed immediately was that reducing the drug dosage made absolutely no difference. In other words, the condition was just as bad on 50% or 25% of the original dose as it was on 100%. Then, once I was free of the drug, very, very slowly at first I began to notice that I was a little better. Within another six months I was back to normal and my life had improved immensely. Even now, more than a decade later, I am convinced that had I just waited a couple of weeks or even a month or two, then my problem would have cured itself naturally without fuss. Once I started on the course of drugs, did they contribute to prolonging the problem by confusing and obstructing my body's natural defences? We will never know conclusively, but one thing is for sure, when I was taking them, they certainly did not help the situation one jot. I have never been back to the doctor (any doctor) for any form of treatment since that time and he certainly did not contact me to see how my condition was progressing without the drugs.

Actually, in July 2011 I did make another visit to see a doctor – accompanied with and on behalf of my recently-bereaved 86 year old father who is registered blind and extremely frail. I went along with an open-mind and prepared to be conciliatory and non-confrontational although I had more than an inkling of what to expect. The reason for our visit was that I had been concerned for a long time that the doctor had been prescribing medication on medication to my father until it had reached the point where he was taking multiple doses of sixteen, yes sixteen different medications every day including 3 different anti-depressants, 3 different pain-killers and 2 different cholesterol-lowering drugs! Is it not absolutely staggering, that a supposedly intelligent, highly-skilled medical practitioner could actually believe that this situation could possibly be in anyone's best health interests?

Anyway, I began by asking him the obvious question and that was… "How could the drug companies actually know that taking all these medications in combination would be guaranteed to be safe? Surely it would be impossible for them to clinically trial every combination of all these drugs and in any case these drugs were provided by many different companies?" If I had not been there to hear his answer in person, I would not have believed it possible, although actually thinking about it; maybe I would, knowing what I know now about how these absolute charlatans in suits operate.

He sat in his expensive leather chair in front of us mere mortals, wearing his £1000 suit, his Rolex watch and his £300 shoes and with a smug, supercilious smile on his 30-something year old face actually said, pointing at his computer screen… "We don't need clinical trials. These days we have a piece of software that tells us whether drug combinations are safe." Pardon me? To be honest, at this point I was dumb-struck. Did I actually hear him correctly? Does he actually believe or even understand the implications of what he just said or was it simply a fob-off for those imbeciles like me who just don't have the intellectual capacity to comprehend these things. My somewhat delayed reply was a little abrupt to be honest. I said, *"Have you never heard of an acronym from the IT world, garbage in, garbage out?"* (Meaning that a computer programme is only as reliable as the data that it has input to it? How can a 'piece of software' possibly come to a reliable conclusion unless the data with which it was working was accurate and how could that data possibly be accurate unless clinical trials had been performed in the first place?)

I could now see by his face that I had definitely outstayed my welcome in his office. This beautifully coiffured, smartly-dressed, 'highly-educated', 'intelligent' young professional whom I dare bet has never had a single independent or semi-radical thought in his entire life was actually being questioned by some scruffy, late-middle-aged oik wearing denim jeans, a T shirt and trainers and worse yet was actually disputing 'facts' upon which he had based virtually all of his highly lucrative career, if not his whole life. I don't believe for a minute he had ever questioned this scenario in his own mind and nor was he prepared to start discussing it now with someone with no medical training whatsoever. We were more or less dismissed with a wave of the hand and an instruction to make an appointment on the way out for a formal 'medication review'. 'Bye then'!

The 'formal medication review' which took place the following week and which I also attended, given by *another* doctor in the same medical practice incidentally, literally consisted of the following exchange (in its entirety):

Doctor to my father: Hello, please sit down. You are here for a medication review I believe?

Me (after a short silence): Yes. (My father did not hear what he had said).

Doctor (briefly perusing his computer screen): Yes, that's all fine.

Me: Is that it?

Doctor: Yes, goodbye and thank you.

The total elapsed time of the meeting from entering his room to leaving it was approximately 30 seconds. I simply could not be bothered questioning this process as to do so would no doubt have antagonised him and possibly jeopardised his professional relationship with my father, whom I judged that at that time of his life would not have benefitted from conflict with his doctor. So we shuffled out of his office and back to the extreme drugs regimen to which my father has now been subjected for the last five or so years. In this time, I have watched him change from someone with a sound mental and physical constitution (for his age) into a frail, bewildered, partially blind and deaf, wreck of a man. Although I concede that some of the deterioration in his condition could be put-down to the natural aging process, the extreme changes in him would seem in every way possible to belie that conclusion, definitively. For my own part, I will never, ever allow myself to ingest a pharmaceutical drug of *any kind*, ever again, whilst still in possession of my full mental faculties.

Please do not misunderstand me. The vast majority of doctors are extremely well-trained, professional, thoroughly competent and knowledgeable in the area of physical, bodily issues such as fractures, sprains and muscular problems, in other words mending physical 'broken' bodies. I would not hesitate to return should I find myself in need of a 'physical' remedy but the track record of first-world doctors in treating or preventing general bodily ailments and diseases is nothing short of scandalous and a disgrace to a so-called civilised society.

We have become so conditioned and propagandised to regard pharmaceutical solutions to health issues as being the 'norm' or the 'only way', that we now regard the treatment or prevention of disease through nutrition and balanced vitamin-rich diets as a form of 'quackery' or witchcraft. Indeed this is how Big Pharma attempts to portray natural health solutions, putting them on a par psychologically with the mediaeval practices of using leeches and the 'bleeding' of patients.

"...doctors and health 'experts' have astonishing gaps in knowledge that should be considered basic health information in any first-world nation. Parents, too, lack any real literacy in nutrition and health. That's largely because medical journals, health authorities and the mass media actively misinform them about health and nutrition issues, hoping to prevent people from learning how to take care of their own health using simple, natural remedies and cures." Natural News, 2009

Pharmaceutical companies are certainly not in business to maintain human health at its optimum levels. They are there to make money for their Elite owners and shareholders and maintain health levels at an appallingly low level in order to further their drug sales agendas. They certainly excel at both of these activities. Big Pharma companies are among the richest if not actually the richest organisations in the world. In recent research conducted to determine the top 100 wealthiest organisations world-wide, 51 were corporations and only 49 were countries, which in itself is truly staggering information. Included in the top 10 were the 'big 4' pharmaceutical companies.

So, here we have a situation where companies that have more disposable income than most countries and are concerned with profits to the detriment of all else are dictating to the medical profession how to conduct a successful health regime and in the process are making colossal profits based on that philosophy. What is wrong with this picture?

"The medical practice of today is anything but a healing modality. It is geared toward maximum profit generated by those for whom disease is a growth industry. They

poison the environment and encourage you to eat bad food, simply because they are invested in your becoming sick." Les Visible, musician and researcher.

Your body never becomes ill because it lacks artificial, pharmaceutical, allopathic drugs. It becomes ill through lack of proper, correct nutrition or because it has become infected with an outside agent such as a bacteria or a virus, often exacerbated by incorrect nutrition. So why do we rush to dose ourselves with more often than not, harmful chemicals at the first sign of any problems or anything untoward with our bodies? I suggest that it is because both we and our doctors alike are conditioned by 'the system' engendered by Big Pharma, so to do.

Sadly, I have to remind you that as I stated in the introduction to this book, that the giant, multi-national pharmaceutical companies have completely infiltrated all of the important healthcare organisations from cancer research charities such as the hugely corrupt American Cancer Society (ACS) to the equally corrupt American Food and Drug Administration (FDA), to the British and American Medical Associations (BMA and AMA) and even medical education establishments across the Western world with the primary intention of deceiving the world about healthcare. Indeed the FDA is provably culpable for allowing highly-profitable yet highly-toxic, substances into the food chain in what can only be described as at best, irresponsible and at worst, criminal activities.

Our healthcare system does not exist to make you well. It exists to profit from your illnesses and keeps you just well enough to stay alive so it can continue to push drugs on you. The last thing the Elite want is a healthy, well-nourished, physically and mentally strong population able to think clearly and look after themselves and their families. What they actually *do* want is a sickly, malnourished society, totally dependent on them and their poisons and unable to act and think freely for ourselves, so they can exploit our helpless situations to the maximum in the cause of reaping their huge annual profits. Unfortunately, over time, this is exactly what they have managed to achieve. As a main thrust of this policy, they also do not want you to understand nutritive disease prevention as there is little or no profit to be had from prevention, but plenty from 'cures'.

When I say 'cures', please be advised that I use the term very loosely. In actual fact most cures to be derived from pharmaceuticals, only treat the symptoms and not the underlying cause of the problem. For example if you have a severe headache, then Big Pharma says you should take a strong painkiller or their migraine formulas. This may well remove the pain, but this ignores the *extremely important fact* that pain exists for a reason and that is to let us know that there is something amiss somewhere. Simply eliminating the pain does not make the reason for the pain go away and could actually be dangerous as it removes the 'alarm call' that pain is designed to be. To use an analogy, imagine your car engine develops a fault and a red warning light appears on the console. Would you remove or cover-up the small red light-bulb to cure the fault and declare it fixed when the light can no longer be seen or would you use that warning signal to actually check under the bonnet (hood) for the real problem?

Almost 100% of pharmaceutical drugs work in this fashion and I include their so-called cancer drugs. All that radiotherapy and chemotherapy does is remove the tumour (sometimes) and kill ALL cells (healthy and unhealthy) whilst destroying one's natural resistance or immune system leaving one open to succumb once more to cancer in other areas of the body and many other deadly ailments. Sadly this is what is happening all the time. Many, many people are delighted to receive the news that their cancer is in remission shortly after a course of radiation. However, what we rarely are told is that the cancer more often than not, returns with a vengeance a few months or sometimes years later, to take advantage of a thoroughly ravaged immune system. Of course even if by luck the cancer does not return, the body's natural defences are in tatters leaving the victim open to all manner of further diseases.

"As clear-thinking people, natural health consumers sometimes look at the actions of the Food and Drug Administration (FDA) and wonder what planet its decision makers seem to be from. It's like the FDA is living in a completely different world than the rest of us - a world where nutrients are dangerous, but synthetic chemicals are perfectly safe for human consumption. In fact, the idea that FDA bureaucrats and modern medicine promoters are living in a different reality is not far from the truth. In my view, FDA decision makers have no connection with reality. They're simply operating on a system of false beliefs and circular reasoning that justifies their efforts to protect Big Pharma profits by exploiting, misleading and directly harming the public." Natural News

So, Big Pharma, in conjunction with Big Food, the FDA and their corporate media whores (all owned by the same bloodline families when you follow the pyramids to the very top) conspire together to wreak havoc on human health so that they can make billions if not trillions out of our misery, whilst pretending that they are spending our millions in the form of charitable donations, to search for cures to diseases that can, in most instances, be treated simply, inexpensively and easily through proper and adequate nutrition.

"The nature of the medical establishment today is unsettling, to say the least. Doctors of all kinds have been trained to prescribe double-edged medical 'solutions' to their patients, draining the finances of patients through side-effect ridden pharmaceuticals and invasive surgeries. Mainstream medical science is increasingly being found to be fraudulent, but many still see doctors and medical officials as 'experts' that can do no wrong." Andre Evans. Activist Post 19th October 2011

Vaccines

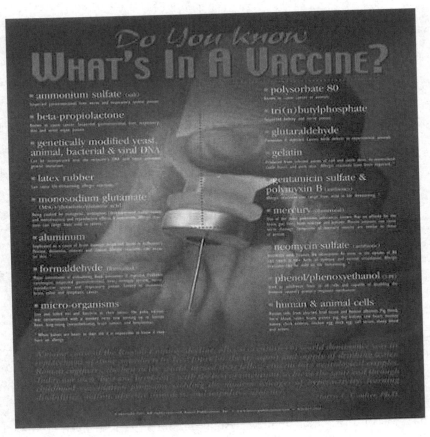

We are so fortunate to live in times where most endemic diseases have been eradicated and we are free to live out our long lives relatively untroubled by the thoughts of succumbing to such horrors as smallpox, poliomyelitis, tuberculosis, whooping-cough (pertussis) or measles.

Of course the main contributory factor to achieving this state of affairs has been the advent of safe and effective vaccines which stimulate our natural defence mechanisms into providing us with a resolute barrier against the ravages of these former killer diseases.

...If only this statement were true.

How can I be actually disputing this proven FACT? Sadly, I have to remind you that the power of persistent, overwhelming propaganda and lies never ceases to amaze, does it? The fact is that not only have vaccines **not** been the great saviour they have been proclaimed to be to our grandparents, parents, ourselves and now our children and grandchildren, but in actuality, the exact opposite is true. Vaccines have been proven over and over again not only to be utterly useless in disease prevention; they are known to be killers and purveyors of disease, misery and destruction on a large scale.

But how can this be? We have been told all our lives by people who 'know' about these things that we *must* have vaccinations if we want to stay healthy. It just simply is not possible that something so basic, so familiar to us, so known as a fact to be true, could be a huge deception and lie.

Is it really so impossible to believe though?

"If I had a child now, the last thing I would allow is his/her vaccination." Retired vaccine researcher

The British Medical Association is a wholly-owned subsidary of Big Pharma, despite its facade of independence and recently, its former chairman, Sir Sandy Macara (significantly, recently out-ed by new GMC disclosure rules as a freemason), called for the highly controversial MMR (measles, mumps and rubella) triple vaccine to be made compulsory.

Big Pharma has been increasing its influence and control over medicine for decade after decade and by funding, cajoling, incentivising and bribing corrupt politicians and senior medical professionals, it has in effect made its own laws and in doing so has become 'above the law'. Now it wants forced vaccinations so that every child, in fact *everyone*, must be injected with its venomous poisons. It is the latest stage in Big Pharma's war on the human immune system designed to cause still more death and disease by devastating the body's natural defences.

These horrendous cocktails of destruction contain toxic chemicals such as thimerasol (mercury), DNA from animal tissue and aborted human foetuses and foreign proteins in the form of live or dead viruses and bacteria. Small babies and toddlers with their immune defences still forming, are now given in some cases twenty five vaccines, including combinations, before the age of two. One simply cannot imagine the havoc it is wreaking on their tiny, immature immune systems. No wonder that once virtually unheard of problems such as Cot Death (Sudden Infant Death Syndrome) and Autism are absolutely rife and increasing exponentially year on year in the Western World.

Dr. Andrew Wakefield, a British vaccine expert was indeed struck-off the medical register for publishing proof and refusing to retract his view that vaccinations were a huge contributory cause in Cot Death and Autism cases. This is what happens when the 'little man' stands-up to these bullies. He is ruthlessly destroyed.

"The world today has 6.8 billion people. That's heading up to about nine billion. Now if we do a **really great job on new vaccines**, health care, reproductive health services, we could lower that by perhaps 10 or 15 percent. But there we see an increase of about 1.3 billion." Bill Gates, founder of Microsoft, eugenicist and Elite 'gofer', speaking in 2010

What more proof do we need that vaccines and 'healthcare' in general are being actively used for de-population?

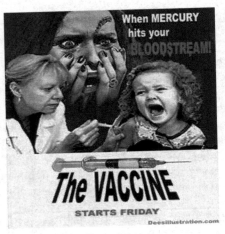

As staggering as it may seem, the Big Pharma octopus has within the grip of its tentacles, the entire mainstream medical profession and industry. It controls what is taught in the medical schools, the drugs that doctors prescribe and it also dictates governmental health policy through its lobbying and a range of techniques that include massive political contributions and bribes to doctors such as all-expenses-paid trips to 'conferences' in exotic places that are nothing more than simply a free holiday.

Mainstream Big Pharma-controlled medicine is a huge morass of corruption and self-interest made even worse by the extraordinary levels of ignorance, incompetence and sadly, corruption among those who are paid large sums to be our so-called medical professionals. Take the example of Dr. Paul Offit at the Children's Hospital of Philadelphia who was paid at least $29 million from his share of royalties for Merck's Rotateq vaccine, which provably causes severe diarrhoea and worse in infants. Despite this outrageous conflict of interest, he used his position with the Centres for Disease Control and Prevention to ensure that childhood vaccination with **his** vaccine became compulsory. The authors of an article exposing Dr Offit said:

"Clearly, based on the distribution of income rights outlined, Paul Offit had a greater personal interest in Rotateq's commercial success than any other single individual in the world and more than any other individual in the world, he found himself in a position to directly influence that success.

Unlike most other patented products, the market for mandated childhood vaccines is created not by consumer demand, but by the recommendation of an appointed body called the ACIP. In a single vote, ACIP can create a commercial market for a new vaccine that is worth hundreds of millions of dollars in a matter of months."

But of course Dr. Offit was 'struck-off' the medical register for corruption and had his medical licence revoked? Wrong. As far as I have been able to ascertain, nothing whatsoever happened to him and this is just one small example and far from an isolated instance. Even had he been stripped of his medical practitioner's licence, would he actually care, with $29m sat in his bank account and no doubt he would have been handed a senior position with Merck, regardless.

However, as a registered medical practitioner, should you attempt to treat people with proven natural remedies, you will firstly get a severe warning and censure and then should you persist in this heinous practice, you will be pretty quickly hauled before the medical boards (GMC in the UK and AMA in the USA) and have your name struck from the medical register. This is not mere supposition on my part, this has happened in literally hundreds of well-documented cases down the years.

The level of ignorance and deceit amongst medical professionals is astounding. Doctors in general have no real idea what is going on behind the scenes in medicine and so they believe their own propagandised education which leads to the killing and maiming of innocents on a monumental scale worldwide. How frightening and disgusting it is to report that doctors are the third largest cause of death in America after heart disease and cancer with upwards of 300,000 people (AMA figures, by the way – so probably under-stated) provably dying in US hospitals every year from unnecessary surgery, medication and other errors, the effects of the drugs and vaccinations given to 'help' them, and infections picked up in hospital. However, I would not wish to be unfair to American health-care professionals, this also holds true of Western Europe as a whole, including the UK. Indeed in the 1980s, there was a strike by doctors in Sweden which lasted around a month and during that period *the death rate actually dropped dramatically.* This is absolutely, provably true.

"Prescription drugs kill some 200,000 Americans every year. Will that number go up, now that most clinical trials are conducted overseas--on sick Russians, homeless Poles, and slum-dwelling Chinese--in places where regulation is virtually non-existent, the FDA doesn't reach, and 'mistakes' can end up in pauper's graves?" 'Deadly Medicine', Vanity Fair magazine, 2011

As people's scepticism about the efficacy of vaccination programmes begins to gain momentum, the medical mainstream fights back with such blatantly fascist tactics as...

"'Local councils could boost immunisation rates among children by making it part of the preparation for going to school. Parents could be asked if their child has been immunised. If they haven't, this could be done by the school nurse as a matter of routine when the child visited their new school before enrolment." Charles Waddicor, writing in the Local Government Chronicle in the UK

And this extremist nonsense, which could have been lifted verbatim from the pages of Huxley's 'Brave New World':

"There also seems to be no way to avoid the conclusion that we need to fight fire with fire - fear with fear. We have to make parents more scared that their children will contract serious preventable infectious diseases than they are about the false fears surrounding vaccines. And I need to emphasize - parents should be more scared of this." Steven Novella, writing in 'Science-based Medicine'

I am not entirely sure what is 'science-based' about that, but nevertheless that is where the quote originated.

"The bloodline families (Elite) and the higher levels of the Big Pharma pyramid couldn't give a damn about protecting the health of the population. Like almost everything else in this crazy world we need to reverse their statements to see their true motivation. They want to cull the global population and reduce human numbers dramatically and there can be few more effective ways to access the body than compulsory vaccination. Once these laws are passed anything goes with regard to vaccine content because you will see the demands increase for another kind of immunity - immunity from prosecution for drug companies who kill and brain-damage people with their witches brew. (Note - this has now already happened in early 2011 and the legislation is now in place protecting these murderers from liability – JH)

Those they don't kill directly they plan to do so indirectly by devastating the immune system and opening people to death by other means that the human defences would otherwise eliminate. This is why the number of vaccines and combinations go on being increased for children under 2 while the immune system, and indeed the brain, is still developing and getting up to speed. They want their immunity to disease and their potential for clear thought dumbed-down and ideally eliminated." David Icke, researcher, 2009

Strong stuff, but absolutely true. Vaccinations are nothing less than part of an elaborate Elite plan to reduce the population of the world to their own stated 'desirable' levels whilst making obscene amounts of profit from their victims in the process.

The 'safety' of vaccines is a complete myth. Under the 1986 National Childhood Vaccine Injury Act, the Vaccine Adverse Reporting System was established. Annually, it reports about 11,000 serious vaccine reactions, including up to 200 deaths and many more permanent disabilities. However, worryingly the FDA estimates that **only 1% of serious adverse reactions are actually reported.** And worse still, several medical school students testified before the US Congress that they are instructed *not to report* these incidents.

According to the National Vaccine Information Centre, only one in 40 New York doctors reported adverse vaccine reactions or deaths yet international studies show vaccines cause up to 10,000 US SIDS (Sudden Infant Death Syndrome or 'cot death') deaths annually and at *least* half of them are from vaccines.

Another American study revealed that 3000 US children die annually from vaccines and that the measured incidence of non-reporting of problems in America suggests that annual adverse vaccine reactions, in fact number from 100,000 to one million!

Since 1988, the US government's *National Vaccine Injury Compensation Program* has paid families of affected children $1.2 billion in damages. It should also be noted though that in settling vaccine damage suits, drug companies impose 'gagging' orders as part of the deal, to keep vital information from the public and additionally, insurers refuse to cover adverse vaccine reactions because of the high potential liability they would face. This of course distorts the true figures in a downward direction.

Vaccinations cause high numbers of severe reactions, permanent disabilities and deaths as well as an enormous personal and public cost. Virtually none of this is reported.

Medical literature documents significant numbers of vaccine failures for measles, mumps, smallpox, pertussis, polio, bacterial meningitis and pneumonia. In 1989, the Middle Eastern country of Oman experienced a widespread polio outbreak six months after completing a population-wide immunisation program. In Kansas in 1986, 90% of 1300 reported pertussis cases were 'adequately vaccinated,' and 72% of Chicago pertussis incidents in 1993 were also similarly vaccinated.

Between the years 1850 to 1940, well before mandatory vaccination programmes, the British Association for the Advancement of Science reported a 90% decrease in childhood diseases due to improved sanitation and hygiene practices. By 1945, US medical authorities noted a 95% drop in deaths from the leading childhood infectious diseases (diphtheria, pertussis, scarlet fever and measles) again well before mass-immunisation programmes began. This is the *real* reason for the decline in mortality, disingenuously attributed wholly to vaccines.

A recent WHO report found that third world disease and mortality rates had no direct correlation with immunisation programmes, but were closely related to hygiene and diet standards. There is no evidence whatsoever that links vaccines with the decline of infectious diseases. Proper hygiene, clean water and diet are proven to be far more effective.

Although some vaccines can stimulate antibody production, no evidence suggests that this alone assures immunity. In 1950 the British Medical Council published a study that found no correlation whatsoever between antibody count and disease incidence. Natural immunisation involves many bodily organs and systems and artificially producing antibodies cannot achieve that.

Research also shows how squalene adjuvants, rife in vaccine serums, actually cause harm to the human immune system, making it susceptible to numerous illnesses and diseases ranging from very irritating to life threatening. In addition, the 'herd immunity' notion of mass-immunisation's effectiveness is totally discredited. In fact the exact opposite is closer to the truth and evidence shows that fully-vaccinated populations have experienced numerous epidemics in the past.

Furthermore, vaccine effectiveness remains 'scientifically unproven' because no double blind studies are ever conducted to test the theory. Significantly, recent disease outbreaks have affected more vaccinated children than un-vaccinated ones and the common practice of 'one size fits all' is worthless, if not downright dangerous as it allows new-born babies to be given the same dosage as a twenty five year old and tolerates dubious quality-control practices.

Shockingly, but maybe not surprisingly knowing what we know about the modus operandi of the FDA, it absolutely refuses to act preventatively against vaccines. In fact, individual vaccine batches have almost never been recalled even when proven to be associated with severe adverse reactions or deaths. Instead, they are administered under the assumption that all recipients respond the same, regardless of age, size, gender, ethnicity, genetics or any other characteristics one can name. There are even reports that suggest that 'bad' vaccine batches that are withdrawn are then sold-on or generously 'donated' to third world countries.

A recent study reported in the New England Journal of Medicine found that a significant number of Romanian children receiving polio vaccine actually contracted the disease. One dose alone raised the polio risk eight-fold.

"Unbeknownst to most doctors, the polio-vaccine history involves a massive public health service makeover during an era when a live, deadly strain of poliovirus infected the Salk polio vaccines, and paralyzed hundreds of children and their contacts. These were the vaccines that were supposedly responsible for the decline in polio from 1955 to 1961! But there is a more sinister reason for the "decline" in polio during those years; in 1955, a very creative re-definition of poliovirus infections was invented, to "cover" the

fact that many cases of "polio" paralysis had no poliovirus in their systems at all. While this protected the reputation of the Salk vaccine, it muddied the waters of history in a big way." Dr. Suzanne Humphries, 'Smoke, Mirrors and the 'Disappearance' of Polio', 17th November 2011

New research may reveal other unknown hazards, but public safety will not be addressed adequately until government health officials act ethically, report accurately and adequately protect their populations from vaccines they never should allow in the first instance. How much chance is there of that coming to pass under the current medical regime? I am afraid the answer is 'none at all'.

Medical institutions tell us that childhood diseases are extremely dangerous or so they would have us all believe. This is absolutely false. Centres for Disease Control (CDC) data shows a 100% pertussis recovery rate during the period 1992-94. One Cincinnati Children's Hospital infectious diseases expert said at the time: *"The disease was very mild, no one died and no one went to the intensive care unit."*

Nearly always, childhood infectious diseases *"are benign and self-limiting. They usually impart lifelong immunity, whereas vaccine-induced immunisation (even when achieved) is only temporary."* In fact, it can increase vulnerability later in life by postponing better tolerated illnesses in childhood, until adulthood when death rates (though still low, relatively speaking) are far higher than would normally be the case. Most importantly, nearly all common infectious diseases are rarely dangerous and in fact, strongly contribute to the development of robust, healthy adult immune systems when they are most needed ie. in adulthood. Additionally, it is commonly known amongst honest medical practitioners that children who did not contract measles in childhood have a higher incidence of skin diseases, degenerative bone and cartilage issues and tumours, while ovarian cancer is higher among childhood-mumps-free adult women. The human immune system benefits greatly from common childhood infectious diseases, so why do we have dangerous and unnecessary vaccine programmes effectively hampering our immune system's natural development process? Freedom from the normal childhood ailments may well be very harmful to us later in life.

It is my firm belief that the dangers of childhood disease are greatly exaggerated to scare parents into having their children vaccinated with dangerous compounds.

What about polio though? Surely that is a classic example of a vaccination programme eradicating a disease? Was it not completely conquered or made almost non-existent by the mass-immunisation programmes in the US and Europe in the late 1950s? Unfortunately the real facts say not, despite the mass hysteria and propaganda generated at the time. In 1955, when Jonas Salk's polio vaccine was introduced, polio was considered the most serious post-war public health problem. One year after the vaccine was widely deployed, six New England states reported sharp rises ranging from more than double in Vermont to a 642% increase in

Massachusetts. Other states also were so badly affected that Idaho and Utah to name but two, halted immunisations due to a greatly increased incidence of adverse reactions and soaring death rates.

In his 1962 congressional testimony, Dr. Bernard Greenberg, head of Biostatistics at the University of North Carolina, reported sharp polio *increases* from 1957 to 1959 but this was completely covered-up and suppressed at the time by a Public Health Service whitewash in order to protect the reputation of vaccinations. In 1985, the CDC reported that 87% of US polio cases between 1973 and 1983 were caused by the vaccine.

Furthermore, misdiagnoses, poor reporting and cover-ups suggest that the actual number of vaccine-associated paralytic poliomyelitis cases *"may be 10 to 100 times higher than that cited by the CDC."* In 1977, even Jonas Salk himself, admitted that mass innoculations had caused most polio cases since 1961. In fact the Salk vaccine proved highly dangerous and truthful information about it was hugely suppressed. The truth is that declines in the disease were well underway when mass-immunisations were commenced. In Europe, the declines occurred in countries that used and then rejected the vaccine proving it was never needed in the first place. By far the biggest contributory factor to the decline of the disease (as with most others) from the turn of the twentieth century to the 1950s was a major improvement in hygiene, nutrition and living standards.

This shows also that the same is true for other diseases, including the fake, non-epidemic of Swine Flu of early 2009 and the pathetic, repeated, probably long-forgotten by the time you read this, attempts of the medical establishment in league with the media to resurrect the scare again in the winter of 2010/11. The World Health Organisation (WHO) and CDC admitted that most cases are mild, unthreatening and generally pass without any form of treatment, let alone risking dangerous and un-needed vaccines.

Does the lack of an initial adverse reaction prove that vaccines are quite safe, really? Far from it, unfortunately. Documented long-term health problems arising from the ingestion or injection of vaccines include arthritis, chronic headaches, skin-rashes indicative of disease, non-healing skin lesions, seizures, autism, anaemia, multiple sclerosis, cancer and many other ingredients common to all vaccines are the real issue. For example, squalene adjuvants are a biological time-bomb that can harm or even destroy the human immune system, long-term.

Other ingredients are known toxins and carcinogens, including thimerasol (a mercury derivative), aluminium phosphate, formaldehyde, phenoxyethanol and numerous gastro-intestinal toxins like liver toxicants, cardiovascular and blood toxicants and reproductive toxicants. Chemical ranking systems rate many vaccine ingredients among the most hazardous substances known to man, even in microscopic doses. Truly staggering.

"Millions of children (and adults) are partaking in an enormous crude experiment and no sincere, organized effort is being made to track the negative side effects or to determine the long-term consequences." Dr. Bart Classen, founder and CEO of Classen Immunotherapies

Dr. Classen's research found vaccines as the cause of 79% of insulin type I diabetes cases in children under 10. The sharp rise in numerous other diseases may also be linked with mass-immunisation programmes. California's autism rate has soared by 1000% in the last 20 years alone, whilst In the 1990s in Britain, MMR vaccine usage (for measles, mumps and rubella) increased and at the same time autism rose sharply in a correlated fashion.   The January 2000 edition of the Journal of Adverse Drug Reactions reported that no adequate testing was done, so in a truly caring, ethical society, the vaccine would never have been licensed for use.

Meanwhile, the Elite-compliant (probably controlled) Autism Society blithely states that; *"Autism is a complex developmental disability that typically appears during the first three years of life and is the result of a neurological disorder that affects the normal functioning of the brain..."*

According to the CDC and National Vaccine Information Centre, one in every 150 US children develops the disease. Tens of millions are affected worldwide, making it more common in children than paediatric cancer, incurable type-1 diabetes and AIDS combined. In the early 1940s, prior to mass immunisations, autism was so rare that few doctors ever encountered it. Today it is a global pandemic.

Long-term vaccination reactions have been suppressed and ignored in spite of the alarming correlation between their use and the rise of auto-immune and other diseases. Vaccines are not for our protection, they are for profit and other nefarious purposes such as depopulation and reducing our ability to fight disease. Avoiding them ALL is absolutely essential to protecting and maintaining human health and well-being.

Had I known 40 years ago what I now know today, my children would never have been subjected to vaccinations. I have met many people with similar views to myself who tell me that their children were never vaccinated at all and they, almost without exception, have never had a single day's illness in their lives.

Natural solutions have proven many times more effective than allopathic (pharmaceutical) medicines in the treatment and prevention of disease. During the 1840s US cholera outbreak, homeopathic hospitals recorded a 3% death rate compared to 50-60% in conventional ones. It is just as true today if not even more so and recent epidemiological studies show that natural remedies are far superior to vaccines in preventing diseases. They are safe, effective and toxin and side-effect-free, yet most health insurers will not even cover them.   Something is very, very wrong with this picture.

Vaccination history shows *"documented instances of deceit, portraying vaccines as mighty disease conquerors, when in fact vaccines have had little or no discernible impact - or have even delayed or reversed pre-existing disease declines...Conflicts of interest are the norm in the vaccine industry."* Government agencies like the FDA and CDC are overloaded with corporate officials who often return to highly paid positions in commerce and industry provided that they place the profit considerations of those corporations over public health and safety issues.

In November 2000, concern over this and adverse reactions prompted the American Association of Physicians and Surgeons to pass a unanimous resolution at its 57th meeting calling for a moratorium on mandatory childhood vaccinations and for doctors to insist on *"truly informed consent for their use..."*

"It is clear...that the government's immunisation policies are driven by politics and not by science. I can give numerous examples where employees of the US Public Health Service...appear to be furthering their careers by acting as propaganda officers to support political agendas. In one case...employees of a foreign government, who were funded and working closely with the US Public Health Service, submitted false data to a major medical journal. The true data indicated the vaccine was dangerous; however, the false data indicated no risk." Dr. Bart Classen, founder and CEO of Classen Immunotherapies, told US Congress in 1999

In addition, Dr. Classen states that *"four letters from the FDA/Public Health Service...clearly revealed that the anthrax vaccine..."* approved for US military personnel was done *"...without the manufacturer performing a single controlled clinical trial."* Honest and ethical trials are essential to determine safety and effectiveness and failure to conduct them proves devastating to the health and well-being of recipients. Besides, all vaccines are unsafe and some are extremely dangerous. In fact, multiple vaccinations for all US military personnel practically assure damage to their immune systems and severe health problems later in life.

It is also unfortunately an undisputable fact that many senior public-health officials approve dangerous vaccines on unsuspecting recipients and profit handsomely for their efforts by way of incentives, bonuses, lucrative job offers with the corporations and 'brown envelope' payments.

All vaccines are biological weapons that weaken or destroy the human immune system. They usually fail to protect against diseases they are designed to prevent and indeed, often cause them.

"The medical authorities keep lying. Vaccination has been a disaster on the immune system and it actually causes a lot of illnesses. We are actually changing our genetic code through vaccination...100 years from now we will know that the biggest crime against humanity was vaccines." Dr. Guylaine Lanctot, Medical Post, December 1994

"There is no evidence whatsoever of the ability of vaccines to prevent any diseases. To the contrary, there is a great wealth of evidence that they cause serious side effects." Dr. Viera Scheibner, internationally known leading expert on adverse vaccine reactions.

Her analysis concluded that "Nonetheless, immunisation programs proliferate because the profit potential is enormous despite growing numbers of reputable scientific figures citing concerns."

Currently, over 200 new vaccines are being developed for everything from birth control to curing cocaine addiction. Many of them are in clinical trials using human 'guinea pigs', thus knowingly and deliberately, seriously jeopardising their health and safety.

New delivery systems are also being developed that include nasal sprays and genetically engineered fruits containing vaccine viruses. With every person and country in the world a potential consumer of these poisons, health and safety considerations are being suppressed and/or ignored for the sake of profits. Unless somehow this madness is stopped, the harm to our children and society will be catastrophic.

"ALL vaccines are causing immediate and delayed, acute and chronic, waxing and waning, impairments to blood flow, throughout the brain and body. This IS causing us all to become chronically ill, sick, and causing brain damages along a continuum of clinically silent to death. This is causing ischemic 'strokes'. In some respects, this is also 'ageing.' Since the damages are microscopic, we cannot see them as they occur. However, we can now see the neurological aftermath of these damages – within hours and days of vaccination – all vaccinations.

If you place your hand on a hot stove element, you will be burned. If you do not experience pain and you cannot see the burn, then you will not learn that touching hot stove elements is harmful.

All vaccines have been causing 'burns' to body and brain. The brain has no pain receptors. You will not feel the pain. You can, however, see the footprints of these 'burns' immediate and delayed, from each vaccination. The evidence was before our eyes all along. We simply did not appreciate what these 'burns' meant let alone that they were emerging, after each vaccination. The 'burns' are largely to internal organ systems. We can ALL now see the damaging effects of these 'burns' with our own eyes.

As a physician, it is my sworn duty to cause no harm. As a human being, it is my duty to watch over my fellow beings. As an educator, it is my responsibility to teach awareness and understanding. As a scientist, it is my duty to separate cause from coincidence. As a Christian, it is my value to do unto others, as I would have others do unto myself. As a man, it is my responsibility to stand up to power, with truth and understanding, when those that wield power are in error.

My statements are not the words of a zealot. These are the words of integrity, couched with understanding that has the potential to reside in every one of you. Seek, and you shall find. Knock, and the door shall be opened unto you. I have sought. I have knocked. The door has been opened. I have found the truths I was seeking. The answers have not come from my own understandings. The answers are simply self-evident – res ipsa loquitur – the thing speaks for itself.

All vaccinations cause brain damage, disease, chronic illness, aging, and death – res veritas loquitur – the truth speaks for itself. If you do not seek, if you do not knock, if you do not look, if you trust your own understandings, then caveat emptor – buyer beware.

We have answers. We have solutions but we cannot provide solutions or treatments to a medical system and model that denies it is sick.

My training has taught me how to translate anecdotal clinical observations into empirically sound clinical measurements in medicine, neurodevelopment, and human physiology. This is especially so in dealing with functions of the human brain and behavior.

...The truth about all vaccinations causing harm is now available for your understanding. The truth is frightening, disheartening, alarming, and now self-evident.

We have made a global medical mistake based on a lack of knowledge and understanding. We have translated forest fires for 1% of the population into chronic brush fires for the entire population. The brush fires are chronic illness and disease, not least of which are the neuro-developmental disorders." Dr. Andrew Moulden, MD. PhD

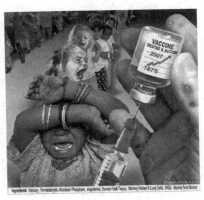

And in early 2011, the US Supreme Court ruled that vaccine producers ie. Big Pharma can no longer be held to account for any damage to anyone's health, whether proven or not to be caused by their hideous, deadly cocktails.

"*The Supreme Court showed the world today that there is nothing supreme or noble about it and that it is as corrupt and cruel as most other governmental institutions. In a 6-3 vote, the high court ruled for Wyeth, saying they could not be sued for vaccine damages. Wyeth is now owned by Pfizer Inc. The U.S. Supreme Court ruled that federal law shields vaccine makers from product-liability lawsuits in state courts seeking damages for a child's injuries or death from a vaccine's side effects. The trial case was a lawsuit by the parents of Hannah Bruesewitz, who suffered seizures as an infant after her third dose of a diphtheria-tetanus-pertussis (DTP) vaccine in 1992. The U.S. Supreme Court ruled on Tuesday the 22nd of February 2011 sustaining the federal law that shielded vaccine manufacturers from desperate parents who seek damages for serious health problems suffered by their children. Today's children are hit with more shots in a day than most of us were hit with in our entire childhood. No doubt certain pharmaceutical madmen fantasize having a permanent tubular hook-up with every child receiving constant (24/7) chemical injection and the Supreme Court would obviously go along with that. Pharmaceutical terrorism and medical madness is alive and well in this world of ours and is part of the backbone of our modern civilization and the legal system has totally bought into it even though they understand nothing about medicine and the consequence of supporting the madness of pharmaceutical companies.*" Mark A Sircus, director of the International Medical Veritas Association, 22nd February 2011

Natural health solutions have been proven time and time again over the years to be far more beneficial to the human body. Why is it then that many governments in conjunction with health authorities are trying their best to make vaccinations mandatory?

The answer is simply that they wish to maximise their profits from us and keep us in a permanent state of unhealthy limbo, which quite frankly, dis-empowers us both physically and mentally. If we can understand that governments and the profit-driven, unethical, genocidal, Elite-owned and run corporations that control them and pull their strings are only interested in two things, then the picture becomes much clearer. The only two things in which the entire corporatocracy are interested are 1) absolute maximisation of profits to the detriment of ALL else and 2) the complete and absolute control of the great majority of mankind by whatever means necessary. Nothing, but nothing else matters at all. Not you, your health or wellbeing, your education, your career, your life, your future, your family, friends or children, absolutely nothing, nil, zero, zilch, nada, zip, nought, nothing at all.

Once you comprehend that one simple fact, everything else falls into place. It is a little similar to completing the outside, straight edges of a jigsaw puzzle in that one then has a 'framework' to operate within and reference points from which one can proceed to gain an even greater understanding of how the world really works by slowly and methodically inserting all the pieces into their correct places.

Bird flu and swine flu 'pandemics'

Bird flu and swine flu are beyond doubt the latest bio-weapons to be used against the human race. In their desperate quest for population reduction, the Elite-run World Health (Homicide?) Organisation (WHO) has deliberately engineered the latest pandemic scares of bird flu and swine flu.

"The bird and mammalian species took hold on the earth approximately 65 million years ago, ie. the same time as the dinosaurs went extinct. So did the flu and other viruses of all the surviving species. Since then, all those viruses have been mating and mutating among themselves without the sky caving in due to any infection. Therefore, any talk of a bird or swine flu pandemic with the probability to kill millions of people is either a purposeful or hallucinogenic nonsense to make profit on the backs of the innocent following." Shiv Chopra, microbiologist, vaccine expert

The swine flu virus was created in a laboratory to generate mass-panic with the specific intention of forcing everyone to be vaccinated. This 'natural' swine flu virus apparently contains genes from humans, birds and pigs from several continents. Ask yourself if true, how can this be? It is impossible. Therefore, if the medical mafia concoct and release a virus and then implement a clearly long-planned mass-vaccination programme, there can be only one sensible conclusion; swine flu is not the biggest danger, it is the *vaccine*.

The scale and speed of the planned vaccination programme is insane given that the overwhelming majority of those who have contracted the virus have had very mild symptoms. Dr Peter Holden of the Elite-controlled British Medical Association said that although swine flu was *not causing serious illness* they were eager to start a mass vaccination campaign, beginning with 'priority groups'. Pardon me? This is not about public health concerns and never was intended to be.

Those actually administering the vaccinations have no idea what is in them or their potential effects. They are just thinking what they are told to think and doing and saying what they are told to do and say. Only those at the core of the conspiracy, and those who bother to research it or read books like this one, know what the real game is.

The WHO absolutely refused to release the minutes of a key meeting of an advisory vaccine group attended by senior executives from Baxter, Novartis and Sanofi that recommended compulsory vaccinations in the USA, Europe and other countries against the artificial H1N1 'swine flu' virus in autumn 2009.

In an email a WHO spokesperson claimed there were no minutes of the meeting that took place on 7th July 2009 in which guidelines on the need for worldwide vaccinations that the WHO adopted were formulated and in which Baxter and other Big Pharma executives participated. Under International Health Regulations, WHO guidelines have a binding character on all of the WHO's 194 signatory countries in the event of a pandemic emergency of the kind that was anticipated in autumn 2009, when the second, more lethal wave of the H1N1 virus which was bio-engineered to resemble the Spanish flu virus, was released.

The WHO actually has the authority to force everyone in those 194 countries to take a vaccine at gunpoint, impose quarantines and restrict travel. Yes you did read that correctly, 'at gunpoint'!

There is verifiable, clear and unambiguous documentary proof that the WHO supplied the live bird flu virus to Baxter's subsidiary in Austria, which was used by Baxter to manufacture 72 kilos of vaccine material in February 2009. Baxter subsequently sent this material out to 16 labs in four countries under a false label designating the contaminated product as vaccine material, so very nearly triggering a global pandemic.

Because Baxter must adhere to strict bio-safety regulations when handling a dangerous virus such as the bird flu virus, the production and distribution of so much pandemic material cannot have been an accident but must have been done by Baxter with criminal intent.

Last year at least 81 people were killed by Baxter International's contaminated blood-thinning product, heparin, which was made in China from, among other things, pig intestines. The contaminated heparin also seriously injured hundreds of people and it was revealed that the factory of Baxter's Chinese supplier had never been inspected by either American or Chinese public 'protection' agencies.

More than 50 dialysis patients died in 2001 because of faults with Baxter International equipment and in 2009 Baxter Healthcare Corporation, a subsidiary of Baxter International, reached an out-of-court settlement of two million dollars with the State of Kentucky. Baxter had been caught inflating the cost of intravenous drugs sold to Kentucky Medicaid by as much as 1,300%.

It is increasingly clear that the WHO and Baxter are just two branches of a much bigger criminal organisation that is moving forward in a synchronised and coordinated way to fulfil the Elite agenda of global population reduction in the coming months and years while putting in place a global government of which the WHO will be an arm.

The WHO, which is a UN agency, appears to play a key role in coordinating the activities of labs, vaccine companies and governments to achieve the goal of population reduction and political and economic take-over of North America and Europe.

Firstly, the WHO gives funds, support and cover to labs such as the CDC to bio-prospect for pathogens, bioengineer them to make them more deadly and also patent them.

Secondly, the WHO gives those same deadly bioengineered pathogens to companies such as Baxter in Austria, so that Baxter could use those viruses to deliberately and systematically contaminate vaccine material. If the contamination of the 72 kilos had not been detected in time by a lab technician in the Czech Republic, millions of people would have caught the 'bird flu' from the injections.

Thirdly, in the event of a pandemic, the WHO orders a compulsory vaccine for all 194 countries, following 'recommendations' by an advisory vaccine group on which executives of Baxter also sit. And fourthly, the WHO awards Baxter, Novartis, Sanofi and other companies lucrative contracts to supply those vaccines.

Furthermore, the WHO acquires new global authority on an unseen scale in the event of a pandemic. Under special pandemic plans enacted around the world including the USA, in 2005, national governments are to be dissolved in the event of a pandemic emergency and replaced by special crisis committees, which take charge of the health and security infrastructure of a country, and which are answerable to the WHO and the EU in Europe and to the WHO and UN in North America.

If the Model Emergency Health Powers Act is implemented on the instructions of the WHO, it will be a criminal offence to refuse the vaccine and police will be allowed to use deadly force against these 'criminal' suspects. Through their control of these special pandemic crisis committees with the power to enact legislation to be set up most countries, the WHO, UN and EU become the de facto government of a large part of the world – a scenario which has been planned for decades as part of the march towards One World Government, the so-called 'New World Order'.

Mass murder and death will also bring economic collapse and disruption, starvation and wars and these events in themselves will lead to a further population reduction.

In summary, the WHO helps create, distribute and then release the deadly pandemic virus and this pandemic virus allows the WHO to assume control of governments in North America and Europe and also order forced vaccination on populations by the very same companies that have distributed and released the deadly viruses in the first place and all under the pretext of protecting populations from a pandemic that they have created in the first place.

The corporate mainstream media owned by the same Elite group which funds the WHO is systematically concealing from the general public the nature of the real danger of these H1N1 vaccinations by withholding from them key information concerning the interrelated activities of this group of organisations for their mutual profit. As a result, most people still believe that the H1N1 virus is a natural swine flu when even the WHO has officially dropped the term "swine" in tacit acknowledgement of its artificial origins.

Most people still believe that the vaccine companies can provide a cure when the vaccine companies are preparing a lethal series of shots containing live attenuated virus, toxic metals and other poisons. The two-dose H1N1 shots are designed to disable the immune system and then load that system with a live virus in a process that mirrors the one described in two of the WHO's 1972 memoranda where the technical means for turning vaccines into killers is outlined.

The Strecker Memorandum also reveals that the WHO has been actively searching for ways to weaken the immune system. How much more evidence does one need than this to prove the 'conspiracy case' against these people? The best protection against the H1N1 virus that has now been released and that will inevitably become more lethal as it mutates is colloidal silver and also vitamins to strengthen the immune system, face masks and other such measures.

However, none of the governments in North America or Europe have stocked up on colloidal silver or announced sensible health measures to contain the coming lethal wave. Instead, there are growing signs, that they will use the panic to terrify people into taking the toxic vaccines which are sure to cause injury or damage due to the presence of heavy metals alone. This mass-vaccination will moreover, allow ever more lethal strains to emerge and also provide a cover for a release of further strains of bird flu virus or other pathogens.

An investigation into this international corporate crime syndicate needs to be conducted in every country because it has its tentacles in every country. There are also reports that Barack Obama has direct financial links with Baxter that need to be investigated by law enforcement. In addition, there is evidence the Austrian Health Minister and other officials have been assisting Baxter in the covering of its tracks.

Also, there is clear evidence that elements of the Austrian media were involved in actively spreading lies and misinformation to lull people into a false sense of security concerning Baxter's manufacture and distribution of pandemic material in Austria in February 2009.

My advice would be not to hold our collective breath, whilst we are waiting for the appropriate authorities to take some much-needed action.

HIV / Aids

Thirty years ago, at the beginning of the 1980s, a small group of homosexual men in San Francisco began dying of a strange, never-seen-before disease.

However, it turns out that there was nothing too mysterious about these deaths, either then or now. The combination of three cultural revolutions, drug, sexual and gay, took a heavy toll on these, its most ardent practitioners. They took part in excessive, anonymous, soulless sex on an industrial scale, copiously administered antibiotics, thinking that this would keep them healthy (useless against viruses but deadly effective against gut-friendly bacteria which are vital to correct immune system function) and imbibed recreational drugs with no consideration of long term effects. This excessive drug use combined with repeated bouts of STDs and parasites and foreign antigens from thousands of other men residing in their bloodstreams took a deadly toll on their bodies. Their immune systems were literally destroyed.

When Ronald Reagan took Presidential office in 1981, he had a mandate to downsize government and the Centres for Disease Control and Prevention (CDC) was an obvious target. The 'war on Cancer' declared by Nixon in 1971, had little to show for all the money spent. The CDC had been acutely embarrassed in 1976 when it attempted to make believe that five soldiers with a mild dose of flu were a potential national 'swine flu' epidemic. A subplot of this charade was their attempt to seize on the completely coincidental outbreak of pneumonia among some visitors to an American Legion convention in Philadelphia. The CDC used this as an excuse to rush out a vaccine that killed dozens of people, which is dozens more than did the flu itself. So-called 'Legionnaire's Disease' as it transpired, turned out to be caused by a known microorganism commonly found in building air conditioners and had absolutely zero to do with swine flu. Thousands of people get infected with it every year, by the way.

So it was very fortunate for them that in 1981, as potential budget cuts were mooted and imminent that the CDC received a report about five young homosexuals dying of immune deficiency disorders. If a 'new' deadly disease could be discovered and promulgated, it could give the CDC a whole new lease of life and raison d'être. The more dangerous and terrifying the better and ideally something a little more deadly than the flu this time would fit the bill nicely.

'Gay Related Immune Deficiency' (GRID), as an initial name for the new disease, was soon discarded. Besides being too 'politically incorrect', it did not sound too threatening to the general (straight) population. So it was eventually replaced with 'Acquired Immune Deficiency Syndrome' (AIDS). The French scientist Luc Montagnier later 'discovered' the Human Immunodeficiency Virus (HIV) and failed American cancer researcher Robert Gallo co-discovered it (if you can call finding it a year later co-discovering. Gallo was later investigated for misconduct, but cleared).

So now today, we have AIDS as the disease and HIV the 'undisputable' cause of it. A press conference by the CDC subsequently launched the idea to the general public, the CDC was saved and a new multi-billion dollar profit-centre for the medical cartel was created.

In the years since the CDC announcement, every scientist or doctor who has tried to question the official story, rather than being applauded for practicing good investigative and stringent science, has instead been attacked and dismissed. That same old MO again – never fails! But now with 30 years of history it is becoming more and more obvious that certain facts do not stand up to scrutiny with the official story.

Filmmaker Brent Leung has recently made a stunning documentary revealing the full story behind the Aids / HIV scam, 'The House of Numbers'. This film is absolutely savaged by the controlled mainstream media film critics (why would it not be?) with one review in particular, likening Leung to someone who would question gravity. In my view and for what it is worth, had the media been complimentary and demanding answers from the medical establishment, then I for one, would have seriously questioned whether or not the film was anti-AIDS or subtle dis-information. If there is one thing that one can virtually guarantee, that is that when the mainstream sharks attack (or indeed defend) anything, there *must* be an ulterior motive for it and you can usually bet your mortgage that the exact opposite of their argument will prove to be truth, upon further research.

In the film, Leung totally debunks HIV testing. But it transpires that HIV testing is almost irrelevant anyway as the WHO has provided a definition for AIDS which lists simple symptoms to use for diagnosing AIDS *without testing*...

"The WHO AIDS surveillance case definition was developed in October 1985 at a conference of public health officials including representatives of the Control CDC and WHO in Bangui, Central African Republic... For this reason, it became to be known as the Bangui definition for AIDS. It was developed to provide a definition of AIDS for use in countries where testing for HIV antibodies was not available." Wikipedia

It stated the following:

Exclusion criteria

Pronounced malnutrition
Cancer
Immunosuppressive treatment

nclusion criteria with the corresponding score	Score
mportant signs	
Weight loss exceeding 10% of body weight	4
Protracted asthenia	4
Very frequent signs	
Continuous or repeated attacks of fever for more than a month	3
Diarrhoea lasting for more than a month	3
Other signs	
Cough	2
Pneumopathy	2
Oropharyngeal candidiasis	4
Chronic or relapsing cutaneous herpes	4
Generalised pruritic dermatosis	4
Herpes Zoster (relapsing)	4
Generalized adenopathy	2
Neurological signs	2
Generalised Kaposi's sarcoma	12

The diagnosis of AIDS is established when the score is 12 or more.

Although it was moderated nine years later with the instruction that testing should really be undertaken, it was instrumental in kick-starting the supposed AIDS epidemic in Africa. How convenient it is though, to create a disease from nothing in this fashion by artificially constructing a score-based system from arbitrary, unconnected symptoms.

But even with testing, it is quite easy to say that there is more HIV in one place than another, as the tests are interpreted differently in different countries. At one point in the film Leung straddles the US / Canadian border and comments, 'No other disease behaves differently when you cross a border.'

He also visits South Africa to examine the 'epidemic' for himself. It is difficult to say what is more shocking about Leung's visit to a poor indigenous village, the ignorance and superstition that people have regarding AIDS or the flies that pass directly from the open sewers to their food plates. Could it possibly be the latter that is the cause of any of the symptoms from the above symptoms table?

Leung interviews several scientists and doctors in the film and they essentially fall into two distinct groups. Those sceptical about the AIDS story include, among others, Kary Mullis, who shared a 1993 Nobel Prize in chemistry, Joseph Sonnabend, a physician who has been involved with AIDS research and treatment since the very beginning and James Chin, an epidemiologist at WHO for five years, whose characterisation of that agency's statistics on the AIDS epidemic in Africa gives the movie its name. And then there is also Peter Duesberg, who was a cancer researcher until he was recently rebuked and subsequently ostracised for questioning the official line on HIV.

On the other side of the debate are, among others, Robert Gallo, Luc Montagnier and Dr. Anthony Fauci. This group, speaking in defence of the AIDS syndrome comprise a curious mixture of the detached and mildly irritated as they relate their weak arguments asserting that the virus exists, that HIV causes AIDS, everyone is at risk and anyone simply not agreeing with their viewpoint is an idiot.

However, when questioned more closely and intensively, they concede there are gaps in the knowledge of how HIV works, but contradict each other and in one instance, the subject actually contradicts *himself*. None of them are able to define AIDS in a simple and consistent phrase, are able to explain satisfactorily or convincingly how HIV works or are willing to address the problem of so many deaths attributed to AIDS that in fact were caused by the incredibly toxic drugs administered to cure it.

Leung himself avoids taking sides, rather playing the annoying devil's advocate, persistently asking probing questions. As the film progresses however, it becomes obvious that the answers are totally inadequate and would not satisfy anyone with anything approaching a semi-functioning brain.

The film also relates the story of a girl by the name of Lindsey Nagel. She was originally a Romanian orphan adopted by Steve and Cheryl Nagel, a couple from Minnesota. Having been tested for HIV in Romania which proved negative, she was then tested again upon arriving in America and this time the test was positive. This is hardly surprising once it is understood that the tests can vary so much from country to country.

Of course, in the beginning, the Nagels followed their paediatrician's recommendations to treat her with anti-retroviral drugs, which at the time meant high dosage AZT (the most common anti-AIDS drug). For months the Nagels watched helplessly as their healthy daughter deteriorated, getting sicker and sicker. Among other things, her growth became stunted. Of course all symptoms were ascribed to her supposed HIV infection and not to the drugs.

After nearly two years of this, the Nagels became aware of Peter Duesberg's dissenting view by a relative who read an article about him. They became intrigued and wrote to Duesberg, who replied immediately, telling them to take Lindsey off the antiretroviral drugs or they would kill her. They did so and for that reason alone, Lindsey is still with us today.

The paediatrician concerned, in 2005 received an award for her leadership in treating HIV patients and in a subsequent interview about the award, had this to say...

"We started on AZT (Retrovir) for a child who was adopted and the parents said it was a poison and they called Peter Duesberg, the man who wrote a book claiming that AIDS isn't caused by HIV and they pulled the child from my care."

However, others were not so fortunate...

"There was nothing you could do years ago. Most children back then did not live past seven to twelve years old. And it was hard; these were children that you got attached to. It was really hard. All we could do was provide some supportive care and treat their opportunistic infections. We had many deaths, ten to twelve in 1994."

The doctor goes on to say that children stand a better chance of survival now, implying that the treatment has improved, but does not mention the fact that this is only because the dosage of retroviral drugs has been **greatly lowered**. However, these drugs are still nonspecific, toxic and eventually still do kill most of those who take them.

Of course, Lindsey Nagel is not the only one who benefitted from ending her intake of AZT, this is also happening in Africa too.

"Recently CNN dispatched a reporter to the West African country of Gambia to do a story on Gambian President Yahya Jammeh, who announced in January that he has discovered a cure for AIDS. President Jammeh has come up with a recipe consisting of seven herbs and spices that is administered to an HIV-positive patient once a day...

...Mr. Sow, according to his own testimony, has been HIV-positive since 1996 and had been taking antiretrovirals for the past four years until he volunteered to try President Yahya Jammeh's new treatment. After only four weeks, he gained 30 pounds and felt like a new person. He feels cured, and has no more 'HIV symptoms.' ...Mr. Koinange is sceptical, though, not so much about the witness's honesty (in fact, he interviewed a lot of patients who made similar statements), but of the scientific basis of the treatment, as the government refuses to provide any medical records that might back the patients' claims.

But the patient, if one will listen carefully, may have provided a full explanation of the efficacy of the dictator's dream-potion. He has been HIV-positive since 1996. What a strange virus this is, that threatened to ravage North America so many years ago, as once a healthy person caught it (which could happen quite easily through normal sexual contact, we were told), the incurable and unstoppable disease AIDS always set in, inevitably killing the patient. Today in North America, the only people who are killed by AIDS are the same people who have always been killed by it, i.e., severe drug abusers and/or homosexual men engaging in a certain sexual practice (usually both). So the AIDS 'disease' has moved on to a new market, Africa, where millions of people are supposedly infected with the HIV virus and are going to start dying any day now. Yet, Ousman Sow had the virus from 1996 until 2003, seven years, before he started taking the antiretrovirals to 'save' his life. It was then, I would be willing to bet, that he started really experiencing his 'HIV symptoms.' Within only four weeks of ceasing the antiretrovirals, he regained lost weight and felt well again.

The cure that our witch doctor has inadvertently found may be nothing more than getting 'HIV positive' patients off their antiretrovirals." James Foye

The treatment for HIV has always been non-specific, DNA destroying drugs. In a supreme irony, the prophecy of a destructive epidemic became on a small scale, self-fulfilling, as tens of thousands died from the very drugs that were supposed to cure them. Of course, they 'officially' died from the disease itself and not the drugs themselves. All of the defenders of the HIV/AIDS orthodoxy are paid, directly or indirectly by government (i.e., they work for the government, or a university that is subsidised by government or a pharmaceutical company whose AIDS drug business depends on people believing what the government says about AIDS and whose drugs are largely paid for by the government). Dissenters like Peter Duesberg, are shut out and disenfranchised, attacked or both.

"HIV does NOT cause AIDS. HIV does not cause anything. This is a staggering statement given the hype and acceptance by the scientific establishment and through them, the public that the HIV virus is the only cause of AIDS. HIV is a weak virus and does not dismantle the immune system. Nor is AIDS passed on sexually. There are two main types of virus. Using the airplane analogy, you could call one of these virus strains a 'pilot' virus. It can change the nature of a cell and steer it into disease. This usually happens very quickly after the virus takes hold. Then there is the 'passenger' virus which lives off the cell, goes along for the ride, but never affects the cell to the extent that it causes disease. HIV is a passenger virus!

So how on earth did it become the big bogeyman virus of the world? The person who announced that HIV caused AIDS was an American, Doctor Robert Gallo. He has since been accused of professional misconduct, his test has been exposed as fraudulent and two of his laboratory executives have been convicted of criminal offences. Tens of millions of people are tested for HIV antibodies every year and Dr Gallo, who patented his 'test', gets a royalty for every single one. Luc Montagnier, Gallo's partner in the HIV-causes-AIDS theory, has since admitted in 1989: 'HIV is not capable of causing the destruction of the immune system which is seen in people with AIDS'. Nearly 500 scientists across the world agree with him. So does Dr Robert E Wilner, author of the book 'The Deadly Deception. The Proof That Sex and HIV Absolutely Do Not Cause AIDS'

Dr Wilner even injected himself with the HIV virus on a television chat show in Spain to support his claims. Other doctors and authors come to the same conclusions, among them Peter Duesberg PhD and John Yiamouyiannis PhD, in their book, 'AIDS: The Good News Is That HIV Doesn't Cause It. The Bad News Is 'Recreational Drugs' and Medical Treatments Like AZT Do'. That's a long title, but it sums up the situation. People are dying of AIDS because of the treatments used to 'treat' AIDS! It works like this. Now it is accepted by the establishment and the people that HIV causes AIDS, the system has built this myth into its whole diagnosis and 'treatment'. You go to the doctor and you are told your HIV test was positive (positive only for the HIV antibodies, by the way, they don't actually test for the virus itself). Because of the propaganda, many people already begin to die emotionally and mentally when they are told they are HIV positive. They have been conditioned to believe that death is inevitable.

The fear of death leads them to accept and often demand, the hyped-up 'treatments' which are supposed to stop AIDS occurring. (They don't.) The most famous is AZT, produced by the Wellcome organisation, owned, wait for it, by the Rockefellers, one of the key manipulating families in the New World Order.

AZT was developed as an anti-cancer drug to be used in chemotherapy, but it was found to be too toxic even for that! AZT's effect in the 'treatment' of cancer was to kill cells - simple as that - not just to kill cancer cells, but to kill cells, cancerous and healthy. The question and this is accepted even by the medical establishment, was: would AZT kill the cancer cells before it had killed so many healthy cells that it killed the body? This is the drug used to 'treat' HIV. What is its effect?

It destroys the immune system, so CAUSING AIDS. People are dying from the treatment, not the HIV. AIDS is simply the breakdown of the immune system, for which there are endless causes, none of them passed on through sex. That's another con which has made a fortune for condom manufacturers and created enormous fear around the expression of our sexuality and the release and expansion of our creative force.

What has happened since the Great AIDS Con is that now anyone who dies from a diminished immune system is said to have died of the all-encompassing term, AIDS. It is even built into the diagnosis. If you are HIV positive and you die of tuberculosis, pneumonia, or 25 other unrelated diseases now connected by the con men to 'AIDS', you are diagnosed as dying of AIDS. If you are not HIV positive and you die of one of those diseases you are diagnosed as dying of that disease, not AIDS. This manipulates the figures every day to indicate that only HIV positives die of AIDS. This is a lie.

Many people who die from AIDS are not HIV positive and the reason that the figures for AIDS deaths have not soared as predicted is that the overwhelming majority of people diagnosed HIV positive have never developed AIDS. Why? Because HIV has nothing whatsoever to do with AIDS!

Anything that breaks down the immune system causes AIDS and that includes so-called recreational drugs. The vast majority of AIDS deaths in the United States involve homosexuals and this perpetuates the myth that it has something to do with sex. But homosexuals in the US are among the biggest users of drugs which genuine doctors have linked to AIDS. Prostitutes who take drugs often get AIDS; prostitutes who do not take drugs invariably do not get AIDS. The rise in the AIDS figures in the United States corresponds perfectly with the increase in the use of drugs - most of which are made available to people on the streets by elements within the US Government, including Bill Clinton and George Bush. In Africa, the breakdown of the immune system, now known as AIDS, is caused by ill health - lack of good food, clean water and the general effects of poverty. Haemophiliacs do not die from HIV-infected blood; they die, as they did before the AIDS scam, from a quirk in their own immune system. Their immune system locks into foreign proteins in the infused blood and on rare occasions it can become confused during this process and attack itself. Their immune system, in effect, commits suicide. HIV is irrelevant to that. Yet how many people today who have been diagnosed HIV positive are having their lives blighted by the fear that the symptoms of AIDS will start any moment?

AZT is the killer. There is not a single case of AZT reversing the symptoms of AIDS. How can it? It's causing them, for goodness sake. The AIDS industry is now worth billions of pounds a year and makes an unimaginable fortune for the drug industry controlled by the Rockefellers and the rest of the Global Elite." David Icke, geo-political researcher, 2007

Interesting is it not, that the AIDS industry refers to those who try to expose the truth as being 'deniers' which has shades of the other great 'denial', that of the holocaust industry? So in effect they are psychologically likening doctors who try to tell the world what is really happening, with Nazis.

"I reported that in early 1987 I had received a telephone call from a researcher for a TV company who had told me that his company (Thames TV) was planning a documentary about AIDS. 'What do you think about AIDS?' he asked me. I told him that I thought that the threat had been exaggerated by some doctors, a lot of politicians and most journalists. The researcher was silent for a moment or two. I could tell by the silence that he was disappointed. It wasn't quite what he'd hoped to hear.
We're planning a major documentary,' he said. `We want to cover all the angles. Haven't you got anything new to say about AIDS?' 'I don't think AIDS is a plague that threatens mankind,' I insisted. I then pointed out that I believed that the evidence about AIDS had been distorted and the facts exaggerated. 'We really wanted you to come on to the programme and talk about some of the problems likely to be caused by the disease,' persisted the researcher. 'I'm happy to come on to the programme and say that I think that the dangers posed by the disease have been exaggerated,' I told the researcher.

The researcher sighed. 'Quite a few doctors have said that to me,' he said sadly. 'But it really isn't the sort of angle we're looking for.' Very gently I put down the telephone. I didn't expect to hear from the researcher again and I didn't. His company produced a networked television programme about AIDS that appeared on our screens a short time after that conversation. And I suspect that most of those who viewed it went to bed believing that AIDS is the greatest threat to mankind since the Black Death. That was by no means an isolated incident. The facts about AIDS were carefully selected to satisfy the public image of the disease - and to satisfy those with vested interests to protect."
Dr. Vernon Coleman, former British 'TV Doctor', dropped from the networks because of his non-compliant views

And whilst we still argue and debate the issues, people are literally dying to know the truth.

Cancer
Everyone should know that the 'war on cancer' is largely a fraud." Linus Pauling, Nobel Laureate

"I keep telling people to stop giving money to 'cancer research' because no one is frigging looking for a cure. We have several and they have been carefully hidden away from public view...this is a multi-billion dollar per year industry and a 'cure' would put a lot of people out of work." Geraldine Phillips, cancer research worker, 2011

"The chief, if not the sole, cause of the monstrous increase in cancer has been vaccination" Dr. Robert Bell, former Vice President, International Society for Cancer Research

Dr. James Watson won a Nobel Prize along with Dr. Francis Crick for discovering and describing the double helix shape of DNA at Cambridge University in the early 1950s and during the early 1970s he served two years on the US National Cancer Advisory Board. In 1975, he was asked his thoughts about the American National Cancer Programme. He declared, "It's a bunch of shit." Blunt and crude though his assessment may be, it also happens to be true.

Cancer, that 'life-threatening disease' and ruthless killer of countless millions of mothers, fathers, sons and daughters in the last 100 years or more, is relatively easy to cure and even easier to prevent.

I am acutely aware of the emotive subject that cancer has become and do not make this glib-sounding statement lightly, but with due deference to the millions who have lost loved ones and / or suffered terribly and had their own lives cruelly cut short for what amounts to no reason at all, unless of course you consider the vast, unimaginable profits made by the purveyors of this great criminal racket, for criminal racket is exactly what it is.

In 1953, a United States Senate investigation reported in its initial findings that there was the strong suspicion of an ongoing conspiracy to suppress and destroy effective cancer treatments. The Senator in charge of the investigation died suddenly in unexplained circumstances, the usual MO (modus operandus or operating method) in these cases, which was obviously very convenient for those with much to lose from his revelations. As a result of his death, the investigation was subsequently suddenly disbanded without further ado and was never resumed. Unsurprisingly, the good Senator was neither the first nor the last of literally hundreds if not thousands of strange, unexplained deaths involving people in positions to threaten the interests of those running the Elite controlled cancer programmes and indeed the Elite controlled anything else. Ethical people who attempt to disrupt the flow of profits into the Elite's coffers have to be silenced one way or another, after all.

But this is only the small tip of a very large and extremely dangerous iceberg. In 1964 the FDA spent millions of dollars to suppress and bury an 'alternative' cancer treatment which had cured hundreds, if not thousands of cancer patients according to well-documented sources. It became apparent and was later disclosed that in the subsequent court proceedings, the FDA had falsified the testimony of witnesses, to suit its own ends. The FDA lost the court case because the jury found the defendants innocent and recommended that the substance be evaluated, objectively. In fact it never was evaluated but instead all the evidence was totally suppressed and then conveniently 'lost'.

For many years (and still to this day), the American Medical Association (AMA) and the American Cancer Society (ACS) co-ordinated their own 'blacklists' of cancer researchers who were regarded as threats to their cancer monopoly and who were to be singled-out for smear campaigns and ostracised by the mainstream. One investigative reporter declared the AMA and ACS to be *"a network of vigilantes prepared to pounce on anyone who promotes a cancer therapy that runs against their substantial prejudices and profits."* The ACS, believe it or not actually makes political donations! A 'charitable organisation' that makes political donations? What does this tell us about them and the system within which they operate?

In the late 1950s, it was learned that Dr. Henry Welch, head of the FDA's Division of Antibiotics, had secretly received $287,000 (a colossal sum in those days) from the drug companies he was supposed to regulate. In 1975, an independent government evaluation of the FDA still found massive 'conflicts of interest' among the agency's top personnel.

And In 1977, an investigative team from the prominent newspaper 'Newsday' found serious 'conflicts of interest' at the National Cancer Institute (NCI) and in 1986, an organized cover-up of an effective alternative cancer therapy, orchestrated by NCI officials, was revealed during Congressional hearings. The list goes on and on and strongly suggest to the reader that they should perform their own Internet research on this topic and not simply take my word for it.

The cancer 'industry' now has a more than 60-year history of vast corruption, incompetence and organised terror against its many detractors and a shameful track record of suppression of cancer therapies which are actually beneficial. Millions, if not billions of people have suffered terrible torture and death because those in charge took bribes, had closed minds to the innovative, or simply were afraid to do what was obviously and ethically correct. Instead, the corporate and individual greed and the desire of the few to profit from the many, as always takes precedence.

The doctor's union (AMA), the cancer bureaucracy (NCI), the public relations fat-cats (ACS) and the cancer cops (FDA) are conspiring to suppress a cure for cancer... It would be easy for any Congressional committee, major newspaper, television network or national magazine to confirm and extend the evidence presented here in order to initiate radical reform of the critical cancer areas--the hospitals, the research centres, the government agencies, and especially state and local legislation regarding cancer treatment.

But that will not happen without a struggle. Neither Congress nor the media desire to lift the manhole cover on this sewer of corruption and needless torture. Only organized, determined citizen opposition to the existing cancer treatment system has any hope of bringing about the long-needed changes. I expect the struggle to be a long, difficult one against tough, murderous opposition. The odds against success are heavy. The vested interests are very powerful... ". Barry Lynes, 'The Healing of Cancer'

There is a veritable mountain of overwhelming evidence and examples which support the theory of collusion between activities of Western governments, especially the United States, along with other prominent members of the 'medical Elite' to prevent an effective cancer treatment being promulgated.

Surgery is a massive shock to the system, uses carcinogenic anaesthesia and increases the risk of cancer in the scar tissue. It has value only where the threat to life processes is immediate, as in digestive obstruction etc. The routine removal of every malignant or sometimes even benign lump, surrounded, by the body with a defensive shield, can be virtually a death sentence, especially in the elderly.

Chemotherapy involves the use of extremely toxic petrochemical drugs in the hope, which is often never realised, of killing the disease before killing the patient. The drugs are designed to kill all fast growing cells, cancerous or not and all cells caught in the act of division are systematically poisoned. The effects include hair loss, violent nausea, vomiting, diarrhoea, cramps, impotence, sterility, extreme pain, fatigue, immune system destruction, cancer and death. According to the government's own figures, around 2 percent of chemotherapy recipients are still alive after 5 years. The term 'alive' is used here in its literal sense, ie. not yet clinically dead. One of chemotherapy's less well-known side-effects is pneumonia. Many cancer patients die of this after undergoing chemo treatment and their cause of deaths are not recorded as 'cancer'.

"Toxic chemotherapy is a hoax. The doctors who use it are guilty of premeditated murder. I cannot understand why women take chemotherapy and suffer so terribly for no purpose." Oncologist, Channel 4 TV, 2010

Radiotherapy likewise is equally, if not more deadly. One person who chose to have treatment with the radiation machine turned-off altogether was the Grand National winning jockey Bob Champion. Convinced by the early detectors, in spite of feeling well, that he was *"... likely to die of cancer of the lymph gland"* he decided that he did not relish the thought of a treatment that *"... could have ruined his lungs"* let alone the rest of him and opted for drugs. He eventually survived the treatment and the 'lymphoma'. His doctor, 'cancer specialist', Ann Barrett, declared *"He is the only patient in my experience who has come through this disease and achieved such a high degree of physical fitness afterwards. His recovery is even more remarkable when you consider that he refused to have the conventional treatment."*! Or not.

The plight of the ever-increasing number of parents of child cancer victims facing 'radiotherapy' was well illustrated in October 1993 *"... after learning of the appalling side-effects of radiotherapy... her anxious mother has opted to take her to America for private treatment... 'I've been told the radiotherapy will cause brain damage knocking forty points off her I.Q... Her growth would be stunted... she would need hormones to help her growth and sexual development. It is also likely she would be sterile'."* Further delights include bone and nerve damage, leading to amputation of limbs, severe burns and of course, death, at a future time, from cancer and leukaemia due to the highly carcinogenic, immune-suppressive effects of the huge doses of radiation.

"Chemotherapy and radiotherapy will make the ancient method of drilling holes in a patient's head, to permit the escape of demons; look relatively advanced... the use of cobalt... effectively closes the door on cure."

The 90/95% death rate within a five year period has not stopped the cancer industry from carrying out the same procedures, day in, day out, for decades with the same deadly, inevitable results. Temporarily suppressing, with the scalpel, drug or radiation, the symptoms of cancer does nothing for the victim's chances of survival.

Adding gross insult to injury, the treatment involves massive doses of carcinogens and super-poisons. The patient is subject to a regime diametrically opposed to that which is needed for survival. Cancer is an acceptable form of suicide for those who have lost the desire to live, this loss being a major factor in the development of the disease in the first place. The great tragedy and scandal is in cases where the victim has a strong determination to live and fight but is then destroyed by the assault from the lethal, useless treatment and not by the cancer.

So why are the vast majority of doctors against alternative cancer treatments and why would they actively encourage you to undergo known-to-be-dangerous treatments such as chemotherapy, radiotherapy and surgery instead of trying natural cures?

Unfortunately, doctors are against these treatments because from the first day of Elite-controlled medical school, they are brainwashed into believing that disease can only be effectively treated by those methods proscribed by Big Pharma. They most certainly will have been led to believe that there are no cures for cancer, when in reality there are several, none of which will enhance the profits of Big Pharma or sustain the payments on a senior hospital consultant's Bentley convertible. Additionally they operate under the severely inhibiting paradox that food is good enough to keep you alive but not sufficiently good to keep you healthy or heal you when you are ill.

Most cancer drugs cost in the region of £25,000 per annum *per patient*. In the US this payable either by the individual or by their health insurer (assuming they are adequately insured) whereas in the UK this is paid by the NHS (National Health Service). However, whichever way, the fact is that this is the amount paid into the coffers of Big Pharma, per person, per annum and when you consider the number of people worldwide who suffer from and die from cancer each year, I am sure you can do the maths. What incentive is there for any organisation whose first responsibility is always to maintain a profit for its shareholders and owners, to discover a cure? I submit that there is none at all and this is the reason for the utter failure (despite the eloquent hype) of Big Pharma in their self-styled 'war on cancer'.

We are even deceived by the so-called professionals in such seemingly beneficial activities as 'cancer screening programmes'. For example, mammograms, heavily promoted as being an integral part of the early detection of breast cancer, provably achieve nothing other than to irradiate the breast and in many cases actually *cause* the cancer it is supposed to be detecting.

Most doctors believe not only that what they were taught in medical school must be true, but they also believe that what they were **not** taught cannot be important and as a result of this are unable to comprehend anything that falls outside of their area of knowledge. Most doctors are still thinking 'inside the box' when it comes to cancer and doctors who do think for themselves instead of regarding their learning as gospel and treat the actual cause of disease rather than the symptoms are regarded as 'quacks' and are subjected to huge pressure, ridicule and threats to conform. One of the FDA's modus operandi is to raid the offices of alternative thinkers and practitioners, destroying their medical records, and putting them in jail.

Additionally, some doctors are afraid of expensive, time consuming lawsuits and their insurer could well refuse to pay out if they use alternative treatments of any kind. Their medical boards may fine them and even revoke their licence to practice or strike them from the medical register, effectively disbarring them from medical practice for ever. Peer pressure is a huge issue too. After all, doctors are only human and their colleagues will not be slow to publicly ridicule them if they use alternative treatments or are seen to be using or endorsing 'non-conventional' medicine.

"Doctors will continue to fail with cancer until they buck the training and accept that a patient is not some collection of malfunctioning cells but a human out of homeostasis. We have cultures alive today who don't get cancer. No stress, no speed cameras, no mobile phones, no Iraq War. Don't get me wrong, I truly believe 21st century civilisation has much to commend it but there are downsides. We're a toxic society and that includes the medicines. If cancer is striking 1 in 3 of us, that means something is going fundamentally wrong and we're either going to be honest about it or continue canoeing down that long river in Egypt called De-Nial, splurfing down the rat-burgers until the meat-wagon comes to collect us." Philip Day, health researcher

Cancer Research UK spends £170 million, annually, on 3,000 research scientists whose brief is to *avoid* any research into holistic, naturopathic, nutritional treatments; therapies which provide the ONLY means to successfully treat a cancer victim.

"Using the guise of "established" medical science, many widely accepted studies are disseminated through medical journals and accepted as the ultimate authority by many. In the case of Professor Sheng Wang of Boston University School of Medicine Cancer Research Center, his cancer research was found to be misconducted, fraudulent and contain altered results. What is unsettling is the fact that his research had been previously accepted and used as a cornerstone from which to base all subsequent cancer research." Andre Evans. Activist Post, 19th October 2011

"The American Cancer Society was founded by the Rockefeller family to act as a propaganda outlet and public relations tool to suck in money and help promote pharmaceuticals for cancer 'therapy'. Gary Null did a fantastic exposé on who and what the ACS is in a series of articles about 10 years ago and he often retold his experiences on

the radio in coming to realize what a fraudulent outfit the ACS actually is. People are simply giving aid and comfort to Big Pharma when they support the ACS." Ken Adachi, political researcher, May 2011

However, not all studies are fraudulent, but when the motivation for these doctors and professors is financial, it turns the current medical paradigm into a war zone. As a consumer, it is important that you undertake your own research on the harsh side effects of traditional cancer treatment methods such as chemotherapy.

There is much evidence that there are in existence literally hundreds of alternative cancer treatments which really do work. Some are even of sufficient potency or are fast acting enough to effectively treat a cancer patient who has been deemed to be 'terminal' by his/her doctor. As untold millions are pumped into the fake cancer industry that thrives on provably fraudulent research, it is important to remember that free, alternative health options do exist. Utilising natural sweeteners, vitamin D therapy and eliminating artificial sweeteners such as aspartame in its many guises, are extremely simple ways to effectively prevent cancer and potentially begin reversing it.

It is not my intention here to relate those cures to the reader as this is outside the remit of this book. It is obviously desirable that everyone become familiar with a few different working methods of *preventing* the disease rather than trying to affect a cure at the eleventh hour, so to speak and these preventative and curative strategies are all available in abundance on the Internet. However, even should the worst happen and you are unfortunately diagnosed with cancer of some kind then it is still not too late to adopt the 'cure rather than prevention' approach in 90% of cases and this is true even in cases where traditional cures have been attempted and apparently failed.

Autism – vaccine-induced brain damage

Controversy has raged for years over whether mercury received through vaccines is sufficient to cause harm to children.   Virtually all studies absolving mercury-containing vaccines of safety deficiencies have been conducted by vaccine insiders with a financial stake in the outcome, rendering them in effect, worthless.

Chronic neurological disorders, especially autism, have increased rapidly during the past two decades in correlation with increases in vaccines and total mercury exposure. In July 1999, CDC, the American Academy of Paediatrics and vaccine companies agreed to remove mercury from all childhood vaccines 'as soon as possible', but at the time of writing it still remains in 16 licensed vaccines, 5 of which are still given to infants.

CDC claims there is 'no convincing evidence of harm' that vaccines cause significant neurological damage or autism and cites a number of studies claiming to exonerate mercury.

"The studies they reference are all deeply flawed, and, as was the case with decades of 'tobacco epidemiology,' were deliberately manufactured to hide the truth," Jim Moody, director of SafeMinds

Data from the CDC's Vaccine Safety Datalink first revealed an association between mercury and brain damage, but these findings were later suppressed and the data were manipulated to exonerate thimerasol. This scientific manipulation was first revealed through documents obtained under the Freedom of Information Act, leading to a best-selling book, Evidence of Harm and to a published retraction of any "no cause" interpretation by the study's lead author Thomas Verstraeten (who by then had left CDC for the vaccine manufacturer, GlaxoSmithKline). The most recent study of VSD data by Young et al. made additional findings that vaccine mercury caused not only autism but several other neuro-developmental disorders. Despite criticism from the Institute of Medicine and Congress, CDC still refuses to grant access to VSD to private researchers and the Justice Department refuses to permit petitioners in Vaccine Courts access to these crucial data.

Big Pharma has been under pressure to remove mercury from all its vaccines for more than a decade now, but still shows no actual intent to do so. What further evidence do we need that there is a conspiracy to maintain the status quo and continue to poison and kill on an industrial scale? The very fact that governments remain complicit and do not intervene also speaks volumes and adds fuel to the fire of conspiracy. It is obviously in everyone's interests (except the general populace of course) that things remain as they are and the cull should continue.

Mercury in dental fillings
The official position of the British Dental Association (BDA) is that 'silver' fillings are safe and that amalgam (containing mercury) is an appropriate material to shore-up decayed teeth. They also state that there is no proven connection with adverse health complaints. This actually conflicts directly with a statement by the Health and Safety Executive which states... *"Mercury forms a large number of organic and inorganic compounds. Mercury vapour and almost all of these compounds are highly toxic. Less hazardous substitutes should be used whenever possible"*.
14,000 scientific papers world-wide have been published which suggest that mercury is a toxic material and should therefore not be used in fillings. However, more recently the BDA has released a statement saying that more research needs to be carried out to ensure safety. The UK Department of Health advises all dentists not to remove or replace amalgam fillings in pregnant women!

It is almost universally agreed that mercury can produce serious side effects. It has become increasingly apparent that a large minority of dentists are no longer happy placing amalgam fillings in patients' mouths or subjecting nursing staff or themselves to further potential toxicity.

"About 3% of the population are estimated to suffer from 'mercury sensitivity'". The British Dental Association (ie. the Elite-controlled and run British Dental Association)

That statement would be hilarious if it wasn't so serious. Who do they really think they are kidding? Everyone is 'sensitive' to Mercury in much the same way as we are 'sensitive' to Sarin nerve gas, hydrochloric acid or a bullet in the head. Mercury, as they well know is a deadly poison causing all manner of unpleasantness to our bodies. Amalgam based dental fillings contain not only mercury but other highly toxic metals which produces vapour that slowly poisons us.

Good health is impossible in the face of constant, low-level mercury poisoning, which occurs in people with mercury based amalgam fillings. As an example, thyroid abnormalities cannot be corrected until amalgams are removed. From the time the mercury is placed in your mouth, until the day you die (or you lose the teeth), chewing causes mercury vapour to escape. It then enters your bloodstream and is delivered to all parts of your body, including your brain.

In California, dentists are required by law to inform patients of mercury risk. Several European countries have outright bans, and the German government reimburses victims for mercury removal. It is commonplace for dental associations to deny the dangers, due to their well-founded fear of being broken by lawsuits from people they have damaged over many decades. Mercury fillings, unfortunately, are still widely used in the UK and are still vehemently defended by many dentists. I leave you to guess their motives in this gross deception.

"The ADA owes no legal duty of care to protect the public... If you are a dentist still using mercury amalgam, be careful. If you tell your patient that it is harmful, you already know that the ADA will come after you. But... if you don't tell your patient, you might be sued for not providing informed consent." American Dental Association in a letter to dentists.

The California State Board of Dental Examiners recently published a warning that mercury is a known toxin that has been shown to escape into the body. The US Environmental Protection Agency classifies mercury filling material, once removed from the mouth, as a toxic waste that must then be carefully handled in special containers, and buried in toxic waste sites.

"When I trained as a dentist some years ago we had no training in nutrition or in the safety of materials. In fact we were told once mercury is mixed into the alloy to make amalgam it is perfectly safe.

However, not long after working in general practice I realised that the suction unit has a filtration device that captures the chunks of amalgam drilled out of a tooth and that the dental nurses would empty this into a jar containing x-ray fixative chemicals at the end of the day so that it could not gas out mercury.

Once the jar was full it would be collected to go away as a hazardous waste material a we are legally not allowed to dispose of it down the sink or in the garbage. Tha material is identical to what I was drilling and placing in teeth yet once out of the mouth was a toxic waste product. How could that be?" Rachel Hall, former National Health Service Dentist in the UK

Mercury toxicity has been linked to the following ailments;

Severe headaches and migraine
Fatigue
Poor Concentration
Irritability
ME
Multiple Sclerosis
Alzheimer's disease

If you have amalgam fillings, my strong advice would be to find a dentist who i capable of and willing to remove them and replace with bio-friendly alternatives. A you have probably gathered by now, our controlled 'healthcare' system does no care about you or your family's health in the slightest. We need to start fighting bac against this insidious group as soon as we can in every way that we can.

Marijuana – the myth

It is said that marijuana or hemp as it was previously known is dangerous, however i is categorically known not to be harmful to either the human body or minc Marijuana does not pose a threat to the general public, but it is very much a dange to the Elite-owned oil companies, alcohol and tobacco industries and a large numbe of chemical corporations. Big businesses with unlimited spending power an influence have suppressed the truth from the people. The truth is that, if marijuan was utilised for its vast array of commercial products and benefits, it would create second industrial revolution all on its own. The truth is again that the super-rich hav conspired to spread disinformation about a plant that, if used correctly, would rui their companies. You may have noticed the same recurring theme here!?

Where did the word 'marijuana' come from? In the mid-1930s, the 'm-word' wa created from an obscure Spanish slang word to tarnish the good image an phenomenal history of the hemp plant. The facts cited here with references, ar generally verifiable in the *Encyclopedia Britannica* which was printed on hemp pape for 150 years:
"All schoolbooks were made from hemp or flax paper until the 1880s." Jack Frazie Hemp Paper Reconsidered 1974

It was legal to pay taxes with hemp in America from 1631 until the early 1800s." LA imes, 12th August 1981

Refusing to grow hemp in America during the 17th and 18th centuries was against the w! You could be jailed in Virginia for refusing to grow hemp from 1763 to 1769". G. M. erdon, Hemp in Colonial Virginia

Benjamin Franklin owned one of the first paper mills in America and it processed emp. Also, the War of 1812 was fought over hemp. Napoleon wanted to cut off oscow's export to England." Jack Herer, Emperor Wears No Clothes

For thousands of years, 90% of all ships' sails and rope were made from hemp. The ord 'canvas' is Dutch for cannabis". Webster's New World Dictionary

eorge Washington, Thomas Jefferson and other founding fathers grew hemp. Washington and Jefferson Diaries). Jefferson smuggled hemp seeds from China to ance and thence to America.

0% of all textiles, fabrics, clothes, linen, bed sheets, etc., were made from hemp until he 1820s, with the introduction of the cotton gin.

he first Bibles, maps, charts and the first drafts of the US Declaration of dependence and the Constitution were made from hemp.

he first crop grown in many states was hemp. 1850 was a peak year for Kentucky hich produced 40,000 tons. Hemp was the largest cash crop until the 20th century.

he oldest known records of hemp farming go back 5000 years in China, although emp industrialization probably goes back to ancient Egypt.

embrandt's, Van Gogh's, Gainsborough's, as well as most early canvas paintings, ere principally painted on hemp linen.

1916, the U.S. Government predicted that by the 1940s all paper would come from emp and that no more trees would need to be cut down. Government studies port that 1 acre of hemp equals 4.1 acres of trees. Plans were in the works to nplement these programs. (US Department of Agriculture Archives.)

Quality paints and varnishes were made from hemp seed oil until 1937. 58,000 tons of emp seeds were used in America for paint products in 1935." Sherman Williams Paint o, testimony before the US Congress against the 1937 Marijuana Tax Act

Henry Ford's first Model-T car was built to run on hemp fuel and the car itself was onstructed from hemp. On his large estate, Ford was photographed among his hemp *fields. The car, 'grown from the soil,' had hemp plastic panels whose impact strength was 10 times stronger than steel."* Popular Mechanics, 1941

William Randolph Hearst and the Hearst Paper Manufacturing division of Kimberly Clark owned a vast acreage of timberlands. The Hearst Company supplied most paper products. Hearst, a destroyer of nature for his own personal profit, stood to lose billions because of hemp.

In 1937, DuPont patented the processes to make plastics from oil and coal. DuPont's Annual Report urged shareholders to invest in its new petrochemical division. Synthetics such as plastics, cellophane, celluloid, methanol, nylon, rayon, Dacron, etc., could now be made from oil. Natural hemp industrialization would have ruined over 80% of DuPont's business.

Andrew Mellon became Hoover's Secretary of the Treasury and DuPont's primary investor. He appointed his future nephew-in-law, Harry J. Anslinger, to head the Federal Bureau of Narcotics and Dangerous Drugs. Subsequently, secret meetings were held by these financial tycoons and as a result, hemp was declared dangerous and a threat to their billion-dollar enterprises. For their dynasties to remain intact, hemp had to be eradicated. These men took an obscure Mexican slang word 'marijuana' and pushed it into the consciousness of America.

A media blitz of 'yellow' journalism raged in the late 1920s and 1930s. Hearst's newspapers ran stories emphasizing the horrors of marijuana. The menace of marijuana made headlines and readers were told that it was responsible for everything from car accidents to low morality.

Films like Reefer Madness (1936), Marijuana: Assassin of Youth (1935) and Marijuana The Devil's Weed (1936) were propaganda hit-pieces designed by these Elites to create an enemy and their purpose was to gain public support so that anti-marijuana laws could be passed. In the film 'Reefer Madness', hemp (marijuana) is referred to as 'a violent narcotic'. It instigates 'acts of shocking violence' and causes 'incurable insanity' and 'soul-destroying effects' and even contains quotes such as 'under the influence of the drug he killed his entire family with an axe' and 'more vicious, more deadly even than these soul-destroying drugs (heroin, cocaine) is the menace of marijuana!'

Reefer Madness did not end with the usual 'the end.' The film concluded with these emotive words plastered on the screen 'Tell your children.' In the 1930s, most people were very naive, even to the point of ignorance. The masses were much like sheep waiting to be led by the few in power and were easily manipulated en masse. They did not often challenge authority and so if the news was in print or on the radio, they believed it just had to be true. This 'knowledge' was passed down to their children and their children grew up to be the parents of the baby-boomers.

"Why is marijuana against the law? It grows naturally upon our planet. Doesn't the idea of making nature against the law seem to you a bit . . . unnatural?" Bill Hicks, comedian

On the 14th April 1937, the prohibitive Marijuana Tax Law, the bill that outlawed hemp was directly brought to the House Ways and Means Committee in the US. This committee is the only one that can introduce a bill to the House floor without it being debated by other committees. The Chairman of the US Senate, Ways and Means Committee at the time, Robert Doughton, was a DuPont puppet and dupe and he ensured that the bill would pass through Congress.

Dr. James Woodward, a physician and attorney, testified too late on behalf of the American Medical Association. He told the committee that the reason the AMA had not denounced the Marijuana Tax Law sooner was that the Association had just discovered that marijuana was hemp. Few people, at the time, realized that the deadly menace they had been reading about on Hearst's front pages was in fact, harmless hemp. The AMA understood cannabis to be a medicine found in numerous healing products sold over the last hundred years.

So, in September of 1937, hemp duly became illegal and the single-most useful crop known to man became a 'drug' overnight and our planet has been suffering ever since. Congress banned hemp because it was said to be the most violence-causing drug known. Harry Anslinger, head of the Drug Commission for 31 years, promoted the idea that marijuana made users act extremely violently and in the 1950s, under the Communist threat of McCarthyism, he then stated the exact opposite, marijuana will pacify them so much that soldiers would not want to fight.

Today, the planet is in a desperate ecological state as large tracts of rain forests disappear at the behest of the corporate Elite. Pollution, poisons and chemicals are killing people but arguably, all this could be reversed if we industrialised hemp once again. Natural biomass could provide all of the planet's energy needs that are currently supplied by fossil fuels. Oil and Gas based fuels are controlled and monopolised by the rich to make extravagant profits to the detriment of the many and we desperately need a renewable resource of energy. Hemp could easily be the solution to soaring fuel prices and scarcity.

Hemp has a higher quality fibre than wood fibre. Far fewer caustic chemicals are required to make paper from hemp than from trees and hemp paper does not turn yellow and is extremely durable. The plant grows quickly to maturity in one season where trees take a lifetime.

All plastic products could be made from hempseed oil. Hemp-based plastics are biodegradable and so over time, they would naturally break-down and not cause harm to the environment, whereas oil-based plastics, the ones we are very familiar with, help ruin nature. They do not break-down easily and remain in the ecosystems for hundreds, if not thousands of years. The process to produce the vast array of natural (hempen) plastics will not ruin the rivers as DuPont and other petrochemical companies have done but unfortunately a caring, sharing, ecologically-based strategy does not fit in with the profit-generation of the oil industry and the political machine. There are no indecent amounts of profit to be made going down that particular road whereas hemp-based products on the other hand are safe and natural.

Medicines could also be made from hemp. It is not that long ago that the AMA supported cannabis-based cures but now 'medical' marijuana is provided legally to only a handful of people while the rest of us are forced into a system that relies on artificial, mostly harmful chemicals. Marijuana is actually beneficial to the human body in so many ways.

A large variety of food products can also be generated from hemp. The seeds contain one of the highest sources of protein in nature and also they contain two essential fatty acids that cleanse the human body. These essential fatty acids are not found anywhere else in nature and consuming raw, uncooked hemp seeds is extremely beneficial for the human body.

Hemp-made clothing is extremely strong and durable over time unlike the cheap artificial fabrics today that tear and wear thin far too easily. Today, there are some companies that make hemp clothing, but hemp fabrics should be everywhere. Instead, they are almost underground and superior hemp products are not allowed advertising space on Elite-owned television stations.

Kentucky, once the top hemp producing state in America, made it illegal to wear hemp clothing. Can you imagine being thrown into jail for wearing quality jeans?

The alcohol, tobacco and oil companies spend billions funding campaigns and propaganda against illegal drugs including marijuana. The lies from the powerful, Elite corporations that began with Hearst are still as numerous today. The brainwashing continues and marijuana is being portrayed more and more as the enemy.

In fact, there is only one enemy, the people to whom we pay our taxes, the war-makers, the corporate and financial gangsters and the destroyers of nature for profit. With our funding, they are destroying the Earth before our eyes. Millions of deaths worldwide each year are caused by tobacco and millions more by alcohol but no-one has ever, ever died from marijuana. In the entire history of the human race, not one death can be attributed to cannabis. Our society has outlawed hemp but condones and promotes the use of the *real* killers, tobacco and alcohol. Why would this be? Because it is all done in the name of profits and the subtle depopulation agenda.

Hemp should be declassified as a drug and its many benefits should be harnessed to help the human race. Stress, hardening and constriction of the arteries are but two examples of conditions that can be cured by the use of hemp and indeed ingesting

THC, hemp's active agent, has a positive effect in relieving asthma and also the nausea caused by chemotherapy.

There is also much evidence to prove that one's creative abilities can be enhanced under the influence of marijuana, but of course that is probably reason enough for it to be banned, if true. It is, in fact the exact opposite state of mind and body as the drunken state, one can be more aware with marijuana. However, as I have mentioned several times, the last thing our Elite rulers want or need is an alert, clear-thinking, creative population. That would be far too dangerous to their ambitions.

Strangely, the hemp plant is thought by many to be an alien plant. There is plenty of physical evidence that cannabis is not like any other plant on this planet and so is it possible that it was brought here for the benefit of humanity, by our ancient alien ancestors? Hemp is the only known plant in which the males and the females appear very different, physically. It is most unusual to speak of males and females in regard to the plant kingdom because plants do not overtly show their sexes. To determine the sex of a normal, earthly plant, its DNA must be examined. A male potato plant, for example looks exactly like a female potato plant. The hemp plant however has a uniquely (amongst the plant kingdom) overt, intense sexuality.

So, in summary, the reason this amazingly useful, very sophisticated, possibly alien plant is illegal has nothing to do with how it physically affects us. Marijuana is illegal because billionaires wish to remain billionaires.

Energy-saving Light-bulbs

These light-bulbs (Compact Fluorescent bulbs or CFLs) are strongly promoted as being a huge contributor to the 'green' economy, even to the extent that it is now no longer possible to buy the standard light-bulb we have been used to all our lives. However, when we examine the reality, it can be seen to be somewhat different to the rosy picture painted of the eco-friendliness of this abomination.

Firstly, eco–friendly or healthy they most certainly are not. CFLs are filled with mercury and furthermore they also emit UV radiation when activated. An average CFL bulb contains 5mg of mercury and considering the fact that ingesting even the tiniest amount of mercury can be very harmful and as the US OSHA (Occupational Safety and Health administration) points out; the permissible level of mercury vapour is 0.1 milligram per cubic metre. A CFL contains 50 times that amount and even more significantly, the threshold limit value for skin contamination is just 0.025mg per cubic metre, 200 times the amount within a CFL!

Should one of these 'eco-friendly' bulbs break open, then anyone within the same room will be exposed to a massive risk of contamination. A study published on the 6th July 2011 showed that once broken, a CFL continuously releases mercury vapour into the air for months and depending on how well-ventilated the room is, can well exceed human safety levels.

The effects of exposure to mercury vapour can be damage to central and peripheral nervous systems, lungs, kidneys, skin and eyes in humans and damage to immune function and perhaps most alarmingly, the release of methyl-mercury, a chemical compound formed in the environment from released mercury that can cause brain damage. This is not exaggeration at all, but simply-stated fact.

CFLs operate in the 24-100 kHz frequency range, classified as Intermediate Frequency 5 (IF5) by the World Health Organisation. This in itself gives rise to fears of biological damage as it has been demonstrated that disturbances in this range cause sufficient interference to raise severe health concerns. In California, a recent study of cancer clusters associated the increased risk of cancer with teachers who taught in classrooms where the GS, a means of measuring dirty electricity, was above 200 GS units. Ironically, a light-bulb which is designed to be eco-friendly and less hazardous is classified as emitting 'dirty electricity', yet the traditional incandescent light-bulb does not.

Also despite the wild claims of CFL's promoters, questions also arise over its life-expectancy. There have been claims suggesting that these bulbs can last up to 10,000 hours whereas 5,000–8,000 hours would probably be closer to the truth. However, it is impossible to accurately determine a specific lifespan due to the large variety of different conditions existing in each individual home. What is known for certain though is that by switching the CFL on and off continually, it unsurprisingly, dramatically reduces the lifespan. Even that Elite propaganda-dispenser *Wikipedia* states, '*In the case of a 5-minute on/off cycle the lifespan of a CFL can be reduced to close to that of incandescent light bulbs*'.

CFLs also take around 2-3 minutes to fully 'warm up' and therefore should light be required purely for a short period, for example quickly entering a room to retrieve an item, far more energy will be used than with conventional bulbs. The U.S. Energy Star program suggests that '*fluorescent lamps be left on when leaving a room for less than 15 minutes to mitigate this problem*'. Is life not already complicated enough without all this to consider?!

A CFL 26 watt bulb is the equivalent of a 100 watt incandescent bulb and costs around £2.50 with a life span of an average of 7000 hours without factoring in the 5 minute on/off cycle. Comparatively speaking, an incandescent bulb costs just around 60p with an average life-span of 800 hours, so according to these figures we would spend around £4.00 more per life-cycle using incandescent eco-friendly, clean bulbs. In effect this then means that we would save a whole £4 over a period of one year.

But, what cannot be excluded from any considerations of the 'value' of this abomination are the severe, potential health risks and the enormous power surges required by CFLs when switching them and also the cost of the quick on/off cycle. These figures are typically always absent from any study on costs and efficiency, creating as usual, a totally false conclusion for widespread consumption by the masses.
In addition, the current price of CFLs reflects their almost exclusive manufacture in China, where labour costs are dramatically less and that will surely change, as the Chinese economy grows and achieves world domination as is widely expected by most commentators. Governments cannot be trusted to control the cost either, as they certainly wish to maximise the import duty on any item. The more expensive the bulb, the more duty they collect is simple mathematics. A good example of this tactic is how we were strongly encouraged to buy diesel cars as the fuel was much cheaper, but now that sufficient numbers of motorists have been 'converted' to the benefits of diesel, we find that the tax on diesel has been miraculously increased and thus we now pay considerably more for diesel than petrol! The game is rigged and the table has most definitely 'tilted'.

Invented diseases
How is it possible to 'invent' a disease - or a syndrome to be more accurate? The answer is quite simple. When you have the financial muscle and the powerful propaganda machine that this kind of extreme wealth can buy, it is fairly straightforward to convince millions that several hitherto unrelated symptoms, when 'grouped' together comprise a new illness, disease or syndrome. Indeed this is exactly the case with AIDS / HIV but as that issue has been covered in another section we will concentrate on other examples.

Psychiatry itself admits *"it has not proven the 'disease theory' or the cause or source of a single mental illness it has classified and the theory of a chemical imbalance in the brain causes mental illness has been thoroughly discredited by the psychiatric industry itself"* mainly because critics pointed out that there isn't even a test for a chemical imbalance, it is complete nonsense. They say psychiatry is the *'original pseudoscience, medical fraud and completely made up'*.

When one delves beneath the surface at the specialty of psychiatry, what is uncovered is so ludicrous it is difficult to believe that it is really true. Prominent psychiatrists from all over the world gather annually for a meeting at which new diseases are invented. There are no objective findings that establish the diagnosis of these diseases. These new diseases are included in the Diagnostic and Statistical Manual of Mental Diseases. Potential new diseases are discussed at these meetings and new diseases are voted in or out by a show of hands, believe it or not.

Among the new diseases are social anxiety disorder (everyone who is uncomfortable in a social setting has this disease) and mathematics disease (anyone who has struggled over a math problem has this disease). Gender identity disorder, passive aggressive disorder, disorder of written expression and sexual disorder are other examples of invented diseases that will follow the individuals tagged with these ridiculous diagnoses the remainder of their lives. Naturally, all these completely fake diseases have a psychoactive drug, which supposedly ameliorates this disease complete with a usually impressive price tag of course.

This may be laughable but unfortunately it has serious consequences. When a child is diagnosed with depression (!) the child is often placed on a potent anti-depressant drug. The manufacturer of one of these leading drugs knew for many years that the drug caused loss of the ability to control violent behaviour, thus increasing violence towards self (suicide) and others (mass murders). This information was covered up because it would have negatively impacted upon sales of the drug. Nearly every teenager involved in the many recent school shooting rampages was taking an anti depressant drug. There is a major fundamental flaw in a system more concerned about sales of drugs than the welfare of its children, but this we know already.

Another subtle ploy is to artificially set a limit on the incidence of certain parameters within the human body and then declare that anything above (or below) that limit is a cause for concern and/or a danger to our wellbeing. By that method it then becomes a simple task to produce a drug that 'cures' that imbalance and make millions for Big Pharma.

High cholesterol is just such a similar scam.

High Cholesterol

"Somewhere along the way however, cholesterol became a household word - something that you must keep as low as possible, or suffer the consequences. You are probably aware that there are many myths that portray fat and cholesterol as one of the worst foods you can consume. Please understand that these myths are actually harming your health. Not only is cholesterol most likely not going to destroy your health (as you have been led to believe), but it is also not the cause of heart disease."
Dr. Joseph Mercola, 10th August 2010

One certainly needs cholesterol. It is present not only in the bloodstream, but also in every cell in the body, where it helps to produce cell membranes, hormones, vitamin D and bile acids that assist in the digestion of fat. Cholesterol also helps in the formation of memories and is vital for neurological function.

The liver makes about 75 percent of a body's cholesterol and according to conventional medicine, there are two types:

High-density lipoprotein or HDL: This is the 'good' cholesterol that helps to keep cholesterol away from the arteries and remove any excess from arterial plaque, which may help to prevent heart disease.

Low-density lipoprotein or LDL: This 'bad' cholesterol circulates in your blood and accumulates in arteries, forming a plaque that narrows arteries and renders them less flexible (a condition called arteriosclerosis). If a clot forms in one of these narrowed arteries leading to your heart or brain, a heart attack or stroke may result.

Please understand that the total cholesterol level is not an indicator of one's heart disease or stroke risk. Health officials in the United States urge everyone over the age of 20 to have their cholesterol tested once every five years. Part of this test is your total cholesterol or the sum of your blood's cholesterol content, including HDL, LDLs, and VLDLs.

The American Heart Association recommends that total cholesterol should be less than 200 mg/dL, but what they do not tell you is that total cholesterol level is just about worthless in determining your risk for heart disease, unless it is above 330. In addition, the AHA updated their guidelines in 2004, lowering the recommended level of LDL cholesterol from 130 to LDL to less than 100, or even less than 70 for patients at very high risk.

In order to achieve these outrageous and dangerously low targets, you typically need to take multiple cholesterol-lowering drugs. So the guidelines instantly increased the market for these dangerous drugs. Now, with testing children's cholesterol levels, they are increasing their potential market even more. So another digit on Big Pharma's bottom line profits there then.

Actually, you may be surprised to hear that cholesterol is neither 'good' nor 'bad'. Now that good and bad cholesterol has been defined, it has to be said that there is actually only one type of cholesterol!

"Notice please that LDL and HDL are lipoproteins - fats combined with proteins. There is only one cholesterol. There is no such thing as 'good' or 'bad' cholesterol. Cholesterol is just cholesterol.

It combines with other fats and proteins to be carried through the bloodstream, since fat and our watery blood do not mix very well. Fatty substances therefore must be shuttled to and from our tissues and cells using proteins. LDL and HDL are forms of proteins and are far from being just cholesterol. In fact we now know there are many types of these fat and protein particles.

LDL particles come in many sizes and large LDL particles are not a problem. Only the so-called small dense LDL particles can potentially be a problem, because they can squeeze through the lining of the arteries and if they oxidize, otherwise known as turning rancid, they can cause damage and inflammation. Thus, you might say that there is 'good LDL' and 'bad LDL.' Also, some HDL particles are better than others. Knowing just your total cholesterol tells you very little. Even knowing your LDL and HDL levels will not tell you very much."   Ron Rosedale MD, a leading anti-aging doctor in the USA

The idea that cholesterol is 'evil' has been very much ingrained in most people's minds; due to the propaganda expounded by the pharmaceutical cartel, but this is a very harmful myth that needs to be eliminated as soon as possible.

Dr. Rosedale further points out, *"First and foremost, cholesterol is a vital component of every cell membrane on Earth. In other words, there is no life on Earth that can live without cholesterol. That will automatically tell you that, in and of itself, it cannot be evil. In fact, it is one of our best friends. We would not be here without it. No wonder lowering cholesterol too much increases one's risk of dying."*

Vitamin D is a much neglected source of wellness and general health and what most people do not realise is that the best way to obtain vitamin D is from safe exposure to sun on one's skin. The UVB rays in sunlight interact with the cholesterol on the skin and convert it to vitamin D.

So therefore, if cholesterol levels are too low it will be impossible to use the sun to generate sufficient levels of health-giving vitamin D. As vitamin D is a major influence in the prevention of many diseases, particularly cancer, this obviously contributes to higher incidences of these diseases, which I am sure is no coincidence.

Essentially, HDL takes cholesterol from the body's tissues and arteries and brings it back to the liver, where most cholesterol is produced. If the purpose of this was to eliminate cholesterol from the body, it would make sense that the cholesterol would be dispatched back to the kidneys or intestines so it could be removed. But, instead it goes back to the liver. *Why should this be?* The reason is because the liver can reuse it.

"It is taking it back to your liver so that your liver can recycle it; put it back into other particles to be taken to tissues and cells that need it," Dr. Rosedale explains. *"Your body is trying to make and conserve the cholesterol for the precise reason that it is so important, indeed vital, for health."*

If cholesterol levels drop too low this can have a devastating effect on the body in so many ways. Remember, every single cell needs cholesterol to thrive including those in the brain. Perhaps this is why low cholesterol wreaks havoc on the psyche. One large study conducted by Dutch researchers found that men with chronically low cholesterol levels showed a consistently higher risk of having depressive symptoms. (Anyone feel a long intensive course of suicide-enhancing anti-depressants coming on?) Seriously though, this could well be because cholesterol affects the metabolism of serotonin, a substance involved in the regulation of moods.

On a similar note, some Canadian researchers found that those in the lowest quarter of total cholesterol concentration had more than six times the risk of committing suicide as did those in the highest quarter. Dozens of studies also support a connection between low or lowered cholesterol levels and violent behaviour. Lowered cholesterol levels may lead to lowered brain serotonin activity, which may, in turn, lead to increased violence and aggression. And one analysis of over 41,000 patient records found that people who take statin drugs to lower their cholesterol as much as possible may have a higher risk of cancer, while other studies have linked low cholesterol to Parkinson's disease.

Probably any cholesterol level reading under 150 is too low - an optimum would be around 200. How strange then that doctors tell us that cholesterol needs to be *under* 200 to be healthy. Or not?

In 2004, the U.S. government's National Cholesterol Education Program panel advised those at risk for heart disease to attempt to reduce their LDL cholesterol to specific, very low, levels. Before 2004, a 130 milligram LDL cholesterol level was considered healthy but the updated guidelines however, recommended levels of less than 100, or even less than 70 for patients at very high risk. It is worth noting that these extremely low targets often require multiple cholesterol-lowering drugs to achieve.

Fortunately, in 2006 a review in the 'Annals of Internal Medicine' found that there is insufficient evidence to support the target numbers outlined by the panel. The authors of the review were unable to find research providing evidence that achieving a specific LDL target level was important in itself and found that studies attempting to do so suffered from major flaws. Several of the scientists who helped develop the guidelines even admitted that the scientific evidence supporting the less-than-70 recommendation was not very strong. So how did these excessively low cholesterol guidelines come about? As if we cannot guess!

Eight of the nine doctors on the panel that developed the new cholesterol guidelines had been taking money from the drug companies that manufacture statin-based cholesterol-lowering drugs – the same drugs that the new guidelines suddenly created a huge new market for in the United States. Coincidence? Probably not, but I will allow the reader to decide.

Now, despite the finding that there is absolutely no evidence to show that lowering one's LDL cholesterol to 100 or below is good for health, what do you think the American Heart Association still recommends to this day? Nothing less than keeping your LDL cholesterol levels to less than 100. And even better for Big Pharma, the standard recommendation to get to that level always includes one or more cholesterol-lowering drug.

If you are personally concerned about your cholesterol levels, taking a drug should be your absolute last resort. The odds are very high, greater than 100 to 1, that you do not need drugs to lower your cholesterol levels.

According to recent data from Medco Health Solutions Inc., more than 50% of health-insured Americans are using drugs for chronic health conditions and cholesterol-lowering medications are the second most common variety among this group, with almost 15% of chronic medication users taking them (high blood pressure medications - another vastly over-prescribed category, were first in the list). This is true as you would imagine for the rest of the Western world, its healthcare systems managed and controlled as it is by Big Pharma's aggressive profit targets.

"Some researchers have even suggested that the [cholesterol-lowering] medications should be put in the water supply." Business Week magazine, 2008

Indeed, cholesterol-lowering drugs are some of the most insidious on the market and please believe me when I say that that is despite the fact they are up against some pretty stiff competition for that particular 'honour'!

Statin drugs take effect by inhibiting an enzyme in the liver that is needed to manufacture cholesterol. What is so worrying about this is that when we try to mess around with the extremely delicate workings of the human body, the major risk is putting the body's natural cycles out of balance, causing a chain reaction of knock-on effects. Big Pharma's answer to that scenario of course is to keep prescribing more and more drugs to counter the side effects of the previous one. Can you even imagine the internal disruption caused by this state of affairs with some patients taking in excess of twenty different medications, each to combat the side-effects of the others? My own father springs to mind. Additionally, do you think that ALL the different combinations of drugs it is possible to have prescribed by your local death-dealer have been tested, even cursorily? The answer has to be 'no' as the permutations would run into many millions if not billions.

"*Statin drugs inhibit not just the production of cholesterol, but a whole family of intermediary substances, many if not all of which have important biochemical functions in their own right,*" Enig and Fallon

Statin drugs deplete the body of Coenzyme Q10 (CoQ10), which is beneficial to heart health and muscle function. Because doctors do not as routine, inform people of this risk and advise them to take a CoQ10 supplement, this depletion leads to fatigue, muscle weakness, soreness and eventually heart failure.

Muscle pain and weakness is actually the most common side effect of statin drugs, which is thought to occur because statins activate the gene which plays a key role in muscle atrophy.

They have also been linked to:

An increased risk of nerve damage
Dizziness
Cognitive impairment, including memory loss
A potential increased risk of cancer
Decreased function of the immune system
Depression
Liver problems
Motor Neurone (Lou Gehrig's) disease

With all of these risks to consider, one would hope that statin drugs were effective. Well, unfortunately this is highly questionable.

Most cholesterol lowering drugs can effectively lower cholesterol numbers, but this does not necessarily make for a healthier individual and there is certainly no available evidence that says that they may help prevent heart disease.

Food and Nutrition

"*Most of what sits in our stores is not really food as we have known it. It is a stew of sorts; chemicals, additives, flavourings, colourings, enhancers, preservatives, aspartame, neotame, and stuff we can't even identify along with residual hormones, vaccines, antibiotics, herbicides and pesticides. It has been irradiated, sprayed with viruses and now covered in ammonia. Reading any label for content makes one think you would be just as well off if you drank floor cleaner and it most likely might be a lot tastier although just as empty of nutrition.*" Marti Oakley, July 2011

"If people let the government decide what foods they eat and what medicines they take, their bodies will soon be in as sorry a state as are the souls of those who live under tyranny." Thomas Jefferson, 1778

"There is no right to consume or feed children any particular food. There is no generalised right to bodily and physical health. There is no fundamental right to freedom of contract." US Dept. of Health & Human Services and FDA, 2010

And there in a neat little nutshell, is everything we need to know about how much these organisations actually care about the welfare of the common herd.

It is an inescapable fact that our food (especially fruit and vegetables, but meat products too) now contains around 50-60% less nutrients and vitamins than was the case as recently as 40 or 50 years ago. What this means in effect is that we have to consume 50-60% more in quantity of the same foodstuffs to achieve the same nutritional benefits as in the past. The reason for this is that modern farming and cultivation methods and food production processes have become such that the only way to compete and survive in the cut-throat world of commercial food, is to foster and encourage faster growth of both animate and inanimate food and this has a knock-on, detrimental effect on its nutritional value as well as other downsides brought about by the widespread use of artificial growth hormones, non-organic fertilisers and pesticides.

The quantities we need to consume have therefore increased hugely and this is partly responsible for the obesity epidemic we see today. I say 'partly', because this does not quite tell the whole story. In addition to consuming ever greater quantities of foodstuffs, it is also the case that much of what we now eat can be classified as 'processed food', that is we no longer tend to buy the basic raw, unadulterated products to make meals as our forebears as recently as two generations ago, would have routinely done. Instead, we rely on the vast supermarket chains kindly provided for our convenience by Big Food where most of us now tend to do our weekly or monthly 'buy-in'. And by far the majority of food products in supermarkets fall under the heading of 'processed food'.

Processed food, whilst undeniably 'convenient' in that it is easily and quickly prepared and served in these days of the instant fix, unfortunately contains many nasty additives, preservatives and colourings which are known in some cases, to have a severe detrimental effect on human health and contribute hugely to the obesity epidemic. The quantity of processed food sold and served these days thus contributes to the overall malaise and generally poor health prevalent today in the Western world.

Aspartame
One of the worst culprits of all food additives is the substance, Aspartame. This is present in much of our processed foodstuff today including *most* carbonated drinks (fizzy pops and sodas) and especially in 'diet', 'lite', 'zero' and 'low-sugar' or 'sugar-free' products as a sweetener.

The story of how this abomination, Aspartame came to be present in our food and drink is a real eye-opener and I am sure you will agree, nothing less than criminal.

In the late 1970s the head of GD Searle, one of the pharmaceutical giants, was a certain Donald Rumsfeld, he of 9/11 infamy amongst many other dubious US government sponsored atrocities. It is well documented that he wanted to get Aspartame, discovered by accident in a laboratory in the 1960s, on to the world markets as a potentially huge money spinner. When I say huge I mean, bigger than you or I could ever imagine. The Aspartame market is worth billions and billions per annum if not trillions, so please do not think I am exaggerating too much.

The substance went through the normal channels of short-term testing by the FDA to determine its safety and efficacy as a sweetener before being accepted and was thus duly rejected due to the health dangers it was found to exhibit. All this took place towards the end of Jimmy Carter's reign as president of the USA, so Rumsfeld as head of a large corporation, duly poured millions of company dollars into Ronald Reagan's presidential campaign coffers which no doubt 'helped' in seeing him elected as the next President. To cut a long story short, as soon as Reagan was installed as President, Aspartame was miraculously approved by the FDA without further tests and rushed on to the market as a sweetener in 1981, within days of Reagan taking office. Just a coincidence though, I'm sure.

"If Donald Rumsfeld had never been born think of how many millions of people the world over would not suffer headaches and dizziness. Thousands blind from the free methyl alcohol in Aspartame would have sight, and there would be much fewer cases of optic neuritis and macular degeneration. Millions suffering seizures would live normal lives and wouldn`t be taking anti-seizure medication that won`t work because Aspartame interacts with drugs and vaccines. Think of the runner, Flo Jo, who drank Diet Coke and died of a grand mal seizure. She, no doubt, would still be alive. Brain fog and memory loss, skyrocketing symptoms of Aspartame disease, would not be epidemic.

Millions suffer insomnia because of the depletion of serotonin. Think of Heath Ledger. He took that horrible drug, Ambian CR for sleep, which makes the optic nerve and face swell and gives you terrible headaches. Plus, he drank Diet Coke (which destroys serotonin) and took other drugs and died of polypharmacy.

Since Aspartame has been proven to be a multi-potential carcinogen, would Farrah Fawcett still be alive?" Hesh Goldstein, 'The Rumsfeld Plague' 2009

Aspartame triggers an irregular heart rhythm (arrhythmia) and interacts with al cardiac medication. It damages the cardiac conduction system and causes sudden death. Thousands of athletes have fallen victim to it. Simply drink a can or bottle of diet drink, perform some vigorous exercise and you too could suddenly die, just as thousands of others provably have since 1981.

As the phenylalanine in Aspartame deletes serotonin, it triggers all kinds of psychiatric and behavioural problems. The mental hospitals are full of patients who are nothing but Aspartame victims. If the FDA had acted ethically, the revoked petition for the approval of Aspartame would have been signed by FDA commissioner Jere Goyan and the mental hospitals would house probably 50% less victims. Jere Goyan would never have been fired at 3.00 am by the Reagan transition team to over-rule the Board of Inquiry. Instead, FDA commissioner Goyan would have signed the revoked petition into law and the FDA today would still be Big Pharma`s adversary instead of being their whore.

For over a quarter of a century there has been mass poisoning of the public in over 100 countries of the world by Aspartame because Donald Rumsfeld, as he put it, *"called in his markers."* The Aspartame industry has bought-and-paid-for front groups and professional organisations to defend them and 'push' it to the very people upon whom it can inflict most harm. How surprising.

If Aspartame had not been approved, Motor Neurone (Lou Gehrig`s) Disease, Parkinson`s and other neuro-degenerative diseases would not be killing-off people in record numbers. Michael Fox, a Diet Pepsi spokesman for several years, would never have contracted Parkinson`s Disease at the age of 30, a ridiculously early age to do so. He would probably still be making films and enjoy robust health. Aspartame interacts with 'L-dopa' a Parkinson drug and another, 'Parcopa' actually contains Aspartame but the pharmaceutical company refuses to remove it despite strong, proven evidence linking it to Parkinson's disease.

Is it not criminal that there is not even a warning for pregnant women? Aspartame triggers every kind of birth defect from autism and Tourettes` Syndrome to cleft palate and is an abortifacient (a drug that induces abortion).

It is of course perfectly normal for young girls to look forward to marriage and children, yet many drink diet drinks or consume Aspartame products not realising that Aspartame is an endocrine disrupting agent, stimulating prolactin, which is a pituitary hormone that stimulates milk production at childbirth, changes and inhibits the menstrual cycle and causes infertility. Many women go through life never knowing why they cannot have children and Aspartame could even be accused of destroying marriages because it causes male sexual dysfunction and prevents the female arousal response.

Clear evidence demonstrates that Aspartame can cause every type of blood disorder from a low blood platelet count to leukaemia. Because it can also precipitate diabetes type II, this disease is epidemic. To make matters worse, it can stimulate and aggravate diabetic retinopathy and neuropathy, destroy the optic nerve, cause diabetics to go into convulsions and interact with insulin. Diabetics lose limbs from the free methyl alcohol; professional organisations such as the American Diabetes Association push and defend this poison because they take large sums of money from the manufacturers. How many millions would not now have diabetes if Rumsfeld had been stopped?

Aspartame (NutraSweet / Equal / Spoonful / E951 / Canderel / Benevia, etc), along with High Fructose Corn Syrup (HFCS) and Monosodium Glutamate (MSG), are responsible for the epidemic of obesity the world over. Why? This is because they instigate a craving for carbohydrates and cause great toxicity in the liver.

An FDA report lists 92 symptoms of Aspartame poisoning, from unconsciousness and coma to shortness of breath and shock. Medical texts list even more: *"Aspartame Disease: An Ignored Epidemic"*, H.J. Roberts, M.D. and *"Excitotoxins: The Taste That Kills"* by neurosurgeon Russell Blaylock, M.D. There is simply no end to the horrors triggered by this literally addictive, excitoneurotoxic and genetically-engineered carcinogenic drug. This chemical poison is so deadly that Dr. Bill Deagle, a respected Virologist once said it was worse than depleted uranium because it is found everywhere in food. He is absolutely correct.

The formaldehyde converted from the free methyl alcohol embalms living tissue and damages DNA according to the 'Trocho' Study done in Barcelona in 1998. Even though this devastating study shows how serious a chemical poison Aspartame is, the FDA has turned a blind eye to it and it continues to flourish everywhere. With Monsanto attorney Michael Taylor now appointed as Deputy Commissioner to the FDA by President Barack Obama, it has now become nothing more than Monsanto's Washington Branch Office. Even before the Ramazzini studies showing Aspartame to be a multi-potential carcinogen were published, the FDA knew that this was the case. Their own toxicologist, Dr. Adrian Gross, even admitted that it violated the Delaney Amendment because of the brain tumours and brain cancer it causes. Therefore, no allowable daily intake ever should have been able to be established. Aspartame causes all types of tumours from mammary, uterine, ovarian, pancreatic and thyroid to testicular and pituitary. Dr. Maria Alemany, who undertook the Trocho Study, commented that Aspartame could possibly kill '*200 million people*'. Damaging DNA could destroy humanity itself.

Dr. James Bowen told the FDA over 20 years ago that Aspartame is mass poisoning the USA and likewise more than 100 countries of the world. No wonder it's called 'Rumsfeld's Plague'.

Big Pharma indeed knows only too well all about Aspartame and its effects and yet they still allow it to be added to drugs, including the ones used to treat the problems caused by Aspartame in the first place. People are so sick from Aspartame and yet this truly criminal organisation continues to sell these dangerous pharmaceuticals at outrageously inflated prices.

Dr. H.J. Roberts said in one of his books that we should *'charge Aspartame with killing children.'* We are talking about a drug that changes brain chemistry. Today children are medicated instead of educated.

Death and disability is what Donald Rumsfeld has foisted on to consumers simply to make money. Charles Fleming used to drink about 10 diet drinks per day and then used Creatine on top of this, which interacts with Aspartame and is thus considered the actual cause of death. Yet his wife, Diane Fleming, remains in a prison in Virginia convicted of his death, despite being the very one who tried to get her husband to stop using these dangerous products containing Aspartame in the first place.

The list goes on and on. At least six American Airlines` pilots, who were heavy users of Aspartame have died, one of them actually in flight, drinking a Diet Coke. So pilots too are sick and dying from Aspartame and when we fly our life is in their hands.

In the Persian Gulf, diet drinks sit on pallets daily in temperatures of over 100 degrees Fahrenheit for as long as 8 weeks at a time before the Allied forces drink them. Aspartame converts to formaldehyde at 86 degrees Fahrenheit; it interacts with vaccines and damages the mitochondria or heart of the human cell, and the whole molecule breaks down to become a brain tumour agent.

Doctors at mortuaries carrying out autopsies know immediately when Aspartame has been the cause of death, because when the skull is opened, they can instantly smell the methanol in the brain tissue and cavity. However it is more than their career is worth to overtly name Aspartame as a cause of death. The hands of physicians are well and truly tied. Most are clueless that a patient is using Aspartame and even that Aspartame is deadly and the drugs they prescribe to treat the Aspartame problem will probably interact negatively and may even contain Aspartame themselves. Those that are aware of the situation also know that there is nothing they can do in the face of strong financial and political pressure.

This is the world for which Donald Rumsfeld is personally responsible.

Of course we will never be told this by our compliant media, who are in any case owned by the same small group of Elite people at the tops of the pyramids. The game is rigged folks. It's a war and we are the enemy under siege.

Genetically Modified Food

The concerted drive to inflict genetically modified food upon us by food corporations such as Monsanto with the compliance with the highly-corrupt FDA in the name of profit is nothing but a disgrace and a sham. Listening to their spokespersons quoting rigged and heavily-massaged trial results and lying about the safety of these substances, is no different to listening to the worst excesses of Nazi propaganda in the 1930s and 40s.

Make no mistake about it, GM foods are nothing short of deadly, to humans and animals alike and the worst news is that they have already infiltrated much of the food chain. According to these Big Food, Elite controlled corporations and their media poodles, GM foods are the answer to the world food crisis and a cheap, efficient way of feeding the starving millions worldwide. Of course they care about the starving millions - we believe them. Of course we do.

The truth is that the reason that genetically modified foods are being produced in the first place is so that the corporations who produce them can patent the genetics and thus control the market for them. Can you imagine owning the sole rights to the genome for a carrot or a tomato or even a strain of cattle? This is a very dangerous situation and very much 'the thin end of the wedge' in the sense that allowing a corporation to own a genome means that they can in effect corner a market and basically charge whatever they then wish for that product. That is really what GM is all about and why it is so insidious. It also gives them the power to make charges for seeds containing *their* genetic blueprint, as opposed to the natural genome, found on other private farms or lands.

There have already been court cases in the US and worldwide where Monsanto have illegally sent their 'agents' into private farmland to gather samples of seeds / plants bearing their genome blueprint, carried in by birds or the wind from neighbouring farms. In all cases the judges have found in Monsanto's favour, declaring that the seeds were 'Monsanto's property' and were being grown illegally. This is not satire by the way, this is the absolute truth.

In addition Monsanto (and other corporation's) GM seeds contain what has become known as the 'terminator gene'. This means that unlike in days gone-by when farmers / growers could save the seeds from one year's crop in order to propagate the following years crop, they are now forced to buy from the Corporations again and again, year on year as the ability of the plants to naturally produce seeds has been 'deleted' from the genome. In my humble view, although this is perfectly legal, it is absolutely, totally immoral and callous profiteering on a grand scale.

Here is a recent case against Monsanto that made the headlines...

"For 40 years Percy Schmeiser grew oilseed rape on his farm in the Canadian province of Saskatchewan. Each year, he would sow each year's crop with seeds saved from the previous harvest. In 1998 Monsanto took Schmeiser to court. Investigators employed by the company had found samples of its GM oilseed rape among Schmeiser's stock. Monsanto's lawsuit alleged that the farmer had infringed on the firm's patent. It even stated that Schmeiser had obtained Monsanto seeds illegally; going so far as to suggest that he might have stolen them from a seed house.

The corporation later admitted that Schmeiser had not obtained the seeds illegally, but said that wasn't important. What did matter, Monsanto argued, was that it had found some of its canola plants in the ditch along Schmeiser's field (note that the plants were not found in Schmeiser's fields); that meant that the farmer had violated the firm's patent.

The judge agreed with Monsanto, ruling that 'the source of (GM) oilseed rape... is not really significant for the issue of infringement'. In other words, it was irrelevant how the patented canola plants got on Schmeiser's land. It could have happened as a result of cross-pollination or by seed movement caused by wind. (The latter is the biggest cause of contamination involving GM crops, and the farm next to Schmeiser's did grow Monsanto's crop.) The judge told Schmeiser that all his seeds, developed over almost half a century, were now the property of Monsanto. The Ecologist May 2004

This is so typical of the immoral behaviour of the Elite corporations. Profit is everything and ordinary, hard-working, decent people and their families count for nothing other the fact that they are considered fair game for extortionate practices or at best regarded as 'profit centres' to be exploited to the maximum.

Worse still, it is a well-documented fact that thousands of farmers in India are committing suicide due to Monsanto's hideously unethical and immoral business tactics. In early 2011 it was estimated that at least 250,000 Indian farmers had committed suicide in the previous decade due to Monsanto's business practices causing their livelihoods to virtually evaporate. Powerful GM lobbyists however are stating that GM crops have transformed India's agriculture, providing greater yields than ever before.

"So who is telling the truth? To find out, I travelled to the 'suicide belt' in Maharashtra state. What I found was deeply disturbing - and has profound implications for countries, including Britain, debating whether to allow the planting of seeds manipulated by scientists to circumvent the laws of nature.

For official figures from the Indian Ministry of Agriculture do indeed confirm that in a huge humanitarian crisis, more than 1,000 farmers kill themselves here each month. Simple, rural people, they are dying slow, agonising deaths. Most swallow insecticide - a pricey substance they were promised they would not need when they were coerced into growing expensive GM crops.

It seems that many are massively in debt to local money-lenders, having over-borrowed to purchase GM seed. Pro-GM experts claim that it is rural poverty, alcoholism, drought and 'agrarian distress' that is the real reason for the horrific toll. But, as I discovered during a four-day journey through the epicentre of the disaster, that is not the full story.

In one small village I visited, 18 farmers had committed suicide after being sucked into GM debts. In some cases, women have taken over farms from their dead husbands - only to kill themselves as well. Latta Ramesh, 38, drank insecticide after her crops failed - two years after her husband disappeared when the GM debts became too much. She left her ten-year-old son, Rashan, in the care of relatives. 'He cries when he thinks of his mother,' said the dead woman's aunt, sitting listlessly in shade near the fields.

In village after village, families told how they had fallen into debt after being persuaded to buy GM seeds instead of traditional cotton seeds. The price difference is staggering: £10 for 100 grams of GM seed, compared with less than £10 for 1,000 times more traditional seeds. But GM salesmen and government officials had promised farmers that these were 'magic seeds' - with better crops that would be free from parasites and insects.

Indeed, in a bid to promote the uptake of GM seeds, traditional varieties were banned from many government seed banks. The authorities had a vested interest in promoting this new biotechnology. Desperate to escape the grinding poverty of the post-independence years, the Indian government had agreed to allow new bio-tech giants, such as the U.S. market-leader Monsanto, to sell their new seed creations.

In return for allowing western companies access to the second most populated country in the world, with more than one billion people, India was granted International Monetary Fund loans in the Eighties and Nineties, helping to launch an economic revolution. But while cities such as Mumbai and Delhi have boomed, the farmers' lives have slid back into the dark ages.

Though areas of India planted with GM seeds have doubled in two years - up to 17 million acres - many farmers have found there is a terrible price to be paid. Far from being 'magic seeds', GM pest-proof 'breeds' of cotton have been devastated by bollworms, a voracious parasite. Nor were the farmers told that these seeds require double the amount of water. This has proved a matter of life and death.

With rains failing for the past two years, many GM crops have simply withered and died, leaving the farmers with crippling debts and no means of paying them off. Having taken loans from traditional money lenders at extortionate rates, hundreds of thousands of small farmers have faced losing their land as the expensive seeds fail, while those who could struggle on faced a fresh crisis.

When crops failed in the past, farmers could still save seeds and replant them the following year. But with GM seeds they cannot do this. That's because GM seeds contain so-called 'terminator technology', meaning that they have been genetically modified so that the resulting crops do not produce viable seeds of their own. As a result, farmers have to buy new seeds each year at the same punitive prices. For some, that means the difference between life and death.

Take the case of Suresh Bhalasa, another farmer who was cremated this week, leaving a wife and two children. As night fell after the ceremony, and neighbours squatted outside while sacred cows were brought in from the fields, his family had no doubt that their troubles stemmed from the moment they were encouraged to buy BT Cotton, a genetically modified plant created by Monsanto.

'We are ruined now,' said the dead man's 38-year-old wife. 'We bought 100 grams of BT Cotton. Our crop failed twice. My husband had become depressed. He went out to his field, lay down in the cotton and swallowed insecticide.' Villagers bundled him into a rickshaw and headed to hospital along rutted farm roads. 'He cried out that he had taken the insecticide and he was sorry,' she said, as her family and neighbours crowded into her home to pay their respects. 'He was dead by the time they got to hospital.'

Asked if the dead man was a 'drunkard' or suffered from other 'social problems', as alleged by pro-GM officials, the quiet, dignified gathering erupted in anger. 'No! No!' one of the dead man's brothers exclaimed. 'Suresh was a good man. He sent his children to school and paid his taxes. 'He was strangled by these magic seeds. They sell us the seeds, saying they will not need expensive pesticides but they do. We have to buy the same seeds from the same company every year. It is killing us. Please tell the world what is happening here.'

Monsanto has admitted that soaring debt was a 'factor in this tragedy'. But pointing out that cotton production had doubled in the past seven years, a spokesman added that there are other reasons for the recent crisis, such as 'untimely rain' or drought, and pointed out that suicides have always been part of rural Indian life. Officials also point to surveys saying the majority of Indian farmers want GM seeds - no doubt encouraged to do so by aggressive marketing tactics.

During the course of my inquiries in Maharastra, I encountered three 'independent' surveyors scouring villages for information about suicides. They insisted that GM seeds were only 50 per cent more expensive - and then later admitted the difference was 1,000 per cent. (A Monsanto spokesman later insisted their seed is 'only double' the price of 'official' non-GM seed - but admitted that the difference can be vast if cheaper traditional seeds are sold by 'unscrupulous' merchants, who often also sell 'fake' GM seeds which are prone to disease.)

With rumours of imminent government compensation to stem the wave of deaths, many farmers said they were desperate for any form of assistance. 'We just want to escape from our problems,' one said. 'We just want help to stop any more of us dying.' Cruelly, it's the young who are suffering most from the 'GM Genocide' - the very generation supposed to be lifted out of a life of hardship and misery by these 'magic seeds'. Here in the suicide belt of India, the cost of the genetically modified future is murderously high." Andrew Malone, UK Daily Mail, 3rd November 2008

Dr. Arpad Pusztai a Hungarian-born protein scientist spent most of his working life at the Rowett Research Institute in Aberdeen, Scotland – a total of 36 years. He was considered to be the world's foremost expert on plant lectins and has authored 270 scientific papers and 3 books on the subject.

However, in 1998 Pusztai publicly announced that the results of his extensive meticulous research showed conclusively that feeding genetically modified potatoe to rats substantially harmed them, leading to his summary dismissal from the institute. The resulting controversy over his dismissal and the attempts to invalidate the conclusions of his research became known as the 'Pusztai affair'.

The rats fed on the genetically modified potatoes showed significant intestinal damage and harm to their immune systems. These effects were not observed in control rats fed on unmodified potatoes, or unmodified potatoes mixed with snowdrop lectin. The team concluded that the effects observed were a result of the genetic modification, not the snowdrop lectin.

Dr. Pusztai commented, *"We had two kinds of potatoes - one GM and the other non GM. I had expected that the GM potato, with 20 micrograms of a component against the several grams of other components, should not cause any problems. But we found problems. Our studies clearly show that the effects were not due to that little gene expression, but it depended on the way the gene had been inserted into the potato genome and what it did to the potato genome."*

In early 2009 I was fortunate enough to briefly meet Arpad's wife, also a scientist, Dr Susan Bardocz at a conference in London. She told me that what *actually* happened although it was obviously distorted in the media, was this;

As soon as the report on the trials was published, at the headquarters of a large corporation primarily concerned with the production and distribution of GM foods alarm bells began to ring and so the head of the corporation involved (no prizes for guessing its name but it begins with M and ends with onsanto) contacted the then US President Bill Clinton to demand some sort of government intervention in order to limit the damage done to GM foods by this worrying turn of events. According to Susan Bardocz who was told this by the director of the institute, Clinton immediately contacted the British PM, Tony Blair and Blair immediately put pressure on the director of the Rowett Institute to dismiss Dr. Pusztai.

In addition to this, the Rowett Institute's director Philip James, who had initially supported Pusztai, suspended him and used misconduct procedures to seize the data. His annual contract was not renewed and Pusztai and his wife were banned from speaking publicly. Phone calls to his office were diverted and his research team was disbanded. Initially the Rowett Institute claimed that they were not performing any research on GM crops but later the Institute claimed that Pusztai had voluntarily retired and apologised for his 'mistake'. According to another version of the 'story the experiments had never been performed in the first place and then yet another version emerged whereby a student had accidentally confused control data with experimental data. This is a typical modus operandus. Confuse the issue as much as possible so that the whole story becomes a total mess and no-one really knows the actual truth any more.

r. Bardocz also said that for the next ten years, Arpad's life became unbearable. His ork, not just the recent work he had done with GM food, but all of his past research oing back 36 years was totally discredited. He was as a result, unable to obtain any ort of position anywhere in the world and all the stress he suffered culminated in im having a stroke in late 2008, severely affecting his health and his life.

cientists who tell the truth revealed by their genuine research projects are really not all welcome in the world of our Elite masters. The truth about most issues, not just ealth is far too dangerous to their position of power to be allowed out in the open d if it should accidentally leak out then a huge, no expense spared propaganda achine immediately cuts-in to discredit the source and cover-up or eliminate the rocess by which it was leaked. This can take the form of anything from a simple lie one extreme, to mass-murder at the other. Either way, it is never a problem.

ese silent killers are deadly, and do not discriminate. They target babies, the derly, teenagers, young adults, middle-aged housewives, and businessmen alike. ey poison livestock, pets and wildlife and the people behind them deny complicity the carnage. These killers are the seemingly beneficial, killing fields of genetically odified (GMO) crops and the people behind them are the US and other Western vernments, the Rockefellers, Monsanto, Dow, DuPont, Syngenta and Bayer Crop ience.

genics is a dirty word, yet particularly applicable to America's GMO killing fields d their inception. In 1974 Henry Kissinger drafted the controversial NSSM-200, lled *"the foundational document on population control issued by the United States vernment."*

ccording to NSSM-200, elements of the implementation of population control ograms could include the legalization of abortion; financial incentives for countries to crease their abortion, sterilization and contraception-use rates; indoctrination of ildren; mandatory population control, and coercion of other forms, such as ithholding disaster and food aid unless an LDC implements population control ograms. NSSM-200 also specifically declared that the United States was to cover up population control activities and avoid charges of imperialism by inducing the United tions and various non-governmental organizations to do its dirty work." Human Life ternational, 2008

1970, Henry Kissinger also said, *"Control oil and you control nations; control food d you control the people."*

w do you control food? By consolidating agricultural interests into what was to be rmed agribusiness, creating genetically modified organisms out of heritage seeds ith funding from the Rockefeller Foundation, patenting the new seeds and making re that these new seeds are force-fed to US farmers as well as the rest of the orld. By holding the patents on these seeds and requiring farmers to purchase new seeds every year, the control is complete. Also, by controlling how these GMO seeds are created, other more sinister uses come to mind. But firstly it is necessary to convince the world of your good intentions. This is accomplished through lies, deception and a modicum of controlled media manipulation. By promising farmers that this technology was safe and would result in increased yields at less cost, they were more than happy to comply. The fact that in most cases this claim was false had yet to be proven by the innocent farmers that believed the lie and by the time independent studies started revealing that GMO is harmful, it was too late, and agri business was on its way to fulfilling its purpose. That is to make as much money as possible by spreading GMO seeds as far as possible and thus gaining control of the population via food.

"In what should amount to a wildly imaginative narrative created by an overzealous science fiction aficionado, the following agencies, their connections, and past actions are real, none-the-less.

Imagine, if you will, a world in which health sciences, disease control, cancer research, bio-weapons research, vaccine development, biotechnology, food and agriculture, national defence, and chemical companies all work together under the military. Then imagine if you will that a certain chemical company under the guise of a life sciences operation, produces an herbicide/defoliant for military use so destructive and highly toxic that contact with it causes cancer, diabetes and birth defects. And then that same chemical/life sciences company partners with a funding corporation whose team members include the ex-partner of the inventor of the world's first completely synthetic organism, which was recently unleashed in the ocean and has since turned its ever hungry sights on human flesh. Then imagine that same company with a monopoly on our food supply...

Sound like an episode out of the Twilight Zone or Dr. Who? Well, it's not. It's history and it's documented." Barbara H Peterson, Farm Wars, June 2011.

High Fructose Corn Syrup (HFCS)

Another product found in much of our processed foods is HFCS which has been added since the early 1970s. In effect a corn-based sweetener, this product is largely responsible for the high incidence of Diabetes type 2 prevalent in much of Western society today. Today, food companies use HFCS, a mixture of fructose and glucose because it is inexpensive, easy to transport and keeps foods moist. And because HFCS is so sweet, it is also cost effective for companies to use small quantities of HFCS in place of other more expensive sweeteners or flavourings.

For these reasons, HFCS isn't going away any time soon. If HFCS is one of the first ingredients listed on a food label, my advice would be to not eat it.

HFCS is a highly refined, artificial product. It is created through an intricate process that transforms cornstarch into a thick, clear liquid. White sugar and HFCS are no the same. Industry advocates for corn growers say that they are the same, but nutritional science studies say that there is a big difference between the two. They say that HFCS is definitely *worse than sugar*.

This manufactured fructose is sweeter than sugar in an unhealthy way, and is digested differently in a bad way. Research has shown that HFCS goes directly to the liver, releasing enzymes that instruct the body to then store fat. This may elevate triglyceride (fat in blood) levels and elevate cholesterol levels. This fake fructose slows fat burning and causes weight gain. Other research indicates that it does not stimulate insulin production, which usually creates a sense of being full, therefore, people are artificially induced to eat much more than they should. Indications also are that the important chromium levels are lowered by this sweetener which contributes to diabetes type 2.

So we have another product that would seem to be harmful in many ways that is allowed indiscriminately into our foodstuffs. Why are we not warned? Why are we not informed about it so that we can make healthy lifestyle choices for ourselves and our families? Once again it would appear to be that profit comes before health. It also says to me that the people in control of our food and thus our health are deliberately deceiving us into disease and obesity for the sake of their own bank balances.

Monosodium Glutamate (MSG)

MSG is an amino acid that affects every organ in the body. There is much evidence also that as with HFCS, MSG is also similarly responsible in large part for the huge epidemic of obesity and diabetes type 2 that the western world is currently undergoing.

It appears in a vast range of processed, tinned and packaged foods from supermarkets and can often be added separately to food in restaurants, cafeterias and institutes such as hospitals and care homes as a 'flavour enhancer'. So in effect we are not safe from it anywhere.

Staggeringly, it is not compulsory for manufacturers of food to specify the exact quantities of MSG that are contained in their products despite the fact that a single 12 gram dose of MSG has been found to be lethal to a 2kg rat, whilst much smaller doses have been shown to cause massive brain damage. Additionally it is now allowed for MSG to be sprayed on to crops and it can also become airborne as a result of this activity.

Study after scientific study has shown MSG to be capable of damaging a multitude of organs and soft tissues and also artificially enhance appetites in a variety of subjects, leading in turn as a by-product of this, to obesity. In other experimental studies using rodents, the food additive has been successfully used to generate diabetes on a large scale.

Perhaps more worryingly, MSG has been proved to pass through the placenta of rodents into the unborn foetus, the implications of this fact for humans, being quite startling. Human foetal development has also been shown to be jeopardised by high quantities of MSG in other studies.

"Children undergoing perinatal brain injury often suffer from the dramatic consequences of this misfortune for the rest of their lives. Despite the severe clinical and socio-economic significance, no effective clinical strategies have yet been developed to counteract this condition. This review describes the pathophysiological mechanisms that are implicated in perinatal brain injury. These include the acute breakdown of neuronal membrane potential followed by the release of excitatory amino acids such as glutamate and aspartate. Glutamate binds to post-synaptically located glutamate receptors that regulate calcium channels. The resulting calcium influx activates proteases, lipases and endonucleases which in turn destroy the cellular skeleton. Clinical studies have shown that intrauterine infection increases the risk of periventricular white matter damage especially in the immature foetus. This damage may be mediated by cardiovascular effects of endotoxins." From the scientific paper, 'Perinatal brain damage from patho-physiology to prevention'. Jensen A, Garnier Y, Middelanis J, Berger R. Eur J Obstet Gynecol Reprod Biol. 22nd September 2003

There are few chemicals that we as a people are exposed to that have as many far reaching physiological effects on living beings as does Monosodium Glutamate. MSG directly causes obesity, diabetes, triggers epilepsy, destroys eye tissues and is toxic to many organs. Considering that MSG's only reported role in food is that of 'flavour enhancer' is that use worth the risk of the myriad of physical ailments associated with it? Does the public really want to be tricked into eating more food and faster by a food additive?

MSG is entering our bodies in record amounts with absolutely no limits. The studies outlined in this report often use a smaller proportional dosage than the average child may ingest daily.

Consider the children of the world who eat MSG in their school cafeterias, hospitals, restaurants and homes. They deserve foods free of added MSG, a substance so toxic that research scientists use it purposely to trigger diabetes, obesity and epileptic convulsions in animals. Perhaps we will see a reduction in obesity, diabetes and other diseases once the excess MSG threat to our health has been removed. We *can* stop the slow, deliberate poisoning of mankind for profits if we all act together.

If you try an Internet search for MSG, be prepared to be bombarded with lies and propaganda. There are literally thousands of websites out there trying to fool you into believing that it really is harmless.

Fluoride

Perhaps the most deadly of all the poisons we are deliberately and deceptively being forced to ingest, Fluoride also comes complete with the biggest hype of these toxins by far.

There is actually no such chemical name as Fluoride. The name stems from the gas 'Fluorine' and from the use of this gas in various different industries, such as Aluminium smelting and the nuclear industry, toxic by-products containing fluorine molecules are created. One example of this is Sodium Fluoride which is the most common and is a hazardous waste by-product of aluminium production. Used for a long time as rat and cockroach poison, it is also an ingredient of anaesthetics and psychiatric drugs as well as deadly Sarin nerve gas.

As we all know, fluoride is used in 99.9% of all proprietary toothpastes and is present in the drinking water (tap and bottled) of much of the first world. Advertised and promoted as protecting teeth, it is unfortunately much, much more sinister than that. Historically, this substance was quite expensive for the worlds' premier chemical companies to dispose of, but in the 1950s and 60s, Alcoa and the entire aluminium industry, with a vast abundance of the toxic waste, somehow sold the FDA and the US government on the insane (but highly profitable) idea of buying this poison at a 20,000% mark-up and then injecting it into our water supply as well as into the world's toothpastes and dental products.

Consider also that when Sodium Fluoride is injected into our drinking water, its level is approximately 1 part-per-million but since we only drink ½ of one percent of the total water supply, the hazardous chemical and the chemical industry not only has a free hazardous waste disposal system, but we have also paid them for the privilege!

You may or may not know or indeed wish to know that Fluoride was used by the Nazis in World War 2 as an intellect suppressant in their many detention camps and also as a way of making the inmates docile and compliant.

Independent scientific evidence over the past sixty plus years has shown that sodium fluoride shortens our life span, promotes various cancers and mental disturbances and most importantly, reduces intelligence and makes humans docile, unquestioning and subservient. There is also increasing evidence that aluminium in the brain is a causative factor in Alzheimer's Disease, and evidence points towards the fact that it has the ability to 'trick' the blood-brain barrier by imitating the hydrogen ion thus allowing this deadly chemical, access to brain tissue.

Honest scientists with no ulterior motive who have attempted to 'whistle-blow' on sodium fluoride's mega-bucks propaganda campaign have consistently been given a large dose of professional 'black-listing' in return and thus their valid points disputing the current vested interests never have received the recognition they deserve in the national press. 'Just follow the money' as the saying goes, to find the source and you will find prominent, Elite families to be the major influence in this absolutely scandalous situation.

In 1952 a slick PR campaign rammed the concept of 'fluoridation' through Public Health departments and various dental organisations worldwide. This slick campaign was far from the objective, scientific, stringently researched programme that it should have been. But as with all these situations, where money is concerned – and billions upon billions of pounds of it in this case – there were no barriers to be seen. It has continued in this same vein right up to the present day and now Sodium Fluoride use has now become the ubiquitous, de facto standard.

"There is a tremendous amount of emotional, highly unscientific 'know-it-all' emotions attached to the topic of 'sodium fluoride' usage - but I personally have yet to find even ONE objective, double-blind study that even remotely links sodium fluoride to healthy teeth at ANY AGE. Instead, I hear and read such blather as '9 out of 10 DENTISTS recommend fluoride toothpaste' etc. etc. etc. Let me reiterate: truly independent (unattached to moneyed vested interest groups) scientists who've spent a large portion of their lives studying and working with this subject have been hit with a surprising amount of unfair character assassinations from strong vested-interest groups who reap grand profits from the public's ignorance as well as from their illnesses.

Do you have diabetes and/or kidney disease? There are reportedly more than 11 million Americans with diabetes. If it is true that diabetics drink more liquids than other people, then according to the Physician's Desk Reference these 11 million people are at much higher risk drinking fluoridated water because they will receive a much deadlier dose because of their need for higher than normal water consumption. Kidney disease, by definition, lowers the efficiency of the kidneys, which of course is the primary means in which fluoride (or any other toxic chemical) is eliminated from the body. Does it not make sense that these people shouldn't drink fluoridated water at all? Cases are on record (Annapolis, Maryland, 1979) where ill kidney patients on dialysis machines died because they ingested relatively small amounts of SODIUM FLUORIDE from unwittingly drinking the 'fluoridated' city water supply? Will adequate warnings be given to people with weak kidneys, or will the real cause of such deaths be 'covered up' in the name of 'domestic tranquillity'?" A. True Ott, August 2000

It is also worth contemplating the fact that in the USA, all toothpaste tubes / packs come with a warning as standard. *'Warning – harmful or fatal if ingested. If swallowed, please consult a doctor immediately'.* Bit of a clue as to its capabilities there I would have thought. How often have you accidentally or absent-mindedly swallowed a toothbrush-full of toothpaste? More importantly, your children and grandchildren love the taste of their special toothpastes with flavour calculated to make them want to brush their teeth more often. How many times might they have swallowed a toothbrush-full over the years and what pernicious harm must it be doing to their immature little bodies?

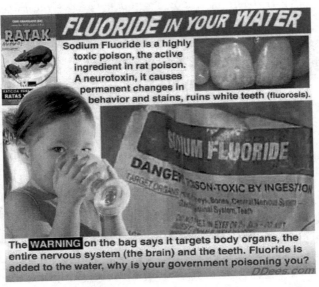

So once again we have a situation where vested interests spend millions, rake in favours or provide financial incentives to get their way and in doing so guarantee themselves billionaire status many times over. And it gets even worse;

"I have your letter of September 29 asking for further documentation regarding a statement made in my book, 'The Truth about Water Fluoridation', to the effect that the idea of water fluoridation was brought to England from Russia by the Russian Communist Kreminoff. In the 1930's Hitler and the German Nazis envisioned a world to be dominated and controlled by a Nazi philosophy of pan-Germanism. The German chemists worked out a very ingenious and far-reaching plan of mass-control which was submitted to and adopted by the German General Staff. This plan was to control the population in any given area through mass medication of drinking water supplies. By this method they could control the population in whole areas, reduce population by water medication that would produce sterility in women, and so on. In this scheme of

mass-control, sodium fluoride occupied a prominent place. Repeated doses of infinitesimal amounts of fluoride will in time reduce an individual's power to resist domination, by slowly poisoning and narcotizing a certain area of the brain, thus making him submissive to the will of those who wish to govern him.

The real reason behind water fluoridation is not to benefit children's teeth. If this were the real reason there are many ways in which it could be done that are much easier, cheaper, and far more effective. The real purpose behind water fluoridation is to reduce the resistance of the masses to domination and control and loss of liberty.

When the Nazis under Hitler decided to go to Poland, both the German General Staff and the Russian General Staff exchanged scientific and military ideas, plans and personnel, and the scheme of mass control through water medication was seized upon by the Russian Communists because it fitted ideally into their plans to communize the world.

I was told of this entire scheme by a German chemist who was an official of the great I.G. Farben chemical industries and was also prominent in the Nazi movement at the time. I say this with all the earnestness and sincerity of a scientist who has spent nearly 20 years' research into the chemistry, biochemistry, physiology and pathology of fluoride - any person who drinks artificially fluorinated water for a period of one year or more will never again be the same person mentally or physically." Charles E Perkins, Chemist, 2 October 1954 writing to the Lee Foundation for Nutritional Research

I somehow do not think that the SS and the Gestapo had the health of children's teeth in mind when they decided upon this course of action, do you? The real reason was as stated, to sterilise and chemically lobotomise their victims. How convenient then for our ruling Elite that this is also the effect it is having today on large swathes of humanity, allowing them even more of a free rein to get on with their plans for a military dictatorship / police state whilst encountering little or no resistance from the medicated masses.

The following letter is also worthy of note;

"It appears that the citizens of Massachusetts are among the 'next' on the agenda of the water poisoners. There is a sinister network of subversive agents, Godless intellectual parasites, working in our country today whose ramifications grow more extensive, more successful and more alarming each new year and whose true objective is to demoralize, paralyze and destroy our great Republic - from within if they can, according to their plan for their own possession. The tragic success they have already attained in their long siege to destroy the moral fibre of American life is now one of their most potent footholds towards their own ultimate victory over us.

Fluoridation of our community water systems can well become their most subtle weapon for our sure physical and mental deterioration. As a research chemist of

stablished standing, I built within the past 22 years 3 American chemical plants and censed 6 of my 53 patents. Based on my years of practical experience in the health food nd chemical field, let me warn; fluoridation of drinking water is criminal insanity, sure ational suicide. DON'T DO IT!!

ven in very small quantities, sodium fluoride is a deadly poison to which no effective ntidote has been found. Every exterminator knows that it is the most effective rat-iller. Sodium Fluoride is entirely different from organic calcium-fluoro-phosphate eeded by our bodies and provided by nature, in God's great providence and love, to uild and strengthen our bones and our teeth. This organic calcium-fluoro-phosphate, erived from proper foods, is an edible organic salt, insoluble in water and assimilable y the human body; whereas the non-organic sodium fluoride used in fluoridating water s instant poison to the body and fully water soluble. The body refuses to assimilate it.

areful, bona fide laboratory experimentation by conscientious, patriotic research hemists and actual medical experience, have both revealed that instead of preserving r promoting 'dental health', fluoridated drinking water destroys teeth before dulthood and after, by the destructive mottling and other pathological conditions it ctually causes in them and also creates many other very grave pathological conditions 1 the internal organisms of bodies consuming it. How then can it be called a 'health lan'? What's behind it?

hat any so-called 'doctors' would persuade a civilized nation to add voluntarily a deadly oison to its drinking water systems is unbelievable. It is the height of criminal insanity! lo wonder Hitler and Stalin fully believed and agreed from 1939 to 1941 that, quoting rom both Lenin's 'Last Will' and Hitler's Mein Kampf: 'America we shall demoralize, ivide, and destroy from within.'

re our Civil Defense organizations and agencies awake to the perils of water poisoning y fluoridation? Its use has been recorded in other countries. Sodium Fluoride water olutions are the cheapest and most effective rat killers known to chemists: colourless, dourless, tasteless; no antidote, no remedy, no hope: instant and complete xtermination of rats. Fluoridation of water systems can be slow national suicide, or uick national liquidation. It is criminal insanity - treason!!" Dr. E.H. Bronner (nephew f Albert Einstein), Research Chemist, Los Angeles, January 1952

he public outcry at the time (now sadly forgotten) was such that the addition of luoride into public water supplies was abandoned for a year. However, the populace lave a very short memory and the topic was resurrected again shortly thereafter, this ime with little to no resistance whatsoever.

luoride, sad to say, has exactly the opposite effect on teeth to that which is promoted to us; strong healthy teeth. There is now, especially in America, an bsolute epidemic of dental fluorosis with up to 80% of children in some cities being ffected. The first visible sign of excessive fluoride exposure according to the US

National Research Council are brownish flecks or spots, particularly on the front teeth, or dark spots or stripes in more severe cases.

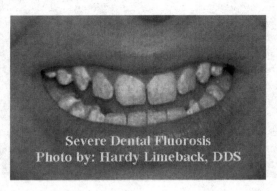

Severe Dental Fluorosis
Photo by: Hardy Limeback, DDS

What is much less known to the public is that fluoride also accumulates in bones.

"The teeth are windows to what's happening in the bones." Paul Connett, Professor of Chemistry at St. Lawrence University, New York.

In recent years, paediatric bone specialists have expressed alarm about an increase in stress fractures among young people in the US. Connett and other scientists are concerned that fluoride-linked to bone damage in studies since the 1930s, may be a contributing factor.

In 1944 a severe pollution incident occurred downwind of the E.I. DuPont de Nemours Company chemical factory in Deepwater, New Jersey. The factory was then producing millions of pounds of fluoride for the Manhattan Project whose scientists were racing to produce the world's first atomic bomb.

The farms downwind in Gloucester and Salem counties were famous for their high-quality produce. Their peaches went directly to the Waldorf Astoria Hotel in New York City; their tomatoes were mainly bought by Campbell's for soup. But in the summer of 1944 the farmers began reporting that their crops were blighted. They said that poultry died after an all-night thunderstorm and that farm workers who ate produce they had picked would sometimes vomit all night and into the next day. The horses looked sick and were too stiff to work, and some cows were so crippled that they could not stand up; they could only graze by crawling on their bellies.

The account was confirmed in taped interviews with Philip Sadtler (shortly before he died), of Sadtler Laboratories of Philadelphia, one of the USA's oldest chemical consulting firms. Sadtler had personally conducted the initial investigation of the damage.

Kidney disease is another hallmark of fluoride poisoning. Multiple animal studies have found that fluoride levels as low as 1 part per million (ppm) which is the amount added to most fluoridated water systems, cause kidney damage. And a Chinese study found that children exposed to slightly higher fluoride levels had biological markers in their blood indicative of kidney damage.

It has also been found that fluoride impairs proper thyroid function and debilitates the endocrine system. Up until the 1970s, fluoride was used in Europe as a thyroid-suppressing medication because it lowers thyroid function. Many experts believe that widespread hypothyroidism today is a result of overexposure to fluoride.

Since fluoride is present in most municipal water supplies in North America and in much of Western Europe, it is absurd to even suggest that parents avoid giving it to their young children. How are parents supposed to avoid it unless they install a whole house reverse-osmosis water filtration system? And even if families install such a system, fluoride is found in all sorts of food and beverages, not to mention that it is absorbed through the skin every time people wash their hands with or take a shower in fluoridated water.

There simply is no legitimate reason to fluoridate water. Doing so forcibly medicates an entire population with a carcinogenic, chemical drug. There really is no effective way to avoid it entirely and nobody really knows how much is ingested or absorbed on a daily basis because exposure is too widespread to calculate. But political pressure and bad science have continued to justify water fluoridation in most major cities, despite growing mountains of evidence showing its dangers.

Is it any wonder that people now after years of ingesting this toxin, have no interest in the world around them and the fate awaiting them and their children and grandchildren? After all, what's more important than who wins the game this weekend or the latest adventures of our favourite soap characters? All as planned of course.

A new study pre-published in December 2010 in the journal 'Environmental Health Perspectives' confirms that fluoridated water definitely causes brain damage in children. The most recent among 23 others pertaining to fluoride and lowered IQ levels, the new study so strongly proves that fluoride is a dangerous, brain-destroying toxin that experts say it could be the one that finally ends water fluoridation. I have severe doubts about that.

I would strongly urge any dentist or doctor reading this to undertake their own research into the efficacy and effects of fluoride and not just parrot the propaganda relayed to them by their own Elite-controlled professional organisations.

However, it is also up to us all to stand up and say 'no' to mass water fluoridation. If someone wishes to voluntarily imbibe fluoride, then let him/her do so. I have no problem with that, but to forcibly administer this poison to an unsuspecting and unwilling populace without prior knowledge or consent is a criminal activity. We are not prisoners....not just yet anyway.

Contaminated Drinking Water

What is actually in our water other than fluoride? Is it pure or does it contain impurities and toxins? If we take heed of the water companies, they will tell us that water is absolutely pure due to being filtered at source. Wrong! This is absolutely untrue.

Have you ever come across a bottle of prescription tablets or a medicine bottle that you no longer needed or perhaps had passed its expiration date? You probably disposed of the substance by flushing it down the toilet, down the sink waste-disposal unit or throwing it in the waste bin?

It is extremely concerning that environmental contaminants originating from industrial, agricultural, medical and common household substances, ie., pharmaceutical waste, cosmetics, detergents and toiletries are being disposed of into the water systems of the world. A variety of pharmaceuticals including painkillers, tranquilisers, anti-depressants, antibiotics, birth control pills, oestrogen replacement therapies, chemotherapy agents, anti-seizure medications etc., are finding their way into the water supplies via human and animal excreta from disposal into the sewage system.

Flushing unused medications down the toilet and pharmaceutical residue from landfills has a tremendously detrimental impact on groundwater supplies and thus drinking water. Agricultural practices are a major source of this contamination and 40% of antibiotics manufactured are fed to livestock as growth enhancers. Manure, containing traces of pharmaceuticals is often spread on land as fertiliser from which it can leach into local streams and rivers and thence into the water table. Conventional wastewater treatments, filtration and recycling as commonly used by our water companies is not even close to being effective in eliminating the majority of pharmaceutical residues.

The prevalence of pharmaceuticals in water is nothing new. In fact, it is reasonable to assume that as long as pharmaceuticals have been in use, they and their metabolites have contributed to overall environmental contamination. What is new is our ability to detect trace amounts of these contaminants in water; hence, we are finding pharmaceuticals in water because we are finally able to detect them.

According to an article published in the December 2002 issue of Environmental Health Perspectives, the amount of pharmaceuticals and personal care products (PCPs) released into the environment each year is roughly equivalent to the amount of pesticides used each year.

During 1999-2000, the US Geological Survey conducted the first nationwide investigation of the occurrence of pharmaceuticals, hormones and other organic contaminants in 139 streams from 30 states. A total of 95 contaminants were targeted including antibiotics, prescription and non-prescription drugs, steroids and hormones, 82 of which were found in at least one sample. In addition 80% of streams sampled were positive for one or more contaminant. Furthermore, 75% of the streams contained two or more contaminants, 54% had greater than five, while 34% had more than ten and 13% tested positive for more than twenty targeted contaminants. There is no valid reason to believe that this is not the case elsewhere in the world.

Pharmaceuticals have since been found in treated sewage effluents, surface waters, soil and tap water. Antibiotics and oestrogens are only two of many pharmaceuticals suspected of persisting in the environment either due to their inability to naturally biodegrade or continued prevalence as a result of continuous release.

Recent monitoring studies fail to address one question: Are the levels of pharmaceuticals in the environment significant? At first glance, one would say 'no' since levels found in the environment are six to seven orders of magnitude lower than therapeutic doses in spite of the fact up to 90 percent of an oral drug can be excreted in human waste. However, low and consistent exposures would not likely produce immediate acute effects but rather subtle impacts such as behavioural or reproductive effects that could very well go unnoticed.

In addition, concern remains over the increasing practice of artificial recharge of groundwater with sewage effluent where pharmaceuticals have been found to percolate into the groundwater. Some common pharmaceutical contaminants are known to persist for more than six years in the sub-surface or groundwater.
The bad news is that conventional water and wastewater treatment methods allow many classes of pharmaceuticals to pass through into our drinking water supplies unchanged and untreated.

So, what is the true risk assessment of pharmaceuticals and other similar contaminants in water? Do they present a health threat to any humans, animals (or even plants) being exposed to them? Many scientists are concerned about long-term, chronic and combined exposures to agents designed to cause a physiological effect in humans and believe we should be very concerned about aquatic ecosystems where sperm levels and spawning patterns in aquatic organisms have been clearly altered in environments heavily polluted with a class of hormone-altering pharmaceuticals known as endocrine disrupters.

With a growing and aging population as well as increased reliance on drug treatments and development of new drugs, the problem with pharmaceutical contamination promises only to increase.

Since we all drink tap and bottled water routinely, every single day in one form or another would it therefore not be unreasonable to conclude that we are all being systematically 'poisoned' on an ongoing basis? Worse still, could any of these substances be cumulative in nature, making the impact on our health and that of our children even more significant? As long as the water corporations continue in denial over this issue, I would suggest that the health of every one of us is at serious long term risk, all through that supposedly most benign of all substances, water.

Junk Food

Many years ago there was a famous story about a man in the USA who accidentally left a McDonald's hamburger in a jacket pocket for a year and when he finally got around to wearing the jacket again, to his surprise, the burger looked and smelled exactly as it did when first bought, twelve months earlier. This took place in 1990. Since then he has bought a McDonald's hamburger every year and saved the results. He now has a veritable 'museum' of McDonald's burgers, complete with bread bun, French fries and associated relishes going back over twenty years and has labelled and dated them. Interestingly, none of them have decomposed – at all. From the one bought in 1989 to the one bought in 2010, they still look virtually identical.

How can this be? Why do fast food burgers and fries not decompose like 'normal' food? The answer is partly that they are treated with so many chemicals that even mould and bacteria will not eat them. This is partially true but not the entire explanation.

Many processed foods do not decompose and are not consumed by moulds, insects or even rodents. Try leaving an open tub of margarine outside in your garden and see if anything bothers to eat it.

Potato crisps (chips) can last for decades. Frozen pizzas are remarkably resistant to decomposition and even some highly processed sausages and meats can be kept for years and they will never decompose.

With meats, the primary reason why they do not decompose is their high sodium content. Salt is a great preservative, as our ancestors have known for thousands of years. McDonald's meat is absolutely loaded with sodium - so much so that it qualifies as 'preserved' meat, without even considering the chemicals you might find in it. However, the real question should be 'why do the bread buns not turn mouldy?' That is the real issue, since normal, healthy bread begins to grow mould within days. What could possibly be in McDonald's hamburger buns that would ward off microscopic life for more than two decades?

Unless you have qualifications in chemistry, you probably cannot even read the ingredients list. McDonalds' website states that these frankly, scary ingredients are contained in their 'bread' buns:

"Enriched flour (bleached wheat flour, malted barley flour, niacin, reduced iron, thiamin mononitrate, riboflavin, folic acid, enzymes), water, high fructose corn syrup, sugar, yeast, soybean oil and/or partially hydrogenated soybean oil, contains 2% or less of the following: salt, calcium sulphate, calcium carbonate, wheat gluten, ammonium sulphate, ammonium chloride, dough conditioners (sodium stearoyl lactylate, datem, ascorbic acid, azodicarbonamide, mono- and diglycerides, ethoxylated monoglycerides, monocalcium phosphate, enzymes, guar gum, calcium peroxide, soy flour), calcium propionate and sodium propionate (preservatives), soy lecithin."

Our old friend HFCS makes an appearance in there as does sugar, partially-hydrogenated soybean oil (real heart-disease inducing fodder) and the long list of chemicals such as ammonium sulphate and sodium proprionate. How appetising!

However, the truly shocking part about all this is...

"In my estimation, the reason nothing will eat a McDonald's hamburger bun (except a human) is because it's not food! No normal animal will perceive a McDonald's hamburger bun as food and as it turns out, neither will bacteria nor fungi. To their senses, it's just not edible stuff. That's why these bionic burger buns just won't decompose. There is only one species on planet Earth that's stupid enough to think a McDonald's hamburger is food. This species is suffering from skyrocketing rates of diabetes, cancer, heart disease, dementia and obesity. This species claims to be the most intelligent species on the planet and yet it behaves in such a moronic way that it feeds its own children poisonous chemicals and such atrocious non-foods that even fungi won't eat it (and fungi will eat cow manure, just FYI)." Mike Adams, Natural News

Do you cook your chicken with dimethylpolysiloxane, an anti-foaming agent made of silicone? How about tertiary butylhydroquinone, a chemical preservative so deadly that just five grams can kill you?

These are just two of the ingredients in a McDonalds Chicken McNugget. Only 50% of a McNugget is actually chicken. The other 50% includes corn derivatives, sugars, leavening agents and completely synthetic ingredients.

The Organic Authority helpfully transcribed the full ingredients list provided by McDonalds:

"White boneless chicken, water, food starch-modified, salt, seasoning (autolyzed yeast extract, salt, wheat starch, natural flavouring (botanical source), safflower oil, dextrose, citric acid, and rosemary), sodium phosphates, seasoning (canola oil, mono- and diglycerides, extractives of rosemary).

Battered and breaded with: water, enriched flour (bleached wheat flour, niacin, reduced iron, thiamin mononitrate, riboflavin, folic acid), yellow corn flour, food starch-

modified, salt, leavening (baking soda, sodium acid pyrophosphate, sodium aluminium phosphate, monocalcium phosphate, calcium lactate), spices, wheat starch, whey, corn starch. Prepared in vegetable oil (Canola oil, corn oil, soybean oil, hydrogenated soybean oil with TBHQ and citric acid added to preserve freshness). Dimethylpolysiloxane added as an antifoaming agent."

Just in case you think I am singling out McDonalds for some unfair treatment here, let me just say that I have no particular 'axe to grind' on this issue. I would include burgers and chicken burgers and any other 'delicious snacks', not just from McDonalds, but from also, take a bow... Burger King, Wendy's, Wimpy, Kentucky Fried Chicken et al. (with sincere apologies to any other manufacturer of this vile filth masquerading as nutrition that I have omitted to mention – you know who you are!).

Until we, as a species, stop buying this dreadful garbage, they will continue to poison us and infect us with disease, while we pay them for the privilege. Let us all let them know that we are not prepared to suffer this any longer by boycotting all such establishments.

However, perhaps the biggest danger we face is not from the Elite corporations who seek to abuse our bodies and health in the name of profits, but from an organisation, truly Orwellian in scope which actively seeks to prevent us from gaining access to healthy eating alternatives. Let me introduce you to...

Codex Alimentarius

Kiss your VITAMINS Goodbye

The United Nations and CODEX ALIMENTARIUS have a plan for you

Codex Alimentarius is the United Nations / European Union plan to destroy organic farming and to eradicate the complementary and natural health care industry which is obviously a threat to the health, welfare and profits of Big Food and Big Pharma.

There would appear to be an almost total lack of awareness (or even interest) with regard to the implications of this pernicious global Commission, particularly amongst those most affected by the excesses of this restrictive legislation. In the words of the National Health Federation, the aims and objectives of Codex Alimentarius are to...

- Allow only low-potency supplements that will do nothing positive for one's health.
- Allow all or most foods to be genetically-modified.
- Make beneficial supplements unavailable or sold by prescription only.

For many people, this agenda is so outrageous, they cannot believe such goals are achievable; yet this may well very soon be reality, if the Codex Alimentarius Commission continues to disregard input from those who offer a counter perspective to the combined forces of Big Food and Big Pharma.

For the past five years the European challenge to Codex has been led by Dr. Robert Vererk, Executive Director of the Alliance for Natural Health and Scientific Advisor to the National Health Federation. Yet despite the efforts of the ANH, the NHF and the Dr. Rath Foundation the Codex agenda lumbers ever closer to the EU statute books.

In April of 2005, the ANH mounted a legal challenge to the Codex Commission; Justice Leendert A Geelhoed, the European Union Advocate General, referred to the arbitrary powers of the Codex-supporting EU legislation as being *"about as transparent as a black box"*. The subsequent 12th July 2005 ruling of the International Court of Justice in Luxembourg followed the July 4th Rome meeting of Codex when the 85 countries present ratified the restrictive guidelines for dietary supplements.

Six days after London was awarded the 2012 Olympics and just five days after the London Bombings, there was little mention of the ICJ ruling in the British media.

Amongst the most disturbing component contained within Article 6 of the EU Directive, is that it strictly prohibits information about diseases being treatable by nutrients and calls for future supplement dosage restrictions. *Such is the power and influence of Big Pharma!*

Today the EU pays an annual fine of $150 million to maintain its ban on the US hormone-fed beef. Clear evidence that WTO rules put *free-trade* interests of agribusiness above national health concerns. Meanwhile, a flood of new GMO products are surreptitiously being introduced into EU agriculture. Monsanto, Syngenta and other GMO multinationals have already taken advantage of lax national rules in new EU member countries such as Poland to get the GMO 'foot-in-the door.' Pro-GMO governments, such as that of Angela Merkel in Germany, abdicate any responsibility by claiming they are only following WTO 'orders', which is exactly the line taken by the FSA and strangely reminiscent of another organisation in history coincidentally from the same part of the world, whose followers used exactly the same defence.

Powerful agribusiness multinationals such as Monsanto, Dow Chemicals and DuPont are working through the WTO-backed Codex Alimentarius Commission in their determination to overrun national or regional efforts to halt the march of GMO.

NHF & ANH resistance to Codex will potentially be little more than an inconvenience to the prime movers behind this pernicious global agenda ... unless and until such time as there is a wider realisation that the organic farming and natural health industries may soon be little more than a memory.

Meanwhile, Big Pharma and Big Food have a very well prepared strategy to ensure the success of the Codex agenda. But our challenge is to demonstrate that no corporate strategy can be effective against the universal desire to retain the basic human right to food and health freedom.

Contrary to popular belief Codex Alimentarius is neither a law nor a policy. It is in fact a functioning body, a Commission, created by the Food and Agricultural Organization and the World Health Organisation under the direction of the United Nations. The confusion in this regard is largely due to statements made by many critics referring to the 'implementation' of Codex Alimentarius as if it were legislation waiting to come into effect. A more accurate phrase would be the 'implementation of Codex Alimentarius guidelines,' as it would more adequately describe the situation.

Codex is merely another tool in the chest of the Elite whose goal is to create a one world government in which they wield complete control. Power over the food supply is essential in order to achieve this. As will be discussed later, Codex

Alimentarius will be 'implemented' whenever guidelines are established and national governments begin to arrange their domestic laws in accordance with the standards set by the organisation.

The existence of Codex Alimentarius as a policy-making body has roots going back over a hundred years. The name itself, Codex Alimentarius, is simply Latin for 'food code' and directly descended from the Codex Alimentarius Austriacus, a set of standards and descriptions of a variety of foods in the Austria-Hungarian Empire between 1897 and 1911. This set of standards was the brainchild of both the food industry and academia and was used by the courts in order to determine food identity in a legal fashion.

Even as far back as 1897, nations were being pushed toward harmonisation of national laws into an international set of standards that would reduce the barriers to trade created by differences in national laws. As the Codex Alimentarius Austriacus gained steam in its localised area, the idea of having a single set of standards for all of Europe began to pick up support too. From 1954-1958, Austria successfully pursued the creation of the Codex Alimentarius Europaeus (the European Codex Alimentarius) and almost immediately the UN directed FAO (Food and Agricultural Organization) sprang into action when the FAO Regional Conference for Europe expressed the desire for a global international set of standards for food. The FAO Regional Conference then sent a proposal up the chain of command to the FAO itself with the suggestion to create a joint FAO/WHO programme dealing with food standards.

The very next year, the Codex Alimentarius Europaeus adopted a resolution that its work on food standards be taken over by the FAO. Then in 1961, it was decided by the WHO, Codex Alimentarius Europaeus, Organization for Economic Co-operation and Development (OECD), and the FAO Conference to create an international food standards programme known as the Codex Alimentarius. In 1963, as a result of the resolutions passed by these organisations two years earlier, Codex Alimentarius was officially created.

Although created under the auspices of the FAO and the WHO, there is some controversy regarding individuals who may or may not have participated in the establishment of Codex. Some anti-Codex organisations have asserted that Nazi war criminals, Fritz ter Meer and Hermann Schmitz in particular, were the principal architects of the organisation. Because many of these claims are made with only indirect evidence or no evidence at all, one might be tempted to disregard them at first glance. However, as the allegations gain more and more adherents, Codex has attempted to refute them. In the Frequently Asked Questions section of its website, the question, 'Is it true that Codex was created by a former war criminal to control the world food supply?' Is answered by stating;

"No. It is a false claim. You just need to type the words 'Codex Alimentarius' in any search engine and you will find lots of these rumours about Codex. Usually the people spreading them will give no proof but will ask you to send donations or to sign petitions against Codex.

Truthful information about Codex http://www.codexalimentarius.net is found on the Internet - there is nothing to hide from our side - we are a public institution working in public for the public - we are happy if people want to know more about our work and ask questions.

There is an official Codex Contact Point

http://www.codexalimentarius.net/web/members.jsp> in each member country who will be pleased to answer your questions on Codex."

But, as one can see from the statement above, Codex's response does very little to answer this question beyond simply disagreeing with it. While it is true that many individuals who make this claim provide little evidence for it, the presentation of the information does not necessarily negate its truthfulness. In fact, Codex offers its own website as a source for accurate information about the organisation; yet, beyond the FAQ section, there is nothing to be found that is relevant to the "war criminal" allegations; furthermore the Codexalimentarius.net website is virtually in-decipherable, almost to the point of being completely useless.

In the end, this response raises more questions than it answers. This is because Codex, if it wished to do so, could put these rumours to rest by simply posting a list of the individuals and organisations that funded or played an integral role in its creation. However, it does nothing of the sort. Beyond mentioning the FAO and the WHO, we are completely unaware of who or how many other individuals and organisations participated in the creation of Codex Alimentarius.

The 'war criminal' claims centre around the chemical conglomerate known as I.G. Farben which was made up of several German chemical firms including, BASF, Bayer, Hoechst and AGFA, that merged together. It was essentially the manufacturing wing of the Third Reich and was the engine behind the Nazi war machine. The company provided the vast majority of explosives and synthetic gasoline used for the military conquest and murder of millions. It also manufactured the now infamous Zyklon-B gas used in the gas chambers. Not only that, but it was influential in the conducting of experiments on concentration camp victims. Indeed, camp victims were often purchased outright at the behest of the company for the express purposes of testing by several different branches of the company, particularly Bayer and Hoechst.

Without I.G. Farben, the German war efforts simply could not have been sustained. During the Nuremberg war trials, the tribunal convicted 24 board members and executives of the company and dissolved it into several different daughter companies. Namely, BASF, Hoechst (later to be known as Aventis), and Bayer. By 1951, virtually all 24 of these executives were released, including Fritz ter Meer and Hermann Schmitz.

Ter Meer had been a member of the I.G. Farben executive committee from 1926-1945 and also a member of the working committee and the technical committee as well as a director of the infamous Section II. He was also the ambassador to Italy given full power by the Reich Minister for armaments and war production and was the industrialist most responsible for Auschwitz. Schmitz was also a member of the I.G. Farben executive committee from 1926-1935, and was chairman of the board and 'head of finances' from 1935-1945. He was also head of military economics and a member of the Nazi party. Both men were found guilty by the Nuremberg war tribunal in 1948, yet Schmitz was released in 1950 and Ter Meer in 1952.

After all this, Schmitz was appointed board member of the German bank of Berlin West in 1952 and in 1956, the honorary chairman of the board of Rheinish steel plants. Ter Meer, however, was even more successful. Upon his release, he was appointed board member of Bayer in 1955 and, in 1956 was appointed chairman. In the years following, he would take on many additional roles such as chairman of the board of Theodore Goldschmidt AG, deputy chairman of the board of Commerzbank and Bank-Association AG, as well as a board member of the Waggonfabrik Uerdingen, Duesseldorger Waggonfabrik AG, the bank association of West Germany and United Industrial Enterprises AG. These are documented connections for both of these men. Indeed, Ter Meer's' connections to the pharmaceutical firm Bayer earned him a foundation named in his honour, the Fritz Ter-Meer Foundation. Through all of this however, this writer could not confirm that either Ter Meer or Schmitz had direct connections to the creation of Codex Alimentarius.

However, Codex does nothing to dispel the allegations besides simply disagreeing with them and the connections are not at all implausible. Codex is very secretive about its beginnings, as evidenced on its website where it only states that it was created at the behest of the FAO and the WHO. It is highly unlikely that such an organisation would be created without the assistance, input, and even funding of privately owned international corporations. Thanks to both the anti-Codex community and Codex Alimentarius itself, there is no evidence that documents which individuals or corporations were involved in its establishment. However, there are other ties that lend more credence to the belief that war criminals played a role in the creation of Codex.

Religion and Spirituality

Mainstream Religion

A substantial part of the control mechanism used as a tool for centuries by the ruling Elite to facilitate the keeping of the masses in their places has always been mainstream religion (as opposed to spirituality). Through Christianity, Judaism, Islam, Hinduism, Sikhism and all the other 'isms' and their minor variations and offshoots, we have been managed very effectively and efficiently and thus prevented from gaining access to the real truths of the Universe.

Indeed, through the ages and even today to a large extent, religious dogma has been largely responsible for the suppression of real truth, real history and even real science in an attempt to prevent the common herds from gaining knowledge of both themselves as spiritual beings and the Universe around them. Of course, that kind of knowledge would be far too dangerous to the control systems and the Elite power-base to allow it to become widespread. The only way that the few can control the many is by deception and deception on an unimaginable scale.

All mainstream religions teach us (broadly speaking) that there are only two courses open to us after death, paradise or the eternal fires of hell. Allegedly, only those of us who are good citizens and obey the religious edicts and civil laws and believe in the one true God (choose any one) will live forever in paradise and the rest will be condemned to a burning pit of fire or similar, for eternity with no hope of redemption. In bygone days when the masses were totally uneducated and illiterate, one can only imagine the impact that this edict had upon the way they conducted their lives. Living in fear of eternal damnation at every turn is a difficult psychological burden to bear, but a wonderfully simple expedient by which the ruling classes, through their brain-washed priests and religious hierarchy could keep the 'great unwashed' in check.

I do not mean to condemn or vilify those many genuine, decent and caring people who follow these religions. Many people find comfort in their religion and there are also caring and charitable people of all religions who are serious about and adhere to their religious values, some of which to be fair, do advocate noble, humanitarian practices. However, it is the imposition of rigidly-structured, restrictive controls by the religious hierarchies that is responsible for the misery and 'imprisoning' of the minds of their adherents that I find problematic.

In order to comprehend the basis upon which all religions were founded, we need to go back in time to the Babylonian and Phoenician eras. All the major religions stem from one great premise – sun worship, the original 'religion' of most of the ancients. If one can understand the original sun worship and its attendant symbolism, then it is possible to understand the basis of all current religious beliefs. All sun symbolism has basis in the Zodiac, representing as it does the Earth's annual journey around the sun. As we may see from the diagram below, the Zodiac can be bisected horizontally and vertically and this I believe is the true origin of the cross symbolism in Christianity.

Many pre-Christian deities had their 'birthdays' as 25th December because of this symbolism. The winter solstice occurs on the 21st/22nd December, the point at which the sun is at its weakest in the Northern hemisphere and the point at which the sun had symbolically died according to ancient traditions. By the 25th December each year, three days later, it became observable that the sun had been 're-born' and had re-commenced its climb back to its absolute zenith on 21st / 22nd June the following year.

Thus, the ancient peoples regarded the sun's 'birthday' as 25th December, the day it was born again, Jesus died on Good Friday, which incidentally has no fixed, definitive date and was resurrected (re-born) three days later on Easter Monday. The Christian Christmas festival is purely and simply a Pagan festival reconstituted, as are they all. Below is a shortlist of other religious 'deities' among many others, whose claimed birthday is 25th December:

Horus (c. 3000 BCE)
Osiris (c. 3000 BCE)
Attis of Phrygia (c. 1400 BCE)
Krishna (c. 1400 BCE)
Zoroaster/Zarathustra (c. 1000 BCE)
Mithra of Persia (c. 600 BCE)
Heracles (c. 800 BCE)

Dionysus (c. 186 BCE)
Tammuz (c. 400 BCE)
Adonis (c. 200 BCE)
Hermes
Bacchus
Prometheus

It is a perhaps little known fact that all the major religions tell us the same stories, myths and legends, albeit using slightly different characters and names which nevertheless are often recycled for mass consumption.

For example, of the above list of commonly known 'deities', many are attributed similar legends to that of the Jesus 'myth' or even the myth of Moses. They are variously and collectively said to have died and been resurrected three days later, become great teachers at the age of 12, been purveyors of 'miracles' some of which are also attributed to Jesus, such as the turning of water into wine, walking on water and the healing of the terminally ill. They all had 12 disciples, fasted for forty days and forty nights in the wilderness, were born of a virgin birth and died at the age of thirty three, whilst yet others were found in a basket in water and brought up by royalty as with the Moses story etc. etc and on and on with broad similarities too numerous to mention.

"There is nothing holy about the Bible, nor is it 'the word of God.' It was not written by God-inspired saints, but by power-seeking priests. Who but priests consider sin the paramount issue? Who but priests write volumes of religious rites and rituals? No one but for these priestly scribes sin and rituals were imperatives. Their purpose was to found an awe-inspiring religion. By this intellectual tyranny they sought to gain control and they achieved it. By 400 BC, they were the masters of ancient Israel. For such great project they needed a theme, a framework and this they found in the Creation lore of more knowledgeable races. This they commandeered and perverted – the natural to the supernatural and the truth to error. The Bible is, we assert, but priestly perverted cosmology." Lloyd Graham, *'Myths and Deceptions of the Bible'*

The Christian religion itself was finally shaped into the format with which we are so familiar today at the conference at Nicaea (in what is now modern-day Turkey) in 325AD. This was achieved amongst much conflict, violent disagreement and compromise until eventually 'modern' Christianity was born and evolved from this event. The conference was also characterised by its lies, distortions and misinformation on a grand scale – all in the name of creating a control mechanism for the masses which was acceptable to all the minor creeds and offshoots of the previous broad base of the religion. In short, Nicaea was a PR exercise and an attempt to sanitise and package for broad consumption, a system of 'belief' that had previously been unacceptable or even unpalatable to so many.

Real consciousness is as much an anathema to religion as critical thinking is to
cademia." Robert Bonomo, activistpost.com 13th October 2011
lease understand that the main function of organised religion is to destroy
pirituality and to prevent people from making the connection to the consciousness
f who we are as a species and as an individual. Given that religions were created in
he first place to enslave the population, is it any surprise that they attempt to
estroy everything for which they purport to stand?

pirituality

Today, a young man on LSD realised that all matter is merely energy condensed to a
ow vibration and that we are all one consciousness experiencing itself subjectively.
here's no such thing as death, life is only a dream and we are the imagination of
urselves. ...Now here's Tom with the weather." Bill Hicks, US comedian, 1961-1994

he humour in this pithy observation is derived totally from the last sentence. The
receding two sentences appear to be the serious observations of someone from
utside the mainstream viewpoint expressing a truly spiritual view of the mysteries
f life. However, this illusion is shattered as we realise the words are being spoken
y a mainstream TV anchor-man character as a link to the next section of the show.
he absurdity of this should be apparent to all – it could never happen in the 'real
orld' as mainstream TV anchors do not says things of that nature and thus the joke
born from the contrast between reality and fantasy, as is much of our humour.

ll Hicks was a unique comedian. Acid-tongued, uncannily accurate observations of
e combined with deep spiritual knowledge and beliefs and a rare understanding of
olitical realities, made him a huge draw with audiences all around the USA and
ventually Britain. Of course, he never became a 'super-celebrity', a mega-star. For
aat to happen one must espouse views that totally conform to the mainstream
herwise one will never be allowed a platform for this 'subversive' approach. Hicks
adly died of cancer at the age of 32 and the world lost a true student of spirituality, a
eep-thinking intellectual and someone who was able to bring an alternative view of
e world to the masses through his insightful comedy shows. He constituted an
xtreme danger to those who try to enslave us all, as he had a huge following who
ung upon his every word. In the light of this fact, could his cancer possibly have
een natural or is it just feasible that it was given to him deliberately. There is no
oubt that the technology to do this, exists and is often used against the overt
pponents of the New World Order. Hicks also said, very aptly...

The world is like a ride in an amusement park. And when you choose to go on it, you
ink it's real because that's how powerful our minds are. And the ride goes up and
own and round and round. It has thrills and chills and it's very brightly coloured and
s very loud and its fun – for a while. Some people have been on the ride for a long
me and they begin to question, is this real or is this just a ride? And other people have

remembered, and they come back to us, they say, 'Hey - don't worry, don't be afraid
ever, because, this is just a ride'... And then we kill those people."

Some years ago, the famous actor Larry Hagman took part in an experiment to
check-out the effects of the (highly illegal) Class A drug, LSD (LySergic acid
Diethylamide). After imbibing the substance and waiting for its effects to manifest
he took an orange from the kitchen and cut it open. Its cellular structure was pulsing
and it looked to him as though the cells were alternating between life and death
which seemed perfectly natural to him in his now highly conscious, altered-state.
Looking up from his scrutiny of the pulsating orange, he saw his reflection in a mirror
on the wall. He too, was pulsating. Cells were dying, whilst others were in the
process of being re-born. An intricate picture of every cell in constant motion
became apparent and he realised that he was a constant flow of energy as indeed
was everything else. The scope of this realisation widened with his conviction that: "I
was part of everything and everything was part of me. Everything was living, dying and
being reborn."

His friend, who had not taken the drug, drove Hagman around Beverly Hills equipped
with a sixteen millimetre camera with which he could zoom-in on plants, flowers and
people and he found that their cells were also constantly pulsating and changing.
This experience shares a number of similarities with near-death, out-of-body and
certain shamanic experiences. These are usually intensely transforming and
empowering and Hagman's own experience was certainly no exception.

Besides self-insight, he also saw much more deeply into people's emotions and how
they were expressed through body and facial language. But most importantly, his
view of life and death were profoundly altered by the experience. He realised that
so-called 'dying' was actually only a transformation into another expression of the
vast creative energy that underlies everything. He concluded that: "Death is just
another stage of our development and we go on to different levels of existence."

He believed he had an understanding of 'God' consciousness. Fear of man-made
concepts of heaven and hell disappeared and he stopped worrying and indeed felt 'at
home' in the universe. It was all so clear and so familiar.

Dangerous knowledge indeed. Can anyone think of a better reason for the illegality
of LSD or any other so-called hallucinatory drug such as Psilocybin (the active
ingredient of 'magic' mushrooms) or Ayahuasca for example?

So what exactly is Spirituality? It extends beyond an expression of religion or the
practice of religion. The relationship between ourselves and 'something greater'
compels us to seek answers about the infinite. During times of intense emotional,
mental, or physical stress, man searches for transcendent meaning, often through
nature, music, the arts, or a set of philosophical beliefs. This often results in a broad
set of principles that transcends all religions.

While spirituality and religion remain different, sometimes the terms are used interchangeably and this lack of clarity in their definitions frequently leads to debates. Through certain actions, an individual may appear outwardly religious and yet lack any of the underlying principles of spirituality. In its broadest sense, spirituality may include religion for some, but still stands alone without a connection to any specific faith. In my view it is simply a belief that this Earth, this Universe, is not all there is. There is an unseen dimension that may or may not contain our God(s) but most certainly contains a spiritual entity or entities of some form of cosmic super-consciousness.

Whether this entity manifests as a 'oneness' or as individual elements, I believe that one thing is certain; we are indeed all one and the same being, part of the overall 'one-consciousness'. We are all literally 'brothers and sisters' and inter-connected at the basic cellular level as is all matter in the Universe, whether sentient or non-sentient.

Consider this; the actual amount of 'solid' matter making up the entire Earth and everything in it, if all the empty space in atoms was removed, would consist of a blob of nuclear material about 1cm (0.4 inches) in diameter. But more mysterious still, the matter in the nucleus is also not solid as it appears, but consists of protons and neutrons with a huge percentage of empty space in-between *them*. And these protons and neutrons are made up of quarks containing yet more space. Quarks consist of neutrinos and even more space, but confusingly this *space* is also 'made of' neutrinos, but vibrating at a different rate to the *matter* that makes up the neutrinos.

Therefore the only difference between substance and nothing at all is the vibratory rate of the neutrinos. When experiments were performed to try to understand why the neutrinos would exist in one specific form one moment and another form entirely in the next, it was discovered that neutrinos always become what they are expected to become. So it has now been confirmed by default by mainstream science, what mystics throughout the ages have said all along; that matter is an illusion created by consciousness. The wave-particle duality model shows us that these particles are waves until they are observed. Simply observing the wave / particle changes the waves into particles and vice versa. The whole universe is nothing but a wave pattern that we make real with **our** awareness. Our bodies are our most personal physical creations, which reflect our thoughts, feelings, beliefs, attitudes, choices and decisions. This phenomenon was first brought to the attention of the world in 1935 by a physicist named Edwin Schrödinger in an hypothesis that has come to be known as 'Schrödinger's Cat' whereby a cat in a box, can be both alive and dead at the same time, depending on the standpoint of the observer.

Every sensory experience, thought and emotion produces an electrical wave, which passes through every DNA molecule in the body. The structure of DNA is a closed spiral, a double-helix, which turns back on itself and also loops back the other way, so any wave that passes through it will travel in both directions simultaneously. The result is a scalar wave, an information wave that has no direction. When this wave is consciously experienced, it moves through the corpus callosum of the brain, which is itself in the shape of a Mobius strip, a strip that is twisted in the middle and coils back on itself, so any wave that passes through it undergoes a 180 degree phase change, which cancels out the wave stored in the DNA coil by destructive interference.

Any thought, feeling or sensory experience that is not fully conscious will remain as a wave within the DNA coil. The electrical wave then draws to itself a melanin-protein complex and forms a crystal. So every suppressed experience, thought or emotion is stored as a crystal in every DNA molecule in the body. So, the body is in effect, a three dimensional hologram, where each part of the DNA affects different parts of the body.

All life is connected and it is through our DNA that we broadcast and receive information. Our entire body is akin to a giant transmission and reception system being constructed through resonant frequencies. The Sun, Earth and 'heavens' are nothing more than illusions. They are frequencies being generated, from which our subconscious constructs and our conscious mind observes what we euphemistically believe to be 'reality'. And this is the whole essence of the imprisonment of our minds as we are led to believe by our lords and masters that this five-sense universe is all there is and anyone who questions that fact must be deluded in the extreme. All dangerous knowledge such as this must be eradicated at all costs so that they can maintain their vice-like grip on our lives.

Reincarnation and 'Life between Lives'

"Earth is a training ground for souls." Les Visible, musician and researcher, 2011.

In the 1970s a prominent psychologist and hypnotherapist in California, Dr. Michael Newton, discovered by serendipitous accident, a completely new phenomenon that was to change his life and that of many thousands of individuals worldwide over the course of the next four decades.

In the process of performing hypnotherapy on a patient and whilst regressing him to a past life to attempt to identify the source of his problem (something he had undertaken many thousands of times previously), to his great astonishment, the patient reached the point of his death in that past life and proceeded to describe a most astounding series of events – the transition of the soul after death into the Spirit World and his 'welcome home' by his 'soul-mates' and spirit guide.

To say he was stunned is a gross understatement. Although he was obviously aware through his vast experience, that the human soul is reincarnated over and over again through the millennia, he had assumed that the soul's life between each life was simply, in his words, a *'hazy limbo that only served as a bridge from one past life to the next'*.   Now here before him was proof that the soul has a true 'life between lives' and the stunning implications of this were now apparent, brought home to him by his client in a vividly described yet matter of factly-related way on his own psychiatrist's couch.

Dr. Newton realised that he simply *had* to find a way to uncover any future subject's memories of this 'spirit world' and unlock them as best he could. Eventually after thousands upon thousands of hours of meticulous recording and collating of the experiences of many subsequent patients he was able to construct a theoretical working model of the structure of the 'spirit world' and this is recounted in fine, jaw-dropping detail in his fascinating books, 'Journey of Souls', 'Destiny of Souls' and 'Memories of the Afterlife'.

During this long, arduous process, he also observed interestingly, that it did not seem to make any difference whether the subject had passionate religious convictions of any kind, was a 'dyed in the wool' atheist or indeed exhibited any other beliefs in-between these two polarities. The outcome was always the same; a clear, coherent, consistent description of the spirit world accompanied by a concise description of the events experienced by souls from death in one life to re-birth in the next.

As Dr. Newton relays in his many case histories, collated over the decades, the consistency of description of the experiences of these transitional souls would appear to be proof positive of not only multiple lives, but possibly even more surprisingly, a life between lives. The impact all this has had on Newton's own life may be summed-up succinctly in his observation that as time went on and more and more subjects relayed to him their past experiences, he realised that his own outlook on life had changed substantially. In his own words, he eventually came to the realisation that he had 'lost the fear of death' and in so doing had rid himself of all the unwanted, associated baggage accompanying this most basic of all human fears.

In addition to this, and importantly I feel, Newton also believes he has uncovered the 'meaning of life' *(my interpretation – not specifically his, JH)*. With every passing instance of his numerous 'visits' to the spirit world courtesy of his subjects' vivid descriptions, it became clearer to him that our purpose in living on this Earth (and the many other worlds populated by souls in this and other physical universes) is simply to learn to achieve perfection. Once we reach this state, we apparently cease re-incarnating and live out a blissful eternal existence without the need to ever again visit this physical realm.

In essence, Earth is a 'school', a training academy for souls. Every lifetime we live, we learn valuable lessons in our quest for perfection and our mentors in the soul world, spirit guides if you will, assist us in this quest in any way they can, often pointing us in the right direction when we struggle with any aspect of the lessons we are here to complete. In addition, immediately prior to each reincarnation, we are encouraged by our spirit guides to choose a specific future life from the options they present to us, that will best fulfil our goals and help us learn from our past mistakes and aberrations thus accelerating our 'growth' as an eternal, immortal being and the gradual progression to ultimate perfection.

Towards the end of his working life, Dr. Newton (who is now in his eighties) founded The Newton Institute in order to train others and provide a tangible platform from which to perpetuate his pioneering work. There are now some 200 practitioners of his methods around the world who through a network of constant communication and training schedules endeavour to keep up-to-date with the latest developments and continue to provide a service to anyone interested in being healed themselves or indeed simply curious about their past lives.

In May 2011, I personally visited one of these practitioners, a hypnotherapist based in the North of England not too far from my home, by the name of Karen Wells, to investigate for myself the concept of 'Life between Lives'. During a pleasant, informal three hour session, alongside four others, I discovered the basics of the theory and the practice behind the process of LBL regression therapy. Karen's passion for the subject was apparent and she kindly agreed to answer a few questions I had, after the session was over.

From this subsequent session, it transpired that Karen had undergone regression herself on many occasions and whilst she quite rightly felt it inappropriate to divulge the precise personal details, she did offer some insights on various aspects of the process in general. For example, she related the fascinating story of one of her clients who came to her for help in ridding himself of severe back pain. Apparently he had tried all the usual routes of doctors, chiropractors and physiotherapists to divest himself of the pain – all to no avail. So, in desperation he decided to try hypnotherapy and visited Karen's practice.

None of the mainstream health professionals he had visited previously could even find a cause for the pain, let alone attempt to affect a cure. However, in being regressed back to a past life in mediaeval times, the subject found himself on a battlefield involved in brutal conflict with a deadly enemy. As the battle progressed he described the scene to Karen vividly as he was captured by the enemy and held down by several of them whilst another of their number 'ran him through' with a sword into his *back*, thus ending his current life.

Obviously there is an element of mild trauma involved in re-living such horrific scenes, but Karen reassured me that the experience is not as bad as it may sound. Although on the surface, it seems to be the stuff of future nightmares for years to come, apparently it is experienced in a detached kind of way, almost as though it was happening to someone else or in a dream, although the pain can sometimes be real enough, albeit relatively short-lived. Then as quickly as it had happened, Karen carefully and sensitively returned him to 'normality'. Upon regaining his senses and 'awakening', the subject immediately noticed that the pain had almost gone, but through re-living the cause and understanding the source of the discomfort, it would appear that the pain had been psychologically and even physically 'exorcised' in some way that no-one can really explain. Shortly afterwards he contacted Karen to let her know that the pain had eventually completely disappeared after an entire lifetime of torment and agony.

Indeed this healing process is the basis and raison d'être of hypnotic regression therapy and has been proven over time to be efficacious in thousands upon thousands of instances.

Karen has also performed regression therapy on several individuals who as it turned-out had experienced life on other, distant planets as non-human life-forms. Some were simply humanoid-type species whilst yet others were non-physical manifestations of life who communicated telepathically. In her experience, it is these troubled souls, having had happy, fulfilling lives in less-demanding environments who find it most difficult to cope with the severe lessons to which we are all subjected on planet Earth and indeed they are the ones most prone to depression and suicide due to their inability to deal with the harshness of life in this world. Some of these poor, sensitive souls unfortunately tend to commit suicide over and over again in desperation and many more of them choose not to return here again after a lifetime of trauma leaves them temporarily damaged and with vivid memories of the utter despair and feeling of 'not belonging here' that they experienced on Earth.

A few years ago, a British TV documentary recounted the story of a small boy in England who could 'remember' a previous lifetime on a remote Scottish island between the two World Wars. His memories were so vivid and persistent and his descriptions of his house and family so clear and consistent that it prompted his family to investigate further. Upon further close investigation they were astounded to discover that the house, the family, the boy and all his siblings as described by their son, actually had existed in the 1920s and 1930s on the island exactly as he had related. The boy himself was too young to have read the story somewhere (and in any case who would have written about an ordinary family living a perfectly ordinary life in a remote outpost of the British Isles, 80 or 90 years ago) and indeed to his parent's knowledge there was absolutely no way that he could have picked up this information without actually having been there at the time. It remains a mystery to this day.

This story is but one of many similar ones that have begun to emerge since the publicity engendered by the documentary. This is food for thought indeed and yet more circumstantial evidence of reincarnation.

To relate an incident from my own experience, very shortly after becoming aware of the work of Dr. Michael Newton and before mentioning it to anyone, I received a phone call from one of my sons, also named John, who proceeded to tell me about what had recently been happening with his daughter, Katy (my granddaughter) who was three years old at the time.

He said that Katy would regularly, when travelling down a particular road in the car come out with statements such as '... there's the house where I used to live with my other mummy and daddy' and '... can I go to my other house today and play with my friends that live there?'

As you may imagine, I was staggered by this revelation and encouraged him to gently question her about it. As a result, he asked her questions such as '... when did you live at your other house, Katy?' and was told 'a long time ago'. Unfortunately it was all very inconclusive, perhaps not unexpectedly and it eventually ceased altogether and she now appears to have no memory of these incidents at all, at the ripe old age of four! Could it be that we all still retain past life memories as infants but over the course of the next few years lose the ability to 'remember' them as we become more and more conditioned into the five-sense world that we are programmed by society to believe is real?

However, mystery notwithstanding, this short anecdote adds further fuel to the fire and as with all the other examples contributes to the now huge mass of circumstantial evidence in favour of multi-life reincarnation that is growing almost daily.

In a broadly related but not entirely similar vein, I spent a weekend in the ancient Roman city of Bath in the South West of England with my wife on a short-break holiday in early 2009. Bear in mind that this was also before I had 'discovered' Michael Newton and his work. Anyway, to cut a long story very short we had had a wonderfully pleasant, relaxing evening with a romantic dinner accompanied by copious glasses of red wine, when I suddenly surprised even myself by saying (and even today, I have absolutely no idea where these words came from) 'I believe that I have been sent here to look after you in this lifetime'. The look she gave me said it all really... a sort of 'what planet are you on?' kind of look and it really broke the spell of the evening. I mumbled something by way of an explanation, but was at a loss to elaborate. Looking back now, it seemed at the time to be such a heap of patronising drivel, but with the benefit of hindsight and the newly acquired knowledge of multi reincarnation, maybe that really is why I am here now. I will probably never know for certain – at least not in this lifetime anyway but maybe, just maybe that is one of the reasons I am here at this time, whilst remaining consciously unaware of the fact (most of the time!).

I believe it is also possible that given the fact that we have all specifically chosen to be here on Earth at this particular time, that we are all here to be part of the battle to ensure the continuity of the human race and fight against the forces of evil that are trying to destroy humanity in its present form. There can be no doubt that the next few months and years are going to be critical if we are to survive as a species and

Some of the greatest challenges the human race has ever had to encounter are just around the corner' in our current lifetimes. If we can all 'wake-up' in time and prove ourselves worthy of these challenges and all play our parts in ensuring the survival of the species against the odds, then the karmic lessons we will have learned in our eternal quest for spiritual perfection, will be more than worth the Earthly sacrifices we will all no doubt have to endure along the way.

It is essential that we ask ourselves the question; why is all this substantial, circumstantial evidence of life after death and previous lives not even considered worthy of discussion in the mainstream and ignored, let alone properly scientifically investigated? There is far less 'proof' than this of, for example, the truth of the *theory* of evolution, but that particular creed has no trouble in gaining widespread, unthinking acceptance as fact by the 'sheeple' of this world. Unfortunately we have to draw the same conclusions once more and that is that certain elements of our society have a serious vested interest in keeping this knowledge from general public consumption whilst promoting other huge lies as the truth. Were the masses to lose their fear of death in great numbers, as did Michael Newton and as I have too, in understanding the real point of life, then the implications of this for our controllers could well be critical. The only way they can remain in control is by maintaining our fear of death whilst presenting us with a totally distorted version of reality and history that maintains the status quo in their favour.

There are perhaps 10,000 of them in total and almost 7 billion of 'us'. Just think of the power we have should we choose to use it and instead of passively accepting slavery as we do now, refuse to be bent to their sadistic wills any longer.

PART 4 – The Epilogue

Why have I spent the last several years of my life attempting to bring this appalling state of affairs to everyone's attention? Why not simply let 'sleeping-dogs lie' and concentrate on procuring the best life I can for myself and my family under the prevailing circumstances, like the other 99.99% of humankind? After all, it is such a thankless task, to be brutally candid and the temptation to 'turn a blind eye' to it all extremely strong. So many people sleep-walk through their entire lives without noticing what is so apparent to those of us who have made the metaphorical leap across the yawning precipice to the truth and so many people will automatically reject as nonsense (often vehemently), virtually every facet of this book without bothering to closely examine the evidence on both sides of the argument. I have been ridiculed and laughed-at and made to feel inadequate many times in trying to get this message across to family, friends and acquaintances, until it reached a point whereby I had to stop talking about what I perceive to be the truth for fear of permanently alienating most people that I know and care about. In fact this has actually happened in more than one instance.

The reason I do not completely give-up however is simply this; I feel a great compulsion to share the truths that I know, not just for the sake of the future of my children and my children's children, but for the future of *all* of mankind and the descendants of all of us. One thing is for sure, we ARE running out of time as the planned endgame approaches rapidly, but it is still not yet quite too late and people are slowly but surely awakening to recognise what is being inflicted upon us as witness the world-wide protests against the Elite banks and corporations in late 2011.

The year 2012 is widely expected in the 'alternative-view' community to be the 'tipping point', the coming to fruition of the 'hundredth monkey syndrome' for humanity whereby the world's population will become spiritually and also politically aware of what is happening now in front of their currently unseeing eyes and we can **all** contribute to this simply by being aware of what is really occurring in the world today and sharing that knowledge wherever and whenever possible. The hundredth monkey syndrome describes a scenario whereby one monkey acquires a new skill and teaches it to its children and peers, who all teach it to their children and so on. After a certain point is reached in this education process (supposedly 100 individuals having the skill – but this is obviously a metaphor), something bizarre happens... monkeys suddenly, no longer need to be taught the skill. They acquire it automatically by some telepathic method or the fact that all matter is connected in some inexplicable way and then in effect the entire species is suddenly endowed 'overnight' with this particular skill. This is a genuine, albeit unaccountable, scientifically-acknowledged phenomenon and not a myth or urban legend. If we can develop our understanding of the truth of our planned fate at the hands of these inhuman-beings and pass on that knowledge to our friends and families, I believe that this will serve to speed-up the hundredth monkey syndrome for humanity, putting to an end, sooner rather than later, the despicable conspiracy that threatens to enslave us all and our descendants forever.

Furthermore, I strongly suspect that this 'tipping-point', will finally arrive when certain sections of the 'middle-classes' who are at the moment fully complicit, albeit in many cases unknowingly, with this monstrous conspiracy, such as for example, BBC, SKY and FOX News and other mainstream networks' TV reporters, police officers at all levels, the military, middle-ranking politicians and senior health-care professionals, finally realise that their own well-being and the future of their own families is in serious jeopardy. Once these people gain awareness of the full impact of what is happening and finally comprehend that they are being egregiously used to usher-in their own destruction or at best, slavery, then a massive 'changing of sides' will commence and without these lackeys on-side, the Elite will ultimately realise there is nowhere to hide.

Many years ago when I worked in the commercial sphere for a large computer software supplier, I was introduced to a client company that had a somewhat radical senior management team. The directors of this organisation, whose name I have long forgotten, instigated a very controversial, yet once accepted by the majority, extremely effective procedure to maximise the efficiency of their working practices. Very simply stated any process at all, from manufacturing through to sales and administration tasks **had** to be scrapped and changed every six months maximum, no exceptions. The effect of this was that the employees were constantly re-assessing existing procedures and examining them critically to determine how they could be improved with a long-term view towards ultimate efficiency. This was, as a result of that policy, the most efficient organisation I have ever seen.

And the point I am making there is that this is how we should look at things in this world and our own lives. Never assume that what is in place at the moment in society is the 'only alternative' or 'just the way it has to be', look at everything with a constructively critical eye and see if you still feel that the way things are currently, are really as they are portrayed to be or indeed as they should be. And please, please do not simply take my word for all that is happening around us. I would actively encourage anyone interested in the subjects covered in the pages of this book, to undertake their own simple research and to go wherever ensuing conclusions may lead. That wonderful tool known as the Internet has made this course of action much easier than in previous decades. I urge you to use it before that avenue is closed to us as it is often threatened to be, in the interests of our 'security'.

The overall outlook, although appearing at first glance to be one of hopelessness against such seemingly insurmountable odds, is actually quite positive. We will not win the war that is to come with violence or bombs and tanks and guns. But, by using our wits and choosing our 'battlegrounds' carefully, there is no doubt that the strength and durability of the human spirit will overcome what may appear at first sight to be vastly overwhelming odds. I firmly believe that we have all chosen to be here at this time in history in order to assist the human race in finally conquering its demons against all odds and having made that choice, we must 'stand up and be counted'.

The over-arching weakness in the make-up of these psychopathic cowards is their inability to love, really deeply, truly love anyone but themselves and thus when they are finally faced with a choice of saving themselves or being loyal to their families their 'comrades' and their cause, it is their own personal safety which will always win through. The solution is certainly in our own hands and with a relatively small degree of co-operation and positive thinking, we (almost) seven billions can surely overcome the tiny minority of sick, deluded, psychopathic individuals who have spent the last several millennia co-opting this planet for their own selfish ends and secure a happy healthy world of plenty for us all and our children, for ever.

And finally, the purpose of this book is not to present answers and solutions to the problems, but to inform and thus provide further impetus to the 'hundredth monkey syndrome' and facilitate its early arrival by appraising people of what is really happening in the world today. I do not profess to be able to answer the question 'what can we do about it, though?' Nor should I, it is not my place so to do, but it is up to each and every individual to follow their own consciences and formulate their own opinions of the best 'solutions' and this humble book is my small contribution to that end. The process of change will occur naturally, eventually when the time is right and it will be as a result of a natural ground-swell of truth and knowledge being made available through education of the masses of the issues that are its ultimate causes and not through anyone, least of all me, saying 'this is what should be done'. Your own personal contribution to the solution, however small and insignificant you feel it may be, *will* make a difference.

This book, although of necessity large and voluminous does not attempt to examine the entire issue in great analytical depth, but rather is meant as an overview, an introduction to this vast subject in order to provide those people who wish to learn more about each individual element, a platform from which to build their own knowledge and thus through that knowledge begin to 'make a difference' in their own ways, no matter how seemingly insignificant that may be.

However, I will now leave the last word of all to George Orwell (real name, Eric Blair) from his interestingly and yet suspiciously perceptive and predictive work, 1984...

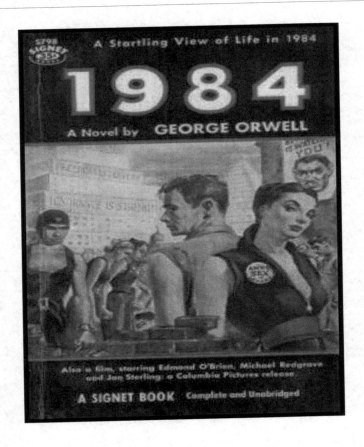

"The frightening thing, he recounted for the ten thousandth time... was that it might all be true. If the Party could thrust its hand into the past and say of this or that event, it never happened – that surely was more terrifying than mere torture and death? And if all others accepted the lie which the Party imposed – if all records told the same tale – then the lie passed into history and became truth. 'Who controls the past' ran the Party slogan, 'controls the future: who controls the present controls the past.' Day by day and almost minute by minute the past was brought up to date. In this way every prediction made by the Party could be shown by documentary evidence to have been correct; nor was any item of news, or any expression of opinion, which conflicted with the needs of the moment, ever allowed to remain on record. All history was a palimpsest, scraped clean and re-inscribed exactly as often as was necessary."

END